GET INTO MEDICAL SCHOOL !

GET INTO MEDICAL SCHOOL !

A Guide for the Perplexed

Kenneth V. Iserson, M.D.

GALEN PRESS, LTD.
TUCSON, ARIZONA

Special bulk purchase terms are available. Please contact our special sales department.

GALEN PRESS, Ltd.
P.O. BOX 64400
TUCSON, AZ 85728-4400
PHONE (520) 577-8363   FAX (520) 529-6459
Orders (U.S. & Canada) 1-800-442-5369

ISBN: 1-883620-23-6

KENNETH V. ISERSON, M.D., M.B.A., FACEP
Professor of Surgery, Section of Emergency Medicine
University of Arizona College of Medicine
1501 N. Campbell Avenue
Tucson, AZ 85724

Library of Congress Cataloging-in-Publication Data

Iserson, Kenneth V.
    Get into medical school! : a guide for the perplexed / Kenneth
V. Iserson.
        p.   cm.
    Includes bibliographical references and index.
    ISBN 1-883620-23-6   (pbk.)
    1. Medical colleges--United States-- Admission.   2. Medical
colleges--United States--Entrance requirements.   I. Title.
R838.4.I84   1997
610 ' 71 ' 173--dc20   96-31926
                                                                        CIP

Printed in the United States of America.

10 9 8 7 6 5 4 3 2 1

Table Of Contents

List Of Figures

Acknowledgments

Those having torches will pass them on to others.

Plato, *The Republic*

This book would not exist but for the significant help I received from others. First and foremost is the fantastic assistance and support from my wife, Mary Lou Iserson, C.P.A. Acting as both a skilled and persistent editor, and the resident computer whiz, she midwifed this book from its outset.

Special thanks to those whose special information and unique insights into the medical school application process has added so much to this book. These include Esther Berren, University Medical Center, Tucson, AZ; Melissa Berren, Tucson, AZ; Ursula Bishop, Health Careers Adviser, California Polytechnic State University; Barb Cheves, Secretary for the Health Professions Committee, Cal Poly, San Luis Obispo, CA; Linda Don, Minority Affairs Coordinator, Office of Minority Affairs, University of Arizona; Shirley Nickols Fahey, Ph.D., Associate Dean for Admissions, University of Arizona College of Medicine; Leonard Finkelstein, D.O., President, Philadelphia College of Osteopathic Medicine; Robert Fisher, M.L.S., Research Librarian, Tucson, AZ; Josephine Gin, M.A., Premed Adviser, University of Arizona; Maggie Gumble, Financial Counselor–Senior, University of Arizona College of Medicine; Francis R. Hall, Asst. Vice President for Student Programs, Association of American Medical Colleges; Jeffrey E. Hanson, Ph.D., Northwestern University; Kerry Hezinger, Assistant to the Dean for Student Services and Preprofessional Programs, College of Science and Technology, University of Southern Mississippi; Lawrence S. Iserson, Lakewood, NJ; Donald Kassebaum, M.D., Vice President, Div. of Educational Research & Assessment, Association of American Medical Colleges; William P. King, Director, AACOMAS, American Association of Colleges of Osteopathic Medicine; T. John Leppi, Ph.D., Associate Dean for Admissions, University of North Texas Health Sciences Center—Texas College of Osteopathic Medicine; Monica Moody Moore, Law and Health Professions Advising, University of Maryland; Stephen M. Payson, M.S., Associate Dean for Student Affairs and Registrar, The University of Health Sciences College of Osteopathic Medicine; Jonathan P. Robles, Recruitment/Retention Coordinator, Office of Minority Affairs, University of Arizona; Marliss G. Strange, Associate Director, Academic Advising and Student Services, University of Oregon; Bonnie A. Saylor, Director of Member Services, American Association of Colleges of Osteopathic Medicine; James Tysinger, Ph.D., Teaching and Learning Skills Consultant, University of Texas, Southwestern Medical School; Donald Witzke, Ph.D., Director of Student Testing and Evaluation, University of Kentucky College of Medicine; and Douglas L. Wood, D.O., Ph.D., President, American Association of Colleges of Osteopathic Medicine.

As always with my books, I owe a debt of gratitude to my friends at the University of Arizona Health Sciences Library, who find sources of information in inscrutable ways. I am especially grateful to Ms. Nga T. Nguyen, B.A., B.S., Senior Library Specialist, and to Ms. Hannah Fisher, R.N., M.L.S., Reference Librarian, who helped to track down some of the invaluable and hard-to-find information for this book.

This book's authenticity and usefulness is greatly enhanced by the many medical students, premedical students, and physicians who contributed their own stories. I owe a special debt to those whose personal statements have been included: Steve Behr, M.D., Arizona class of 1996;

Robert G. Bonillas, Arizona class of 1999; Tracy L. Davis, M.D.-Ph.D. student, Arizona class of 2002; Brian D. Fitch, M.D., Arizona class of 1996; Benjamin Gonzalez, M.D., Arizona class of 1996; Steve Hocheder, Arizona class of 1999; Gina M. Jansheski, M.D., Arizona class of 1996; Priscilla Madsen, UT-Southwestern class of 1999; Molly Roberts, Arizona class of 1999; and William Segalla, (applying for 1997).

Other physicians, medical students, and premed students who contributed to this book include: James Adams, M.D., Georgetown 1988; Digna Acosta, M.D., UCSD 1996; Jeff Baker, M.D., Colorado 1993; Patricia Barreto, M.D., Arizona 1996; Kirsten Bourke, Arizona 1999; Peter Brown, M.D., Vermont 1994; Ellen Dillavou, M.D., Arizona 1996; Christine Farris, M.D., Indiana 1993; Miguel Fernandez, M.D., Medical College of Wisconsin 1985; Albert Fiorello, M.D., SUNY–Buffalo 1995; Charles B. Fooe, M.D., North Carolina 1993; Zoe Forester, Arizona 1998; Bruce Friedman, Arizona 1998; Barbara L. Garcia, M.D., USC 1996; Kurt Glaesser, Arizona 1997; Linda Heckler, Arizona 1999; Pamela Hite, Arizona 1998; Gretchen Hull, Arizona 1998; Heather Isaacson, M.D., Arizona 1996; Ross Lamb, Tucson, AZ; Margarita Loeza, UCSD 1997; John Micaels, Tucson, AZ; Martha Miller, M.D., Arizona 1996; Joy Mockbee, M.D., Arizona 1996; Cyndee Price, Arizona 1997; Karen Randall, D.O., Univ. of Osteopathic Medicine and Health Sciences 1982; Craig Stump, Arizona 1997; Kristin Thom, U AZ 1998; Mary Jo Villar, D.O., Nova-Southeastern 1994; Cheryl L. Waterkotte, Arizona 1999; Jennifer Lynn Weber, Arizona 1999; Warren Withers, M.D., Creighton 1994; and Antonia M. Zazueta, UCSF 1997.

I would be remiss if I did not also thank the people at Galen Press, especially Mary Lou Sherk and Chris McNellis, who have been wonderful in supporting this project. While I greatly appreciate the fine help from the many knowledgeable people who helped me to refine this book, in the end, I am responsible for what has been included and omitted.

I have diligently attempted to amass the best data possible, especially about the various medical schools which were often reluctant to part with the information. I am, however, willing to emend incorrect information if any medical school or medical organization wishes to forward it to me.

KVI
December 1996

FEEDBACK FORM

Medical schools and other agencies: Please use this form to update or correct your contact information.

Please return to: Kenneth V. Iserson, M.D.
Section of Emergency Medicine
University of Arizona College of Medicine
1501 N. Campbell Avenue
Tucson, AZ 85724 USA

I would like to pass on the following information or personal experience for inclusion in the next edition of *Get Into Medical School! A Guide for the Perplexed.* Or, I have a suggestion about what to add to the next edition.

_____

_____

_____

_____

_____

_____

_____

_____

_____

_____

(If you need more space, continue on the back or use another sheet.)

(Optional)   Name: _____

Address: _____

_____

Phone Number: _____

Thanks for your feedback.

1: A Medical Career

Do all the good you can,
By all the means you can,
In all the ways you can,
In all the places you can,
At all the times you can,
To all the people you can,
As long as ever you can.

John Wesley, *Rules of Conduct*

YOU WANT TO BE A PHYSICIAN? First, ask yourself why you want to put yourself through the ordeal of

- a prolonged and arduous premedical education,
- a highly competitive medical school admissions process,
- a demanding medical school education,
- an exhausting postgraduate (residency and fellowship) training,
- the tough licensing examinations, and
- board certification examinations.

Then after you go through all of this, you end up in a career with long hours, increasing government and insurance company interference, and lots of stress. Clearly, only those individuals who are very dedicated (or foolish) would put themselves into this situation. If you have spoken to practicing physicians who question whether "any sane person should go into medicine," you might reflect on why these individuals went into medicine in the first place. Have they lost their real motivation amidst a flurry of bad career choices? Or did they go into medicine for the wrong reasons?

Why do *you* want to be a physician? Examine your answer carefully. If you can't come up with a good reason, then forget it—the sacrifices are not going to be worth it to you. If, however, you think you have good reasons and the dedication needed to enter the field, research medical careers in depth. Learn about what opportunities are available and what physicians' lives and practices are really like. Then, if you still want to become a physician, become familiar with the rules needed to get through the system successfully. This book is designed to guide you through this process.

Remember, however, that the goal is not to get into medical school. No matter how difficult, getting into (and through) medical school is only an interim, short-term objective. The real goal is to be a practicing physician. Is that the goal you really want to work and sacrifice for? Think about it very hard. There is a lot of work; there will be many sacrifices.

Should You Be A Physician?

Deciding why you really want to commit your life to a medical career is the most important step on the road to getting into and through medical school (and residency and medical practice)—and the one most people omit. The beginning of any path offers the most opportunity for changing course. Later, as you travel down the road, you may not have as many options. Before you start your own journey (whether you are an undergraduate, a postgraduate, or a high school student) take the time to really study your own motives for choosing this career. No one else can peek into your mind, so be honest with yourself.

Most physicians love their work (at least most of the time) and wouldn't trade what they do for anything else. Unfortunately, there are some physicians who hate their careers and who dream of doing something else. These are the ones who didn't spend time assessing their own wants, needs, and motivations. Better to assess yourself now and make a well-considered decision to enter or bypass a medical career. That way, you will not become one of those decidedly patient-unfriendly doctors who fifteen or twenty years down the road are bitter, frustrated, and feel hemmed in by careers and lives that they neither expected, nor really wanted.

A well-known general practitioner from Georgia, nearing the end of his career, recently said,

> I have not advised anybody to *go* into medicine. And I have not advised anybody *not* to go into medicine. I personally feel like "what else is there?" Coming to the end . . . of a career as a general practitioner, I still feel that this is The Queen of all professions. That this is something that is so much greater than the sum of all its parts. That you can serve medicine but you can never conquer medicine, and all you can be is a walking disciple. And I wouldn't do anything else if I could.

Another physician put it more succinctly, answering her own question by saying,

> Are you sorry you went to medical school? Yes, I would still do this . . . and, NO, I'm not sorry I went to medical school. I thank God for the privilege of having a chance to experience those rare sweet natural highs. Just one or two of those in a lifetime make the strenuous battle worthwhile.

Frequently, bright high school and college students tell me that they won't consider a medical career because they "can't stand the sight of blood." Actually, it is an unusual individual who is not initially made uncomfortable by the sight of someone's blood (especially his own). As a high school senior, I joined our local volunteer rescue (ambulance) squad, although I was somewhat concerned about how I might react when I saw lots of blood or someone badly hurt. A very wise officer told me that it was all right if I felt queasy when I saw some of the horrible sights. And, it was okay to be sick—after I finished doing my job and helping the patient in any way I could. As an example, he pointed out that the biggest, loudest, and strongest person in our organization had, after a recent call, gotten sick from what he saw. But this was after he did his job.

Many people react badly to the sight of (other people's) injuries because they are uncertain about what they will actually see when the skin opens up. Part of a physician's training (in anatomy and surgery courses) is to learn exactly what he will see when different parts of the body are exposed in different ways. Physicians aren't generally repulsed by what they see because they know what to expect and have seen it before. It's simply a matter of knowledge and experience, and such fear is certainly no reason to abandon the thought of a medical career.

Give the idea of a medical career lots of thought. If you decide you really want it, you will be able to get through the rough spots. You will also be a physician who loves his or her work.

What Are Your Motivations?

Most people want jobs that provide excitement and meaning to their lives. Medicine fulfills these desires, and it gives practitioners

- an opportunity to *help* people.
- *respect.*
- an *action-oriented,* rather than a desk-bound, job.
- an *exciting* job. (Just how exciting depends upon the specialty you choose.)
- the chance to *change locations,* since physicians are in demand almost everywhere.
- the *flexibility* to follow many paths at different career stages.
- a good *income* with a secure future.

Most people who seek careers as physicians are basically idealistic. They want to help others. Perhaps this idealism is necessary to carry aspiring physicians through their many years of often-grueling education and residency training.

Unfortunately, many students (and residents) become disheartened when some medical "educators" try to demolish their idealism. Sadly, in many cases they succeed. Others get disillusioned later when they find that they cannot save the world or even a large part of it. Rather, they discover that the physician's role in medicine is to be an important cog in the health-care-delivery system; they relieve pain and suffering for a relatively small number of people.

Individuals who seek medical careers because of the lure of a substantial income should do some simple calculations. Getting an master of business administration (M.B.A.) degree from a good school may be easier and may result in a better income than becoming a physician, for those who have the aptitude and interest. An M.B.A. degree takes only two years and, for the first decade after they graduate, these business people often have higher incomes than those who pursue medicine. Some will make more money than most physicians will during their entire careers.

Self-Test

If you are thinking about medicine as a career, but are not quite sure if it is right for you, ask yourself the following questions developed by the Association of American Medical Colleges (AAMC):

- Do I care deeply about other people, their problems, and their pain?
- Do I enjoy using my skills and knowledge to help people?
- Do I enjoy learning and gaining new understanding?
- Do I often dig deeper into a subject than my teacher requires?
- Do I enjoy and value learning, not just making good grades?
- Am I interested in how the human body functions?
- Am I intrigued by the ways medicine can be used to improve life?

If you answered "Yes" to most of these questions, your interests and personality are most likely similar to those of practicing physicians. Now you must ask yourself whether you have the motivation to pursue the studies necessary to achieve that goal.

Premedical advisers suggest that if you don't know whether you want to be a physician or whether you "have what it takes," do two things: take some required premed science courses and spend some time getting clinical experience. The science courses will demonstrate to you whether you have the interest in, aptitude for, and ability to perform well learning material that is similar to basic science courses taught in medical school. The clinical experiences will show you whether you have a real interest in a medical career.

Formal Tests

Career counselors have tests available to help you decide what career direction to take. While these tests are far from perfect, they provide you with a mirror in which to see your current likes and dislikes related to a career choice. If you are uncertain about whether you really want to go into medicine, you may want to take one or more of these tests. You may not believe what they tell you, but they are one of the most objective tools you have.

This episode certainly sticks with me: As a ninth-grade student, I took the Kuder Preference Record-Occupational Test along with my classmates. It was supposed to give us an idea of what career we were best suited for. I took it, although I already knew I was going to be an attorney. When we got the results back, I knew the test was a ridiculous waste of time. It said that I should be a fireman, a forest ranger, or of all crazy things, a physician. As it turned out, I later spent five years as a volunteer fireman, have spent the last fifteen years as a member of a wilderness search and rescue team, and, of course, practice medicine.

Sometimes these tests can tell you things about yourself that you either don't know or don't yet recognize. If you're in doubt, give them a try.

Why You May *Not* Want To Be A Physician

Nearly two-thirds (61%) of those applying to medical school decide to pursue a medical career while still in high school, and another 11% decide while they are college freshmen. Many of their peers also consider medical careers but decide not to pursue them. While all groups seek job satisfaction, those who apply to medical school differ from their peers in that they are usually more idealistic and have a strong desire to help others. Other striking differences are that medical school applicants want to be constantly challenged in their jobs and have time for friends, family, and other interests; but they do not want to move frequently because of their job.

Students who seriously consider medical careers take the MCAT examination, do well on it, and plan to apply to medical school. Of these students, about 10% change their minds and never apply. It is instructive to look at their reasons for not applying and at their attitudes toward medicine to see if you agree with them.

- Physicians must give up too much time and freedom.
- Another career seems more satisfying.
- My science interests are better served in another field.
- The future of medicine is bleak, according to physicians.
- I can help others better in another field.
- The financial rewards do not justify the time and money invested.
- Medical education is too stressful.
- Physicians have too many legal liabilities and their malpractice insurance costs too much.
- Physicians' independence has been impaired by changes in the health-care-delivery system.

As you consider a medical career, ponder these statements from those who chose not to take that path. If you agree with two or more of them, you should seriously reassess whether you really do want to become a physician. If you have doubts, now would be a good time to find an alternative career path—the route to medicine is long, tortuous, and demanding.

Also be wary of going into medicine because of family pressures. The premed adviser at a large Midwestern school tells this story:

> I had a student who came in to get the MCAT application materials. "Why?" I asked, since I had never seen this student before. "To prove to my parents (his mother is a physician) that I shouldn't be a doctor. I plan on being a computer scientist." He explained that he had started undergraduate school as a premed, but while taking a computer course in his first semester, he knew he had found his niche. His physician-mother, however, couldn't understand that. He subsequently got appropriately dismal scores on the MCAT and went on to follow his own dream, rather than his mother's.

Experienced admission officers view applicants whose parents are physicians with a wary eye, being very careful to question the students' own motivations for entering medicine. If these students have their own reasons for pursuing medicine, there is no problem. If they are following this course to fulfill their parents' dreams, it's a danger signal.

What Are The Steps To Take To Become A Doctor?

You have undoubtedly had contact with physicians. They often seem wise, unflappable, and able to work magical feats with their medicines, scalpels, and other devices. You can hardly imagine them struggling though the rigors of medical school and residency, let alone high school and college. Don't let yourself be intimidated by the image. They were once in your situation, just hoping that they would get into medical school. If you have the motivation to be a physician, you can do it. It just takes a lot of time and effort.

Figure 1.1 is a flow chart which lists the sequence of events for premed students. Few people follow this course exactly, but whenever you "jump in," it provides a rough guide to where you are in the process.

The Challenge

Although entering medical school is now quite difficult, before World War I medical schools accepted nearly anyone who could pay the entry fees. At that time, U.S. medical schools were of inconsistent quality and, for the most part, not regarded very highly. Subsequently, one of the major reforms in medical education was to require accepted students to have at least minimum requirements to prepare them for their medical studies. With this change, the difficulty of getting into medical school slowly increased. As one example, the following is a description of (1934 Nobel Prize winner) George Minot's entry into Harvard Medical School:

> The two cousins felt little urgency to make a decision, and so they separated for the summer of 1908, with George sailing for Europe. When he returned at the end of the summer, he and his cousin talked more about going to the medical school. In their world there was only one medical school to be considered. So they decided to go to medical school on Monday in late September. On that day, they ran some errands and watched football practice; the next day, they picked up their college credentials in Cambridge and on Thursday, 1 October 1908, were among the 65 men who began their medical studies in the Harvard Medical School Class of 1912. (Brieger GH. Getting into medical school in the good old days: good for whom? *Ann Int Med* 1993;119:1138-43.)

Figure 1.1: Typical Premed Activities

HIGH SCHOOL

- ❑ Get good grades
- ❑ Take biology (1-year minimum)
- ❑ Take chemistry (1-year minimum)
- ❑ Take physics (1-year minimum)
- ❑ Take an advanced science course (1-year minimum)
- ❑ Take mathematics (4 years)
- ❑ Take English (4 years)
- ❑ Take a foreign language (3-year minimum)
- ❑ Take speech
- ❑ Take psychology/sociology
- ❑ Take computer science
- ❑ Do volunteer community service
- ❑ Shadow a physician
- ❑ Participate in premed club
- ❑ Take SAT or ACT exam
- ❑ Get college/university information
- ❑ Get medical school Accelerated Program information
- ❑ Do Must/Want Analysis for schools you consider
- ❑ Apply to colleges
- ❑ Apply to Accelerated Program (if you want to)

COLLEGE: Freshman Year

- ❑ Meet with premed adviser/learn premed requirements
- ❑ Develop a premed course of study
- ❑ Plan a tentative schedule for the next 3½ years
- ❑ Think about a major and minor courses of study
- ❑ Get AAMC's *MCAT Student Manual* for subject outlines
- ❑ Develop study skills
- ❑ Maintain excellent GPA
- ❑ Work/volunteer in medical area
- ❑ Begin extracurricular activities
- ❑ Participate in premed club
- ❑ Subscribe to medical student journals (see *Bibliography*)
- ❑ Read interesting books about medicine (see *Bibliography*)
- ❑ Review medical school admission requirements
- ❑ Consider what you will do this summer
- ❑ Apply to MMEP (minorities only)
- ❑ Apply to Accelerated Program (if desired)
- ❑ Talk to premed upperclassmen to get a reality check
- ❑ Contact senior medical students or residents and ask if you can "shadow" them for a 24- or 36-hour shift

Figure 1.1: Typical Premed Activities, cont'd.

COLLEGE: Sophomore Year

- ❏ Work/volunteer in medical area
- ❏ Read some interesting books about medicine
- ❏ Meet with premed adviser to discuss your program
- ❏ Select your major and minor courses of study
- ❏ Maintain excellent GPA
- ❏ Check medical schools' entry requirements
- ❏ Fine-tune your planned college schedule
- ❏ Consider participating in research
- ❏ Consider what you will do this summer
- ❏ Apply to MMEP (minorities only)
- ❏ Study for MCAT (summer before junior year if you will take the MCAT early)
- ❏ Apply for MCAT (if you will take it early)
- ❏ Plan for any special junior-year program (e.g., junior year abroad)

COLLEGE: Junior Year

- ❏ Study for MCAT (if not yet taken)
- ❏ Apply for MCAT (if not yet taken)
- ❏ Take MCAT:
    1. August before junior year
    2. April of junior year
    3. August after junior year
- ❏ Meet with premed adviser
- ❏ Meet with minority premed counselor, if applicable
- ❏ Maintain the best GPA you can
- ❏ Gather information about medical schools
- ❏ Complete Must/Want Analysis forms for schools in which you are interested
- ❏ Get AMCAS/AACOMAS/other applications
- ❏ Begin preparing AMCAS/AACOMAS essay
- ❏ Work/volunteer in medical area
- ❏ Meet with premed committee
- ❏ Request reference letters
- ❏ Obtain/send/review transcripts
- ❏ Complete AMCAS/AACOMAS/Texas/ & other applications
- ❏ Visit nearby school in which you are interested
- ❏ Apply for Early Acceptance Program (optional)
- ❏ Consider what you will do this summer

Figure 1.1: Typical Premed Activities, cont'd.

COLLEGE: Senior Year

- ❑ Work/volunteer in medical area
- ❑ Take MCAT in August to improve scores or if not yet taken
- ❑ Confirm that schools have received your application materials & letters
- ❑ Maintain the best GPA you can
- ❑ Complete secondary medical school applications
- ❑ Interview at medical schools
- ❑ Revise Must/Want Analyses for schools visited
- ❑ Complete GAPSFAS financial aid form
- ❑ If wait-listed, send letter confirming interest
- ❑ Consider what you will do this summer (keep options open)
- ❑ ACCEPT OFFER (By May 15)
- ❑ Accept additional offers if higher on your Must/Want Analysis list; withdraw previous acceptances
- ❑ Write to thank references and tell them of your success
- ❑ *Thank premed adviser for all of his/her help*

Initially, changes in medical school curricula and the institution of accreditation led to a decrease in the number of medical students who graduated. Many failed the more difficult courses. Today, however, nearly all students who enter medical school graduate—which is appropriate, since they are so highly qualified. Medical schools have also added numerous support systems to assist students through their medical education, both academically and emotionally.

Number of Applicants

The number of individuals applying to U.S. medical schools waxes and wanes (figure 1.2). In the 1970s, large numbers of students applied. At that time there were about 2,000 fewer positions than there are today. Subsequently, the number of applicants decreased, to a low in 1988-89. Since then, however, the number of applicants has risen dramatically. There were about 47,000 applicants for 1996-97.

You may wish you had applied to medical school in the least-competitive years—1988 and 1989. Unfortunately (or fortunately), we cannot live in the past and do not know what the future will bring. The cycle that reduced the number of medical school applicants may well repeat itself. Medicine may become less attractive to students due to major changes in health-care-delivery systems or the lack of media hype (television shows and books) glamorizing the career.

If you want to look on the bright side, be thankful that you are not applying to medical school in many European countries where the ratios of first-year medical students to applicants is extraordinarily low (e.g., Norway 1:19.8; Greece 1:16.4; Turkey 1:12.2; France 1:7.8; Portugal 1:7.5; Sweden 1:7.4). This means, for example, in Norway, one out of 19.8 applicants is accepted to medical school.

For the present, however, it is important for you to know the reality of the application process so that you can accurately assess your chance of getting accepted to medical school.

Figure 1.2: Applicants and Acceptance Ratios to U.S. (M.D.) Medical Schools

	Number of Applicants	Number of Applications Submitted	Avg. Number Applications per Person	Number of Accepted Applicants*	Applicant: Acceptance Ratio
1974-75	42,624	362,376	8.5	15,066	2.8
1984-85	35,944	331,937	9.2	17,194	2.1
1985-86	32,893	307,427	9.3	17,228	1.9
1986-87	31,323	295,744	9.4	17,092	1.8
1987-88	28,123	266,900	9.5	17,027	1.7
1988-89	26,721	258,442	9.7	17,108	1.6
1989-90	26,915	262,426	9.7	16,975	1.6
1990-91	29,243	290,489	9.9	17,206	1.7
1991-92	33,301	354,017	10.6	17,436	1.9
1992-93	37,410	405,720	10.8	17,464	2.1
1993-94	42,808	482,788	11.0	17,362	2.5
1994-95	45,365	561,593	12.4	17,317	2.6
1995-96	46,968	595,975	12.8	17,385	2.7

* Some accepted applicants decide not to enter medical school.

Adapted from: Barzansky B, Jonas HS, Etzel SI. Educational programs in U.S. medical schools, 1994-95. *JAMA* 1995;274(9):716-22, and other information.

Number of Positions

There are 20,201 first-year medical school positions available in U.S. and Canadian M.D. schools and U.S. Osteopathic medical schools (figure 1.3).

Medical schools granting M.D. degrees anticipate that the number of available positions will be reduced slightly over the next few years (figure 1.4). The Pew Commission, however, recommends reducing the size of first-year medical school classes by 20% to 25%. If the number of applicants continues to rise, competition for a position will become even greater than it is now.

Medicine—The Promise And The Reality

The Potential Future

It is difficult to predict either the need for or the supply of U.S. physicians in the future—in total or by specialty. While many experts predict an oversupply of physicians around the year 2000, especially in the specialty areas, some suggest that there will be an increasing physician shortage, which will become serious by the year 2011. Factors cited in support of this hypothesis are: (1) the aging of the population; (2) the decreasing workload required of residents; (3) the increasing number of women in medicine (who are documented to spend fewer total lifetime years working in the profession); (4) the increasing number of AIDS and other unknown disease cases; and (5) shorter working hours for all physicians due to the increase in alternative health plans, legislative requirements, and changing life styles.

Figure 1.5 shows estimates of the growth rate over the next ten and twenty years in the major specialties. Note that the number of pathologists and general surgeons is expected to remain

Figure 1.3: Number of Schools and First-Year Positions at U.S. and Canadian Medical Schools

Type of School	Number of Schools	Number 1st-Year Positions[#]
U.S.-M.D.	124 + 1*	16,253
U.S.-Osteopathic	17	2,329
Canadian	16	1,619
Total	**157 + 1**	**20,201**

* The University of Minnesota-Duluth School of Medicine offers only a 2-year curriculum. Students then transfer to the University of Minnesota–Minneapolis to complete their degrees.

[#] The number of available first-year positions for new entrants. There are approximately 800 positions for those repeating the first year.

Adapted from: Barzansky B, Jonas HS, Etzel SI. Educational programs in U.S. medical schools, 1994-95. *JAMA* 1995;274(9):716-22, and other information.

relatively constant between 2000 and 2010. But again, these are only estimates. And, while they are based on projected future needs, they are highly speculative. While a decreasing birth rate may suggest a need for fewer pediatricians, a new health care system that would allow children greater access to care may increase their need. No one knows whether advances in the treatment of coronary artery disease will favor a need for more invasive cardiologists (those who pass catheters under x-ray guidance) rather than for more thoracic surgeons. Changes in both the treatment of chronic renal disease and the government's and public's attitude toward chronic renal dialysis programs will profoundly affect the need for nephrologists. Finding an organic basis for more major psychoses may reduce the need for psychiatrists, while increasing the need for (and effectiveness of) neurologists. And if history is any guide, AIDS will be only one of many epidemics requiring more internists, family physicians, and specialists in infectious diseases. Primary-care physicians will also be gobbled up by health maintenance organizations which, by 1998, will need all residents graduating in primary-care specialties to fill their positions.

Figure 1.4: Anticipated Number of First-Year Positions and Graduates at M.D. Schools–1995-1996 through 1999-2000

	First-Year Class	Graduates
1995-1996	16,156	16,324
1996-1997	16,140	17,274
1997-1998	16,150	16,524
1998-1999	16,142	16,191
1999-2000	16,137	16,106

Adapted from: Barzansky B, Jonas HS, Etzel SI. Educational programs in U.S. medical schools, 1994-95. *JAMA* 1995;274(9):716-22, and other information.

Figure 1.5: Estimated Percentage Increase in Physician Specialties–1991-2000 and 1991-2010

Specialty	Physicians		% Change	
	1991	1995	1991-2000	1991-2010
Pediatric Subspecialties	5,762	6,700	36.5	71.9
Emergency Medicine	15,580	17,800	31.0	58.1
Medical Subspecialties	57,879	64,900	26.0	47.6
Gen Pediatrics	41,038	44,600	20.0	40.3
Anesthesiology	28,901	31,800	21.4	39.9
Gen Internal Medicine	87,658	95,200	19.3	38.2
Radiology	30,178	32,800	18.2	32.6
Obstetrics/Gynecology	35,881	38,400	15.7	30.7
Surgical Subspecialties	73,335	77,900	12.6	19.8
Family/General Practice	73,156	75,700	8.1	17.0
Psychiatry	41,945	43,800	9.4	16.3
Pathology	18,057	18,600	6.4	10.0
Other Specialties	50,341	51,000	3.3	6.7
General Surgery	34,976	35,500	3.2	5.3

Data supplied by the Policy Development Section, American Medical Association, February 1996.

Basically, medicine does not remain static. Rather, it is an ocean of care with many storms and currents. The storms are the major new medical discoveries, new diseases, and changes in the demographics of the population. The currents are the changes in attitudes by both the medical community and the public concerning the popularity of various medical practices. (Yes, unfortunately medicine is guided by more than pure science.) If you become a physician, your ship will sail this ocean. Care, foresight, and a willingness to occasionally alter your course slightly will keep you afloat.

Length of Training

The length of the training required to become a physician may affect your decision about pursuing a medical career. But, the majority of medical students do not make specialty choices based on the length of required training. The pleasure they get out of practicing a specialty in which they are interested generally pays them back for the added preparation.

The length of training does seem to influence some medical students, however, particularly those selecting generalist or support specialties. This influence increases as the student's debt rises, becoming particularly noticeable at debt levels above $75,000. While this may be understandable, it is sad that after so much effort, a life-long career decision may be made on such a flimsy basis.

One point worth noting, however, is that longer training does not always yield higher income. In the medical subspecialties, for example, while gastroenterologists have large incomes because they spend some time specializing, rheumatologists make scarcely more than general internists. This doesn't mean that those who have a calling in rheumatology should not pursue this specialty, only that extra education does not always equal extra income.

Hours Worked

Work hours and lifestyle may also affect your decision whether to become a physician and, later, your decision about which specialty to enter. Medical students often work very long hours during their clinical (third and fourth) years of school. The hours worked during the intern year (now officially called the "first year of residency") can be unbelievably horrible. This varies depending upon the specialty (psychiatry, radiology, and pathology can be pretty easy) and the institution (public hospitals usually have the toughest schedules). During residency, the hours spent in a specialty often mimic the hours practitioners work in that specialty. Although there are official rules that limit the amount of time most residents can work, many programs do not follow the rules.

The hours physicians work markedly influence their family life and extracurricular activities. If you expect to have any life outside of medicine, consider this carefully. Note that much of the time a surgeon or obstetrician spends at work may be "down time" waiting (usually in the middle of the night, on weekends, and on holidays) for an available operating room or for a woman in labor. However, as figure 1.6 shows, the hours worked by different specialists do not correlate with their incomes.

Many specialists now join group practices to decrease their work hours and on-call (available in the hospital or by pager for patient care) time. This has resulted in a large variation in work hours not only among specialties, but also within each individual specialty. Therefore, work hours should not be your only consideration when choosing a career in medicine or a specialty—but do not totally ignore this factor.

Figure 1.6: Average Weekly Work Hours of Specialists Compared to Income*

Specialty	Patient Care	All Professional Activities	Salary
Obstetrics/Gynecology	58.1	63.0	$200,000
Gen Internal Medicine	56.6	63.1	150,000
General Surgery	53.4	59.6	225,000
Radiology	51.9	56.8	240,000
Family Practice	51.9	56.5	110,000
Pediatrics	51.6	58.4	120,000
Anesthesiology	50.5	57.4	220,000
Psychiatry	43.0	50.4	120,000
Pathology	41.2	48.2	170,000

* Median annual income after expenses and before taxes.

Adapted from: American Medical Association. *Socioeconomic Characteristics of Medical Practice, 1995.* Chicago, IL: AMA, 1995, pp. 44, 48, & 148.

Basic Rules For Success

If you decide to pursue a medical career, you can anticipate setbacks and obstacles along the way. One way of mentally preparing yourself for the grind is to consider the following rules that military officers use to survive when in hostile territory:

- Get control of your mind before panic sets in.
- Mentally motivate yourself.
- Think about what you already know about solving the problem.
- Break the problem down into a set of smaller, prioritized steps.
- Don't dwell on past mistakes; concentrate on solving the current problem.
- Mentally prepare yourself for the long haul.
- Negative thinking is a dead end.

The world is generally hostile to premed students. You must have the personal motivation and be willing to repeatedly overcome personal, academic, and bureaucratic obstacles to succeed. If you are willing to do that, you can become a physician.

2: Medicine's Scope: The Specialties

Medicine is the most difficult art to acquire.
All the college can do is teach the student principles based on facts
. . . they simply start him in the right direction;
they do not make him a good practitioner.
That is his own affair.

Sir William Osler

THE MEDICAL PROFESSION IS DIVIDED into numerous areas of expertise, known as "specialties" and "subspecialties." Each of these areas describes a group of physicians with in-depth training in a unique medical field. As you can see from figure 2.2, the array of medical specialties and subspecialties is vast. The list would be even longer if some, such as trauma surgery, were officially approved.

The various specialties are often divided up in several ways that may not be readily apparent: primary care specialties; hospital-based specialties; and the medical and surgical specialties.

Primary care (sometimes called "continuous care") specialties officially include general internal medicine, family practice, general pediatrics, and obstetrics & gynecology. These physicians are supposed to provide first-contact care to patients and then continue that care over time. This area is important because of the federal and state financial support that flows to schools and residency programs that train these specialists. Figure 2.1 lists the factors that indicate if a medical school applicant will probably enter a primary care specialty.

Hospital-based (sometimes called "support") specialties are those which are primarily practiced in hospitals and which often provide assistance to other physicians. These mainly include anesthesiology, emergency medicine, pathology, and radiology. At large institutions, this category also includes critical care, neonatology, and nuclear medicine.

Most physicians have practices that are mainly *medical*, *surgical*, or a combination of the two. Surgical specialties include all areas in which physicians do surgery on an inpatient or outpatient basis (all surgical subspecialties) and neurosurgery, orthopaedic surgery, otolaryngology, and urology. Medical specialties include pediatrics and internal medicine, with all their subspecialties, plus neurology, dermatology, anesthesiology, physical medicine & rehabilitation, psychiatry, and radiation oncology. Emergency medicine and, sometimes, family practice combine the two areas of practice. (See figure 2.3.)

Figure 2.1: Characteristics Associated with Entering a Primary Care Specialty

- Behavioral science/liberal arts major
- Married
- Older
- Preference on admission
- Attended public school
- Received federal scholarship
- Self or spouse from a small town
- "Sensing, feeling, judging" type on Meyers-Briggs-Type Indicator Test
- Tolerance for ambiguity

Medical students often determine which specialty to enter by deciding whether they want to do a medical specialty, a surgical specialty, neither, or both. Once they graduate from medical school, most medical students do a one-year internship (officially called the "first year of residency"), either in a specialty or rotating among several specialties (called a "transitional internship"). If they want to be qualified in a specialty area, this first year is followed by between two and four more years of residency in that specialty. Following their residency training, they may elect to enter a fellowship to get subspecialty training. These fellowships last between one and three years.

Jobs—The Ultimate Goal

Completing medical school and residency seems pointless if you cannot ultimately get a position in your specialty. Some recent graduates, especially in pathology, plastic surgery, and anesthesiology are having that problem (figure 2.4). For multiple reasons, jobs in these and other specialties are becoming harder to find, especially in certain parts of the United States. Physicians now find it most difficult to find positions in the Pacific states (Washington, Oregon, California). The Rocky Mountain and the New England states also seem to need fewer full-time physicians than elsewhere in the nation.

In response, many residency programs plan to reduce the number of training positions over the next few years, although the decrease in positions does not directly correlate with the difficulty in finding jobs. In some cases, these decreases may be due to local funding cuts for residency positions. The specialty may decrease its number of graduates nationally to insure that future graduates will have jobs.

When reviewing these numbers, it is vital to remember that everything, including the need for most specialties, will follow a cycle. Your future cannot be based solely on what is happening now. Rather, you must also anticipate what may happen in the future. Since this is not a very easy task, your ultimate specialty selection will probably be influenced both by changes in health care delivery and by which parts of medical practice you find you like the most.

Figure 2.2: Approved Specialty Boards, Certification and Special Qualification Categories

AMERICAN BOARD	CERTIFICATION	SUBSPECIALTY
Allergy & Immunology	Allergy & Immunology	Clinical & Lab Immun
Anesthesiology	Anesthesiology	Critical Care Medicine Pain Management
Colon & Rectal Surgery		Colon & Rectal Surgery
Dermatology	Dermatology	Dermatopathology Clinical & Lab Derm Immun
Emergency Medicine	Emergency Medicine	Medical Toxicology Pediatric Emergency Med Sports Medicine
Family Practice	Family Practice	Geriatric Medicine Sports Medicine
Internal Medicine	Internal Medicine	Adolescent Medicine Cardiovascular Disease Clin Cardiac Electrophysiology Clinical & Lab Immun Critical Care Medicine Endocrine, Diabetes & Met Gastroenterology Geriatric Medicine Hematology Infectious Diseases Medical Oncology Nephrology Pulmonary Diseases Rheumatology Sports Medicine
Medical Genetics	Clinical Biochemical Genetics Clinical Cytogenetics Clinical Genetics (M.D. only) Clinical Molecular Genetics Medical Genetics	
Neurological Surgery	Neurological Surgery	
Nuclear Medicine	Nuclear Medicine	
Obstetrics & Gynecology	Obstetrics & Gynecology	Critical Care Medicine Gynecologic Oncology Maternal and Fetal Medicine Reproductive Endocrinology
Ophthalmology	Ophthalmology	
Orthopaedic Surgery	Orthopaedic Surgery	Hand Surgery
Otolaryngology	Otolaryngology	Otology/Neurotology Pediatric Otolaryngology

Figure 2.2: Approved Specialty Boards, cont'd.

AMERICAN BOARD	CERTIFICATION	SUBSPECIALTY
Pathology	Anatomic & Clinical Pathology Anatomic Pathology Clinical Pathology	Blood Bank/Transfus Med Chemical Pathology Cytopathology Dermatopathology Forensic Pathology Hematology Immunopathology Medical Microbiology Neuropathology Pediatric Pathology
Pediatrics	Pediatrics	Adolescent Med Clinical & Lab Immun Medical Toxicology Neonatal-Perinatal Med Pediatric Cardiology Ped Critical Care Med Pediatric Emergency Med Pediatric Endocrinology Pediatric Gastroenterology Ped Hematology-Oncology Ped Infectious Diseases Pediatric Nephrology Pediatric Pulmonology Pediatric Rheumatology Sports Medicine
Physical Medicine & Rehabilitation	Physical Medicine & Rehabilitation	Spinal Cord Injury Medicine
Plastic Surgery	Plastic Surgery	Hand Surgery
Preventive Medicine	Aerospace Medicine Occupational Medicine Public Health & General Preventive Med	Medical Toxicology Underseas Med

Psychiatry & Neurology	Psychiatry
	Neurology
	Neurology with Special
	  Qualifications in
	  Child Neurology
		Addiction Psychiatry
		Child & Adolescent Psych
		Clinical Neurophysiology
		Forensic Psychiatry
		Geriatric Psychiatry

Radiology	Radiology Diagnostic Radiology Radiation Oncology Radiological Physics	Neuroradiology Nuclear Radiology Pediatric Radiology Vascular/Interventional Rad
Surgery	Surgery	General Vascular Surgery Pediatric Surgery Surgical Critical Care Surgery of the Hand
Thoracic Surgery	Thoracic Surgery	
Urology	Urology	

Adapted from: American Board of Medical Specialties. *1995 Annual Report & Reference Handbook.* Atlanta, GA: ABMS, 1995.

Figure 2.3: Practicing Physicians' Specialties

Specialty	Total Physicians
Aerospace Medicine	63
Allergy & Immunology	3,729
Anesthesiology	31,816
Cardiovascular Disease	18,437
Child Psychiatry	5,212
Colon & Rectal Surgery	965
Dermatology	8,353
Emergency Medicine	17,744
Family Practice	54,829
Forensic Pathology	472
Gastroenterology	9,087
General Practice	18,454
General Preventive Medicine	1,266
General Surgery	37,902
Internal Medicine	111,427
Medical Genetics	74
Neurology	10,921
Neurological Surgery	4,710
Nuclear Medicine	1,469
Obstetrics & Gynecology	36,649
Occupational Medicine	2,999
Ophthalmology	17,144
Orthopaedic Surgery	21,533
Otolaryngology	8,785
Pathology–Anat/Clin	17,781
Pediatrics	48,113
Pediatric Cardiology	1,244
Physical Medicine and Rehabilitation	5,224
Plastic Surgery	5,206
Psychiatry	37,702
Public Health	1,910
Pulmonary Diseases	7,189
Radiology (All)	27,107
Radiation Oncology	3,493
Thoracic Surgery	2,308
Urology	9,727
Other Specialties	7,643
Others in Practice	21,869

Adapted from: American Medical Association. *AMA Physician Characteristics & Distribution in the U.S.* Chicago, IL: AMA, 1996.

Figure 2.4: Specialties Where New Residency Graduates Have Difficulty Getting Full-Time Jobs* and Specialties That May Reduce Residency Positions

Specialty	Percentage Without Full-Time Jobs in Their Specialty	Percentage That May Reduce Residency Positions[#]
Urology	0.0 %	10.5 %
Emergency Medicine	0.6	1.4
Obstetrics & Gynecology	1.2	3.2
Psychiatry	1.3	19.6
Family Practice	1.4	1.7
Internal Medicine	1.5	10.9
Otolaryngology	1.5	13.4
Geriatrics	1.5	1.9
Pediatrics	2.1	12.1
Critical Care Medicine	2.4	30.2
Diagnostic Radiology	2.6	16.3
Infectious Diseases	3.2	22.9
Hematology	3.3	15.6
Ophthalmology	3.6	18.6
Gastroenterology	3.7	36.4
General Surgery	5.0	6.6
Oncology	5.1	15.6
Endocrinology	5.2	15.2
Nephrology	5.3	13.6
Cardiology	5.4	43.5
Rheumatology	5.5	24.7
Orthopedic Surgery	5.9	5.1
Pulmonary Diseases	6.2	19.2
Anesthesiology	6.6	60.6
Plastic Surgery	9.9	30.7
Pathology	10.8	19.3

* These percentages are only of those who sought full-time positions in their specialties.

[#] Reducing residency positions is anticipated within three years.

Adapted from: Miller RS, Jonas HS, Whitcomb ME. The initial employment status of physicians completing training in 1994. *JAMA* 1996;275(9):708-12.

3: Specialty Descriptions

Legend for Specialty Descriptions

* Entry into a training program is VERY EASY

** Entry into a training program is EASY

*** Entry into a training program is DIFFICULT

**** Entry into a training program is VERY DIFFICULT

***** Entry into a training program is EXTREMELY DIFFICULT

(F) FELLOWSHIP training is required following completion of an initial residency.

ADMINISTRATION *

Administrative medicine, also called Medical Management, designates those physicians whose primary role is as a manager at the departmental, group, clinic, hospital, managed care organization, or health system level. This, as yet unofficial, specialty is developing into a major, and often quite lucrative, field for many physicians. Although some physicians have always assumed administrative duties in helping to run hospitals, medical schools, and private practices, they have done this while continuing to practice medicine. Now, however, physicians are, in increasing numbers, entering the administrative arena exclusively. In part, this is due to the markedly expanded bureaucracy associated with managed care, vertically integrated health-care-delivery systems, and for-profit health care institutions. Some of these physicians are nearing the end of their careers and see this option as a way of "winding down." Others enter these positions to seek a new challenge, because they find that they have untapped talent in these areas, they seek a route to power or increased income, or because clinical medicine is not for them.

Few formal training programs exist for budding physician-managers. Many either have on-the-job training or have advanced degrees, such as a Master of Business Administration (M.B.A.), a Master of Public Health (M.P.H.), or a law degree (J.D.). Some students in combined-degree programs obtain this additional training while in medical school.

For more information, contact:

- American College of Physician Executives, Two Urban Center, Suite 200, 4890 West Kennedy Blvd., Tampa, FL 33609.

AEROSPACE MEDICINE ***

Aerospace medicine is a specialty within preventive medicine. Practitioners are responsible for the medical care and safety of individuals involved in aviation and space travel. This includes both crew members and ground personnel. Most flight surgeons or aviation medical examiners are employed by the Federal Aviation Administration, NASA, the military, or the aerospace industry. They are usually engaged in clinical medicine, research and development, or administration. Medical certification of pilots for flight duty often constitutes a large part of their clinical practice, and most physicians in this field are pilots themselves.

Two years of residency training are required after internship. One of these years must be spent obtaining an advanced degree in a relevant area, usually a master of public health. The second residency year devotes more time to clinical aerospace medicine. A fourth year of training, teaching, practice, and/or research is required to take the board examination. There are two military aerospace medicine programs (Brooks Air Force Base, Texas and Pensacola Naval Air Station, Florida) and one civilian program (Wright State University, Ohio). To be considered as an applicant to the military programs, an individual must already be in the military and be practicing as a flight surgeon.

For more information, contact:

- Aerospace Medical Association, 320 S. Henry Street, Alexandria, VA 22314-3579.

- American College of Preventive Medicine, 1660 L Street, N.W., Suite 206, Washington, DC 20036.

- American Osteopathic College of Preventive Medicine, 1900 The Exchange, Suite 160, Atlanta, GA 30339-2022.

ALLERGY AND IMMUNOLOGY (F) *

Allergy and Immunology is a subspecialty of both internal medicine and pediatrics devoted to the diagnosis and treatment of allergic, asthmatic, and immunologic diseases. The patients seen most frequently by specialists in this field are those with asthma and chronic or seasonal allergies. There is a great deal of art, as well as science, in the practice of the allergist-immunologist. Practitioners get most of their patients through referrals; there is usually very little emergency or night call. Practice opportunities are more restricted than in the past, due to an increasing number of physicians who do allergy testing and treatment. Allergist-Immunologists are mainly office-based and are concentrated in metropolitan areas. Research opportunities in this field are increasing dramatically because of the growing recognition of immunology's role in diseases.

The training in the subspecialty lasts two years after completing either a pediatric or an internal medicine residency. It includes both pediatric and adult diseases. A special qualification in clinical & laboratory immunology requires an extra year of training.

For more information, contact:

- American Academy of Allergy, Asthma, & Immunology, 611 E. Wells Street, Milwaukee, WI 53202.

- American College of Allergy, Asthma, & Immunology, 85 W. Algonquin Road, Suite 550, Arlington Heights, IL 60005.

- American College of Osteopathic Internists, 300 Fifth Street, N.E., Washington, DC 20002.

ANESTHESIOLOGY *

Anesthesiologists give general and regional anesthesia during surgical, obstetric, diagnostic, and therapeutic procedures; function as critical care physicians; and give anesthetic blocks in conjunction with pain clinics. They often specialize in pediatric, neurosurgical, obstetric, cardiothoracic, or ambulatory anesthesiology, although critical care and pain management are the only formal subspecialties. Anesthesiology is a hospital-based specialty with frequent night call. Research is continuing to push the practice of Anesthesia into an ever more elegant and scientific realm. The growing use of less-expensive nurse-anesthetists and a declining number of surgeries has decreased the need for Anesthesiologists. This trend is expected to continue.

Residency programs in anesthesiology start either at the first or second postgraduate year. Training consists of a "base" year, followed by three years of training in clinical anesthesia and critical care. The training is essentially the same for Osteopathic physicians. Training in the subspecialties of anesthesia critical care medicine and anesthesia pain management take a minimum of one year after completing an anesthesia residency.

For more information, contact:

- American Osteopathic College of Anesthesiologists, 17201 E. Highway 40, Suite 204, Independence, MO 64055.

- American Society of Anesthesiologists, 520 N. Northwest Highway, Park Ridge, IL 60068-2573.

CARDIOLOGY (F) **

Cardiologists deal primarily with patients who have diseases of the heart and circulatory system. They both diagnose and treat these diseases. The core of their practice is the medical history and physical diagnosis, frequently augmented by the latest medical technology and medications. Recently, cardiologists have become involved with the angiographic (catheters in arteries) treatment of obstructions of vessels, primarily the coronary arteries. This will be a rapidly expanding area of their practice. Cardiologists are generally office-based, but spend about one-third of their professional time in hospitals. This frequently includes long hours and significant night call.

Between 1965 and 1995, there was more than a seven-fold increase in the number of cardiologists; at this rate the number will nearly double again by 2010. However, since cardiology has been targeted as a specialty with too many practitioners, especially in the highly paid area of invasive cardiology, the number of available training positions will decrease in the future.

Training in cardiology is currently a three-year fellowship following completion of an internal medicine residency. One year is devoted to research. Additional training is necessary for pediatric cardiology or electrophysiology. Post-fellowship training is also available in nuclear cardiology and cardiac catheterization. For Osteopathic physicians, cardiology training follows internship and two years of internal medicine residency.

For more information, contact:

- American College of Cardiology, 9111 Old Georgetown Road, Bethesda, MD 20814-1699.

- American College of Osteopathic Internists, 300 Fifth Street, N.E., Washington, DC 20002.

CHILD AND ADOLESCENT PSYCHIATRY (F) *

Child and Adolescent Psychiatrists diagnose and treat mental, emotional, and behavioral disorders in children, adolescents, and their families. Child psychiatrists work with pediatricians, courts, schools, and social service agencies. They often have both inpatient and outpatient practices, and frequently work as part of multidisciplinary teams.

Fellowships in child and adolescent psychiatry, for both M.D.'s and D.O.'s, consist of two years of child and adolescent psychiatry in addition to at least two years (following internship) of general psychiatry. Child and adolescent psychiatry training can start any time after the internship year, but generally begins after the second year of psychiatry training.

For more information, contact:

- American Academy of Child & Adolescent Psychiatry, 3615 Wisconsin Avenue, N.W., Washington, DC 20016.
- Pediatrics-Psychiatry Joint Training Committee, 111 Silver Cedar Court, Chapel Hill, NC 27514-1651.

CHILD NEUROLOGY (F) *

Child Neurologists diagnose and manage neurological disorders of the infant, child, and adolescent. They treat diseases of the brain, spinal cord, and neuromuscular system. Many such problems are congenital or developmental in nature. Child neurology specialists, most often based at academic medical centers, usually see patients in consultation for primary care physicians.

Before entering this training, applicants must have completed at least two years of a pediatric residency. Training in child neurology then takes an additional three years.

For more information, contact:

- American Academy of Neurology, 2221 University Ave., S.E., Ste 335, Minneapolis, MN 55414.
- Child Neurology Society, 3900 Northwoods Drive, Ste 175, Saint Paul, MN 55112-6966.

COLON AND RECTAL SURGERY (F) ****

Colon and Rectal surgeons diagnose and treat disorders of the intestinal tract, rectum, anal canal, and perianal areas that are amenable to surgical treatment. They are involved not only in operative treatment, but also in diagnostic procedures, including colonoscopy. Most patients seen by these specialists are referred by other physicians. Most practitioners in this specialty are found in medium to large cities. The training consists of a complete residency in general surgery followed by a one-year fellowship in colon and rectal surgery.

While there are no training programs in this specialty for Osteopath physicians, the more limited specialty of proctology, consisting of two years of training after internship, is available.

For more information, contact:

- American Osteopathic College of Proctology, 1020 Galloping Hill Road, Union, NJ 07083.
- American Society of Colon & Rectal Surgeons, 85 Algonquin Road, Suite 550, Arlington Heights, IL 60005.

CRITICAL CARE (F) **

Critical Care physicians work in hospital intensive care units managing critically ill medical and surgical patients. The practice requires both a broad knowledge of the medical and surgical conditions that cause patients to be in the intensive care unit, and a specialized knowledge of the respiratory, fluid, and cardiovascular management needed to maintain these patients. Many critical care physicians alternate their duties in the critical care unit with practice in their primary specialties. The majority of critical care physicians in adult units are Internists, most commonly specialists in pulmonary diseases. Night call or night duty in the intensive care unit is common. Most individuals in this specialty are located in large cities.

Training ranges from a six-month (not eligible for any certification) to a three-year fellowship following completion of the primary residency. At present, there appears to be a much greater need for critical care specialists than the number available.

For more information, contact:

- American College of Osteopathic Internists, 300 Fifth Street, N.E., Washington, DC 20002.
- Society of Critical Care Medicine, 8101 E. Kaiser Blvd., Anaheim Hills, CA 92808-2259.

DERMATOLOGY *****

Dermatologists deal with patients who have both acute and chronic disorders of the skin. They diagnose skin lesions and use both chemotherapeutic agents and surgery to effect cures. Dermatologists get referrals from other physicians and from patients who refer themselves. There is very little night call and very rarely an inpatient service associated with a dermatology practice. Under managed care plans, many patients who once would have been referred to dermatologists are now being treated by primary care practitioners, decreasing the need for dermatologists. Dermatology residencies are three years following initial training. Several programs require the prior completion of a residency in another specialty.

For more information, contact:

- American Academy of Dermatology, 930 N. Meacham Road, Schaumburg, IL 60172-4965.
- American Osteopathic College of Dermatology, P.O. Box 7525, Kirksville, MO 63501-7525.

EMERGENCY MEDICINE *****

Emergency physicians deal with the entire spectrum of acute illness and injury in all age groups. Hands-on physical diagnosis and the use of both medical and surgical therapeutic modalities are an integral part of the specialty. Emergency physicians are trained to stabilize patients with acute injuries and to deal with life-threatening conditions. Hours are long, but schedules are fixed in advance. There is rarely a call schedule outside of assigned working hours. Emergency physicians are mainly hospital-based. Most practitioners in the specialty work in medium to large cities. Many new emergency medicine opportunities are available at academic centers and in research. All sources agree that there will still be a shortage of emergency physicians in the year 2025.

Training is three to four years in length. Students can also enter five-year combined-training programs in emergency medicine-internal medicine and emergency medicine-pediatrics. Fellowships following residency include medical toxicology, pediatric emergency medicine, and sports medicine.

For more information, contact:

- American College of Emergency Physicians, P.O. Box 619911, Dallas, TX 75261-9911.
- American College of Osteopathic Emergency Physicians, 142 East Ontario Street, Suite 218, Chicago, IL 60611-2818.
- Society for Academic Emergency Medicine, 901 North Washington, Lansing, MI 48906-5137.

ENDOCRINOLOGY, DIABETES AND METABOLISM (F) *

Endocrinologists treat patients with diseases of the endocrine (glandular) system and with a wide variety of hormonal abnormalities. The most common diseases include diabetes mellitus, high lipid (blood fats or cholesterol) levels, and thyroid disorders. Patients are often referred to endocrinologists for failure to grow, early or late puberty, excess hair growth, high calcium levels, osteoporosis, pituitary tumors, or reproductive problems. Endocrinologists also consult in the rapidly growing areas of nutrition and metabolism. This includes helping with post-operative and chronic-disease patients who need extra nutritional support. Many endocrinologists also participate in clinical or basic science research. Training is two years following an internal medicine residency. For Osteopathic physicians, training follows internship and two years of internal medicine residency.

For more information, contact:

- American College of Osteopathic Internists, 300 Fifth Street, N.E., Washington, DC 20002.
- Endocrine Society, 9650 Rockville Pike, Bethesda, MD 20814.

FAMILY PRACTICE **

Family physicians treat entire families, as did the general practitioners of the past. They spend more than 90% of their time in direct patient care. Their practice varies with the extent of their training, interests, area of the country, the number of other medical practitioners in their locale, and the rules of their local hospitals. Family physicians practice medicine mostly in an outpatient setting. They provide primary care to a diverse population, unlimited by the patient's age, sex, organ system affected, or disease. They usually have a significant number of both pediatric and geriatric patients. Delivering babies, although always a part of the training, is not always a part of the practice: due to the rising cost of professional liability insurance and the irregular hours involved, among other factors, many family physicians now severely limit this aspect of their practices. They also address the behavioral aspects of medicine, including family life-cycle events (birth, stress, grief), and render other psychological services.

Most family physicians enter group practices, and nearly three-quarters participate in some type of managed health-care-delivery system (HMO, PPO, IPA). Many have assumed the often-uncomfortable role of "gatekeeper" or "case manager" within these systems and end up allocating services to patients. The average family physician works 57 hours per week, with 69% of their time spent on office visits, 13% on hospital rounds, 14% on other patient visits, and 4% doing surgical/manipulative procedures. There is currently a shortage of family physicians, who are increasingly in demand in managed-care systems and rural areas. Part of the reason for this shortage is that the specialty suffers from a lack of recognition, both publicly and professionally. And, while many family physicians work longer hours than their colleagues and often must know how to treat a broader range of medical problems, their remuneration is lower. Physicians in this field get satisfaction from providing continuity of care to patients, in the context of their entire family, throughout the various stages of life.

The training requires three years. (Ten medical schools now have programs in which students in special tracks can combine three years of medical school with three years of residency, decreasing the total time spent training by one year.) Osteopathic residencies are generally two years following internship. About ten percent of family physicians specialize. Family practice graduates (M.D.'s) can take geriatric medicine or sports medicine fellowships following initial residency training. Osteopathic graduates can take a two-year geriatrics fellowship after their first year of family practice residency, or a two-year osteopathic manipulative medicine fellowship after completing residency.

For more information, contact:

- American Academy of Family Physicians, 8880 Ward Parkway, Kansas City, MO 64114.
- American College of Osteopathic Family Physicians, 330 East Algonquin Road, Suite 2, Arlington Heights, IL 60005.

GASTROENTEROLOGY (F) **

Gastroenterologists are internists who specifically deal with diseases of the esophagus, stomach, small and large intestines, liver, pancreas, and gallbladder. A large number of their patients have ulcer disease or chronic diseases of the liver, intestinal tract, or pancreas. Recent advances in endoscopy have increased the number of procedures that gastroenterologists perform. Gastroenterologists are predominantly office-based. They do take some night call and many have active inpatient services. The field of gastroenterology grew about eleven-fold between 1965 and 1995; it is still growing rapidly and has been targeted as an over-populated specialty. The specialty's leaders are considering a 50% decrease in available training positions.

A subspecialty of internal medicine, its training consists of a two-year fellowship following completion of an internal medicine residency. For Osteopathic physicians, training follows internship and two years of internal medicine residency.

For more information, contact:

- American College of Gastroenterology, 4900-B South 31st Street, Arlington, VA 22206-1656.
- American College of Osteopathic Internists, 300 Fifth Street, N.E., Washington, DC 20002.

GERIATRIC MEDICINE (F) *

Geriatric medicine is a primary care subspecialty that deals with the complex medical and psychosocial problems of older adults. Due to the significant growth of the country's elderly population, the demand for geriatric physicians is rapidly increasing. Conservative projections estimate the need for up to 2,100 academic geriatricians and up to 30,000 geriatric clinicians by the year 2000. Currently, only about 1,300 physicians have completed geriatrics fellowship training. There are far fewer geriatricians than are needed currently and the demand is expected to vastly increase.

While one-third of all patients that Internists see are over sixty-five years old, nearly half of geriatricians' patients are older than seventy-five years old.

Opportunities exist in academic medicine and research, corporate (HMO) medicine, community medicine, long-term care, and private practice. At present, however, most graduates of geriatric medicine and geriatric psychiatry fellowships hold academic faculty appointments, although relatively few do research or publish. The specialist in geriatrics must be able to work within a multispecialty team consisting of both medical and non-medical personnel. Most specialists begin from a base of training in family practice, internal medicine, or psychiatry. Some of the programs operate jointly, with both the internal medicine and family practice programs participating. Fellowships of varying length, either in geriatric medicine (programs accredited by the Accreditation Council for Graduate Medical Education [ACGME] must currently be two years in length) or geriatric psychiatry are now being offered at many sites.

For more information, contact:

- American Academy of Family Physicians, 8880 Ward Parkway, Kansas City, MO 64114.
- American College of Osteopathic Internists, 300 Fifth Street, N.E., Washington, DC 20002.

- American Geriatric Society, 770 Lexington Avenue, Suite 300, New York, NY 10021.
- American Association for Geriatric Psychiatry, 7910 Woodmont Avenue, 7th Floor, Bethesda, MD 20814.

HAND SURGERY (F) **

Hand surgeons primarily treat diseases of and injuries to the hand and forearm. Nearly all hand surgeons have training in either orthopaedic surgery or plastic surgery. Advances in the specialty have come with development of new microsurgical techniques. Some hand surgeons do reimplantation surgery after traumatic amputations. One benefit of hand surgery is that it is usually done sitting down. Much of the surgery is now done on outpatients. Fellowship training in hand surgery lasts one year after a residency in orthopaedic surgery, plastic surgery, or general surgery.

For more information, contact:

- American Academy of Orthopaedic Surgeons, 6300 N. River Road, Rosemont, IL 60078-4226.
- American College of Osteopathic Surgeons, 123 N. Henry Street, Alexandria, VA 22314-2309.
- American Association for Hand Surgery, 444 East Algonquin Road, Suite 120, Arlington Heights, IL 60005.
- American Society for Surgery of the Hand, 6060 Greenwood Plaza Blvd., Suite 100, Englewood, CO 80111-4801.

HEMATOLOGY-ONCOLOGY (F) **

Although separate specialties, hematology (the diagnosis and treatment of diseases of the blood) and oncology (the diagnosis and treatment of patients with cancer) are often combined in both training and practice. This specialty's patients, once seen as victims of hopeless diseases, now can frequently be offered significant life-extending treatments.

The specialty is predominantly office-based, but practitioners often have a large primary or consultative inpatient service. Night call and emergencies can be frequent. Most specialists in this field reside in medium to large cities. Hematologists and oncologists are drawn from the specialties of pediatrics and internal medicine. Training in either hematology or oncology is usually a two-year fellowship following completion of an Internal medicine or pediatric residency. Many programs combine the two specialties into three-year fellowships. For Osteopathic physicians, training follows internship and two years of internal medicine residency.

For more information, contact:

- American College of Osteopathic Internists, 300 Fifth St., N.E., Washington, DC 20002.
- American Society of Clinical Oncology, 435 North Michigan Avenue, Suite 1717, Chicago, IL 60611-4067.
- American Society of Hematology, 1200 19th St., N.W., Ste 300, Washington, DC 20036-2412.

INFECTIOUS DISEASES (F) *

Infectious disease specialists deal with the diagnosis and treatment of contagious diseases. With the introduction of antibiotics, the specialty was thought to be on the edge of extinction. It is now making a large comeback due to the great diversity of drug-resistant bacteria and the AIDS epidemic. Infectious disease specialists act as consultants to other physicians. Many are also involved in research, and most work in major medical centers. With the increased incidence of nosocomial infections, many infectious disease specialists now work part-time as hospital infection control officers. Physicians in this subspecialty generally receive lower salaries than those in specialties which are more procedure-oriented. Many infectious disease specialists also practice general internal medicine. Training consists of a two-year fellowship following completion of an internal medicine residency. For Osteopathic physicians, training follows internship and two years of an internal medicine residency.

For more information, contact:

- American College of Osteopathic Internists, 300 Fifth Street, N.E., Washington, DC 20002.
- Infectious Disease Society of America, 1200 19th Street, N.W., Ste 300, Washington, DC 20036-2401.

INTERNAL MEDICINE **

Internists (specialists in Internal Medicine, not to be confused with interns) are divided into general internists and subspecialists in internal medicine (see the subspecialties listed under "Internal Medicine" in figure 2.2). The general internist provides longitudinal care to adult patients with both acute and chronic diseases. In rural areas, the general internist often acts as a consultant to other practitioners on complex medical cases. In suburban and urban areas, however, other primary care practitioners frequently consult with internal medicine subspecialists; surgical specialists consult with both General and subspecialty internists. urban general internists provide primary health care and treat non-surgical diseases such as diabetes, hypertension, and congestive heart failure on both an inpatient and an outpatient basis. They are also very active in managed care plans, such as HMOs.

Students attracted to general internal medicine seek an intellectual challenge, have an interest in primary care, and often have had positive experiences during their third-year internal medicine rotations. The field of general internal medicine has recently become of more interest to graduating medical students, although internists' incomes remain lower than that of either the average physician or internal medicine subspecialists. Many students avoid general internal medicine because they perceive that practitioners have relatively low prestige, mainly care for chronically ill patients, and are overworked, unhappy, and underrewarded. At the same time, growth of managed care plans and societal pressure to enhance primary care have led to increased job opportunities for general internists.

Internal medicine is often described as "less procedural and more cerebral" than other specialties. While this may be true for general internists, it is not true of the procedurally oriented subspecialists in gastroenterology, critical care, pulmonary diseases, and cardiology. The average internist (general and subspecialists) has a 63-hour work week, with 49% of the time spent in office visits, 27% spent on hospital rounds, 21% on other patient care activities, and 3% spent doing surgical/manipulative procedures.

Training in internal medicine takes three years. If an Osteopathic graduate enters an internal medicine (specialty-specific) internship, his internal medicine training time is shortened by one year. One of the advantages of internal medicine training is the number of options available following residency. About 58% of all internal medicine residency graduates go on to subspecialize. Many physicians do not finalize their decision to practice as either general internists or subspecialists until well into their residency. Following residency, fellowships are available in: adolescent medicine; cardiovascular disease; clinical cardiac electrophysiology; critical care medicine; clinical & laboratory immunology; endocrinology, diabetes & metabolism; gastroenterology; geriatric medicine; hematology; infectious diseases; medical oncology; nephrology; pulmonary diseases; rheumatology; and sports medicine.

For more information, contact:

- American College of Osteopathic Internists, 300 Fifth Street, N.E., Washington, DC 20002.
- American College of Physicians, Independence Mall West, Sixth Street at Race, Philadelphia, PA 19106-1572.
- American Society of Internal Medicine, 2011 Pennsylvania Avenue, N.W., Suite 800, Washington, DC 20006-1808.
- Society of General Internal Medicine, 700 13th Street, N.W., Suite 250, Washington, DC 20005.

INTERNAL MEDICINE–PEDIATRICS ***

Combined internal medicine–pediatrics training programs are designed for the individual who wishes to practice primary care without offering obstetric and surgical services. The training is four years in length, with a minimum of twenty months of internal medicine. Programs, for the most part, integrate blocks of internal medicine and pediatrics. This often demands nearly two years of internship. Completion of combined programs makes the individual eligible to take the specialty board examinations in both pediatrics and internal medicine.

For more information, contact:

- American Board of Internal Medicine, 3624 Market St., Philadelphia, PA 19104-2675.
- American Board of Pediatrics, 111 Silver Cedar Court, Chapel Hill, NC 27514.

MEDICAL GENETICS *

Medical genetics is the newest medical specialty. Currently, relatively few physicians have been certified in clinical genetics or a laboratory subspecialty (clinical biochemical genetics, clinical molecular genetics, clinical cytogenetics, and M.D. clinical genetics) practice in the field. Most of them come from pediatrics, obstetrics & gynecology, or internal medicine. While the field is still quite small, rapid changes occurring in clinical genetics suggest that the future demand for these practitioners will be greater. Training in the specialty requires two years in another medical specialty before admission to two or more additional years of training in medical genetics.

For more information, contact:

- American Society of Human Genetics, 9650 Rockville Pike, Bethesda, MD 20814-3998.

MEDICAL INFORMATICS *

Medical informatics specialists, who deal with the interaction of medicine and computers, are just coming into their own as in-demand practitioners. Most physicians in this area have "day jobs," although some now work full time in the area. In the near future, though, more physicians with computer expertise will choose medical informatics as their full-time specialty. They are needed in nearly every area of medicine, but there are few who are truly qualified. Medical informatics is becoming an essential part of every physician's practice and continued learning. Its effects are already being seen in computer-assisted diagnosis and therapy, and in patient-data-retrieval systems. Revolutionary computer-aided educational systems will, in the future, completely change the nature of medical education. This specialty will be at the forefront of dramatic changes in research, including ways of gathering and handling more accurate epidemiological data. It will also provide new ethical dilemmas as previously private personal medical records become ever more public.

For more information, contact:

- Center for Applied Medical Informatics, MSU-Kalamazoo Center for Medical Studies, 1000 Oakland Drive, Kalamazoo, MI 49008-1284.

MEDICAL TOXICOLOGY (F) **

Medical toxicologists diagnose, treat, and consult on a wide variety of intentional, accidental, and industrial poisonings. Many work with regional poison control centers, supervising and monitoring their work. They consult with other physicians whose patients have unusual or complicated poisonings or envenomations. Some also care for their own patients, often in intensive care units or in toxicology clinics. Toxicology clinic patients often need complicated evaluations for industrial exposures. Toxicology fellowship programs are usually administered by emergency medicine or pediatric departments, and residents may enter these fellowships after completing training in either of these specialties or a preventive medicine residency.

For more information, contact:

- American Board of Pediatrics, 111 Silver Cedar Court, Chapel Hill, NC 27514-1651.
- American Board of Preventive Medicine, 9950 W. Lawrence Avenue, Suite 106, Schiller Park, IL 60176.
- American College of Emergency Physicians, P.O. Box 619911, Dallas, TX 75261-9911.
- Society for Academic Emergency Medicine, 901 North Washington, Lansing, MI 48906-5137.
- Society of Toxicology, 1767 Business Center Drive, Suite 302, Reston, VA 22090-5332.

NEONATAL–PERINATAL MEDICINE (F) **

Neonatologists treat the problems associated with premature births. They practice in neonatal intensive care units on those neonates who do not yet have the capacity to live without medical assistance. As with other critical care specialists, they must be able to skillfully perform procedures—but they must do them on *very* tiny babies: The size of the infants they work with has progressively decreased. Neonatologists work closely with specialized teams of nurses, social workers, and respiratory therapists. They also work closely with families to sort out both medical and ethical issues of care. These fellowships are two years in length following a pediatric residency.

For more information, contact:

- American Academy of Pediatrics, P.O. Box 927, 141 Northwest Point Road, Elk Grove Village, IL 60009-0927.
- American College of Osteopathic Pediatricians, 5301 Wisconsin Avenue, N.W., Washington, DC 20075.

NEPHROLOGY (F) *

Nephrologists diagnose and treat diseases of the kidney and the urinary system. Most of their patients have chronic diseases requiring long-term care. Managing dialysis, and treating dialysis and renal transplant patients form a large part of most nephrologists' practices. The specialty is predominantly office-based, however, practitioners may have large primary or consultative inpatient services. Night call can be frequent. Training is generally a two-year fellowship following the completion of an internal medicine residency. For Osteopathic physicians, training follows internship and two years of an Internal medicine residency.

For more information, contact:

- American College of Osteopathic Internists, 300 Fifth Street, N.E., Washington, DC 20002.
- American Society of Nephrology, 1200 19th Street, N.W., Suite 300, Washington, DC 20036.

NEUROLOGICAL SURGERY *****

Neurosurgeons provide operative and non-operative management of lesions of the brain, spinal cord, peripheral nerves, and their supporting structures (skull, spine, meninges, and CNS blood supply). Many are also involved in pain management. This requires much manual dexterity and a willingness to accept both dramatic successes and long-term failures in patient care. New developments in autologous and fetal tissue transplantation and in stereotactic surgery for epilepsy, Parkinson's Disease, and tumors may increase the need for neurosurgeons during the next decade. Patients range in age from neonates to the elderly. Night call and emergency surgery are frequent.

Residency training lasts five years following one year of general surgery. A minimum of 36 months of training must be spent in clinical neurosurgery and 3 months in clinical neurology. The balance of time can be spent in the study of relevant basic sciences, such as neuropathology and neuroradiology, or of other related fields, such as pediatric neurosurgery or spinal surgery. The areas covered during these extra months are the key differences among this specialty's training programs.

For more information, contact:

- American Association of Neurological Surgeons, 22 S. Washington Street, Suite 100, Park Ridge, IL 60068.
- American College of Osteopathic Surgeons, 123 N. Henry Street, Alexandria, VA 22314-2903.
- Society of Neurological Surgeons, 750 Washington Street, Suite 178, Boston, MA 02111.

NEUROLOGY *

Neurologists diagnose and treat patients with diseases of the brain, spinal cord, peripheral nerves, and neuromuscular system. Much of their practice deals with the diagnosis, and increasingly the treatment, of patients seen in consultation. Many of these patients have headaches, strokes, seizure disorders, or chronic neuromuscular diseases. It is anticipated that the need for neurologists will increase as the population ages. The specialty is predominantly office-based. Neurologists may, however, have large primary or consultative inpatient services. Night call can be frequent, especially in solo or small group practices.

Training is three years after an internship, most often in internal medicine, pediatrics, family practice, or a transitional program. Some neurology programs have their own first year and so are four years long. Training programs are similar for Osteopathic physicians.

For more information, contact:

- American Academy of Neurology, 2221 University Ave., S.E., Ste 335, Minneapolis, MN 55414.
- American Neurological Association, 5841 Cedar Lake Road, Suite 108, Minneapolis, MN 55416-1491.

- American Osteopathic Board of Neurology & Psychiatry, 104 Hardin Lane, Suite B, Somerset, KY 42501.

NUCLEAR MEDICINE*

Specialists in nuclear medicine use radioactive materials to both diagnose and treat diseases by imaging the body's physiologic function. The field combines medical practice with certain aspects of the physical sciences, including physics, mathematics, statistics, computer science, chemistry, and radiation biology. Specialists in nuclear medicine, unlike those in radiation oncology, use radioactive materials that are "unsealed," i.e., free in the bloodstream, for their diagnostic studies and treatments. At some institutions they are also responsible for performing radioimmunoassay tests. Practitioners in the specialty have no primary patient care responsibility and little night call. Many individuals who are currently practicing nuclear medicine have been neither formally trained nor certified in the specialty. However, anyone currently entering the field is expected to have been fully trained. The specialty may become either very dynamic or rather static in the future, depending upon how rapidly some currently innovative techniques become available to it.

Training consists of two years of nuclear medicine following, interspersed with, or, in a few cases, preceding two years of initial training in a clinical specialty. These are most commonly radiology, internal medicine, or pathology. Osteopathic programs also accept two years of initial training in family practice. Nuclear medicine is a specialty distinct from nuclear radiology.

For more information, contact:

- American College of Nuclear Medicine, 1200 19th St., N.W., Ste 300, Washington, DC 20036.
- American Osteopathic Board of Nuclear Medicine, 5200 S. Ellis Avenue, Chicago, IL 60615.
- Society of Nuclear Medicine, 1850 Samuel Morse Drive, Reston, VA 22090-5316.

OBSTETRICS & GYNECOLOGY ****

Obstetrician-Gynecologists manage pregnancies and treat disorders of the female reproductive tract. Obstetricians deal with pregnancy and fertility in women. Gynecologists deal with medical and surgical diseases of the female reproductive tract not involving pregnancy. While some specialists in this field work primarily in one or the other area, most work in both. This specialty has been affected more than any other by the increasing cost of medical liability insurance and the increasing propensity to sue physicians. Due to this increased legal risk, most obstetricians are eliminating deliveries from their practice or are reducing the provision of care to patients who have, or are likely to have, high-risk pregnancies. As the population ages and awareness of women's health care needs increases, there will be a greater need for gynecologists. The specialty combines both surgical and non-surgical approaches to disease. The average obstetrician-gynecologist, in a 63-hour week, spends 53% of the time seeing patients in the office, 30% in surgery or deliveries, 10% on hospital rounds, and 7% on other patient visits. Obstetrics & gynecology is primarily office-based, but there can be a sizable inpatient-service load. A busy obstetric practice has considerable emergency and night call. An increasing number of women are entering this field.

The basic training in obstetrics & gynecology is four years following medical school. If Osteopathic graduates enter an obstetrics-gynecology (specialty-specific) internship, their obstetrics & gynecology training time is shortened by one year. Following residency, physicians can take subspecialty fellowships in reproductive endocrinology, more commonly known as fertility, or in gynecologic oncology, which requires extra surgical training. Maternal and fetal medicine is the newest of the subspecialty areas, in which physicians treat the developing child *in utero*.

For more information, contact:

- American College of Obstetricians & Gynecologists, 409 12th Street, S.W., Washington, DC 20024-2188.
- American College of Osteopathic Obstetricians & Gynecologists, 5200 South Ellis Avenue, Chicago, IL 60615.

OCCUPATIONAL MEDICINE **

Occupational medicine is one of the specialties of preventive medicine. It focuses on the effects that specific occupations have on health. Occupational physicians work in industry, teaching hospitals, government, and occupational health clinics. As positions in industry have decreased, those trained or interested in occupational medicine have increasingly opted for private practice within occupational health clinics. Specialists rarely take night call or have inpatient responsibilities. Training consists of two or three years following internship. Part of the time is used to earn a graduate degree in an appropriate area, usually a Master of Public Health. A fourth year of training, teaching, practice, and/or research is required to take the board examination.

For more information, contact:

- American College of Occupational and Environmental Medicine, 55 W. Seegers Road, Arlington Heights, IL 60005.
- American College of Preventive Medicine, 1660 L St., N.W., Ste 206, Washington, DC 20036.
- American Osteopathic College of Preventive Medicine, 5200 S. Ellis Ave., Chicago, IL 60615.

OPHTHALMOLOGY ***

Ophthalmologists prevent, diagnose, and treat the diseases and abnormalities of the eye and periocular structures. A combination of office-based medical practice and surgical treatment of eye diseases makes this one of the most popular and competitive specialties. Ophthalmologists treat patients of all ages, often using high-technology equipment in both diagnosis and therapy. Patients are usually seen on an outpatient basis. Many ophthalmologists take some night call, but they rarely have to go into the hospital after hours. Inpatient services represent a small proportion of their practice. Since optometrists now do many of the functions once reserved for ophthalmologists, the field is rapidly becoming over-staffed.

The training consists of three years following an internship. Fellowship positions are offered in cornea, glaucoma, neuro-ophthalmology, pediatric ophthalmology, and retina-vitreous, among others.

For more information, contact:

- American Academy of Ophthalmology, 655 Beach Street, San Francisco, CA 94109.
- American Osteopathic Colleges of Ophthalmology, Otorhinolaryngology, and Head & Neck Surgery, 3 MacKoil Ave., Dayton, OH 45403.

ORTHOPAEDIC SURGERY *****

Orthopaedic surgeons treat diseases and injuries of the spine and the extremities. They use surgery, medications, and physical therapy to preserve maximal function of the musculoskeletal system. Much orthopaedic surgery that was once done on an inpatient basis is now done as ambulatory surgery. Individuals who go into this specialty like to work with their hands. Many have hobbies such as woodworking that emphasize this, and the majority are sports-oriented. Many orthopaedic surgeons continue to take night and emergency call during their entire careers.

Training consists of one year in a broad medical specialty followed by four years of orthopaedics. Both subspecialty training and certification are available in hand surgery. One-year fellowship positions also exist in musculoskeletal oncology, orthopaedic sports medicine, pediatric orthopaedics, orthopaedic trauma, adult reconstructive orthopaedics, and surgery of the spine.

For more information, contact:

- American Academy of Orthopaedic Surgeons, 6300 N. River Road, Rosemont, IL 60018-4226.

- American College of Osteopathic Surgeons, 123 N. Henry Street, Alexandria, VA 22314-2903.

OTOLARYNGOLOGY *****

Otolaryngologists, or Head and Neck Surgeons, specialize in the evaluation and treatment of medical and surgical problems of the head and neck region, including disorders of the ears, upper respiratory tract, and upper GI tract. The specialty is frequently referred to as ENT (Ear, Nose, & Throat). Physicians in this specialty have substantial office practices, with varying amounts of surgery. The majority of head and neck surgery is now performed in an ambulatory surgery setting, so most practitioners have few inpatients. Since managed-care organizations have targeted some of this specialty's common procedures, such as tympanotomies, for decreased use, this field may quickly become over-staffed.

Training consists of one or two years of general surgery followed by three or four years of ENT training. Fellowships and certification are available in otology/neurotology and pediatric otolaryngology. Additional fellowships are available in facial plastic and reconstructive surgery and in head and neck cancer surgery. About 25% of all residency graduates take additional fellowship training.

Most Osteopathic programs combine otolaryngology and facial plastic surgery.

For more information, contact:

- American Academy of Otolaryngology–Head and Neck Surgery, 1 Prince Street, Alexandria, VA 22314-3357.

- American Osteopathic Colleges of Ophthalmology, Otorhinolaryngology, and Head & Neck Surgery, 3 MacKoil Ave., Dayton, OH 45403.

PATHOLOGY *

Pathologists are laboratory-based physicians who are often referred to as the "doctor's doctor." They act as consultants for other physicians, helping them to determine the nature of disease in tissue, body fluids, or entire organism. They apply basic scientific methods to the detection of disease, but generally have little or no direct contact with (live) patients. Their interactions are with other physicians. Pathologists' lives are generally low-key and there is little in-hospital night call.

The field is divided into the areas of *anatomic pathology* (i.e., autopsies), cytopathology, surgical pathology (gross and microscopic pathology), and *clinical pathology*, i.e., hematology, microbiology, clinical chemistry, and blood banking/transfusion medicine. Most pathologists, especially the anatomic pathologists, are hospital-based. Many pathologists are also researchers and teachers in university medical centers/medical schools—frequently while maintaining active pathology practices. In the past, the income has been very generous—especially for clinical pathology. However, changes in reimbursement have decreased their incomes. Many recent pathology residency graduates have had difficulty finding desirable positions.

A residency can be taken separately in either clinical pathology or anatomic pathology (three years), or the two can be combined (four years). Positions available for subspecialty training following the initial residency include: neuropathology, immunopathology, forensic pathology, dermatopathology, blood banking/transfusion medicine, chemical pathology, hematology, selective pathology, cytopathology, and medical microbiology.

For more information, contact:

- American Osteopathic College of Pathologists, 12368 NW 13th Ct, Pembroke Pines, FL 33026.
- American Society of Clinical Pathologists, 2100 W. Harrison St., Chicago, IL 60612.
- College of American Pathologists, 325 Waukegan Road, Northfield, IL 60093-2750.

PEDIATRIC SURGERY (F) *****

Pediatric surgeons diagnose and treat surgical diseases in children. Depending upon their training, they deal with abdominal, urological, and thoracic problems, as well as multiple trauma. Because of the volume of patients that is needed to support such a specialized practice, most pediatric surgeons live in moderate- or large-size cities, and are associated with major medical centers. Since this is a subspecialty of general surgery, applicants for training must first complete a general surgery residency. The training in pediatric surgery is two years in length.

For more information, contact:

- American Pediatric Surgical Association, 750 Terrado Plaza, Ste. 119, Covina, CA 91723-3619.

PEDIATRICS ***

Pediatricians take care of pediatric patients. While that may sound circular, it is the only way to describe many pediatric practices. Pediatricians may at one time have dealt primarily with children, but they have now expanded their scope of practice to include adolescents and young adults. Patients from 12 to 21 years old make up 22% of the average pediatrician's practice. And in some cases, pediatricians provide continuing care to patients with illnesses, such as cystic fibrosis, that were in the past uniformly fatal during childhood. They do a great amount of well-child and preventive care. And recently, they have the often uncomfortable role of "gatekeepers" or "case managers" for prepaid health plans. In this position, they determine their patients' access to care.

Due to the shrinking pediatric population, this specialty may become over-populated. Today, fewer pediatricians opt for private practice, and two-thirds work in group practices. Pediatricians rarely experience the intensive exposure to ill children seen by residents and medical students during their training. Office-based for the most part, they rarely use surgical techniques such as suturing or fracture reduction. The average pediatrician, in a 58-hour work week, spends 55% of the time in office visits, 21% in non-clinical care activities, 16% on hospital rounds, 6% on other patient visits, and 2% doing surgical/manipulative procedures. Pediatrics is one of the lowest paid medical specialties, averaging about $100,000 per year before taxes. Most pediatricians choose this field, nevertheless, because they love working with children.

Initial pediatric residency training is three years. Following that, about 38% of all graduates go on to specialize. Subspecialty training (each two to three years long) is available in: medical toxicology, neonatal-perinatal medicine, pediatric cardiology, pediatric critical care, pediatric emergency medicine, pediatric endocrinology, pediatric gastroenterology, pediatric hematology-oncology, pediatric nephrology, and pediatric pulmonology. Fellowships are also available in adolescent medicine, allergy-immunology, pediatric infectious diseases, and pediatric rheumatology. Pediatric neurology training can be started after two years of pediatric residency.

Combined internal medicine–pediatrics training programs are described under "Internal Medicine–Pediatrics". There are also programs lasting five years in emergency medicine–pediatrics and pediatrics–psychiatry–child psychiatry.

For more information, contact:

- American Academy of Pediatrics, 141 Northwest Point Rd., Elk Grove Village, IL 60007-0927.
- American College of Osteopathic Pediatricians, 5301 Wisconsin Avenue, N.W., Suite 630, Washington, DC 20015.
- American Pediatric Society, P.O. Box 675, Elk Grove Village, IL 60009-0675.

PHYSICAL MEDICINE AND REHABILITATION *

Physiatrists (specialists in physical medicine and rehabilitation, or PM&R) diagnose, evaluate, and treat patients with impairments or disabilities which involve musculoskeletal, neurologic, cardiovascular, or other body systems. These patients include those with: (1) musculoskeletal pain syndromes, industrial and sports injuries, degenerative arthritis, or lower back pain; and (2) severe impairments amenable to rehabilitation, from strokes, spinal cord and brain injuries, amputations, and multiple trauma. Physiatrists also perform electrodiagnosis (i.e., EMG, nerve conduction, somatosensory-evoked potentials). The physiatrist's goal is to maximize the patient's physical, psychosocial, and job-related recovery, as well as to alleviate pain. Depending upon their practice, they may have frequent or no night call. Physiatry is one of the specialties in which there are many more positions available for graduates of residency training programs than there are graduates to fill them.

Residency training is four years. There are also combined programs in internal medicine-PM&R, pediatrics–PM&R, and neurology–PM&R.

Osteopathic physicians can also train in osteopathic manipulative medicine, also called osteopathic principles and practice (OPP), or osteopathic manipulative treatment (OMT). Many D.O.'s with advanced training in these techniques are in great demand. Training lasts two years after internship or one year following completion of a primary care specialty. Family practice programs still have two-year fellowships.

For more information, contact:

- American Academy of Physical Medicine & Rehabilitation, One IBM Plaza, Suite 2500, Chicago, IL 60611-3604.
- American Congress of Rehabilitation Medicine, 4700 W. Lake Avenue, Glenview, IL 60025.
- American Osteopathic College of Rehabilitation Medicine, 9058 West Church, Des Plaines, IL 60016.
- Association of Academic Physiatrists, 7100 Lakewood Building, Suite 112, 5987 E. 71st Street, Indianapolis, IN 46220.

PLASTIC SURGERY (F) ***

Plastic surgeons operatively treat disfigurements of the body, whether they are congenitally or traumatically induced, or are caused by aging. This area of surgery is as much an art as a science, and an artist's vision is said to be necessary to excel in the field. Microsurgery and liposuction are two techniques being used both in reconstructive and cosmetic surgery. The practice consists of a large amount of night call to the emergency room, especially early in a practitioner's career. Much of plastic surgery is done on an ambulatory basis. While the field is quite lucrative at present, plastic surgery is expected to become overcrowded in the near future.

Training in plastic surgery lasts at least two, and often three, years after completion of at least three years of general surgery or an entire otolaryngology or orthopaedic surgery residency. Individual programs vary in their preferences regarding previous training. All programs accept applicants who have completed general surgery training, and most accept those who have completed otolaryngology or orthopaedic residencies. Many programs will consider candidates with four years of general surgery; some three-year programs accept applicants having only three years of general surgery training.

Additional training in plastic surgery, and fellowships in craniofacial surgery, microsurgery, and burn surgery are available following completion of plastic surgery training.

For more information, contact:

- American Academy of Facial & Reconstructive Surgery, 1101 Vermont Avenue, N.W., Suite 220, Washington, DC 20005.
- American Association of Plastic Surgeons, 888 Glenbrook Avenue, Bryn Mawr, PA 19010.
- American College of Osteopathic Surgeons, 123 N. Henry Street, Alexandria, VA 22314-2903.
- American Society of Plastic & Reconstructive Surgeons, 444 East Algonquin Road, Arlington Heights, IL 60005.

PREVENTIVE MEDICINE * to **** (see individual areas)

Preventive medicine, unlike most other primary specialties, requires that those entering the field do so through one of three specialty areas: public health and general preventive medicine, occupational medicine, or aerospace medicine. All programs require completion of a Master of Public Health or equivalent degree. Some family practice programs arrange for concurrent training in preventive medicine. Subspecialty certifications are available in medical toxicology and underseas medicine.

For more information, contact:

- American College of Preventive Medicine, 1660 L Street, Suite 206, N.W., Washington, DC 20036.
- American Osteopathic College of Preventive Medicine, 1900 The Exchange, Suite 160, Atlanta, GA 30339-2022.

PSYCHIATRY *

Psychiatrists diagnose and treat disorders of the mind, from mild situational problems to severe, incapacitating psychotic illnesses. They practice in a variety of settings, including private offices, community mental health centers, psychiatric hospitals, prisons, and substance abuse programs. The majority are office- rather than hospital-based. While they may take night call, many psychiatrists use other health care workers to screen their calls. The wide diversity of potent psychotropic medications has given psychiatrists a powerful pharmacological armamentarium, which has resulted in their increased effectiveness. Many more disease-specific drugs are anticipated in the future. This may strengthen the ties between psychiatry and other types of clinical practice. Many job openings for psychiatry residency graduates exist.

Students choose to specialize in psychiatry because they seek an intellectual challenge, want to return to a humanities/social science background, want novel and unique problems, and want to treat the "whole person."

Training is three years following a clinical internship which is usually very similar in structure to a transitional year. The residency consists of not only training in psychiatry, but also includes a significant amount of neurology training. Combined programs exist in internal medicine–psychiatry. Subspecialty fellowships and certification are available in addiction psychiatry, forensic psychiatry, clinical neurophysiology, and child & adolescent psychiatry.

Fellowships in child & adolescent psychiatry, for both M.D.'s and D.O.'s, consist of a minimum of two years of child and adolescent psychiatry and at least two years (following internship) of general psychiatry. The child psychiatry training can start any time after the internship year. There are also programs with five years of training combining pediatrics, psychiatry, and child psychiatry.

For more information, contact:

- American Osteopathic Board of Neurology & Psychiatry, 2250 Chapel Avenue West, Suite 100, Cherry Hill, NJ 0800-2000.

- American Psychiatric Association, 1400 K Street, N.W., Washington, DC 20005.

PUBLIC HEALTH AND GENERAL PREVENTIVE MEDICINE *

Specialists in public health and general preventive medicine (1) assess information about the community's health, (2) develop comprehensive public health policies, and (3) assure the provision of services necessary to achieve the public health goals. They work in governmental and private health agencies, academic institutions, and health service research organizations. They manage health problems both of entire communities or countries and of individual patients. Their goals are to promote health and to research the risks of disease, injury, disability and death. They frequently engage in the administrative and political sides of medicine. These specialists rarely have night call and command very low (usually government) pay. Preventive medicine practitioners allocate their time among administrative duties (32%), patient care (29%), research (20%), teaching (8%), consulting (8%), and other activities (3%). The dearth of residency programs (a number have closed in the past few years due to lack of funding) have made these specialists among the most sought-after in medicine.

Training in general preventive medicine consists of two years following a clinical internship. One of these years is spent obtaining an advanced degree, usually a Master of Public Health. A fourth year of training, teaching, practice, and/or research is required to take the board examination. Some programs in family practice, internal medicine, and pediatrics have dual training with preventive medicine.

For more information, contact:

- American Association of Public Health Physicians, 777 S. Mills Street, Madison, WI 53715.

- American College of Preventive Medicine, 1660 L Street, N.W., Suite 206, Washington, DC 20036.

- American Osteopathic College of Preventive Medicine, 1900 The Exchange, Suite 160, Atlanta, GA 30339-2022.

PULMONARY DISEASES (F) **

Pulmonologists diagnose and treat patients with diseases of the lungs such as lung cancer, asthma, and chronic lung diseases. Pulmonologists, because of their background, often act as full-

or part-time critical care physicians. The specialty combines patient care and manipulative procedures with a strong underlying base of physiology. The major manipulative procedures performed by pulmonologists are bronchoscopy, endotracheal intubation, management of mechanical ventilators, and placement of pulmonary artery catheters. They practice with both inpatients and outpatients. Night call depends upon the type of practice.

Training consists of a two- or three-year fellowship following completion of an internal medicine residency. Many three-year programs fulfill the requirements for certification in critical care as well as pulmonary diseases. For Osteopathic physicians, training follows internship and two years of an internal medicine residency.

For more information, contact:

- American College of Chest Physicians, 3300 Dundee Road, Northbrook, IL 60062.

- American Thoracic Society, 1740 Broadway, New York, NY 10019-4374.

RADIATION ONCOLOGY ***

Radiation oncologists use radiation therapy to treat malignancies and other diseases. Until about twenty-five years ago, training in radiation oncology was combined with diagnostic radiology. A flood of new information about radiation and cancer biology has made radiation oncology a rapidly changing field. Many radiation oncologists become the primary physician for their cancer patients.

Although radiation oncologists have previously been in high demand, the specialty is now close to equilibrium. Radiation oncologists have relatively little night call. Training lasts three years after internship.

For more information, contact:

- American Osteopathic College of Radiology, 119 E. Second Street, Milan, MO 63556.

- American Society for Therapeutic Radiology & Oncology, 1891 Preston White Drive, Reston, VA 22091.

- Association of Residents in Radiation Oncology, Dept. of Radiation Oncology, Massachusetts General Hospital, Boston, MA 02114.

RADIOLOGY, DIAGNOSTIC *

Diagnostic radiologists use x-rays, ultrasound, magnetic fields, and other forms of energy to diagnose patients. Although they still learn to read basic radiographs, they now also learn how to interpret nuclear scans, PET scans, ultrasonography images, CT scans, and MRI images. Additionally, they are trained to perform diagnostic and interventional procedures, such as angiography, guided biopsy and drainage procedures, and non-coronary angioplasty.

This is an enormous task for the four years of training following internship which make up most programs. Osteopathic training is four years after internship. Some diagnostic radiology programs provide an additional year of training in nuclear radiology. This should not be confused with a residency in nuclear medicine—a distinct specialty with training only in that area.

Most practitioners are hospital-based, although there is a growing movement among radiologists to practice out of free-standing diagnostic facilities. Because of the increased demand for emergency CT and ultrasound studies as well as interventional procedures, diagnostic radiology night call has become frequent in many hospitals. Radiology has also joined obstetrics & gynecology as a frequently sued specialty.

The field of diagnostic radiology is rapidly filling up, with the number of available positions for residency graduates decreasing each year. Many residents, to gain an edge for employment, are taking year-long fellowships in interventional-, cardiovascular-, neuro-, and other areas of radiology following their residencies. Positions in post-residency fellowships exist for neuroradiology, nuclear radiology, pediatric radiology, and vascular and interventional radiology.

For more information, contact:

- American College of Radiology, 1891 Preston White Drive, Reston, VA 22091.
- American Osteopathic College of Radiology, 119 E. Second Street, Milan, MO 63556.

RHEUMATOLOGY (F) **

Rheumatologists diagnose and treat patients with a wide variety of diseases of the joints, soft tissues, and blood vessels, including the various types of both chronic and acute arthritides. The field has grown in recent years with the increased interest in the autoimmune diseases which underlie many rheumatologic conditions. Rheumatology is one of the quieter subspecialties of internal medicine. Yet rheumatologists often care for very ill patients with various autoimmune and acute joint diseases. There is usually little night call and small primary or consultative inpatient services for those not mixing their rheumatology practice with general internal medicine. Training consists of a two-year fellowship following completion of an internal medicine residency. For Osteopathic physicians, training follows internship and two years of internal medicine residency.

For more information, contact:

- American College of Osteopathic Internists, 300 Fifth Street, N.E., Washington, DC 20002.
- American College of Rheumatology, 60 Executive Park South, Suite 150, Atlanta, GA 30329.

SPORTS MEDICINE (F) **

Sports medicine is divided into two types of training programs and practice: primary care sports medicine and orthopaedic sports medicine. Primary care sports medicine specialists prevent, diagnose, and treat non-operative sports-related injuries. Primary care sports medicine specialists emphasize prevention and rehabilitation in addition to acute treatment. Some perform epidemiological studies to determine the best preventative methods. Many practitioners incorporate sports medicine into their existing practices—usually those in emergency medicine, family practice, internal medicine, or pediatrics. They offer fitness evaluations, act as team physicians, and work with recreational athletes. Training is one year after completing the initial residency.

Orthopaedic sports medicine is a subspecialty of orthopaedic surgery. It uses the same preventive and therapeutic measures as primary care sports medicine physicians, but treats injuries surgically when necessary. Training in orthopaedic sports medicine is a one-year fellowship following the completion of an orthopaedic surgery residency.

For more information, contact:

- American College of Sports Medicine, P.O. Box 1440, Indianapolis, IN 46206-1440.
- American Orthopaedic Society for Sports Medicine, 6300 N. River Road, Suite 200, Rosemont, IL 60018.
- American Osteopathic Academy of Sports Medicine, 7611 Elmwood Avenue, Suite 201, Middletown, WI 53562.

SURGERY ****

General surgeons primarily diagnose and treat diseases and injuries to the abdominal organs, and the soft tissues and vasculature of the neck and trunk. They are also called in to manage, often with other surgical specialists, patients suffering injuries to more than one body area. In rural settings, the general surgeon may still be "general," doing orthopaedic, urological, and, occasionally, thoracic or neurosurgical procedures. But, for the most part, today's general surgeon primarily works in the abdomen, on the breasts, on the peripheral vasculature, on the skin, and in some cases, on the neck. In the average 60-hour work week of all surgeons in private practice, 47% of their time is spent on office visits, 29% in surgery, 16% on hospital rounds, and 8% on other patient visits.

The field of general surgery is overcrowded; job opportunities for residency graduates are relatively scarce. Yet there are still many areas of the country that are underserved by surgeons. Training in general surgery usually requires five years after medical school. It takes four years after internship for Osteopathic physicians. Subspecialty fellowships and certification are available in surgery of the hand, pediatric surgery, surgical critical care, and general vascular surgery.

For more information, contact:

- American College of Surgeons, 55 E. Erie Street, Chicago, IL 60611.
- American College of Osteopathic Surgeons, 123 N. Henry Street, Alexandria, VA 22314-2903.

THORACIC SURGERY (F) ***

Thoracic or cardiothoracic surgeons operatively treat diseases and injuries of the heart, lungs, mediastinum, esophagus, chest wall, diaphragm, and great vessels. The most common surgery that they perform is coronary artery bypass grafting. Other common procedures include cardiac surgery for acquired valvular disease or for congenital cardiac defects, pulmonary surgery for malignancies, and surgery for trauma to intrathoracic organs. Thoracic surgeons are responsible for the post-operative care of all these patients. As might be expected from the nature of the patients whom thoracic surgeons treat, very long and erratic hours are often necessary. Thus, thoracic surgery is one of the most time-consuming and stressful of all the specialties. Those in the field, though, generally feel that the rewards are worth the price.

Thoracic surgery is a subspecialty of general surgery, and certification in general surgery is required to take the thoracic surgery boards. Training lasts at least two years after completion of a general surgery residency. Since the process of going through a general surgery residency is itself grueling, this acts as a major deterrent to many individuals who might otherwise enter this field. Osteopathic programs are two years in length after three years of general surgery and one year of internship.

For more information, contact:

- American College of Osteopathic Surgeons, 123 N. Henry Street, Alexandria, VA 22314-2903.
- Society of Thoracic Surgeons, 401 N. Michigan Avenue, Chicago, IL 60611.

TRAUMA SURGERY (F) ***

While not yet an official subspecialty, trauma surgery is one of the fastest growing areas in surgery. With the widespread institution of trauma centers, there is an increasing need for surgeons with training in the treatment of the multiple-injury patient. Trauma surgeons generally perform surgery on patients with major injuries, and also help coordinate the large teams responsible for both initial and postoperative care. In-hospital call with long hours is usually required on a frequent basis, making family life difficult. Trauma surgeons must be able to immediately go full speed from a dead halt. Most trauma surgeons are in medium- to large-sized cities. Training normally consists of a one- or two-year fellowship at a major trauma center following a general surgery residency. At the present time, few trauma surgeons have completed such fellowships. Their necessity in the future is currently unknown. Fellowships are arranged on an individual basis during the third or fourth year of general surgery training. Many fellowship are combined with training in critical care or with research opportunities.

For more information, contact:

- American Association for the Surgery of Trauma, Harborview Medical Center, Dept. of Surgery, 325 9th Avenue, P.O. Box 359796, Seattle, WA 98104-2499.

- American Trauma Society, 8903 Presidential Parkway, Suite 512, Upper Marlboro, MD 20772.

UROLOGY ****

Urologists diagnose and treat diseases of and injuries to the kidneys, ureters, bladder, and urethra. In males, they also treat disorders of the prostate and genitals. Often they work with nephrologists (internists) and have both surgical and non-surgical practices. Research into fertility and male sexuality, and the use of non-invasive techniques, such as lithotripsy, are expanding areas within the field. Urologists have a moderate amount of night call. They often have small inpatient services, since much urologic surgery is now done in an ambulatory setting.

Urology training generally consists of two years of general surgery followed by at least three years of urology. Fellowship training exists in pediatric urology.

For more information, contact:

- American College of Osteopathic Surgeons, 123 N. Henry Street, Alexandria, VA 22314-2903.

- American Urological Association, 1120 North Charles Street, Baltimore, MD 21201.

VASCULAR SURGERY (F) ***

As subspecialists of general surgery, vascular surgeons diagnose and treat diseases of the arterial, venous, and lymphatic systems. Unless they are associated with very large medical centers, specialists in this field often must perform general surgery as well in order to make a living. This is, in part, because so many general surgeons also continue to perform vascular surgery as a routine part of their practice. Training for both M.D.'s and D.O.'s is generally one year following completion of a general surgery residency.

For more information, contact:

- American College of Osteopathic Surgeons, 123 N. Henry Street, Alexandria, VA 22314-2903.

- Society for Vascular Surgery, 13 Elm Street, P.O. Box 1565, Manchester, MA 01944.

4: Osteopathic Medicine—The Other Degree

What's in a name?
That which we call a rose
by any other name
would smell as sweet.

Shakespeare, *Romeo and Juliet, II, 2*

What Is A "D.O."?

A D.O., OR DOCTOR OF OSTEOPATHIC MEDICINE, is a physician, although his or her degree is less familiar to most people than the M.D. degree. As Gertrude Stein said, however, a "rose is a rose is a rose." Both D.O.'s and M.D.'s are licensed to practice medicine and surgery, may prescribe drugs, usually hold appointments on hospital staffs, and legitimately use the title "Doctor," as in "Is there a doctor in the house?" (Ph.D.'s consider themselves the only "real" doctors, but they often get a bit squeamish when they see sick people.) About 5% of all U.S. physicians have D.O. degrees. Historically, more than 60% of all Osteopathic physicians choose to practice in primary care fields.

Why Are There Two Different Degrees?

In nineteenth-century America, many types of medical practitioners existed. These included homeopaths, eclectics, hydropaths, magnetic healers, allopaths (a term now often incorrectly applied to M.D.'s), osteopaths (D.O.'s), and M.D.'s. None of these different disciplines tolerated each other, leading to bitter professional rivalries. The outcome of this internecine warfare resulted in M.D.'s dominating American medicine, with D.O.'s being the only other type of physician still existing in any appreciable number. The bitterness and misunderstanding between these two physician groups continues and is only slowly ebbing as new generations of M.D.'s and D.O.'s work side by side.

Originally, D.O.'s concentrated on curing patients by manipulating their spines and other joints. Later, they adopted many techniques used by M.D.'s, although they still frequently used spinal manipulation, now known as osteopathic manipulative medicine (OMM). In the mid-twentieth century, D.O.'s began emphasizing their role as general practitioners, especially to smaller communities. This is a role that they naturally grew into when, after World War II, smaller communities could find no other physicians to serve their needs. Their expansion into primary care was enhanced when D.O.'s were banned from virtually all M.D. residency (graduate) training programs. (This total ban no longer exists.) Today, most colleges of Osteopathic medicine still emphasize treating the whole patient and encourage their graduates to enter family practice.

Why Choose A D.O. Versus An M.D. School?

Students may have any of four reasons for applying to D.O. schools in preference to M.D. schools: D.O. role model, the Osteopathic philosophy/primary care orientation, ease of entry into the school, or the desire to learn osteopathic manipulative treatment.

D.O. Role Model

Individuals' role models often strongly influence their career decisions. Many students apply primarily or solely to D.O. schools due to the memorable contacts they had with one or more Osteopathic physicians as they grew up. These "Marcus Welby-like" physicians demonstrated a caring, as well as curing, attitude that these students wanted to emulate. Many of these D.O.'s also acted as the students' mentors as they progressed through undergraduate school.

If you have such a mentor, it will be important to get a letter from him or her when applying to Osteopathic school. Most schools require or strongly suggest that applicants send a letter from an Osteopathic physician. In part this is so that they can be assured that the applicant really knows something about Osteopathic medicine.

Philosophy/Primary Care

Osteopathic medicine has always concentrated on the entire patient, rather than simply the disease process. While this is now considered the modern basis of all medical practice, especially family practice, D.O.'s have held this attitude from the beginning. Osteopathic medical schools still try to instill this attitude into their students. This is in contrast to M.D. schools, where they may "talk the talk" about the "whole patient," but they don't "walk the walk" where it counts—in the clinical setting.

Andrew Taylor Still, M.D., used the following principles as a foundation for Osteopathic medicine in the late 1800s:

- The body is an integral unit, a whole. The structure of the body and its functions work together, interdependently.

- The body systems have built-in repair processes which are self-regulating and self-healing in the face of disease.

- The circulatory system or distributing channels of the body, along with the nervous system, provide the integrating functions for the rest of the body.

- The contribution of the musculoskeletal system to a person's health is much more than providing framework and support. Improper musculoskeletal functioning can impede essential blood and nerve supplies.

- While disease may be manifested in specific parts of the body, other parts may contribute to a restoration or a correction of the disease.

About two-thirds of all Osteopathic physicians are in generalist/primary care practices, which include family practice, internal medicine, obstetrics & gynecology, osteopathic manipulative treatment, and pediatrics.

At the present time, the Osteopathic profession is struggling with the issue of how deeply they hold the belief that the musculoskeletal system is central to disease processes. Many Osteopathic residencies, especially in non-primary care specialties, barely mention manipulative techniques, and many Osteopathic physicians do M.D. residencies that, of course, do not include these procedures. Some within Osteopathic medicine believe that losing this touchstone with their professional heritage will eventually dissolve any remaining differences between M.D.'s and D.O.'s.

Easier To Enter

For the above reasons, many students pick Osteopathic training as their first choice. Osteopathic medical schools have, however, over the past decade, often admitted students that M.D. schools rejected. These included older students and those with slightly lower GPAs (3.33 in 1995) or slightly lower MCAT scores (8.3 Biological Sciences, 8.0 Physical Sciences, 8.1 Verbal Reasoning, "O" Writing Sample in 1995). As evidence of the vagaries of medical schools' admission procedures, some D.O.'s are now on the faculties of M.D. schools. Many Osteopathic medical schools will admit applicants with an interest in primary care in preference to those with higher grades and scores who do not express such an interest. As the qualifications (if not the quality) of applicants to medical schools increase, entering Osteopathic school will become more difficult. (For additional information about Osteopathic medical schools, see figure 15.1, figure 15.2, and figure 15.3.)

Unlike M.D.-granting schools, which have been combining, the number of Osteopathic medical schools has been increasing. In 1996, the Arizona College of Osteopathic Medicine held its first classes and a new school in eastern Kentucky may begin in 1997.

The number of applicants to D.O. schools has increased by about 19% per year over the past decade. There are now over four applicants for each first-year position at Osteopathic medical schools. The percentage of women applying to D.O. schools has also increased. The number of women in Osteopathic medical schools varies markedly by school, from the University of Health Sciences where only about 25% of the students are women, to the UMDNJ College of Osteopathic Medicine where women account for 52% of students. Most have only about 39% women—far behind the percentage at M.D. schools. All underrepresented minorities compose only about 9% of first-year Osteopathic students. The number of minority students also varies markedly among schools, with minority students accounting for less than 10% of the students at three schools (West Virginia, Philadelphia, and University of New England), but more than 25% at two others (College of Osteopathic Medicine of the Pacific—now Western University of Health Sciences—and Texas College of Osteopathic Medicine). Both women and underrepresented minorities have a lower-than-average record of acceptance.

Some Osteopathic medical schools serve mostly state residents, while others draw from the entire country. Those that primarily take in-state students are: Texas (92%), New Jersey (91%), New York (90%), Oklahoma (85%), and West Virginia (82%). Those accepting the most out-of-state students are: Kirksville (89%), University of Osteopathic Medicine and Health Sciences (84%), New England (81%), and the University of Health Sciences (85%).

Osteopathic Manipulative Medicine

A unique part of Osteopathic medical schools' curricula is osteopathic manipulative medicine (OMM). This is the manipulation of the spine to relieve painful conditions. Medical school applicants with a background in physical therapy or related fields have often seen the extraordinary relief that patients can obtain with OMM and want to learn to use it in their own practices. While there are some D.O.'s who do not use OMM, especially if they go into non-generalist specialties, others use it to supplement standard medical treatments. A few D.O.'s even specialize in OMM after completing an OMM residency or fellowship. Some M.D.'s now take special courses to learn the simpler OMM techniques.

Less than 4% of all Osteopathic school faculty specialize in OMM. And, while on average, more than one-fourth of students' clinical experiences in their "preclinical" years (usually years one and two) are spent learning OMM, students only spend an average of one week doing OMM during their clinical (usually third and fourth) years.

Osteopathic Curriculum

Osteopathic medical schools have essentially the same curricula as do M.D. schools (figures 4.1 and 4.2). Osteopathic medical schools' curricula and teaching methods vary, as they do among M.D. schools. D.O. students may take the same licensing examination (USMLE) as M.D. students, although most take a separate D.O. examination which covers the same material and is administered by the National Board of Osteopathic Medical Examiners.

Figure 4.1: Average Osteopathic Curriculum—Basic Sciences (Preclinical)

Subject	Average Number of Hours	Percent of Time
Clinical Medicine	393 hrs.	23 %
Gross Anatomy	210	12
Osteopathic Principles/Practice	197	11
Pathology	137	8
Physiology	130	8
Biochemistry	112	6
Pharmacology	106	6
Microbiology	104	6
Microanatomy	74	4
Neuroanatomy	70	4
Applied Medicine	36	2
Miscellaneous	26	2
Immunology	25	1
Behavioral Medicine	15	1
Histology	10	1
Physician Skills	10	1
Epidemiology/Biostatistics	9	1
Embryology	9	1
Genetics	8	<1
Cardiovascular System	8	<1
Psychiatry	5	<1
Endocrinology/Metabolism	5	<1
Gastrointestinal System	5	<1
Musculoskeletal System	5	<1
Respiratory System	5	<1
Community Medicine	4	<1
Nutrition	4	<1
Radiology	4	<1
TOTAL	1,726 hrs.	

Adapted from: American Association of Colleges of Osteopathic Medicine. *1995 Annual Statistical Report.* Rockville, MD: AACOM, 1995, p. 22.

Figure 4.2: Average Osteopathic Curriculum—Clinical Years

Subject	Average Number of Weeks	Percent of Time
Electives	19 weeks	23 %
Family/Community Medicine	15	18
Internal Medicine	13	16
Surgery	8	9
Pediatrics	5	6
Obstetrics & Gynecology	5	6
Psychiatry	4	5
Radiology	1	2
Surgical Subspecialties	1	2
Neurology	1	1
Osteopathic Manipulative Treatment	1	1
Other (Emergency Medicine, Geriatrics, & Anesthesiology were the most common.)	11	13
Total	**84 weeks**	

Adapted from: American Association of Colleges of Osteopathic Medicine. *1995 Annual Statistical Report.* Rockville, MD: AACOM, 1995, p. 23.

While most Osteopathic medical schools have strong basic science courses, some schools' clinical training is weaker than that at comparable M.D. schools. Some Osteopathic medical schools do not have their own teaching hospitals nor do they have strong ties with large busy teaching hospitals where their students can do clinical rotations. This is, in part, because M.D.'s have long controlled the teaching hospitals in many large communities. They have often been reluctant to allow Osteopathic students to do clinical rotations alongside M.D. students.

Even with this caveat, students at any Osteopathic school should be able to get as good a medical education (or better) as do students at comparable M.D. schools. As in M.D. schools, success depends upon the student's ability to assertively seek out clinical opportunities and to strive to get the best possible rotations.

Impact of an Osteopathic Degree on a Medical Career

Osteopathic physicians face three obstacles during their careers, which may or may not be of importance to you: confusion about what a D.O. is, hostility and discrimination within the physician community, and the unwieldy and user-unfriendly Osteopathic bureaucracy. First, many individuals, both within the medical profession and among the lay community, do not know what D.O.'s are. Many confuse Osteopathic physicians with chiropractors, and others do not know that D.O.'s are physicians, albeit with a different degree. Some Osteopathic physicians, to avoid this confusion, wear name tags with "Dr. S. Victory," rather than "S. Victory, D.O."

Second, Osteopathic physicians still face hostility within segments of the M.D. community. They feel it the most when applying to residencies. While in many areas, Osteopathic physicians are warmly welcomed into undersubscribed M.D.-run residency programs in primary care specialties, they are less commonly accepted into difficult-to-match-with specialties, such as emergency medicine and dermatology. Because of long-standing animosity at the national level, few D.O.'s are accepted into M.D.-run surgery programs.

D.O.-Run Residency Training

Third, specialty training in Osteopathic residencies is currently difficult to obtain due to a lack of available positions. The increase in Osteopathic medical students now far outpaces the increase in students at M.D. schools. Between 1970 and 1990, the number of D.O.'s doubled, the number of Osteopathic medical schools increased from nine to fifteen (a sixteenth opened in 1993 and a seventeenth in 1996), and the number of graduates more than *tripled*. Additional Osteopathic medical schools are in the planning stages. There are now about 1,800 D.O. graduates annually. The number of Osteopathic residency slots, however, barely increased. Those programs that do exist cannot accommodate the increasing percentage of new Osteopathic physicians who want to pursue specialties other than primary care. While the more than 1,800 funded Osteopathic internships would be barely sufficient to meet the needs of Osteopathic graduates (if they all entered D.O. internships), the 1,137 funded entry-level residency positions are far too few to accommodate the current number of Osteopathic graduates (figure 4.3). This means that many Osteopathic graduates must look to the M.D. side of the profession for their training.

One detail about residency programs still seems to elude the Osteopathic community. While most M.D.-run residency programs and their applicants use a national matching program, D.O.'s who want to enter D.O.-run specialty training must still scramble around trying to match themselves up with training sites. (Just recently, Osteopathic medicine has established a matching program, but only for their internship programs—more than forty years after M.D. students began using matching programs.)

D.O.'s in M.D.-Run Training

Osteopathic graduates say they "jump ship" to M.D. programs because they believe these programs provide better training, have more positions, supply better salaries, have more full-time and better qualified faculty, and include specialty training unavailable in Osteopathic programs. That is not surprising since only 13 Osteopathic teaching hospitals in the United States have more than 300 beds. Osteopathic educators fear that AOA-approved postgraduate programs will become a haven only for D.O.'s interested in surgical or other non-internal medicine or non-family practice specialties. As one said, when defending students who do M.D. residencies, "students do not see anything distinctive in what Osteopathic graduate medical education training programs have that would differentiate them from [M.D.] programs. . . . these choices may be the result of enlightened decision making and not necessarily an indication of disloyalty."

If you enter Osteopathic school intending to pursue M.D. training, as did 2,464 D.O.'s (56% of all D.O.'s in residency programs) in 1993, you will have to deal with both the American Osteopathic Association (AOA) and the programs themselves. If you change your mind after you have completed an M.D. internship and want to do an Osteopathic residency, they will not accept you. Also, even though you will generally be eligible to take the AMA's specialty board examination upon successful completion of an M.D. training program, you will not be allowed to take the AOA's specialty examination in the same field unless you pay the AOA to site-visit your residency program. Even if you pay this significant cost, they may not approve the program. This may mean that you will not be eligible for specialty staff privileges at some Osteopathic hospitals. (You may also be unable to obtain a license in some states. See below.)

Figure 4.3: Osteopathic Specialties—Programs and Funded Entry-Level Positions *

Specialty	Number of Programs	Annual Number of Funded Entry-Level Positions
Anesthesiology	23	29
Cardiology	9	18
Child Psychiatry	2	1
Critical Care	4	5
Dermatology	11	9
Diagnostic Radiology	20	32
Emergency Medicine	28	125
Emergency Med–Fam Practice	1	1
Emergency Med–Internal Med	7	12
Endocrinology	3	3
Family Practice	101	467
Gastroenterology	6	11
Geriatrics	3	4
Hematology/Oncology	2	2
Infectious Diseases	2	4
Internal Medicine**	43	126
Internal Medicine–Pediatrics**	1	<1
Nephrology	2	3
Neurological Surgery	8	5
Neurology	5	7
Obstetrics/Gynecology**	32	51
Occupational Medicine	2	2
Oncology	1	<1
Ophthalmology	11	14
Orthopaedic Surgery	29	51
Osteopathic Manipulative Med	7	14
Otolaryngology	2	1
Otolaryngology/Facial Plastics	18	17
Pathology	3	3
Pediatrics	6	10
Physical Med & Rehabilitation	1	1
Proctology	2	2
Psychiatry	5	20
Pulmonary Medicine	8	10
Radiation Oncology	1	<1
Rheumatology	1	<1
Sports Medicine	1	1
Surgery [General]	37	59
Thoracic Surgery	1	2
Urological Surgery	11	6
Vascular Surgery [General]	4	5
Internships **	144	1,820

* Many programs list positions for which they do not have funding. This chart lists only funded (real) positions available for Osteopathic physicians going through the Match.

** An internship is required before any Osteopathic residency training can be started. Taking a specialty-specific internship in Internal Medicine and Obstetrics/Gynecology can shorten the total residency length by one year.

Information from: American Osteopathic Association. *Opportunities—1995-96 Directory of Osteopathic Post-doctoral Education Programs.* Chicago, IL: AOA, 1995.

More Osteopathic graduates are entering M.D. training programs each year. An obvious reason for this is that the numbers of Osteopathic graduates has been steadily increasing, while the number of Osteopathic training positions has remained fairly constant. However, you must recognize that, for whatever reason, M.D. training in some specialties is almost completely off-limits to Osteopathic physicians (figure 4.4). Chief among these are diagnostic radiology, general surgery, and various surgical specialties, such as colon and rectal surgery, neurosurgery, otolaryngology, thoracic surgery, and urology. Even in the military, it is nearly impossible for an Osteopathic medical school graduate to obtain a position in, and be allowed to finish, a surgical residency program. This is controlled by the "powers" granting accreditation to residency programs. It may change in the future, but don't hold your breath.

Finally, there is the Osteopathic hierarchy itself with which you have to contend. While bureaucracy exists throughout medicine, the (often-justified) paranoia of Osteopathic medicine's leadership places great strains on young practitioners. First is the problem of getting a medical license. In some states (such as Florida and Michigan), D.O.'s cannot get a medical license unless they complete an internship approved by the American Osteopathic Association. (Osteopathic medical boards change these rules without notice.) Unfortunately, these internships do not count toward any M.D.-run specialty training, and they count as a specialty-training year only for selected D.O. specialties. Most individuals who want to enter a D.O.-run residency, and all who want to enter an M.D.-run residency, must repeat the year. The duration of D.O.-run residencies is usually the same as M.D.-run residencies.

While I was in the military, I first experienced the M.D. establishment's often-shabby treatment of Osteopathic physicians. In one incident, a very competent physician was booted out of a general surgery residency when the program director was told that they could lose their accreditation if they graduated an Osteopathic physician. This physician went on to become an excellent flight surgeon (although these "surgeons" do not do surgery).

In another case, an excellent Osteopathic student of mine, who wanted to do an internal medicine residency at the premier military hospital, was originally told that they would not take any D.O.'s. Only after several M.D.'s intervened did they, very reluctantly, agree to take him. (Of course, he was so good that he was later appointed Chief Resident; some years later he became Head of the department.)

More recently, a well-trained (one D.O. and two M.D. residencies) Osteopathic physician was told by the director of an M.D. medical school's residency program, who was seeking faculty members, that they "would never accept a D.O. on our school's faculty." She is on the faculty at another prestigious (M.D.) medical school in the same specialty.

The animosity, unfortunately, cuts both ways. When I attended my protégé's graduation from a D.O. school, physicians "hooded" many of the students during the ceremony. With a rather narrow view of the professions, they did not recognize an M.D. as a physician for this purpose. (She is finishing an internal medicine residency and will shortly begin a hematology-oncology fellowship in Miami. Both are M.D. programs.)

Some areas of the country, such as the Midwest, have large numbers of Osteopathic physicians and Osteopathic training facilities, so these problems may be somewhat minor there.

Osteopathic Medical Practice

States with the largest numbers of Osteopathic physicians are Pennsylvania and Michigan (more than 4,500 each). Other states with large numbers of Osteopathic physicians are Florida, New Jersey, Ohio, and Texas (each with more than 2,000). Arizona, California, Illinois, Missouri, New York, Oklahoma, and the military services each have more than 1,000 practicing D.O.'s.

Figure 4.4: Osteopathic Graduates in M.D. Programs

Specialty	Number in M.D. Training Programs	% of all Available M.D. Positions
Allergy/Immunology	6	2 %
Anesthesiology	244	5
Cardiovascular Disease	75	3
Child/Adolescent Psychiatry	35	5
Colon & Rectal Surgery	0	0
Critical Care Medicine	31	3
Dermatology	4	1
Emergency Medicine	149	5
Endocrinology	3	1
Family Practice	786	9
Gastroenterology	26	3
Geriatrics	8	4
Hematology/Oncology	15	3
Infectious Diseases	8	1
Internal Medicine	697	3
Internal Med–Pediatrics	43	4
Nephrology	16	3
Neurological Surgery	2	<1
Neurology	71	5
Nuclear Medicine	5	3
Obstetrics & Gynecology	145	3
Ophthalmology	9	1
Orthopaedic Surgery	18	1
Otolaryngology	6	1
Pathology	50	2
Pediatrics	222	3
Pediatric Surgery	0	0
Physical Med/Rehabilitation	120	11
Plastic Surgery	3	1
Prevent Med/Pub Hlth (all)	25	6
Psychiatry	191	4
Pulmonary Diseases	15	5
Radiation Oncology	8	1
Radiology, Diagnostic	61	2
Rheumatology	4	1
Surgery	74	1
Thoracic Surgery	1	<1
Urology	7	1

Adapted from: Appendix II, Table 1. *JAMA* 1996;276(9):739-40.

Where To Get More Information

More information and current application materials can be obtained from the American Association of Colleges of Osteopathic Medicine (AACOM), 6110 Executive Boulevard, Suite 405, Rockville, MD 20852-3991. You may want to read the publications listed below.

- *Osteopathic Medical Education,* a pamphlet about the field.

- *Osteopathic Medical College Information*, an annual listing of each Osteopathic school, including contact information, curricula, entrance requirements, application procedures selection factors, class sizes, deadlines, and tuition.

- *Annual Statistical Report*, AACOM's comprehensive overview of Osteopathic medical education in table and chart form.

- *Debts and Career Plans of Osteopathic Medical Students*, a periodic publication that gives another perspective on Osteopathic medical education.

5: Preparation in High School

When I was a child,
I spake as a child,
I understood as a child,
I thought as a child;
but when I became a man,
I put away childish things.

I Corinthians, XIII, 11

High School Academics

IDEALLY, POTENTIAL PHYSICIANS SHOULD TAKE enough high school math and science courses to be able to "test out" of them in college. If you do this, you will have the advantage of taking advanced science courses earlier in your curriculum. Also, if you decide to major in a non-science area, it gives you more leeway to pursue studies in that area while still completing the required premed courses.

The most important thing you can learn in high school is *proper study skills*. Many students who consider becoming a physician find that they have not had to study very hard throughout their schooling. Because of this, they do not develop the discipline or the vital time-management skills necessary to learn the vast amount of material required to get good grades in college, let alone in medical school. When you get to college, you will probably work twice as hard as you did in high school to achieve the same or lower grades. Studying in medical school is harder than in college, particularly because there is no such thing as asking "What's on the test?" The answer, at least for a medical career, is that everything is on the test. This is the nature of medical practice. It therefore pays to develop the discipline needed to set time aside every day to study the required (or extra) course material. The following are some of the study habits that successful students use:

- Study *at least* one hour outside of class for every hour spent in an academic class. The time you spend on each subject will vary from day to day.

- Plan your daily study schedule based on the class requirements and how well you are doing in various courses. Don't skimp on those courses in which you are doing poorly.

- Study your least-favorite subject first. That way you can't keep putting it off, and the rest of your studying becomes easier.

- Spend time reviewing your notes from previous classes in each subject during the term. The midterm and final exams are usually comprehensive.

- Study alone, unless you are working on a group project. Studying with friends provides an excellent way to waste time. (The exception may be if you are specifically trying to improve your problem-solving skills, where group interaction often helps.)

- Study in a quiet, well-lit place. Turn off the stereo, radio, and television.

- When in the library, face a wall or use a study cubicle. The library's distractions are noise and people (especially friends).

- If you have any breaks between classes, use them to study.

Over time, you will undoubtedly develop your own techniques to improve your studying. By developing these study habits now, you will have a much easier time in both college and medical school. Both are far less structured than high school, have many more distractions, and require you to learn much more material in much less time.

A Taste Of Medicine: Volunteer And Work Opportunities

Once you think you have decided on medicine as a career, why don't you give it a try? Would you buy a car without taking it for a test drive? Of course not! Then why consider investing time, effort, money, and the risk of disappointment to pursue a medical career without first testing your decision?

If you can get any type of clinical experience, it will help you to determine whether you really want to pursue a medical career. If your parents or your parents' friends are physicians, it may be easy to get them to let you "shadow" them as they work. If not, your high school's counselors can sometimes arrange the opportunity for you. Watching a physician at work in an office, in the operating room, or doing hospital rounds allows you to see both the exciting and the routine sides of medical practice. It also dispels some of the myths perpetuated by medical television shows and movies.

Although you may not be able to practice medicine, you can certainly observe what physicians do, talk to them about their careers, and see how happy they are with their decision to enter medicine. Over the years I have met a number of medical students who claimed that they had not been in a hospital since birth. And, while hospitals are not the only arena where medicine is practiced, since so much physician training and medical practice occurs in them, I had to assume that these individuals had not taken the effort to become familiar with the career they were entering. This is not a very intelligent way to proceed with your life. Be smart. Test your career choice before you invest too much of yourself in it. (For more information about volunteering, see "Extra-curricular activities" in chapter 7.)

Special Programs

Some high schools have special programs for potential physicians. MedStart, which gives underrepresented minority and disadvantaged students interested in medicine a chance to learn about the science and practice of medicine while in high school, is one example.

A key to using MedStart and similar programs effectively is to maintain contact with the faculty you meet in these programs. As Linda Don, the University of Arizona's minority premed counselor, says, "once a MedStarter, always a MedStarter." Maintaining these contacts allows you to learn about additional programs available to you as you later progress through your undergraduate schooling.

Information about Medicine: Realism Versus Reality

Many sources describe medical careers. Many of them are not only wrong, but they also give a much too glamorized view of a physician's life. You may want to check out some of the sources listed in the *Bibliography* to get a more realistic (and vivid) picture of what the medical career you are contemplating is like.

Physicians go through different stages in their careers. For the majority, these stages are education, residency training, practice, and retirement. Many others modify their careers at some stage to enter medical management (part- or full-time), switch into other medical areas or, occasionally, enter other careers. Some of the alternative paths physicians have taken (either before or after their "official" retirements) include

- Working with disabled physicians
- Reviewing malpractice cases
- Processing peer-review organization claims
- Creating medical computer applications
- Doing utilization review or quality assurance for hospitals, insurance agencies, or the government
- Publishing medical material
- Working with home-health agencies
- Performing aeromedical examinations
- Doing *locum tenens* for other physicians (replacing them when they are away on vacation or at meetings)
- Getting law, business, or other degrees
- Working with pharmaceutical companies
- Counseling alcoholics and drug abusers
- Going into a medically related business
- Entering politics (medical or non-medical)
- Writing fiction, non-fiction, and technical pieces

It must be obvious by now that medicine has an enormous number of opportunities, and physicians have many opportunities once they want to slow down or stop their clinical practices.

You Haven't Blown It Yet

If you did poorly in high school, you can still get into medical school. It will just take more effort than if you were an academic star. Since you are reading this book, if you didn't do well, it was probably due to a lack of effort and motivation on your part (and probably a lack of any encouragement from your teachers).

A student in my high school class performed dismally, barely squeaking by to graduate. Her perpetual expression was one of boredom. She drifted off to a small college—probably getting in purely by chance. Yet, once she reached college, she found a goal (medicine) and teachers who could inspire her to achieve her real potential. It gave me quite a start to see her in the crowd of new medical students on my first day at school. She had found a goal, decided to aggressively pursue it, and didn't let her marginal high school performance weigh her down.

If you now have the motivation and are willing to put out the effort, you still can make the grade.

6: Unique Opportunities—Accelerated Programs

Fortune favors the bold.
(Audentis Fortuna juvat.)

Virgil, *Aeneid*, X

IF YOU ARE A MATURE, STELLAR HIGH SCHOOL STUDENT who is aiming for a career in medicine, you may want to investigate the accelerated programs that some medical schools offer. These programs accept high school seniors or college freshmen and sophomores into a combined Bachelor of Science/Arts–Medical curriculum. The undergraduate portion usually lasts two or three years, while students take their "premed" courses at the medical school's undergraduate campus. If they do well in these courses, students then enter the associated medical school as regular students. (Although it is classed as "accelerated," one program at Brown University lasts eight years.)

These programs usually reduce the amount of formal schooling needed to become a physician by one to three years. They are, of course, heavily weighted with the premed requirements. Some students find that they do not have time either to complete enough credits to graduate or to take other courses they find interesting. However, most programs allow students to defer their entrance into medical school one or two years to spend more time on undergraduate studies if they desire. If a student in an accelerated program does not acquire enough credits to get an undergraduate degree by the time he or she enters medical school, the school normally awards a Bachelor of Medical Sciences after the student's first year in medical school.

Studies suggest that, for students with equivalent records before college, accelerated students do as well in medical school and in postgraduate (residency) training as do those who complete a more traditional premedical course. But a greater percentage of accelerated students take more than four years to graduate from medical school. (Does this mean they become "decelerated"?)

Although they may appear to be the best way to pursue a medical education, accelerated programs are not perfect. Before you leap into one of these programs, consider these factors:

Positive Aspects

1. Greater chance of completing the program than "normal" premed students. Students in combined bachelor's degree–medical degree programs have been shown to be eight times as likely to become physicians as other premed students, even when the SAT scores for the groups were controlled. For underrepresented minority students, the differences are a little less dramatic, but still impressive.

2. Stress reduction. As long as participants do well in the undergraduate program (and for some programs, also on the MCAT), they are guaranteed a slot in medical school.

3. As long as they take the premed curriculum, students can choose any major they want. Unlike other students who must gear their majors toward possible employment alternatives in case they don't get into medical school, students in accelerated programs can major in any area which interests them.

4. Some programs offer accelerated students summer courses or research opportunities at the medical school. Since these students are (almost) in the profession, the medical school's faculty takes a kinder view of their participation in the school's activities.

5. Since they have had experiences at the medical school, students have an easier time adjusting. Unlike many other new medical students, they will probably know other students in their class and in the upper classes. They may also know some of the faculty.

Negative Aspects

1. Entering an accelerated program weds you to a medical career, often well before you have had a chance to have many other life experiences. (You can, of course, always divorce yourself from this decision, but like all divorces, it can be a soul-wrenching process.) A major concern should be *who* made your decision to enter medicine and *why* it was made. Think hard before you commit yourself.

2. Each program has minimum requirements to meet during the undergraduate years. These may include a specific GPA (or subsets, such as a minimum GPA in science or humanities courses), a minimum grade in any course (for example, nothing less than a "C"), and, in some cases, minimum scores on the MCAT. Each program has different requirements, so it is important to check to see if you are willing and able to meet them.

3. You will probably have a different undergraduate experience than most of your peers. First, you may have less time to participate in extracurricular activities, since you will take a very heavy load of science classes, usually involving extended laboratory time. Second, in some programs, you will live with other students in the accelerated program. This can lead to less interaction with other undergraduates than students normally would have. In some cases, it also has caused friction between these students and other premed students who aren't getting the "free ride" into medical school.

4. Accelerated-program students often feel that they have missed out on the wider life-perspective that a liberal arts education offers. While they may compensate for that with self-study and courses in later life, few physicians find that they have the time for this. (In fairness, however, many regular-curriculum "gunner" premed students also miss out on these opportunities.)

5. Since students in these programs have proven that they have the intelligence and motivation to be physicians (at least up to this point in their schooling), they can apply to and probably get into many medical schools. Yet in many of these programs, students lose their guaranteed

place in medical school if they apply to other schools. Also, since these students often do not have bachelor's degrees when they are ready to enter medical school, they are at a competitive disadvantage when applying to other schools.

To mangle an old expression, if you have seen one accelerated program, you have seen *one* accelerated program. The programs vary considerably. Some of the programs are rigid, others are highly flexible. In some, the students form a distinct and isolated group within the college; in others, they are fully integrated into the school and student body. There are programs at small colleges and at large universities. Few are linked to the most prestigious (not necessarily the best) medical schools. Since there are so many variations among the accelerated programs, be sure to investigate the details thoroughly.

The section below has a list of schools offering combined undergraduate-medical school programs. The American Association of Medical College's annual book, *Medical School Admission Requirements,* also has a section describing schools with these programs. The listings include each school's entrance requirements; selection factors; curriculum; expenses; available financial aid; application policies; and the number of in-state and out-of-state applicants, interviewees, and matriculants during the prior year.

Note that "accelerated programs" and "early admission programs" (described in chapter 7) are two different animals.

Schools with Combined Undergraduate–M.D. Programs

Programs marked with an asterisk (*) have programs combined with undergraduate schools at other institutions. The medical school (MD) and the undergraduate campus (UG) are both listed.

ALABAMA

University of South Alabama
Office of Admissions
Administrative Building, Room 182
Mobile, AL 36688-0002
(334) 460-6141; (800) 872-5247
http://www.usouthal.edu

CALIFORNIA

University of California, Los Angeles,
    School of Medicine (MD)*
University of California, Riverside (UG)

Student Affairs Officer
Division of Biomedical Sciences
University of California, Riverside
Riverside, CA 92521-0121
(909) 787-4333
http://www.medsch.ucla.edu (UCLA)
http://www.ucriverside.edu (Riverside)

University of Southern California
Office of College Academic Services
College of Letters, Arts, and Sciences
University of California
Los Angeles, CA 90089-0152
(213) 740-5930
http://www.usc.edu

FLORIDA

University of Miami
Office of Admissions
P.O. Box 248025
Coral Gables, FL 33124
(305) 284-4323
http://www.miami.edu
(state residents only)

ILLINOIS

Chicago Medical School (MD)*
Midwestern University
Illinois Institute of Technology (UG)

Director of Admissions
B.S./M.D. Program
10 West 33rd Street
Chicago, IL 60616
(312) 567-3025; (800) 448-2329
http://www.iit.edu

Northwestern University
Office of Admission & Financial Aid
1801 Hinman Avenue
Evanston, IL 60204-3060
(847) 491-7271
http://www.nwinfo.nwu.edu

MASSACHUSETTS

Boston University
Associate Director, Admissions
121 Bay State Road
Boston, MA 02215
(617) 353-2330
http://web.bu.edu/

MICHIGAN

Michigan State University
College of Human Medicine
Office of Admissions
A-239 Life Sciences
East Lansing, MI 48824
(517) 353-9620
http://www.msu.edu

University of Michigan
Inteflex Program
Wing "C"
5113 Medical Science I Building
Ann Arbor, MI 48109-0611
(313) 764-9534
http://www.umich.edu

MISSOURI

University of Missouri–Kansas City
School of Medicine
Council on Selection
2411 Holmes
Kansas City, MO 64108
(816) 235-1870
http://www.umkc.edu

NEW JERSEY

UMDNJ–New Jersey Medical School (MD)*
Boston University (UG)
Drew University (UG)
Montclair State University (UG)
New Jersey Institute of Technology (UG)
Stevens Institute of Technology (UG)
Richard Stockton College of New Jersey (UG)
Trenton State College (UG)

Office of Admissions
C-653 MSB
UMDNJ–New Jersey Medical School
185 South Orange Avenue
Newark, NJ 07103-2714
(201) 982-4631
http://njmsa.umdnj.edu/umdnj.html (NJMed)
http://www.bu.edu (BU)
http://www.drew.edu (Drew)
http://www.montclair.edu (Montclair)
http://www.njit.edu (NJIT)
http://www.stevens-tech.edu (Stevens)
http://loki.stockton.edu (Stockton)
http://www.trenton.edu (Trenton)

UMDNJ–Robert Wood Johnson Medical
School (MD)*
Rutgers University (UG)

Bachelor/Medical Degree Program
Nelson Biological Laboratory
Rutgers University
P.O. Box 1059
Piscataway, NJ 08855-1059
(908) 445-5270
http://www.umdnj.edu/rwjms.html (UMDNJ–
RWJ)
http://www.rutgers.edu (Rutgers)

NEW YORK

Albany Medical College (MD)*
Rensselaer Polytechnic Institute (UG)

Admissions Counselor
Rensselaer Polytechnic Institute
Troy, NY 12180
(518) 276-6216
http://www.rpi.edu

Albany Medical College (MD)*
Siena College (UG)

Office of Admissions
Siena College
Route 9
Loudonville, NY 12211
(518) 783-2423

Albany Medical College (MD)*
Union College (UG)

Associate Dean of Admissions
Union College
Schenectady, NY 12308
(518) 388-6112

Combined New York Medical Schools (MD)*
Sophie Davis School of Biomedical
  Education (UG)

Office of Admissions
Sophie Davis School of Biomedical
  Education
City University of New York
Y Building, Room 205N
138th Street & Convent Avenue
New York, NY 10031
(212) 650-7707 or -7712
(state residents only)

New York University
Admission Office
College of Arts & Science
22 Washington Square North
Room 904 Main Building
New York, NY 10003
(212) 998-4500
http://www.nyu.edu

SUNY–Brooklyn College of Medicine (MD)*
Brooklyn College (UG)

Director of Admissions
1602 James Hall
Brooklyn College
Brooklyn, NY 11210
(718) 951-5044
http://www.hallux.medschool.hscbklyn.edu/student
  (SUNY)
http://www.brooklyn.cuny.edu (Brooklyn Coll)

SUNY–Syracuse College of Medicine (MD)*
Binghamton University (UG)

Rural Primary Care Recruitment Programs
SUNY College of Medicine
Health Science Center at Syracuse
P.O. Box 1000
Binghamton, NY 13902
(607) 770-8515

University of Rochester School of Medicine &
  Dentistry
Program Coordinator
Rochester Early Medical Scholars
Undergraduate Admissions—Meliora Hall
Rochester, NY 14627
(716) 275-3221
http://www.rochester.edu

OHIO

Case Western Reserve University
Assistant Director of Admissions
Office of Undergraduate Admission
10900 Euclid Avenue
Cleveland, OH 44106-7055
(216) 368-4450
http://www.cwru.edu

Northeastern Ohio Universities College
  of Medicine (MD)*
Kent State University (UG)
University of Akron (UG)
Youngstown State University (UG)

Associate Director of Admissions
Northeastern Ohio Universities
College of Medicine
4209 State Route 44, P.O. Box 95
Rootstown, OH 44272-0095
(216) 325-2511
http://www.kent.edu (Kent)
http://www.uakron.edu (Akron)
http://www.ysu.edu (Youngstown)

PENNSYLVANIA

Jefferson Medical College (MD)*
Pennsylvania State University (UG)

Undergraduate Admissions
Pennsylvania State University
201 Shields Building—Box 3000
University Park, PA 16802
(814) 865-5471
http://www.tju.edu (Jefferson)
http://www.psu.edu (Penn)

Allegheny University of the Health
  Sciences (MD)*
  (Formerly the Medical College of
  Pennsylvania & Hahnemann University
  School of Medicine)
Lehigh University (UG)

Office of Admissions
Lehigh University
27 Memorial Drive West
Bethlehem, PA 18105
(610) 758-3100
http://www.medcolpa.edu (Allegheny UHS)
http://www.lehigh.edu (Lehigh)

Allegheny University of the Health
  Sciences (MD)*
  (Formerly the Medical College of
  Pennsylvania & Hahnemann University
  School of Medicine)
Villanova University (UG)

Office of Undergraduate Admissions
Villanova University
800 Lancaster Avenue
Villanova, PA 19085-1699
(800) 338-7927
http://www.medcolpa.edu (Allegheny UHS)
http://www.vill.edu (Villanova)

RHODE ISLAND

Brown University
College Admission Office
Box 1876
Providence, RI 02912
(401) 863-2378
http://www.brown.edu

TENNESSEE

East Tennessee State University
Director, Premedical–Medical Program
Office of Medical Professions Advisement
P.O. Box 70,592
Johnson City, TN 37614-0592
(423) 439-6905
http://www.etsu.east-tenn.st.edu

Meharry Medical College (MD)*
Fisk University (UG)

Associate Vice President
College Relations and Lifelong Learning
1005 D.B. Todd, Jr. Boulevard
Nashville, TN 37208
(615) 327-6425

TEXAS

Baylor College of Medicine (MD)*
Rice University (UG)

Office of Admissions
One Baylor Plaza
Room 106A
Houston, TX 77030
(713) 798-4841

University of North Texas Health
  Science Center
Texas College of Osteopathic Medicine
Office of Medical Student Admissions
3500 Camp Bowie Boulevard
Ft. Worth, TX 76107-2699
(817) 735-2204; (800) 535-8266

VIRGINIA

Eastern Virginia Medical School
Office of Admissions
721 Fairfax Avenue
Norfolk, VA 23507-2000
(804) 446-5812

WASHINGTON, D.C.

George Washington University (MD)*
Columbian College (UG)

School of Medicine
Office of Admissions
2121 T Street, N.W.
Washington, DC 20052
(800) 447-3765

Howard University School of Medicine
Director, Center for Preprofessional
  Education
P.O. Box 473
Administration Building
Howard University
Washington, DC 20059
(202) 806-7231
http://www.howard.edu

WISCONSIN

University of Wisconsin–Madison
  Medical School
Medical Scholars Program
1300 University Avenue, Room 1250
Madison, WI 53706
(608) 263-7561
http://www.biostat.wisc.edu
(state residents only)

7: Undergraduate Preparation

MEDICAL EDUCATORS DON'T HAVE a high opinion of most medical school applicants' undergraduate experiences. This was best expressed by Robert Petersdorf, the Association of American Medical Colleges' president emeritus, when he said,

> We must face the fact that the U.S. medical education system has, in fact if not by design, been guilty of stifling intellectual growth and exploration. All too often a career in medicine is launched in the rigid premedical educational environment that prevails in colleges and universities. Students become study machines, characterized as hypercompetitive and narrow-minded at best, and greedy and dishonest at worst. They are thought to be interested only in courses they believe will help ensure their admission to medical school. Students in college should be broadening their educational background, exploring various disciplines, and broadening their minds to new intellectual horizons. Instead, we hear too often of students who will not consider an intellectually challenging course for fear of getting a poor grade and hurting their chances of admission to medical school. [Petersdorf RG, Turner KS. Medical education in the 1990s—and beyond: a view from the United States. *Acad Med* 1995;70(7) Supp:S41-S47.]

Being motivated, disciplined, goal-oriented, and getting good grades are positive attributes. But don't let the negatives of "premed syndrome" overwhelm you and obscure the positive aspects of your undergraduate education. As you peruse this section of the book, decide what type of premed student you want to be: grade greedy or educationally enlightened.

"Best" Preparation For Medical School

Everyone always asks about the "best" preparation for medical school. "Is this college the best?" they ask. Or, "What major is best?" There is no universal "best" answer, since each student is unique. But there are some guidelines to follow. In the end, each of you must choose what is right ("best" if you must) for yourself—whether you are choosing an undergraduate school, a medical school, or especially, a major course of study.

Choosing a Major

A lot of scuttlebutt exists about which major to choose. As you ponder your selection, think about this: If you like a subject area, you will be happy taking in-depth courses in it, and consequently you will do better than you would if you did not enjoy the subject. Remember that you will spend a lot of time, over four or five years, studying in your major field. If you select a major in a field that interests you, learning will be enjoyable, and you will be less stressed as an undergraduate. The best answer is to major in an area that you would choose even if you did not have the goal of getting into medical school.

What if you either don't get into medical school or change your mind about going? Will your major be something that was worthwhile studying? Will it prepare you in any way for anything else you might want to do? Is it something that will help you with the rest of your life? Also (but least important), if you are a premed non-science major, you will stand out from the crowd of biochemistry and molecular biology applicants when you apply to medical school. It might just give you an edge in getting accepted. (Perish the thought!)

When choosing a major, make sure you will have enough time to complete your basic premed requirements. Some premeds may have difficulty completing their majors and also fulfilling premed requirements. This most frequently occurs in those majors with few electives, such as engineering or architecture. If you wish to pursue either of these majors, you will need an understanding adviser and a superb knowledge of your school's systems (e.g., registration, administration) so that you can complete all the courses you need in a timely manner. (Note also that, at some schools, students majoring in "difficult" areas, especially engineering, may be near the top of their class even though they have a "B" average. Medical school admission officers do take this into *account* if your reference letters confirm this situation.)

Most premeds "play it safe" by majoring in the biological sciences. (This must really bore most medical school admission officers. All majors are, however, evaluated equally.) Less than 20% of all medical students majored in the physical sciences as undergraduates, with more than half of these majoring in chemistry or biochemistry. Sadly, fewer than 17% majored in non-science subjects, with only a negligible number in the humanities. In contrast, only 20% of non-premed students major in the natural sciences, with most students majoring instead in the social sciences, business, or the humanities.

One of the top students in my medical school class majored in French literature. It amazed everyone that a premed would pick this major. He explained that he actually had an easier time as an undergraduate than many of his compatriots. Since he really enjoyed his major subject area, he did not feel stressed when studying for those courses. Therefore, he found it much easier to put in the "drudge time" studying organic chemistry than other premed students did.

A survey of medical students about their undergraduate experiences yielded this "top five" list of recommendations about premed education.

1. You don't have to major in science.

2. Take classes dealing with people, society, communication, ethics, and life—they are all helpful in clinical medicine.

3. Biochemistry and upper-level biology are the science courses that help you the most in medical school. (A recent study suggests that taking biochemistry as an undergraduate provides the most help to first-year medical students.)

4. Concentrate on developing your critical-thinking, problem-solving, and scientific-thinking skills.

5. Realize that courses such as physics and organic chemistry help you prepare for the MCAT, but they are of little or no use to you during medical school.

Other comments they made about their majors were:

I majored in chemistry. While I'm not sure if it helped or hurt getting into medical school, and while I loved chemistry, I think it's totally useless. If I had to do it over, I would major in something pertinent to medicine and health, such as medical anthropology, health education, political science, or economics. (She got an M.P.H. while in medical school.) The liberal arts classes I did take gave me skills and perspectives that have been useful in medicine.

My major may have helped me get into medical school. As a theology major, it's hard to say—maybe God was on my side.

My major was history, and at first I was afraid that it would hinder my chances of being accepted. But it was actually kind of an advantage. I was different from the average applicant and it really helped in interviews because we could discuss a variety of topics. Admissions personnel seemed glad not to see another biology/chemistry major.

Two caveats: First, even if you choose not to major in the sciences, it is still important to take more than one laboratory course during some semesters. If you don't do this, you may extend your undergraduate career interminably. Medical schools specifically look at performance during these semesters for a clue to how well you will do in medical school. Second, studies suggest that, on average, students with a broad-based (non-science) undergraduate education don't do as well initially in medical school as those with science majors. However, the performance for both groups evens out during their clinical years.

Keep Your Options Open—You May Change Your Mind

Not everyone who enters college as a "premed" goes to medical school. (And some who enter college without any expectation of going to medical school eventually "see the light" and become physicians. I was one of those.) In any case, plan several alternative routes as you progress through school. If you find that you do not like the courses offered in your major, are you prepared to switch fields without losing too much time or too many credits? If the courses you need are not open when you go through registration, do you have alternatives to take? Finally, if you find that your goals have changed and you really don't want to go to medical school, have you considered other options? If so, do you know how to get there from here?

Life is uncertain. Your life plan is just a guide. These facts won't change once you graduate, once you go to medical school, or once you are a practicing physician. It's always an excellent idea to have alternative plans at every stage of your life. As the Scouts say, "Be prepared."

Length of Premedical Education

Most premeds now take five years to complete their undergraduate degrees. They often choose this longer course so that they can pursue non-science majors or minors, work to pay for school, or pursue extracurricular activities. At some schools, it is difficult to get the necessary classes at the right time and that hinders students from advancing through their programs.

Choosing an Undergraduate College

After you have given at least some thought to your major field of study, it's time to choose your undergraduate college. If you know your major, you can look for schools known for their expertise in that field. If you are still unsure of your major, look for schools that allow you many areas of study while you complete premed requirements.

Choosing a college is tough. Choosing a college based on whether you can get into medical school after graduation is even tougher.

In the past, men had the best chance of entering medical school if they attended private universities with associated medical schools, previously all-male colleges that had recently become coeducational, or traditionally coeducational colleges. Women's entry rates were highest for students from women's colleges, distantly followed by private universities having associated medical schools. However, these rates are changing due to the increasing numbers of women entering medical schools and the decreasing number of all-women colleges.

Medical schools reportedly give preference to applicants from "top name" colleges and universities. Some such students have even been offered interviews at medical schools before they submitted secondary applications. Yet attractive as this sounds, it is not reason enough to pick such a school for your undergraduate work. Students get into medical schools from all U.S. undergraduate schools. You can too.

Undergraduate schools can be very expensive. In the United States, the annual tuition at community colleges averages less than half the cost of tuition at public four-year colleges, and only about 10% of that at private four-year colleges (figure 7.1). Since you will probably incur large debts for your medical school education, you may want to limit the amount you spend (or owe) for undergraduate school.

Although community colleges are relatively inexpensive, medical schools want applicants to have taken at least their upper-level science courses at four-year colleges. They believe that four-year schools have more rigorous standards, have less "grade inflation," and better measure a student's ability to perform well in medical school. This means that if you start out at a community college, you should immediately begin planning your transfer to a four-year school.

Your primary goal when selecting an undergraduate school is to get a good education. Hopefully, while you complete your course of study, you will also mature as an individual, enjoy your experience, and not go broke doing it. To meet all these goals, you should consider many factors to find the "best" school for you to attend.

Is There A "Best" College?

Must/Want Analysis (Undergraduate Schools)

One way to determine which undergraduate (and later which medical) school to attend is to use the Must/Want Analysis (see also chapter 16). This method allows you to analyze which factors are important to you and to determine which schools meet your needs. By forcing you to examine what you really need and want in a school, it helps you to see past a school's reputation and the "best college" pronouncements of your advisers and family.

To use the Must/Want Analysis, first make a list of all the factors that could possibly influence your decision about which undergraduate school you would like to attend. (See figure 7.2 for an example.) Let's first see how you will use the list in your Must/Want analysis.

Once you have your list, assign "Weights" to each factor based on its importance to you. (Refer to figure 7.3 and figure 7.4 to see how a sample student assigned "Weights" to the factors important to her.) In giving "Weights" to each factor, remember that the total of the weights must equal "100". Therefore, apportion each item's weight in relation to its importance to all the other factors you are considering.

Figure 7.1: Average Cost of Undergraduate School Tuition (Per Year)

	Community College	Public 4-Year School*	Private 4-Year School		Community College	Public 4-Year School*	Private 4-Year School
AL	$ 1,123	$ 2,234	$ 7,404	MT	$ 1,329	$ 2,346	$ 6,993
AK	1,320	2,502	7,950	NE	1,097	2,294	8,897
AZ	734	1,943	6,076	NV	842	1,830	7,494
AR	1,123	2,062	6,162	NH	2,316	4,537	12,143
CA	365	2,918	12,748	NJ	1,755	3,649	12,951
CO	1,279	2,458	11,710	NM	678	1,938	11,549
CT	1,520	3,828	15,704	NY	2,152	3,697	12,892
DE	1,266	3,962	7,187	NC	582	1,622	10,406
DC	None	974	13,367	ND	1,689	2,211	6,653
FL	1,112	1,790	9,941	OH	2,164	3,664	11,782
GA	1,015	1,076	9,571	OK	1,153	1,741	8,078
HI	500	1,524	5,951	OR	1,324	3,241	12,969
ID	990	1,714	11,246	PA	1,751	4,693	13,457
IL	1,194	3,388	11,070	RI	1,686	3,619	14,445
IN	1,854	3,040	11,848	SC	1,048	3,103	9,122
IA	1,699	2,565	11,430	SD	3,430	2,549	8,574
KS	1,044	2,110	8,079	TN	945	2,001	9,210
KY	1,080	2,160	7,038	TX	680	1,832	8,410
LA	1,027	2,139	11,769	UT	1,640	2,007	2,814
ME	2,137	3,582	15,383	VT	2,877	5,521	15,032
MD	1,848	3,111	13,762	VA	1,984	3,965	10,309
MA	2,441	4,178	15,685	WA	1,314	2,726	12,412
MI	1,432	3,789	8,739	WV	1,312	1,997	9,889
MN	1,928	3,108	12,233	WI	1,649	2,555	10,835
MS	935	2,443	6,289	WY	893	2,005	None
MO	1,203	3,007	9,607				
				USA	$2,779	$2,537	$11,522

Adapted from the *National Center for Education Statistics, 1994-95 Report*, and *U.S. General Accounting Office data for 1995.

To assign weights, it is easiest to first select those factors that are not at all important to you and rate them "0." These may be eliminated from your list. Next, look over your list to find those items that are absolute necessities for you, such as a special premed curriculum. *If an item is an absolute, a "Must," you have decided that the factor is so important that it must be present or else it will eliminate a school from consideration, regardless of its other qualities.* If a factor is a "Must," instead of assigning it a number value, put the word "Must" in the weight column.

Now you are ready to decide the relative importance of the remaining factors by assigning each factor a "Weight." Choose factors of minimal importance, rating them "1." Then choose those with more importance and rate them a "2." Continue in this fashion until the total for all assigned "Weights" equals "100." *You will use your same weighting of the same factors to rate all the schools that you consider.* For example, you might want to live in the midwest, if possible, and might rate "geography" a "1." But you are much more interested in schools' academic programs than their location, so you would rate that factor (academic programs) a "4."

In evaluating a school, assign a "Score" to each factor you consider. The "Score," on a 1-10 scale, is your estimate of how well that school fulfills your initial expectations for that category (10 is "perfect"). Multiply the "Weight" by the "Score" to give the factor "Total" for that school. All factor "Total"s are added to give your "School Evaluation Score." If an element that you have rated as a "Must" is not present at the school, you should drop that school from consideration.

Figures 7.3 and 7.4 are examples of one student's Must/Want Analyses for two schools she was considering. Notice that in figure 7.4, although the school got high marks in some factors this student considered important, two of her "make or break" factors (indicating a strong computer science department) were not present. Therefore, she did not continue completing the form and eliminated that school from consideration. Therefore, even if this school offers her admission, she will not accept. When making factors a "Must," be sure that they are so important that you are willing not to go to an otherwise excellent school that lacks that factor. (She also deleted any factors she rated "0," or not at all important to her, from her lists. This considerably shortened the forms she used to rate the schools.)

As shown in figure 7.3, this student will use Hometown University's "School Evaluation Score" of 613 to compare this school with other schools in which she is interested. If there is no change in her situation, she will go to the school with the highest score that accepts her.

Figure 7.2: Must/Want Analysis

SCHOOL _____

PROGRAMS	WEIGHT	X SCORE	= TOTAL
Broad Range of Courses			
Special Premed Curriculum			
Strong in Your Major & Minor			
Has All Required Premed Courses			
Strong Science Departments			
Flexibility (Times, Year-Round)			
Enough Positions in Courses			
Class Sizes			

GEOGRAPHIC LOCATION			
Inner City, Suburb, Rural			
Part of Country			
Specific City			
Spouse/Family/Dependent Needs			

REPUTATION			
School's Reputation			
High Academic Standards			
School's Age and Stability			
Percentage On-Time Graduations			
Attitude Toward Women, Minorities			
Success Getting Into Medical School			

FACULTY			
Availability			
Teach Introductory Courses			
Teach Advanced Courses			

CURRICULUM			
Curriculum Structure			
Innovative Curriculum			
Time to Degree			
Combination Degrees			
Self-Paced Learning			
Computer Education			
Pre-School Orientations			
Specialty-Selection Counseling			
Case-Based Teaching			
Small-Group Learning			
Large/Small Classes			
Student-Teacher Ratio			
Types of Examinations			

ESPRIT DE CORPS			

Figure 7.2: Must/Want Analysis, cont'd.

RESEARCH OPPORTUNITIES/TRAINING	WEIGHT	X SCORE	= TOTAL
Knowledge			
Materials			
Time			
Funding			
LOCAL JOB PROSPECTS			

FACILITIES			
Easy Registration Process			
Campus Size			
Student-Body Size			
Strong Computer Use/Orientation			
Up-To-Date Lecture Facilities			
Good Laboratory Facilities			
Library/Media			
Parking			
Bookstore			
Safety/Security			

HEALTH CARE			
Medical Insurance			
Student Health Service			
Psychiatric Counseling			

MISCELLANEOUS			
Child Care			
Premed Counseling			
Mentoring			
Available Housing			
Available/Affordable Food			
Student-Learning Center			

EXTRACURRICULAR ACTIVITIES			
Social Life			
Medically-Related Activities			
General Atmosphere			

FINANCIAL			
Tuition Costs			
Housing Costs			
Other Cost-of Living			
Scholarships			
Loans			
Jobs			

TOTAL OF ALL WEIGHTS =   <u>100</u>

SCHOOL EVALUATION SCORE =   _____

Figure 7.3: Undergraduate School Must/Want Analysis—Example 1

SCHOOL ___HOMETOWN UNIVERSITY___

PROGRAMS	WEIGHT	X SCORE	= TOTAL
Broad Range of Courses	8	5	40
Strong in Your Major & Minor	6	9	54
Has All Required Premed Courses	10	10	100
Strong Science Departments	5	4	20
Flexibility (Times, Year-Round)	1	7	7
Enough Positions in Courses	7	3	21

REPUTATION			
School's Reputation	1	4	4
High Academic Standards	8	7	56
Percent On-Time Graduations	1	5	5
Attitude Toward Women, Minorities	3	7	21
Success Getting Into Medical School	2	6	12

FACULTY			
Availability	7	3	21
Teach Introductory Courses	1	1	1
Teach Advanced Courses	3	8	24

CURRICULUM			
Curriculum Structure	3	2	6
Time to Degree	1	4	4
Self-Paced Learning	1	2	2
Computer Education	MUST	YES	✓

ESPRIT DE CORPS	2	7	14

FACILITIES			
Easy Registration Process	2	1	2
Strong Computer Use/Orientation	MUST	YES	✓
Good Laboratory Facilities	1	4	4
Library/Media	3	9	27
Safety/Security	2	6	12

HEALTH CARE			
Student Health Service	1	1	1

MISCELLANEOUS			
Premed Counseling	1	5	5
Available Housing	3	9	27

EXTRACURRICULAR ACTIVITIES:			
Social Life	1	4	4
Medically-Related Activities	3	7	21
General Atmosphere	2	5	10

FINANCIAL			
Tuition Costs	5	9	45
Other Cost-of Living	1	7	7
Scholarships	2	9	18
Jobs	3	6	18

TOTAL OF ALL WEIGHTS =   __100__

SCHOOL EVALUATION SCORE =   __613__

Figure 7.4: Undergraduate School Must/Want Analysis—Example 2

SCHOOL ___NEVERMORE COLLEGE___

PROGRAMS	WEIGHT	X SCORE	= TOTAL
Broad Range of Courses	8	8	64
Strong in Your Major & Minor	6	1	6
Has All Required Premed Courses	10	10	100
Strong Science Departments	5	9	45
Flexibility (Times, Year-Round)	1	6	6
Enough Positions in Courses	7	8	56
REPUTATION			
School's Reputation	1	8	8
High Academic Standards	8	9	72
Percent On-Time Graduations	1	5	5
Attitude Toward Women, Minorities	3	7	21
Success Getting Into Medical School	2	7	14
FACULTY			
Availability	7	6	42
Teach Introductory Courses	1	5	5
Teach Advanced Courses	3	10	30
CURRICULUM			
Curriculum Structure	3	5	15
Time to Degree	1	6	6
Self-Paced Learning	1	3	3
Computer Education	MUST	NO	STOP!!
ESPRIT DE CORPS	2		
FACILITIES			
Easy Registration Process	2		
Strong Computer Use/Orientation	MUST	NO	STOP!!
Good Laboratory Facilities	1		
Library/Media	3		
Safety/Security	2		
HEALTH CARE			
Student Health Service	1		
MISCELLANEOUS			
Premed Counseling	1		
Available Housing	3		
EXTRACURRICULAR ACTIVITIES:			
Social Life	1		
Medically-Related Activities	3		
General Atmosphere	2		
FINANCIAL			
Tuition Costs	5		
Other Cost-of Living	1		
Scholarships	2		
Jobs	3		

TOTAL OF ALL WEIGHTS = 100

SCHOOL EVALUATION SCORE = NO SCORE (Does not have a "Must" Requirement)

Medical School Requirements

The requirements to enter medical school have changed somewhat since 1894 when the Association of American Medical Colleges (AAMC) first standardized them. At that time, they listed the application requirements as:

1. An English composition in the handwriting of the applicant, of not less than 200 words, said composition to include construction, punctuation, and spelling.

2. Arithmetic—fundamental rules, decimal fractions, and ratio and proportion.

3. Algebra—including quadratics.

4. Physics—elementary.

5. Latin—an amount equal to one year of study as indicated in *Harkness's Latin Reader.*

It wasn't until 1900 that medical schools required a high school diploma or the equivalent as demonstrated by examination.

Medical school admission requirements vary from school to school. *Medical School Admission Requirements* (*MSAR*), an annual book from the AAMC, lists the specific requirements for each (M.D.) medical school in the United States and Canada. The Association of Canadian Medical Colleges also publishes a more detailed description of Canadian schools in its *Admission Requirements to Canadian Faculties of Medicine and Their Selection Policies.* The American Association of Colleges of Osteopathic Medicine issues a similar book annually, *Osteopathic Medical College Information.* These books are vital for everyone considering applying to medical school, so that they can plan their undergraduate courses of study. Most college libraries have a copy of at least the AAMC book, usually in the reference section; all college bookstores carry this book. For the Canadian and Osteopathic books, write to the respective associations (addresses in Appendix B).

Most medical schools expect applicants to take the Medical College Admission Test (MCAT) and to have completed *at least* course work in:

- Biology (1 year)
- Physics (1 year)
- English (1 year)
- Chemistry—through Organic Chemistry (2 years)

Since you don't know where you will apply to medical school, the safest course is to meet at least these minimum requirements. Some medical schools will not accept advanced placement (AP) credits in lieu of their required courses (figure 15.5). They expect students to still take the same amount of the subject in college, even though they may begin their college studies with higher-level courses. For example, if you get AP credit for chemistry, you may need to not only take organic chemistry in college, but also another year of chemistry, such as biochemistry. Although having AP credits may not decrease the number of classes you need to meet premed requirements, it is still worth taking AP classes in high school, since they will better prepare you for college-level work.

Also, consider taking a foreign language in college. Although a language may not be explicitly required (except for Puerto Rican and French Canadian schools), students who can converse in another language (especially Spanish) are given preference at schools where many patients speak that language.

How Much Science and Math Must (Should) You Take?

Science majors will need to take lots of math and science courses to complete their course requirements. For them, this question is moot. How about non-science majors? While you can get by with only the basic premed courses, most medical schools recommend that you also take some upper-level science courses to prepare you for the preclinical basic science courses. I recommend that you take, if possible, biochemistry and molecular biology. Taking these courses as an undergraduate allows you time to grasp the basics so that you can better assimilate additional information during medical school. Unlike many other parts of the premed curriculum, these courses are relevant to medicine and are, on the first pass, often difficult to learn. (Making your first term in medical school just a bit easier by allowing you more time to study anatomy also is worthwhile.)

For those who do not need math courses for their major (or minor), note that many medical schools suggest or require calculus. While not specifically required, computer skills and statistics are an integral part of medical education (in medical school and beyond). Try to acquire at least basic knowledge in these areas. (See figure 15.1 for each school's specific requirements.)

Most medical schools encourage students to take honors courses, complete independent study, and do research. All of these allow students to explore specific subject areas in-depth. Even if they are not related to the sciences or to medicine, these types of independent learning are vital to a physician's continuing education.

Extracurricular Activities

You will never have as much free time to try new activities and explore your world as you do during undergraduate school. Take advantage of this time. Use extracurricular activities to unwind from class work, to stretch your mind, and perhaps, to make money. Getting involved in activities and sticking with them throughout college shows others that you have the maturity and commitment needed to succeed in a medical career. It is important to try to have fun, but don't sacrifice your school work to extracurricular activities.

A big mistake some budding premedical students make is to think that their summer "vacation" is really a vacation. Admission committees often closely scrutinize an applicant's summer activities. Did he or she use the time to earn money for school, to do new and interesting things, to take additional course work, or just to "goof off"? The choices one makes during these free periods offer excellent insight into his or her basic personality.

Service

What extracurricular activities "look best" on your application? While there are no particular activities that stand out, those you engage in should encourage your personal growth and show that you are both altruistic and people-oriented. These activities should also demonstrate that you are a well-rounded individual. Any activities in which you spend time helping others will be beneficial to your application. More importantly, however, such activities correlate with the life of service to others that epitomizes the medical profession.

When seeking out activities, find something you like to do, not just something that enhances your résumé. For the activities to "count," they need to be done over a prolonged period of time. If you don't like doing something, you won't be able to stick it out. What are some examples? If you like teaching, mentor high school students. If you like community service, help out at a food or clothing bank. If you are more organization-oriented, work with your campus premed group, the student government, the first-responder team, or join the service-oriented fraternity or sorority (Alpha Phi Omega, ΑΦΩ; Gamma Sigma Sigma, ΓΣΣ).

Even if you must work to finance your schooling, try to engage in some other activity. Can you help your church or synagogue with their fund-raising events? How about becoming a student guide for incoming freshmen?

Clinical Experiences

Currently, nearly all applicants admitted to medical school have some experience with the medical profession. They may have been health care workers (nurse, P.A., EMT, nurses aide, orderly, technologist), volunteers (on an ambulance; in a hospital, hospice, or nursing home), or ancillary workers in a health facility (clerk, housekeeper). Any of these experiences put you in close contact with physicians, patients, and their interactions. Such health-related experiences are carefully scrutinized by both premed committees and medical school admission officers. They want to know how intense the experience was and when you had it. As one medical student says, "It's not how much experience you have that matters, but the quality of it. If you've never experienced anything clinical, saying 'I know I want to do medicine,' during your interview isn't going to cut it."

If there has been too much time (e.g., three years) between a less-than-intense experience (e.g., a short stint as a part-time volunteer) and your medical school application, evaluators may wonder if you had enough clinical experience to know what you are getting into and whether you have a real interest in medicine. With more intense experiences (such as several years working as a clinical nurse), the timing may be less important.

Sometimes working in clinical settings also solidifies an individual's desire to become a physician, as one student's story shows.

> I really decided to go to medical school in my sophomore year of college when I tried out all of the "easier" careers that combine science and service. I say "easier" meaning better hours, less stress, more conducive to having a family, less time for training. I volunteered in a state hospital working with occupational therapists, shadowed physical therapists, and took an education class (to see if I wanted to be a biology teacher). After trying these and considering nursing, I decided that training as a physician would teach me about all the illnesses that these specialists look at incompletely. Basically, I wanted to know it all. I decided to pursue what I considered the ultimate in education and service. And if I didn't get in, I would fall back on one of the other professions I had considered.

Volunteering

This is an excellent time to volunteer your services in a medical area. You generally have time to spare. If you are asking yourself "When?" the answer is that you have time to do anything that is important to you. *And this is important.* Certainly you can arrange to spend a couple of hours a week to learn about the field you wish to enter. How about Saturday mornings? This experience can help you determine if you really want to become a physician. This must, after all, be *your* choice, not your parents', teachers', or friends' choice for you. And in volunteering, you will be able to see the amount of dedication, hard work, and commitment to continued learning that the profession requires. If a medical career is really what you want, this experience will renew your motivation. If not, it may save you a lot of frustration and help you to redirect your energies.

How do you volunteer now? First, determine what you are interested in and what you are willing to do. Ask yourself the following questions:

- What am I seeking in a volunteer experience?
- What do I want to accomplish through volunteering?
- Who (patients, clinicians, others) do I want to work with?
- What setting would be ideal?

- How much time am I willing to commit?
- What skills do I have?

Volunteers can work either through an organization or with an individual physician, or both. Most premeds, because more opportunities are usually available, volunteer through organizations, such as hospitals, nursing homes, hospices, and ambulance services. When thinking about medically related organizations in which to volunteer your time, you may want to consider the following:

- What is the organization's purpose and who does it serve?
- What time commitment does it require? (This may vary depending upon the specific activity you choose.)
- Will I have patient contact?
- Will I have any responsibility?
- Does the organization provide training? If so, how much and of what quality?
- Does it provide the type of volunteer activity I am seeking?
- How will this activity help me to improve myself as an individual?

Another option is to volunteer with an individual practitioner. Since you may have few contacts in the medical field, your best bet is to first approach your own family's doctor or a physician at your college's health center. Tell him or her of your interest in the medical profession and of your desire to experience medicine firsthand by "tagging along and helping out." Usually the clinician will be flattered that you asked, and will let you participate in at least a limited fashion. After a few months of this (stick it out, you are learning vital information on which to base life-long decisions) it may become obvious that you have experienced most of what this practitioner is willing to offer you. If he does not spontaneously suggest it, you should inquire as to whether a colleague can offer you more in-depth (read "active") medical experiences. If you know him really well, you might even address the possibility in your first meeting. In many cases, of course, working with a practitioner will be interesting and intriguing. If that is true for you, stick with it.

Working In Medicine

If you have the opportunity and the time, you might consider seeking employment in a medical setting. Paid positions are often available in hospitals, hospices, nursing homes, and physicians' offices for individuals with little or no health care experience. These jobs are usually not very glamorous. They may involve being housekeepers, nurses aides, or clerical personnel. The positions, however, have three advantages: they give you an excellent inside view of medical practice, they offer you a "bottoms-up" look at physicians, and they give you a paycheck. (And they introduce you to those who can help you in your future career.)

As a real part of the "team" you will often interact with the clinicians, patients, and their families. You will also be able to observe physicians at work—warts and all. If you have an idea that medicine is all glamour and kudos, this should disabuse you quickly. Additionally, students who have worked their way up from one of these jobs to eventually go through medical school have, in my experience, been among the finest physicians. They interact well with nurses and patients, and generally are sensitized to patient's concerns. Getting paid for this learning experience is just an added bonus.

The Emergency Medical System

Since many medical schools now expect applicants to have medically related experience, paid positions on ambulances have become much more difficult to get than they once were. Also, the requirements for even volunteer ambulance personnel now often include at least Emergency Medical Technician (EMT) certification, if not training at a higher level. If you can get such a position, however, it provides one of the best clinical experiences available to non-licensed individuals. It also allows you to interact with physicians in a variety of settings, and may be itself an entrée into a paid part-time hospital job. I am particularly fond of the Emergency Medical System (EMS), since that is how I began my medical career, and I still practice medicine "in the field" as a member of the Southern Arizona Rescue Association (wilderness search and rescue).

My own introduction to medicine was through a volunteer ambulance service, the Wheaton Rescue Squad in Maryland. At the time, the training requirements were Red Cross Advanced First Aid, the "new-fangled" American Heart Association's CPR course (not yet approved by the Red Cross), and an emergency childbirth class. This limited training was considered the best in the country at that time (1967). Most ambulance crews had far less first-aid training. My experiences on the ambulance enamored me with the practice of medicine (and especially Emergency Medicine). It also demonstrated that you don't have to have either a heart of stone or a cast-iron stomach to deal with many of the terrible events physicians must witness. Based on these experiences, I quietly switched to a premed curriculum (from pre-law). Since I went into medicine with firsthand knowledge of the field, I have never regretted the decision.

Some undergraduate schools now have their own first-responder teams to provide first aid for on-campus accidents and illnesses. These groups provide care at campus gatherings, including sporting and large social events, until ambulances arrive. While it usually provides a somewhat lightweight medical experience, this activity may be a desirable introduction to the world of medicine.

Research

Opportunities exist for undergraduates to do summer research, either in the laboratory or elsewhere. Research need not be in the "hard" sciences, and may simply be independent investigations supervised by a professor. Medical schools look for individuals who can work independently to expand their interests, abilities, and work habits. When considering a project, ask yourself if it accomplishes these goals.

Special research programs are also available through national research organizations, such as the National Institutes of Health and the Howard Hughes Foundation. Some medical schools also offer a limited number of research opportunities to undergraduates. See chapter 9, *Minority Applicants,* for additional opportunities available for minority and disadvantaged premed students.

Relaxation

Okay, so you are a good citizen. You have served mankind through clinical, research, and community service. What do you do to relax? This is a very individual decision and reveals a lot about your personality.

Medical schools are interested in how you relax because medical careers are often stressful. (Medical school and residency are definitely stressful!) If you don't know how to relax now, what will you be like when you are a physician? Will you be prone to abuse drugs or alcohol? Will you decompensate? If you engage in relaxing pastimes, you will be less likely to have these problems. So they want to know, can you relax?

There is absolutely no optimal avocation, but whatever yours is, you should do it regularly. If you are sports-oriented, have you developed a fondness for particular sports, especially those which you will still be able to play in five or ten years? (Tackle football is probably out, although many physicians now play rugby.) If you have a more sedate hobby, such as woodcarving or yoga, do you make time to do it regularly? Do you enjoy it? Do you have goals for yourself within the discipline? If you do, you have an avocation that may last you a lifetime, or that will at least give you something to fall back on when you need stress reduction.

Is your family your avocation? Excellent! Just ask yourself if you have any time for them or for yourself, and what do you do then. Watch television? Not a good answer. Read mystery novels or go hiking? Okay.

What GPA Do You Need?

Medical schools vary in the minimum GPAs they require of applicants and in the mean GPAs of those they accept (figure 15.4). Each also views transcripts differently. While some schools have rigid and high GPA requirements, others will overlook earlier marginal performance if there is an improvement in upper-level, graduate, or postbaccalaureate course work.

When evaluating GPAs, admission committees realize that in some majors, such as engineering, few students can maintain "B" averages; in others, such as biology, "A"s and "B"s are the norm. Also, admission committees usually recognize that some undergraduate schools require more from their students to get good grades than do others.

As you review the mean GPAs of the students entering different medical schools, realize that while the mean may be high, it is only a mean. About half of their students are admitted with lower GPAs—often much lower.

Interacting With Your Professors

As a premed student, you will take some very challenging courses. Think of your premed curriculum as a triathlon. In this three-event race (swimming, running, biking), not all competitors excel in every event. But to succeed, they must finish every event in a reasonable manner. Similarly, not every student excels in every course. You may have difficulty with a science course, a lab, or a non-science course. Where do you turn for help?

Believe it or not, you go to your professor. All professors have office hours, but few students know how to use their help effectively. Here are some tips to effectively use your time with a professor.

- Visit your professors during office hours if you are having difficulty with a course or need other assistance.

- Go as soon as you begin having trouble, even if it is early in the course. Do not wait until the situation seems to be beyond help.

- Few situations are actually beyond help—again, ask for it.

- Write your questions ahead of time in case you have trouble thinking or speaking when you are there.

- Ask the professor to watch you work a problem or to listen while you answer a question, so he or she can spot and help correct your errors.

- Don't simply accept a hard-to-understand answer to your question and plan to read more later. That's what got you into this situation in the first place. If you don't understand, ask for clarification. Keep asking until both you and the professor know that you really understand.

- Be assertive. (This might not be in your nature, but do it for your own good.)

- Make frequent (not constant) eye contact. Although it may not be culturally correct for you, this shows the professor that you are interested and alert.

- If you want a recommendation letter from this professor, meet with him or her early in the course to ask for it. The professor can then pay more attention to how you do—and possibly help you sooner if you have trouble in the course.

While many undergraduates complain that they don't see their professors enough, it is often their own fault. Professors are there to help you—let them do their job.

Premedical Advisers: The Good, The Bad, And The Ugly

Premed advisers are available at most U.S. and Canadian four-year undergraduate schools, although some smaller colleges have recently dropped the position to save money. Few exist at junior colleges, and many junior college students often first learn the specifics about premed requirements when they transfer to four-year schools. Nationally, about 30% of all undergraduate students who begin the premedical curriculum and are advised by their premedical education offices are eventually accepted into medical schools.

Premed advisers are either volunteers or draftees. Volunteers are often individuals for whom advising is their sole responsibility (professional advisers), although some very committed volunteers balance this job with their teaching and research responsibilities. Draftees get their advising job due to their administrative position, because they were unlucky in the faculty lottery, or simply because it was their turn to accept it. They are generally not too happy about being premed advisers and often view this as an additional chore for which they are not rewarded, either professionally or financially. More than half of them get no time off from their other duties to advise students. Premeds who believe that their adviser does not have his or her "heart" in the job must rely on other sources of information, such as knowledgeable faculty members or, if available, medical school faculty.

Volunteers, of course, are preferable as premed advisers, but only larger schools can generally afford to fund them. Nationally, the premed advisers are 67% tenure-track faculty, 31% professional advisers, 1% full-time hourly staff, and 1% part-time hourly staff. The numbers are the same for public and private schools. The chance of getting a professional premed adviser increases when the school has more than 100 medical school applicants each year.

Although there are no standard training or background requirements for premed advisers, they usually do have unique information about the medical school application process, and few other college advisers are willing to substitute for them when they are absent. This means that you should, early on, develop a close working relationship with your school's premed adviser. Depending upon the individual, he or she can be extremely helpful, or can hurt good applicants' chances of getting into medical school, or can simply be a very irritating annoyance to students.

The average premed adviser counsels nearly 300 students a year, with those at the larger schools or those at schools with a high percentage of premed students counseling 500 to 600 students each year. These include premed students who seek advice during their freshman (34%), sophomore (22%), junior (25%), and senior (20%) years. Premed advisers also counsel alumni. Forty-five percent of students counseled by premed advisers at public colleges, and nearly 60% at private schools, eventually apply to medical school. Many premed advisers also act as liaisons to high schools, junior colleges, and some medical schools. In some cases, university premed offices have calendars of interesting events for premed students. Web pages for a campus' premed students are becoming common.

Premed advisers' activities include:

- Provide initial contact with and orientation of students at freshman registration.

- Advise students and alumni on an individual basis, before, during, and after the application and acceptance processes.

- Hold group meetings several times a year to disseminate new or updated information.

- Organize premed clubs and bring in speakers.

- Supply information on special awards, summer jobs and fellowships, minority intern programs, non-U.S. medical schools, Medical Scientist Training Programs, and alternative career pathways.

- Maintain a library of relevant information.

- Coordinate the distribution of application materials.

- Distribute recommendation letters and produce a composite/premed committee letter.

- Advise rejected students and alumni about their options.

The best premed advisers do not tell students whether they will get into medical school. Rather, they show students the average achievement levels of those accepted by medical schools, determine the level of their advisee's achievements, and then let the student decide if the goal is worth the effort. A premed adviser's role is to inject common sense, realism, and information into the process of getting into medical school. If the student decides to pursue this goal, the adviser can then help him or her go through the necessary steps without getting delayed, discouraged, or dismayed by the details. As Josephine Gin, the University of Arizona's premed adviser says, "Each student is unique. They all have different paths to achieve their goals. My job is to help them."

Premed advisers have a very powerful position. One former premed student relates that, after taking some chemistry classes, she went to her premed adviser saying that she had decided to major in chemistry. "You don't want to do that," said the adviser. So she didn't. Subsequently, after doing well in school and on the MCAT, this student decided to take another career direction. Her adviser said to her, "Go ahead and apply to medical school anyway. You are certain to get in." This time, however, she didn't listen to this (bad) advice. This former premed student is now the premed adviser at a large university—and remembers well the damage that an adviser's ill-timed words can wreak.

Unfortunately, studies show that about 60% of premed advisers try to discourage some potential medical school applicants. This may be due partly to the fact that more than half of them view medical education as rigid, physically demanding, and excessively costly, as well as believing that the subsequent medical career requires too much of a time commitment. Discouraging marginal applicants also makes the school look better to prospective students (and their parents) when the advisers talk about the percentage of their students applying to medical schools who are accepted.

The ideal premed adviser has the following qualities, which you might want to compare with those of the premed adviser you have:

- Is flexible when working with various types of students.

- Presents information non-judgmentally.

- Has accurate and verifiable information about their school, about medical schools, and about medicine.

- Cares about students. (They must not be so caring, however, as to dissuade qualified students from applying to medical school.)

- Provides options for school and career.

- Stays attuned to student attitudes, interests, and activities.

- Remains open to new ideas, including re-trying old ideas.
- Doesn't serve as a pre-screener for medical schools!

As the following anecdotes demonstrate, premed advisers vary greatly in their skill and their willingness to help students. The first story is from a physician who graduated from a University of California school and is now a senior emergency medicine resident. The second is from a physician who graduated from a large Eastern state's school and is now a medical school professor. The others are from current medical students from a wide spectrum of undergraduate schools.

I met my premed adviser my first week of school. She was wonderful! She helped me to develop an appropriate course of study, assisted me over some rough spots, and showed me the best way to use the application system for medical schools. She knew a great deal about medicine and medical schools. In my senior year, I helped her out by orienting new premeds.

We had one premed adviser for a student body of about 35,000. He was a chemistry professor who had failed to get into medical school as an undergraduate. He was very clear about detesting medicine as a career and physicians as a group. He met with most premeds. The story was that he always gave one of two speeches. If you were an excellent science student, he tried to convince you to go into something intellectual, particularly the "hard" sciences. If you were majoring in anything other than science or you were not the top student in the class, he would say that you had no chance of ever becoming a physician and you were wasting his time. I was in the latter group. Fortunately, I had enough self-confidence to ignore his "advice."

My premedical advisor was very valuable to me when I applied after being out of school for five years. Without him I would not have had a clue how to pursue this goal, since I'm the first person in my entire family to go to medical school. I saw him each semester when making up my schedule, and knew him fairly well from being around the Chemistry Department and being active in the school's premedical club.

Looking back on it, I feel that my premedical advisor didn't have a clue. I made my decision to pursue medicine late, and the advisor didn't give me good advice, didn't take me seriously, and basically left me completely on my own.

My premedical advisor gave me great advice, great preparation, and great follow-up after graduation. She helped dissuade me from some rather crazy plans.

One suggestion about advisers: Even if the system insists that you keep an inadequate "formal" premed adviser, nothing prevents you from securing your own "informal" adviser who meets most or all of the above criteria. As one physician (now a hematology-oncology fellow) says:

This was such a large school with so many premeds they used almost anyone as a premed adviser. None of them seemed to have any interest in our career goals or any real knowledge of the process. The premed adviser assigned to me was called "the drill sergeant." She was nasty to all premeds, told all of us we wouldn't get into medical school, and really didn't have a clue about the entire process. After she told me that I couldn't ever get into medical school, I didn't even bother asking her to write the "official" premed adviser's letter. I simply got recommendation letters from other faculty who knew me well.

She was not the only one who used another adviser. As these comments from two medical students demonstrate, sometimes it works and sometimes it doesn't.

The "official" pre-medical advisor at my school is a dinosaur with outdated information. He had little information about or experience with minority admissions. He was full of stereotypes and myths about medical school, but you had to work with him to get a cover letter. I had lots of "surrogate" advisors.

My school had no pre-medical advisor, so I sought out an instructor who I thought could help. He did give me information about a summer research fellowship I took, but misinformed me about when to take the MCAT (in the *senior year!*). That set me back an entire year.

The national organization for premed advisers is the National Association of Advisors for the Health Professions (NAAHP). They sponsor a premed organization that you might find useful— The National Prehealth Student Association (NPSA). The organization's purpose is to provide premeds (and other prehealth students) with timely, accurate, and pertinent information, as well as a means to influence the issues affecting their future careers. Three services they currently provide are quarterly newsletters, guidebooks, and a travel program offering discounted airfares for interview trips. Initial membership is $45 (and includes three valuable publications), with annual renewals costing $20. For further information, contact: NPSA, P.O. Box 1518, Champaign, IL 61824-1518; telephone (217) 355-0063.

Peer Advisers

Some schools use students as the first advisers other premed students encounter when they have questions. Most often these are the best of a school's junior and senior premed students and are personally selected by the official premed adviser. Their roles are to answer many of the routine questions, give other students pointers they have gained from personal experience, run special programs for other premed students (such as premed stress reduction, women in medicine, and awareness of Osteopathic medicine), maintain a section of the premed library, and talk to high school students and incoming freshman premeds. Some schools only have a few paid peer advisers. At others, this is a volunteer activity spread among a larger group. Some schools have both. Peer advisers have variable training and knowledge. If you question their information, ask to see the official adviser.

One premed adviser offered to fix any trouble premed students encountered by following incorrect advice from his office—whether it was from him or a peer adviser. This is a great (although not always doable) offer. Although he found such problems rarely occurred, not many advisers offer to correct the damage their bad information causes. In the future, the use of peer advisers will probably increase dramatically, since they cost much less than professional advisers.

For information about special advisers or counselors for minority students, see chapter 9, *Minority Applicants*.

Mentors

You may be able to weave a path through the premed jungle on your own, but it will be much easier if you have help and support. This is where a mentor comes in. Selecting a mentor is one of your most important career decisions. Most students, however, don't have one—they only have "advisers." These faculty members, usually officially designated, often have multiple advisees and little time for any of them. They may not even have any interest in actually helping students advance their careers in the right direction. *You need a mentor!*

Selecting a mentor is serious business. When Odysseus went on his travels, Mentor was the person he entrusted with caring for his house and son. He looked for a wise and faithful counselor. That is also what you seek.

Ideally, the qualities to look for in a mentor are:

- *Experience.* Has the individual helped other premeds get through the system and enter medical school? Can he or she give you advice that is sound, valid, and verifiable? (Ask the individual or find out from your peers.)

- *Knowledge.* Does the individual know the current rules of "the game"? If not, is he or she willing to learn them (just as you will) so that you don't make a mistake? (Ask the individual what the MCAT, AMCAS-E®, or AACOMAS by Computer® is all about. Anyone who knows the answers or says she will find out is fine. If she just shrugs her shoulders, watch out.)

- *Empathy.* You will probably experience insecurity at various points in your journey. Will this individual take enough interest in you to encourage you during these tenuous times? (Your first meeting should give you a good idea.)

- *Compatible personality.* Will you enjoy working with this individual? Is he or she warm and open, or rigid and standoffish? The better you interact with your mentor, the more you will gain from the relationship. (Both his reputation and a brief meeting should confirm this.)

- *Role model.* Is this someone you can use as an example of how to live your life (at least in some areas)? Does he or she exemplify some of the characteristics that you admire in people? Role models are useful, since you can see excellent characteristics demonstrated "in the flesh." (Reputations can sometimes be misleading. Check for yourself.)

When you were born, you could not choose your parents. You now, however, have a choice of mentors. At best, your mentor can simplify the whole process of deciding upon a medical career; selecting an appropriate curriculum; locating appropriate summer work, awards, and clinical opportunities; identifying the best study plan for your classes and for the MCAT; choosing appropriate medical schools; and then applying to these schools. At worst, a mentor can obstruct your path by lowering your self-confidence, providing erroneous or incomplete information, sitting on your paperwork, and generally putting roadblocks in your way.

An optimal mentor helps you make the most of your education. He or she gets you over the rough spots, shows you opportunities that you otherwise might miss, guides your career, and generally thinks of your interests above those of other students. Your mentor is your guide, your teacher, and your role model. But finding one is up to you. It takes effort, initiative, and assertiveness to locate the right individual. The choice is yours—you can either find a mentor or resign yourself to struggling through on your own.

Choose Early

You should select your mentor early to have the widest possible selection and to fully use his or her expertise. "I'm only a freshman," you say. "I'll wait until I have had some clinical experience." Baloney! The longer you wait, the less likely it is that your mentor will be: (1) your first choice; (2) a mentor, rather than a standard "adviser"; and (3) able to actually help you very much.

What Type of Person?

How do you find a mentor? This will take some effort on your part. Generally you should choose a faculty member at your school. (Even if your professional mentor is a physician with whom you have worked, your parent, or your family physician, you also need someone on your school's faculty.) These are the individuals who know not only "the system" at the school, but also how to help you if you have difficulties with the system (getting necessary classes, avoiding administrative hassles). Start by making contacts with upper-level (junior, senior, and graduate) students. You may find them in the premed club, in your dorm, or acting as teaching assistants for a laboratory course. Introduce yourself as a fellow premed student and tell them that you need some advice. They will generally be honored that you have asked them for advice, and will probably give you honest answers since you will not be competing with them for a medical school position. Ask them who they consider the best teachers at the school. Ask several students for their opinions. This will get you started.

Pick a Known Teacher

Now you have a list of teachers that other students consider excellent. Why did they choose these people? Being an excellent teacher takes effort. This effort stems from an interest in helping students to learn. It is also based on a deep and abiding interest in student welfare. Doesn't this sound like the type of person you want for a mentor? Of course, since they are considered excellent by other students, some of them may already have many students whom they are counseling. If they cannot add another student, ask if they can recommend someone else to be your adviser. These people can usually spot the gems among their colleagues, so take their suggestions seriously. If one of them feels that she can add you to her group, go for it. You already stand out by showing initiative so early. You can now do several other things to enhance that positive image.

First, *be visible.* This means showing up with some regularity at your mentor's doorstep. The best and most productive way to accomplish this is to spend time with him or her. This could mean working together in the laboratory or on a project. This will provide you with the opportunity to learn potentially valuable skills, interact with people on a professional level, and demonstrate your personality to someone who will eventually write you a letter of recommendation for medical school.

Second, *develop an image* in your mentor's mind of a likable, courteous, and considerate individual. It is always pleasant to have a cheerful person around. But fawning and flattery generally have a negative effect. Mentors can see through these false habits in a minute.

Be respectful of your *mentor's time.* Once a professor has agreed to be your adviser/mentor, make an appointment to see that individual whenever necessary. This is the professional thing to do and your mentor will appreciate your consideration of his or her valuable time. Ask if you should use their scheduled office hours or make appointments at a different time so you and their other students aren't short-changed.

Finally, be *clear about what you desire* from your mentor (advice) and what your mentor can expect from you (hard work and dedication). Don't push for anything else. If you demonstrate the hard work and dedication, all else will follow.

Transferring From A Junior/Community College

Students often go to junior or community colleges to save money, to avoid enormous class sizes in the introductory or survey courses, or to see if they are able to do college-level work. If you plan, or have already begun, to study at a junior college, you can do several things to smooth your passage into a university and, subsequently, into medical school.

As early as possible, contact the premed adviser at the college you plan to transfer to (if you already know) or the premed adviser at the local four-year college. Find out which courses will transfer, what the college requires for various degree programs, and what they recommend as their premed curriculum. Also, find out what grades, courses, and paperwork are required to transfer to their school. In general, medical schools want students to take upper-level science courses at four-year institutions, where the competition is generally much stiffer and the grading scale less inflated than at junior colleges.

Accelerated And Early-Assurance Programs

Accelerated programs take both high school seniors and those in their first or second year of undergraduate school. They are one way to shorten the time it takes to complete undergraduate and medical school curricula. These programs are described more fully in chapter 6.

Early-assurance programs guarantee students admission to a particular medical school (usually the school associated with the undergraduate school) if they do well in their course work. They may accept students during either their first or second year of undergraduate school. One interesting aspect of the early-assurance programs is that, while they require accepted students to maintain their GPAs, they often don't require the MCAT—so these students don't take it. Some cynics who have gone through such programs wonder if these schools don't require the MCAT so that their students will not be able to apply to other medical schools. (Medical school admission officers wouldn't think that way, would they?)

Early Admission

If you are a stellar sophomore student with a clear and convincing desire to become a physician, you may qualify for early admission to certain medical schools. Medical schools vary in their willingness to admit students without bachelor's degrees. (See figure 15.2 for schools that don't require bachelor's degrees.) Fewer than 10% of all first-year medical students lack an undergraduate degree, so the odds are not favorable. But you should certainly try for early admission if you have the qualifications, are willing to cut your undergraduate career short, and are willing to expend the time and energy to go through the application process.

Applying for early admission and failing to get in does not harm your chance of getting accepted later as a regular admission. The major down-sides to the process are the amount of work it takes, the possible deleterious effect this effort will have on your class work, and the disappointment that most students have when they are rejected. If it works and you are accepted, however, it will be worth the effort.

The specific process of applying for early admission varies with each school. If this appeals to you, contact the schools you are interested in to find out if they have this program.

Undergraduate school can provide students with many educational opportunities. Many premeds, however, mistakenly see their undergraduate training as simply a barrier to cross to get into medical school. This diminishes the quality of what can be learned and makes the work much more difficult than it should be. The best course is to view undergraduate school as an opportunity to expand your horizons. You may never have this chance again.

8: Women—No Longer Unusual

*If men cannot cope with women
in the medical profession,
let them take a humble occupation
in which they can.*

Emma Hart Willard, *Godey's Lady Book* (1853)

Women Physicians

IN 1995-96, WOMEN MADE UP 42.5% of all medical school applicants, 42.8% of accepted students, and 42.7% of those who began medical school (figure 8.1). These numbers represent a steady rise in medical schools' acceptance rates since 1960-61 when women formed only about 7% of all applicants and accepted students. In 1994-95, women composed 42% of all first-year medical students, 41% of all medical students, and 39% of all new medical school graduates. (The difference between the first-year and graduating percentages reflects the increasing number of women entering, rather than any difficulty completing, medical school.) Women constitute over half of all underrepresented minority medical students.

Contrary to popular thought, having large numbers of women physicians in the United States is not a new idea. In the latter half of the nineteenth century, about 5% of all physicians were women, and at least seventeen women's medical schools existed in the United States. Other medical schools were not tolerant of women. In 1893, for example, the new Johns Hopkins Medical School, because it needed the funds that women were raising, agreed (under duress) to accept qualified women as medical students. Sir William Osler wrote of this, "It is always pleasant to be bought, when the purchase price does not involve the sacrifice of an essential—as was the case in the happy purchase of us [Johns Hopkins School of Medicine] by the Women's Education Association." By 1910, all but three of the women's medical schools had closed, had become co-educational, or had merged with other schools, thus severely limiting women's' access to the schools. Boston University and the Medical College of Pennsylvania both began as women's medical schools. The attitude toward women physicians was generally negative within the profession, typified by Osler's more characteristic statement that "There are three classes of human beings: men, women, and women physicians." At the beginning of the twentieth century, medical schools imposed quotas on the number of women they accepted—usually no more than four women per year. These quotas remained in effect (except during World War II when there was a shortage of male applicants) until at least the 1960s.

Figure 8.1: Number of Women and Men Accepted into Medical Schools

	Men Accepted	% of Male Applicants	Women Accepted	% of Female Applicants
1975-76	11,699	35.8	3,666	38.1
1981-82	11,953	47.7	5,333	45.7
1985-86	11,370	53.3	5,858	50.7
1991-92	10,493	53.5	6,943	50.7
1995-96	9,920	37.0	7,437	37.6

Adapted from Association of American Medical Colleges. *AAMC Data Book: Tabulations of Statistical Information Related to Medical Education.* Washington, DC: AAMC, December 1995 Update, Table B7.

At graduation, many more women physicians (nearly one-third) than men (less than one-fifth) plan to go into generalist practices. Women tend to enter pediatrics, obstetrics & gynecology, family practice, psychiatry, dermatology, pathology and preventive medicine, while men tend to enter the other hospital-based specialties and surgical specialties. Perhaps for this reason, women expect to earn one-fourth to one-third less than their male counterparts once they enter practice. An equal proportion of men and women plan academic careers. Although as recently as 1977 there were female residents in fewer than two-thirds of all specialties, by 1995 women were training in every accredited area except hand surgery and the subspecialties of adult reconstructive orthopaedics, chemical pathology, and orthopaedic trauma.

All medical schools, and many teaching hospitals, have designated a "Women's Liaison Officer" to address the concerns of women in medicine. To identify the Women's Liaison Officer at a particular institution, contact: Staff, Women Liaison Officers, Division of Institutional Planning and Development, Association of American Medical Colleges, 2540 N Street, N.W., Washington, DC 20037-1127; telephone (202) 828-0521. These liaisons may often be able to answer women applicants' questions during the interview visit better than some of their colleagues. Other medical women's organizations can be contacted using the information in *Appendix B.*

Women As Premeds And Applicants

Not all schools admit women equally. Figure 8.2 lists those schools at which women compose 50% or more of the first-year class.

The large number of women premedical students and medical school applicants represents a wide and diverse group. Characterizing any such group is difficult, but at least one study suggests that there are some common motivating factors among women who pursue medical careers. These include:

- One or both parents who emphasized intellectual success
- Parental support for traditional feminine values (helping, nurturing, marriage)
- Positive maternal attitude toward female employment
- Interest in science
- A desire to work with people
- Emphasis on vocational flexibility or autonomy
- Need for intellectual stimulation
- Parental, teacher, and peer encouragement

Figure 8.2: Schools where Women Compose 50% or More of the First-Year Class

U. New Mexico (63%)	Michigan State U. (52%)
Brown U. (60%)	Wright State U. (52%)
U. Missouri–Kansas City (59%)	UC–San Francisco (51%)
Yale (56%)	U. Miami (51%)
Morehouse (55%)	Northwestern (51%)
U. Texas–Houston (55%)	Harvard (51%)
George Washington (54%)	Washington U. (51%)
U. of Arizona (53%)	Mt. Sinai (51%)
U. Hawaii (53%)	East Carolina (51%)
Johns Hopkins (53%)	U. Chicago (50%)
U. Massachusetts (53%)	U. Maryland (50%)
U. Puerto Rico (53%)	Albany (50%)
U. of Connecticut (52%)	Cornell U. (50%)
Howard (52%)	U. North Carolina (50%)
U. Florida (52%)	E. Tennessee State (50%)

While at least as many women as men begin premed studies, more men complete these programs and apply to medical school. This has been termed the "premed persistence gap." Why does it occur? What happens to the women who fall by the wayside?

One prior explanation, shown to be too simplistic, is that sex discrimination keeps women out of medical school. (Since the early 1980s this has not been true at most schools, and such discrimination is now virtually non-existent.) Another oft-cited reason is that women have lower expectations for their own achievement, especially in science-related areas, and this leads to failure. They don't, although women are slightly more likely to attribute failure to "bad luck" than are men. Also, while women have, on average, not done as well as men on many measures of science accomplishment, the difference cannot explain the large numbers of women who do not continue to pursue medical careers. Women with the highest GPAs (3.5 to 4.0) have equally good or better science grades than do comparable men. Other explanations have been that women receive less encouragement to pursue medical careers. (They actually receive as much or more support from parents, friends, lovers, and professors than do men.) It is also claimed that women have difficulty seeing themselves in the potentially conflicting roles of physician, wife, and mother. Women who continue and those who drop out of premed curricula plan to marry in nearly equal numbers and plan to have an equal number of children, although those who persist plan to marry and have children slightly later in life.

One explanation that has gained credence over the years is that women, because of their socialization (how they were raised), view pursuing a high-status career as transgressing cultural norms. Normative barriers may exist, but not in exactly the way most people expect (see below).

The gap between men and women applicants begins in high school. While the very top women students (those with A averages) are as likely as their male counterparts to continue to pursue their career goals, women with lower grades are from 1½ to 2 times less likely to continue than are men with the same grades.

In college, women seem to drop out of premed curricula because they are not as persistent as their male peers. Men are more likely to pursue medical careers until they either succeed or unequivocally fail (and sometimes beyond this point), but women tend to pursue the goal only until they see that they *might not succeed*. The result is that many marginally competitive women who might not get into medical school on the first pass (or who think they might not) abandon their dreams of becoming physicians. The men stick it out and many get accepted.

Why do women have this attitude? Sociologists believe the reason is that, while women are no longer barred from medical school through quotas, there exists no societal mandate (norm) for women to strive for career success. They are permitted to, but do not need to, pursue lucrative or prestigious careers.

Women In Medical School And Beyond

The last U.S. medical school to begin admitting women was Jefferson Medical College in Philadelphia in 1960. The last U.S. medical school to become co-educational (by admitting men), however, was the Women's Medical College of Philadelphia, which first admitted men in 1970. It then changed its name to the Medical College of Pennsylvania and, in 1994, merged with Hahnemann University Medical School to form the Allegheny University of the Health Sciences.

Once in medical school, women do not do as well as men of the same racial/ethnic background on the first part of the national licensing examination—the part primarily testing basic-science knowledge. Not surprisingly, this seems to parallel performance on the MCAT examinations. It appears, however, that this difference does not persist into the second and third (clinical) parts of the licensing examination.

Perhaps because of their multiple life roles, sexism, and difficulty resolving issues of intimacy and career, women medical students experience more distress than their male cohorts. Medical school counselors see this in an increased incidence of stress, depression, daily alcohol use, and personal problems among women students.

As mentioned, most women physicians specialize in internal medicine, pediatrics, or family practice (46% of all women residents, but only 34% of men in 1995). Another 15% of women (8% of men) go into obstetrics & gynecology and psychiatry. However, only 53% of women physicians are Board-Certified in their specialties, as opposed to 65% of men. (Most well-paying positions and nearly all academic appointments require physicians to be certified by their specialty Boards after completing residencies, taking specialty-specific examinations, and fulfilling additional requirements.) Figure 8.3 shows which specialties have the greatest numbers of women residents.

However, this does not mean that there is no longer discrimination against women trying to get residency positions—especially in the surgical fields. While the match (acceptance) rate for women is better than for men in family practice, internal medicine, anesthesiology, emergency medicine, and diagnostic radiology, the reverse is true in some other specialties. In obstetrics & gynecology, pediatrics, psychiatry, pathology, general surgery, and orthopaedic surgery men have consistently higher match rates than women. It has been suggested that in the first four of the latter set of specialties, a form of reverse discrimination is occurring. Program directors may be attempting to reverse the preponderance of women in those specialties by giving preference to male applicants.

In surgery, though, only 5% of all residents are women. Twenty-five percent of women applying to general surgery residency programs have failed to match in recent years, compared with about 15% of men. Women account for less than 2.5% of new physicians entering the field of general surgery, and for less than 3.7% of those entering surgical subspecialties. A recent survey of both male and female physicians cited general surgery, orthopaedic surgery, and urology as the specialties that most restrict opportunities for women. Respondents cited family practice, obstetrics & gynecology, pediatrics, and internal medicine as having more opportunities for female physicians. In internal medicine, a much higher percentage of women than men practice general internal medicine, regardless of whether or not they have had subspecialty training.

Figure 8.3: Percentage of Women Residents and Fellows in Selected Specialties

Specialty	% of Women	Specialty	% of Women
Pediatrics	61	Nuclear Medicine	30
Obstetrics & Gynecology	58	Radiology	28
Dermatology	52	Emergency Medicine	27
Child/Adolescent Psych.	52	Ophthalmology	26
Rheumatology	47	Anesthesiology	25
Child Neurology	45	Critical Care Medicine	25
Neonatology	44	Pulmonary Diseases	20
Psychiatry	44	Nephrology	20
Pathology	43	General Surgery	18
Family Practice	42	Otolaryngology	18
Geriatrics	41	Plastic Surgery	17
Preventive Medicine	41	Gastroenterology	15
Endocrinology	39	Cardiology	13
Allergy & Immunology	39	Colon & Rectal Surgery	13
Infectious Diseases	36	Pediatric Surgery	9
Physical Medicine/Rehab	35	Neurosurgery	9
Internal Medicine	33	Vascular Surgery	8
Hematology/Oncology	33	Urology	8
Radiation Oncology	31	Orthopaedic Surgery	7
Neurology	30	Thoracic Surgery	4

Adapted from: Appendix II, Table 1. *JAMA* 1996;276(9):739-40.

If a woman candidate for medical school (or residency) presents herself as firm and assertive, she is often labeled "strident and aggressive." If she demonstrates a milder, more traditionally feminine image, she runs the risk of being labeled "meek and wimpy." In essence, it is often a lose-lose situation.

Greater awareness of federal laws prohibiting discrimination against women in hiring and during employment, as well as a change in social attitudes toward professional women, have made discriminatory practices more complex and subtle. These practices are often based upon the irrational fears of potential employers, who often are not only unfair but also arbitrary. These employers are frequently disturbed by the idea of working with women as equals. One possible result is the underrepresentation of women on medical school faculties.

The percentage of women faculty members varies greatly by specialty, and their academic ranks are lower than those of their male colleagues (figures 8.4 and 8.5). This has become so egregious that, in mid-1996, the AAMC launched its "Increasing Women's Leadership in Academic Medicine" initiative. Their initial report shows that the percentage of women full-professors at medical schools has remained stable since 1980, despite the marked increase in the number of women physicians. Women constitute only 5% of medical school department heads and fewer than 10% of major teaching hospital CEOs. Only four women are medical school deans.

One example of widespread discrimination is seen in the discrepancy between the average male and female physicians' incomes. Women physicians in practice (and not working for the federal government) receive an average of 40%, or about $75,000, less annual net income than

Figure 8.4: Gender of Medical School Faculty (by Rank)

Academic Rank	Men		Women	
	number	percentage*	number	percentage*
Professor	13,232	22 %	2,010	9 %
Associate Professor	15,345	26	3,979	17
Assistant Professor	21,401	36	10,212	44
Instructor	4,207	7	3,358	14
Other	4,849	8	3,785	16

* Percentages do not total 100% due to a small amount of missing data.

Adapted from: Association of American Medical Colleges. *AAMC Data Book: Tabulations of Statistical Information Related to Medical Education.* Washington, DC: AAMC, November 1995 Update, Table C7.

---

their male counterparts. This is only partially explained by differences in specialty, practice setting, age, and productivity. Although women physicians average about 10% fewer work-hours per week than do men, their hourly income is significantly lower. The exact amount varies by specialty, but this trend pervades medical practice.

Sexual Harassment

Unfortunately, more than 25% of female medical students and residents report sexual harassment or discrimination by patients, nurses, peers, residents, or attending physicians. Most incidents involved residents and attending physicians. More than half the members of the American Medical Women's Association reported gender discrimination, and 27% reported sexual harassment within the past twelve months.

The United States Equal Employment Opportunity Commission states:

Unwelcome sexual advances, requests for sexual favors, and other verbal or physical conduct of a sexual nature constitute sexual harassment when:

1. submission to such conduct is made either explicitly or implicitly a term or condition of an individual's employment;

2. submission to or rejection of such conduct by an individual is used as the basis for employment decisions affecting such individual; or

3. such conduct has the purpose or effect of unreasonably interfering with an individual's work performance or creating an intimidating, hostile, or offensive working environment.

The frequency of sexual harassment varies by specialty. Among those in residency or in practice, the reported rate of women saying they were sexually harassed was: general surgery 50%, internal medicine 37%, and about 25% in family practice, obstetrics & gynecology, and pediatrics. Only 12% of women in psychiatry recount having had this problem. The same rate applies to medical students rotating through these clinical specialties' services. Harassment included gender-specific and general sexual comments, being touched or pinched, and being pressured for dates. Married women and those with children suffered less harassment than single women without children. Most women say they don't report harassment because they fear the

Figure 8.5: Women Faculty in Various Specialties

Specialty	% of All Specialty Faculty Who Are Women	% of Women Faculty Who Are Full Professors	Number of Women Dept. Chairs
Physical Medicine	39 %	5.9 %	7
Pediatrics	38	9.5	11
Public Health	35	12.2	0
Obstetrics/Gynecology	34	6.0	8
Family Practice	32	5.8	12
Psychiatry	32	7.0	3
Dermatology	30	10.1	2
Anesthesiology	25	4.3	5
Pathology (all)	26	14.7	9
Emergency Medicine	22	3.1	3
Internal Medicine	22	7.1	1
Neurology	21	9.0	0
Ophthalmology	19	9.4	1
Radiology	21	10.6	6
Otolaryngology	18	13.1	0
Orthopaedic Surgery	10	4.3	0
Surgery	10	8.2	0

Not all specialties or faculty are included in the data.

From: Association of American Medical Colleges. *AAMC Data Book: Statistical Information Related to Medical Education*. Washington, DC: AAMC, November 1995 Update, Table C4; Association of American Medical Colleges. *Directory of American Medical Education 1994-1995*. Washington, DC: AAMC, 1994; and other sources.

---

negative impact and they believe that no action would be taken anyway, even though virtually all teaching hospitals have policies regarding sexual harassment. While male medical students and residents have also reported being sexually harassed, this occurs at a much lower rate than with women. (Nine times as many women as men are subjected to unwanted sexual advances by school personnel.) Women more frequently suffer physical harassment. Those who harass them generally have a higher professional status than the harassed woman.

During medical school interviews, women are often asked sexist, blatantly illegal questions. See "Illegal Questions" in chapter 25 for more information.

Even without discrimination, women in medicine have unique personal problems which have no easy solutions. Medical school and residency cut directly across the childbearing years. This results in women physicians having fewer children, and at a later age, than other women. Only 60-70% of married women physicians have children, compared to 90% of their married male counterparts.

Additional information for and about women in medicine can be obtained from the American Medical Women's Association (AMWA), 801 N. Fairfax, Suite 400, Alexandria, VA 22314. This organization also provides student members with educational loans, scholarships, awards, a bed-and-breakfast program, and a bimonthly journal. Another source of information is the Department of Women in Medicine, American Medical Association, 515 N. State St., Chicago, IL 60610. This section of the AMA serves as an information resource on issues relating to women physicians.

Many individual specialties also have separate societies for women physicians. You can locate them through the main specialty society, through the AMWA, or through the AMA.

Relationships And Marriage

The problems associated with adjusting to marriage and having children during medical training were once thought to be solely a woman's concern. Not any longer. While women do have unique biological concerns regarding pregnancy, *both men and women physicians* are now more frequently basing career decisions on how they will affect their families. The major concerns include maintaining the family relationship, pregnancy, and child care. [This section is located here simply for convenience.]

Relationships

Studies show that women and men seek different attributes in potential mates. This impacts on the available partners for both. Women generally seek mates with an occupational status equal to or higher than their own. They also want an intelligent partner whose ambitions and achievements they can respect. They generally want to get married during their last year of medical school or during residency because they either are concerned about fertility or about their chances of marrying if they wait much later. Men generally seek mates with equal or lower occupational status and income, and who are physically attractive. They prefer to marry during or after residency training. Women medical students overwhelmingly believe that, as their status increases, the pool of acceptable partners decreases, while for men, exactly the opposite situation occurs. In general, unmarried women and men medical students have equivalent support from their significant others.

Marriage

Upon entering medical school, only 13% of women students and 15% of men are married, while at graduation, 30% of the women and 34% of the men have achieved "wedded bliss."

Nearly half (48%) of all married women physicians are married to other physicians, and nearly all the rest are married to non-health professionals (22%), those in business or creative areas (17%), or other health professionals (6%). Nearly 82% of women physicians' spouses have graduated from college or graduate school.

Three times as many married women medical students as men report stress in their personal relationships. It has been suggested that this may be due to the fact that women do not have the "work first" attitude that men generally take.

Marriages and relationships take effort to maintain, and up to 70% of medical marriages are dysfunctional. In part, it is because physicians often hold positions of unquestioned authority at work and it can be difficult to relinquish this role at home. Medical students and residents don't have much personal time, and those in relationships wage a constant tug-of-war between their personal and professional lives. Does this mean that your partnership is doomed? No! All new professionals have the same stresses. The relationships that work are those in which both partners give each other emotional support for their careers. The key is to lend your partner as much support for his or her career as you desire for your own.

Balancing personal and professional goals, and the responsibilities accompanying each, can be a major challenge for both men and women—although women have more stressors. Significant social expectations for women physicians apart from their medical careers can create tension between their private and professional lives. This contributes to the fact that only 66% of women physicians marry, compared to 90% of both non-physician women and male physicians. In addition, since so many married women physicians are married to other physicians, the complications mount. Compared to women physicians partnered with non-physicians (usually other professionals), the women in physician-physician relationships are more likely to bear the primary responsibility of caring for their children and home. Many do this by working fewer hours and subordinating their careers to those of their partners. As many as half of all women physicians change their career plans because of marriage or family responsibilities.

Male physicians' marriages (including those to other physicians) are often dysfunctional because of the average male physician's compulsive personality. While fewer physicians are divorced than the general public, they are generally unhappy in their marriages. The (mostly male) physician's compulsive personality limits emotional intimacy or avoids it altogether. In marriages to women physicians, many male physicians assume that their spouses have fewer emotional needs than other ("regular") women. Several traits are related to this compulsive personality: perfectionism, a susceptibility to self-doubt and feelings of guilt, a chronic sense of emotional impoverishment, difficulties managing dependency and aggression, and a limited capacity for emotional expression. While these traits may be useful in medical practice, the resulting rigid and emotionally flat method of relating to others helps destroy relationships. Physicians blame their lack of emotional commitment on their time commitments—often promising to have more time "later" to spend with the family.

In spite of everything, studies show that marriage enhances well-being. Married men and women are generally happier and less stressed than single people. Male physicians benefit more from marriage than do women physicians, primarily because women often must shoulder the triple role of professional, wife, and mother. They often, as a result, stretch themselves too thin. However, both married men and women physicians exhibit decreased stress, which can help to enhance their lives.

Pregnancy, Children, and a Medical Career

Two of the most stressful personal situations that medical students must deal with are pregnancy and child-rearing. On entry to medical school, 6% of women and 7% of men have children. By graduation, however, 11% of women and 16% of men have at least one child. Approximately 3,000 women currently in residency have at least one dependent—usually a child. Most medical schools do not have formal policies dealing with parental leave. Despite this, however, some are quite flexible when dealing with the situation, while others are not. A model family leave policy for medical students is shown in figure 8.6.

With ingenuity and foresight, successful pregnancies can take place at any time during medical school, although there will be unavoidable stresses and compromises. Some students who are pregnant during their preclinical years find that the classroom seats are too small to accommodate them, and they need special chairs. (This is also true during their board examinations, so special arrangements must be made in advance.) Many medical schools now allow any student, on a case-by-case basis, to take a leave of absence of from one term to an entire year. While many students take leaves of absence to do research or pursue other studies, such as for an M.P.H. degree, some women have used this opportunity for childbearing. (Some have simultaneously pursued research or other studies while pregnant.)

The advice from women physicians who have had children during their training varies. Most physicians who have been pregnant during their clinical medical school years or during residency training report receiving inequitable treatment, ranging from unconscious slights to actual harassment. Most suggest avoiding (if possible) having children during the third year of medical school and the intern year, since these are the most time-intensive and stressful training periods. To lessen stress, some women physicians suggest planning pregnancies for the time between the second and third year of medical school, during the fourth year of medical school when electives

Figure 8.6: Model Family Leave Policy for Medical Schools

1. Family leave is available for all medical students for birth, adoption, or for a child's severe illness.

2. An independent-learning option is available for pregnant students during the basic science years.

3. Pregnant students may be allowed to postpone their education or take leaves of absence, with the option of making up the work during the summer, if such courses are available.

4. Vacation time during the clinical years can be lumped together to permit adequate family leave time.

5. During family leave, students are considered enrolled in school and receive the same benefits students normally receive.

6. Following family leave, students must return on a full-time basis. If in their preclinical years, they need not attend lectures, but they must attend laboratory sessions and take all examinations. If in their clinical years, returning students may take elective clerkships or research, postponing their required clerkships.

7. All students will fulfill all school requirements prior to graduation.

Adapted from: Justin I. Parental leave policies. *Colorado Medicine* 1994;91(1):22-3.

---

can be scheduled to accommodate the pregnancy, during the senior year of residency (not a surgical residency), during a year off, or after residency. (Of course, pregnancies are often not "planned.") Also, it helps to give your (hopefully supportive) colleagues adequate notice that you will be on leave. Women medical students (and residents) have survived having children at all stages of training. This illustrates their tenacity, strength, and motivation.

Pregnant medical students and residents usually have lifestyles that they would not recommend to their patients—long hours, rigorous physical activity, poor eating and sleeping habits and, during the clinical years, exposure to disease. Fortunately, studies have shown that these stressors have had little effect on the physical success of their pregnancies, although there appears to be a higher-than-expected incidence of preeclampsia and preterm labor, but not preterm delivery (figure 8.7). Additionally, female residents (and presumably medical students in their clinical years) have the same rate of induced abortions as their non-physician counterparts.

Family leave, previously called maternity leave or parental leave, policies have been problematic for at least two reasons. First, women physicians-in-training who have been pregnant feel that the leave, if less than six weeks long, is inadequate. Second, since these policies only apply to a subset of medical students (parents, usually mothers), extended leave can wreak havoc on schedules and on the baseline educational requirements that must be met for graduation. The Federal Family and Medical Leave Act, which took effect in August 1993, applies to most residents, but not to medical students (since they are not yet employees).

Figure 8.7: Women Physicians' Pregnancy Complications

Complication	Women Physicians	Non-Physicians*
Preterm labor requiring bed rest	11.3 %	6.0 %
Preeclampsia or eclampsia	8.8	3.5
Premature ruptured membranes	6.4	6.7
Placenta previa	0.8	1.2
Placental abruption	0.4	0.7
Miscarriages	13.8	11.8

* In this study, physicians' wives were used as the control group.

Adapted from: Klebanoff MA, Shiono PH, Rhoads GG. Outcomes of pregnancy in a national sample of resident physicians. *N Engl J Med* 1990;323(15):1040-45.

Children

Child care can be an enormous burden for medical students, especially if both parents work or are in school. Child-care facilities, although relatively common in the business world, have yet to routinely exist in the medical field. Even hospitals which offer child care rarely include medical students' children.

Women carry most of the burdens of child-rearing in our society. They cannot be medical students and parents without some help. Whether they enter school with children or have them while in school, they must arrange for help in caring for their children, whether they are well or ill, in order to successfully continue their careers. Some resources containing helpful tips for men and women are listed under "Parenting" in the *Bibliography*.

Once they finish residency, most women physicians plan to work part time for at least the first two to three years after their children are born. Some take part-time or "shared-schedule" residency programs to spend more time with their children during their residency training.

9: Minority Applicants

It is never too late to give up your prejudices.

Thoreau, *Walden*

The night is beautiful
So the faces of my people.
The stars are beautiful
So the eyes of my people.
Beautiful also is the sun.
Beautiful also are the souls of my people.

Langston Hughes, *My People*

MEDICAL SCHOOL MINORITY RECRUITMENT focuses on four groups that are underrepresented in the medical field when compared with their percentages in the general U.S. population: Mexican-Americans (Chicanos), Blacks (African-Americans), Puerto Ricans (in mainland U.S.), and Native Americans/Alaskan Natives. While other groups, such as non-Chicano Hispanics, are also minorities, only the listed groups may receive consideration for special premed and medical school programs, funding, and, in some cases, admission.

Many medical schools have minority admission offices that seek out qualified students, help them through the admission process, and provide assistance to them during medical school. They often identify qualified candidates through the Medical Minority Applicant Registry (Med-MAR; see below for more information). Nearly one-third of all underrepresented minority applicants come from California, New York, and Texas.

Medical admission officers generally look at a minority applicant's entire history rather than simply at grades and scores. This doesn't mean that good grades and high MCAT scores aren't important; only that admission officers are more likely to make some allowances for merely adequate grades and test scores if an applicant demonstrates other personal factors that are associated with success in medical school. Schools understand that minorities, as a group, may not perform as well as others on standardized examinations and that such applicants, for many reasons, may have spotty academic records. They seek applicants who have demonstrated the capability to succeed academically, even if they are not consistently successful in their attempts.

Admission officers seek minority applicants who demonstrate leadership and who have strong culturally based support systems. They also seek individuals who have realistic views of their own capabilities. Specific qualities they look for include the determination and motivation to be a physician, social interest, maturity, the ability to cope with adversity, and good communication skills. The AAMC runs a three-hour-long Expanded Minority Admissions Exercise (EMAE) at member schools annually to explain these factors to admission officers, admission committee members, and other faculty members who participate in the admission process. Individual schools then use the EMAE for their admission committee staff and interviewers. The program is designed to teach faculty how to look beyond a student's GPA and MCAT scores to assess how well a minority applicant will do in medical school. To do this, they are taught to evaluate "non-cognitive" factors, such as the individual's realistic self-appraisal, ability to communicate, leadership, determination, maturity, emotional support, and social commitment.

The reasons minority students give for choosing a medical career differ only slightly from those other students give. However, minority medical students often have a greater desire to serve their community and to educate patients about health. They generally put less value on working independently.

Don't let financial fears keep you from medical school. Minority students often feel that they can enter medical school only if they can afford to pay the fees. As you can see from chapter 18, *Financial Information*, few students can afford the ever-increasing tuition and fees that medical schools charge (and don't forget about living expenses). Rest assured that medical schools work closely with the students they accept to ensure that they get the necessary funds to see them through.

Project 3000 By 2000

In 1991, the AAMC began a project aimed at increasing the number of underrepresented minority physicians. They hope to do this by annually admitting 3,000 underrepresented minority students to U.S. medical schools by the year 2000. They are still far from reaching this goal.

A consistent pattern through the 1990s shows that applicants from the underrepresented minority groups have a statistically better chance of being accepted to medical school than do their cohorts. In 1995-96, for example, while about 38% of the 46,591 applicants to medical schools were accepted, 39% of the 3,595 Black (African-American) applicants, 44% of the 305 Native American/Alaskan Native applicants, 54% of the 917 Mexican-American (Chicano) applicants, and 42% of the 329 mainland-Puerto Rican applicants were accepted. As a result, these minorities compose slightly less than 14% of the first-year class. The total percentage of underrepresented minority students in all years of medical school has steadily risen from 2.4% in 1968-69 to 12% in 1995-96. However, Project 3000 by 2000 fell short of its goal for the first time in 1995: the expected enrollment of 2,500 underrepresented minority first-year students was not met. In fact, 1995 saw only 2,010 enrolled—slightly fewer than in 1994.

According to the AAMC, the average underrepresented minority *applicant* to medical school has the following characteristics:

- Female, 25½ years old, Black[#] ([#] Black women constitute the largest group of applicants, rather than an "average.")
- Biological Sciences major
- First-time applicant
- Science GPA: 2.73
- Other GPA: 3.17
- Total GPA: 2.92

- Average MCAT scores:
  - Verbal: 6.4
  - Physical Sciences: 6.2
  - Biological Sciences: 6.3
  - Writing Sample: N
- Applications submitted: 11.3
- Average parental income: $51,300
- Both parents have business or professional/managerial occupations and some college or post-high school training

How do other ethnic groups compare? In 1995, approximately 38% of all White applicants (29,294), 32% of all Asian-American applicants (9,644), 47% of all Commonwealth Puerto Rican applicants (412), and 31% of all other Hispanic applicants (1,066) were accepted to medical school. Thus Whites composed 64% of the first-year class; Asian-Americans, 18%; Commonwealth Puerto Ricans, slightly more than 1%; and other Hispanics, nearly 2%. (The ethnic background of 1% is unknown.) Admissions for all minorities decreased by 5% in 1996.

There is one thing to keep in mind: Project 3000 by 2000 and many similar local initiatives to increase the number of underrepresented minority physicians were developed at a time when the courts were sympathetic to affirmative action plans. Beginning with Allan Bakke's successful U.S. Supreme Court challenge to the University of California–Davis' use of special standards as the sole criteria to admit some students, affirmative action plans have rested on a shaky legal base. Recently, courts throughout the United States have aggressively altered their stance on affirmative action, making medical schools' admission committees very nervous. In the future, it may be very difficult for some medical schools to maintain their high level of minority admissions. The California Board of Regents recently removed race from the list of factors that schools could consider when admitting students. Because of recent court decisions, a note on the Texas A&M College of Medicine's application now reads, "Based on the United States Court of Appeals, 5th Circuit, in its *Hopwood v. University of Texas School of Law* opinion, the self-description section on page one of the [application] . . . is not a factor in admission selection." The 5th Circuit's decision was affirmed by the U.S. Supreme Court in July 1996.

Are You a "Minority" Student?

This is not as unusual a question as you might imagine. If you have always identified yourself with a minority culture, there is no problem. However, many students who come from "underrepresented minority" populations don't consider themselves to be minorities. They have been "mainstreamed" their entire lives and don't identify with a minority culture. According to several minority premed advisers, many such students "find" their cultural heritage only after they discover that it gives them an advantage when applying to medical schools. These students are often called "check-box" minorities, in reference to the boxes on forms where they designate themselves as minority students.

These advisers suggest that minority applicants should ask themselves whether they feel comfortable identifying themselves with the culture and as "minority" students—many don't. Some will have to struggle with the decision about whether to classify themselves as minorities. Minority affairs counselors suggest that you examine your family-derived values to see how strongly you have been influenced by the culture, even if you have not consciously thought of yourself as a minority. Although they considered themselves "mainstream" students, some Native American students, for example, have returned to their family gatherings for traditional ceremonies or have been strongly influenced by stories of how the government treated their parents. This may indicate a strong cultural identity. Often, talking with the staff at a medical school's minority affairs office can clarify this issue.

With the increasing diversity of the American population, some applicants have trouble deciding which box to check. One student who is part Native American, part Mexican, part Scot, and part Puerto Rican said, "Okay, so I'm an underrepresented minority—which one?" The Association for Multi-Ethnic Americans (AMEA) reports that many people now confront this problem when they must complete forms, such as MCAT or medical school applications. If you have not ever truly identified with a particular culture, you may find yourself in a bind when asked to "check a box." If so, you also may want to consult with your minority affairs office for advice. You can also contact AMEA at P.O. Box 191726, San Francisco, CA 94119-1726; telephone (800) 523-AMEA.

At some medical schools, the minority affairs office has the unenviable task of determining which students really do qualify as minorities. Most schools, however, have wisely avoided this no-win trap, allowing applicants' self-designations to prevail.

The "Minority Attitude"

Minority applicants have unique cross-cultural insights that they can contribute to medical schools and, eventually, to medical care. Practitioners with this quality have been described as delivering "culturally competent" health care. (Non-minority students with intense cross-cultural experiences, such as from working with the Peace Corps, may also have similar insights which may help them when applying to medical schools.) Minority applicants do best if they view their cultural heritage as a strength—an asset that other applicants may not have, rather than as a crutch to lean on to excuse poor motivation or performance.

Many individuals from underrepresented minorities have, however, felt themselves "marginalized." If they voice their desires to become physicians, they often get negative feedback, not only from advisers but also from their peers and families. This only reinforces the message that they will remain marginalized. When non-minority students receive similar feedback stating they "can't do it" or "lack what it takes," they more often see it as an affront (the "Oh yeah? I'll show them!" or "Says who?" response), and try even harder to reach their goals.

Many minority applicants avoid announcing their intention to apply to medical school too early because they fear a negative response. They wait until the last possible moment to meet with premed or minority advisers, to apply for or take the MCAT, and to submit applications. These are big mistakes. Most minority (and many premed) advisers will be supportive. In fact, they can actually ease the way for students progressing through the complex system of applying to medical schools. They can also offer specific assistance with special programs, such as the MMEP. Minority affairs offices themselves are often viewed by minority applicants, students, and residents as "safe havens" in the midst of a relatively unfriendly environment.

It is never too early to contact your minority adviser, even if you are still in high school. The earlier you make contact, the more information you can obtain about learning the rules, improving the quality of your application packet, and improving your medical school application "game." Once you contact your minority adviser, you may be put on mailing lists and receive a variety of useful information concerning academic opportunities at every stage of your education. This is especially true if you participate in some of the special programs put on by the minority affairs office.

In those cultures in which extended families are important, minority advisers often speak to applicants and, if they wish, their families. Advisers can explain the importance of family support throughout the stressful years of premed, medical, and graduate medical (residency) education. An applicant's (and a medical student's) family must be flexible and understanding for an individual to succeed. Early input from a knowledgeable source, such as a minority adviser, can ease the way for both the student and his family. Medical students often find it useful for an influential family member to spend a day with them observing their time constraints and other stresses they must handle.

The "I'm Not a Minority" Attitude

A schism often exists between minority premed and medical students who identify with other minority students and those who don't. Some students do not want to be identified with other minority students because they want to "make it on their own," they don't want to be stigmatized and stereotyped, or they are tired of being outside of mainstream student culture. They may distance themselves from other minority students implicitly (for example, by sitting or socializing with non-minority students) or explicitly (openly stating that they do not want a "minority medical school experience"). Medical schools' minority affairs offices adopt differing attitudes toward these students. Some are openly hostile, believing that those who don't identify with their own cultures have abandoned them. Others are more tolerant, offering their help, but accepting that people may choose different paths and have different goals. Many minority affairs counselors, however, feel that those who remain committed to their heritage usually tread an easier road and have happier and more peaceful lives. This sometimes leads to stress when individuals from multi-ethnic backgrounds feel that they are being forced to identify more with one part of their heritage than another.

Successful Minority Applicants

Those who work with minority medical school applicants (and students) say that the one quality that most distinguishes those who succeed from those who don't is *persistence*. Even though the students themselves may be the only ones who believe that they can get into or succeed in medical school, those who are successful search out the resources to get help and stick to their goal. Persistence is vital, since more minority medical students make their career choices before or during high school (62%) than do other medical students (42%).

For students to be successful, they must be flexible when pursuing their goal. If one route doesn't work, they should adjust their thinking and try others. According to the AAMC, the *average underrepresented minority student entering medical school* has the following characteristics:

- Female, 24 years old, Black[#] ([#] Black women constitute the largest group of applicants, rather than an "average.")

- First-time applicant

- Acceptances received: 2.2

- Science GPA: 2.97

- Other GPA: 3.31

- Total GPA: 3.12

- Average MCAT scores:

  - Verbal: 7.8

  - Physical Sciences: 7.3

  - Biological Sciences: 7.7

  - Writing Sample: N

- Applications submitted: 12.0

- Average parental income: $61,952

- Both parents having business or professional/managerial occupations and some college or post-high school training

The median parental income of first-year medical students, of all ethnicities, is higher than that of similar families in the United States. For example, in 1993 the median family income of Blacks ($22,000) and of all Hispanics ($24,000) was significantly lower than the median income of families with applicants accepted to medical school who were Black ($41,000); "Other Hispanic" ($60,000); mainland-Puerto Rican ($45,000); or Mexican-American ($40,000). Similarly, median incomes for all White ($39,000) and Asian-American ($44,000) families were below the median incomes of the families of White and Asian-American first-year medical students (both $65,000).

One predictor of how well minority premed students will do on the MCAT is the Developing Cognitive Abilities Test (DCAT), a measure of scholastic aptitude. Some premed advisers, university teaching offices, and summer minority premed programs use this test to help students assess their own abilities.

The MCAT scores and GPAs of applicants from various ethnic groups accepted to medical school in recent years is shown in figure 9.1.

The MCAT scores and GPAs for applicants not accepted to medical school from various ethnic groups in recent years is shown in figure 9.2.

Of particular note, a significant percentage of premed minority students (including Asians and Pacific Islanders) don't apply to medical school, although their MCAT scores are high enough to make them competitive candidates. Many of these students believe (incorrectly) that their MCAT scores are too low. If you have questions about this, ask your minority affairs counselor or a medical school admission officer.

Office Hours and Getting Help

Many minority students earn lower grades than other students and are thus thought to be less intelligent. Often the lower grades are due to culturally related behavior, such as deferring to professors or not asking questions because of a respect for elders or more-learned people. Sometimes, students don't think they should ask for help. When they do, perhaps during a professor's office hours, they often don't know how to interact effectively to get the most out of these sessions. See chapter 7, *Undergraduate Preparation,* for some helpful tips.

Other help with your course work is also available. Tutors can often be arranged through your minority counselor or premed adviser. If you need a tutor, get one early, both to establish rapport and to keep from falling behind in your classes.

Unique Information For Different Minorities

Once minority applicants are accepted into medical school, special programs are often available to them.

One program open to all of them is the Minority Mentor Recruitment Network (MMRN). This national program pairs minority medical students with faculty physicians from the same cultural background. Some schools also have their own programs that predate the MMRN.

Figure 9.1: Average MCAT Scores and GPAs of Accepted Applicants By Race/Ethnicity

	Black	Native American	Mexican American	Mainland-Puerto Rico	Asian/ Pacific Isle	Other Hispanic	C'wlth Puerto Rico	White
WOMEN								
MCAT								
Verbal Reasoning	7.7	8.9	8.3	7.7	9.5	9.2	6.0	9.9
Physical Sciences	7.0	7.6	7.8	7.7	10.0	8.9	6.5	9.4
Biological Sciences	7.4	8.2	8.4	7.9	10.1	9.4	7.2	9.8
Writing Sample*	O	O	O	O	P	P	L	P
GPA								
Science	3.03	3.17	3.13	3.16	3.52	3.35	3.21	3.55
Other	3.42	3.45	3.38	3.53	3.69	3.56	3.64	3.65
Total	3.19	3.29	3.23	3.34	3.59	3.45	3.40	3.59
MEN								
MCAT								
Verbal Reasoning	7.6	8.9	8.3	8.2	9.6	9.0	6.0	9.8
Physical Sciences	7.7	8.7	8.6	8.3	11.0	9.7	6.5	10.3
Biological Sciences	7.9	8.8	9.1	8.7	10.7	9.7	7.2	10.3
Writing Sample*	N	N	O	N	P	P	L	P
GPA								
Science	3.00	3.17	3.14	3.13	3.56	3.38	3.09	3.53
Other	3.31	3.34	3.34	3.37	3.62	3.49	3.43	3.57
Total	3.13	3.25	3.22	3.22	3.58	3.43	3.23	3.54

* Median score

Adapted from: Association of American Medical Colleges Section for Student Services. *Final National Admission Action Summary Report.* Washington, DC: AAMC, 1995.

Figure 9.2: Average MCAT Scores and GPAs of Applicants By Race/Ethnicity Who Were Not Accepted

	Black	Native American	Mexican American	Mainland-Puerto Rico	Asian/ Pacific Isle	Other Hispanic	C'wlth Puerto Rico	White
WOMEN								
MCAT								
Verbal Reasoning	5.5	7.4	6.5	5.3	7.6	7.3	4.2	8.3
Physical Sciences	5.2	6.4	6.0	5.4	8.0	6.8	5.0	7.5
Biological Sciences	5.1	6.9	6.3	5.3	8.2	7.4	4.9	7.9
Writing Sample*	M	N	N	M	O	M	K	O
GPA								
Science	2.54	2.82	2.64	2.65	3.09	2.89	2.65	3.16
Other	3.13	3.27	3.16	3.27	3.44	3.35	3.39	3.45
Total	2.80	3.03	2.86	2.92	3.24	3.09	2.97	3.29
MEN								
MCAT								
Verbal Reasoning	5.2	7.3	6.4	5.4	7.6	7.3	4.0	8.4
Physical Sciences	5.7	7.5	6.7	5.9	9.0	7.8	5.3	8.6
Biological Sciences	5.4	7.3	6.8	5.9	8.9	8.0	5.0	8.7
Writing Sample*	M	M	M	M	N	N	K	O
GPA								
Science	2.52	2.81	2.63	2.60	3.15	2.94	2.55	3.14
Other	2.97	3.09	3.02	3.13	3.34	3.18	3.10	3.33
Total	2.71	2.92	2.80	2.82	3.22	3.04	2.79	3.21

* Median score

Adapted from: Association of American Medical Colleges Section for Student Services. *Final National Admission Action Summary Report.* Washington, DC: AAMC, 1995.

Native Americans/Alaskan Natives

As of 1996, there were 501 Native American/Alaskan Native students attending U.S. medical schools. This represents 0.7% of all medical students, but it shows a marked increase during the past 25 years. In 1969, only 9 Native American students were in U.S. medical schools.

The seven universities which produce the largest number of Native American/Alaskan Native applicants accepted at U.S. medical schools are: University of Arizona, University of Oklahoma,

UC–Berkeley, Stanford, UC–Davis, Pembroke State University, and University of Southern California.

Some medical schools have more Native American students than others. Leading the pack, in terms of their percentage of all medical students, is the University of North Dakota, where nearly 15% of medical students are Native American. Most come from the school's very successful "Indians into Medicine" (INMED) program. This program, which primarily draws students from Montana, Wyoming, Nebraska, and North and South Dakota, runs a six-week Summer Institute to encourage junior and senior high school students to consider health-related careers. The Indian Health Service or the Health Careers Opportunity Program pays for participants' travel, room, and board, as well as a small stipend for each student. During the admission process, INMED recruits Native American students to the University of North Dakota and conducts a preliminary review of their records before referring them to the admission committee.

Harvard Medical School has its own eight-week "Four Directions" summer research program for Native American premed students. This program includes opportunities not only to participate in research, but also to gain clinical exposure. For more information, contact your minority counselor or the Harvard Medical School. The University of Oklahoma College of Medicine's Native American Center of Excellence sponsors similar programs for high school and college students.

The twenty-six medical schools with five or more Native American medical students (in all four years) in 1995 were: Alabama, Arizona, UC–Davis, UC–San Francisco, USC, Colorado, Dartmouth, South Florida, Harvard, Kansas, Michigan State, Minnesota–Duluth, Minnesota–Minneapolis, New Mexico, North Carolina, North Dakota, Oklahoma, Stanford, UT–Galveston, Tufts, Tulane, Uniformed Services, Utah, University of Washington, and University of Wisconsin.

Blacks (African-Americans)

In 1996, U.S. medical schools had 5,337 Black students. Although this number shows a marked increase since 1969, when only 783 Blacks were enrolled in U.S. medical schools, Blacks still account for only 8% of all medical students.

The undergraduate schools which produce the largest numbers of Black medical students are: Xavier, Howard, Spelman, Morehouse, University of Michigan, Harvard, University of Virginia, Yale, UCLA, Cornell, Hampton, Duke, and Johns Hopkins.

A number of historically Black undergraduate schools were analyzed to determine why their graduates have been so successful. Undergraduate schools with active premed programs, a broad range of externally sponsored enrichment activities, and a high proportion of premeds majoring in biology or chemistry produced the strongest applicants. The most successful premed programs provided premed offices and clubs, active premed advisers, early career planning assistance, and curriculum development to their students. Undoubtedly, the presence of all of these factors increases the chance of medical school acceptance for all applicants, regardless of their undergraduate school.

The thirteen schools with twenty or more Black first-year medical students in 1996 were: UCLA, George Washington, Harvard, Howard, Illinois, LSU–New Orleans, Meharry, Morehouse, North Carolina, Medical University of South Carolina, Temple, UT–Galveston, and Wayne State.

Studies show that once they enter medical school, Black medical students' performance (at least on the USMLE) is strongly related to their perception of the amount of control they have over their lives. Those who believe that they control their own destinies do better than those who believe that external forces control them. To encourage self-esteem among Black students, some schools (such as Wright State and the Medical College of Georgia) pair Black students with Black faculty mentors, with excellent outcomes.

Mexican-Americans (Chicanos)

In 1996, U.S. medical schools had 1,769 Mexican-American students. This represented 2.6% of all medical students. It is a marked increase from 1969, when only 59 Mexican-Americans attended U.S. medical schools. Still, Hispanics now constitute nearly 9% of the U.S. population, but they only compose 4% of all physicians.

The AAMC indicates that there is currently a lack of qualified Hispanic candidates for medical school. Only 9% of Hispanics hold college degrees, compared to 25% of non-Hispanics. (This ratio has not changed since 1980.)

The undergraduate schools that generate the largest number of successful Mexican-American medical school applicants are: Stanford, Texas A&M, the University of Arizona, UC–Berkeley, UCLA, UC–Riverside, UC–San Diego, University of St. Mary's–San Antonio, UT–Austin, UT–El Paso, and UT–San Antonio.

The twenty-two schools with twenty or more Mexican-American medical students (in all years) in 1995 were: Arizona, Baylor, UC–Davis, UC–Irvine, UCLA, UC–San Diego, UC–San Francisco, USC, Colorado, Harvard, Iowa, Michigan State, Michigan, New Mexico, Stanford, Texas Tech, UT–Galveston, UT–Houston, UT–San Antonio, UT–Southwestern, University of Washington, and the University of Wisconsin.

The National Hispanic Mentor Recruitment Network (NHMRN), a cooperative effort of the Interamerican College of Physicians and Surgeons and the National Health Service Corps, establishes links between Hispanic medical students and practicing Hispanic clinicians. This program helps the students develop their own professional networks, provides supportive role models, and gives them opportunities for early clinical exposure. For more information, contact: the National Hispanic Mentor Recruitment Network, Interamerican College of Physicians and Surgeons, 1612 K Street, N.W., Suite 1000, Washington, DC 20006; or call (800) 559-3707.

Mainland-Puerto Ricans

As of 1996, U.S. medical schools had 455 mainland-Puerto Rican students. This represents 0.7% of all medical students. In 1969, only 3 mainland-Puerto Ricans were in U.S. medical schools.

The eight undergraduate schools generating the largest numbers of mainland-Puerto Rican medical students are: University of Puerto Rico–Rio Piedras, Harvard, Miami University, Rutgers–New Brunswick, SUNY–Buffalo, Florida International University, University of Puerto Rico–Mayaguez, and NYU.

Surprisingly, the three approved Puerto Rican medical schools do not accept mainland-Puerto Ricans in large numbers. The University of Puerto Rico accepts only eight to ten mainland-Puerto Rican applicants each year, Ponce accepts only two to four, and Caribe only one or two. For the most part, such applicants have as good or better chances of being accepted at many of the New York-/New Jersey-/Philadelphia-area schools.

The twenty-eight schools with five or more mainland-Puerto Rican medical students (total) in 1995 were: Albany, Albert Einstein, Baylor, Caribe, Columbia, Cornell, South Florida, Georgetown, Allegheny UHS, Harvard, Illinois, Michigan State, Michigan, Mount Sinai, UMDNJ–NJ Medical, UMDNJ–RWJ, New York Medical, SUNY–Buffalo, SUNY–Brooklyn, SUNY–Stony Brook, SUNY–Syracuse, Ponce, Puerto Rico, Temple, UT–San Antonio, Tufts, University of Wisconsin, and Yale.

Other Minorities

Other Hispanics

Other Hispanics, including Cuban-Americans and those of Central and South American heritage, constitute 1.9% (1,247) of all medical students. As recently as 1978, there were 426 "other Hispanics" in U.S. medical schools, which was only 0.7% of all students.

Native Hawaiians

Native Hawaiians apply primarily to Hawaii's medical school. In 1967, when the John A. Burns School of Medicine was established, there were only ten Native Hawaiian physicians practicing medicine in Hawaii. In 1972, the school developed the *Imi Ho'ola* postbaccalaureate program to channel qualified Native Hawaiians, Filipinos, Samoans, and residents of Guam, the Commonwealth of the Northern Mariana Islands, the Federated States of Micronesia, the Republic of Palau, and the Republic of the Marshall Islands into the medical school. The program accepts up to twenty students annually, and 49% of its graduates have been accepted by the medical school. Of those, 88% have graduated from medical school or are still enrolled. More than one-third of the medical school's graduates are Native Hawaiians. At present, 14% of the John A. Burns' medical students and 7% of students at the University of Hawaii's Manoa campus are Native Hawaiian. This contrasts with an estimated 20% of Native Hawaiians among Hawaii's population.

Asian-Americans

Asian-Americans, while not an underrepresented minority in medicine, may be judged by different criteria when they apply to medical school. Asian-American students normally do very well in math, physics, and other science courses, and have high MCAT scores. Studies suggest that, all other things being equal, the main predictor for how well Asian-Americans will perform in medical school is the MCAT Verbal Reasoning section (and probably the Writing Sample, although the studies were done before this section was added). Since many Asian-American students now applying to medical schools are first- or second-generation citizens, they may have learned English as a second language. And, since medical education is very language intensive, English-language ability plays a large part in a student's performance. Asian-Americans whose first language is not English should keep this in mind and concentrate on honing their English-language skills.

Special Preparation Programs For Minorities

Medical Minority Applicant Registry (Med-MAR)

Medical schools often identify qualified candidates from underrepresented groups through the Medical Minority Applicant Registry (Med-MAR). The AAMC compiles this list of financially disadvantaged and minority medical school applicants from the demographic information provided by those taking the MCAT. When applicants take the MCAT, they indicate whether, at no cost, they want to be included in the Registry. The AAMC circulates the list among medical schools twice a year, usually in July and November. The Registry provides schools with the following information about each student: name, address, birth date, social security number, undergraduate college and major, racial or ethnic self-description, state of legal residence, and MCAT scores. Schools contact the applicants in whom they are interested. Highly qualified applicants listed in the Registry may expect to receive many phone calls and letters from medical schools throughout the country.

Once minority students graduate from medical school, the AAMC enters them into the Minority Physicians Database (MPDB) and tracks their practice patterns. For more information about Med-

MAR, contact: Minority Student Information Clearinghouse; Division of Minority Health, Education, and Prevention; AAMC; 2450 N Street, N.W.; Washington, DC 20037-1126.

Minority Medical Education Program (MMEP)

Minorities have long been underrepresented in medicine. To help correct this imbalance, the Minority Medical Education Program (MMEP) was developed to identify and assist promising Black (African-American), Native American/Alaskan Native, Mexican-American (Chicano), and mainland-Puerto Rican undergraduate students who are interested in medical careers. Although these four groups make up about 19% of the U.S. population, they represent only about 6% of U.S. physicians. Since 1989 when the program began, more than 4,000 students have participated. More than half of them applied to medical school and about 60% of those have been accepted.

The six-week summer program (supported by the Robert Wood Johnson Foundation and with direction from the AAMC) gives these students an intimate understanding of the personal and academic requirements needed to become a physician. It also gives them a chance to associate with other students who share their dreams of a medical career. According to the MMEP's director, "The program provides a 'handbook' on how to transform a dream into reality." As one former participant testified,

> An important factor that helped me get into medical school was that I attended the Minority Medical Education Program (MMEP). This program gave me a better understanding of the medical school application process, and helped me to prepare for the MCAT. In addition, this program gave me additional educational and practical experiences to improve my competitiveness in the medical school application process.

The program has four components: academics, MCAT preparation, laboratory exposure, and counseling. Each of the MMEP sites, however, has a slightly different curriculum. They all include formal assessments of participants' academic strengths and weaknesses, and have academic reviews of MCAT topics. All programs also pair students with laboratory or clinical mentors for the duration of their stay. Some sites have "work-shadowing" programs, in which students follow physicians while they work, observing and questioning what they do and participating when possible. Participants have found work-shadowing to be a valuable experience.

Many programs work very closely with those who plan to apply to medical schools in the coming year. Counselors make certain that students are familiar with the application process and help them complete their paperwork.

The application packet for MMEP contains descriptions of the programs available at each site. When deciding which three programs (the maximum) to apply to, applicants are encouraged to contact either the national MMEP office (see below) or the individual programs.

Although exceptions can be made on a case-by-case basis, in order to be eligible for the MMEP, students must

- be a U.S. citizen or permanent resident;
- be a member of one of the underserved minorities listed above;
- have completed at least one year of college by the time they start the program (those with bachelor's degrees may apply);
- have an overall GPA of 3.0 (on a 4.0 scale) with at least a 2.75 in the sciences;
- have combined scores of at least 950 on the SAT or 20 on the ACT; and
- demonstrate a serious interest in a medical career.

Think about your summer plans during the winter break from school. That will give you enough time to investigate your options, complete the paperwork, and still send everything to the programs in a timely manner. (The application deadline for transcripts is in early April.) Treat the process as if you were applying to medical school. The two are very similar. If you are not constrained by geographical limitations, apply to three programs. This will give you the best chance of being accepted by at least one of them. Currently, there are eight programs:

UNIVERSITY OF ALABAMA SCHOOL OF MEDICINE
Marlon L. Priest, M.D.
P-100 Volker Hall
Birmingham, AL 35294-0019
(800) 707-3579: (205) 934-8724 Fax
mmep@uasom.meis.uab.edu

BAYLOR COLLEGE OF MEDICINE/RICE UNIVERSITY
William A. Thomson, Ph.D.
1709 Dryden, Suite 545
Houston, TX 77030
(713) 798-4841 or (800) 798-8244; (713) 798-8201 Fax
wthomson@bcm.tmc.edu

CHICAGO SUMMER SCIENCE ENRICHMENT PROGRAM
Larry Goodman, M.D.
Rush Medical College
600 S. Paulina, 0524 AcFac
Chicago, IL 60612
(312) 942-6914; (312) 942-2333 Fax
baier@bstat.pvm.rpslmc.edu

Consortium member sites:
LOYOLA UNIVERSITY
NORTHWESTERN UNIVERSITY
RUSH UNIVERSITY
UNIVERSITY OF CHICAGO/PRITZKER

CASE WESTERN RESERVE UNIVERSITY SCHOOL OF MEDICINE
Rubens J. Pamies, M.D.
10900 Euclid Avenue
Cleveland , OH 44106-4920
(216) 368-2212; (216) 368-8597 Fax
rjp9@po.cwru.edu

UNITED NEGRO COLLEGE FUND PREMEDICAL SUMMER INSTITUTE
at Fisk University and Vanderbilt University
Mary E. McKelvey, Ph.D.
Fisk University
1000 Seventeenth Avenue North
Nashville, TN 37208-3051
(615) 329-8796; (615) 329-8636 Fax
mckelvey@dubois.fisk.edu

UNIVERSITY OF VIRGINIA SCHOOL OF MEDICINE
Moses Kwamena Woode, Ph.D., D.I.C., FAIC
Box 446, HSC
Charlottesville, VA 22908
(804) 924-2189; (804) 982-1870 Fax
gas2v@virginia.edu

UNIVERSITY OF WASHINGTON SCHOOL OF MEDICINE
Charlie Garcia, M.S.W.
Health Sciences Center, SC-64
Seattle, WA 98195
(206) 685-2489; (206) 543-9063 Fax
cgarcia@u.washington.edu

Consortium member site:
UNIVERSITY OF ARIZONA COLLEGE OF MEDICINE
Linda Don, M.Ed.
1501 North Campbell Avenue, Rm. 1119-B
Tucson, AZ 85724
(520) 621-5531; (520) 626-2895 Fax
ldon@ccit.arizona.edu

YALE UNIVERSITY SCHOOL OF MEDICINE
Stephen J. Huot, M.D., Ph.D.
Alex Ortiz, M.D.
87 LMP 333 Cedar Street
New Haven, CT 06520-8033
(203) 785-7249; (203) 785-7258 Fax

Individuals may participate in MMEP only once. The application form is remarkably similar to the AMCAS® application. Simply having to go through the steps will benefit most applicants. Applications and descriptions of the programs can be obtained from your premed adviser or directly from the Minority Medical Education Program, Association of American Medical Colleges, Section for Student Services, 2450 N Street, N.W., Suite 201, Washington, DC 20037-1126; telephone (202) 828-0401 or (202) 828-1125; E-mail: MMEP@AAMC.ORG.

Laboratory Internships

The National Institutes of Health (NIH) funds the Minority High School Summer Research Apprentice Program (MHSSRAP). This program annually provides stipends for 3,000 students to work with biomedical research mentors. High school counselors should have information about this program.

The NIH also sponsors, and provides funding for, minority and disadvantaged undergraduate and graduate students to engage in research projects to help prepare them for biomedical careers. The NIH Undergraduate Scholarship Program awards a limited number of scholarships, up to $20,000 per academic year, to excellent students from minority or disadvantaged backgrounds with an interest in a biomedical research career. During summers, awardees spend ten weeks as paid employees in NIH research laboratories, where they work with mentors and attend various programs. After graduation, or after subsequently finishing medical or postgraduate education, each awardee must work in an NIH research laboratory one year for each year of scholarship support. For more information, contact the NIH Educational Loan Repayment and Scholarship Programs, 7550 Wisconsin Avenue, Bethesda, MD 20892-9121; tel. (800) 528-7689.

The Howard Hughes Foundation has set up a program to enrich minority students' science and research backgrounds. All participants must be under twenty-one years old. Participating undergraduate schools include Xavier (LA), Humboldt State (CA), Georgetown University (DC), and the University of Arizona. A program for high school students from San Antonio, Texas, is held at Carleton College (MN), and for students from the Philadelphia area at Haverford College (PA).

Some American Heart Association chapters also sponsor summer research in cardiovascular diseases. Contact your local chapter for more information.

Several national programs exist to encourage underrepresented minority medical students to choose biomedical research careers. Medical school Deans of Students can assist in locating such programs and funding.

Individual Medical Schools' Programs

Nearly two-thirds of all medical schools, and some undergraduate schools, have their own summer enrichment programs for minority high school and undergraduate students interested in medical careers. Examples of such programs include: the Gateway to Higher Education Program for junior and senior high school students and the Bridge to Medicine program for high school seniors (New York Medical School); the Student Educational Enrichment Program (SEEP) for incoming high school seniors (Medical College of Georgia); multiple programs at all educational levels (Baylor College of Medicine); the Science and Technology Education Program (STEP) for junior and senior high school students (New York's state medical schools); College-STEP Program (C-STEP) for college undergraduates (Mt. Sinai School of Medicine and Albany Medical College); the Med-Start Summer Program for high school students (University of Arizona); and the Summer Science Academy, a series of four summer seminars, for 9th through 12th graders (Xavier University, New Orleans). One undergraduate school, Southern Illinois University, has a medical exposure/preparation program built into its curriculum, with college credit given for participation (MEDPREP). (See also Appendix D, *Medical School-Sponsored Summer Programs for Undergraduates.*)

Many individual medical schools, such as Creighton (NE), Harvard (MA), Mayo Clinic (MN), Meharry (TN), Ohio University College of Osteopathic Medicine (OH), SUNY–Buffalo (NY), Tufts (MA), UMDNJ–Newark (NJ), UC–San Francisco (CA), University of Cincinnati (OH), University of Colorado (CO), University of Connecticut, (CT), Cornell (NY), and the University of Rochester School of Medicine and Dentistry (NY), offer research opportunities to minority undergraduate students. Contact local medical schools for information about their programs.

Many other schools have similar programs. To find out about them, contact your high school counselor, premed adviser, or local medical school's minority affairs office.

Designing Your Own Summer Program

If you cannot travel to an MMEP program site, were not accepted, or have already gone through the program, you can still use the summer to improve your chance of entering medical school. Work with your counselor or premed adviser to develop a combination of classes, self-study programs, and clinical experiences that will improve your academic performance and enhance the other factors that medical school's admission committees seek.

Medical Association Programs

Native Americans may go to the premedical advisory workshops sponsored annually by the Association of American Indian Physicians. At these conferences, Native American premed students meet with practicing American Indian physicians who help familiarize them with the medical school application and interview processes. The Association pays for students' expenses to attend this conference.

Nearly all local, state, and national medical organizations have annual conferences. Most of these organizations, especially the ethnic physician groups, will allow you to attend. In some cases (but only if you ask), they may even be willing to pay some of your expenses.

Many large undergraduate campuses have minority premed organizations that often sponsor their own special programs. The minority or premed adviser will know about whether such organizations exist on your campus.

Applying To Medical School

Choosing A Medical School

Minority applicants use somewhat different criteria when choosing medical schools than do other applicants. A school's curriculum is much more important to minorities, as are the school's teaching methods. With regard to the educational programs, minority applicants are more interested than other applicants in whether schools provide community experiences, a medical ethics program, family medicine experiences, and problem-based learning.

Also, minority applicants pay close attention to a school's success in placing its graduates in residency programs they desire. Given that, on average, minority students incur larger debts than their cohorts, a school's cost and financial-aid programs play a major role in their decision. More than sixty percent of minority applicants evaluate the quality of a school's minority programs and services, and half consider faculty mentor programs when they choose schools.

Two Admission Strategies

Applicants from underrepresented minorities may want to consider applying to medical schools that have not recently admitted many applicants from their ethnic group. If you are willing to brave it as an "ethnic rebel," this may provide your best chance for admission to medical school. How do you find out which schools these are? The AAMC includes a list, by school, of the numbers of "new entrants," "first-year students," and "total students" from the four underrepresented minorities in *Medical School Admission Requirements*. (By comparing the "new entrant" and "first-year student" categories you can determine if any of the minority students from the previous year's class were held back.) Be aware, however, that some medical schools (those in Puerto Rico, for example) see themselves as having a special mission (in their case, educating physicians for Puerto Rico) with little interest in other students.

Another strategy, just as valid for minority as for non-minority applicants, is to apply to Osteopathic medical schools. Although traditionally minorities have not "gone the D.O. route," increasing numbers are doing just that. In 1994-95, for example, the number of enrolled minority Osteopathic medical students reached 7.9% of all D.O. students. Given that the number of positions at Osteopathic medical schools is increasing and the number at M.D. schools is decreasing, you may want to seriously consider this option.

Once You Get Into Medical School

More than half of all U.S. medical schools offer optional summer enrichment programs for newly admitted students from underrepresented minorities and non-traditional backgrounds. Most programs are solely for students accepted to that school, but six schools (Medical University of

112

South Carolina, New York Medical College, University of California–Irvine, University of Colorado, University of Miami, and University of Minnesota–Duluth) offer programs for students accepted to any medical school.

These programs offer information and develop skills valuable for first-year medical students. While they vary in structure and content, they usually include academic material, study-skills enhancement, familiarization with available support resources (personal, academic, and financial), and early clinical exposure. The programs are designed to help students succeed in medical school. Studies show that most students who complete these summer "pre-matriculation" programs do significantly better in their first- (and often their second-) year course work than they would have done without the program. Performance in these sessions has also been used to identify participants' academic weaknesses so that they can get additional assistance as they need it. Participants usually adjust to the medical school environment much better than do similar students who do not participate.

Some schools also offer special tutorial, counseling, and advising sessions throughout the first and second years of medical school for students who participated in the pre-matriculation program. Again, these are generally optional, but are worth investigating.

Take all the help that the schools offer if you think you may need it—and the statistics suggest that you may. While nearly 92% of non-minority and nearly 90% of other minority medical students graduate in *five* years or less, fewer than 78% of underrepresented minority students graduate within this time period. Of those underrepresented minority students who don't graduate, 3.5% withdraw, nearly 4% are academically dismissed, and nearly 13% are still in medical school. An even larger difference exists for *four*-year graduations. At the end of four years, nearly 83% of non-minority, 78% of other minority, and 56% of underrepresented minority students graduate.

Once you begin medical school, you next want to think about residency programs. Some medical schools offer special summer clinical fellowships in an attempt to attract additional minority residents to their programs. Duke University has one such program. Many of these offer stipends and special clinical opportunities. They are worth investigating.

Many minorities will, for the foreseeable future, remain underrepresented among both the populations of practicing physicians and physician-researchers. Individuals from these backgrounds often need additional support to overcome the social, financial, and educational barriers to entering the medical profession. The key is to look for that help early and to persevere toward your goal.

10: Unconventional Premed Students

*To do easily what is difficult for others
is a mark of talent.
To do what is impossible for talent
is the mark of genius.*

Amiel, *Journal*, Dec. 17, 1856

Physically Challenged/Disabled Applicants

DATA ON DISABLED PHYSICIANS AND MEDICAL STUDENTS is sparse and incomplete. The only available information suggests that about 3,000 practicing U.S. physicians have major physical disabilities. Nearly all became disabled after entering, and usually after completing, medical school. Of those medical students with known physical impairment (only about 0.25% of all medical students), approximately 25% have visual disabilities, 42% are neurologically or musculoskeletally impaired, 8% have auditory disabilities, and 14% have learning disabilities. (The remainder do not specify their disabilities.) The subgroup of physically impaired medical students is unique. The individuals in this group are singular both among medical students for their tenacity and drive to overcome the obstacles to get where they are, and among the physically impaired, since they are able enough to complete medical school's clinical requirements.

Who Is "Disabled"?

Under the Americans with Disabilities Act of 1990, "disability" is defined as a physical or mental impairment that substantially limits one or more major life activities (e.g., limitations to caring for oneself, performing manual tasks, walking, seeing, hearing, speaking, breathing, learning, and working). Under the Act, persons are considered disabled if they have a record of such an impairment or if they are regarded as having such an impairment. The Act requires potential employers to make "reasonable accommodations" for the known physical or mental disabilities of an otherwise qualified individual, as long as these accommodations do not impose an "undue burden" on the institution (e.g., cause "significant difficulty or expense" given the circumstances) or the individual does not pose a direct threat to the health or safety of others. If you are a medical school applicant and are disabled, that applies to you. In addition, if you are not currently disabled, but become disabled once you are a medical student or a resident, the school must make reasonable accommodations for you.

Various contagious diseases (such as tuberculosis or HIV) are considered impairments under the Act. However, current illegal- or excessive legal-drug use, alcoholism that interferes with performance, sex-related behavior and disorders, and certain behavioral disorders (including pyromania, kleptomania, and compulsive gambling) are not covered by the Act.

Learning Disabled

Learning disabilities cover a wide spectrum of disorders, including dyslexia, dyscalculia, and attention-deficit disorders. Individuals with recognized learning disabilities successfully apply to medical school, including those whose disabilities have not been diagnosed. It is estimated that up to two percent of all medical students have learning disorders. Special programs have been developed for those students who need help in passing their courses and the USMLE.

One of my brightest residents took our specialty's national in-service examination and scored in the lowest 1%. In our faculty's estimation, this did not come close to reflecting his true abilities. Upon questioning, he admitted that he could only learn material when he read things aloud to himself—usually two or three times. In classes, he simply memorized everything the professor said. He had not yet taken a licensing examination (since at that time physicians could take the one-part FLEX test) and had had trouble taking tests in medical school. In some cases professors had given him oral, instead of written, examinations without examining the problem further. When I referred him to our university's learning center for evaluation, they found that he was severely dyslexic—but had developed unique coping mechanisms. After working with specialists for a year, he successfully took and passed both his licensing and specialty board examinations without any special accommodations.

Unfortunately many, if not most, medical schools lack skilled personnel to either diagnose or support learning-disabled students. Those who know they are learning disabled may find it useful to quietly determine whether a medical school has such services. You can do that by writing to their Dean of Students, who is not usually involved in the application process.

A unique program exists to help medical students with learning disabilities—the Medical H.E.L.P. Program. For information about the two-week Medical H.E.L.P. Program for medical students with learning disabilities and dyslexia, contact Marshall University in West Virginia at (304) 696-6315.

Physically Disabled

Physical disabilities are diverse in their scope and severity. Many seemingly preclude individuals from performing many physician-related tasks, while others simply pose a hindrance for which alternative practice methods must be found. In most cases, it is the person, rather than the disability, that determines whether or not he or she can become a physician, as the story below illustrates.

> A gowned patient with cerebral palsy came to a medical school class on a stretcher. The patient had a speech impediment and severe ataxia (inability to coordinate muscle movements). After the instructor took the medical history and did a physical examination, the patient was wheeled out of the room. The class was asked to evaluate the patient's job potential; they thought it was extremely poor. A few minutes later, the "patient" reappeared, now in his suit and white coat, and was recognizable as the physician-director of a large rehabilitation hospital.

While medical schools, in general, are willing to make accommodations for those whom they feel can complete the cognitive and most of the procedural parts of a medical curriculum, they take a pretty tough stance against accepting students who cannot do so. As the envelope continues to be stretched, medical schools are being asked to accept individuals that they feel cannot, even with reasonable accommodations, complete their basic curricula or ultimately perform a physician's basic job functions. Recent examples have involved a quadriplegic man (admitted to medical school with great reluctance because of significant outside pressure) and a blind woman (not admitted despite extensive court challenges).

Infectious diseases represent another physical disability. While medical schools in the United States don't discriminate against individuals with infectious diseases that don't pose a danger to others, nearly all schools require immunization against Hepatitis B, and about half of all schools have policies regarding students who become HIV or Hepatitis-B positive. Elsewhere in the world there is discrimination against those with infectious diseases. In Britain, for example, some schools reject applicants if they test positive for specific diseases.

Other Disabilities

Some disabilities may not be obvious, and can be recognized only if you are tested for them. One such disability (or potential disability) is a genetic predisposition to lethal or devastating diseases, such as early-onset cancer or Huntington's Disease. Another more common (at least for the present) set of disorders are unrecognized physical impairments that can prevent medical school graduates from entering certain medical specialties. For example, at least one-third of the ophthalmology programs, all aerospace medicine programs, and a smattering of other programs test applicants for color vision and stereognosis. (This is perfectly legal if all applicants are screened and it can be shown that the examination is job-related.) Some applicants, especially men who never knew they were "impaired," fail.

Admission Requirements—An Equitable Playing Field

Medical schools are now struggling to piece together policies ("technical standards") that meet the requirements of the federal laws governing the disabled (Americans with Disabilities Act of 1990 and Section 504 of the 1973 Rehabilitation Act).

Their first question is whether MCAT scores for the increasing numbers of applicants taking the MCAT "with special accommodations" are equivalent to those on tests taken under routine conditions. Special accommodations, such as separate rooms or increased examination time-limits, for students with disabilities can be arranged. If you have special needs due to a documented disability, contact the MCAT administrators as early as possible. They will then supply you with additional information. If applicants request special accommodations, current policy is to report the special testing circumstances to the medical schools. Special accommodations for non-physical disabilities, such as learning disorders, will only be granted if there is documentation of the disability from a licensed professional. This, in itself, can be problematic, since the range of learning disabilities is both wide and still being debated among professionals.

The second and much tougher question is, What is the body of knowledge and skills that define a physician's academic qualifications? Put another way, what is it that is *essential* for every graduating medical student to know and to be able to do, without regard for how they achieve these goals? The key word is *essential*. This is where the debate becomes strident.

Must all medical school graduates have the potential to enter any specialty? Must they have the ability to perform, at the least, such lifesaving interventions as CPR, IV placement, and mouth-to-mouth resuscitation? Or can some of the knowledge and techniques be foregone given an agreement by the student to enter only areas where these procedures will not be needed? Some disabled applicants want to use "trained intermediaries" to help them do some tasks they cannot physically accomplish, such as parts of the physical examination. It's unclear how expansive the role of a trained intermediary can be and what part such intermediaries should take. Most schools find that the use of trained individuals who interpose themselves between the physician and the patient is unacceptable, because it may color the physician's judgment. (However, unskilled intermediaries, such as individuals who use the telephone for deaf physicians when they communicate with non-deaf patients and colleagues, seem to be acceptable.)

If applicants disclose their disabilities, medical schools may request further information about whether they will require special accommodations. On a case-by-case basis, admission committees must decide whether an applicant is otherwise qualified for admission. They ask whether, without the disability, the individual's qualifications meet their acceptance criteria. Only if the answer is yes does the school then need to determine what accommodations they can reasonably make to provide the student with an education equivalent to that of his or her classmates.

The "reasonable accommodations" medical schools must make for disabled medical students are alterations in the learning or physical environment that would not fundamentally change the educational program, do not impair public safety, and do not impose insurmountable financial burdens on the school (based on the school's entire budget). Sometimes these accommodations take only minor ingenuity, rather than major expense. An interesting example of special accommodations one school uses for colorblind students is to use special stains for hematology and histology specimens they must examine. Another school uses transparent surgical masks as one way of helping hearing-impaired students work in the operating room, delivery suite, and emergency department.

What Barriers Do You Face?

Federal law requires that medical schools "provide an equal opportunity for an individual with a disability to participate in the . . . application process and to be considered [for admission]." This means that applications must not include questions about an applicant's health, medical history, or disability status. If requested, schools must provide applicants with materials (applications, forms, brochures, catalogs, and curriculum descriptions) that accommodate a disabled applicant's needs, such as large-print versions. They must also have these materials in locations accessible to disabled applicants. Interviews must be conducted in accessible locations and special accommodations must be made (e.g., sign-language interpreters) upon request. While the law prohibits asking questions about an applicant's disability, expect this rule to be broken.

To test whether you will need special accommodations, get some health-related experiences. How you perform in patient-care situations will help you determine what, if any, accommodations you may need. Talk to some disabled physicians. If you don't know any, contact your local medical society to find some names. You will be surprised at how many are in successful practices. Finally, once you are in the process of applying to medical schools, try to visit the campuses before you apply to see whether the facilities necessary for your life are currently accessible to you. While the school may fulfill the requirements, for example, by having wheelchair-accessible facilities, the parking, living, and geographic situations (e.g., hills) may not be as good.

Medical schools accept students on the condition that they fulfill certain expectations (such as successfully completing current course work). One of these requirements can be to complete a medical-history form for the school's records. A school can legally withdraw its acceptance if an applicant's history reveals that he could not fulfill the *essential* requirements for graduation, if accommodating his special requirements would cause the school undue hardships, or if he would need unreasonable accommodations.

While in the past a few blind applicants have been admitted to medical school and at least one graduated (Temple University in the 1970s), medical schools are now reluctant to repeat this experience. Recently, after being sued, Case Western Reserve University Medical School was ordered to admit a blind applicant. They refused and appealed the decision, saying that it is "not possible for any blind person to complete medical school unless the curriculum and requirements are significantly altered." The Ohio Supreme Court agreed with the medical school.

Admission Committee Attitudes

Admission committees understand the need to evaluate disabled applicants in a reasonable and thoughtful manner. The question committees now face is, how much "reasonable accommodation" can they make for students and still be assured that they will be qualified to practice medicine when they graduate? Since they see producing practicing physicians as their ultimate goal, they are concerned about applicants who may not be capable of "going the distance."

The official (and oft-repeated) policy is to "focus on the individual, not the disability." According to several Deans of Admission, many schools remain hesitant to voluntarily enter into situations requiring large financial outlays to accommodate disabled students or to fill a precious medical school position with a student who will either not be able to meet minimum requirements to practice medicine (as set by the school or state licensing boards) or even live long enough to finish training. Once accepted, it is the student's responsibility to notify the medical school of any special accommodations he or she requires.

Committee members, however, often have inaccurate perceptions of disabled applicants' limitations and of what tasks they can really do. As one deaf physician who spent seventeen years trying to enter medical school said, "They just assumed that I couldn't do it. I would explain technical advances, I would bring pictures of my instruments, and I would explain how to do it. Even after I answered, they felt uncomfortable. They didn't want to say yes, but they had a hard time saying why not." This applicant also admits that she failed to appreciate her own limitations. Her speech was difficult to understand in interview situations. After several years of trying, and failing, to be admitted to a medical school, she finally brought an interpreter to the interview and was accepted.

Disabled Medical Students, Residents, and Physicians

By 1995, more than one-third of all teaching hospitals had made accommodations under the Americans with Disabilities Act for disabled residents. While some residency programs may hesitate to take a physically impaired individual, this attitude is normally due to ignorance.

The medical specialties that disabled physicians enter generally depend upon when their disability occurred. Those who became disabled before or during medical school usually are drawn to physiatry (physical medicine and rehabilitation), psychiatry, pathology, and anesthesiology. Those whose disabilities occurred later tend to remain in their original specialty, but modify their working environment to accommodate their needs.

For more information about resources and referrals for physically impaired physicians, write: The American Society of Handicapped Physicians, c/o Mr. Will Lambert, 105 Morris Dr., Bastrop, LA 71220; or The Committee on Physically Challenged Physicians, Los Angeles County Medical Association, 1925 Wilshire Blvd., Los Angeles, CA 90057; or the Equal Employment Opportunity Commission, Review and Appeals Division, 1801 L Street, N.W., Washington, DC 20507.

Older Applicants

If you are reading this book, chances are that you are probably not too old to begin a medical career. At our medical school, one student began his first year at age forty-nine. (As a joke, his medical-student classmates, all dressed in black, presented him with a black cake for his 50th birthday.) In another case, one of my residents began her internship the same year her oldest son began college. She is now not only a practicing physician, but also the state's medical director for emergency medical services. Older medical students have done very well. Ask yourself whether you *feel* young enough to change your career, to learn a mass of new information, and to radically alter your lifestyle. If so, go for it!

Perhaps the best known "older medical student" story is that of Albert Schweitzer. He first earned a Ph.D. in philosophy at age 24 and then a doctorate in theology at 25. He soon became a world-renowned theologian while simultaneously becoming recognized as an accomplished organist. Not content with this, he graduated from medical school when he was 38 years old and went off to Africa as a medical missionary. Based on his remarkable accomplishments as a physician, he won the 1952 Nobel Peace Prize for his efforts on behalf of "the Brotherhood of Nations." If anyone gives you grief about your age, tell them about Dr. Schweitzer.

You don't have to be a potential Nobel laureate to enter medical school as an older student. A friend, and one of my former residents, Jeff Baker (Colorado, Class of '93) describes his experience:

I was a "ski bum" until I was 27 years old. I lived from paycheck to paycheck, working at lots of different jobs, including heavy-equipment operator and clinic "gopher" in the off seasons. I took the clinic job because I thought I might be interested in physical therapy as a career. By that time I knew I would eventually have to give up the vagabond's life. What I saw there convinced me that I wanted to be a doctor. Then, I simply had to apply to undergraduate school, complete the requirements, get into medical school, and graduate. No problem. (Jeff now practices medicine near the Aspen ski slopes.)

In 1995, Tufts University School of Medicine graduated a 58-year-old former computer manufacturer. He will complete his residency at age 61. He says, "Only perseverance has kept my dream alive." His mother graduated as a physician from Tufts in 1927. Another student, at Michigan State University College of Human Medicine, entered (in 1991) at age 59.

One out of fifty first-year students at M.D.-medical schools in the United States is 36 years old or older, and 7% of medical students begin their medical education after age 30. Nearly 7% of medical students received their bachelor's degrees seven or more years before entering medical school.

You, your inertia, and your fears are the barriers to following your desire to practice medicine. If you really want to do it, go for it *now*. Four years from now, you will still be four years older—whether or not you will also have a medical degree is your choice. As the old saying goes, "It is better to wear out than to rust out."

Why Medical School Now?

You have your own reasons for considering medical school now, but they probably fall into one of the following categories. Each has its pitfalls.

- *Mid-life career change.* Most often found among lawyers, architects, and engineers, this desire to change represents dissatisfaction with their current career. Having shown that they have talent in an area in which they have not found personal fulfillment, they seek another life path. Admission personnel ask: How do you know you will be happier in medicine? Are you running toward medicine or away from your prior career and lifestyle?

- *After child-rearing.* Rather than suffering from the "empty-nest" syndrome, many women find that their lives improve when they have fewer household-based restrictions. They discover that they can use their talents to achieve personal and professional recognition. Admission personnel ask: Are you just casting about for something to do now that your children are out of the home?

- *Mixing careers.* Some individuals seek to introduce a new aspect to their current profession through medical school. These may include lawyers, engineers, artists, and others who may foresee being able to successfully combine their talents in one profession with a physician's skills and knowledge. In a (very) few cases, individuals can continue their old careers while pursuing medical studies—but no one should count on being able to do this. Admission personnel ask: How serious are you about medicine? Aren't there much easier ways to pursue your goals? Are you more interested in the degree than in the knowledge?

- *Retirement.* Usually, individuals who retire think that they are too old to enter medical school. Especially for those with some government jobs ("20 years and out"), this is not the case. In any event, increasing numbers of older individuals are applying. Some, essentially because of their age, must abandon their dreams of going to medical school or else go to non-U.S. medical schools. Admission personnel ask: Do you have the (fill in the blank) to keep up with the younger students? What they really mean, of course, is, "Aren't you too old to be applying?" But, of course, they can't legally ask it that way.

Issues To Consider

Older applicants must consider several issues which do not concern younger applicants. Upon reflection, you may find that they either present impossible barriers to your attending medical school or can be overcome with understanding and patience.

Many older applicants have been away from school so long that their study habits have grown rusty. However, your study habits can be honed while preparing to take the MCAT. If you did (or do) well on the MCAT, don't worry about your study habits. (As shown in figure 15.5, many schools require that the MCAT be taken within 2 to 3 years of applying.) Part of developing good study habits is building good time-management skills. If life and work experiences have helped you in this area, you have little to worry about.

Part of your identity is the job you do now. Very few people can deftly and successfully manage to continue in their present careers while going to medical school. Medical school is not a part-time experience; it is difficult enough going full time. Consider whether you are willing to give up your current position to take the leap into medicine.

Medical school will place a double financial burden on you. Not only will you incur the same large debt as other medical students, but you will also lose the income you receive from your current job. Unless you are among the lucky few who are independently wealthy, this will probably lead to a radical change in your lifestyle—for at least *seven years* (residents make about $30,000 to $40,000 a year). Think about that while you eat pâté de foie gras. (It isn't good for you anyway.)

If you are determined to go to medical school, you may have to relocate. This can wreak havoc on you, your family, and your friendships. You may even have to move out of the country if you cannot get accepted to a U.S. school and decide to go the foreign route. A number of older applicants have done just that. Are you ready for such a significant readjustment? Is your family?

Speaking of family, you probably have more people depending upon you than do younger applicants. Do they support your decision? Are they willing to subsist at a much lower living standard (and work harder) to help you reach your dream? If so, you can probably do it. If not, you will have a very rough time. Personal problems compounding the rigors of medical school (and residency) make awfully tough sledding.

Since you are "older," who do you think will be your bosses on the clinical services when you are a medical student and resident? That's right! The "kids." In one extreme case, an older medical student was supervised by his own son, who was the attending on one service during his medical school rotations. Now that's a real role reversal. Is your ego strong enough to take it? If not, quit now.

Finally, there is the question of stamina. Will you be able to keep up with the younger folks? While this concern is undoubtedly at the forefront of most interviewers' minds, they won't voice it. But ask yourself, "Can I pull 'all-nighters' to study for exams if necessary? Can I work 36-hour shifts?" And, while you probably can do anything that younger students can do, the real question is, Do you want to? If you do, go forth and pursue your dream.

You and the Premed Adviser

Even though you may have graduated from college many years ago, you are still welcome at your undergraduate school's premed office. They will feel that they still have a connection to you, since you have now decided to pursue a medical career. They have materials and information that may prove invaluable to you. Most will not charge you for their services, although some will if you did not graduate within the past five to seven years. If you are too far away to easily interact with your alma mater's adviser, contact her by mail. Also contact the premed adviser at a local college. You should be able to review her information and get her advice.

Of course, if you are still an undergraduate or have returned to school to pick up or retake premed courses, simply seek out your current school's adviser.

Some Different Criteria

You may be nervous about competing against younger applicants, but as an older, presumably more experienced, applicant you are expected to excel in certain areas. The interview is where you should really shine. Interviewers expect older applicants to be more self-assured, poised, and articulate than their younger compatriots. Excelling in the interview may not score you as many points as a youngster's equivalent performance, but being only mediocre can be devastating. One technique to use not only to excel, but also to make a positive impression, is to draw the interviewer into interesting discussions about what you have done when you weren't in school.

Admission officers can be sticklers about grades. They want to know if you can "hack it" in competition with kids with sharp study skills who are right out of undergraduate school. Excellent grades in postbaccalaureate programs or graduate school may not be a big help, but mediocre grades will hurt you badly, as one applicant found out, but overcame.

> An interviewer told me my numbers weren't good enough to get in, blah, blah, blah. I finally got mad and told him to ask me what I *could* do instead of telling me what I couldn't do. By the end of the interview, he was president of my fan club and was off to the Dean of Admissions to tell her to take me. [This student graduated from medical school in 1996.]

Studies have shown that while older medical students had slightly lower GPAs than did their younger cohorts, they had equivalent MCAT scores—and ultimately did nearly as well in medical school. The biggest difference in medical school performance was in the first-year basic sciences, as might be expected.

As their age increases, there is a gradual decrease in the percentage of applicants accepted to medical school. This is true for both men and women (figure 10.1). The really dramatic difference is after the age of twenty! Of course, 98% of all medical school applicants have already passed over that hill.

While only one U.S. medical school explicitly discriminates against older applicants (Uniformed Services University, which takes civilians up to age 30 and military personnel up to age 35), admission officers want to know whether you still have the neurons and the drive to go the distance in medical school and to complete residency training. Show them you've got both! Remember, as Bernard Baruch said, "Old age is always fifteen years older than I am."

Figure 10.1: Acceptance Rates To First-Year Class By Age*

AGE	MEN		WOMEN	
	Percent of Applicants	Percent Accepted	Percent of Applicants	Percent Accepted
20 or less	2 %	73 %	2 %	75 %
21 to 23	52	45	56	43
24 to 27	29	31	26	31
28 to 31	10	29	8	30
32 to 34	4	28	3	30
35 to 37	2	24	2	25
38 or over	2	20	3	22

* Sums may not add up to 100% due to rounding.

Adapted from: Association of American Medical Colleges: *Women in U.S. Academic Medicine—Statistics.* Washington, DC: AAMC, 1995, Table 3, and other sources.

Postbaccalaureate Premed Programs

Postbaccalaureate premed programs are those courses individuals who already have at least a bachelor's degree take either to complete premed requirements or to improve their scholastic records so that they are competitive applicants. Many students only decide to pursue medical careers after they have received their bachelor's degrees. They may have done badly in undergraduate school, so use postbaccalaureate programs as a method of "academic renewal," knowing that admission committees often give more weight to the most recent courses. Other students do not have the required preparatory courses, so they must complete these before taking the MCAT or applying to medical schools.

If you are interested in postbaccalaureate education, there are three ways to proceed. Many students simply take the necessary premed courses at their local colleges. Others enroll in graduate degree programs that will improve their GPAs or give them the required course work. Some, however, go to special premed programs designed for those who already have their bachelor's degrees. Usually, individuals enter these programs because they have been out of school awhile, they were originally non-science majors, or they have already tried and failed to enter medical school.

Students seeking a postbaccalaureate premed program (*Appendix C*) should realize that these programs differ markedly in their entry requirements, length, curricula, and costs. They also vary in what they promise students—and in what they deliver. Selecting a postbaccalaureate program is much like deciding on a medical or undergraduate school. Therefore, the Must/Want analysis (figures 7.2 and 16.1) will be very useful in deciding among programs.

Some of these programs only accept minorities, women, or state residents, while others accept only graduates of specific schools. There are programs that take only those who were science majors and others which only take non-science majors. Some require minimum GPAs or MCAT scores, while others are less rigid. A number of programs only accept students who have tried and failed to enter medical school, while others only take students who have not yet applied. It is vital to review the entry requirements carefully before applying to one of these programs.

Postbaccalaureate premed programs vary in length from one to more than two years. Their curricula range from only basic premed courses to the entire course-load of a first-year medical student. The cost ranges from nothing (scholarships are provided) to well above the normal cost for a year at most medical schools. Most programs offer assistance in obtaining loans and other financial aid.

Most schools only promise to give students a good premed education, although a few guarantee medical school admission if students do well in the program. Many medical school deans admit that they take relatively few students out of these programs. They may, however, take many more students who complete premed requirements on their own after earning their bachelor's or graduate degrees.

One benefit of these programs is the immediate close ties students have with the premed (and often a separate minority premed) adviser. Postbaccalaureate students who take premed classes on their own should also tie into the premed advising system on campus even before classes begin. This will give them support, a window into the medical school application process, and an experienced individual to guide them through that process.

Postbaccalaureate students generally have unique qualities that, for better or worse, you may recognize in yourself. They

- feel under pressure from significant personal and financial responsibilities.

- see themselves in a win-lose situation, with this program being their last chance at reaching their goal.

- are focused and goal-oriented.

- have employers who may not be sympathetic to their goals.

- need both moral and practical support to succeed.

- have high anxiety when they move from a comfortable and known situation, to an uncomfortable and unknown situation and future.

- waiver between confidence and self-doubt.

- have high expectations for themselves, the faculty, and their advisers.

- have little tolerance for glitches in the program.

Overall, they act like "adult learners," who want to know what they need to know, to get that information without any extraneous garbage thrown in, to receive positive feedback for good work, and to get through as quickly as possible. Does that describe you correctly? It also describes many medical students.

Studies suggest that, while postbaccalaureate students who enter medical school do a little worse in their first year (as do older students in general), their overall medical school performances are on a par with traditionally prepared students.

Other Unconventional Students

Special Programs For Ph.D.'s

In the 1970s and 1980s, special programs existed at the University of Miami and at Washington University for entering medical students who already had Ph.D.'s. These programs shortened the length of medical school training. Although the faculty seemed pleased with graduates of these programs, both have been discontinued. Some medical schools, especially those with active M.D.-Ph.D. programs, say that they will give applicants with Ph.D. degrees advanced standing on a case-by-case basis. This, unfortunately, means contacting each medical school, determining which ones will be willing to give you advanced standing if accepted, and then applying to those schools. Since each applicant has a unique background, this onerous process seems to be the only way to shorten your medical education by getting credit for your Ph.D. experiences.

Special Programs For Dentists

Some medical schools allow a few dentists or dental students to transfer into their school, usually with "advanced standing," meaning that they enter at the second-year level. Mayo Medical School, SUNY–Brooklyn and Wayne State University School of Medicine accept dentists whose goal is to get M.D. degrees so they can pursue careers in oral and maxillofacial surgery. The University of North Carolina School of Medicine occasionally accepts transfers into their medical school from their own oral surgery residency program. Other schools admit general dentists, dental students, or oral surgeons without these restrictions. (See figure 15.5.) Overall, however, very few dentists or dental students are admitted. Those who are often have stellar records in dental school and very convincing reasons why they want to enter medical school.

Rural Americans

If you grew up in a rural area, you probably overcame quite a few educational and social obstacles to complete college and apply to medical school. You are an (unofficial) underrepresented minority. Since medical schools are being pushed to increase the number of their graduates who enter primary care, especially in inner-city and rural areas, they may see you as a "diamond in the rough." Since you have a rural background, they believe that you will return to a similar area to practice. They're generally wrong about this, though.

Most medical students come from large cities or their suburbs (figure 10.2). To take full advantage of your background, make it clear to the admission committees that you're from America's hinterlands. Some specifically ask if you are from a rural area, and then give such applicants special consideration if they complete the appropriate forms (giving the specifics of your rural background) that the medical school supplies.

In some states, special programs exist to pay the medical school expenses of students agreeing to return to practice medicine in a rural part of the state for a specific period of time once they finish residency. This means that, in some cases, students leave medical school with little or no debt. Medical schools with these programs are constantly seeking applicants who are willing to participate. If you are, let them know it.

Transfers With Advanced Standing

In 1994-95, 123 students transferred to M.D.-granting U.S. medical schools from "other" graduate or professional degree programs. Most of these students transferred from foreign medical schools. They represent only a tiny portion of the U.S. citizens training at non-U.S./Canadian medical schools, since transferring from a non-U.S. medical school to a U.S. medical school is extremely difficult. (See chapter 17 for more details.)

Foreign-Born U.S. Citizens

This category includes anyone who spent much of his life speaking a language other than American English. This includes our English-speaking cohorts in Britain and the many countries that once made up the British Empire. You may speak English and write excellent English, but it is not American English, and that may be where you get tripped up.

Figure 10.2: Locale of Medical Students' High Schools *

Locale	% of High Schools
Suburb of large city	25 %
Large city (population 500,000+)	18
Moderate-sized city (50,000 to 500,000)	17
Small city (10,000 to 50,000)—not suburb	13
Suburb of moderate—sized city	9
Town (2,500 to 10,000)—not suburb	9
Small town (<2,500)	4
Rural/unincorporated area	2

* Percentages do not add up to 100% due to rounding and missing data.

Adapted from: Association of American Medical Colleges. *AAMC 1992 Graduating Student Survey Results.* Washington, DC: AAMC, 1992, p. 25.

American English is full of colloquial expressions that make no sense unless you memorize them. Use one of the books listing these expressions to build your vocabulary, such as Spears' *Essential American Idioms,* and then practice on your friends.

Your accent may also be problematic. Speaking with a mild British or Australian accent may be considered very fashionable. But if your accent is too difficult for Americans to understand, you will be at a disadvantage during your interviews—as well as subsequently in class, on the wards, and when applying to residency programs. Many colleagues have said that they improved their American-English accents through attending special classes where, rather than teaching English grammar, the concentration was on the students' accents and being understood. Many colleges offer such courses at night or on weekends. Audiotapes are also useful (if you actually listen to them) since you can use them whenever it's convenient.

Foreign Nationals

Permanent U.S. residents who hold "Green Cards" (actually, they are pink) may apply to U.S. medical schools on the same basis and through the same mechanisms as any other applicants. In Canada, landed immigrants may apply on the same basis as Canadian citizens.

Although they may apply, very few foreign nationals are admitted to U.S. medical schools, since qualified U.S. citizens receive preference. In 1995, for example, only 481 (3.6%) graduating medical students were not U.S. citizens. Of these, 350 (72.8%) were permanent residents, i.e., had "Green Cards." Many of the others undoubtedly were Canadian citizens. Some schools are more willing to enroll foreign nationals than others (figure 15.5).

Foreign nationals must be ready to supply medical schools with complete visa information. They must have a visa that allows them to complete their studies at a U.S. graduate school. Since medical schools are not generally able to provide foreign nationals with scholarships or loans, these applicants must arrange to finance their own medical school education—and to demonstrate, to the school's satisfaction, how they will do it. Some schools require that a portion of these monies be placed in an escrow account before the student begins classes.

Foreign nationals applying to transfer with advanced standing to U.S. medical schools should contact individual schools directly. They should also contact the ECFMG for information about taking the USMLE Step 1. The chance of non-U.S. citizens or permanent residents getting advanced standing at U.S. medical schools is very small. (For additional information, see figure 15.5 and Louise B. Ball's *International Medical Graduates' Guide: Negotiating the Maze*.)

Gays, Lesbians, and Bisexuals

Gay, lesbian, and bisexual medical school applicants, medical students and physicians are a largely invisible minority, although they are becoming more visible in the medical profession as our society changes. Maturing societal attitudes now acknowledge alternative lifestyles and many individuals feel more comfortable identifying themselves as gay, lesbian, or bisexual. Medical organizations of gay, lesbian, and bisexual physicians have thousands of dues-paying members, and membership is growing at the rate of 10% annually. The medical problems of this group, including AIDS, have forcefully gained the profession's attention. Yet, as mentioned in other sections, medical practitioners generally have conservative attitudes toward their life and work.

Organized medicine has not felt comfortable accepting gay, lesbian, and bisexual physicians, as exemplified by the difficulty that many national physician organizations have approving resolutions banning discrimination on the basis of sexual orientation. One study showed that 30% of physicians would refuse applicants admission to medical school based solely on the fact of their being gay or lesbian, and 40% would discourage them from entering pediatric or psychiatric residencies on that basis alone. This suggests that gay, lesbian, and bisexual medical students may not want to broadcast their sexual orientation when applying for residency positions.

As one medical student, Lydia Vaias, wrote in *JAMA*, "Interviews are uncomfortable, scary processes for everyone. They are particularly terrifying for lesbian and gay people, because we must grapple with telling who we are, without revealing an integral aspect of ourselves."

Gay and bisexual applicants may also encounter medical school faculties' fears that, if accepted, they may join the estimated 5,000 HIV-infected physicians. This fear represents more than mere homophobia; it denotes concerns about having students who need prolonged absences, have disabilities, and have other problems with which admission directors and faculty do not want to deal if they can avoid them.

As with any applicant, you may doom your application by demonstrating to interviewers that you are not "mainstream." Wearing triangle or rainbow jewelry or any other trapping of gay culture will most likely decrease the probability of your getting into many medical schools. If you feel, however, as some people do, that it is essential to demonstrate your sexual orientation to potential teachers, be forewarned that it may cost you the medical school slot you desire. On the other hand, if this is the reason you don't get into a school, you may not want to go there anyway.

Two national groups now lend assistance and support to gays, lesbians, and bisexuals in medicine: American Association of Physicians for Human Rights, 273 Church Street, San Francisco, CA 94114; and for medical students: Lesbian, Gay & Bisexual People in Medicine, American Medical Student Association, 1902 Association Drive, Reston, VA 22091-1502. There are also a number of local groups in larger cities.

Summary

There are many paths into medical school and many types of individuals constitute the medical profession. The key for any successful applicant is to persist, know your own strengths and weaknesses, and improve yourself however possible. Many individuals get into medical school because others drop by the wayside and don't pursue their dream. It's up to you.

11: The Medical College Admission Test (MCAT)

Genius is one percent inspiration and
ninety-nine percent perspiration.

Thomas A. Edison

THE MEDICAL COLLEGE ADMISSION TEST, commonly referred to as the "MCAT," represents a major hurdle for most applicants to medical school. The seven-plus-hour (including breaks) multiple-choice examination, administered by the MCAT Program Office, measures your knowledge of the biological and physical sciences, your ability to read and interpret information, and your ability to write coherently. The MCAT is not designed to test your ability to regurgitate information, but rather it tests your ability to think, read, and process information quickly. Nearly all U.S. medical schools require applicants to take the MCAT before applying for admission (figure 15.2). Even the U.S. medical schools, such as Dartmouth, that don't require applicants to take the MCAT, say that those who have not taken it may be at a competitive disadvantage. Nearly all schools require applicants to have taken the test after 1991, when a new format was introduced, and many require that the test be taken within two to three years of applying (figure 15.5).

The MCAT is designed to put applicants with different backgrounds, and from different schools with disparate grading systems and grading stringency, on an "even playing field" for comparison. The test supposedly measures how well students will do in medical school. In fact, it primarily indicates who will be outstanding (the top MCAT performers) and who will do miserably (the worst MCAT performers). Those scoring in the middle can go either way. Above all, the MCAT is an endurance test, leading one student to suggest that medical schools might do just as well having students run a marathon, with those who finish first having the first pick of schools to attend.

Although you need to do well on the MCAT, good scores on this test will not substitute for a poor GPA. For those with borderline grades that have improved over time, however, excellent MCAT scores can suggest to medical schools that you have enough potential for them to take a chance on admitting you.

Your premed adviser has detailed information about MCAT schedules and, usually, also has samples of useful study materials.

When To Take The MCAT

The MCAT is administered twice a year, on a Saturday in April and in August. For an additional $10 fee and with advance notification, special Sunday administrations (on the same weekend as the Saturday administration) can be arranged for those with religious or other unavoidable conflicts.

Many undergraduates take the test either in April of their junior year or in August of their senior year. Most medical schools suggest that students take the MCAT in April, about 18 months before they plan to enter medical school. This makes sense for several reasons. Taking the test in April allows you to apply to medical school early. If you wish, you can participate in the early-decision program (see chapter 26). If you don't do well in April, you also have a chance to retake it in August. Finally, since few students benefit from taking additional course work between the April and August administrations, why not take it in April and get it over with? The exceptions are those students who use the summer to take science courses or MCAT prep courses.

Still, most people continue to take the MCAT in the "fall" (actually August). In 1995, for example, out of 67,436 examinees, 30,042 took the test in April and 37,394 took it in August. The major problem with taking the April administration is that you will have to prepare for the exam while you are also studying for your regular classes. Even if you lighten your class schedule during that time period, this is not a particularly easy endeavor, and can be quite stressful.

Another option, which is not frequently mentioned, is to take the MCAT in August after your sophomore year. The advantages of this strategy are that you will probably have completed the basic science courses covered on the test and you will have an entire summer to study (assuming you don't have to work) or to take an MCAT prep course. If you entered college with advanced standing in some of your premed courses, you may even have taken upper-level science courses by the time you take the MCAT. Taking the test in your sophomore year also gives you the opportunity to apply to an early-decision program if you do well, or to retake the test if you do poorly. The main reason not to take the MCAT at this time is that you have not yet completed the course work covered on the exam.

Some postbaccalaureates take the MCAT before they have completed the required premed subjects covered on the exam. In that case, they have to find alternative ways of studying, as one student did:

> The only courses I needed for medical school were my science requirements. I realized that if I took the MCAT before taking all the classes, I could shave a whole year off the admissions process. I learned organic chemistry and physics in the Test & Tape library of the Kaplan course and did very well on the MCAT.

Another student with a similar situation tried the same tactic, but at the end barely made it to the exam:

> I used a prep course, since I hadn't taken physics or organic chemistry when I took the MCAT. When I took the MCAT, I was an active duty military officer and for a month prior to the exam had been playing war games in a remote area of Washington State. I had to be helicoptered out of the mountains to take the test and then flown back. A bit stressful. (I'll bet!)

Description Of The MCAT

The MCAT is a grueling, multiple-choice examination developed by medical school admission officers, premed instructors, medical educators, practicing physicians, AAMC staff, and testing experts, all working under the auspices of the Association of American Medical Colleges (AAMC). While the test's format was revised in 1991 to emphasize a broader knowledge of the natural and social sciences and the humanities, it still concentrates on subjects near-and-dear to the premed curriculum.

Rather than simply asking for a regurgitation of memorized facts, the exam is designed to test how well you can scan information, synthesize data, and solve problems. It tests information processing, rather than information collecting.

The Test Day

A typical test-day schedule (figure 11.1) includes 5¾ hours of testing plus time for breaks. The day of the test, you *must* arrive on time, since you will not be allowed to take the test if you come late. Normally, you must be there no later than 8 A.M. What time the test actually begins will depend upon the number of registrants at that site and the amount of time needed to check in all of them. Therefore, when you arrive to take the test, realize that there will be delays while proctors check individuals against their registration photos and complete other preliminary paperwork. Stay calm!

Verbal Reasoning Section

The Verbal Reasoning section tests examinees' ability to read and comprehend information while under pressure, as well as their ability to critically reason and assess the material. There are 9 or 10 long passages (totaling 500 to 600 words), each associated with 6 to 10 multiple-choice questions. All information necessary to answer the questions is presented in the passages. The passages are drawn from the humanities, natural sciences, and social sciences, but the subject content itself is not tested. The passages are "arguments," in which the author presents and defends a controversial position, trying to persuade the reader to accept his viewpoint. The passages are taken from previously published material, so they are often truncated versions of the originals. This sometimes makes them sound rather awkward, but the questions can still be answered based on the material presented.

Four types of questions generally accompany these passages. *Comprehension* questions require examinees to identify, justify, and synthesize the central concepts of the passage. For example, what is the writer saying, how is the position justified, what assumptions are made, and what conclusions are drawn? They may also ask for comparisons of information or for the definitions of terminology contained in the passage. If the question begins, "According to the author," the answer should be in the passage. *Evaluation* questions ask whether the author's reasoning, information sources, claims, and conclusions can be supported by the evidence presented in the passage. *Application* questions ask examinees to apply the information contained in the passage to hypothetical or real-world situations. *Incorporation* questions require examinees to decide how the writer's argument is affected by new information supplied in the question. Although MCAT study materials break down these question types even further, independent experts suggest that doing so is not particularly useful.

Some people suggest that you critically read newspaper editorials to prepare for this section since they are about the same length as the passages. (It is also useful to get into this habit, since you will be asked about current topics during your medical school interviews.) Others suggest taking courses that use argument and reasoning skills, such as rhetoric, logic, and composition. In fact, many medical schools require or recommend that applicants take these courses (figure 15.1). (These courses also will help to improve your score on the MCAT Writing Sample.)

When taking the Verbal Reasoning section, don't leave any questions blank expecting to return to them later. Answer each question when you get to it. You won't have enough time to reread the long passage and answer the question. You can, of course, skip an entire item (a passage and its questions) and return to it later, since that does not take any more time than it

Figure 11.1: Typical MCAT Test Schedule

Section	Number of Questions	Time (minutes)
Morning Session		
Verbal Reasoning	65	85
(Break)		10
Physical Sciences	77	100
(Lunch Break)		60
Afternoon Session		
Writing Sample	2	60
(Break)		10
Biological Sciences	77	100

would have initially. Also, while reading the passage, systematically "highlight" important words or phrases. (Highlighters are not permitted.) Some examinees use a double line under the passage's main theme, a single line under principal details supporting the theme, and place brackets around [secondary details].

Physical Sciences Section

The Physical Sciences section covers information, divided equally, from the introductory undergraduate courses in general chemistry and general non-calculus physics. Questions consist entirely of science problems and may include data presented in graphs, tables, or charts. The questions test examinees' knowledge of basic biological concepts, their ability to interpret data, and their problem-solving abilities. There are 10 or 11 long medically relevant passages to read (each about 250 words), each having 4 to 8 associated multiple-choice questions. In addition, there are 15 stand-alone multiple-choice questions not based on a descriptive passage.

Passages may include descriptive information with diagrams, problems to solve, or persuasive arguments. They may describe experiments, instruments (often with diagrams), or study designs. Passages in this section are presented in one of the four formats listed below.

1. *Information*, in which problems are presented from material previously published. A good place to find this type of passage, with the turgid writing style, is *The New England Journal of Medicine*. It can be found in most public and all medical libraries.

2. *Problem-Solving,* which is similar to the word problems found in many science texts.

3. *Research Study,* which describes all or part of a scientific experiment.

4. *Persuasive Argument* passages, in which the writer tries to convince the reader that particular results are correct, or that specific methods, evidence, or conclusions are appropriate.

Some questions, especially those dealing with organic chemistry, may require multiple mathematical calculations or the understanding of abstract and integrated concepts when answering them. However, a knowledge of calculus is not needed, nor is memorization of unusual constants, formulas, and conversion factors, which are all provided if needed. (A periodic table is provided in the test booklet.) The questions in this section often resemble those in textbooks.

Writing Sample Section

The Writing Sample section comes at the start of the afternoon session. Examinees have one hour to complete two essays on different topics (30 minutes for each essay). This portion of the test examines your critical thinking, ability to organize ideas, and writing skills. The topics do *not* include: the technical content of biology, chemistry, physics, or mathematics; the medical school application process; why you chose medicine as a career; social or cultural issues that are not within the general experience of MCAT examinees; and religious or other emotionally charged issues.

The "topic" provided for each essay consists of a statement that expresses an opinion, discusses a philosophy, or describes a policy. They are usually quotations (see examples below). You must accomplish three basic tasks in each essay. *First,* you must explain or interpret the quotation. Your explanation should be as complete as possible. The statements are not straight facts or self-evident, so they cannot generally be explained in a single sentence. Your *second* task is to oppose the concept by finding an instance in which it might be contradicted or not be applicable. Here, a specific example is required, along with further exploration of the statement's meaning. *Finally,* you must resolve the conflict between the initial statement and the contradiction that you have described. In doing this, you should attempt to apply your understanding of the topic to more general issues raised by the conflict between the opposing views.

Two graders independently score each essay. (A third is used if there is a discrepancy.) They expect an essay to flow logically from one point to the next. The score is determined by the depth, cohesiveness, and clarity with which each task is addressed and by the extent to which ideas are developed. The essay should be in correct English, but at "first-draft level," so don't waste valuable time polishing your writing and thereby ending up with incomplete essays. *Do* take the time to make your handwriting legible, since real people have to read it. If they cannot decipher your scratching, the essay will be graded "X" for "Not Ratable." A real danger lies in the fact that this MCAT section comes just after lunch. Overeating may make you sleepy (i.e., ineffective, sloppy), so don't have a big lunch.

The following examples are typical of the essay questions (and the examples the AAMC uses in seminars to explain this test section):

1. John F. Kennedy made the following comment: "The credit belongs to the man who is actually in the arena. Whose face is marred by dust, sweat and blood: who knows the enthusiasm, the great devotion, and spends himself in a worthy cause. Who at best if he wins knows the thrill of high achievement and if he fails at least fails while daring greatly so that his place shall never be with those cold and timid souls, who know neither victory nor defeat."

   Explain what the author means when he comments on the man in the arena. Relate the concept of the passage to an area with which you are familiar.

2. An American statesmen said: "In matters of principle, stand like a rock; in matters of taste, swim with the current."

   Explain what the statesman means. Include a description of a situation in which it is hard to distinguish between principle and taste. What criteria should one use to distinguish between principle and matters of taste?

The key to answering these questions appropriately is to first read them carefully and note what they are asking you to do. Both of these questions, for example, ask you to *explain*. The first then asks you to *relate* the concept to an area you know. The second asks you to *describe* a specific situation and then *list criteria* to distinguish between the two concepts. Similar key words might include *define, cite, identify, name,* or *give.* Knowing this, the successful essay writer will quickly jot down an outline covering the points requested and then write them in prose. Those who begin to write without these few minutes of advance planning doom themselves to sloppy, disorganized essays. An essay's quality, not its length, determines its score.

Biological Sciences Section

The Biological Sciences section covers information contained in undergraduate first-year, introductory general biology and organic chemistry courses. It consists entirely of science problems and may include data presented in graphs, tables, or charts. The questions test examinees' knowledge of basic biological concepts, and their ability to interpret data and solve problems. There are 10 or 11 long, medically relevant passages (each about 250 words), each with 4 to 8 multiple-choice questions. Passages may include descriptive information with diagrams, problem-solving, or persuasive arguments. They may describe experiments, instruments (often with diagrams), or study designs. The problem-based questions often require an advanced understanding of research methods and result interpretation in biology or organic chemistry. Passages in this section are in one of four formats, which are the same as those described in "Physical Sciences Section," above. In addition, there are 15 stand-alone multiple-choice questions which are not based on descriptive passages.

More information on specific test content can be found in the *MCAT Student Manual* and the various commercial MCAT preparation materials.

MCAT Test Items

To reassure you that the MCAT is assembled with considerable care, here is an outline of how each test item is prepared.

1. Undergraduate and medical school faculty, at an MCAT editor's request, write test items for a specific content area.

2. MCAT's editors review and revise these items for technical accuracy and clarity. They often request up to three times the number of items they will finally need, since so many are rejected.

3. MCAT technical editors, who are content experts in the tested areas, review the questions for technical accuracy. "Bias editors," who represent various racial and ethnic groups, also review the questions for potentially objectionable or inaccessible material. (Examples of item bias include a question about facial flushing that was considered biased against Blacks, and an item about air pressure and scuba diving that was thought to favor men, who might have more experience with the sport.) Both groups suggest improvements.

4. MCAT test editors review the suggestions and revise the items.

5. Acceptable items are field-tested during actual MCAT administrations. (There is no way to tell which are the "real" questions and which are not.)

6. Field-test results are examined for validity and for bias. Acceptable items are added to subsequent tests.

7. Following each MCAT administration, the staff usually gets more than 150 letters from examinees describing items they consider flawed. These letters are evaluated before the tests are scored. If the staff finds that any of these comments detected previously

unnoticed flaws in a test item, an individual question or even all the questions associated with a passage, can be left unscored.

Preparing For The MCAT

Almost anybody can do well on the MCAT as long as he or she develops a sound study plan and begins preparing for the exam as early as possible. Start by obtaining the AAMC's *MCAT Student Manual* during your freshman year. This book lists the topics tested on the MCAT (and has some sample questions). As students take their course work, they can compare each class syllabus with the *Manual*, and highlight those topics that are very important to learn well the first time. That makes it easier to review the material before the MCAT.

Then, get into the mindset that you plan to take the test only once. That way, you will give it the preparation it deserves. If you entered college determined to become a physician, you should have included those courses necessary to do well on the exam. It's best to complete at least the minimum premed curriculum (including biochemistry even if it isn't part of the curriculum) before you take the test. Then you will at least be able to recognize the questions, even if you do not exactly know all the answers. Beginning your preparation early will also allow you the freedom to choose the time when you want to take the exam, rather than having it thrust upon you.

Keep all your textbooks, laboratory manuals, and laboratory notebooks for the courses that cover any topics covered in the MCAT outline. Use these books not only to later review for the MCAT, but also to help you link topics between various courses. For example, if you encounter the Krebs cycle in your biochemistry course, see how it was discussed in the biology course you already completed. This provides a better insight into important topics and gives you the necessary cross-linkage of concepts between the subject areas.

Although mathematics is not a separate MCAT section, you will need to know basic math, including algebra and trigonometry, to solve some questions. Also, many of the questions incorporate tables, graphs, or diagrams which you will have to interpret.

Since the test heavily favors those who read quickly with good comprehension, and since it relies so heavily on problem-solving ability, taking courses to improve these skills will help you as much as learning the specific test content will. For example, many of the basic-science principles with which you should be thoroughly familiar will be buried within complex paragraphs to make them harder to recognize.

You should take a writing course. Most premed students concentrate on the science portions of the MCAT, and then do relatively poorly on the writing section. Most physicians (and presumably premeds) can write a coherent sentence. It does not, therefore, take very much skill to do well on the MCAT writing section. You simply have to prepare for it as you do for the science sections.

The best preparation for the Writing Sample section is to write essays. Write at least one essay per week under the same time constraints (30 minutes) as on the test. Use sample questions from the *MCAT Student Manual, Examples of MCAT Writing Sample Responses and Explanations of Their Scores,* commercial MCAT books, or books with provocative quotations, such as *Bartlett's Familiar Quotations,* that are available in all libraries.

Since the MCAT is a long series of examinations, consider it a "test marathon." Runners train for a marathon by progressively running longer distances. When training for the MCAT, take as many "diagnostics" (old or simulated tests) as you possibly can. Take the tests under the same time constraints as you will have during the real test, since that will help you to figure out how to best approach different types of test questions.

You need to determine your plan of action. First, decide whether to study alone (or with a study group) for the MCAT or to enroll in a commercial prep course. Then, obtain all available

MCAT materials from the AAMC. If you develop a good study plan and follow that plan closely, you have an excellent chance of scoring well on the MCAT.

A recent national survey of medical students found that 90% felt that individual study was important to their success on the MCAT. Nearly two-thirds felt that studying old MCAT examinations and preparatory books benefited them the most. One-fourth believed that formal preparatory courses were important to their success; but, of course, everyone learns a little differently. Those who seemed to benefit from structured courses included students who had been out of school for a while, non-science majors, and even some who had not yet taken all of the required premed courses (usually postbaccalaureate students).

Most students know the study techniques that work best for them. Use this knowledge to determine how you will prepare for the MCAT. Sometimes it's hard to fit the studying in, but if you're serious about it, you can do it, as this student showed:

> I had a seven-month-old daughter at the time I was preparing for the MCAT and was working about 50 hours a week as an engineer (as was my wife). I was also taking two premedical courses and an MCAT prep course on the weekends. The only time I had free to study was from 3 A.M. to 6 A.M. I did that every morning for three months. (Now, that's dedication!)

Materials For Self-Study

A wide variety of materials are available to help students prepare for the MCAT. The most important ones to get are those produced by the Association of American Medical Colleges, the folks who run the MCAT. (Good source, right?) These include the following:

- *MCAT Student Manual.* This book contains detailed outlines and descriptions of each MCAT subsection. These outlines are the essential building blocks to use to prepare for the test.

- *MCAT Practice Test I.* This practice test contains test items used during the experimental phase of the new MCAT. This manual comes packaged with the *MCAT Student Manual.*

- *MCAT Practice Test II.* Similar to *Practice Test I,* it provides additional test items from prior MCAT administrations.

- *MCAT Practice Test III.* This practice test contains test items actually used in MCAT examinations. In addition to the test questions, it also contains tables that allow students to analyze their strong and weak subject areas.

- *Scoring the MCAT Writing Sample–Examples of MCAT Writing Sample Responses and Explanations of Their Scores.* This book not only discusses the requirements for a good essay, but also contains twelve sample essays, both good and bad, with evaluations of each. An excellent guide for how, and how not, to write your essays.

- *Preparing for the MCAT.* A 24-minute videotape describing the knowledge and skills that the MCAT tests, as well as preparation strategies for each of the four test sections. Since it is inexpensive ($12), you may want to purchase it. Otherwise, your premed adviser or library probably has a copy you can view. Be prepared to take notes; it contains valuable information.

Many other books describing the MCAT, prepared by commercial sources, also exist. Since their formats vary and they are updated regularly, ask your premed adviser for suggestions about which ones other students have recently found most helpful.

If you plan to study on your own, you also need reference materials containing the subject matter that the MCAT tests. Textbooks, especially ones you've used, are excellent. Highlight the important parts of your books when you take your courses, so you can more effectively review them. Lecture notes may be less helpful, because they are often too detailed for MCAT preparation. It is important to methodically review the following texts:

- Biology text and laboratory manuals

- General Chemistry text and laboratory manuals

- Physics (without calculus)

- Mathematics (without calculus)

Use your textbooks along with the subject outlines provided in the *MCAT Student Manual*. Using an MCAT workbook, do at least 20 problems in each of the Verbal Reasoning, Physical Sciences, and Biological Sciences sections every day.

When reviewing for the MCAT, remember that you need not recall specific facts, but rather, you must be familiar with how to apply various concepts. (When necessary, specific facts are provided in the questions.) Even so, one medical student claims that his success on the MCAT came from watching *Jeopardy* for three months prior to the test. Sure it did!

Commercial Preparation Courses

Commercial "prep courses" do not replace personal study plans. They only supplement and help structure such plans. Even if you use a prep course's study guides, you still must review other reference materials on relevant MCAT topics. It is best to use such courses to map out your study schedule and to supplement your weak subjects. Always keep commercial courses and aids in perspective. *You* are the key ingredient in doing well on the MCAT. Unless you put forth the effort, no course or study aid will help you.

One problem with commercial courses is that, because they must cater to large audiences, their course schedules are relatively rigid. For example, Kaplan's courses (1-800-KAP-TEST) are designed around five- or ten-week periods. The Princeton Review Courses (1-800-2REVIEW) and Columbia Review (1-800-300-PREP) work similarly. These time frames may not work for you.

A prep course only succeeds for those who are willing to put in the time to do the assigned work. It is important not only to attend all their classes, but also to visit their "Test Center" as often as possible to work on practice tests and to review the correct answers. These courses aren't cheap—they often cost about $1,000—so get your money's worth.

Test-Taking Hints

These hints have been gathered from successful MCAT examinees (those who got into medical school). Use them to good advantage.

- Bring your admission card, lots of *pre-sharpened* number 2 pencils, a good eraser, and some high-carbohydrate snacks to eat during the breaks. Also, remember to bring a watch to help pace yourself (you may not use the alarm since it will disturb others), and two ballpoint pens with black ink for the essays. You need two pens, because Murphy's Law says that if you bring only one, it won't work.

- Calculators, computers, and, of course, notes may not be taken into the exam room. Other banned items include beeping or calculator watches, pagers, cellular phones, slide rules (does anyone still use them?), cameras, radios, tape recorders, highlighters, colored pencils, scrap paper, lapboards/deskboards, or other aids. If you bring any of these, the proctors will hold them during the test. Earplugs are also forbidden during the test.

- Get a good night's sleep before the exam. If necessary, find someplace other than the dorm, fraternity, or sorority house to sleep. (Remember, it will be a Friday night.)

- Don't study the morning of the exam, or even the night before. Do something relaxing (but not mind-altering). Reducing stress will help you on the test.

- Some examinees feel better if they visit the examination room before the test. You can generally do this until the exam day, but understand that the room may be changed to accommodate additional examinees or for other reasons. You will not be able to select your seat; the proctors will assign one to you.

- Dress very comfortably. Bring a sweater, sweatshirt, or jacket in case the room gets too cold—a common problem.

- Allow enough time to transfer your answers from the test booklet to the answer sheet, because if answers aren't on the answer sheet, they won't be scored. This must be done within the time allotted for each section, because no additional time is allowed to transfer answers.

- Don't discuss the test during breaks—it will only serve to distract and depress you. Do stretching exercises, meditate, and check out the bathroom.

- After the test, go out and celebrate with people who have not taken it. You don't want to rehash the test or go over the "right" answers with anyone.

Test Disruptions

Premed advisers report that there are disruptions at about one hundred MCAT testing sites each year. While many of these are minor and affect relatively few test-takers, others have literally been disasters. In recent years, they report that marching bands practiced and athletic events occurred just outside of the testing rooms, fire alarms required the rooms to be evacuated, and tornadoes blew through the area panicking everyone. My own story is somewhat dated, but certainly sticks with me.

The night before I took the MCAT, civil unrest (a riot) took place on campus. Although Vietnam protests were occurring regularly, this was somewhat unexpected. What began with a rather unruly protest march quickly gave way to a massive police presence, including the widespread use of tear gas. The tear gas was liberally deposited not only among the protesters, but also in the dorms, the chapel, and of course, in the large lecture hall where the MCAT was to be given the next day. Since my dorm was one of those tear-gassed, I spent a very uncomfortable night in a classroom building far enough away from the melee so only some of the tear gas seeped in. The next morning when I showed up for the test, I was understandably depressed, since I felt my performance would suffer due to my lack of rest. Only when I arrived did I discover that my limited exposure to the tear gas had built up my tolerance enough so that I wasn't bothered by the residual gas in the room. Most of my fellow test-takers weren't so fortunate. No adjustments to anyone's scores were made.

Other, more recent, test-takers have also endured disruptions during the MCAT.

The night before a recent administration, a huge storm shut down the air conditioning at an Arizona test site. As the test began, the temperature hovered over $100°$F. Water from a burst pipe flooded the front row where examinees were sitting. They reported that it was so hot that they could see steam rising from the pooled water. Vapor curled their test booklets and answer sheets. Just outside the exam room, workers used chain saws to dismember trees felled in the storm.

Nevertheless, the exam continued. However, this was not the end of the saga for these hapless examinees. About a month later they were notified that their Writing Sample essays had been lost and they would have to retake that portion of the test. Unfortunately, some students were not notified (they were out of the country) and their entire tests were voided. The AAMC sent an explanatory letter with all these students' scores. No one knows if medical schools considered these letters, but at least some of these students are now in medical school.

One of the other test-takers broke the thermostat [at another student's exam] and the room's temperature rose to more than 100°F. The proctors had to wedge open the doors—and there was jackhammering and construction just outside. Not a very conducive environment. Imagine my astonishment on the first day of class when I found that bozo was one of my classmates!

In August 1996, a gunman burst into a San Francisco test center just before the last MCAT section began. Waving his gun, he screamed "I want the test. I want the test." Many examinees ducked on the floor, fearful for their lives. The would-be robber, supposedly wanting the test to sell on the black market, was subdued by angry proctors and test-takers after a violent struggle. "After I saw blood around his head and on the floor, it was hard to finish the test," said one man, who nevertheless completed the exam. Some examinees did not complete the test. All were offered an opportunity to take a different version of the test the following weekend.

If you have a disruption at your test site, immediately write a letter to both the MCAT Program Office (the test administrators at P.O. Box 4056, Iowa City, IA 52243) and the Association of American Medical Colleges (who owns the test). Detail the disruption and specifically ask that a letter describing the incident be included with your scores. Have all of your friends who took the test do the same thing. Also, immediately contact your adviser, describe the incident, and give her a copy of the letters you sent. The response in the past from the AAMC and ETS has varied depending on the nature of the incident and the number of people complaining. In some instances, especially where it was "an act of God," they included a letter explaining the circumstances with the scores they send from that site. In some cases, however, they have not responded at all. The best that can be said is that their policy on dealing with test disruptions is inconsistent.

MCAT Scores

You cannot "pass" or "fail" the MCAT, although you can do relatively well or "bottom out." Examinees score points for correct answers. There is no penalty for incorrect answers. Once you take the MCAT, the scores remain on your record; you may not cancel or delete them.

Four separate MCAT scores are reported: Verbal Reasoning, Physical Sciences, Writing Sample, and Biological Sciences. Examinees receive both a "raw score," the number of correct answers, and a "scaled score" for each test section. Scaled scores are graded on a 1 (worst) to 15 (best) scale except for the Writing Sample. The Writing Sample is graded from "J" through "T," with "J" equating to the bottom eight percent and "T" to the top nine percent. Most people's scores are scattered in the "M" through "R" range. Medical schools receive the scaled scores and the Writing Sample letter score.

What's a Good Score?

The average MCAT scaled scores are about "8" for Verbal Reasoning, Physical Sciences, and Biological Sciences, and "N" for the Writing Sample. The scores needed to be a competitive applicant vary with each medical school (figure 15.4).

Figure 11.2: Percentages Correlating To MCAT Raw and Scaled Scores.

Score	Verbal Reasoning		Physical Sciences		Biological Sciences	
	# Correct	Percentile	# Correct	Percentile	# Correct	Percentile
≧12	60-65	97-99	67-77	94-99	66-77	95-99
10-11	52-59	73-96	57-67	75-93	60-65	71-94
8-9	44-51	42-72	48-56	44-74	49-59	38-70
7	41-43	30-41	42-47	28-43	44-48	27-37
6	35-40	17-29	36-41	15-27	40-43	16-26
5	32-34	11-16	32-35	6-14	35-39	9-15
≦4	0-31	0-10	0-31	0-5	0-34	0-8
Mean Score	7.8		8.0		8.0	
Std. Dev.	2.4		2.3		2.4	

Adapted from: Association of American Medical Colleges. *MCAT Practice Test III.* Washington, DC: AAMC, 1995, p. 99.

Figure 11.2 gives the approximate number of correct test items needed to get a particular scaled score on the three numerically scored sections. It also shows the percentage of test-takers who get that score. The exact distribution will vary slightly with each test administration, but the chart roughly approximates what your scores mean. (A similar chart for your MCAT administration will come with your scores.)

Some medical schools use a formula that combines applicants' GPAs with their MCAT scores. If you ask, some schools will tell you how they weigh each, so you can better evaluate your chances of acceptance.

Statistical Breakdown of Applicant and Matriculant Scores

The following chart (figure 11.3) gives an overall view of how all applicants to (M.D.) medical schools and those who were accepted (matriculants) scored on the MCAT. Note, however, that students' average MCAT scores (figure 15.4) vary widely among individual schools.

Only about two-thirds of those who take the MCAT actually apply to medical school. Some apply to other health-related schools. Many, however, do not score well and thus never apply. This self-screening increases the average of all applicants'—and, subsequently, matriculants'—scores.

Reporting Scores

Examinees receive their MCAT scores about ten weeks after taking the exam. The notice comes by first-class mail—scores are never given out over the phone. As one recipient noted, it's "a bit like waiting for the death notice of a terminally ill relative. Even though you expect to hear at any time, you are always unprepared when word actually comes."

Examinees may opt *at the time they take the MCAT* to have their scores sent directly to the American Medical College Application Service (AMCAS). AMCAS will then automatically forward the two most recent MCAT scores with the examinee's application materials to all AMCAS-participating schools to which he or she has applied or will apply. At the time of the test,

Figure 11.3: Average MCAT Scores for Applicants and Matriculants

		1992*	1993	1994	1995	1996
Biological Sciences	Applicants	8.2	8.3	8.5	8.7	8.3
	Matriculants	9.3	9.5	9.6	9.8	NA
Physical Sciences	Applicants	8.1	8.2	8.3	8.6	7.9
	Matriculants	9.2	9.3	9.4	9.7	NA
Verbal Reasoning	Applicants	8.3	8.3	8.3	8.5	7.8
	Matriculants	9.2	9.4	9.4	9.5	NA
Writing Sample	Applicants	O	O	O	O	O
	Matriculants	O	P	P	P	NA

* The year medical schools first used the "New" MCAT test results.

examinees may also designate, at no additional cost, six non-AMCAS institutions (i.e., non-AMCAS M.D.-granting medical schools and schools of osteopathic, podiatric, and veterinary medicine) and their current premed adviser as score recipients. Additional MCAT-score reports can be sent to non-AMCAS destinations by completing an *MCAT Additional Score Report Form* and paying the extra fee. Information and the forms are available by writing to: Additional Score Reports, Section for Student Services, Association of American Medical Colleges, 2450 N Street, N.W., Washington, DC 20037-1131 (AMCAS will no longer forward scores from pre-1991 MCAT administrations.)

Note that, if they wish, schools getting your MCAT scores can also request the essay from your Writing Sample. Although many are satisfied with simply seeing your scores, more than half review the essays of marginal applicants, as well as those of applicants having a discrepancy between their Writing Sample score and the quality of writing in their personal essay. A few schools do not consider the Writing Sample when evaluating applicants.

There are only two ways to avoid having your MCAT scored—and both must occur on the day you take the test. The first is simply to leave before the test is over. This automatically voids your test, no matter what your reason for leaving. The second is to personally ask the proctor to void your test. Once you take the entire MCAT and leave the test center, the test cannot be voided.

Registering For The MCAT

Students can obtain current MCAT registration materials from their premed advisers in February. The packet includes a registration card, information about the test itself, test dates for the current year, testing locations, score distributions, and the application deadlines. Others can obtain this information from: MCAT Program Office, P.O. Box 4056, Iowa City, IA 52243; telephone (319) 337-1357.

Examinees must pre-register for the MCAT. There is no walk-in registration. You must register on time and, preferably, as early as possible. There may be limited space available at the test site nearest to you, and spots are assigned on a first-come, first-served basis. If you miss the deadline, tough luck—there are no extensions, no matter how good your sob story. Submit registration materials by certified, return-requested mail. While it is a pain to go to the post office and wait in line, it is worth the time and a little extra money to be sure that your registration materials arrive safely. Don't send your registration fee in cash; use a check or money order.

If you have taken the MCAT three or more times, you will also probably need to submit evidence that you really are applying to medical schools. This evidence can be in the form of a rejection letter, a current completed application, or a letter from a medical school or premed adviser.

Cost

Taking the MCAT costs $150 (in 1996).

Applicants with financial hardships can apply to the Association of American Medical Colleges' MCAT Fee-Reduction Program. Apply early, and expect to be approved only if you show extreme financial hardship. If approved, applicants pay only $55 to take the test. The procedure for applying to this program and a request form is included with the MCAT registration materials. For more information about this program, contact the AAMC's Section for Student Services.

How Many Times Should You Take The MCAT?

Since the MCAT is so important, some students think that they should take the test once for practice and then again "for real." Bad move. The MCAT report sent to medical schools includes not only your most recent MCAT scores, but also *all previous scores*. Some schools average all your scores when they evaluate your application.

Medical schools don't normally like to see students take the MCAT more than three times. Unless you really do miserably on your first try, don't retake the test unless you have to re-apply to medical schools.

The data show that if you score a "10" on the numerically scored sections or an "O" on the Writing Sample and retake the examination, you are just as likely to get a worse score on the retake as to get a better one. (The score was unchanged for just under one-third of repeaters who had initially scored at these levels.) The farther below this you score, the better your chance of improving your score, although even with the lowest scores some people don't improve their scores with retesting. The higher you score above these levels, the better the chance that you will score lower if you retake the MCAT.

You should, however, retake the test if: (1) there is a marked discrepancy between your undergraduate performance and the test scores, (2) you took the test before you were prepared for it (meaning that you *will* be prepared before you take it again), (3) you were ill or had a distracting personal situation when you took the test, or (4) a medical school's admission committee recommend that you retake the test.

If you must retake the MCAT, register the same way you did the first time.

Test Security

How carefully does AAMC protect the exam? *Very* carefully. For example:

- During each MCAT administration, several forms of the test, each with different questions, are issued. Each of these forms has several versions with the questions in different order.

- Photographs, photo-IDs, and thumbprints are used to detect impersonators. Obvious impersonators are not admitted, and suspicious cases are investigated after the test, often by using handwriting analysis.

- Proctors assign examinees to widely scattered seats, with adjacent examinees receiving different forms of the test.

- Prior test-takers will not be issued the same form of the test they previously took.
- The tests are transported by bonded courier, and two people must always be present when the tests are out of secure storage. These individuals may not break the test seals or examine the test contents.
- If there are test violations, the episodes are investigated. If fraud is proven, the scores are voided and all medical schools are notified.

The MCAT is well protected, ensuring that all those who invest the time, money, and grief to take the test are likewise protected.

12: Applying To Medical School

For the want of a nail the shoe was lost,
For the want of a shoe the horse was lost,
For the want of a horse the rider was lost,
For the want of a rider the battle was lost,
For the want of a battle the kingdom was lost—
And all for the want of a horseshoe-nail.

Benjamin Franklin, *Poor Richard's Almanac,* 1758

THE MEDICAL SCHOOL APPLICATION PROCESS can be daunting. Knowing how it works is the key to alleviating anxiety and doing well. Most premed students are, in the words of one adviser, "wound so tight that I have to unscrew them from the ceiling." You can reduce your stress by learning the steps in the application process and developing an effective strategy to complete all of them on (or ahead of) time. To learn about the process, read the information below and then talk with your own premed adviser.

Think of the admission process as a series of screens with progressively smaller holes. Premed students, potential applicants, and applicants are filtered out at every step. As you will see below, however, just how small the holes get for you will, in part, depend upon whether you can "get your act together" in a timely manner.

Timing—It's Your Future

The American Medical College Application Service (AMCAS) and the Association of American Colleges of Osteopathic Medicine Application Service (AACOMAS®) begin accepting applications on June 1, and the University of Texas System Medical and Dental Application Center begins accepting applications on May 1. It is wise to submit your materials to them as close to these dates as possible. Even though it is very advantageous for applicants, especially those who are marginal, to submit their applications early, very few are received in the first few weeks after the deadlines.

Many schools use "rolling admissions" systems in which applicants who submit their materials first get the first interviews. These schools then select acceptable candidates for admission from those interviewed, and continue this process until the class is filled. Many of these individuals will be admitted to medical school before other applicants are even interviewed. Therefore, it is to your advantage to get your application materials in early. Don't hinder (and often delude) yourself by waiting to submit your applications before the medical schools' official deadlines. That's often too late.

One of the most common reasons that good applicants don't get into medical school is because they fail to submit the required materials on time. Medical schools have, in the past, allowed applicants some leeway with their deadlines, but since they now get an overwhelming crush of applications, they rigidly stick to their rules. One school reported that they received fifty completed secondary applications after their deadline in one year. Those students wasted their time completing the applications and had to, if they were still interested, re-apply in subsequent years.

Late applications usually come from students whose credentials will barely get them through the interview screen. Such students have a habit of tardiness and often sloppiness in all their work. As one admission officer said, "They can't seem to get *anything* done on time." People in this group don't make the best physicians. If you want to be labeled as part of this group, now you know how to do it. If you want to get into medical school, send all your materials in on time—and check to make certain they have been received.

Keep a copy of *everything* you submit to the schools, whether they are your applications, transcripts, reference letters (if you can get copies), or other materials. File them in a safe place, using a system that allows you to easily retrieve any document. A sturdy cardboard file-box (sometimes called a "bankers box") works fine, is inexpensive, and doesn't take up too much room. A 12" x 15" x 10" box can hold about 35 files. Since medical school admission staff, college records offices, MCAT staff, and national application-service staff, as well as their systems, are fallible, some of your vital materials may go astray. If you have duplicates, you can quickly mail or fax them another copy. (And since nearly two out of three applicants don't get accepted to medical school the first time they apply, these materials are useful if you must re-apply.)

Keep track of any material you get (and when you got it) from schools. Likewise, keep track of what materials you send (and when) to each school or service bureau. Modify figure 12.1 to fit your needs.

Using a Résumé

Although you don't need a résumé to apply to medical school, spending the time to prepare a good one does three things: *First,* it forces you to gather the facts, names, and dates you will need to complete your applications. *Second,* it helps you organize your thoughts about what is and is not important in your history. *Third,* and most importantly, it will be the basis of the ongoing résumé that you will keep and update throughout your career, to use when you apply for residencies and post-residency jobs.

Putting your first résumé together can be an onerous project. If you prepare one before you complete your medical school applications, it will make completing these applications easier and faster. A résumé also allows premed committees, mock interviewers, reference-letter writers, and occasionally medical school interviewers, to quickly see who you are and what you have accomplished.

For help preparing your résumé, see Tysinger's *Résumés and Personal Statements for Health Professionals* (see *Annotated Bibliography*).

Medical School Applications

Medical schools use three types of applications: *uniform* applications (AMCAS; AACOMAS; University of Texas System Medical and Dental Application Center; Ontario Medical School Application Service), *school-specific primary* applications, and *school-specific secondary* applications. A student applying to twelve medical schools may complete up to *sixteen* applications. (This, of course, doesn't include the forms used to apply for financial aid.) Whew! Lots of paperwork.

Figure 12.1: Application Record

Schools	U of A	B Med	UC Med	D School	U of E
Application Deadline!!	Nov 1	Nov 15	Nov 15	Oct 15	Oct 15
Receive Catalog	Feb 20	April 8	March 6	May 16	May 3
Receive Application	May 12	May 10	May 12	May 16	May 12
Application to Typist	NA	May 15	NA	May 22	NA
Application Mailed	May 30*	June 3	May 30*	June 5	May 30*
Receipt Confirmed	June 8	June 9	June 8	June 18	June 8
Receive 2° Materials	None	None	Rejected	Aug 7	July 14
Returned 2° Materials	NA	NA	NA	Aug 10	July 17
Receipt Confirmed	NA	NA	NA	Aug 14	July 22
School Got Rec. Letters	June 20	June 12	NA	Aug 14	July 28
Interview Date	Oct 22	Dec 12	NO	Jan 12	Sept 6
Accepted? Y = Yes N = No W = Waiting List	Y March 3	W Feb 15	N July 30	N Feb 20	Y Oct 15

* Designates a uniform application; NA = Not Applicable.

About half of all medical schools require that applicants submit both uniform applications and school-specific applications. Another 20% use a uniform application as a screen and then send the school-specific secondary application to applicants meeting their screening criteria (figure 15.5). Just over 10% require only a uniform application or only their school-specific primary application. A few require that students who apply to special programs or declare minority status submit a supplemental form. Nearly all applicants for combined-degree curricula (e.g., medical degree plus Ph.D., M.P.H., or J.D.) must submit a separate application for entry into the additional program.

The AMCAS Application (M.D. Schools)

The AMCAS (American Medical College Application Service) Application is a single form used by all but sixteen U.S. M.D.-granting medical schools. In recent years, about 95% of all applicants used AMCAS to apply to at least one medical school. *For AMCAS-participating schools, applicants for first-year positions may apply only through AMCAS.* Those applying to such schools for "admission with advanced standing" or who are transferring from other schools should contact each school directly. The primary benefit of applying through AMCAS is the reduction of paperwork, since students send out only one set of material as their initial application to most medical schools.

The AMCAS form becomes available each spring (usually in April, but occasionally as late as mid-June). It is used to apply for medical school positions beginning the following year (about sixteen months after the form is issued). The four-page application is detailed and difficult to complete. It consists of three parts: a General Information Page (Education, Work, Activities, Honors), the Personal Statement, and a list of Course Work and GPA Calculations. For help completing the Personal Statement portion, see Tysinger's *Résumés and Personal Statements for Health Professionals* (*see Annotated Bibliography*). For help listing your courses and grades, carefully read the *AMCAS Instruction Booklet* (and have a lot of white-out on hand). If you have difficulty interpreting the instructions or completing the form, go to your premed office. They have had lots of experience with these forms.

Make multiple copies of the application so that you can try several drafts before you submit the final product to the typist. You won't be able to include everything, so you must choose those items that admission committees look for—honors, public service, and health-related work experiences.

Most students hire professional typists to complete the form from their draft copy. The submitted application must look professional, without any errors, stains, or sloppiness. Obtain copies of the AMCAS Application from your premed adviser or from AMCAS, Section for Student Services, Association of American Medical Colleges, 2501 M Street, N.W., Lbby-26, Washington, DC 20037-1300; telephone (202) 828-0600 (then dial 1-1-2 and you go to voice mail). You can also contact AMCAS using e-mail (amcas@aamc.org).

AMCAS does not make admission decisions. Its only responsibility is to process, duplicate, and send your application, MCAT scores, and transcripts to the participating medical schools to which you apply. Use the *AMCAS Designation Form* to indicate which schools should receive your information.

AMCAS accepts applications beginning June 1. Apply as close to this date as possible. (Material submitted before this date, except for school transcripts, will be returned.) If you do this, you may begin receiving secondary applications from some schools during the summer, and interview in early October. As mentioned previously, applying early gives you an advantage at schools having a "rolling" admission policy. Also, be sure to include the correct fees or Fee Waiver Cards (for up to ten schools), since AMCAS will not process applications with insufficient payment (including unapproved credit cards and checks with insufficient information, with incorrect information, denominated in non-U.S. funds, or drawn on accounts with insufficient funds) or from applicants who owe the AAMC money for any reason. They notify you in writing if this applies to you.

Other reasons that AMCAS frequently returns applications include not completing the bottom of the last page (including signing the form), exceeding the allowable space for comments, submitting a copy rather than the original form, submitting a prior year's form, illegible print, Academic Record completed incorrectly (not in chronological order, information incomplete, or incorrect information or codes), no official transcripts submitted, School Designation Form incomplete or inconsistent, and more than one school is designated in conjunction with an Early Decision Declaration.

You can hand-deliver, mail, or express mail/courier your application to AMCAS. If you hand-deliver or mail your application, use the official envelope in which you originally received your AMCAS materials. If you use an express, overnight, or courier service, seal your application in the AMCAS-supplied envelope with your name on the outside. Put this envelope in the mailing service's envelope. AMCAS can receive mailings from these services Monday through Friday, 9 A.M. to 5 P.M. (Eastern Time) except on holidays. Do not send these materials "collect" or "bill receiver," since AMCAS will refuse them. Also, do not send reference letters, photographs, résumés, or other material that AMCAS does not specifically request.

Once AMCAS receives your application and enters it into their database, you can check your application status through an automatic phone system that is operative 24-hours a day. To do this, telephone (202) 828-0600, 1-1-3-1-(your Social Security number)-(your birth date). Once your materials have been sent to the schools, AMCAS sends you a "Transmittal Notification." It includes your identifying information, the schools you attended, GPA, hours, MCAT date(s) and score(s), and the schools to which you applied.

Transcripts

Before you send your application to AMCAS, you must send them your transcripts. They must receive an official transcript from every one of the following schools that you have attended in the United States, Canada, or U.S. Territories, whether or not you earned any credits: junior or community college, college, university, graduate school, U.S. medical school, trade school, and professional school. (You must repeat this process each year that you apply, even if you sent transcripts to AMCAS for prior application cycles.) You should simultaneously ask each school to *send you a copy of your transcript,* since you will need these transcripts to complete the AMCAS application. AMCAS does not require transcripts from: foreign schools (except Canada, U.S. Territories, and U.S. colleges overseas), CEGEP/Grade-13 programs, course work you are currently taking at a new institution, non-credit premed summer enrichment programs, credits recorded in clock-hours or continuing-education-units without an official conversion to semester/quarter hours, and consortium/cross-registration programs where there is no separate transcript. If you claim any of the last three listed "transcript exceptions," you generally must provide a contact name and phone number so that AMCAS can verify that no transcript exists.

AMCAS uses the official transcripts to verify the information you list on your application. They will not forward your application materials until they verify this information.

Deadlines

AMCAS application deadlines vary depending on the schools to which you apply. They can be found under each school's listing in the AAMC's annual publication, *Medical School Admission Requirements,* at the front of the annual *AMCAS Instruction Booklet,* and in the AMCAS-E program. These deadlines are the dates by which AMCAS must *receive all* of an applicant's materials except transcripts. AMCAS accepts transcripts from March 15 until two weeks after their deadline for receiving your AMCAS application. The deadline for AMCAS to receive all materials, including the transcript, for students using the early-decision program is August 1.

Cost

AMCAS charges are based on the number of AMCAS-participating schools to which you apply. The current fee is listed in the *AMCAS Instruction Booklet.* Individual schools charge additional fees, normally in conjunction with submission of a secondary application (figure 15.2).

The AMCAS Fee Waiver Program allows applicants who cannot afford the fee to have it waived for applying to up to ten schools. The Fee Waiver Request Form comes with the AMCAS application packet, can be printed from AMCAS-E (see below), or can be downloaded from the AAMC Web site (http://www.aamc.org). The deadline for Fee Waiver Requests is December 1, although it is best to apply three to four weeks before the earliest medical school deadline you have to meet, since you must include the Fee Waiver Form (if approved) with your AMCAS application. They begin processing Fee Waiver Request Forms on May 15, and stop accepting them on December 1. Students must contact medical schools directly to have supplemental fees waived, although some will automatically waive their fees if the applicant has been granted an AMCAS fee waiver.

The AMCAS-E Application (M.D. Schools)

Beginning in mid-1996, the AMCAS Application became available in electronic form. It can be accessed through either computer disks or on-line at the AAMC's web site. Both medical schools' admission offices and applicants benefit from the electronic format. The program is configured and looks like a typical Windows™ program. It automatically calculates some of the grade and course-hours information that applicants had to compute manually in the past. The program automatically knows the grade conversion factors applicable to most U.S. and Canadian colleges. For applicants, this is the program's greatest benefit. Lesser benefits are that changes on the form are made with the computer's Delete key, rather than with white-out, and that you can initially write the "Honors/Awards," "Extracurricular," "History" (volunteer experiences and employment), and "Personal Comments" sections in your word processing program, with its spell checker and grammar checker, and then import the text to the form.

Before you are ready to complete the AMCAS-E application, you can use the program to print transcript-request forms and requests for an AMCAS Fee Waiver. For each school, you can designate whether transcripts should be sent to you, to AMCAS, or to both (the best course for most applicants).

Applicants have a choice of having the program use its "interview" mode to guide them, step-by-step, through many of the AMCAS questions. For most questions, they can also use the faster, "free-form" mode. An interesting feature is that medical schools can be selected based on their admission deadline dates, in cases where applicants have procrastinated in sending their applications. The program also has extensive "help" menus. The program has an "audit" feature that will not permit an applicant to save the file without completing vital information. It lists those items that have not been completed, marking those that are required with an "R." If a section has been suitably completed, the master checklist places a check (✓) next to it. Finally, the program automatically calculates the fee owed to AMCAS. It can be paid by personal check, money order, cashier's check, Visa or Mastercard. Fifty dollars of the fee is non-refundable.

Although applicants can preview the final form and print out copies of their AMCAS-E application on their local printer, they should submit only the data diskette to AMCAS. AMCAS then prints the data in a standardized format to distribute to medical schools. This means that admission officers will no longer have to try to read 7-point type, as they often had to do in the past. (The program requires at least 10-point type.) In the future, AMCAS plans to have applicants complete forms on the World Wide Web, eliminating the need for diskettes.

Before running AMCAS-E, print the "Readme.txt" file to get the latest information on how to avoid some of the program's peculiarities, such as special problems listing dual majors or dual degrees from the same institution. Software for the electronic AMCAS application, called AMCAS-E is available for MS-Windows™ and will be available for the Macintosh™ platform in April 1997. Students can install AMCAS-E on their personal computers either from disks obtained from their undergraduate prehealth advisers or the AAMC, or by downloading it from the AAMC's World-Wide Web site (http://www.aamc.org) and selecting the "Student & Applicant Info." option, by writing the AAMC, calling the AAMC at (202) 828-0600, or by sending them a request via e-mail (AMCAS@aamc.org). If you run into problems downloading, installing, or using the program, check out the "frequently asked questions" section at the AAMC Web site.

The formatted 1.44 MB diskette, on which you save the final version of your AMCAS-E application and which you send to AMCAS, contains two files: AMCAS.AMC and [your file name].WIP. Do not change the name of the AMCAS.AMC file, since that is the one that the AAMC processes. Before sending your disk, affix a standard diskette label with the following *legible* information:

AMCAS-E   Entering Year: _____

Name: _____

Telephone: _____

E-Mail: _____

SSN: _____

_____ Check/Money Order Attached

_____ Windows™   _____ Macintosh™

Place your diskette into a standard computer-disk mailer. If you are paying by check or money order, include that. Do not include anything else, since it might damage the disk. Send it to AMCAS, Association of American Medical Colleges, Section for Student Services, 2501 M Street, N.W., Lbby-26, Washington, DC 20037-1300.

You may only submit one disk each year to AMCAS. If, once you submit it, you want to either designate additional schools to receive the application or need to amend the information on your application, you may only do so in writing. AMCAS-E allows you to re-enter your computer file to print a *Post-Submission Change Request* and an *Additional Designation* form. Mail these to the same address you used to mailed your disk.

AMCAS-E Capabilities

- Allows completion of all AMCAS application materials using a personal computer.

- Prepares and prints transcript requests.

- Applies for an AMCAS Fee Waiver.

- Prepares additional medical school designations.

- Prepares biographic and academic change requests.

- Obtains information for minority applicants.

- Obtains medical school addresses.

- Obtains information on the MCAT and AAMC financial-aid programs.

- Provides special information for those applying to "Early Decision" programs.

AMCAS-E Software Features

- Network or stand-alone installation.

- Context-sensitive help for all instructions and medical school information.

- Provides a "quick tour" of the program.

- Pull-down menus, and print and print-preview capabilities.

- Complete reference files.

- Audits for required information.

- Password protection and file encryption to ensure confidentiality.

- One-time entry of data.

- Automated semester-hour and grade conversion—updated annually.

- Ability to import personal comments from an external word processor.

- Warning for impending or past application deadlines.

- Telephone technical support.

System Requirements
Microsoft Windows™ Minimum Requirements

- Windows™ 3.1 or higher

- 386-SX, 4 megabytes RAM

- 3.5" diskette capability and two blank, formatted disks

- Mouse, printer (recommended), and 30 sheets of paper

Macintosh™ *Requirements (Available April 1997)*

- 68020 or higher processor, 4 megabytes RAM
- System 7 or greater (7.1 or higher for Power Macintosh)
- 3.5" diskette capability and two blank, formatted disks
- Mouse, printer (recommended), and 30 sheets of paper

Non-AMCAS M.D. Schools

Sixteen M.D.-granting U.S. medical schools, all foreign medical schools, and Osteopathic medical schools do not participate in AMCAS. The application procedure for non-AMCAS schools is described below.

University of Texas (UT) Schools

The four University of Texas medical schools (UT–Southwestern, Dallas; UT–Galveston; UT–Houston; and UT–San Antonio) use their own uniform application. The application consists of two parts, the "Application Information Form," and "Personal Data and Record of College Work" booklet. The Application Information Form requests all the typical personal information, and essentially requires you to reproduce most of the material from your résumé. One page is devoted to a chronological listing of all your activities since graduating from high school. There are 1½ pages for an essay. Regular M.D. applicants must discuss "why you want to study medicine and why you think you should be accepted to medical school." M.D.-Ph.D. applicants must also, in a separate essay, discuss "why you want a dual degree (M.D.-Ph.D.), your future goals relevant to that degree, and your research background." This section of the application must be typed using black ink. (Sorry, they haven't produced a "Texas-E" application yet.)

The Personal Data and Record of College Work form is mainly devoted to reproducing your college transcripts, just as on the AMCAS application. But rather than typing in the data, you simply fill in the ovals on a computer-readable form. This part is simpler than on the paper AMCAS application.

Instead of forwarding reference letters with this application, your health professions advisory committee, health professions advisor, or academic professional supervisor completes a single "Health Professions Evaluation Form" which is sent directly to the University of Texas System's (UT-system's) Application Center. In addition, you must submit enough 2" x 3" photographs of yourself so that the Center can keep one and also distribute one to each school to which you apply (maximum of five photos). You arrange for each undergraduate school you attended to send the Center an official transcript. If you have reference letters, send them directly to each school. The Center notifies students when all of their application materials been have received.

The Application Center begins accepting applications on May 1. For Texas residents, the cost to apply is $45 for the first school plus $5 for each additional school. For non-residents, it is $80 for the first school plus $10 for each additional school. If you don't know whether you are a Texas resident, the application packet includes a questionnaire to complete so they can determine your status. There is no fee-waiver policy.

Applicants may rank (or re-rank) the order in which they would prefer attending UT-system schools after completing interviews at each school. On January 15, the Application Center runs a computer match to determine who gets initial acceptances to each UT-system medical school. Applicants are matched with the school they ranked the highest. After they receive an acceptance, they may later receive an acceptance from a school they prefer. In that case, they are responsible for withdrawing their initial acceptance and accepting the second offer.

A University of Texas application packet can be obtained from: the University of Texas System Medical and Dental Application Center (UTSMDAC), 702 Colorado, Suite 620, Austin, TX 78701.

OMSAS—Ontario (Canada) Application Service

The five medical schools in Ontario, Canada, use the Ontario Medical School Application Service (OMSAS). *Applicants for first-year positions may only apply through OMSAS (or its computerized version, COMA).* The primary benefit of applying through OMSAS is the reduction of paperwork, since students send out only one set of material to these medical schools.

The OMSAS form becomes available each summer (usually in July). It is used to apply for medical school positions beginning the following year (about fourteen months after the form is issued). The four-page application is detailed and difficult to complete. Applicants may complete the form in either French or English. It consists of three parts: a General Information Page, two pages on which to list Course Work and GPA Calculations, and a page for an "Autobiographic Sketch" (actually an abbreviated résumé). McMaster, Toronto, and Queen's Universities also have supplemental pages for essays. Note that McMaster requires that any activities cited in the essays have references listed who will corroborate these activities. For help completing the Personal Statement portion, see Tysinger's *Résumés and Personal Statements for Health Professionals* (*see Annotated Bibliography*). For help listing your courses and grades, carefully read the *OMSAS Instruction Booklet* (and have a lot of white-out on hand). If you have difficulty interpreting the instructions or completing the form, go to your premed office. They have had lots of experience with these forms.

Make multiple copies of the application and the essay pages so that you can try several drafts before you submit the final product to the typist. Most students hire professional typists to complete the form from their draft copy. The submitted application must look professional, without any errors, stains, or sloppiness.

Obtain copies of the OMSAS Application from your premed adviser or from: Ontario Universities' Application Centre, 650 Woodlawn Road West, P.O. Box 1328, Guelph, Ontario N1H 7P4, Canada; telephone (519) 823-1940; e-mail (omsas@netserv.ouac.on.ca); World Wide Web site (http://ouacinfo.ouac.on.ca).

OMSAS does not make admission decisions. Its only responsibility is to process, duplicate, and send your application, MCAT scores, premed committee recommendation letter or Confidential Assessment Forms, and transcripts to the participating medical schools to which you apply. If U.S. applicants use a premed committee letter, they should *not* also submit Confidential Assessment Forms. There is a place on the application to indicate which schools should receive your information.

Unless the mail service is disrupted, applications must be mailed to OMSAS. The deadline for submitting the application is November 1 (4:30 P.M. EST). All supporting academic documents, Confidential Assessment Forms, and transcripts must be received at OMSAS by December 2. If applying to any school except McMaster, have MCAT send a copy of your results to OMSAS.

Once OMSAS receives your application and enters it into their database, they send applicants a Verification Report listing the information to be sent to medical schools. If required data or transcripts are missing, these will be noted so the applicant can correct the omission.

Ontario medical schools begin notifying accepted applicants on May 1 by telephone or telegram. To accept an offer, applicants must respond to OMSAS by telegram or courier. While applicants can hold only one acceptance to an OMSAS-participating school at a time, they may provisionally accept an offer pending acceptance by another school where they would rather go. If they notify OMSAS, their other applications can remain active until August 1.

Transcripts

OMSAS must receive transcripts directly from every college, university, junior college, or graduate school you attended. (You must repeat this process each year that you apply, even if you sent transcripts to OMSAS for prior application cycles.) You should simultaneously ask each school to *send you a copy of your transcript,* since you will need these transcripts to complete the OMSAS application. If the university does not issue transcripts, OMSAS must receive, directly from the school, an official statement of attendance designating any degrees granted. They will not accept transcripts from graduate departments.

OMSAS uses the official transcripts to verify the information you list on your application. They will not forward your application materials until they verify this information.

Confidential Assessment Form

Three Confidential Assessment Forms come with each application. They have code numbers that match the application. These one-page forms ask the "Referee/Répondant" to rate the applicant from "1" (Excellent) to "10" (Poor) in fourteen areas: intellectual capacity, initiative, maturity, cooperation, integrity, problem-solving ability, spoken and written English, communication ability, emotional stability, ability to relate to others, self-directed-learning ability, and tolerance of others.

The Referee must also provide an "Overall Rating," using the same scale, to describe how well and in what capacity he or she knows the candidate. There is also a space to describe an applicant's "motivation and desire to enter medicine, ability to relate to people in a compassionate and caring manner, moral and ethical development, and strengths and weaknesses." That's an awful lot to write in one-third of a page.

OMSAS acknowledges, to the sender, their receipt of this form.

Cost

The cost is $225 (Canadian) to apply to one participating school, and $75 (Canadian) for each additional school. The application fee is not waived. Payment can be by check, money order, Visa, or Mastercard. If the check does not clear the bank or the credit card information is invalid, OMSAS assesses an additional $25 fee.

COMA—Computerized Ontario Medical Application

Beginning in mid-1996, the OMSAS Application became available in electronic form, called COMA. It can be accessed through a computer disk sent by OMSAS. Both medical schools' admission offices and applicants benefit from the electronic format. The program is configured and looks like a typical Windows™ or Macintosh™ program, *although it runs only under DOS.* The program automatically calculates some of the grade and course-hours information that applicants had to complete manually in the past. Changes on the form are made with the computer's Delete key, rather than with white-out. This is particularly helpful when completing the essays within the program that some schools require. Each McMaster essay allows 1,300 characters per essay, Queen's allows 1,500 characters, and Toronto's essay allows 8,000 characters. (Unfortunately, there are not advanced editing features.)

Before you are ready to complete the COMA application, you can use the program to print transcript-request forms. For each school, you can designate whether the forms will request a transcript be sent to you, to OMSAS, or to both (the best course for most applicants). You should also print the Confidential Assessment Forms to send to your references (unless you are using a premed committee letter).

OMSAS has simple-to-understand pull-down menus for each item. Every section is self-explanatory. The program has an "verification" feature that informs the applicant when required information is missing or when information in several sections is not consistent. A "Warning" message is issued if information is missing, listing what information needs to be supplied. An "Error" message is for inconsistent data and prevents saving the information to disk. Finally, the program automatically calculates the fee owed to OMSAS. It can be paid by check, money order, Visa, or Mastercard. All fees are non-refundable.

Although applicants can preview the final form and print out copies of their COMA application on their local printer, they submit only the original diskette to OMSAS. OMSAS then prints the data in a standardized format to distribute to medical schools.

Before running COMA, install it on your hard drive. Do not allow anyone else to use your program, since it has an embedded unique applicant-code number tied to your name. (If more than one person using the same computer is applying using COMA, each must have his or her own disk and install the program in directories with different names. The instructions for this are in the manual accompanying the program.)

When returning your OMSAS computer disk, use the mailer it came in. Applicants must also include a signed Certification Clause, the Remittance/Payment Form found on the last page of the manual, and, if Permanent Resident status is indicated in the program, a Canadian Immigration Record. If you are paying by check or money order, include that. Send it to Ontario Universities' Application Centre, 650 Woodlawn Road West, P.O. Box 1328, Guelph, Ontario N1H 7P4, Canada. If you have any difficulties, you can also contact COMA staff at: telephone (800) 277-5979 (in North America, 8 A.M. to 4 P.M. Ontario time); or e-mail (coma@netserv.ouac.on.ca).

You may only submit one disk each year to OMSAS. Once you submit your disk, if you either want to designate additional schools to receive the application or need to amend the information on your application, you may only do so in writing. COMA allows you to re-enter your computer file to print a *Post-Submission Change Request* and an *Additional Designation* form. Mail these to the same address as you mailed your disk.

System Requirements–DOS

- IBM or IBM-compatible computer, 80386 or higher processor
- DOS version 5.0 or higher
- 1 megabyte RAM
- 590 KB free memory
- VGA monitor
- 3.5"–1.44 MB diskette capability
- Hard drive with 5 MB free space
- Dot matrix or LaserJet printer
- Mouse (recommended)

Other M.D.-Granting Schools

Obtain applications for other non-AMCAS M.D.-granting schools (that are not part of the UT-system) directly from the medical schools. Each has a different deadline, so be sure to read their instructions carefully. If you expect serious consideration from them, do not simply send a copy of your AMCAS Application! For Osteopathic medical schools, use the AACOMAS Application (see below).

The U.S. medical schools that do not use any of the uniform applications are:

Baylor	Johns Hopkins	U. MO–Kansas City
Brown	New York Univ.	U. North Dakota
Columbia	Texas A&M	Univ. Rochester
Harvard	Texas Tech	Yale

Many of these schools do not make applications for the next school year available until after July 1. The state-supported schools on this list require out-of-state applicants to make a second application request after they receive the school's initial information. Yale's application is available in May, either by mail or on the Internet (http://info.med.yale.edu/medadmit/).

AACOMAS Application (D.O. Schools)

The AACOMAS (American Association of Colleges of Osteopathic Medicine Application Service) Application is a single form used by all seventeen D.O.-granting U.S. medical schools. *Students applying for first-year positions at Osteopathic medical schools must use AACOMAS.* (Those applying for "admission with advanced standing" or who want to transfer from other schools should contact each school directly.) The benefit of using AACOMAS is that it reduces paperwork, since students send out only one set of materials for their initial applications.

The AACOMAS form, very similar to the paper AMCAS form, becomes available in early spring. It is used to apply for medical school positions for the following year (about sixteen months after the form is issued). The ten-page application is detailed and difficult to complete. (Most applicants only have to complete six pages, however.) It consists of three parts. The first is the Main Application Form, which requests general information, a listing of Course Work and GPA Calculations, MCAT scores, and a half-page of "Personal Comments." Unless you have to use part of this Personal Comment space to explain prior questions, you may use it to "provide your motivation for applying to the field of Osteopathic medicine." You may even prepare this statement on another sheet and paste it into the space provided. For help with this personal statement, see Tysinger's *Résumés and Personal Statements for Health Professionals* (see *Annotated Bibliography*). For help listing your courses and grades, carefully read the *AACOMAS Instruction Booklet*. If you have difficulty interpreting the instructions or completing the form, go to your premed adviser's office. They have had lots of experience with these forms.

The second part of the application, similar to the portion of the main application in which you list your course work, is the "Professional School Academic Record." (Most applicants will not have to complete this form.) On this form, you list all course work taken at professional schools leading to a certificate or license that did not directly contribute to your receiving a bachelor's, master's, or doctorate degree. Also include course work from institutions that are not regionally accredited. Which courses to list on which form can be quite confusing—and if you list courses on the wrong form, AACOMAS will return it to you, thus delaying the processing of your application. If you have any questions about which form to use, call them at (301) 468-2037.

The third, and simplest, part of the application is the "College Designation Form." Use this form to designate which Osteopathic medical schools should receive your information. AACOMAS will then send your application materials to them. This part of the application also contains the fee schedule.

As with any application forms, make multiple copies of each part so that you can try several drafts and get it right before you submit it to a professional typist to complete the final product. Your submitted application must look professional, without any errors, stains, or sloppiness. Obtain copies of the AACOMAS application from your premed adviser or from the American Association of Colleges of Osteopathic Medicine, 6110 Executive Boulevard, Suite 405, Rockville, MD 20852; telephone (301) 468-2037.

AACOMAS does not make admission decisions. Its only responsibility is to process, duplicate, and send your application, MCAT scores, and transcripts to the participating medical schools to which you apply.

AACOMAS accepts applications beginning June 1. Apply as close to this date as possible. If you do so, you may begin getting secondary applications from some schools in the summer, and be able to interview in early October. This gives you an advantage at schools having "rolling" admissions policies, which select students from each group as they interview them until they fill their class.

AACOMAS returns the confirmation card included in the application packet when they receive your application. They send another one when either all your transcripts have arrived or processing of your application has been delayed due to missing transcripts. *Remember to put postage and addresses on these cards before you return them to AACOMAS.* If everything goes smoothly, you should receive an "Applicant Profile" about six to eight weeks after AACOMAS receives all your application materials. This form includes: your identifying information; disadvantaged or ethnic self-description; a list of family members who are physicians; any misdemeanor or felony convictions; your prior application to Osteopathic medical schools; how you learned about Osteopathic medicine; the schools you attended, major, total GPA and credit-hours; individual courses, hours and GPAs (with lists of school-specific deficiencies in their prerequisites and of courses with grades less than 2.0 or "C"); MCAT date(s) and score(s); the schools to which you applied; and your "Quality Points."

Quality Points equals the total of the numeric value of your grades (for example, 3.7 or an A-) multiplied by the number of semester-hours in which you received that grade. For example, in your freshman year, suppose you took 32 semester-hours of credit, and got an "A" for 18 of those hours, a "B" for 15 hours, and a "C" for 3 hours. For that year, the Quality Points you earned would be: $(4.0 \times 18) + (3.0 \times 15) + (2.0 \times 3) = 123$.

If you don't receive your confirmation card, transcript acknowledgment, or your Applicant Profile, call AACOMAS to discover what has gone wrong. Once you get your Applicant Profile, check it carefully to make sure that it is correct. (AACOMAS makes this *your* responsibility.) This form is what the schools use to decide whether to interview you and to accept you as a student.

Once you submit your application, you must notify AACOMAS, in writing, if you wish to have them stop processing it or change the information. If there are new or updated grades to enter, you must also send a transcript reflecting these grades.

Transcripts

Before you send your application to AACOMAS, arrange for them to receive your transcripts. They must receive an official transcript from every one of the following schools that you attended within the United States, Canada, or U.S. Territories, whether or not you earned any college credits: junior or community college, college, university, graduate school, U.S. medical school, trade school, and professional school. You should simultaneously ask each school to send you a copy of your transcript, since you will need them to complete the AACOMAS application. (You must repeat the process each year that you apply, even if you already sent transcripts to AACOMAS for prior application cycles.) If AACOMAS does not receive all your transcripts, they send you a "Missing Transcript Notification" card.

Be careful when you complete the application! If AACOMAS finds *major* discrepancies between your data and information contained in the transcripts, they may return your application to you or file an "AACOMAS Report" with the colleges to which you are applying and with the AAMC (which also files similar reports with AACOMAS).

If an official transcript is unavailable, AACOMAS requires a letter of explanation from the school. If transfer credits are noted on a transcript, you also need to supply AACOMAS with the original transcript for these courses. Grade-13 and Canadian college-level courses are not included on the AACOMAS Applicant Profile, but if a transcript of this work is provided, it will be sent to the designated medical schools. List any summer-study programs that you have attended, such as a Health Careers Opportunity Program, in the Personal Comments section. Have a copy of your Certificate of Completion sent to AACOMAS for distribution to the schools to which you apply.

Undergraduate course work taken at foreign institutions can be evaluated for U.S.-institution equivalence. If you want foreign course work to be included on the Applicant Profile, you should contact either: World Education Services, Inc., P.O. Box 745 Old Chelsea Station, New York, NY 10113-0745; tel. (212) 966-6311; or Josef Silny & Associates, Inc., International Educational Consultants, P.O. Box 248233, Coral Gables, FL 33124; tel. (305) 666-0233. Work done at foreign schools that has not been evaluated by one of these two groups will not appear on your Applicant Profile.

The AACOMAS application packet comes with two "AACOMAS Transcript Matching Forms." Use these to request your transcripts. Make additional copies if you need them. The registrars sending the transcripts will normally include these forms when they return the transcripts to AACOMAS. AACOMAS uses the official transcripts to verify the information you list on your application. They forward your application materials to the schools only after they verify the information.

MCAT Scores

You must supply your MCAT scores to complete the AACOMAS application. To have your MCAT scores sent to AACOMAS, designate "code 600" on the appropriate form the day you take the MCAT. If you failed to do this, contact the AAMC (2450 N Street, N.W., Suite 201, Washington, DC 20037-1131; tel. (202) 828-0600-1-2-3-2) to obtain an Additional Score Report (ASR) form. When you return the completed form and fees, AAMC will forward your scores to AACOMAS.

AACOMAS keeps MCAT scores on file for three years. If you have previously submitted these scores and have not retaken the test, you do not need to resubmit them.

Deadlines

The deadline for receiving your AACOMAS Application and all transcripts varies from December 15 to February 15, depending upon the schools to which you are applying. Check the *AACOMAS Instruction Booklet* for the specific date for each school. If AACOMAS receives your materials after the deadline for a school to which you want to apply, but not for others, they will only forward your materials to the schools whose deadlines have not passed.

It takes AACOMAS from six to eight weeks to process applications. You should check on your application's status about two weeks after you receive the Acknowledgment of Receipt card.

Cost

AACOMAS charges applicants based on the number of Osteopathic medical schools to which they apply. (The current fees can be found in the *AACOMAS Instruction Booklet,* but they generally range from $50 for one school to $370 for all seventeen schools.) Individual schools charge additional fees, normally in conjunction with submitting secondary applications. AACOMAS accepts only checks or money orders. If your check does not clear the bank, you are assessed an additional $15 and must then pay the total amount by money order or certified check within ten days or your application's processing stops.

The AACOMAS Fee Waiver Program allows applicants who cannot afford the fee to have it waived for applications to up to three schools. To apply to more than three schools, you must pay the standard additional fee. To apply for a fee waiver, submit the College Scholarship Service's Profile and have the Needs Analysis Report for the current year ("Renewal Version" or, if the Report is current, the "Additional Needs Analysis Report") sent to AACOMAS. (Use "code 7363" to designate that the report goes to AACOMAS.) All available waivers are granted by August 1. Wait to submit your application until you receive notice about your Fee Waiver. Those granted fee waivers, and those who qualify for them but do not receive them only because funding no longer exists, have their names forwarded to Osteopathic medical schools to be considered for waivers of the schools' supplemental application fees. Additional information about AACOMAS fee waivers is in the *AACOMAS Instruction Booklet* as well as on the AACOMAS By Computer program.

The AACOMAS By Computer Application (D.O. Schools)

Beginning in 1996, the AACOMAS application became available in electronic form. (Either this form or the paper form can be used to apply to Osteopathic medical schools.) The entire computer package also includes a "Viewbook" that contains information about Osteopathic medicine and the individual Osteopathic colleges. Either the entire program or just the application can be obtained from your premed adviser or from AACOMAS, 6110 Executive Boulevard, Suite 405, Rockville, MD 20852-3991; telephone (301) 468-2037. Both the program and the application can be downloaded from the AACOM homepage (http://www.aacom.org). If you want the entire program, you must download it to your hard drive. (It takes about 40 minutes.) If you want only the application (1.3 megabytes), you can download it to a disk.

The first thing to do when using the AACOMAS By Computer application is to follow the directions and try to print the sample application included in the program using a Hewlett-Packard-compatible laser or deskjet printer. (If using a deskjet, turn off the Windows Print Manager®.) If the print quality is good, continue with the program. You can then use this printout as a model while you complete your own form. If the print quality is not good or if the program is not compatible with your printer, *STOP.* Request a paper AACOMAS application by calling (301) 468-2037. Since you have to submit both the paper and disk versions for your AACOMAS By Computer application to be processed, it is vital that you are able to print a good quality application.

Be sure to read all the instructions. There are some special instructions for those using Windows 95® and for dealing with commonly encountered setup and printing problems.

AACOMAS By Computer can be completed "free-form" (like the written form) or by using drop-down boxes that help complete certain sections. It also has context-sensitive pull-down help menus, which can all be printed. Validation checks tell you what is missing from the application, so you don't accidentally forget something. If you run into difficulties, there are people who can help you. Contact them at (301) 468-1596 for their hours of operation.

Both medical schools and applicants benefit from the electronic format. The program automatically calculates some of the grade and course-hours information that applicants had to compute by hand in the past. For applicants, this is the program's greatest benefit. It also allows you to easily import your personal statement and other information from a Windows™-based word processor. (Since AACOMAS By Computer does not have a spell checker or grammar checker, this option may considerably improve the quality of your essay.) For now, AACOMAS only plans to supply the program in a Windows™ version.

AACOMAS By Computer Capabilities

- Complete all AACOMAS application forms using a personal computer.
- Prepare transcript requests.
- Learn how to apply for an AACOMAS Fee Waiver.

- Import personal essay to application from word processor.
- Obtain information about Osteopathic medical schools, including their addresses and phone numbers.

System Requirements—Microsoft Windows™ Only

- Windows 3.1 or higher
- 486 or higher processor
- Super-VGA Monitor (256 colors)
- 4 MB RAM (8 MB recommended)
- At least 5 megabytes of free hard-drive space
- 3.5" floppy disk drive and two formatted 3.5" diskettes
- Mouse
- Hewlett-Packard-compatible laser or DeskJet-type printer and at least 35 sheets of plain white paper

Bad Options—The Desperate Application

Some people fail to get accepted into medical school and then try some pretty bizarre things to get in. As an example, in April 1996, *USA Today* ran this classified ad under the heading "In search of"

> Looking for U.S. Medical School to
> accept me! BSN, St. Louis Univ. 4 yrs
> exper. in telemetry, ICU, ER, L&D. 3.7
> GPA (cum), 3.80 Science GPA, 30
> MCAT. Excellent letters of recomm.,
> Alpha Sigma Nu honor society. U.S.
> Army Reserve Nurse. [Telephone number]

Sounds like a good candidate for medical school. This, however, is not the way to get accepted to a U.S. or Canadian medical school. Follow the rules, get your application materials, complete them, and send them in early. That's how to have the best chance of being accepted into a medical school.

13: Essays, Recommendations, And Secondary Applications

Personal Statements And Essays

PERSONAL STATEMENTS AND ESSAYS cause more anguish among applicants than almost anything else in the application process. Many applicants spend a great deal of time and effort polishing these epistles—and their work often pays off in interviews and acceptances. Admission officers carefully scrutinize personal statements and supplementary essays. ("Personal Statement" generally refers to the composition on the Uniform Application, while "essay" refers to the themes on school-specific primary or secondary applications—usually on specific topics.)

If admission committee members read your essay, they have already determined that you can handle the academics of medical school. They look at your essay to decide if you will make a good physician. So think about what qualities a good physician should have (e.g., motivation, self-assurance, altruism, leadership, ability to work well with others). Then show them that you possess these traits with stories from your life, not by saying, "I have motivation as demonstrated by . . ."

In addition to using them to select potential students, committee members also use poor personal statements to eliminate those individuals who clearly stand out as being: (1) relatively illiterate, (2) pompous or tactless, or (3) outside the reasonable norm for medical students and physicians. The key to writing a good personal statement is to *be honest, but not shy* about trumpeting your virtues. Describe why you are motivated to be a physician. Rather than simply repeating your résumé in prose, *describe yourself as a person,* using personal anecdotes wherever possible. Many students find this hard to do.

Uniform Applications

The AMCAS, AACOMAS, University of Texas, and Ontario applications consist mostly of fairly straightforward questions. You only need to find and transcribe your information. But one page (half a page on AACOMAS) labeled "For Personal Comments," is blank. This is your opportunity to speak directly to the admission committee in your own words—for better or for worse. (Many secondary applications also have blank pages for essays, often on specific topics.) The task of writing these compositions can be quite daunting, so plan ahead to produce essays that represent you well. You should begin to write them early, so you have time to think about them, write several drafts, and have them competently proofed for content, spelling, and grammar.

While there is no "ideal" essay, some of the best personal statements and essays are interesting stories about the applicant that reveal the writer's personality, thought processes, and motivations. If you have a story, perhaps about how you became interested in medicine or why you want to pursue this career, then tell it. If it catches the eye of a jaded admission officer and conveys your message about why you want to enter medical school, it is a good personal statement. See the sample essays used by some successful applicants (who are now medical students or physicians) on the following pages.

Assuming that you are not a writer and that you have no one to help you, the elements of a "safe and sane" personal statement include:

1. *Who are you?* Give a brief (two or three sentences) sketch of yourself and where you are in life.

2. *How did you get where you are?* Briefly explain what has drawn you to a medical career. If you have a noteworthy story to tell, tell it. Describe any particular event or person that stands out as markedly influencing your career decision. If you are a minority applicant, you may want to indicate that here, as in "I want to provide care to my fellow (fill in the minority)." Do not state that you are interested in medicine because of the influence of pop culture (e.g., current movies or television shows), the prestige of the profession, or the monetary rewards you anticipate. These reasons are usually considered evidence of a shallow personality. You may mention other things you have done if they fit into your story. Discussing your family, sports, and community activities are safe. Admission officers look for applicants who have enough time, interest, and academic skills to take their noses out of their books and to spend quality (i.e., helpful) time with their compatriots. Medicine is a helping profession and most physicians spend lots of time with people. Are you a "people" person?

3. *What do you intend to do during your medical career?* Be general. It is always safe to say that you plan on pursuing a primarily clinical career with some clinical research and teaching. Many schools now actively seek individuals who want to enter primary care specialties, such as general internal medicine, family practice, general pediatrics, or obstetrics & gynecology. It is unrealistic and patronizing for you to say that you are sure you want to go into a particular specialty (unless you can back this up with reasons grounded in experience), but it is safe to say that you are interested in caring for the same patients over a long period. Try to demonstrate that you like to work with people. If you have any reason to honestly say that working in inner cities or rural areas also interests you, this comes across very positively. *If possible, tell your own story explaining why you want your medical career to take this path.*

4. *Ideals.* How do your values fit into a medical career, and vice versa? Wrap up your essay by briefly mentioning how some of the things you have already discussed illustrate these values or motivations. Talk is cheap, so admission committees are interested in seeing evidence that you really have these ideals (and have acted on them).

Additional points that may be addressed in the statement include explanations of any major problems, or deficiencies that may appear in your application or transcript. You might want to mention something particularly outstanding from your undergraduate career or your life outside of school. *Avoid discussing politics or religion.* Neither has any place in your application materials. Also, do not say "I want to relieve the world's suffering," or anything similar. Admission committees don't seriously consider applicants who have lost touch with reality. Review your statement for grammar, spelling, and format (figure 13.1) as you do all other materials you send to medical schools, before you have the final copy typed. There is no one perfect style.

As a final check, have someone else read your statement aloud to you. If it makes sense, use it. Otherwise, try again.

Occasionally students ask whether they should try to make their personal statements unusual enough to stand out. This is not a good idea and you take a big risk in doing so. Remember that physicians, in general, are conservative animals. Anything odd or unusual will ordinarily be regarded negatively. "Unusual" in a personal statement is normally interpreted by those reading the statement as something that is cute, flippant, or crass. These are not the impressions for which you are striving. It is true that some applicants have gotten interviews and even positions based, in part, on unusual personal statements. But it is very rare. Unless your life story by itself is unusual, stick with using personal anecdotes to illustrate and individualize your points. The question you should ask yourself when you have completed your personal statement is, "If I were on an admission committee, would I be interested in talking with the person who wrote this essay?" If not, perhaps you need to rewrite it.

Sample Essays

The following essays were used by applicants who were accepted to medical school. Each of them shows aspects of the individual's personality, motivation, and background that suggest why they were accepted into medical school.

Alternative Essay Style

Although not suitable for everyone, occasionally an applicant may decide to use an alternative form of personal statement rather than the typical prose style. (See *Personal Statement #10.*) The advantage of using a unique format is that it will stand out from the other similar essays; this is also its primary drawback. The example given, *Personal Statement #10*, was written by a medical school applicant with an unusual educational background. However, while his premed adviser encouraged him to use this format, his school's premed committee discouraged him from submitting it. (He did submit it and is now busily completing a slew of secondary applications.)

Figure 13.1: Requirements for Personal Statements

- Sized to fit on form. One page for most uniform applications and a half-page for AACOMAS. It *must* fit on the form or the application will most likely be returned to you.

- Laser or inkjet printer, if not done on electronically (submitted on disk).

- Proper grammar, spelling, and composition. (Get help with this if you need it.) Import from word processor if using AMCAS-E or AACOMAS BY Computer, so you can use the spell checker and grammar checker.

- 10-point font (type size) or larger.

Personal Statement #1

I was raised in a low-income, bilingual family (Spanish and English). My parents did everything possible to expose me to all the things that make a well-educated, well-rounded individual. Because of their limited income, one of the most valuable lessons I learned from them was to be resourceful in obtaining those opportunities. I sought what they could not offer. I began violin lessons at the age of eight and by the time I started high school I had performed as soloist with both the Mesa and Phoenix Symphonies. I performed at various social functions as Concert Master for my high school's chamber orchestra. I enjoyed the traveling and the opportunities to meet new people that my musical pursuits offered. It was during a music tour to Egypt, where I was exposed to Arabic, that I learned of my affinity for languages.

After high school, I joined the Air Force to pursue language studies and to earn money for college. On my own, I learned some basic Arabic from a self-paced program. The Air Force sent me to the Defense Language Institute (DLI) to learn Hungarian. After completing the DLI course, I was sent to join a special airborne unit attached to the National Security Agency in Maryland. There I traveled in high-performance aircraft to different parts of the world translating and transcribing various languages. During the six years I served in the Air Force, I also learned Italian and a limited amount of Russian. I also competed as the Air Force's representative in the triathlon at national and international levels. I thoroughly enjoyed learning and using the languages, traveling to meet new people, and learning about their cultures. However, something was missing: a complete education.

I took evening college courses while in the Air Force. In many instances though, I was ordered on missions out of the country with little advance notice. This forced me to withdraw from many classes. This was the case during my first psychology class at Anne Arundel when I was not able to return until after the class had ended. This resulted in an irrevocable grade of F. However, I later repeated the class and earned an A. As time passed, I realized the only way to complete my undergraduate degree was to leave the Air Force and go to school full-time. At first my intentions were to continue my linguistic studies, but it was during my secondary jobs as the unit Medical Records clerk and a CPR/First Aid instructor that my interest in health and human physiology began.

My first year out of the Air Force was a difficult one. I encountered many financial difficulties which required me to work part-time. I chose to work as a Resident Assistant representing the non-traditional student body, including hearing-impaired students. To better assist the hearing-impaired students, I learned sign language and translated at sporting events and social functions. I derived great satisfaction in bridging the gap between the hearing and the hearing-impaired students. Also, while at Western Maryland College (WMC), I began a CPR training program for Resident Assistants that is still used today. Teaching CPR and First Aid, and knowing that there are now many more people with the basic skills to save a life, is very rewarding to me. It became even more personal when, toward the end of my first semester at WMC, my father suffered a heart attack. I flew home a few weeks before finals and returned to school just after the beginning of the January term. I was allowed to take the finals when I returned, which accounts for the grades I earned that year.

To gain exposure to the field of human physiology, I completed a January-term internship in the Sports Medicine Clinic at Union Memorial Hospital in Baltimore. However, instead of working with the clinic's physiologists, I ended up working with their orthopedic surgeons. I had the opportunity to scrub and be at the operating table during surgery. I administered stress tests, drew blood, and assisted patients undergoing neuromuscular assessments and rehabilitations. I enjoyed being directly involved with the patients and watching their progress. It was then that I put together my interest in science and physiology, my ability to work well with people, my desire for promoting a healthy lifestyle, and my recent experience working alongside surgeons, and realized that I should become a physician.

I knew that I had some catching up to do academically and that my financial troubles would not go away. I earned an Army ROTC scholarship which helped my financial situation and I continued to work as a Resident Assistant. My grades improved and I ended my senior year on the Dean's List with a 4.0. I earned a commission as an officer in the Army's Medical Service Corps. I am currently responsible for running a health clinic that supports 595 people. I am not only responsible for the administrative management of the clinic, but also conduct initial patient screening and assessment. My work has only increased my interest in becoming a primary health care provider. I feel I am focused and confident in my commitment to study medicine and become a physician.

Benjamin Gonzalez, written in 1992

Personal Statement #2

I want to provide medical care for the financially indigent. For years I have worked with low-income people, those who struggle with haunting memories of past abuse, and those who live with one emotion which overrides all others: fear. My interest started when I was an EMT. Working on an ambulance gave me access to difficult situations in people's lives. I, who had been raised with unusual privilege, was shocked by the conditions under which people do live. Later, as a Parent/Counselor/Aide, I visited mothers each week in their homes, listening to their problems, and helping them to provide for their families' physical and emotional needs. I interviewed over 100 women, reporting their stories of many types of abuse, neglect, and just plain bad luck. For two years, I volunteered as a crisis counselor for the H.E.L.P. child-abuse hotline. This work did not tire me, as it did some. Instead it created a new energy inside me to find out more, to change things. I had had an abusive marriage where I lost all hope in the future, all interest in my own self-worth. I had been through bankruptcy and the loss of my home and possessions, and inevitably, my pride. The fact that over a ten-year period I was able to struggle out of that way of life leaves me with no less compassion for those still in it.

My children have given me a perspective on life beyond academia or personal satisfaction. I would not have understood so many of the hardships families face without having experienced motherhood. Perhaps it is this that causes me to be consistently drawn to helping those who do not know how to overcome their struggles. Over the years, I learned that I have the ability to leave the emotional residue from my sometimes frustrating occupations at work.

Three years ago, I returned to school with the express desire to become a physician. I had seen that the service I was able to provide as a lay person was limited. Continuing to work in those areas of need was important to me, even as a premedical student, because I did not want to lose my perspective. I have organized three women's resource fairs on campus and volunteered much time to community efforts for women. Presently, I continue to visit families as a genetics counselor for the Sickle Cell Anemia Society.

My past experiences have helped me to discover the type of work I am interested in pursuing as a physician. I have seen that there is a definite and increasing need for medical care in rural and low income areas. I know that as a physician I will be able to do much more to serve and teach those with limited resources.

Gina M. Jansheski, written in 1992

Personal Statement #3

I haven't always been interested in medicine, but during high school I took an anatomy class in which the semester project involved dissecting fetal pigs. I wasn't too enthusiastic about cutting up pigs in the first place, and so, when I discovered that our field trip to see a human dissection was mandatory, you can imagine my enthusiasm. Not sure how I would stomach the ordeal, I waited as they wheeled the first cadaver out. Upon seeing the body, I took a deep breath and after the initial shock, opened my eyes to the world of medicine. The body before me seemed a pure miracle, a work of art, and it thoroughly fascinated me. That night, I excitedly told my parents what I had witnessed and, although their reaction at the dinner table didn't match my excitement, they were glad to see my newfound enthusiasm.

No one in my family has ever gone into medicine, so when I decided to major in biochemistry, my mother lovingly suggested that I shoot myself instead, a much faster way to the same end. Yet I have never taken the easy road and have constantly searched for something new and exciting to do. Early in high school, I began my long career of volunteering in the community. First I started in the transport department of a local hospital. Soon I was staffing city carnivals with the parks and recreation division, helping out the Special Olympics in tennis, demonstrating dissections of the eye at an elementary school, and working in a homeless shelter during the winter holidays as part of the Mayor's Youth Committee. It didn't stop when I came to college. I got involved with clubs and found myself Christmas caroling in the children's ward of the University Medical Center, tutoring fellow students, staffing an annual university carnival, helping with a Halloween party for a retirement home, serving as a peer mentor in the honor's college, volunteering in a child crisis center, and taking groups of children on camping trips with Camp Wildcat while working as the Donations Coordinator for the club.

My interest in volunteering is partially selfish, for there's an unexplainable satisfaction in helping someone in need. For example, during my senior year in high school, I was with a group delivering Christmas food baskets and a man in his upper 80s was the last delivery of the day. He had no family to speak of, except for three very large dogs which roamed his tiny, barren home. Although we had brought the basket of food, he was still in need of something more. We were the first company to have visited in a long time and he desperately wanted just to talk to someone. We stayed and visited until late in the evening while this man poured out his life story, including the fact that he had bone cancer. If I have ever been in need of a goal for my life, it was clarified that night talking to that lonely man. Volunteering has allowed me to mature in ways that ordinary school life could not possibly facilitate.

At the University of Arizona, I continue to participate, as well as excel in my studies, by becoming involved in a variety of activities. It must be dedication when you find yourself attending Monday morning 8 A.M. meetings out of interest. I joined honors clubs such as the Honors Student Association, Phi Eta Sigma, and Golden Key National Honor Society; medically-oriented clubs: HIV Advisory Committee; Student Health Advisory Committee; and interest clubs: Camp Wildcat, Relate Crew (a freshman orientation organization), Manzi-Mo Funhouse (a theater group), and even the Kazoo Band (the volleyball pep club)! In addition, I continued to pursue personal interests in piano, tennis, and private aviation.

Personal Statement # 3, page 2

Since my freshman year, I have been involved in research. My first experience was in an entomology lab where I studied the mechanisms of olfactory reception in *Triatoma rubida*, commonly known as the Kissing Bug. I spent most of my time gathering data on the insects, tracking pathways in response to various odors. The following year, I entered a chemistry laboratory where I had the challenging responsibility of synthesizing butadiene-iron-tricarbonyl, an uncharacterized chemical. After trial and error, I was the first in our group to successfully obtain the pure compound, and presented my work at the 1992 Honors Mini-Symposium. A summer later, I was hired for a full-time job in the neuro-oncology laboratory of Barrow Neurological Institute in Phoenix. There I was exposed to a hard-core, fast-paced research lab where I studied the bFGE signal-transmission pathway mechanisms in neuroblastomas, basically how a cancerous brain cell imports a growth hormone, using immunochemistry and tissue culture techniques. In addition, I studied the effects on normal tissues of chemicals secreted by cancerous cells. I presented my work during the 1993 Summer Cancer Biology Seminar series. The director of the lab invited me back to work the following summer during which I pursued research involving cell migration of malignant gliomas by the use of immunofluorescence. After performing this cancer research, I felt a need to see the clinical aspect of cancer. I observed in the Oncology Radiation Center of Desert Samaritan Hospital. I interacted with patients and learned how to read bone scans, MRIs, and CT scans. It didn't take long for me to reaffirm my interest in medicine. This past fall I worked as a student-assistant in a neuroanatomy laboratory at the University Medical Center. The primary focus of the lab was studying the developmental organization of glycine receptors in embryonic rat neurons. I compared various aged neurons using fluorescent microscopy techniques.

After a great deal of research experience, and spending two full summers working in an oncology lab, I am just as interested in medical research as I am in clinical medicine. For this reason, I am applying to M.D.-Ph.D. programs and am confident that I will succeed in both the world of medicine and the sphere of research. As a physician and a scientist, I will be able to bridge the gap between the two disciplines and not only help people help themselves, but also teach them how to stay healthy, rather than to just merely care for them. I want this more than anything and with determination like mine, I know that I am going to enter an M.D.-Ph.D. program and succeed.

Tracy L. Davis, written in 1994

Personal Statement #4

I am a woman truly blessed. My husband, a physician, is my soul mate and partner in all things. I have three wonderful children that I have the great honor of raising. My parents' love for me has never been in question and they are now two of my closest friends. I have a lot for which to be thankful. So why would I want to put myself through the long, grueling task of becoming a physician? I do not see this as something I am putting myself through but, rather, as a process toward becoming fully who I am.

I have wanted to be a doctor for as long as I can remember. As a little girl, I would buy first-aid books and watch all the medical shows on TV. I took First Aid and CPR courses at the Red Cross. I had a very special woman doctor during my childhood whom I always identified with because "I was going to be doctor too." As a teenager, I volunteered at the local hospital as a candy striper. In high school, I majored in math and science, took all the advanced classes, and won both the National Honor Society's Award and the Harvard Award for all-around excellence during my junior year. I enrolled in two college courses during my senior year through a merit scholarship and graduated a semester early with a Regents diploma.

I began college as a premed major on two academic scholarships and did very well in my first semester. However, three traumatic events changed my life path. First, my brother, who had been the "genius" of the family, was diagnosed with acute paranoid schizophrenia. He was hospitalized for six months and was ill for another two years. At the time, the biochemical causes of schizophrenia were not understood and a Freudian approach was taken in which our family was repeatedly blamed for my brother's illness. This greatly heightened the pain experienced by everyone involved. I now realize they were doing their best with the knowledge available at that time. However, it is clear to me that healing involves more than knowledge and that knowledge changes. The caring and support of the physician are essential ingredients that must remain constant. My brother's experience sparked my interest in the psychiatric aspects of both physical and mental illnesses and had a profound impact on my sense of priorities and values. (My brother was one of the lucky ones who recovered completely and is now a happily married tax attorney.)

In the next event, I was injured in a car accident, which made me contemplate my own mortality. Did I really want to spend the next ten years in medical school and training?

The final blow came when I contracted mononucleosis. I missed a third of that semester and I contracted multiple infections during the next year due to my weakened immune system. Despite all of this, I always took more than a full load of classes, worked from 30 to 40 hours a week as a waitress, fit in time for socializing, and graduated a year early. My grades, however, had suffered. I ended up with a 3.4 GPA and felt that my grades were not adequate to fulfill my dreams of going to medical school. I worked for a year after college to replenish my financial reserves, which had been put toward the family's basic needs during my brother's illness.

I then completed a Master of Science degree a semester early with a double major in Rehabilitation Counseling and Vocational Evaluation at the University of Arizona. I worked 30 to 40 hours a week during this time as a Rehabilitation Counselor, helping clients who had been injured on the job to find alternative employment or retraining. My internship and subsequent year in San Diego turned out to be one of the most important periods of my life. Being alone and in an unsupportive environment, I learned a great deal about creating my own happiness and sense of self-worth.

Personal Statement # 4, page 2

I next took to a transition job in insurance and financial investments, where I had the highest sales of any "rookie" in the history of that office.

As time went on, however, I knew that I would not be fulfilled by a job outside the medical profession. I returned to the University of Arizona to obtain a Ph.D. in Rehabilitation Psychology. I also worked as a Psychiatric Crisis Worker at Kino Community Hospital. This job involved evaluating and treating suicidal, homicidal, and psychotic patients, both in the emergency department and with police out in the field. I felt totally at home working with the patients, the medical staff, and the police, and felt a great sense of fulfillment.

During this time, I married and chose to put my work on hold while starting a family. I had more difficulty deciding what to do about my education. I had only a few more classes to complete before my internship and dissertation. However, I had three children in three years and was not sure how to incorporate my school work with my duty to my children. After some false starts, I decided to go ahead and finish my degree. However, during my three years of absence, the Rehabilitation Department had reorganized the course requirements. Instead of a few classes, it would now take five more years of course work to complete my Ph.D. This gave me an opportunity to re-evaluate my path. My husband, a psychiatrist and former family practitioner, asked me where my passion truly lay and I immediately knew that I wanted to become a doctor. This was no surprise to him, and we set out together to determine how I could "have it all."

I returned to the University of Arizona to compete the premedical requirements and have maintained a 4.0 GPA. (In evaluating my MCAT scores, it may be helpful to know that I had not yet taken the second semesters of organic chemistry and physics at the time of the test.) After my circuitous route, I am back on the path I feel is mine. In my heart, I am a doctor, a healer. I have absolutely no regrets about the time or the energy I spent in other pursuits. Each experience has provided learning and growth, and I truly believe that I will make a much better doctor now than if I had followed the more conventional path.

Molly Roberts, written in 1994

Personal Statement #5

Growing up in a small town, I have always felt the support of the families in my community. As neighbors and friends, they offered me emotional support. As professionals, they offered me services, including those of a small but vital medical community. As a child, I watched our town's physicians resolve situations with what seemed to me then to be an almost mystical knowledge of the sciences. I envied physicians for their mastery of that knowledge and their ability to use it to effect a positive change in others. That introduction, along with my continually developing love for science and for the community, has fostered in me a commitment to become a physician. I want to be able to affect other's lives with the same substantial, positive influence these physicians had on my life. I want to be the very foundation of a small rural community, as they were.

This now-firm commitment was not one I made immediately. In the early seventies, I allowed a personal situation to affect my grades. After my first year, my advisor informed me that my grades would not enable me to get into medical school, so I temporarily discontinued my studies. I also married and started a family. Determined to take control of the situation, I returned to school and changed majors to pursue a career in which I could make a fresh start. I earned a Bachelor of Business Administration in 1978.

I secured a sales position with a large corporation and established myself professionally. Then, ready for a challenge and more confident of my own skills, I returned to school for postbaccalaureate work in 1980-81 and earned a second degree, Bachelor of Science, with a strong GPA of 3.92.

I spent the next seven years both as a commercial insurance underwriter and a marketing representative. As an underwriter leading a team of four, I learned the importance of interpersonal communication skills in reaching defined objectives. As a marketing representative, I was the mediator in frequently antagonistic contract negotiations between outside brokers and company underwriters. This responsibility further developed my interpersonal skills by teaching me the art of negotiating a common agreement through compromise. These skills will prove invaluable to my future work with patients and colleagues.

Although I had learned a great deal in business, I was not fully satisfied with my professional life. I still wanted to become a physician. I wanted to push myself to the limit of my talents, not only for self-enrichment, but also for the benefit of my family and community. Over the past two years, I completed the medical school prerequisites, earning a 3.92 GPA.

While fulfilling these prerequisites, I enrolled in a course entitled Student Pre-Med Internship (HES 394) which allowed me to observe and assist emergency physicians at a level-one trauma center. This work, along with my current volunteer work in the emergency department of my neighborhood hospital, has enabled me to witness the ability of physicians to apply their knowledge to practical, vital work. This opportunity has reinforced my original impressions of the responsibilities and rewards of being a medical doctor and reconfirmed my decision to pursue medicine.

The pressures of being a physician are at an all-time high. Life-support technology demands answers to the right-to-die question. AIDS tests the wills of even the strongest physicians because of its terminal certainty. Litigation threatens careers as it moves toward becoming a form of social insurance against accidental outcomes. Government intervention threatens to reduce the physician's role from that of patient advocate to industrial technician. Although each of these considerations is serious, they have not acted as deterrents to me. Each challenge reinforces my desire to be among those who determine the eventual solutions and compromises.

In all my assessments, my conclusion is always the same as it was when I was that small youth watching our family physician work. Fifteen years have passed since my earlier attempt to study medicine. I now have even more of the dedication and maturity required to become a physician.

Brian D. Fitch, written in 1992

Personal Statement #6

Throughout my life, the most rewarding feelings have come from helping others. Whether it was sharing a meal with a small boy in a Rwandan village or playing a game of chess with a lonely rehabilitation patient on the road to recovery, the satisfaction of helping someone, if only in a small way, is very fulfilling. It is my hope that this essay serves to highlight those experiences which have solidified my desire to become a physician.

My love of science and a strong personal desire to improve the quality of medical care helped me to overcome my fear of leaving the security of a familiar and well-paying profession to enter the medical field. A physicist, I first learned about the vital role of technology in medicine while earning my bachelor's degree from the Institute of Optics at the University of Rochester. Not long after graduation, when my uncle was diagnosed with macular degeneration, I learned that technology, with its limitations, must complement compassion and never just substitute for it. The ophthalmologist told my uncle that no treatment had been proven successful in stopping his rapidly deteriorating vision. My uncle was devastated. Upon hearing this, I did a comprehensive document search at UCLA's medical library. It appeared that laser treatment offered the only hope of halting the blindness. The laser treatment which my uncle subsequently received slowed, but did not halt, the condition. The doctor was right, but I believe my efforts gave my uncle time to come to terms with his loss of sight. The feeling of having made a difference in someone's life was tremendous. I recall thinking that a physician probably enjoys that feeling quite often. However, it wasn't until five years later, upon returning from a trip to central Africa, that I began to pursue a medical career in earnest.

While backpacking through central Africa, I met a young French doctor from the organization Doctors Without Borders. He invited me to his clinic—a thatched-roof hut in a remote Rwandan village. Many of his patients were children suffering from dehydration brought on by dysentery. Without the antibiotics and rehydration therapy which this doctor administered, many of these children would not have survived another week. That evening, I shared my rice and beans with a small boy, and while I watched him eat I reflected on what I had witnessed that day. I had seen how a small amount of primary care—just some pills and rehydration solution—could save the lives of no fewer than five children just like the one sitting next to me. I decided then to become a physician.

When I returned to the United States, I began taking medical school prerequisites while maintaining the full-time engineering responsibilities I had had for six years. I combined my MCAT preparations with my duties as an engineer and a new father, making use of the only quiet time left, 3 AM to 6 AM! My efforts paid off for me and coffee bean growers around the world.

Three years ago I turned my desire to help into action and began my first volunteer position. The Harbor-UCLA Medical Center's emergency room and intensive care unit taught me the importance of comforting patients in stressful environments. This usually meant just lending an attentive ear while the staff was busy. The chief trauma surgeon befriended me and, upon hearing of my plans to go to medical school, invited me to observe his activities. In time, I became familiar with the entire acute-care process, from examination to post-operative recovery. I also saw that the emergency room has become a costly bottleneck of care, the default method many people use to obtain medical attention for minor ailments. This exposure to emergency medicine and to the acute setting strongly supported my decision to pursue medical school.

One year ago, I began another volunteer position, which I continue to this day, at the Rehabilitation Institute of Tucson. It was here that I really began to understand and appreciate the patient's perspective of day-to-day care. As a volunteer, I have an abundant supply of time to listen. Because of this, I have gained a unique insight into medical care from patients. Frequently, a patient, who at first is quiet and withdrawn, ends up talking for hours about his home, his grandchildren, or his youth. Sometimes, as I listen to his story, I know that he is not sitting in that wheelchair, he is at home or with his grandchildren. When I am a part of this, I am happy.

Most recently, I have also begun a research project at the Arizona Health Sciences Center's Department of Radiology. The project involves evaluating spiral CT technology in the area of cervical spine trauma. The ultimate objective is to minimize patient discomfort, handling, and exposure to multiple, costly procedures. This must be accomplished without compromising the effectiveness of the current means of establishing diagnoses and prescribing courses of action.

I am fully aware of the scope of commitment and responsibility necessary to become a physician and I look forward to the day when I will be able to combine my knowledge and my compassion in a whole-hearted effort to help others. I want to make a difference. I hope that you will share my confidence that I will be an asset to the medical community and to the people it serves.

Steve Hochader, written in 1994

Personal Statement #7

In February 1992, I was accepted into the 1992 entering class of the College of Medicine. Shortly afterwards, I failed the Human Neuroscience course in which I was enrolled. I informed the Admission Committee of the College of Medicine of my grade, and subsequently my acceptance was withdrawn. I was devastated and humiliated. However, I have accepted full responsibility for my choice to prioritize my full-time research position as a Research Technician in Anesthesiology over the class.

I missed class whenever there was an eligible patient for one of the protocols. I also remained at the hospital late at night for heart transplants and post-surgical blood draws for the drug study protocols. These choices compromised my academic performance. I simply did not spend enough time studying the course material and preparing for the exam. Since the withdrawal of my application, I have learned much about responsibility, and I am determined to erase any doubts about my academic ability and commitment to a medical career. I have reduced my hours per week for my job, and I took considerable time off from work in the weeks leading up to the September 1992 MCAT. I have retaken the MCAT and also enrolled in two upper-division biology courses to demonstrate my academic ability in science.

I became interested in medicine years ago when, as a child, doctors appeared to me as a source of immediate comfort and trust. As a teenager, I watched my grandfather succumb to emphysema and wished I could have been in a position to help him. At the same time, my high school anatomy and physiology class confirmed my interest in the complexities of the human body. I tried to understand, through this new knowledge, the reasons behind my grandfather's deterioration. These experiences awakened my desire for an active role in health care.

I enrolled at the University of Arizona as a premed student, and I declared a history major with a biochemistry minor with an eye to obtaining a broad liberal arts education. In retrospect, my work in history has served me far better than I had anticipated, particularly as it relates the development of individuals and their communities to the expanding field of health care. In order to gain practical knowledge about medicine, I volunteered in the Department of Anesthesiology at the University of Arizona College of Medicine, and two months later took a job as a student investigator. This position exposed me to the clinical aspects of medicine with the first project: evaluation of implicit memory during general anesthesia. I discussed the study with surgical patients, played them a tape during their operation, and tested their recall post-operatively. Through this experience I realized that patients with confidence and trust in their physician were relaxed and confident going into surgery.

Our research team became involved in studies of cardiac surgery and anesthesia, and this work allowed me to make my first quantifiable contribution to the field of medicine. We examined the effect of altered hemoglobin-oxygen affinity during cardiopulmonary bypass. We also tested the effectiveness of the beta-blocker esmolol to lower cellular oxygen demand and protect cardiac tissue from damage caused by oxygen debt during cardiopulmonary bypass. I recorded numerous surgical parameters and drew blood for blood gases, drug concentrations, and various plasma levels. I realized that I was an active part of a research project designed to give cardiac patients hope for improvement in the quality and duration of their lives. Our research expanded into the investigation of human heart tissue, and I became responsible for obtaining a sample of left atrium from the hearts of transplant recipients. Seeing a successful transplant of a diseased heart with a stronger, healthier one gave me even deeper appreciation for life and the advances of medicine.

Personal Statement #7, page 2

In sharp contrast, I witnessed the death of a cardiac patient during a seemingly routine procedure. As the operating room team frantically attempted to sustain life, I could only wait and watch. The pressures dropped, the heart ceased, and a thick silence replaced the commotion. As with my grandfather, I was frustrated by my inability to help, and questioned how and why the death occurred. I wondered what could have been done to make the outcome different, and what new therapies the future will provide.

At that point in my senior year, I was so eager to enter medical school that I took another job to finance the MCAT and the application process. Ironically, my performance in biochemistry suffered as a result. Unexpected reconstructive knee surgery and rehabilitation the following spring further complicated my academic efforts while I maintained my research position to support myself. After graduation I was promoted to Research Technician, and my responsibilities were augmented to include study development and design, research grant applications, and supervision of the research team. Our team has since continued the esmolol and memory-during-anesthesia projects and studied the narcotic mirfentanil for conscious sedation, the anti-nausea drug ondansetron for use in the post-operative setting, and the narcotic agonist-antagonist dezocine for use during gall bladder removal and conscious sedation during endoscopic colonoscopy.

In the last four years of work in clinical research I have had patient, physician, and other staff interactions that have shown me the reality of medicine as it exists today. However, no greater lesson has slapped me in the face than my failure last spring. I have learned that my research position is a transitional role, and responsibilities in the lab should never interfere with my goal of admission to medical school. I have taken steps to prove my academic potential, and to remove any doubts about my dedication to my goal of becoming a physician. Temporary setbacks, rejections, and detours are all a part of the process of being human. My goal to become a physician remains strong, and I will continue to strive for it.

Steve Behr, written in 1993

Personal Statement #8

With the ever-changing field of medicine, many people wonder what medicine will be like in the future. For example, will we still have to live in fear of contracting an incurable and deadly disease, like AIDS? Or will medicine in the future have the capability of handling such threats to our lives? Answering these questions and having the proper education and training to help prevent such threats has been my major ambition. I feel that I can best fulfill this ambition by becoming a physician. I never really thought of going to college until the tenth grade. Just like my father, I had always thought I would be a mechanic and own my own shop because I enjoyed the challenges that arose while diagnosing different problems in cars. It wasn't until I was at my doctor's office that I realized the similarities between the work of physicians and mechanics. Both require one to diagnose and solve problems. That was when I became interested in medicine. As time went by, I started to develop a fascination with the anatomy, physiology, and biochemistry of the human body. Furthermore, I was amazed with how physicians were able to use medication to alleviate pain and heal individuals. Consequently, these attractions to the workings of the human body and the physician's job led me to pursue a career in medicine.

During my first semester at the University of Arizona, my interest in medicine was further intensified by attending the Minority PreMed Club meetings in which several physicians came and spoke to us about their roads to medical school and their current positions in the medical field. The following semester, I accepted an offer by the president of the Minority PreMed Club to help organize and implement community service projects and special events for the club. This gave me the chance to use my skills and interests in helping out the community and fellow premed students.

During the spring of 1993, I started tutoring mathematics and chemistry for the Minority Student Services Math & Science Learning Center at the University of Arizona. Through comprehensive tutor training, I further developed my interpersonal skills and knowledge of the concepts and procedures gained from previous course work to help students in their classes. Not only was this a valuable learning experience for the students I tutored, but it was also a worthwhile learning experience for me. In particular, I found working with students from different cultural backgrounds very broadening and personally rewarding.

In the summer of 1993, I volunteered in the transportation department at St. Mary's hospital in Tucson, Arizona. This gave me the opportunity to communicate with many patients and observe physicians. I will never forget the faces of those severely ill patients. The importance of medicine and physicians in our society became even more clear and compelling to me.

The following summer I participated in the first Minority Medical Education Program (MMEP) held at the University of Arizona College of Medicine. The purpose of this program was multifaceted. It gave me a better understanding of what is expected in medical school and the responsibilities and characteristics of a commendable physician. For example, through my involvement with MMEP, I have been shadowing an orthopedic surgeon at University Medical Center for more than twelve months. I observe his special skills with his patients and fellow physicians. I also get to watch him work in the operating room. In one case, as a scrubbed observer in the operating room, I felt I was part of the medical team that gave an infant with deformities the chance to walk. It was the climax of my premedical experiences. I will never forget the trust and confidence this physician had in my ability to give him a helping hand in surgery. More important was the fact that I was part of a team that made a significant difference in the patient's life. This is a feeling nobody can take from me. I absolutely knew after this that I wanted to be a physician more than anything in my life.

I know that one day when I am a physician, I will provide the experience that was given to me in an effort to help a premedical student. Without mentors, premedical students will never get the proper experiences and may never be certain whether medicine is the suitable career for them.

I am the first in my family to attend college. Luckily, I have a family that has supported and encouraged my success in college. I have also been fortunate enough to have made it this far on my road to medical school with the help of my premedical advisor, premedical programs (MMEP), and my mentor. I know that with their continued support, I will be able to successfully complete the curriculum needed to become a physician. I know, however, that the road to a medical degree will be hard and long, but I will never give up my dreams of becoming a physician. I am determined to help fight the war against those life threatening diseases like AIDS, and by becoming a physician, I can be on that special team that will make a difference in a patient's life.

Robert G. Bonillas, written in 1995

Personal Statement #9

I have wanted to be a doctor since I was a senior in high school. I worked for a doctor to pay my tuition to a private church school, and my contact with her sparked my interest in medicine. To pay for my medical school tuition, I became an Emergency Medical Technician. This allowed me to take a good look at the medical profession and decide exactly what I wanted to do. During EMT school, I felt like I really found my niche, and when I began working on the ambulance, I knew that I belonged in medicine. I enjoyed patient care, I found that I enjoyed explaining medical conditions to people even more than I enjoyed the adrenaline rush of responding to calls. I still do. Two years later, I was the valedictorian of my paramedic class.

I knew when I finished paramedic school that I had just gotten a taste of medicine and wanted more. Also, I wanted to be a flight medic on a helicopter and began pursuing that. Two years later, I began flying for Flight for Life, out of Mother Francis Hospital, in Tyler, Texas. Even though aeromedical transport is viewed as the pinnacle of EMS, it still was not enough for me. One day as we were flying in a critical patient and I was giving my report to the doctor over the radio, it struck me that I was on the wrong side of the radio. It was time to go back to school and continue my education.

That day on the radio, I realized that I wanted the leadership role in medicine that a physician has. A physician has more autonomy and the depth of care that she performs is much greater than any other member of the health care team. Most of all, a physician has the opportunity to be involved in the doctor-patient relationship, and I believe that this relationship has a greater effect on peoples' lives. I want to be a part of that.

I have been pursuing my education while a paramedic at Life Star Ambulance. These last ten years on an ambulance have been highly educational for me. I have become ACLS-certified, a BTLS instructor, EMD-certified, and am currently working on becoming a pediatric prehospital-life-support instructor. More importantly, however, I have learned how to talk with patients, how to listen to them, and how to care for them and their families.

In 1989, I attended a class on pediatric prehospital trauma. I watched videotapes of a doctor from the University of Florida talking about the number of pediatric trauma-related deaths that could have been prevented by the caregivers at the hospital. I began to get interested in pediatric critical care. A few years later I began volunteering at Cook-Fort Worth Children's Medical Center holding sick babies in the Special Care Unit. I am now interested in working with critical pediatric patients, either in an emergency department or in oncology. I want to spend the rest of my life caring for sick children and, when possible, making them better.

I think I should be accepted into medical school for many different reasons. I have been working on an ambulance for ten years, and I know what I am getting into. I have worked full time while obtaining my prerequisites for medical school, and keeping my GPA high, and I did well on my MCAT. I consider myself to be a highly motivated, goal-oriented, altruistic person who could make a difference in my patients' lives. I believe I have the intangible qualities of a good doctor: the desire to educate, to serve, and to heal.

Priscilla Madsen, written in 1994

Personal Statement #10

What can I offer to medicine?

I can offer a passion for life, my own as well as others'. I also bring to medicine an analytical mind attached to a compassionate heart.

What does medicine offer me?

The simple smile of a 9-year-old when his sister signs his cast. The swell of warmth as I guide a patient to health. The rewards are indescribable. There is something magical in working with people to better their health. It is the interaction with people intertwined with the pursuit of science in a way that will bring a common goal: a healthier and happier lifestyle.

What kind of person am I?

Eclectic. I am a student-athlete graduating with a degree in Electrical Engineering and a Philosophy Minor. To me, life is engaging. Throughout my education and career, I hope to never stop growing. I have always struck a natural balance of mind, body, and spirit when striving for academic excellence, when competing in sports, or in understanding my place in this universe.

Why Electrical Engineering?

Electronics have amazed me since I first played with a 30-in-1 Heath Kit at age eight. Although I found my career direction (medicine) early in college, I knew that I still wanted to study engineering in school. I've learned how to critically analyze a situation and solve problems efficiently and discovered that health care can be improved with electronics. For my senior project, I am designing a hearing aid that shifts spoken sounds to lower frequencies where the ear is usually less damaged. While practicing medicine, I expect to find further applications of electronics to health care.

Why a Philosophy Minor?

I'm a reflective person, and philosophy examines the "whys" and "hows" that underlie everyday life. One must be able to think critically and logically, yet there is creativity in conjuring abstract notions. My philosophical background has opened my mind to countless ways of thinking.

Have I experienced health care?

My motivations have been reinforced by my experiences in health care. As a volunteer, I help admit and discharge patients. I can see the change in expression as they go from sick to well. I see nervous families waiting for their loved ones in surgery. When the physician comes out, there is a wave of relief. I see the caring, knowledgeable way in which physicians interact with patients, and I aspire to eventually be in that position.

I am also prepared for the other side of health care: the embittered patient, the terminal case of cancer. Serving as a volunteer in General Hospital Emergency Room, I see how difficult it can be to deal with the patients who are physically and/or mentally ill. It is a part of life to face its harshness with patience, perseverance, and love.

Will I be a good physician?

Yes. My strength lies in the balance of qualities of a complete physician: an intelligent person who evaluates a situation effectively; a human being with the humility and compassion to relate with patients; a health advocate asserting that healthiness and happiness are really the same word.

William Segalla, 1996

Essays For School-Specific Applications

The essays that medical schools require applicants to submit with their secondary applications often are mixtures of several themes: What experience led you to pursue a medical career? What personal goals do you have? What motivates you? and other personal themes seeking to better describe applicants' values and attitudes. While mulling over ideas for your initial personal statement, jot down ideas for parallel essays. If you can, write standard essays in advance so you can polish them before they are due. Since you will want to return your secondary applications as soon as possible, pre-writing some essays will markedly speed the process. Even if the schools ask for something different in their essays, you will probably be able to cut-and-paste material from the essays you already wrote to answer most essay questions. Some schools are notorious for requesting numerous essays. Queen's University, for example, asks for four additional essays, McMaster for seven, and Stanford for eight! By itself, this requirement dissuades many fine students from applying.

Most schools with a specific primary-care mission ask about this in their essay questions. They may ask questions that correlate with a primary care career, such as: "To what extent have your past experiences, goals, and/or accomplishments demonstrated your understanding of and commitment to this school's mission?"; "Discuss the type of medical practice in which you see yourself."; or "What other career possibilities have you considered?" Studies suggest that, aside from discussing their prior contact with a specialty, the content of applicants' essays has little to do with their final specialty choices. Loma Linda specifically asks how the school's "theological perspective" relates "to your personal, educational, and career goals."

Other examples and a detailed method for writing personal statements and essays can be found in *Résumés and Personal Statements for Health Professionals,* by J.W. Tysinger (see *Annotated Bibliography*).

An additional point about your personal statement. Before you submit it to your prehealth committee, ask if they will allow revisions, if necessary, before they forward it to medical schools. Such revisions, of course, should only be made if you have pertinent new experiences to add.

Reference Letters

The reference letters sent to medical schools describe you from other people's perspectives. They play an important part in your being asked for a medical school interview. Obtaining good reference letters, however, takes advance planning, hard work, and initiative. The steps outlined below will help you to get the best possible reference letters. They will also help you make the most of the ones you do get.

Medical schools generally expect to see letters from: (1) a science professor (or your major adviser for graduate students), (2) a responsible person who can comment on your clinical or research experience, and (3) your premed committee or adviser. If you are currently employed, some schools also want a letter from your supervisor. Some schools request specific letters; others have a limit on the number of letters they wish to see. (Figure 15.5 gives an approximation of each school's preferences.) Carefully read all the information you receive from the schools and that comes with the uniform applications. If you don't follow their rules exactly, the schools may be just peeved enough to deny you an interview.

You will also need reference letters when you apply for scholarships. You may be able to ask the same individuals who wrote letters for your application for these letters as well. (You may even be able to use the same letters.) This makes it doubly important to go about the process of obtaining reference letters correctly.

Reference Letters From Premed Advisers And Committees

About 94% of premed advisers at private undergraduate schools and 75% at public schools write reference letters for their medical school applicants. While most write these letters for all premed students, about 15% require applicants to meet minimal standards (such as a prehealth committee recommendation, specific faculty support for their application, or a minimum GPA) before they will write such letters. About 1% require all students to pay for such letters, even though this seems to produce a major conflict of interest and diminishes these letters' significance to medical school admission committees.

Most colleges and universities also have premedical committees that will produce composite reference letters if students request them. Typically, the committee is comprised of faculty members representing both the sciences and the non-sciences. Prior to writing the letters, they review students' records and then, as a group, interview each student. (At some schools, the committees do not interview students. These committees write letters highlighting the comments and accomplishments taken from other reference letters and from the school's records.) In general, committee members evaluate the student's undergraduate performance and activities to see if he or she has: realistic goals based on the record, considered alternatives to medical school, and had clinical experience. This is a very important process.

For most students, being interviewed by this committee will be the first "live" part of their application process. Preparation for this interview is the same as that for an interview at a medical school. (See chapters 22, *Interview Preparation;* 23, *The Interview;* and 25, *The Questions—The Answers.*)

Medical schools take these committees' recommendations very seriously. Admission committees know that these are objective evaluations from individuals who are experienced in judging undergraduates applying to medical schools. Although students can choose their individual references, they cannot choose committee members. And since committee members are not pressured by individual students, they are more willing to write critical letters, if it is appropriate. Many premed committees use standard language to summarize their evaluations, such as "Highly Recommended," "Recommended," or "Recommended With Reservations." *Take these interviews very seriously.* They can either help you immensely or hurt you badly.

Many medical schools accept a premed committee's recommendations in lieu of additional reference letters (figure 15.5). Most prefer to see premed recommendations, and some schools will contact an applicant's undergraduate school if it has a premed committee, but the student did not use it. Experience has shown that most applicants also benefit from additional excellent reference letters from individuals they know. (Some schools, however, instruct you not to add them. Follow their instructions.) If your committee gives you an unenthusiastic evaluation, these additional letters may still give you a shot at getting medical school interviews.

Some medical schools require student applicants to provide statements in their committee's or adviser's letter that they are "in good standing" at their school. If this is the case, tell the committee or adviser that this statement needs to be included.

Some committees (and faculty members) don't actually send letters, but rather send forms that rate each student on a variety of factors. A typical example of such a form, used by the University of Mississippi's Premedical and Health Professions Office, is shown in figure 13.2. Several faculty members rate a student and a composite of the ratings is sent to medical schools.

Premed committee interviews have one additional benefit. Committee members often provide feedback to students about qualities to stress, how to act, and what deficiencies should be explained during medical school interviews. Of course, you usually have to do well at the committee's interview to get as far as a medical school interview. In general, students don't see the committee's letters.

Figure 13.2: Rating Sheet for Applicants to Medical School

Applicant: _____

FACTORS:
For each factor below, please indicate with a check mark (✓) your opinion of this applicant's rating on that factor relative to other students you have observed.

RANKING STANDARDS:
1. Exceptional, top 5%.	**3.** Good, next 20%	**5.** Reservation, next 30%	**7.** No basis for judgment
2. Excellent, next 10%	**4.** Average, middle 30%	**6.** Poor, low 5%	

FACTORS	1	2	3	4	5	6	7
EMOTIONAL STABILITY performs under pressure; mood stability; constancy in ability to relate to others							
INTERPERSONAL RELATIONS ability to get along with others; rapport; cooperation; attitude towards supervision							
JUDGMENT ability to analyze problems; common sense; decisiveness							
RESOURCEFULNESS originality; skillful management of available resources and time; initiative							
RELIABILITY dependability; sense of responsibility; promptness; conscientiousness							
PERSEVERANCE stamina; endurance (physical and psychological)							
COMMUNICATION SKILLS clarity in writing and speech; articulation							
SELF CONFIDENCE assuredness; capacity to achieve with awareness of own strengths and weaknesses							
EMPATHY consideration; tact; sensitivity to the needs of others							
MATURITY personal development; social consciousness; ability to cope with life situations							
INTELLECTUAL CURIOSITY realness and intensity of desire to learn and extend beyond course expectations							
SCHOLARSHIP ability to learn (quality of study habits plus native intellectual ability)							
MOTIVATION genuineness and depth of commitment; intensity, reality and maturity of expressed reasons to enter medicine							

EVALUATION SUMMARY:
Compare with other premed students you (have) know(n) and provide an overall evaluation.

( ) Exceptional Candidate, top 5%   ( ) Average Candidate, middle 30%
( ) Excellent Candidate, next 10%   ( ) Weak Candidate, bottom 35%
( ) Good Candidate, next 20%   ( ) No basis for judgment

Adapted, with permission, from the form used by the University of Southern Mississippi.

Other Reference Letters

Whom To Ask

Most of the reference letters you send to medical schools will come from individuals you have personally asked to write them. It is essential for you to know whom to ask.

When considering whom to ask for reference letters, remember to select people who know you well and who are credible. Remember that you also want the letters to complement and reinforce what you say about yourself in your personal statement.

The Ideal Reference

The ideal reference letter is written by an individual who is well-known to the members of admission committees—usually a nationally recognized physician, researcher, or scholar who: (1) has worked closely with you in school or elsewhere; (2) thinks you are a "star"; and (3) came from the institution to which you are applying. If the individual is on a medical school's faculty, it is best if the letter says that you have been strongly encouraged to apply to his or her school. All this may be difficult to achieve in one letter. But you should think of such a reference as the "gold standard."

Faculty

Faculty members, especially senior faculty, are good references But choose someone with whom you have worked closely in some capacity and who thought you did a great job. For example, you may have worked with a professor in the laboratory, or on extracurricular activities, or been part of his or her small seminar. If those are in a "medically related" area, such as molecular biology, so much the better. Try to get one letter from a faculty member outside of your major area. For example, if you are a science major, get a letter from a faculty member in the humanities, and vice versa. This helps to demonstrate that you are the well-rounded person many medical schools now seek.

If you have cultivated a mentor early on, whether or not he or she is in a health care field, have him or her write you a letter. If your mentor has worked closely with you (and if they haven't it is *your* fault), his or her opinion will carry a great deal of weight. Letters, even from prominent faculty members, hold much less weight if they cannot show that they know you well.

Non-Academic References

You may have played an active role in non-school activities, for example as a Scout leader, a Little League coach, or a volunteer firefighter. The overall supervisor for the activity (such as the fire chief) can write a reference letter detailing your selfless effort, explaining how well you get along with people, and even citing specific outstanding events that he or she has witnessed. If chosen wisely, such references add spice to your application, making you a memorable, and often desirable, applicant.

If you have worked in a medical setting, ask a physician who worked closely with you to write a letter. Such an individual is qualified to assess your behavior in a medical setting. Admission committees look for this type of information, as well as details about an applicant's work style, personality, and stamina. Most Osteopathic schools require or strongly suggest that you get a letter from an Osteopathic physician.

Your boss at work can also be an excellent reference. Hopefully, he or she will say that you are a diligent, hard-working employee, or that you are innovative and demonstrate commonsense, honesty, or other positive attributes.

Counterproductive References

Do not get letters from: (1) teaching assistants; (2) friends or school alumni (if not in one of the above categories); (3) relatives; (4) clergymen; (5) politicians; or (6) people who just don't like you. You think I'm being funny? Not a bit. Medical schools often receive reference letters from

177

individuals in all these categories. Letters from these sources do not normally help your application. Why do people request letters from such references, especially from those who don't like them? Usually students feel obligated to ask such individuals for letters because they have worked with them or mentioned them in their résumé or personal statement. Don't fall into this trap! Concentrate on finding people who think you're great.

Many students ask teaching assistants for letters. But even if they know you better than professors, they come across as very weak references. (If they are so inclined, ask them to write the letter for the professor's signature.) Teaching assistants may, in fact, be detrimental. Admission officers are interested in how well you will do in school and in the profession. They want consistent information from reputable, knowledgeable sources. That means your professors. "If she can't get these letters, there must be something wrong with her," they say. Don't make the admission committee think that!

When To Ask

Don't be a wimp! If you want a letter from a particular individual, ask for it. But ask at the right time and in the right way. When is the right time? If you do a great job in a class and you want the professor to write a reference letter, ask near the end of the term, or soon afterwards. Don't wait until six months or a year later. Even if the faculty member's memory of you does not fade with time, he or she may have moved away, be on sabbatical, or be otherwise unavailable. Ask if the letter can be drafted immediately, explaining that you will subsequently give him or her a list of schools where to send the letters.

Ask your mentor or adviser during a counseling session. If your adviser has been arbitrarily selected by someone other than you, for example by the Dean of Students, first think about whether he or she knows you well enough to write a good reference letter.

If you want a letter from someone you have worked with on the job, as a volunteer, or in the laboratory, just ask the individual if he or she can "write you an excellent reference letter." If you will be working with several such individuals over an extended period of time, ask each of them in advance if they will write you a letter when you are ready to apply. Then, provide the final information needed to write it to those individuals whose letters you think will be the strongest.

Be certain to ask for your reference letters no later than the spring before you submit your AMCAS Application. If you wait longer than that, some of the faculty you want to write letters will be busy giving final exams and afterwards, they will most likely be away from campus until the fall. Ask for these letters early.

How To Ask

Don't send coded messages. Ask for a reference letter directly. But phrase it in such a way that neither you nor the faculty member will be saddled with either a negative or a neutral (read: "negative") letter. One way of doing this is to ask if the faculty member "would feel comfortable writing me a *strong* letter of support?" If you note any hesitation, forget it and try elsewhere. Avoid getting a letter from someone who may be uncomfortable writing you a superior reference letter. Be thankful that this person did not just say "yes," and then send a negative or even a lukewarm reference. Such letters can demolish your chance of getting into medical school. One of our wisest and most experienced faculty members, Douglas Lindsey, M.D., D.P.H., offers to write letters for every student. He writes them honestly. He then shows the student the letter. It is up to the student to decide whether it is sent. This is an excellent policy of a great teacher. Unfortunately, it is probably unique.

If someone agrees to write a reference letter for you, assist him (and yourself) by supplying him with the information he needs to make it an outstanding letter. Give him a copy of your résumé, your personal statement, your "goals" statement if you have one, and perhaps a picture.

A picture? Sure! If he is one of your professors, he may have from three to five hundred students, or more, each term. Remind him of who you are—give him a picture.

One way of circumventing the problem of a poor reference letter is to ask for a copy of the letter for your files. This gambit is somewhat tricky. If you firmly believe that the individual you have asked will write a superlative letter but will not give you a copy, go ahead—at some risk. If the individual agrees to give you a copy of the letter, then you stand a good chance of, at least marginally, upgrading the quality of the letter because they often write a more positive letter if they know you will see it. Only a few people in academia make it a policy to send copies of the reference letters they write to the individuals for whom they write them. In the business world, this is standard practice and common courtesy. Too bad the practice isn't yet widespread in academia.

Many medical school admission committees prefer "confidential letters," which means that you have waived your right to ask the prehealth office to show them to you. This doesn't mean, however, that your letter writers cannot send you a copy. If possible, you do want to see those letters before they go out. Ask your references to send you copies, explaining (if it is true, as it is in most cases) that the prehealth committee will not allow you access to your file.

The Format

While letters from your premed adviser are usually professionally typed or printed on the school's stationary, the same may not be true for other reference letters. It is almost unbelievable that faculty and other professionals often send out reference letters that are not on letterhead, done with dot matrix printers, or handwritten. This is a negative reflection not only on these individuals, but also on you. Other references, such as the coordinator of the Little League team you coach, may not use letterhead or a computer. Physicians working for some branches of the federal government and those in solo or rural practice also seem to have difficulty producing professional reference letters. If you believe that any of your references will have difficulty producing professional-appearing documents, either offer to have the letter typed and printed for them or just ask someone else. The best format to use is a laser- or inkjet-printed letter on letterhead stationery with a handwritten note from the writer. That gets attention.

Few people have been taught what goes into a good reference letter. They might find it useful if you give them a copy of figure 13.3, Elements of a Reference Letter, when you ask them to write one for you. Better still, especially with older or more experienced individuals, first ask if they would like you to send them a copy of the figure. Whether or not you send this to them, do provide them with the materials mentioned above to help them when they write the letter. Be sure to tell them where to send the letters. Also, tell them, and include prominently in the materials you give them, the deadline for the letters' receipt. (You might want to give them pre-addressed and stamped envelopes in which to send the letters.) Use one or more copies of figure 13.4 if your premedical committee does not send out your letters.

Follow-Up

Once an individual says a reference letter has been sent on your behalf, you have two more jobs—ensuring that the letter arrives and thanking the letter writer. Your first duty is to ensure that the letters actually got where they needed to go—either to the medical schools or the premed office. It's surprising how many reference letters seem to get lost in the mail, in an office, or most commonly, on the letter-writer's desk. About two weeks after the writer says the letter was sent (or after you received a copy) call the offices that were to receive the letter and ask if it arrived. If it hasn't, recontact your reference, explain the situation, and ask him or her to send another copy.

Your second duty is to send a thank-you note to each person who wrote a letter on your behalf. This is the professional and courteous thing to do. It also increases the probability that this person will willingly write letters for future medical school applicants. That's a gift you can give to those students who are behind you in the process.

Figure 13.3: Elements of a Reference Letter

You have been asked to write a reference letter for medical school. Medical schools heavily weigh these letters when considering applicants. If possible, please consider including the following items in your letter:

Please address the letter to: **"Dear Admission Committee"**

A. How and How Long You Have Known the Individual?

B. Who are You?
  Brief, one sentence description.

C. Individual's Scholastic Record
  1. Standing in graduating class
  2. Honors/Commendations in courses
  3. Other honors
  4. Any extenuating circumstances that should be considered when interpreting the individual's grades

D. Individual's Personal Characteristics
  (List strongest points first. Give specific examples.)
  1. Relations with peers, faculty, ancillary staff
  2. Willingness to assume responsibility
  3. Ability and methods for handling stressful situations
  4. Consistency of working up to potential
  5. Dependability
  6. Integrity; moral and ethical qualities
  7. Industriousness
  8. Initiative
  9. Motivation
  10. Interest in medicine and learning
  11. Emotional maturity
  12. Flexibility
  13. Sense of humor

E. Summary
  1. Of all premedical students with whom you have dealt, how would you rate this applicant on the basis of his or her personal characteristics (e.g., Top 1%, 5%, 50%)?
  2. Are there any personal characteristics that might interfere with this individual's career in medicine?
  3. May the Admission Committee members contact you with any questions about your letter?

Figure 13.4: Request For a Reference Letter

[Type or neatly print all information.]

NAME: _____   DATE: _____

ADDRESS: _____   PHONE: _____

Schools must receive these letters by: _____

SCHOOL   ADDRESS

_____   _____

                                 _____

                                 _____

_____   _____

                                 _____

                                 _____

_____   _____

                                 _____

                                 _____

_____   _____

                                 _____

                                 _____

_____   _____

                                 _____

                                 _____

_____   _____

                                 _____

Secondary Applications

About five weeks after you submit all your AMCAS or AACOMAS materials, you should begin receiving secondary applications from some schools (figure 15.5). Each medical school has its own forms. Read the cover letters accompanying the secondary applications very carefully. While most schools *actively screen* applicants by eliminating individuals whose Uniform Application clearly indicates they are not competitive, some use a *passive screen*. A passive screen means that all applicants receive secondary applications, although applicants get different cover letters depending on how competitive they are. Either the cover letter will say that you "still merit consideration" but must first complete the secondary application, or it will say that "your credentials are not competitive with other applicants." While you may still complete the secondary application if you get the second message, it is probably not worth your effort.

In most cases, secondary applications request the same material you included on your uniform application plus some additional details, additional essays—and an additional $15 to $100. (The University of British Columbia charges out-of-province applicants $185 to evaluate their applications and transcripts. Do you think they are trying to tell you not to apply?) It doesn't take long for these sums to mount up—often to over $1,000.

If the schools ask for one or more additional essays, they will provide you with particular topics to write about, rather than the general description covered in your personal statement. (Hopefully you have written all or some of these essays in advance.)

Since your uniform application is sent to the schools simultaneously, your secondary applications may arrive in batches. The worst possible move is to procrastinate in filling them out and generating any requested materials. Set a time limit for completing each one, for example, two days after its arrival. Write this deadline on the envelope in which you receive the material, and try very hard to meet it. To spur you on, note that some schools will not consider secondary applications returned more than three weeks after they were sent to the applicant. When you return the application material to the school, use a fast delivery method (U.S. Priority or Express Mail or an overnight service) with a way to track it. (Use "return-requested" if by U.S. mail. Overnight services automatically track packages.)

Letter-File Services

Your reference letters are sent to schools only with secondary applications (not with the uniform application). About 77% of undergraduate schools have a "letter-file service," often through their premed offices, that keeps your reference letters on file and mails them when you provide your list of medical schools. The larger the school, the more likely they are to offer this service. About 12% of schools charge a fee for this service, with schools having more than 100 medical school applicants per year being the most likely to charge. The cost ranges from $20 to $160 for those with a one-time charge. Those that charge per letter sent average $5 per letter. (Some only charge individuals who are not current undergraduates.)

Most (about 72%) of these services have no maximum number of letters that they will file for a student. If an applicant needs to re-apply in a subsequent year, nearly all permit additional reference letters to be added. Most services automatically send all letters in a student's file, although about 29% allow the student to select the letters from their file they want sent. Nearly half of these services store students' letter files permanently. The rest destroy the letters sometime after the student's graduation.

If you don't have such a service available or if you elect not to use it, inform your letter writers of the medical schools' addresses. If at all possible, give them adhesive labels to attach to their envelopes to speed the process. Many secondary applications also have special forms for your letter writers to complete. Make sure that they receive these. *Check back within two weeks to be sure that the letters or forms have been sent.*

Unlike the AMCAS-E or AACOMAS By Computer applications, secondary applications are not (yet) in electronic form. So, after completing copies of these forms as carefully as possible, you will need to find a professional typist to prepare the final drafts.

Although these secondary applications are a hassle to complete, they indicate that you have cleared the first obstacle in your pursuit of a medical school education.

Photographs

About half of the school-specific applications and the University of Texas' uniform application either require or give the applicant the option of including a passport-size photograph. Requesting or requiring such pictures happens to be illegal under civil-rights legislation, since photos reveal race, gender, and age. The legal point is that since schools cannot discriminate against individuals based on race, sex, age, and national background, there is no reason for a picture. If pictures are optional, don't include one. Let your application materials speak for you.

However, once you have been granted an interview, have a photograph for the school to include with your application materials. Why should you do this? For a very obvious reason. You want to be remembered. Do you really think that an interviewer will remember anything specific about Jerry Glover or Mary Smythe after seeing forty applicants? Probably not. But with a photograph to jog their memory during final selection, the good impressions that you left with the interviewers will come flooding back.

What kind of photograph do you give them? As with everything else you do in the application process, your photograph should look professional. Have it professionally done. Don't sit in the drugstore photo machine which gives you five pictures for one dollar (as I foolishly did as a destitute undergraduate). This is your career at stake. Go to a real photographer and explain that you need a portrait photo. Unless you are specifically asked for a black and white picture, get it in color. The benefit of using a skilled photographer is that no matter what you really look like, you will appear much better in the picture. To get the best price, shop around. The differences, especially if you are in a large city, can be enormous.

Finally, before handing the picture to the admission secretary for your file, put a gummed label on the back with your name, address, telephone number, and the date that you are interviewing.

Oh yes, remember to say "cheese."

Assessing Your Chance For Acceptance

There is a rather simple formula that seems to be a good barometer for measuring each student's chance of being accepted to medical school, although its validity is based only on anecdotal evidence. Developed by Dr. William Hussey at Brooklyn College, that formula is:

(Total GPA X 10) + (Science GPA X 10) + MCAT Score = ADMISSION SCORE

Using the admission score, applicants can be divided into three groups according to their chance of admission to medical school. Applicants with scores of 100 or greater have an excellent chance of acceptance to medical school. Those with scores in the high 90s have a reasonable chance of acceptance, and those scoring in the low 90s will probably not be accepted. Note that this scale is shifted down by 15 points for minority and disadvantaged applicants, by 5 to 10 points for Osteopathic medical schools, and variable amounts for selected medical schools (see figure 15.2).

Example: Jane Smith has a total GPA of 3.6, a science GPA of 3.5, and a total MCAT score (excluding the essay) of 29. Her "admission score" is 100. Based on her admission score, Jane Smith has an excellent chance of getting into medical school.

With the increase in applicants to medical school, those in the middle category have suffered the most. Those in the high-acceptance group still get in and those in the low-acceptance group generally do not. Those with scores in the high 90s are the "swing" group, and are eliminated if the number of applicants in the high-acceptance group enlarges, as it has in the past few years.

Several problems exist with this formula. One is that many medical schools say they weigh the MCAT scores more heavily than the GPA, while other schools don't even require the MCAT or barely consider the scores. So there is a great deal of variation among the schools. As for MCAT scores, you may be delighted (or saddened) to learn that, in 1994, about 2% of those who scored "1" on the Verbal Reasoning section were accepted to M.D.-granting medical schools, while about 22% of those who scored "13" and above were rejected. About 2% of those who scored "2" on the Physical Science section were accepted, and about 18% of those who scored "15" were rejected. About 2% of those who scored "2" on the Biological Science section were accepted, while about 5% of those with a score of "15" were not. On the Writing Sample, about 12% who scored a "J" were accepted, while about 26% of those scoring a "T" were rejected. (The Writing Sample is the portion of the MCAT most frequently ignored or downplayed by medical school admission committees.)

In terms of GPAs, in 1994 about 5% of applicants with a science GPA of 1.50 to 1.99 were accepted to M.D.-granting medical schools and about 10% of applicants with a non-science GPA at this level were accepted. About 22% of those with a science GPA of 3.90 to 4.00 were rejected, as were about 30% of those with a non-science GPA in the same range.

Communicating With The Schools

Once you send in your initial application packet, you will communicate with the schools primarily by telephone.

The first time you should call the schools is about a month after you have requested that all of your material be sent to them. Find out if everything has arrived. If not, what is missing? It is your responsibility, not theirs, to assure that they have all your materials.

How you communicate with schools is very important. It is amazing that the nicest, most sophisticated individuals often have a terrible telephone "presence." Your voice over the telephone and your attitude on it will make a big impression on the admission staff. Don't think that you can behave any way you want to on the telephone because you are *only* talking to the secretary! And don't express your frustration at being put on hold in crude terms.

As in many businesses, a secretary who interacts with applicants often has a major impact on who is selected—both for interviews and for final positions. Many admission officers ask their secretaries for input. And most take this input very seriously. Refine your telephone technique. Be very pleasant to those Admission secretaries. They can be either your allies or your enemies. Make them think of you as a nice person, someone who they want as a student at *their* medical school.

Once you are in a medical school's admission system, stay in touch with the Dean of Admissions or the admission committee. Unless your premed advisor or the school's application materials tell you that they do not want additional information from you, write to tell them about anything interesting or relevant to your future medical career that you have done since you submitted your application. Continue to do this even after your interview. If something particularly noteworthy happens, give them a call. Some schools keep track of these "interest communications." Your message to them is that you are the right choice for their medical school!

14: Admission Committees And Procedures

Though this be madness, yet there is method in 't.

Shakespeare, *Hamlet*, II,

ADMISSION COMMITTEES AND ADMISSION PROCEDURES vary among medical schools. General information is provided below, but each school's system has individual quirks.

Committee Composition

The average admission committee consists of about fifteen people, usually including the Dean of Admissions and both basic-science and clinical faculty. About two-thirds of the schools also have at least one medical student on the committee, in either a voting or non-voting capacity. About one-fourth have alumni or members of the admission staff, and one in eight schools has residents (physicians in postgraduate training) serving as committee members.

As Randall Ziellinski says in *The Medical School Interview,* "The committee must compare apples with oranges, and predict which, when fed to the cow, will make the tastiest steak four years down the road." It's not an easy task. Of course, being human, they do it imperfectly.

Screening Process

The admission committee sets the criteria which members use to screen applications. These criteria often differ for in-state (in-Territory, in-Province) and out-of-state residents, even at some private schools. In addition, their criteria also usually vary for underrepresented minority candidates. A small subcommittee, often just two or three committee members, usually screens the initial applications and supporting materials to decide which applicants will be interviewed. They generally place applicants into one of four categories: interview, possible later interview (depending upon the quality of other applicants), re-review (often by a larger subcommittee or the entire committee), and reject. At some schools, the subcommittee alone makes this determination, while at others the entire admission committee makes all these decisions or just those decisions that are difficult or borderline. Most take this task very seriously, since they understand that most applicants can ill-afford the expenses for travel, lodging, and often, time off work or school that an interview entails. Therefore, they try to offer interviews only to applicants whom they are seriously considering.

At some schools, after the initial screening, applicants who rate high enough to meet preset criteria are sent secondary applications. Otherwise, they can be rejected at this stage. (Schools that use a "passive screen" send cover letters saying that an applicant is not competitive, but still include a secondary application.) Some schools, especially state-supported medical schools, are quite liberal in sending secondary applications. A few schools skip the secondary-application step altogether.

The secondary applications are then screened by a few members of the admission committee who generally place applicants into one of four categories: interview, possible later interview (depending upon the quality of other applicants), re-review (often by a larger subcommittee or the entire committee), and reject.

After interviews, the entire admission committee reviews each applicant's admission packet. While only one or more members of the subcommittee will generally have interviewed the applicant, other committee members review the application materials and the interviewer's oral or written comments. Normally, all committee members vote on each applicant's acceptability. Those applicants with the highest number of votes (in any admission cycle) are accepted to the medical school, while those with a lower number are either put on a waiting list or rejected. If an applicant is rejected, no appeals mechanism exists (except for the courts, which is a long, costly, tiresome, and often fruitless process). The only option is to be accepted at another medical school or to re-apply in a subsequent year.

The flow chart on the next page is the committee's selection process at one medical school. Each school's criteria are different. The numbers given are different (both higher and lower) at many schools.

Selection Criteria

Lots of scuttlebutt exists about what information admission committees consider important in selecting medical students. When these committees were actually surveyed, they divided the information into three categories: very important, moderately important, and (by implication) not important.

The VERY IMPORTANT factors are:

- Ratings from the medical school interview
- Undergraduate, postbaccalaureate, and/or graduate school GPAs
- MCAT scores
- Recommendation letters from premedical committees, undergraduate advisers, or faculty members
- Knowledge about health care issues
- Commitment to a health care career

The MODERATELY IMPORTANT factors are:

- Number of incompletes, withdrawals, or repeated undergraduate or graduate courses
- Community and campus citizenship
- Health-related (volunteer or paid) work experience
- Extracurricular activities
- Recency of relevant course work
- Quality of the school(s) attended
- Number and quality of science courses

- Compatibility between candidate's characteristics or professional goals and the school's mission
- Personal statement(s) on centralized and institution-specific applications

Since these are the factors they do consider important, other factors, by implication, are not important. Note that, although admission committees do use these criteria and sources of information, exactly how each piece of information is evaluated may differ among applicant categories.

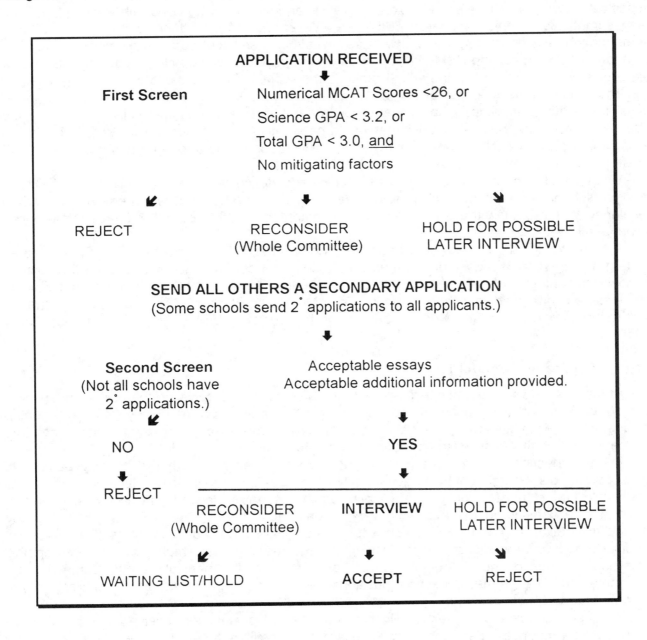

How Good Are The Selection Criteria?

While this question may seem obvious and easily tested, the real question is, "What are the committees selecting for?" As Drs. Coombs and Paulson wrote in the *Journal of Medical Humanities*, "The typical recruitment process favors applicants who are emotionally inexpressive, grade-conscious, competitive and narrowly specialized in science. They are . . . self-sacrificing and bookish rather than broadly experienced, and trust in a hard science quantifying approach that disregards less readily measurable psychosocial factors, such as feelings."

Although the current criteria seem to favor these individuals, most admission committees specifically *don't* want this type of person, but rather an individual who will be an excellent clinician (and sometimes a clinical researcher/educator). What type of individual do they look for? Is it someone who will do best in the first two (preclinical/basic science) years of medical school? Is it someone who will pass the USMLE? (It probably must include this, for without passing this test, or an equivalent test for D.O.'s, they can't practice medicine.) Is it applicants who will be accepted into the most competitive residency? Or is it, in the end, someone who will make the "best" physician—who is intelligent, has compassion for patients, and has the ability to survive the stresses of medical practice? Ideally, that would be what medical schools want to test applicants for. Unfortunately, we still cannot identify or test for what constitutes (or who has qualities of) the "best" physicians.

What we do know is that some selection criteria do correlate with preclinical and clinical medical school performance, with passing Steps on the USMLE, and with performance during residency. We also know that some measures commonly thought to be indicators correlate poorly or not at all.

Applicants' MCAT scores, their science and overall GPAs, and the selectivity of their undergraduate schools (based on the mean SAT scores for entering students) are good predictors of how well students will perform in their preclinical years. This seems to be true for both traditional and less-traditional medical school curricula. Their MCAT scores and GPAs also seem to correlate (but not as strongly) with how well students do on the first two USMLE Steps and in their clinical rotations.

Special Applicants—School Ties

At many schools, applicants with special ties to the school receive preference for interviews, and sometimes, for acceptance. Some schools say that they waive residency (state or country) requirements. At others, they give the applicants preference for interviews, and if they are "borderline" or on the waiting list, special preference for admission.

Such connections offer no guarantees, but since every advantage helps, it would be wise to apply to schools where you have a connection. If you have a tie to a medical school, it is worthwhile noting that fact on your application or in a separate letter to the school's admission office. Those considered to have "ties" vary among the schools. Categories that schools use include the children, grandchildren, spouses, or significant others of: current medical students, medical school and resident alumni, faculty, staff, volunteers, former employees, any Osteopathic physician, "friends of the school," or current applicants to the medical school. Some schools designate a number of medical school positions each year for graduates of their undergraduate school.

In most instances, however, applicants with these special ties receive only a "courtesy interview" or a "counseling session" if their file is not competitive. If you do have a tie to a medical school that invites you for an interview, before you go you may want to check to see whether it is a regular interview. While the courtesy interview or counseling session may prove useful to you, you may not want to spend the money (and time) if it isn't a "real" interview with a real chance of admission to that medical school.

Selecting Applicants To Be Generalist Physicians

Educators have tried to determine which applicant characteristics lead to physicians who will become generalists (general internal medicine, family practice, general pediatrics), rather than specialists. Some schools have a mission, often designated by their primary funding sources (the legislatures), to produce a large number of generalists, so they take this goal very seriously. They have found, as could have been predicted, that many of the current admission criteria select for specialist, rather than generalist, physicians.

Medical students who subsequently have subspecialty or research careers usually have high MCAT Science scores, extensive science backgrounds, and an interest in intellectual achievement. They also have higher "Machiavellian scores" (i.e., they prize devious behavior and flattery as a means of getting ahead, and devalue homosexuals, people with low IQs, patients with self-inflicted problems, and individuals who don't contribute to society).

Individuals who enter the generalist specialties usually have high MCAT Verbal Reasoning scores, are more tolerant of ambiguity, are primarily interested in patient problems related to social issues and psychology, are non-science majors, have a more acute sense of social responsibility, and are women. They usually have taken a wide variety of undergraduate courses and shown a strong commitment to community service in their prior activities and in their essays. The likelihood of an applicant's entering a generalist specialty seems to be inversely related to her socioeconomic status, but it is not related to the type or number of her non-service extracurricular activities. (However, it does relate to a strong leadership role.)

About one-fourth of those who eventually enter a generalist specialty envision that career path at the time they take the MCAT, while only about one in twelve of those who think they will be specialists eventually enter a generalist specialty. Medical school applicants, savvy to what admission committees want to hear, tend to answer questions about career choice in a "politically correct" manner. To counteract this, some schools train their interviewers to ask about applicants' medically related experiences to determine whether they are oriented toward generalist specialties. To increase the number of their graduates entering generalist specialties, some medical schools accept students specifically for primary care tracks, even though they may have lower test scores or GPAs than the average medical student.

Some medical schools have tried recruiting students from rural areas with the hope that they will return to practice in these medically underserved regions. But these students generally don't return, preferring instead to follow the same paths as their classmates. (As the 1919 song goes, "How You Gonna Keep 'Em Down on the Farm After They've Seen Paree?")

A More Perfect Application System?

You don't look so great on paper, but you have all the personal qualities needed to be a great physician. "Why don't they look at me as a person?" you ask. Some leading medical educators and policy makers are asking the same thing. They know that the majority of the applicants they reject from medical schools would make good physicians, perhaps better than many of those they currently accept. With that in mind, they would like to see medical schools select students who have a tolerance for ambiguity and an ability to function with uncertainty, individuals who want to care for and not just cure their patients, those who can tolerate the increasing oversight and regulation within medicine, those with interpersonal skills, and those who are comfortable with cultural diversity. They would, of course, like to see these qualities in those who have also demonstrated intellectual achievement, diverse academic interests (demonstrated by taking courses in the humanities, ethics, and social sciences), computer literacy, a capacity for self-education, and critical-thinking skills. Figure 14.1 lists some of the positive and negative personal qualities which admission committees seek—usually in the interview, personal essays, and recommendation letters.

Admission officers repeatedly say that committees could be replaced by computers if all they had to do was "crunch the numbers." The recent deluge of applications combined with the limited time committee members have to devote to the process (rarely, if ever, are they acknowledged or compensated for this work) does not let them really assess applicants' subjective qualities—especially in the first cut, when they decide whom to interview. As Dr. John Bruhn wrote in the *Journal of Medical Education*, "The admission committee often bows to the following rationale: Why belabor noncognitive factors in the biography of an academically borderline applicant when there are so many applicants with strong academic credentials (grades and MCAT scores) irrespective of noncognitive factors?"

If committees begin to use subjective criteria more heavily, though, rejected students will have cause for legal action under the U.S. Constitution's 5th Amendment's guarantees of due process and the 14th Amendment's guarantees of equal protection under the law. (The schools are quite aware of the cases, especially in California and Texas, where rejected students have successfully sued on these bases.) Schools violate these Constitutional rights when they publish their admission criteria in their brochures and in the AAMC's *Medical School Admission Requirements*, but then fail to apply those criteria equally to all applicants. If they use extended, personality-related criteria, they must explicitly say this in the information all applicants receive.

The bottom line, then, is to strive to improve your "numbers," and then demonstrate your other qualities in your essays and interviews.

What They Want: The "Perfect" Applicant

Everyone wants to know who makes the "perfect" applicant. That, of course, is neither the right question to ask nor a question with a unique answer. Why shouldn't you ask this question? First, because it is demoralizing. No one is perfect, and striving for perfection can only produce headaches.

Second, the person you compete against is nearly always yourself. Have you done the best you could? Are you doing it now? Since you can only do your best, it really doesn't matter that much what others do. Contrary to popular belief, it does not take a genius to be a physician; it takes the willingness to work hard over the long haul. Nearly anyone who can graduate from college has the ability to become a physician. The question is whether an individual has the necessary motivation to put forth the effort.

Third, you really don't compete against "perfect" applicants. If anyone comes close to these criteria, they have no difficulty getting into medical school. It is the other ninety-nine percent of applicants, imperfect like you and me, who compete for the remaining slots.

The question of what is the "perfect" applicant also has no universal answer. Different medical schools, especially those with special missions or with novel curricula, have different criteria for choosing their medical students. If you don't believe that, see figure 14.2, a composite of the GPAs, MCAT scores, etc. of the students who *do* get into medical schools.

Figure 14.1: Positive and Negative Personal Attributes in Medical School Applicants

Positive Attributes

Self-motivation
  Positive attitude toward self-education
  Spirit of inquiry and curiosity
  Imagination and creativity

Compassion, tolerance, empathy, and patience

An appropriate view of the physician's changing roles
  Realistic expectations
  Tolerance of others' beliefs
  Ability to work as part of a team
  Willingness to subordinate one's own needs to those of patients
  Flexible outlook

Social responsibility
  Self-confidence
  Altruism

Intellectual honesty

Optimism

Maturity

Verbal communication ability

Negative Attributes

Neurotic

Rigid and intolerant of other ideas and people

Dishonest

Extreme traits
  Introvert/Extrovert
  Compulsive/Disorganized
  Obsessed/Poorly motivated
  Manic/Apathetic

Adapted from: Powis DA. Selecting medical students. *Medical Education* 1994;28:443-69.

Figure 14.2: The "Imperfect" (Real) Medical School Matriculant

Grade Point Average	• 3.5 on a 4.0 scale (mean)
MCAT Score	• 9.5 scores; "P" on Writing Sample (mean)
Experience	• Clinical: Recent • Research: Minimal or none (except those applying to combined-Ph.D. programs)
Reference Letters	• Excellent, from premed committee or adviser, undergraduate/graduate faculty, or clinicians • Say that applicant is personable, insightful, and understands what a medical career entails
Interview	• Articulate and outgoing • Demonstrates understanding of medical profession
Abilities	• Walks on land, swims through water, and falls through the air (will float gently over land after medical school and fall through the air a little slower after residency)

Having said that, I'll succumb to the temptation and list the criteria for the "perfect" applicant, knowing that such individuals exist in remarkably small numbers. See figure 14.3 for the qualities of those who "walk on water."

No one set of criteria, however, is acceptable to all medical school admission committees. In the end, the question is whether your qualities match those selection factors being sought by the schools to which you apply. The key is to read the schools' materials carefully and then apply to the schools that want people like you.

Figure 14.3: The "Perfect" Medical School Matriculant

Grade Point Average	• 3.9+ on a 4.0 scale
MCAT Score	• 13+ scores; "T" on Writing Sample
Experience	• Clinical: Recent and significant • Research: Published research related to medicine
Reference Letters	• From dynamic, well-known people • Say that applicant is personable, insightful, and understands what a medical career entails
Interview	• Articulate and personable • Demonstrates compassion and understanding
Abilities	• Walks on water, flies through the air, catches bullets with hands (will catch them in teeth after medical school and stop them by using telepathy after residency)

15: Picking The Right Schools

See one promontory, one mountain,
one sea, one river, and see all.

Socrates

M.D. and D.O. Schools in the United States and Canada

MEDICAL SCHOOLS DIFFER in their teaching methods, facilities, ambiance, costs, faculty, curricula, admission processes and requirements, reputations, special programs, locations, and the types of students they take. There are, however, more similarities than differences among them all. Some of factors you may want to consider before applying to specific schools are found in figures 15.1, 15.2, 15.3 and 15.4. Note that an empty box in figure 15.1 indicates that the school does not require that element for admission.

Figure 15.1: Medical School Admission Requirements—Courses
(The amount of each subject varies with individual schools.)

School	Biol	Gen Chem	Organ Chem	Physics	Math	English	Other
Alabama	E	L	L	L	●	C & Lit	
Alabama, South	L	L	L	L	Clc*	C/Lit	H
Albany	E,L	L	L	L			
Albert Einstein	L	L	L	L	●	●	H*,S*
Alberta+	●	●	●	●	St	●	
Allegheny UHS^c	L	L	L	L		●	B*
Arizona	E	●	●	●		C & Lit	
Arizona Osteo+	●	●	●	●		●	H,S,ψ
Arkansas	●	●	●	●	●	●	G*,Q*,ψ*
Baylor	L	L	L	L		●	
Boston	L	L	L	●	Clc*	C/Lit	H
Bowman Gray	●	●	●	●			
British Columbia+	●	●	●			L,C	B
Brown (prog)##	●	●	●	●	Clc,St		S,ψ,B
Calgary+	*	*	*	*	Clc*	*	B*,AB*,M*,S/ψ*
Calif.–Davis	L	L	●	●	Clc	●	
Calif.–Irvine	E	●	●	●	Clc		B
Calif.–San Diego	●	●	●	●	Clc/Cm/St	●	
Calif.–San Francisco	E,L	L	●	L			
Calif.–UCLA	●	L	L	L	Clc*	C	AB,Q,B*
Calif., Southern	L	L	L	L		C	M,S,H,St*,Cm*
Caribe^S	E	●	●	●	●	●	H/S/ψ,Sp
Case Western Res.	●	●	●	●		C	
Chicago–Pritzker	E,L	L	L	L			B*
Chicago Medical	E,L	L	L	L			O*
Chicago Osteo+	●	●	●	●		●	
Cincinnati	*	*	*	*	*		
Colorado	E,L	L	L	L	●	C & Lit	Clc*
Columbia	●	●	●	●		●	
Connecticut	E	L	L	L			
Cornell	E	●	●	●		C/Lit	AB*
Creighton	L	L	L	L		●	
Dalhousie+	*	*	*	*			S*,H*
Dartmouth	●	●	●	●	Clc		
Duke	●	●	●	●	Clc	●	B*
East Carolina	E,L	L	L	L		E	H*,S*
Emory	L	L	L	L		●	H/S/ψ,B*
Florida	L	L	L	L			B
Florida, South	L	L	L	L	●	●	
Geo. Washington	E,L	L	L	L		C & Lit	

Figure 15.1: Medical School Admission Requirements—Courses, cont'd.

School	Biol	Gen Chem	Organ Chem	Physics	Math	English	Other
Georgetown	L	L	L	L	●	●	B*,H*,Cm*
Georgia, Med. Coll.	L	L	L	L		●	B*
Harvard	L	L	L	●	Clc	C*	B*,M*
Hawaii	L	L		L			B,M,H*
Howard	E	●	●	●	●	●	
Illinois, Southern	E*	*	*	*	St*	C*	
Illinois, University of	*	*	*	*	Clc*		ψ*
Indiana	L	L	L	L			
Iowa	E,L	L	L	L	●	Lit*	Rh*,AB*,S*,ψ*
Jefferson	L	L	L	L	*		
Johns Hopkins	L	L	L	L	Clc		H,S,ψ
Kansas	L	L	L	L	Clc/St/Cm	●	B*,S*,H*
Kentucky	L	L	L	L		●	
Kirksville Osteo.♣	E,L	L	L	L		●	B*,A*
Lake Erie Osteo.♣	L	L	L	L		C,Lit	ψ
Laval+F	L	L	●	L	Clc		H,S,ψ,Fr
Loma Linda	E,L	L	L	L		●	
Louisville	L	L	L	L	●	●	
Loyola–Stritch	E,L	L	L	L			B*
LSU–New Orleans	E,L	L	L	L			
LSU–Shreveport	E,L	L	L	L		●	B
Manitoba+						C,Rh	S/ψ
Marshall	E,L	L	L	L		●	
Maryland	●	●	●	●		●	B*,Clc*,St*,S*,ψ*
Massachusetts	L	L	L	L			B
Mayo	E	●	●	L			M/B
McGill+	L	L	L	L			
McMaster+	+	+	+	+	+	+	+
Meharry	E,L	L	L	L		C,Lit	
Mercer	L	L	L	L			B*
Miami	E	L	L	L		●	B*,O
Michigan St. Osteo.♣	L	L	L	L		●	ψ,B*,A*,M*,G*
Michigan State	L	L	L	L		C,Lit	S/ψ
Michigan, University	L	L	L	L		C,Lit	B,H
Minnesota–Duluth	E,L	L	L	L	Clc/St	C	H,ψ,B*
Minnesota–Minneap.	E,L	L	L	L	Clc/St	●	B*,ψ*,G*,H*
Mississippi	E,L	L	L	L	●	●	AS,H*,ψ*
Missouri–Columbia	L	L	L	L	●	C	B*,H*,S*,Com*
Missouri–KS City	#	#	#	#	#	#	

Figure 15.1: Medical School Admission Requirements—Courses, cont'd.

School	Biol	Gen Chem	Organ Chem	Physics	Math	English	Other
Montréal⁺ᶠ	●	●	●	●	Clc	●	Fr,S,ψ,Phil
Morehouse	L	L	L	L	●	C	ψ*
Mount Sinai&	●	●	●	●	●	●	
Nebraska	L	L	L	L	Clc/St	C	H/S
Nevada	●	●	●	●	Cm*	C,Lit*	AB,ψ,H*,Phil*
New England Ost.*	L	L	L	L		C,Lit	
New Mexico	L	L	L	●	Clc*		B*,Sp*
New York Coll Ost.*	L	L	L	L		●	
New York Medical	L	L	L	L		●	
New York Univ.&	L	L	L	L		●	B*,AB*
Newfoundland⁺						●	
North Carolina	E,L	L	●	L		●	
North Dakota	E	●	●	●	●	C,Lit	S/ψ,Cm*
Northwestern	*	*	*	*		*	
Nova Univ. Osteo.*	L	L	L	L		C,Lit	
Ohio Osteo.*	●	●	●	●		●	
Ohio State	●	L	L	●			ψ,AB*
Ohio, Medical Coll.	●	●	●	●	●	●	
Ohio, Northeast. ##			●	●	●		AB*
Oklahoma	E,L	●	●	●	●	●	S/ψ/H,AB
Oklahoma St. Ost*	●	●	●	●		●	B*,M*,A*
Ontario, Western⁺	L		L		*		++++
Oregon	●	L	L	L		C	G*,H,S,B*
Ottawa⁺	E	●	●				B,H
Pacific Osteo.*	●	●	●	●		●	ψ
Pennsylvania State	●	●	●	●	●,Clc*,St*		H,ψ,G*,S*
Pennsylvania, Univ.	*	*	*	*	*	*	Com*
Philadelphia Ost.*	L	L	L	L		C,Lit	B*
Pittsburgh	L	L	L	L	*	C,Lit	H*,ψ*,S*
Ponce^S	●	●	●	●	●	●	H,Sp
Puerto Rico^S	●	L	L	L		●	S/ψ,Sp
Queen's⁺	●	+++	+++	+++			H/S
Rochester	L	●	●	L	Clc*, St*	C	B*,H/S/ψ
Rush	E	●	●	●			B*,H*
Saint Louis	E,L	L	L	L		●	H,ψ,B*
Saskatchewan⁺	L	L	●	L		L,C	H/S
Sherbrooke⁺ᶠ	L	L	L	L	Clc	L	Phil,S,ψ
South Carol., Med U	+	+	+	+	+	+	+
South Carol., Univ.	E,L	L	L	L	●	C,Lit	Clc*

196

Figure 15.1: Medical School Admission Requirements—Courses, cont'd.

School	Biol	Gen Chem	Organ Chem	Physics	Math	English	Other
South Dakota	E,L	L	L	L	●		Clc*,AB*,Cm*,G*
Stanford	L	L	L	L	Clc*		B*,P*,ψ*
SUNY–Brooklyn	L	L	L	L	*	●	B*,O*
SUNY–Buffalo	L	L	L	●		●	S*,H*
SUNY–Stony Brook	L	L	L	L		●	B*
SUNY–Syracuse	E,L	L	L	L		●	
Temple U.	L	L	L	L			H
Tennessee State, E.	L	L	L	L			Com
Tennessee, Univ. of	L	L	L	L		C,Lit	
Texas A&M	L	L	L	L	Clc	●	AB
Texas Coll Ost ♣	L	L	L	L		C	H/ψ
Texas Tech	E,L	L	L	L		●	
Texas, U–Galveston	L	L	L	L	Clc	●	H*
Texas, U–Houston	L	L	L	L	Clc	●	H*
Texas, U–San Anton	L	L	L	L	Clc	●	H*
Texas, U–Southwest	L	L	L	L	Clc	●	H*
Toronto ⊕	●				St*		H/S
Tufts	L	L	L	L			
Tulane	E,L	L	L	L		●	
UMDNJ-Coll Ost. ♣	L	L	L	L	●	C	ψ/S,H*,Phil*
UMDNJ-NJ Med	E,L	L	L	L	*	●	
UMDNJ-RWJ	E,L	L	L	L	●	C	
Uniformed Serv. U.	L	L	L	L	Clc	●	
Univ Health Sci Ost ♣	L	L	L		*	C, Lit	B*,G*,A*,S*,Phil*,ψ*
Univ. Ost. Med/Hlth ♣	L	L	L	L		C	B*
Utah	●	L	L	L		C/Com	M,H,S
Vanderbilt	E,L	L	L	L		C	
Vermont	E,L	L	L	L			
Virginia, Eastern	L	L	L	L			
Virginia, Med. Coll.	L	L	L	L	●	●	
Virginia, Univ. of	L	L	L	L			
Washington U. (MO)	●	●	●	●	Clc		
Washington, Univ of	●	++	++	●	*	*	O
Wayne State	E,L	L	L	L		●	
West Virginia	L	L	L	L		●	S/ψ,B*,M*
West Virginia Ost. ♣	E,L	L	L	L		●	B*,M*,A*,AB*
Wisconsin, Med Coll	L	L	L	●	●	C	
Wisconsin, Univ. of	E,L	L	L	L	Clc*	●*	AB,B*,H*,S*,Q*
Wright State	●	●	●	●	●	●	
Yale	E,L	L	L	L			

Figure 15.1: Medical School Admission Requirements—Courses, cont'd.

◇: Canadian medical school
♣: College of Osteopathic Medicine
◉: Non-U.S./non-Canadian medical school
F: Classes taught in French
S: Classes taught in Spanish
C: Formerly the Medical College of Pennsylvania/Hahnemann Medical Schools
&: New York University and Mt. Sinai are merging into a single medical school
L: Required with laboratory
●: Required
*: Recommended
/: Alternative courses (e.g., H/S = Humanities or Social Sciences)
ψ: Behavioral Sciences/Psychology
A: Anatomy
AB: Advanced Biology course
AS: Advanced Science course
B: Biochemistry
Clc: Calculus
C: Composition
Com: Communications Skills courses
Cm: Computer-literate or courses
E: Biology or Zoology
Fr: French language course
G: Genetics
H: Humanities
Lit: Literature
M: Molecular & Cellular Biology
O: Other sciences (Biology, Chemistry, or Physics)
P: Physical Chemistry
Phil: Philosophy
Q: Quantitative Analysis
Rh: Rhetoric
S: Social Sciences
Sp: Spanish language course
St: Statistics course
#: Only accepts high school graduates
##: Most students admitted directly from high school
+: No specific prerequisite courses for admission
++: Requires 12 semester-hours of Chemistry
+++: Any combination of Physical Sciences
++++: Other science courses

Information obtained from: Association of American Medical Colleges. *Medical School Admission Requirements, 1997-1998.* Washington, DC: AAMC, 1996; American Association of Colleges of Osteopathic Medicine. *1995 Annual Statistical Repor.t* Rockville, MD: AACOM, 1995; and other sources.

Figure 15.2: Medical School Admission Requirements—Other

School	AMCAS	Applic Deadline[1]	Early Dec Prog	Applic Fee ($)	% Out-of-State Stud	MCAT Req[++]	Bach Deg Req[+]
Alabama	●	Nov 1	●	65°	14	●	
Alabama, South	●	Nov 15	●	25°	11	●	●
Albany	●	Nov 15		70	61	●	
Albert Einstein	●	Nov 1	●	75	53	●	
Alberta[+]		Nov 1	●	60	9	●	
Allegheny UHS[C]	●	Dec 1	●	55	44		
Arizona	●	Nov 1		None	0*	●	
Arizona Osteo*	A	Feb 1		40°	NA	●	
Arkansas	●	Nov 15		10°	2	●	
Baylor		Nov 1	●	35	24		●
Boston	●	Nov 15	●	95	68	●	
Bowman Gray	●	Nov 1	●	55	44		●
British Columbia[+]		Dec 15		105/185◇	2	●	
Brown (prog)##		March 1		60	NA		
Calgary[+]		Nov 30		60	38	●	
Calif.–Davis	●	Nov 1		40°	3	●	●
Calif.–Irvine	●	Nov 1		40°	0	●	●
Calif.–San Diego	●	Nov 1		40°	7	●	●
Calif.–San Francisco	●	Nov 1		40°	23	●	●
Calif.–UCLA	●	Nov 1		40°	10	●	●
Calif., Southern	●	Nov 1	●	70	NA	●	
Caribe[S]	●	Dec 15	●	50	15	●	
Case Western Res.	●	Oct 15	●	60	40		●
Chicago–Pritzker	●	Nov 15	●	55°	60	●	●
Chicago Medical	●	Dec 15	●	65	72	●	●
Chicago Osteo*	A	Feb 1		40°	51	●	●
Cincinnati	●	Nov 15	●	25	18	●	●
Colorado	●	Nov 15	●	70	18	●	
Columbia		Oct 15		65	74	●	●
Connecticut	●	Dec 15	●	60	12	●	●
Cornell	●	Oct 15	●	65	40	●	●
Creighton	●	Dec 1	●	50	84	●	●
Dalhousie[+]		Nov 15		55	10	●	●
Dartmouth	●	Nov 1		55	87		●
Duke	●	Oct 15		55	68	●	●
East Carolina	●	Nov 15	●	35°	0	●	●
Emory	●	Oct 15		50	47	●	●
Florida	●	Dec 1		20°	5	●	●
Florida, South	●	Dec 1	●	20	0	●	●
Geo. Washington	●	Nov 1	●	55	88		

Figure 15.2: Medical School Admission Requirements—Other, cont'd.

School	AMCAS	Applic Deadline[1]	Early Dec Prog	Applic Fee ($)	% Out-of-State Stud	MCAT Req[++]	Bach Deg Req[+]
Georgetown	●	Nov 1		60	99		●
Georgia, Med. Coll.	●	Nov 1	●	None	2	●	
Harvard		Oct 15		70	92	●	●
Hawaii	●	Dec 1	●	50°	5	●	
Howard	●	Dec 15		25	96	●	
Illinois, Southern	●	Nov 15	●	50°	0		●
Illinois, University of	●	Dec 1	●	30°	6	●	●
Indiana	●	Dec 15	●	35°	6	●	●
Iowa	●	Nov 1	●	20°	13	●	●
Jefferson	●	Nov 15	●	65	59	●	
Johns Hopkins		Nov 1	●	60	86		●
Kansas	●	Oct 15	●	40◇	9	●	●
Kentucky	●	Nov 1	●	30°	5	●	●
Kirksville Osteo.♣	A	Feb 1	●	50°	89	●	
Lake Erie Osteo.♣	A	Feb 1		50°	57	●	
Laval+F		Feb 1		55	8		
Loma Linda	●	Nov 1	●	55	47	●	●
Louisville	●	Nov 1	●	15°	9		
Loyola–Stritch	●	Nov 15	●	50°	50	●	●
LSU–New Orleans	●	Nov 15	●	50°	0⌃	●	
LSU–Shreveport	●	Nov 15		50	0	●	
Manitoba✦		Nov 15		45	1	●	●
Marshall	●	Nov 15	●	30/50◇	6	●	
Maryland	●	Nov 1	●	40°	17	●	●
Massachusetts	●	Nov 1	●	50	0	●	●
Mayo	●	Nov 1	●	60	74✗	●	●
McGill +		Nov 15		60	21	●	●
McMaster +	O	Nov 1		150	6		
Meharry	●	Dec 15	●	25	89	●	
Mercer	●	Dec 1	●	25	0	●	●
Miami	●	Dec 1	●	50	1	●	
Michigan St. Osteo.♣	A	Dec 1	●	30+60°	28	●	
Michigan State	●	Nov 15	●	50	24		●
Michigan, University	●	Nov 15	●	50	39	●	●
Minnesota–Duluth	●	Nov 15	●	50°	12	●	●
Minnesota–Minneap.	●	Nov 15	●	50°	8		●
Mississippi	●	Nov 1	●	None	0	●	●
Missouri–Columbia	●	Nov 1	●	None	1		
Missouri–KS City		Nov 15		25/50◇	16		
Montréal+F		March 1		55	6		

Figure 15.2: Medical School Admission Requirements—Other, cont'd.

School	AMCAS	Applic Deadline[1]	Early Dec Prog	Applic Fee ($)	% Out-of-State Stud	MCAT Req[++]	Bach Deg Req[+]
Morehouse	●	Dec 1	●	45	26	●	
Mount Sinai[&]	●	Nov 1	●	100	37	●	●
Nebraska	●	Nov 15		25	0	●	
Nevada	●	Nov 1	●	45°	10	●	●
New England Ost.[♣]	A	Jan 2		55°	81	●	
New Mexico	●	Nov 15	●	25°	10	●	
New York Coll Ost.[♣]	A	Feb 1		60°	10	●	●
New York Medical	●	Dec 1	●	75	78	●	●
New York Univ.[&]		Dec 1		75	52	●	
Newfoundland[+]		Nov 15		50	20	●	
North Carolina	●	Nov 15	●	55	11	●	●
North Dakota		Nov 1		35	25[&]	●	●
Northwestern	●	Oct 15	●	50°	53	●	●
Nova Univ. Osteo.[♣]	A	Jan 15	●	50°	47	●	
Ohio Osteo.[♣]	A	Jan 2		25°	15	●	●
Ohio State	●	Nov 1	●	30	19	●	
Ohio, Medical Coll.	●	Nov 1	●	30	14	●	●
Ohio, Northeast. ##	●	Nov 1	●	30	4	●	
Oklahoma	●	Oct 15		50	11	●	
Oklahoma St. Ost[♣]	A	Dec 1		25°	27	●	
Ontario, Western [+]	O	Nov 1		150	19	●	●
Oregon	●	Oct 15		60	24	●	
Ottawa[+]	O	Nov 1		150	11	●	
Pacific Osteo. [♣]	A	Feb 1		50°	28	●	●
Pennsylvania State	●	Nov 15	●	40	52	●	
Pennsylvania, Univ.	●	Nov 1		55	73	●	
Philadelphia Ost.[♣]	A	Feb 1	●	25/50°◇	28	●	●
Pittsburgh	●	Nov 1	●	60	40	●	
Ponce[S]	●	Dec 15	●	50	23	●	
Puerto Rico[S]	●	Dec 1		15	1	●	
Queen's [+]	O	Nov 1		150	20	●	
Rochester		Oct 15		65	65		●
Rush	●	Nov 15	●	45	13	●	
Saint Louis	●	Dec 15	●	100	72	●	●
Saskatchewan[+]		Dec 1		40/75◇	2	FUT	
Sherbrooke[+F]		March 1		30	10		●
South Carol., Med U	●	Dec 1	●	45	9		●
South Carol., Univ.	●	Dec 1	●	20	11	●	●
South Dakota	●	Nov 15		15	20	●	●
Stanford	●	Nov 1	●	55°	44	●	●

Figure 15.2: Medical School Admission Requirements—Other, cont'd.

School	AMCAS	Applic Deadline[1]	Early Dec Prog	Applic Fee ($)	% Out-of-State Stud	MCAT Req[++]	Bach Deg Req[+]
SUNY–Brooklyn	●	Dec 15	●	65	4	●	●
SUNY–Buffalo	●	Nov 1	●	65	1	●	●
SUNY–Stony Brook	●	Nov 15	●	65	8	●	●
SUNY–Syracuse	●	Nov 1	●	60	5	●	●
Temple U.	●	Dec 1	●	55	43	●	●
Tennessee State, E.	●	Dec 1	●	25	10	●	
Tennessee, Univ. of	●	Nov 15		25	6	●	
Texas A&M		Nov 1		45	2	●	
Texas Coll Ost *	A	Dec 1	●	NA	8	●	●
Texas Tech		Nov 1	●	40	1	●	
Texas, U–Galveston	T	Oct 15		45/80◇	5	●	
Texas, U–Houston	T	Oct 15		45/80◇	8	●	
Texas, U–San Anton	T	Oct 15		45/80◇	5	●	
Texas, U–Southwest	T	Oct 15		45/80◇	12	●	
Toronto+	O	Nov 1		150	17	●	
Tufts	●	Nov 1	●	75	70	●	●
Tulane	●	Dec 15	●	95	77	●	
UMDNJ-Coll Ost. *	A	Feb 1		50°	9	●	●
UMDNJ-NJ Med	●	Dec 1	●	50	94	●	
UMDNJ-RWJ	●	Dec 1	●	50	13	●	●
Uniformed Serv. U.	●	Nov 1		None	NA	●	●
Univ Health Sci Ost*	A	Feb 1		35°	85	●	
Univ. Ost. Med/Hlth*	A	Feb 1		50°	84	●	●
Utah	●	Oct 15	●	50	25	●	●
Vanderbilt	●	Oct 15	●	50	91		●
Vermont	●	Nov 1	●	70	68	●	●
Virginia, Eastern	●	Nov 15	●	80	24		●
Virginia, Med. Coll.	●	Nov 15	●	75	68		●
Virginia, Univ. of	●	Nov 1		50	29	●	●
Washington U. (MO)	●	Nov 15		50	90	●	●
Washington, Univ of	●	Nov 1		35	8	●	●
Wayne State	●	Dec 15	●	30	7	●	●
West Virginia	●	Nov 15	●	30	3	●	●
West Virginia Ost. *	A	Feb 1		35/75°◇	18	●	
Wisconsin, Med Coll	●	Nov 1	●	60	54	●	
Wisconsin, Univ. of	●	Nov 1	●	38	17		●
Wright State	●	Nov 15	●	30	13	●	●
Yale		Oct 15	●	55	89	●	●

Figure 15.2: Medical School Admission Requirements—Other, cont'd.

⁺: Canadian medical school
ᵃ: College of Osteopathic Medicine
ᶠ: Classes taught in French
ˢ: Classes taught in Spanish
ᶜ: Formerly the Medical College of Pennsylvania/Hahnemann Medical Schools
&: New York University and Mt. Sinai are merging into a single medical school
1: Latest due date for primary application. Some Canadian schools have later dates for in-Province applicants.
●: Required
◇: Fee for non-residents
◔: Fee requested after application screened
◈: Includes INMED program, Minnesota, and WICHE applicants who are actually considered as "in-State"
✕: Minnesota, Arizona, and Florida residents considered "in-State"
∧: Students from special program with Univ. of New Orleans considered "in-State"
*: WICHE applicants considered "in-State" (Alaska, Montana, Wyoming)
**: WAMI applicants considered "in-State" (Alaska, Montana, Idaho)
++: MCAT not required of students entering accelerated programs
+: At many schools that do not require Bachelor's degrees, 95% to 99% of entrants have such a degree (except for students in accelerated programs).
##: Most students admitted directly from high school
A: Osteopathic school requiring the AACOMAS application
NA: Data not available
O: Application through the Ontario Medical School Application Service (OMSAS)
T: Application through the University of Texas System Medical and Dental Application Center
FUT: MCAT may be required for 1998-99

Information obtained from: Association of American Medical Colleges. *Medical School Admission Requirements, 1997-1998.* Washington, DC: AAMC, 1996; American Association of Colleges of Osteopathic Medicine. *1995 Annual Statistical Repor.t* Rockville, MD: AACOM, 1995; and other sources.

Figure 15.3: Medical School Specifics

| School | TUITION ($) | | Fees ($) | Class Size | Start Date | Deferred Accept[э] |
	In-State	Out-of-State				
Alabama	5,708	17,124	2,159	165	Aug	●
Alabama, South	5,808	11,616	567	64	Aug	6/1-R
Albany	24,074	25,346	None	135	Aug	●
Albert Einstein	24,550	24,550	1,200	180	Aug	6/1-R
Alberta[+]	3,885[C]	8,120[CX&]	350[C]	103	Aug	●
Allegheny UHS[C]	22,500	22,500	500	240	Aug	●
Arizona[N]	6,960	——	66	100	July	4/15
Arizona Osteo[♣]	20,800	20,800	NA	100	Sept	
Arkansas	7,334	14,688	783	143	Aug	7/15
Baylor	6,550	19,650	1,559	168	Aug	●
Boston	30,300	30,300	375	135	Aug	
Bowman Gray	18,500	18,500	None	108	Aug	●
British Columbia[+]	3,937[C]	3,937[C]	243[C]	120	Aug	●
Brown (prog)##	23,840	23,840	1,603	62	Sept	●
Calgary[+]	4,512[C]	9,024[CX]	323[C]	69	Aug	
Calif.–Davis	None	7,699	7,837	93	Sept	6/15
Calif.–Irvine	None	7,699	8,282	92	Sept	7/15
Calif.–San Diego	None	7,699	8,239	122	Sept	7/1
Calif.–San Francisco	None	7,699	7,696	141	Sept	5/1
Calif.–UCLA	None	7,699	7,864	145	Aug	5/1
Calif., Southern	26,520	26,520	1,232	150	Aug	6/1
Caribe[S]	17,800	24,000	789	60	Aug	
Case Western Res.	23,100	23,100	790	138	Aug	5/15
Chicago–Pritzker	21,660	21,660	1,645	104	Sept	7/1
Chicago Medical	29,106	29,106	100	166	July	●-R
Chicago Osteo[♣]	16,620	20,200	NA	150		●
Cincinnati	10,533	18,861	504	160	Aug	●-R
Colorado	10,382	47,794	1,768	129	Aug	●-R
Columbia	23,740	23,740	1,597	150	Aug	●
Connecticut	8,050	18,400	3,300	81	Aug	6/1-R
Cornell	22,365	22,365	560	101	Aug	6/1
Creighton	23,434	23,434	402	112	Aug	●
Dalhousie[+]	4,725[C]	7,425[CX]	229[C]	86	Aug	●
Dartmouth	22,810	22,810	3,900	91	Aug	6/15
Duke	22,400	22,400	1,341	101	Aug	6/15
East Carolina	1,952	20,466	833	72	Aug	
Emory	20,280	20,280	430	114	July	5/15
Florida	8,173[&]	21,172[&]	NA	85	Aug	●
Florida, South	7,142	20,141	1,120	96	Aug	●
Geo. Washington	30,200	30,200	732	158	Aug	●

Figure 15.3: Medical School Specifics, cont'd.

School	TUITION ($)		Fees ($)	Class Size	Start Date	Deferred Accept⊃
	In-State	Out-of-State				
Georgetown	23,625	23,625	None	165	Aug	7/15
Georgia, Med. Coll.	4,755	14,976	249	180	Aug	6/1
Harvard	23,200	23,200	1,519	165	Sept	6/1
Hawaii	5,996	21,030	87	56	Aug	●
Howard	14,400	14,400	788	111	Aug	●
Illinois, Southern	10,035	30,105	1,260	72	Aug	●
Illinois, University of	9,520	27,740	1,218	317	Aug	8/1
Indiana	9,990	22,866	187	280	Aug	●
Iowa	8,428	22,248	172	175	Aug	●
Jefferson	24,500	24,500	None	223	Aug	8/1
Johns Hopkins	21,800	21,800	1,828	119	Sept	51
Kansas	8,572	20,756	230	175	Aug	7/15
Kentucky	8,479	18,699	389	95	Aug	6/1-R
Kirksville Osteo. ♣	21,300	21,300	1,000	145	Aug	●-R
Lake Erie Osteo. ♣	20,400	20,400	600	100	Aug	
Laval ♣F	1,964^C	7,696^C	200^C	137	Sept	
Loma Linda	22,788	22,788	None	159	Aug	●
Louisville	8,300	18,520	0	137	Aug	●
Loyola–Stritch	25,600	25,600	409	130	July	6/1-R
LSU–New Orleans	6,776	14,676	150	175	Aug	●
LSU–Shreveport	6,776	14,676	151	101	Aug	●
Manitoba ♣	4,197^C	4,197^C	41^C	69	Aug	
Marshall	7,784	18,210	450	49	Aug	4/15-R
Maryland	10,751	20,851	1,833	146	Aug	●-R
Massachusetts[N]	8,792	——	1,720	100	Aug	71-R
Mayo	9,925♣	19,800	None	42	Aug	5/15
McGill ♣	1,845^C	7,635^C	823^C	119	Aug	●
McMaster ♣	5,012^C	22,936^{CX}	None	100	Aug	●
Meharry	16,500	16,500	1,896	80	June	●
Mercer[N]	18,890	——	None	55	Aug	
Miami	23,040	23,040	110	138	Aug	
Michigan St. Osteo. ♣	14,058	29,904	NA	125	Aug	
Michigan State	14,556	31,038	856	104	Aug	●
Michigan, University	16,040	25,140	176	165	Aug	●
Minnesota–Duluth	14,616	29,112	586	50	Aug	8/15
Minnesota–Minneap.	14,616	29,112	586	185	Sept	●
Mississippi	6,600	12,600	115	100	Aug	●
Missouri–Columbia	13,216	26,579	528	92	Aug	●
Missouri–KS City	12,460	25,654	480	104	Aug	
Montréal ♣F	2,260^C	7,455^C	30^C	161	Sept	

Figure 15.3: Medical School Specifics, cont'd.

School	TUITION ($) In-State	TUITION ($) Out-of-State	Fees ($)	Class Size	Start Date	Deferred Accept⊃
Morehouse	15,750	15,750	1,933	35	July	●
Mount Sinai[&]	21,000	21,000	825	115	Aug	●
Nebraska	10,500	20,300	1,141	119	Aug	
Nevada	6,821	17,976	1,894	52	Aug	●
New England Ost.[♣]	19,075	19,075	NA	80	Sept	
New Mexico	4,867	13,954	32	73	Aug	●
New York Coll Ost.[♣]	18,250	18,250	NA	180		No
New York Medical	25,150	25,150	465	188	Aug	●
New York Univ.[&]	20,900	20,900	3,720	159	Sept	●
Newfoundland[+]	2,312[C]	30,000[C]	200[C]	60	Sept	●
North Carolina	1,952	20,466	733	160	Aug	6/15
North Dakota	8,460	22,588	318	57	Aug	4/15
Northwestern	25,446	25,446	None	174	Sept	●
Nova Univ. Osteo.[♣]	15,800	19,950	NA	150	Aug	No
Ohio Osteo.[♣]	8,907	13,014	NA	100	Sept	8/1
Ohio State	9,174	26,460	234	210	Aug	●
Ohio, Medical Coll.	9,534	12,963	279	135	Aug	●
Ohio, Northeast. ##	9,717	19,434	699	25	Aug	
Oklahoma	7,550	18,658	325	149	Aug	
Oklahoma St. Ost[♣]	6,567	16,226	NA	88	Aug	No
Ontario, Western [+]	3,496[C]	3,496[C]	None	96	Sept	
Oregon	13,466	28,339	2,997	96	Sept	
Ottawa[+]	3,116[C]	14,670[CX]	239[C]	84	Sept	●
Pacific Osteo. [♣]	19,060	19,060	630	176	Aug	●
Pennsylvania State	15,708	22,615	1,048	119	Aug	●
Pennsylvania, Univ.	24,530	24,530	1,183	151	Aug	5/15
Philadelphia Ost.[♣]	20,500	20,500	NA	250	Aug	No
Pittsburgh	18,170	24,300	415	139	Aug	●
Ponce[S]	16,973	25,304	1,813	60	July	
Puerto Rico[S]	5,500	10,500	580	115	Aug	
Queen's [+]	3,118[C]	14,402[CX]	539[C]	75	Sept	●
Rochester	22,700	22,700	1,680	99	Aug	●
Rush	22,944	22,944	1,536	120	Sept	●
Saint Louis	24,200	24,200	1,024	152	Aug	●
Saskatchewan[+]	5,000[C]	5,000[C]	105[C]	55	Aug	●
Sherbrooke[+F]	2,942[C]	11,624[CX]	None	91	Aug	
South Carol., Med U	6,496	17,416	2,796	138	Aug	●
South Carol., Univ.	7,290	18,620	25	72	Aug	●
South Dakota	8,841	19,687	2,841	50	Aug	●
Stanford	24,375	24,375	607	86	Sept	6/15

Figure 15.3: Medical School Specifics, cont'd.

School	TUITION ($)		Fees ($)	Class Size	Start Date	Deferred Accept^ɔ
	In-State	Out-of-State				
SUNY–Brooklyn	10,840	21,940	220	186	Aug	●
SUNY–Buffalo	10,840	21,940	350	135	Aug	●
SUNY–Stony Brook	10,840	21,940	130	100	Aug	●
SUNY–Syracuse	10,840	21,940	215	148	Aug	6/1
Temple U.	19,416	24,555	358	187	Aug	●
Tennessee State, E.	8,750	15,468	408	60	Aug	7/1-R
Tennessee, Univ. of	8,690	16,120	858	165	Aug	7/15
Texas A&M	6,550	19,650	1,400	64	Aug	●
Texas Coll Ost ♣	6,550	19,650	NA	100	Aug	6/1
Texas Tech	6,550	19,650	1,101	116	Aug	●-R
Texas, U–Galveston	6,550	19,650	427	200	Aug	●
Texas, U–Houston	6,550	19,650	250	200	Aug	
Texas, U–San Anton	6,550	19,650	375	201	Aug	
Texas, U–Southwest	6,550	19,650	696	199	Aug	●
Toronto ✦	3,883^{C&}	16,369^{CX&}	—	172	Sept	●
Tufts	28,800	28,800	330	176	Aug	●-R
Tulane	25,791	25,791	1,341	144	Aug	●
UMDNJ-Coll Ost. ♣	12,795	16,791	NA	75	Aug	●
UMDNJ-NJ Med	13,295	17,445	1,100	170	Aug	
UMDNJ-RWJ	13,295	17,445	1,187	138	Aug	715
Uniformed Serv. U.	0	0	None	165	July	●
Univ Health Sci Ost♣	19,740	19,740	NA	180	Aug	
Univ. Ost. Med/Hlth♣	20,000	20,000	NA	205	Sept	
Utah	6,927	14,760	435	100	Sept	
Vanderbilt	20,000	20,000	1,202	103	Aug	●
Vermont	14,150	26,650	535	93	Aug	7/1
Virginia, Eastern	13,000	23,000	1,283	101	Aug	●
Virginia, Med. Coll.	9,552	23,317	1,008	174	Aug	7/1
Virginia, Univ. of	8,484	20,458	922	139	Aug	6/1
Washington U. (MO)	25,170	25,170	None	122	Aug	6/15
Washington, Univ of	7,752	19,686	None	120	Sept	●
Wayne State	9,566	19,061	350	247	Aug	
West Virginia	7,980[&]	19,714[&]	NA	88	Aug	●
West Virginia Ost. ♣	8,400	20,654	NA	65	Aug	No
Wisconsin, Med Coll	12,894	22,985	35	204	Aug	7/1-R
Wisconsin, Univ. of	13,041	18,895	None	143	Aug	●
Wright State	12,244	17,332	672	90	Aug	●-R
Yale	23,300	23,300	175	101	Sept	7/15

Figure 15.3: Medical School Specifics, cont'd.

✧: Canadian medical school
♣: College of Osteopathic Medicine
●: Non-U.S./non-Canadian medical school
♣: College of Osteopathic Medicine
●: Tuition is listed for comparison only, it changes yearly
F: Classes taught in French
S: Classes taught in Spanish
C: Formerly the Medical College of Pennsylvania/Hahnemann Medical Schools
&: New York University and Mt. Sinai are merging into a single medical school
N: Do not take out of state students, so have no listed out-of-state tuition.
##: Most students admitted directly from high school

R: Restrictions on reapplication.
Ↄ: Date by which deferred acceptance must be requested
◈: Non-resident
✦: Applicants from AZ, FL, and MN considered "in-State"
&: Tuition plus fees
C: Canadian dollars
X: Non-Canadians

Information obtained from: Association of American Medical Colleges. *Medical School Admission Requirements, 1997-1998.* Washington, DC: AAMC, 1996; American Association of Colleges of Osteopathic Medicine. *1995 Annual Statistical Repor.t* Rockville, MD: AACOM, 1995; and other sources.

Figure 15.4: Medical School Admission Requirements—Grades, etc.

School	Applicants		% of Applicants Interviewed		Accepted Students		
	In-State	Out-of-State	In-State	Out-of-State	Mean GPA	Mean MCAT*	% Women
Alabama	578	1,738	70	9	3.6	29.0	40
Alabama, South	550	957	41	1	3.6	28.4	40
Albany	2,496	7,596	11	8	3.5	29.7	50
Albert Einstein	2,385	6,750	23	18	3.5	30.0	47
Alberta[+]	400	416	58	28	NA	NA	NA
Allegheny UHS[C]	1,442	12,160	29	7	3.5	28.8	43
Arizona	540	602	95	2[W]	3.6	28.2	53
Arizona Osteo[+]	New[G]	New[G]	New[G]	New[G]	3.4	26.0	31
Arkansas	400	505	94	3	3.5	25.4	40
Baylor	1,473	1,750	34	10	3.7	33.0	40
Boston	774	10,989	32	9	3.3	27.3	40
Bowman Gray	830	7,457	32	4	3.4	29.1	41
British Columbia[+]	497	210	71	2	NA	NA	NA
Brown (prog)##	NA	NA	NA	NA	H	H	60
Calgary[+]	367	518	25	19	3.6	29.7	54
Calif.–Davis	4,612	879	NA	NA	3.5	33.0	42
Calif.–Irvine	4,656	533	NA	NA	3.6	30.9	41
Calif.–San Diego	4,178	1,386	NA	NA	3.7	33.0	45
Calif.–San Francisco	3,221	2,665	NA	NA	3.7	33.0	51
Calif.–UCLA	4,266	1,845	16	15	3.7	31.5	38
Calif., Southern	4,346	2,142	NA	NA	3.5	30.0	42
Caribe[S]	435	644	43	3	3.1	18.0	47
Case Western Res.	1,168	6,540	35	7	3.5	30.0	44
Chicago–Pritzker	1,165	7,242	12	5	3.6	30.9	50
Chicago Medical	1,342	11,456	11	5	3.3	27.0	40
Chicago Osteo[+]	605	4429	34	5	3.3	24.0	40
Cincinnati	1,489	3,730	30	5	3.5	28.5	33
Colorado	755	2,320	69	11	3.6	29.1	43
Columbia	1,009	3,257	33	35	3.5	32.1	41
Connecticut	446	2,890	61	4	3.5	29.0	52
Cornell	1,747	5,682	49	7	3.5[#]	30.9	50
Creighton	273	8,799	NA	NA	3.7	26.4	32
Dalhousie[+]	200	392	78	10	NA	NA	NA
Dartmouth	80	7,966	33	6	3.6	28.8	41
Duke	480	7,013	NA	NA	3.6	32.4	46
East Carolina	981	990	66	<1	3.3	24.4	51
Emory	716	7,896	29	8	3.7	29.5	45
Florida	1,449	1,105	24	2	3.7	28.0	52

Figure 15.4: Medical School Admission Requirements—Grades, etc., cont'd.

School	Applicants		% of Applicants Interviewed		Accepted Students		
	In-State	Out-of-State	In-State	Out-of-State	Mean GPA	Mean MCAT*	% Women
Florida, South	1,433	560	26	0	3.7	28.9	34
Geo. Washington	81	12,290	43	8	3.4	28.2	54
Georgetown	62	12,386	NA	NA	3.6	30.0	42
Georgia, Med. Coll.	978	933	48	3	3.5	28.2	35
Harvard	698	3,216	31	26	3.8	34.3	51
Hawaii	259	1,372	69	4	3.6	28.5	53
Howard	67	6,094	19	8	3.0	21.0	52
Illinois, Southern	1,439	665	16	<1	3.5	26.4	45
Illinois, University of	2,123	4,532	X	X	3.4	27.9	35
Indiana	739	2,385	94	9	3.7	28.2	40
Iowa	368	3,145	41	<1	3.6	28.2	45
Jefferson	1,407	10,287	NA	NA	3.4[#]	29.7	34
Johns Hopkins	339	3,371	22	19	3.7	33.0	53
Kansas	445	2,029	81	4	3.6	27.3	39
Kentucky	555	1,743	53	4	3.6	27.0	38
Kirksville Osteo.♣	212	4,365	15	10	3.4	29.0	33
Lake Erie Osteo.♣	206	1,831	48	52	3.2	23.1	38
Laval+F	1,598	102	19	28	NA	NA	NA
Loma Linda	2,572	2,480	NA	NA	3.6	26.7	48
Louisville	548	1,419	46	3	3.6	26.7	47
Loyola–Stritch	1,676	8,670	13	4	3.5	28.5	45
LSU–New Orleans	891	521	45	<1	3.4	25.8	38
LSU–Shreveport	783	294	27	0	3.5	26.4	33
Manitoba+	178	207	81	6	NA	NA	NA
Marshall	305	1,159	83	2	3.4	24.6	24
Maryland	1,078	3,567	34	5	3.5	27.0	50
Massachusetts	930	596	45	0	3.5[#]	30.0	53
Mayo	423	3,482	13	11	3.7	30.0	46
McGill+	757	245	32	43	3.5	32.3	49
McMaster+	1,714	624	21	7	3.5	NA	59
Meharry	268	5,280	12	7	3.1	22.5	45
Mercer	733	738	56	0	3.3	25.8	44
Miami	1,406	1,867	22	<1	3.6	29.8	51
Michigan St. Osteo.♣	NA	NA	NA	NA	3.2	24.0	41
Michigan State	1,266	2,453	23	6	3.4	27.9	52
Michigan, University	1,123	4,750	28	7	3.6	32.1	40
Minnesota–Duluth	609	996	31	3	3.6	27.7	48

Figure 15.4: Medical School Admission Requirements—Grades, etc., cont'd.

School	Applicants		% of Applicants Interviewed		Accepted Students		
	In-State	Out-of-State	In-State	Out-of-State	Mean GPA	Mean MCAT*	% Women
Minnesota–Minneap.	816	2,101	70	6	3.6	29.1	48
Mississippi	308	322	68	0	3.6	27.0	29
Missouri–Columbia	572	761	45	<1	3.6	27.9	49
Missouri–KS City	419	348	66	26	H	H	59
Montréal[+F]	2,057	146	22	26	NA	NA	NA
Morehouse	400	2,530	32	45	3.0	21.0	55
Mount Sinai[&]	1,747	3,671	25	12	3.5	27.3	51
Nebraska	399	1,255	100	4	3.6	27.6	38
Nevada	241	981	71	3	3.6	28.2	40
New England Ost.[♣]	NA	NA	NA	NA	3.2	22.5	38
New Mexico	352	931	98	2	3.5	27.0	63
New York Coll Ost.[♣]	1100	3500	50	5	3.3	23.6	41
New York Medical	2,581	9,708	13	11	3.3	30.0	33
New York Univ.[&]	NA	NA	NA	NA	3.6	32.1	42
Newfoundland[+]	132	425	79	21	NA	NA	NA
North Carolina	1,042	2,378	72	4	3.4	27.0	50
North Dakota	145	177	68	28[☑]	3.6	26.6	42
Northwestern	1,371	8,151	14	4	3.5	29.1	51
Nova Univ. Osteo.[♣]	720	3110	62	38	3.4	26.0	40
Ohio Osteo.[♣]	547	3429	24	2	3.4	25.6	44
Ohio State	1,376	4,535	32	5	3.5	30.6	34
Ohio, Medical Coll.	1,349	3,469	37	6	3.5	27.5	39
Ohio, Northeast. ##	767	611	14	2	3.6	27.3	44
Oklahoma	477	1,224	66	5	3.6	27.6	42
Oklahoma St. Ost[♣]	365	1999	60	3	3.5	26.2	32
Ontario, Western [+]	1,201	572	NA	NA	3.5	25.0	NA
Oregon	394	1,689	57	8	3.6	29.7	45
Ottawa[+]	1,123	534	NA	NA	NA	NA	NA
Pacific Osteo.[♣]	1074	2933	NA	NA	3.2	23.5	31
Pennsylvania State	1,385	5,900	NA	NA	3.6	27.3	45
Pennsylvania, Univ.	1,004	7,923	15	12	3.6	32.1	39
Philadelphia Ost.[♣]	790	4694	46	4	3.3	23.3	44
Pittsburgh	1,233	5,454	21	11	3.6	31.5	43
Ponce[S]	368	606	48	5	3.3	18.3	45
Puerto Rico[S]	365	619	41	1	3.5	22.0	53
Queen's [+]	910	502	26	35	3.5[A]	32.3	NA
Rochester	1,082	2,877	20	17	3.5	26.4	40

211

Figure 15.4: Medical School Admission Requirements—Grades, etc., cont'd.

School	Applicants		% of Applicants Interviewed		Accepted Students		
	In-State	Out-of-State	In-State	Out-of-State	Mean GPA	Mean MCAT*	% Women
Rush	1,736	3,891	23	3	3.4	27.3	43
Saint Louis	398	4,909	46	23	3.7	30.0	36
Saskatchewan+	205	196	85	9	86[P]	NR	58
Sherbrooke+F	1,592	139	5	5	3.8	NR	NA
South Carol., Med U	498	2,919	62	3	3.4	27.0	45
South Carol., Univ.	398	1,480	53	9	3.4	27.0	41
South Dakota	115	1,135	100	5	3.6	26.1	42
Stanford	2,858	4,148	10	8	3.6	32.0	42
SUNY–Brooklyn	2,818	3,323	25	3	3.5	27.9	42
SUNY–Buffalo	2,817	969	16	2	3.6	29.4	47
SUNY–Stony Brook	2,887	1,095	NA	NA	3.5	30.0	40
SUNY–Syracuse	2,884	1,205	19	10	3.5	27.3	49
Temple U.	1,409	7,375	30	7	3.4[#]	28.2	41
Tennessee State, E.	637	1,453	35	6	3.4	27.4	50
Tennessee, Univ. of	723	1,614	46	4	3.5	27.0	35
Texas A&M	1,382	137	34	8	3.7	28.8	38
Texas Coll Ost +	848	1371	42	3	3.4	25.1	42
Texas Tech	1,579	17	22	12	3.5	27.9	24
Texas, U–Galveston	2,601	615	46	27	3.5	27.9	46
Texas, U–Houston	2,618	745	40	7	3.4	26.1	55
Texas, U–San Anton	2,722	553	32	24	3.4	27.9	43
Texas, U–Southwest	2,521	833	26	15	3.6	30.9	38
Toronto+	1,136	411	NA	NA	3.5[A]	NA	NA
Tufts	788	10,746	23	6	3.5	27.6	41
Tulane	618	10,528	22	7	3.5	30.0	43
UMDNJ-Coll Ost. +	543	2,668	33	2	3.5	25.1	51
UMDNJ-NJ Med	1,410	2,911	38	9	3.4	28.8	30
UMDNJ-RWJ	1,452	3,184	41	5	3.5	28.2	44
Uniformed Serv. U.✪	3,238		17		3.5	30.3	30
Univ Health Sci Ost+	226	4,583	42	6	3.5	24.8	37
Univ. Ost. Med/Hlth+	134	4,356			3.3	24.3	32
Utah	436	973	68	15	3.5	31.5	33
Vanderbilt	332	6,556	15	11	3.7	33.0	29
Vermont	86	8,561	70	5	3.3	27.0	41
Virginia, Eastern	1,075	6,279	28	4	3.3	27.0	51
Virginia, Med. Coll.	1,183	4,114	37	10	3.5	28.8	34

Figure 15.4: Medical School Admission Requirements—Grades, etc., cont'd.

School	Applicants		% of Applicants Interviewed		Accepted Students		
	In-State	Out-of-State	In-State	Out-of-State	Mean GPA	Mean MCAT*	% Women
Virginia, Univ. of	1,041	4,395	23	5	3.5	30.6	48
Washington U. (MO)	301	6,713	20	14	3.8	34.2	51
Washington, Univ of	975	2,948	70	3	3.6	30.4	47
Wayne State	1,417	2,992	47	6	3.5	26.7	43
West Virginia	278	1,514	85	3	3.6	27.2	45
West Virginia Ost. *	258	2165	94	4	3.3	20.2	40
Wisconsin, Med Coll	525	7,247	34	5	3.5	27.0	37
Wisconsin, Univ. of	635	2,399	27	2	3.6	28.5	49
Wright State	1,341	2,332	29	2	3.5	24.0	52
Yale	146	3,286	23	23	3.6	33.0	56

✦: Canadian medical school
♣: College of Osteopathic Medicine
F: Classes taught in French
S: Classes taught in Spanish
C: Formerly the Medical College of Pennsylvania/Hahnemann Medical Schools
&: New York University and Mt. Sinai are merging into a single medical school

*: Mean MCAT = total of three numerical scores
NA: Not Available
W: Certified WICHE applicants from Alaska, Montana, Wyoming
G: New school in 1996. Future plan is for 50% of class to be from Arizona. Percentage of interviewed applicants
    expected to be similar to Chicago College of Osteopathic Medicine
✦: Percentage of class; percentage interviewed not available
X: This school does not conduct interviews
#: Science GPA
A: lowest GPA of applicants considered for acceptance
H: Students accepted from high school
☑: Includes INMED, MN, and certified WICHE applicants
◐: Considers residents of all states and territories equally
P: Grades calculated on 100-point scale
NR: MCAT not required

Information obtained from: Association of American Medical Colleges. *Medical School Admission Requirements, 1997-1998.* Washington, DC: AAMC, 1996; American Association of Colleges of Osteopathic Medicine. *1995 Annual Statistical Repor.t* Rockville, MD: AACOM, 1995; and other sources.

Figure 15.5: Medical School Application Information

School	% 2° Appl. In-State /Other	Recom. Letters	AP Credit OK?	Last MCAT Date	Transfers Accepted? Into Which Years?	Admit Non-U.S. Citizen /Non-Perm Resident	When Fin. Aid Info Sent?
Alabama[R]	●	C+2	Yes	2 Yr	M,D,O^Σ	Rare	April
Alabama, South	●/20	C/5L	+/-	3 Yr	M,D,I^Σ	No	Accept
Albany	100	C/2L	Yes[S]	?	Rare	Yes	Jan
Albert Einstein	100	C/2L	Yes[S]	?	No	Yes	Spring
Alberta[◆]	No 2°	2L	NA	New	M→2,3	Non-Can	Accept
Allegheny UHS[CR]	NA	C+A+L/L	Yes	2 Yr	M→2,3,O	Yes	Feb
Arizona	●	C+2/3L	No	2 Yr	$Rare^\Sigma$	No	Jan
Arizona Osteo[♣]	100	C+L(D)/A+L(D)	NA	New	D→3	Yes	Intvw
Arkansas	●	C/3L	Yes[S]	3 Yr	No	Rare	Accept
Baylor	No 2°	C+2L/A+2L	Yes[S]	5 Yr	M→3	Yes	NA
Boston	No 2°	C/3L	No	3 Yr	M,D,I[ﬁ]→2,3	No	Accept
Bowman Gray	50	C/A+L/2L	+/-	3 Yr	M→2,3	Yes	April
British Columbia[◆]	No 2°	NA	NA	New	M	No	NA
Brown (prog)##	No 2°	C+L/A+L	Yes	NA	M,D,I,O^Σ→3	Yes	NA
Calgary[◆]	No 2°	3L	NA	New	M→3	Non-Can	Accept
Calif.–Davis	20/5	Inst	Yes[S]	3 Yr	No	Rare	Jan
Calif.–Irvine[R]	25/0	2-6L	Yes	3 Yr	No	NA	Intvw
Calif.–San Diego	20	C+1L/3L	Yes[S]	3 Yr	No	Yes	NA
Calif.–San Fran.[R]	25	A+2L/3L	Yes	2 Yr	No	Rare	May
Calif.–UCLA	No 2°	C+3-5L/A+3L	No	2 Yr	M→3	Yes	NA
Calif., Southern	100	C/2L	Yes	2 Yr	M→3,O	Yes	NA
Caribe[S]	100	C/L	Yes	3 Yr	M,D,I→2,3	Yes	Accept
Case Western Res.	50	C/3-5L	Yes[S]	2 Yr	M→3	Yes	Intvw
Chicago–Pritzker	100	C or A/3L	Yes[S]	?	M	Yes	March
Chicago Medical	100	C/3L	+/-	3 Yr	M,D,I→2/3,O	Yes	Accept
Chicago Osteo[♣]	100	C/2L(D)	Yes[S]	3 Yr	D→3	Yes	Intevw
Cincinnati[R]	●/NA	Inst	Yes	2 Yr	M^Σ	Yes	Accept
Colorado[R]	100	3-5L	Yes[S]	New	M,D,I^Σ	Rare	NA
Columbia	No 2°	C+L/L	Yes[S]	New	M→2,3;I→3	Yes	Accept
Connecticut	100	C+4L	Yes[S]	?	M→3	Yes	Accept
Cornell	100	C/2L	Yes[S]	5 Yr	M→2,3	Yes	May
Creighton[R]	NA	C/A+3L	Yes[S]	3 Yr	No	Yes	Accept
Dalhousie[◆]	NA	NA	NA	NA	NA	NA	NA
Dartmouth[R]	100	C/A+2L	Yes	3 Yr	M,D→2,3;I→2	Yes	April
Duke[R]	40	C+4-5L/4-5L	Yes	4 Yr	M,D[ﬁ]	Yes	April
East Carolina	●/NA	Inst	Yes	2 Yr	M,D,I	No	NA
Emory	NA	C/A+3L	Yes[S]	New	M→2/3	Yes	April
Florida	40/0	3L/C+3L	Yes[S]	3 Yr	M→2/3	No	Feb
Florida, South[R]	90/0	C+3L/6L	Yes	3 Yr	M→2/3	No	Jan

Figure 15.5: Medical School Application Information, cont'd.

School	% 2° Appl. In-State /Other	Recom. Letters	AP Credit OK?	Last MCAT Date	Transfers Accepted? Into Which Years?	Admit Non-U.S. Citizen /Non-Perm Resident	When Fin. Aid Info Sent?
Geo. Washington	100	C+3L/3L	Yes[S]	3 Yr	M,D,I→2/3	Yes	Jan
Georgetown	100	C/3L	Yes	3 Yr	M,D,I→2/3,O	Rare	NA
Georgia, Med. Coll.	●	C+2L/3L	Yes[S]	3 Yr	M,I$^\Sigma$→2/3	Yes	Jan
Harvard	NA	C+3L/4L	Yes[S]	5 Yr	M$^{\&}$→3	Yes	Intvw
Hawaii	50	NA	Yes[S]	3 Yr	No	Yes	NA
Howard	100	C/2L	No	3 Yr	M→3	Yes	April
Illinois, Southern	NA	C/4L	Yes	2 Yr	M→2,3,D,I,O→2	No	Intvw
Illinois, University of	35	C/3L	Yes	3Yr	M→3,D,I$^\Sigma$→2[&]	No	NA
Indiana	NA	4L	+/-	4 Yr	M,D,I	Yes	Accept
Iowa[R]	●/50	C+2L	Yes	New	No	No	NA
Jefferson	100	C/L	Yes[S]	New	M→3	Yes	Accept
Johns Hopkins	No 2°	C or A+L/2L	Yes[S]	NR[J]	M→2,3	Yes	March
Kansas	NA	C+3L/3-5L	Yes	3 Yr	M→2,3	No	April
Kentucky	●/10	C/3L	Yes[SP]	2 Yr	M→2,3	Yes	Jan
Kirksville Osteo.[+ R]	NA	C+L/A+2L	Yes	3 Yr	M,D→2,3,4	Yes	NA
Lake Erie Osteo.[+]	100	C+2L(D)/3L(D)	No	3 Yr	No	No	Accept
Laval[◇F]	No 2°	None	NA	NR	NA	Yes	NA
Loma Linda	100	Inst	No	3 Yr	M→3	Yes	Accept
Louisville	NA	C/3L	Yes[S]	2 Yr	M$^\Sigma$→2,3	No	Jan
Loyola–Stritch	80	NA	Yes	?	M,D,I→3	No	Jan
LSU–New Orleans[R]	●	C+5L/5L	Yes[S]	3 Yr	M→2,3,4	No	Jan
LSU–Shreveport[R]	●	C+L/3-5L	+/-	3 Yr	M→2,3,4	No	Feb
Manitoba[◇]	60/15	Special Forms	Yes	3 Yr	M→2,3	Can	NA
Marshall[R]	100	C/3L	Yes[S]	3 Yr	M→2,3; I→3$^\Sigma$	No	Feb
Maryland	NA	C+L/3L	Yes[S]	3 Yr	M,I$^\Sigma$→3	Yes[Dip]	Jan
Massachusetts	100	C/3L	Yes[S]	2 Yr	M→3	No	June
Mayo	No 2°	C+L/3L	Yes	2 Yr	O	No	Accept
McGill[◇]	No 2°	C/L	Yes	3 Yr	No	Yes	NA
McMaster[◇]	No 2°	Special Forms	No	NR	No	Yes	Req
Meharry[R]	NA	C+3L/A+3L	+/-	?	M→3	Yes	Intvw
Mercer	70/0	C/A+1L	No	2 Yr	M→3$^\Sigma$	No	NA
Miami[R]	70/30	C+2L/3L	Yes	3 Yr	M,D,I$^\Sigma$	No	Accept
Michigan St. Osteo[+ R]	●/25	D/2L	Yes	3 Yr	D→3	Yes	Jan
Michigan State[R]	NA	C/3L	Yes	?	M	Yes	Jan
Michigan, University	100	L/C+L	Yes	3 Yr	No	No	Accept
Minnesota–Duluth	NA	Inst	Yes	3 Yr	No	C(Man)	Accept
Minnesota–Minneap.	25	C+3L/5L	Yes[S]	3 Yr	M→3	Yes	Accept
Mississippi	●	Inst	No	3 Yr	M→2,3$^\Sigma$	No	Feb
Missouri–Columbia	●/NA	3L/C+L	Yes[S]	New	M→3$^\Sigma$	Yes	Jan
Missouri–KS City Ⓖ	No 2°	Special Forms	NA	NA	No	No	Accept
Montréal[◇F]	No 2°	Not used	Yes	NR	No	Non-Can	NA

215

Figure 15.5: Medical School Application Information, cont'd.

School	% 2° Appl. In-State /Other	Recom. Letters	AP Credit OK?	Last MCAT Date	Transfers Accepted? Into Which Years?	Admit Non-U.S. Citizen /Non-Perm Resident	When Fin. Aid Info Sent?
Morehouse	87	C/3L	+/-	2 Yr	M→2	Rare	Intvw
Mount Sinai[♣]	100	C/L	Yes[S]	All	M,I→3	Yes	NA
Nebraska[R]	NA	Inst	No	New	M→3	No	NA
Nevada	●/NA	C/3L	No	3 Yr	M,D→3[Σ]	No	NA
New England Ost.[♣]	80	C(D)/2L(D)	Yes[S]	2 Yr	D→2,O	Yes	Accept
New Mexico	●/NA	C/A+3L	Yes	New	M,D,I[Σ]	No	NA
New York Coll Ost.[♣ R]	NA	C(D)/A+3L(D)	Yes	?	Rare	No	Intvw
New York Medical	100	C+L/3L	Yes	3 Yr	M,I→3	Yes	March
New York Univ.[♣]	NA	C/2L	Yes	New	M,D	Yes	April
Newfoundland[◊]	No 2°	2L	NA	New	M	Non-Can	NA
North Carolina	75/5	C/A+L	Yes	New	M→3	Yes	Intevw
North Dakota	No 2°	C/4L	Yes	3 Yr	M→2,3	No	Jan
Northwestern	75	C/3L	Yes	3 Yr	No	Yes	NA
Nova Univ. Osteo.[♣]	100	C+2L(D)/3L(D)	Yes	NA	D	Yes	Intvw
Ohio Osteo.[♣ R]	60	C or A+2L(D)	Yes	3 Yr	D	No	Jan
Ohio State	75/30	Inst	+/-	2 Yr	M→3	Yes	April
Ohio, Medical Coll.[R]	80/70	Inst	Yes	?	M→2,3	Yes	Accept
Ohio, Northeast. ##	30	Inst	Yes[G]	2 Yr	M,D,I[Σ]→2,3	Yes	Intvw
Oklahoma St. Osteo[♣]	100	C+2L(D)/3L(D)	Yes[S]	NA	D	No	NA
Oklahoma[R]	100	C/L	Yes[S]	New	M[Σ]→3	No	NA
Ontario, Western[◊]	NA	Special Forms	NA	New	M[CanSch]	Can	NA
Oregon	75/NA	C/A+L/L	Yes	3 Yr	No	No	Intvw
Ottawa[◊]	No 2°	Special Forms	No	New	No	Can	NA
Pacific Osteo.[♣]	100	NA	Yes	3 Yr	M,D	Yes	Intevw
Pennsylvania State	100	C+3-4L/3L	NA	2 Yr	M→3	Yes	May
Pennsylvania, Univ.	100	C/L	NA	New	M	Yes	May
Philadelphia Ost.[♣]	100	C or A+(D)/L+(D)	Yes[S]	New	M,D→2,3	Yes	Accept
Pittsburgh	NA	C+3L	NA	3 Yr	M→3	No	May
Ponce[S]	NA	C/A+3L	Yes	2 Yr	M,I→2,3	Yes	Accept
Puerto Rico[S]	●/NA	C/3L	+/-	3 Yr	M[Σ]→3	Yes	NA
Queen's[◊]	No 2°	Special Forms	Yes	New	No	Can	Aug
Rochester	No 2°	C/3-5L	Yes[S]	NR	M	Yes	Intvw
Rush	NA	C/3L	Yes[S]	?	M→3	No	Accept
Saint Louis[R]	NA	C+L/3L	Yes[S]	New	M→2,3	Yes	Accept
Saskatchewan[◊]	NA	L	No	NR	M	Can	NA
Sherbrooke[◊ F]	NA	NA	NA	NR	No	Yes	NA
South Carol., Med U	●/NA	A+3L/C/3L	Yes	5 Yr	No	No	Jan
South Carol., Univ.	90/20	C+6L/3-6L	Yes	NA	M→2,3	Yes	Jan
South Dakota	●/NA	Inst	Yes[S]	3 Yr	M[Σ]→2,3	No	Accept
Stanford[R]	50	A+3L/3L	Yes	3 Yr	No	Yes	Accept

Figure 15.5: Medical School Application Information, cont'd.

School	% 2° Appl. In-State /Other	Recom. Letters	AP Credit OK?	Last MCAT Date	Transfers Accepted? Into Which Years?	Admit Non-U.S. Citizen /Non-Perm Resident	When Fin. Aid Info Sent?
SUNY–Brooklyn[R]	100	C/2L	Yes[S]	3 Yr	M→3, O	Yes	NA
SUNY–Buffalo	100	C+3-5/3-5	Yes[S]	New	M,D,[I]→3	No	Jan
SUNY–Stony Brook	100	C+L/2L	Yes	5 Yr	M	Yes	March
SUNY–Syracuse[R]	100	C/2L	Yes	?	M,D,[I]	Yes	Accept
Temple U.	100	C/2L	+/-	3 Yr	No	No	Spring
Tennessee State, E[R].	25	C/L	Yes[S]	2 Yr	M→2,3	No	Spring
Tennessee, Univ. of	NA	C/3L	Yes[S]	5 Yr	M	No	April
Texas A&M	No 2°	C+2L/2L	Yes	5 Yr	No	No	Intvw
Texas Coll Ost ♣ U	33/23	C/3L	Yes[S]	3 Yr	D$^\Sigma$→3	No	Intvw
Texas Tech	No 2°	A+2L/2L	Yes[S]	5 Yr	M,I$^\Sigma$	No	Intvw
Texas, U–Galveston[U]	No 2°	C/2L	Yes	1 Yr	M$^{\bowtie}$	No	NA
Texas, U–Houston[U]	No 2°	C/2L	Yes	1 Yr	No	No	NA
Texas, U–San Anton[U]	No 2°	Inst	Yes	New	M	Yes	Accept
Texas, U–Southwest[U]	No 2°	C/2L	Yes	5 Yr	M$^{\bowtie}$	No	Accept
Toronto ♦	No 2°	Special Forms	NA	New	No	Yes	NA
Tufts[R]	100	C+L/L	Yes[S]	3 Yr	M	Yes	May
Tulane	100	C+3-5L/3-5L	Yes[S]	3 Yr	M,I→2,3	Yes	Jan
UMDNJ-Coll Osteo. ♣	NA	C/2-4L	Yes[S]	3 Yr	D→2,3	No	Accept
UMDNJ-NJ Med	No 2°	C+2-3L/3L	Yes[S]	All	M,D,I→2,3	No	Accept
UMDNJ-RWJ	NA	C+L/3L	Yes[S]	4 Yr	L,D,I→3	No	Accept
Uniformed Serv. U.[R]	NA	C/3L	Yes[S]	3 Yr	No	No	NA
Univ Health Sci Ost ♣	NA	C/3L(D)	Yes[S]	2 Yr	D	Yes	Accept
Univ.Ost. Med/Hlth ♣ R	85	C+A+2L/2L	Yes	2 Yr	M,D→2	Yes	Accept
Utah	95/30	Inst	No	4 Yr	M$^\Sigma$→2,3	Yes	Accept
Vanderbilt	14	C/3L	Yes[S]	New	M→3	Yes	April
Vermont[R]	NA	C+2-4L/3-4L	NA	3 Yr	M,D,I→1,2	Yes	Feb
Virginia, Eastern	50/30	A+L/C+1L/3L	Yes	2 Yr	M→2,3	No	NA
Virginia, Med. Coll.	75/30	A+L	Yes	3 Yr	M→3	No	Intvw
Virginia, Univ. of[R]	NA	2L	+/-	3 Yr	M→3	Yes	May
Washington U.(MO)[R]	NA	C/3L	Yes	3 Yr	M→3	Yes	April
Washington, Univ of[R]	NA	C/L	Yes[S]	3 Yr	NA	No	NA
Wayne State	75/50	3L	Yes[S]	?	M,D,I,O→2,3	C	Accept
West Virginia	●/NA	C	Yes[S]	New	M,D→3	Yes	Intvw
West Virginia Ost. ♣	NA	(D)	Yes[S]	New	M,D→1,2	No	Intvw
Wisconsin, Med Coll	No 2°	Inst	Yes[S]	3 Yr	M→2,3	Yes	Intvw
Wisconsin, Univ. of	●/20	4L	Yes[S]	4 Yr	M→3;I$^\Sigma$→3	No	Jan
Wright State	100	C+3L/3L	NA	3 Yr	M,D→2,3	No	Feb
Yale	No 2°	C/A+3L	Yes[S]	4 Yr	M$^{\bowtie}$→2/3	Yes	Jan

Figure 15.5: Medical School Application Information, cont'd.

✧: Canadian medical school

♠: College of Osteopathic Medicine

⊕: Non-U.S./non-Canadian medical school

F: Classes taught in French

S: Classes taught in Spanish

C: Formerly the Medical College of Pennsylvania/Hahnemann Medical Schools

R: School has a "rolling" admission policy

U: School has a uniform admission date and thereafter uses a "rolling" admission policy

&: New York University and Mt. Sinai are merging into a single medical school

⑥: Information is about 6-year program for high school students

##: Information is primarily for those not applying through the eight-year program

●: All state applicants get secondary application

C: Premed Committee letters preferred

L: Individual recommendation letters required with/or instead of Premed Committee letter. If no number is specified, it indicates that several letters should be sent.

A: Premed Adviser cover letter

Inst: Use the format for recommendations normally used at your undergraduate institution

(D): At least one letter must be from a D.O.

S: Supplement premed courses with advanced courses in same areas

P: Physics not accepted as an Advanced Placement (AP) credit

G: Organic Chemistry not accepted as an Advanced Placement (AP) credit

New: MCAT scores must be from the "New" MCAT, administered since 1991

NR: MCAT not required

J: Does not require MCAT, but requires results of either SAT, ACT, GRE, or MCAT

M: Transfers accepted from U.S. M.D.-granting schools

D: Transfers accepted from U.S. D.O.-granting schools

F: Transfers accepted from non-U.S. medical schools

I: Transfers accepted from non-U.S. medical schools

[I]: Transfers accepted from foreign schools approved by the NY Dept. of Education

Σ: State residents only or preferred

O: Oral surgeons or general dentists accepted—into second-year class, unless otherwise noted

⅋: Transfer considered if there is a personal relationship with a student or staff at the school

&: Applicants for transfer must take a special University-administered examination

CanSch: Transfers from other Canadian medical schools only

Dip: Non-U.S. citizens/non-permanent residents on diplomatic visas considered

C: Accepts Canadian citizens

C(Man): Accepts Canadian citizens from Manitoba

Can: Only Canadian citizens or landed immigrants admitted

Non-Can: Non-Canadian citizens/landed immigrants admitted

Accept: Financial information sent when applicant is accepted or shortly thereafter

Intvw: Financial information distributed at interview

Req: Financial information distributed on request only.

Information obtained from: Association of American Medical Colleges. *Medical School Admission Requirements, 1997-1998*. Washington, DC: AAMC, 1996; American Association of Colleges of Osteopathic Medicine. *1995 Annual Statistical Repor.t* Rockville, MD: AACOM, 1995; and other sources.

Differences Among Medical Schools

Most applicants, for better or for worse, use a school's general reputation and its geographic location as their two most important selection factors. Women are more concerned about a school's teaching methods and curriculum than are men. They are also more frequently dissatisfied with the course of study upon graduation.

Size

Many people compare medical schools by citing differences in their sizes. You can measure medical school sizes two ways: by the number of students in each year of the curriculum and by the total number of students in the school. Class size varies greatly (figure 15.3), from the minuscule 25 students per year at Northeastern Ohio University to a gargantuan 317 students per year at the University of Illinois. The total number of medical students can be approximated by multiplying the class size by the number of years for the typical curriculum. The University of Illinois, for example, has about 1,268 students in all four years (give or take some to account for decelerated, dismissed, combined-degree, and transfer students).

There are three reasons why neither of these numbers may be terribly helpful. First, some schools, such as Indiana University and the University of Nevada, have more than one preclinical campus. Preclinical students at such schools rarely, if ever, see their compatriots on the other campuses. Second, some schools, such as Texas A&M, have their preclinical campus far removed from their clinical campus, so preclinical students rarely see the upperclassmen. Third, most schools have many clinical sites where medical students train. The number of sites is usually in direct proportion to the number of medical students at the school. Therefore, the total number of students should not, in itself, prevent you from applying to a medical school. It is probably much more important to know about the faculty-to-student ratio in the preclinical years and whether adequate positions are available for training during the clinical years.

Curriculum (Changing)

How the faculty imparts the information necessary to practice medicine (and what information the faculty deems "necessary") varies among schools. If you are a self-directed learner, you may be uncomfortable at schools using the rigid curriculum/lecture method. If you prefer that method, you will certainly have difficulty at schools using independent-study or problem-based learning. The evaluation methods used by each school (and departments within each school) also differ significantly. Find schools with curricula, teaching philosophies, and evaluation methods that mesh with your needs. Many students do not consider this, and they suffer the consequences.

Nearly one in twenty medical school graduates is dissatisfied with the quality of her medical education. Worse (and this is sort of scary), more than 16% of graduating medical students are not confident that they have learned the clinical skills required to begin a residency program! This may, however, have more to do with individual students than with the schools they attended.

Time To Complete Medical School

The typical medical school curriculum lasts four years, although the actual time varies from 129 to 177 weeks. (Note that, according to the LCME, the official minimum is 130 weeks, preferably spread over four years.) On average, this breaks down to 37 weeks in the first year, 35 weeks in the second year, 46 weeks in the third year, and 35 weeks in the fourth year. These numbers do not include the time periods devoted to studying for mid-term and final examinations, or time set aside to study for the licensing examinations. Over the past decade, the average number of hours that first- and second-year medical students meet with their instructors has decreased by about 10%, in part due to the introduction of computer-assisted instruction.

More than 10% of the medical students enrolled in four-year programs take five years to graduate. Students most likely to take longer than four years to graduate are women, those 28 years or older when they apply, those with undergraduate GPAs of 2.5 or less, and those with MCAT Science Composite Scores less than 8. The last two factors are the most significant predictors. Minority students are least likely to graduate in four years. The percentage of medical students who graduate in four years, by ethnicity, are: Whites (85%), Asian-Americans (80%), Hispanic-Americans (70%), Native Americans (60%), and Blacks (52%).

Medical School Courses

Medical students spend their first two years primarily studying the basic sciences. The first year, they concentrate on learning normal or healthy conditions in anatomy and histology, neuroanatomy, physiology, and biochemistry. The second year concentrates on abnormal conditions and on medical treatment: pathology, microbiology, and pharmacology. Other courses, including behavioral sciences, medicolegal topics, introductory physical diagnosis, and public health/epidemiology, also are taken during the first two years. About 25% of medical schools include time for electives in the first and second years.

The second two years are primarily spent on the clinical services, with third-year students normally "rotating" through pediatrics, surgery, internal medicine, obstetrics & gynecology, psychiatry (and sometimes neurology), and, in an increasing number of schools, through family practice. This clinical time is usually divided between hospitals and clinics. Students are given varying amounts of responsibility for evaluating patients, devising courses of evaluation and treatment, and performing procedures. They go on "rounds" from one to three times a day, attend lectures, and participate in the operating room. An increasing amount of time, rather than being spent in the hospital, is spent in ambulatory settings—where most physicians really practice (figure 15.6). Students are supervised primarily by residents, with a varying amount of faculty input. These rotations always have final written examinations and often an oral examination. One-third of schools allow third-year students to take electives, although the available options may be very limited.

Figure 15.6: Weeks of Required Third- and Fourth-Year Rotations

Specialty (number of schools requiring)	Average Weeks Spent	% Time Spent in Ambulatory Care (Average)
Internal Medicine (all schools)	12	22
General Surgery (all schools)	9	16
Obstetrics & Gynecology (all schools)	7	30
Pediatrics (all schools)	7	39
Family Practice (89 schools)	6	95
Psychiatry (all schools)	6	21
Surgical Subspecialties (55 schools)	5	—

Data derived from: Barzansky B, Jonas HS, Etzel SI. Educational programs in U.S. medical schools, 1994-1995. *JAMA* 1995;274(9):716-22.

At most medical schools, there are few, if any, required rotations during the fourth year. Most students spend their fourth year doing elective rotations, taking vacation, and looking for a residency position. On average, schools allow 25 weeks of elective time. Some schools limit the amount of time (averaging 15 weeks maximum) that students may spend away from the school and its affiliated facilities. While students are required to successfully complete a certain number of rotations, they usually get to select where, when, and what rotations they take. The quality of each student's fourth-year curriculum depends, therefore, on his willingness to be challenged by new experiences and on the insight of his advisers.

Special Tracks

In an effort to produce more primary care practitioners, some medical schools have added family practice to their required curricula, often increasing the amount of time on Family Practice rotations to six weeks. Others have developed special primary care "tracks" that allow participants to substitute an extended rural family practice experience for the usual third-year rotations. A few schools, such as the University of Kentucky (FP and IM), East Carolina University (FP), New York Medical College (IM), and Nova Southeastern College of Osteopathic Medicine (FP) condense medical school and family practice (FP) or internal medicine (IM) residencies into a total of six, rather than seven, years.

Medical schools will probably continue to experiment with similar programs in an attempt to maintain the increased interest in primary care specialties. (Graduates of internal medicine residencies have, in the past, mostly entered subspecialty training rather than practicing primary care.)

Teaching Methods

When surveying medical schools, ask yourself which schools use teaching approaches that work for you?

Medical schools' teaching methods vary. Problem-based learning (PBL), small-group sessions, integrated learning, and computer-assisted instruction are the newest buzzwords in medical education. Except for computer instruction, most schools only pay lip service to these methods and continue to use traditional teaching methods. In part, this is because, so far, no one has convincingly shown that using the new methods leads to better physicians. (Some educators suggest that medical schools have not implemented these methods correctly and that if they did so, they would produce better physicians.)

Problem-Based Learning (PBL)

This method (also described in chapter 24, *Your Questions*) makes students work through problems, which are usually clinical, using all the resources at their disposal. In solving the problem, students must integrate basic sciences and clinical knowledge, much as practicing physicians do. By doing this with adequate faculty leadership, they are supposed to learn both the factual knowledge and the problem-solving skills necessary for clinical practice. Many schools that have experimented with PBL are uncertain whether students really do "get" the information they need, and so they supplement these sessions with formal lectures. The push nationally is to make most medical education follow the PBL model. Early studies suggest that students taking only PBL courses do worse on the first parts of their licensing examination (mainly basic-science oriented) than their cohorts who take "standard" courses. However, PBL-trained students do better on the last part (clinical-practice oriented) of these exams.

Small-Group Sessions

Similar to PBL, these sessions hone students' communication, teamwork, and learning skills. However, small-group sessions require an enormous amount of faculty time—which has become scarce in these days of shrinking medical school funding. During the first year of medical school, students currently spend 50% of their class time in traditional lectures and only 13% in any type of small-group session. Unfortunately, many of these sessions deteriorate into formal lectures, defeating the purpose of small-group teaching. Most frequently, small-group learning occurs on the clinical services, since only a small number of medical students and residents are on a service at any one time.

Integrated Teaching/Learning

Ideally, medical students should simultaneously learn normal anatomy, pathology, and physiology with the associated pharmacology, ethical and legal dilemmas, and epidemiology for the same body areas or systems. This, however, would require an enormous restructuring of the curriculum, as well as extraordinary cooperation among faculty from the various disciplines involved. Even with the best intentions, this is almost impossible to accomplish. Also, a fail-safe mechanism for medical students may be lost in the process. While there is an enormous amount of information thrown at medical students, the truism is that anything that is really important will be taught at least three times in various parts of the curriculum (or on the wards or during residency). Integrating the curriculum may lessen this effect. Since it is so difficult to do, even at the medical schools that attempt to do it, only a minuscule part of students' instruction involves integrated learning.

Computer-Assisted Instruction

Nearly all medical schools now use computer-based instructional programs in one or more courses. Most often they are used as part of the basic-science courses. Computer programs can be used as the primary instructional method, as supplementary study aids, and for students to self-test their understanding of previously presented material. More than half of all medical schools use computer-based simulations to teach or to evaluate students' diagnostic or therapeutic decision-making skills. More than 73% of all medical students now use computer-based programs as study aids, and more than half use them as a formal part of their courses. (More than 80% of medical students use computers for bibliographic searches—that number probably increases to nearly 100% for residents.)

Other Methods And Programs

Many medical schools have unique programs. They are usually used in parallel with the "regular" program, with some students electing to follow the "special" program. Examples of these are the University of Wisconsin's Independent Study Program, the University of Kansas' Docent System, and the State University of New York–Brooklyn's Generalist Physician Track. Many other schools also have experimented with different teaching methods. Read each school's material carefully to locate programs that interest you.

Evaluation Methods

Medical schools primarily use six testing methods: multiple-choice examinations, oral examinations, structured-patient examinations, computer-based simulations, and direct observation. The most stringent of these are the multiple-choice United States Medical Licensing Examination (USMLE) and the Objective Structured Clinical Examination (OSCE).

To advance from the preclinical to the clinical portion of medical school, 87 M.D.-granting schools require their students to pass Step 1 of the USMLE. The USMLE is a national standardized test given in three separate parts, called "Steps." Step 1 primarily tests basic-science information. Another 53 schools require students to pass Step 2 before either advancing to their third year or graduating. Step 2 tests information necessary to begin practicing medicine as a first-year resident, and requires students to integrate basic sciences with clinical medicine. Step 3 is taken during or after internship.

Relatively new in medical schools, the OSCE tests a student's clinical abilities over a wide range of patient problems commonly seen in primary care. The OSCE uses "standardized patients"—either patients with stable physical findings (e.g., arthritis, heart murmurs) who describe disease symptoms, or staff members trained to describe such symptoms and to simulate the relevant physical signs. The standardized, 6- to 8-hour-long OSCE evaluates how well students deal with real patients' problems, not just how well they score on multiple-choice tests, in class, or on licensing examinations. Ideally, the OSCE tests whether a student can

- perform a focused history and physical examination,
- recognize pathological processes,
- interpret laboratory data,
- establish a relevant differential diagnosis,
- develop a treatment plan, and
- clearly document these clinical findings and plans.

More than fifty schools now use the OSCE, and several require their students to pass it before graduation. In the future, more schools will undoubtedly use this test.

In the preclinical years, multiple-choice examinations following the USMLE style are common. Computer-based testing is becoming more common, and it also often follows the multiple-choice format.

During the clinical years, the testing modalities most frequently encountered are: either school-generated multiple-choice examinations or USMLE-type "Subject Exams" (86% of students experience this); oral examinations (69%); standardized patients or OSCE (59%); observed history-taking and physical examinations (77%); and computerized case simulations (24%).

Grading Systems

Medical schools primarily use two grading systems: Pass/Fail or numeric/letter grades. Some schools mix the two systems, depending upon the courses. When they do this, the least-significant courses are usually graded using the Pass/Fail system.

In the 1960s and 1970s, there was a big push toward placing less emphasis on grades, resulting in Pass/Fail grading systems springing up at most medical schools. Gradually, however, most schools succumbed to using a three-grade system (Honors/Pass/Fail) as their faculty and students found that the simple Pass/Fail system was not discriminating enough, that there was little motivation to work harder (since students had been conditioned to the "carrot" of better grades), and that residency directors began relying heavily on scores from licensing examinations to compare applicants, since usable grades and class rankings were no longer available.

Today, most schools use the Honors/Pass/Fail grading system. "Honors" grades have become very important for students applying to the most competitive residencies. Everyone realizes this system is simply a modification of the old numeric/letter grading system—essentially reduced to "A", "C", and "F." Only a few medical schools still use a true Pass/Fail system and their graduates are at a disadvantage when they apply to highly competitive residencies.

Figure 15.7: Median Annual Medical School Tuition And Fees

| | Private Schools | | Public Schools | | | |
| | | | RESIDENT | | NON-RESIDENT | |
	Cost	1960 $*	Cost	1960 $*	Cost	1960 $*
1960-61	$1,050	$1,050	$498	$498	$830	$830
1970-71	2,000	1,526	683	521	1,300	922
1980-81	7,910	2,841	2,079	747	4,118	1,479
1990-91	18,930	4,287	6,115	1,385	13,839	3,134
1995-96	23,695	4,583	8,715	1,686	20,133	3,894

* Indicates cost in 1960-adjusted "real" dollars.

Adapted from: Association of American Medical Colleges. *AAMC Data Book: Statistical Information Related to Medical Education.* Washington, DC: AAMC, 1996, Table E1.

Costs

The average charges for medical school tuition and fees vary markedly among schools (figure 15.3). These charges, especially at public schools, may be different for students who are in-state or out-of-state residents. The average yearly costs for tuition and fees are shown in figure 15.7. If you compare the amounts in the "1960 $" column, you can see the real change in costs over time.

Location

There are medical schools throughout the United States, its Territories, Canada, and in most other countries. How do you decide where, geographically speaking, to go? Students normally consider five factors when choosing geographic locations: their "state-residency" status, where they want to live and practice permanently, the location of their "support systems," unique personal or family requirements, and their "gestalt" for that locale.

The first factor you should consider is your "state of residence." Being considered an "in-state" student is one of the few ways to still get a (relatively) inexpensive medical education. You don't necessarily have to live in the state where the medical school is located to be considered "in-state." Several states have made special arrangements so that their citizens can be considered "in-state" applicants at specific medical schools located in other states. (See chapter 16 for more information.) You also, of course, have a better chance of acceptance at your state school(s) than at most other medical schools. Note that many private schools also give some preference to in-state residents. See figure 15.4 for school-specific information. Overall, about 75% of all medical students go to school in the state where they are legal residents.

Some students pick a medical school on the basis of where they want to live permanently. This is a mistake. Most physicians do not ultimately practice in the city where they attended medical school. Rather, physicians tend to settle near the city where they complete their residencies. It is often more important for medical students to be near their personal "support systems." Your support system may include your family, friends, co-religionists, mentors, or teachers. If you're married, you can usually take your support system with you wherever you go. If not, it is very helpful to have people close by who can bolster your spirits during the difficult times you will inevitably encounter while in medical school. You or your family members may also have special needs that require you to be in a certain place during school. Among these are your spouse's job, children's medical needs, or parents who need special attention.

Finally, you need to feel comfortable at the medical school. Would you feel safe, comfortable, and "at home" in that area of the country, that city, or that part of the city? Just because you are not familiar with a particular type of locale, however, is no reason to dismiss it out of hand. Locations often grow on you.

For some schools, actual physical safety may be a concern. The federal Campus Security Act requires all U.S. colleges and universities to publish an annual security report containing campus security policies and procedures, campus crime statistics, campus programs to prevent sexual-assault, and procedures to report sex offenses. These reports must be distributed to current and prospective students. Few medical schools spontaneously send out such information; but they will if you ask for it.

Success in "Competitive" Residencies/Specialties

A school's reputation does play a role in how easily its graduates obtain some competitive residency positions. How much of a role is uncertain and varies with the specialty. Students from schools known for graduating excellent clinicians, for example, often have an easier time than those from "big-name" schools in obtaining the most competitive primary care residencies. To see how graduates of a particular school have done in getting residencies, ask the Dean of Students to show you a list of the residency sites and specialties for students from the last one or two classes. While many graduates, especially from state schools, opt for in-state residencies, look to see if some graduates matched in the competitive specialties (even if you don't think you will want to) and whether some went to competitive training sites. (You may have to rely on physician mentors to help you decipher these lists.)

However, when schools tell you how many of their students "got their first or second residency choice," ignore it. That is a bogus figure. Many students who do not believe they are competitive erroneously put their "sure bet" programs high on their list so they will be certain to get a position in the Match. This vastly inflates some schools' number of students who get the programs "they wanted."

The Faculty

Medical school faculties are comprised of full-time, part-time, and volunteer instructors in both the preclinical and clinical areas. How a school's faculty compares to the average faculty may give you an idea of their orientation: teaching, clinical work, or research. See figure 15.8.

At the average medical school, about 10% of school's faculty, and more than 18% of full-time faculty, are in the preclinical (basic) sciences. About 5% of the preclinical faculty are part-time and 29% are volunteers (unpaid).

About 90% of the average medical school's faculty, and about 82% of full-time faculty, are clinicians. About 6% of the clinical faculty are part-time and 61% are volunteers.

The average ratio of full-time faculty members to medical students is about 1.3 to 1.0. This is a marked increase from ten years ago. In 1984-85, for example, the ratio was only 0.88 to 1.0. Most of this increase stems from the need for more clinicians to generate income to keep the schools financially viable. This is mirrored by the overall decrease in preclinical faculty during this same period.

Only 29% of preclinical faculty and only 25% of clinical faculty are women, with very few full professors among them. Only 22% of women preclinical faculty are full professors versus 45% of men. Among the clinical faculty, only 8% of women are full professors, while nearly 29% of men hold that rank. (See figures 8.4 and 8.5.)

Figure 15.8: Average Medical School's Full-Time Faculty in Various Areas#

PRECLINICAL	Percent of Faculty		Percent of Faculty
Anatomy/Cell Biology	2.6%	Other	1.6 %
Biochemistry	2.3	Pathology*	5.3
Biomedical Engineering	0.1	Pharmacology	2.0
Genetics	0.5	Physiology/Biophysics	2.0
Microbiology	2.0	Neuroscience	0.3

CLINICAL			
Anesthesiology	5.0	Otolaryngology	1.2
Dermatology	0.7	Pediatrics	10.4
Emergency Medicine	1.0	Physical Med/Rehab	1.0
Family Practice	3.3	Plastic Surgery	0.1
Internal Medicine	22.6	Psychiatry	8.4
Neurology	3.0	Public Health/Prev Med	1.3
neurosurgery	0.7	Radiology	6.3
Obstetrics & Gynecology	4.1	Surgery	6.9
Ophthalmology	1.7	Urology	0.6
Orthopaedic Surgery	1.7	Other	1.3

Percentages do not add up to 100% due to rounding.
* Many pathologists work both as preclinical and as clinical faculty.

Adapted from: Barzansky B, Jonas HS, Etzel SI. Educational programs in U.S. medical schools, 1995-96. *JAMA* 1996;276(9):715-19.

Type of Physicians Produced

A key question to ask that reveals both the school's curricular strengths and the opportunities that will be available to you during school is, "What type of physicians does the school produce?" Do their graduates enter primary care or other specialties? What is the school's mission? You can find current answers to these questions in the AAMC's annual *Medical School Admission Requirements,* from the school's Web site (Internet addresses in *Appendix E),* or from the material the schools send you. Many have specific missions to produce primary care providers. Some even have special primary care "tracks," which may also allow students to shorten their residency training by one year if they enter the track.

There are two other questions you may want to consider: Does the school have a reputation for producing researchers or clinicians? Are their graduates educators or in non-teaching practices? You often can get this information from the school's published materials, but if it is unclear, ask these questions during interviews. Most medical school graduates are non-teaching clinicians (yes, even from the "big name" schools), but you may want to know if the school is known for producing either researchers or educators in case you decide to follow one of these paths. If you are interested in research, you should probably investigate combined Ph.D. or M.P.H. programs. If you want to be an educator, it really does not matter that much which medical school you attend, only that you get a good education, pattern yourself after the best role models, and pick up good teaching techniques along the way.

Attrition Rates

The common wisdom has been, for at least three decades, that once you enter medical school, you graduate. In this case, conventional wisdom is as close to the truth as it ever gets.

For example, in the 1993-94 academic year, less than 1% of medical students withdrew or were dismissed. Of those, more than half were dismissed for academic deficiencies. Others withdrew for personal, financial, or health reasons. Some left to pursue other careers or because they became disenchanted with medicine. About 40% of those who left medical school were first-year students.

While students don't usually get dismissed from medical school, in 1993-94, 1.7% of all medical students had to repeat academic years because of poor performance. Repeating students made up 3% of the first-year class! Another 1.9% of medical students took reduced course loads. Approximately one-third of these students were first-year students, and another third were second-year students.

In addition, 2.4% of all medical students that year were on leaves of absence, most commonly to pursue research or another degree (41%), but also for personal, financial, or health reasons (36%); academic deficiencies (14%); and other reasons (9%). Of those on leaves of absence, first-year students accounted for 21%; second-year students, 26%; third-year students, 37%; and fourth-year students, 16%.

Instructional Language

Nearly all U.S. and Canadian medical schools teach their classes in English. There are, however, some exceptions.

Three LCME-accredited schools teach their courses in French: Université Laval, Université de Montréal, and University of Sherbrooke—all located in Quebec, Canada. These schools require fluency in French. Students at the University of Ottawa may write their examinations in French, although instruction is in English.

Some or all of the teaching is conducted in Spanish at the three Puerto Rican schools: Universidad Central de Caribe, Ponce, and University of Puerto Rico. Students must be fluent in Spanish and in English. Most Caribbean medical schools that cater to U.S. students teach in English, as do, of course, medical schools in Britain, Ireland, New Zealand, and Australia. Other non-U.S./non-Canadian medical schools may teach their classroom work in English, but clinical work will generally be in the host country's language.

16: Which Medical Schools? The Must/Want Analysis

Anyone can make a decision given enough facts.
A good manager makes decisions without enough facts.
A perfect manager operates in perfect ignorance.

Corollary to Murphy's Law

Must/Want Analysis

ONE WAY OF DECIDING WHICH MEDICAL SCHOOL to attend is to use the Must/Want Analysis. (Also see chapter 7.) This method allows you to first determine which factors are important to you and then to figure out which schools meet your needs. It allows you to look past the glitter (or dullness) of a school's reputation and forces you to examine what you really want (and need) from a school.

To use the Must/Want Analysis, first make a list of all the possible factors that could influence your decision about the medical school you would like to attend. (See chapter 15 for some factors to consider and figure 16.1 for an example.) Some of the items may be absolute necessities for you, such as a problem-based curriculum or computer instruction. *If an item is an absolute necessity, a "Must," you have decided that the factor is so important that it must be present or else it will eliminate a school from consideration, regardless of its other qualities.* Other items will be relatively important. For example, living in the Midwest might be more important to you than living on either coast or the quality of the school's research program. In that case, you will rate (as explained below) each item based on its relative importance to you. Use the examples as a guide, and add items that are of particular interest to you. Some factors, of course, will not matter to you at all and can be eliminated from your list.

Once you have made your list, assign "Weights" to each factor based on its importance to you. In giving "Weights" to each factor, remember that the total of the weights must equal "100". Therefore, apportion each item's weight based on its importance in relation to all the other factors you are considering. It is easiest to first select those factors that are not at all important and rate them "0." Then move on to those of minimal importance, rating them "1." Continue in this fashion until the total for all assigned Weights equals "100." However, if a factor is a "Must," instead of assigning it a number value, you should assign it the word "Must." *You will use your same weighting of the same factors to rate all the schools that you consider.* Refer to figures 16.2 and 16.3 to see how a sample applicant assigned "Weights" to the factors on her list.

Following this, you will assign a "Score" for each factor at every school you consider. If an item that you have rated as a "Must" is not present, you will drop the school from consideration (as in figure 16.3). The "Score," on a 1-10 scale, is your estimate of how well the specific school fulfills your initial expectation in that category (10 is "perfect").

Once you have entered all Scores, calculate each factor's "Total" by multiplying the "Weight" by the "Score." All factor "Totals" are added to give your "School Evaluation Score." Use this score to decide the ranking of the schools on your list.

The information for scoring the factors can first be obtained from the schools' written materials, their Web sites, and the AAMC or AACOM's annual school listings. The interview provides a chance to verify this information and add any information (such as an evaluation of faculty interest, espirit de corps, and the quality of the food) that can only be obtained from visiting the school.

Figures 16.2 and 16.3 are examples of how one student completed her Must/Want Analysis for two schools she was considering. She has shortened the list given in figure 16.1 to eliminate those factors which are not important to her (and which she gave "0" for the Weight). Among the factors she eliminated are: all the Research Opportunities, "Pre-school Orientation" and other Curriculum factors, the Non-Health Benefits except for "Meals" and for "Parental Leave," which is a Must for her, and all the Health Benefits.

This student will use U. of M.'s "School Evaluation Score" of 546 (figure 16.2) to compare this school with other schools that interest her. If there is no change in her situation, she will go to the school with the highest score that accepts her.

Although U. of C medical school (figure 16.3) got high marks in some factors this student considered important, the school did not have a formal parental-leave policy. This was her "make or break" factor which she considered essential and that she rated "MUST." Since this factor was not present, she did not complete the form and eliminated that school from consideration. Therefore, even if this school offers her an interview (or a position if she only found out this information when she interviewed), she will not accept. When making factors a "Must" be sure that they are so important to you that you are willing not go to an otherwise excellent school if it lacks that factor.

Figure 16.1: Must/Want Analysis for Medical School

SCHOOL _____

CLINICAL EXPERIENCE	WEIGHT	X SCORE	= TOTAL
In Preclinical Years			
Patient Population			
Responsibility			
Clinical Settings			
Elective Time			
Range of Local Specialties			
Exposure to Managed Care			
Time in Ambulatory Setting			

GEOGRAPHIC LOCATION

Inner City, Suburb, Rural			
Part of Country			
Specific City			
Spouse/Family/Dependent Needs			

REPUTATION

School's Reputation			
School's Age and Stability			
Percent On-Time Graduations			
Success on USMLE, Steps 1 and 2			
Attitude Toward Women, Minorities			
Success Getting Desired Residency			

FACULTY

Availability			
Interest			
Stability			

CURRICULUM

Curriculum Structure			
Innovative Curriculum (PBL)			
Time to Degree			
Combination Degrees			
Self-Paced Learning			
Computer Education			
Pre-School Orientations			
Specialty-Selection Counseling			
Case-Based Teaching			
Small-Group Learning			
Large/Small Classes			
Student-Teacher Ratio			
Types of Examinations			
Grading System			
Amount of Elective Time			
Graduation Requirements			

Figure 16.1: Must/Want Analysis for Medical School, cont'd.

ESPRIT DE CORPS	WEIGHT	X SCORE	= TOTAL
Friendliness			
Cooperation Among Students			

RESEARCH OPPORTUNITIES/TRAINING			
Knowledge			
Materials			
Time			
Funding			

FACILITIES			
Clinical Laboratory Support			
Computerized Records/Lab Results			
Lecture Hall/Lab Age, Atmosphere			
Hospitals' Ages, Atmosphere			
Library/Media			
Parking			
Medical Bookstore			
Safety/Security			
Recreation Facilities			
Easy, Affordable Transportation			
Cafeteria/Food			

BENEFITS

Health Benefits:

Health Insurance			
Health Promotion			
Psychiatric Counseling			

Non-Health Benefits:

Child Care			
Educational Counseling			
Residency Applic. Counseling			
Mentoring			
Family Educational Benefits			
Uniforms/Scrubs			
Parental Leave			
Meals			
Photocopying			
Vacation			
Student-Learning Center			
Dorms/Subsidized Housing			

Figure 16.1: Must/Want Analysis for Medical School, cont'd.

FINANCIAL

Costs:	WEIGHT	X SCORE	= TOTAL
Tuition			
Housing			
Other Costs-of-Living			
Employment for Spouse/Family			

Assistance:			
Scholarships			
Loans			
Jobs			

TOTAL OF ALL WEIGHTS =   __100__

SCHOOL EVALUATION SCORE =   _____
(Total of Weights x Scores)

Figure 16.2: Must/Want Analysis—Example 3

SCHOOL: <u>U. of M. Medical School</u>

CLINICAL EXPERIENCE	WEIGHT	X SCORE	= TOTAL
In Preclinical Years	6	8	48
Patient Population	1	6	6
Responsibility	4	8	32
Clinical Settings	3	7	21
Elective Time	2	2	4
Range of Local Specialties	1	5	5
Exposure to Managed Care	2	2	4
Time in Ambulatory Setting	3	2	6

GEOGRAPHIC LOCATION			
Inner City, Suburb, Rural	0	—	—
Part of Country	3	6	18
Specific City	0	—	—
Spouse/Family/Dependent Needs	0	—	—

REPUTATION			
School's Reputation	3	3	9
School's Age and Stability	0	—	—
Percent On-Time Graduations	1	7	7
Success on USMLE, Steps 1 and 2	3	8	24
Attitude Toward Women, Minorities	2	7	14
Success Getting Desired Residency	3	6	18

FACULTY			
Availability	6	6	36
Interest	4	3	12
Stability	0	—	—

CURRICULUM			
Curriculum Structure	1	3	3
Innovative Curriculum (PBL)	3	2	6
Time to Degree	0	—	—
Combination Degrees	0	—	—
Self-Paced Learning	0	—	—
Computer Education	3	2	6
Pre-School Orientations	0	—	—
Specialty-Selection Counseling	1	1	1
Case-Based Teaching	0	—	—
Small-Group Learning	0	—	—
Large/Small Classes	0	—	—
Student-Teacher Ratio	0	—	—
Types of Examinations	0	—	—
Grading System	0	—	—
Amount of Elective Time	0	—	—
Graduation Requirements	0	—	—

Figure 16.2: Must/Want Analysis—Example 3, cont'd.

ESPRIT DE CORPS

	WEIGHT X	SCORE =	TOTAL
Friendliness	2	3	6
Cooperation Among Students	2	3	6

RESEARCH OPPORTUNITIES/TRAINING
None important to this student

FACILITIES (only those shown are important to this student)

Clinical Laboratory Support	0	—	—
Computerized Records/Lab Results	0	—	—
Lecture Hall/Lab Age, Atmosphere	3	4	12
Hospitals' Ages, Atmosphere	1	6	6
Library/Media	3	4	12
Safety/Security	3	3	9
Cafeteria/Food	2	7	14

BENEFITS

Health Benefits: (all not important to this student)

Health Insurance	0	—	—

Non-Health Benefits: (only those shown are important to this student)

Parental Leave	MUST	YES	√
Meals	2	8	16

FINANCIAL

Costs: (only those shown are important to this student)

Tuition	10	9	90
Housing	0	—	—
Other Cost-of-Living	3	5	15
Employment for Spouse/Family	0	—	—

Assistance:

Scholarships	8	5	40
Loans	4	6	24
Jobs	2	8	16

TOTAL OF ALL WEIGHTS = <u>100</u>

SCHOOL EVALUATION SCORE = <u>**546**</u>

Figure 16.3: Must/Want Analysis—Example 4

SCHOOL: <u>**U. of C. Medical School**</u>

CLINICAL EXPERIENCE	WEIGHT	X SCORE	= TOTAL
In Preclinical Years	6	6	36
Patient Population	1	8	8
Responsibility	4	7	28
Clinical Settings	3	7	21
Elective Time	2	6	12
Range of Local Specialties	1	8	8
Exposure to Managed Care	2	5	10
Time in Ambulatory Setting	3	7	21

GEOGRAPHIC LOCATION			
Inner City, Suburb, Rural	0	—	—
Part of Country	3	7	21
Specific City	0	—	—
Spouse/Family/Dependent Needs	0	—	—

REPUTATION			
School's Reputation	3	5	15
School's Age and Stability	0	—	—
Percent On-Time Graduations	1	4	4
Success on USMLE, Steps 1 and 2	3	7	21
Attitude Toward Women, Minorities	2	6	12
Success Getting Desired Residency	3	8	24

FACULTY			
Availability	6	5	30
Interest	4	5	20
Stability	0	—	—

CURRICULUM			
Curriculum Structure	1	6	6
Innovative Curriculum (PBL)	3	3	9
Time to Degree	0	—	—
Combination Degrees	0	—	—
Self-Paced Learning	0	—	—
Computer Education	3	3	9
Pre-School Orientations	0	—	—
Specialty-Selection Counseling	1	3	3
Case-Based Teaching	0	—	—
Small-Group Learning	0	—	—
Large/Small Classes	0	—	—
Student-Teacher Ratio	0	—	—
Types of Examinations	0	—	—
Grading System	0	—	—
Amount of Elective Time	0	—	—
Graduation Requirements	0	—	—

Figure 16.3: Must/Want Analysis—Example 4, cont'd.

ESPRIT DE CORPS	WEIGHT	X SCORE	= TOTAL
Friendliness	2	6	12
Cooperation Among Students	2	6	12

RESEARCH OPPORTUNITIES/TRAINING
None important to this student

FACILITIES (only those shown are important to this student)

Clinical Laboratory Support	0	—	—
Computerized Records/Lab Results	0	—	—
Lecture Hall/Lab Age, Atmosphere	3	7	21
Hospitals' Ages, Atmosphere	1	3	3
Library/Media	3	3	9
Safety/Security	3	5	15
Cafeteria/Food	2	3	6

BENEFITS
Health Benefits: (all not important to this student)

Health Insurance	0	—	—

Non-Health Benefits: (only those shown are important to this student)

Parental Leave	MUST	NO	X
Meals	2		

FINANCIAL
Costs: (only those shown are important to this student)

Tuition	10		
Housing	0		
Other Cost-of-Living	3		
Employment for Spouse/Family	0		

Assistance:

Scholarships	8		
Loans	4		
Jobs	2		

TOTAL OF ALL WEIGHTS =   <u>100</u>

SCHOOL EVALUATION SCORE = <u>NO SCORE (Does not have a "Must" Requirement</u>

Playing The Odds: To How Many Schools Should I Apply?

If you look at the long list of medical schools, you can be overwhelmed. However, you don't have a real chance of getting into most of those schools. Most medical schools are publicly funded state schools. They take few or no out-of-state applicants, although many people foolishly apply with no hope of getting in. (See figure 15.4 for the percentage of out-of-state residents accepted by schools.) This wastes your time, energy, and, of course, money. So, first you should consider applying to your state's schools and to schools that consider you to be an in-state resident through a cooperative program, such as WICHE (see "Interstate Cooperative Programs" in this chapter). Next, pick the private schools where you have the best chance of success. At most, your preliminary list will have about 25 schools, and probably fewer.

Once you have a list, look at figure 15.3 for the tuition and fees for each school and figure 15.4 for the average GPA and MCAT scores of the students they accept. Select those schools for your "short list" that you can afford and to which you have at least a reasonable chance of being admitted based on your GPA and MCAT scores.

Don't be too pessimistic about your personal or financial assessment, however. Professional photographers constantly tell amateurs to go ahead and take lots of pictures. "So what if you blow a few shots? You may end up with some beautiful pictures you wouldn't have gotten if you had been more conservative. Remember," they say, "the film is the least expensive part of system." Just so with the application process. Applying to a few extra schools, especially those to which you really want to go but are afraid that they won't accept you, makes good sense for at least two reasons. First, you will never have to say to yourself, as so many physicians do in their later years when they meet up with a moronic graduate from a medical school where they really wanted to go, that "I could have gotten in if only I had applied." Second, you actually may get an interview (and then a position) at that school. It takes very little extra effort to apply to *a few* more carefully selected schools. If the school's costs are a reason for not applying, see chapter 18, *Financial Information*. Follow your dreams—they may come true!

One thing to consider when applying to medical schools is that most schools with secondary applications charge between $40 and $100 to file these applications. Also, it takes lots of time (three to eight hours each) to complete the secondary applications, generate the required essays, and send the additional materials. How much time (and money) do you have? Perhaps it is wiser to spend more time answering the following questions: (1) To which schools you want to go? (2) At which schools do you have the best chance of admission? and (3) Which schools can you afford? Then, put your efforts toward completing the materials for these schools instead of dithering away (and driving yourself crazy) trying to complete extraneous paperwork.

Medical Schools and In-State Applicants

Although you should try to follow your dreams, be realistic about your chances when applying to out-of-state schools. While the number of applications medical schools receive has increased dramatically, many seem to be submitted only to kill trees, waste money, and give the U.S. Postal Service something to do. Most public medical schools accept few or no students who are not official residents of their state. Applying to these schools is like spitting in the wind—you think you have done something constructive but, in the end, you find out that you haven't (and it just ends up annoying you). Private schools may also give preference to in-state residents, since many receive state funds or support from foundations or endowments within their states.

Most applicants have a definite state-of-residence. If your state has one or more medical schools, you should apply to these schools. If your state doesn't have a medical school, find out which medical schools treat your state's applicants as in-state students. Every state without a medical school has at least one such arrangement. See "Interstate Cooperative Programs," below, and contact your premed adviser for additional information. (See also *Appendix E* for a list of medical schools by state.)

Definition of "In-State" Applicants

Each state has its own requirements for determining who is an "in-state" applicant. Often these definitions stem from the state's tax code. In general, to be considered an "in-state" resident, an individual must:

- Have lived in the state at least one year,
- Have a state drivers license,
- Be registered to vote in the state,
- Have a car (if one is owned) registered in the state, and
- Pay (or qualify to pay) income tax as a state resident. Or
- Own property (usually a house) in the state, or
- Live permanently in the state.

If, for example, you move to a new state, but are still registered to vote in your old state and complete that state's resident income-tax forms, you will probably be considered a resident of your old state. Even if you complete the above requirements, if you are a college student the entire time you live in a new state, you may not be considered a resident there. This can get very tricky, and every state is different, so if you have a question about your residency status, check with the schools in question before applying. (It is so difficult that the University of Texas Application includes a special form to submit so they can help you determine your residency status.) You may have to demonstrate your in-state eligibility to the school during the selection process.

Residency requirements also extend to medical schools in Canada and Puerto Rico. Few U.S. citizens are accepted to Canadian medical schools, except for McGill University in Montreal. Similarly, few non-Puerto Ricans are accepted to that island's three accredited medical schools.

Interstate Cooperative Programs

Some states do not have medical schools. Others states want to provide special medical school opportunities, so they will underwrite the costs of a private medical education for some students. If you live in such a state, your state has a contract with public and private medical schools in other states that requires them to treat you as an "in-state" student when they consider your application and tuition, or to subsidize the tuition at private schools in their own or other states. These programs exist throughout the country and are managed by regional agencies. Contracts change from year to year, so it is important to check with your state's Department of Education or regional agency (listed below) to find out with which M.D.- or D.O.-granting institutions your state currently has a contract. If there is such a contract, you must fulfill certain residency and academic requirements to be eligible for (and have the state support the non-resident part of your tuition under) these programs. Some states (e.g., Montana) also have other programs run by state agencies. You must apply to your state or regional agencies to be certified as a qualified student *before* you apply to the medical schools. The regional agencies are:

SOUTHERN REGIONAL EDUCATION BOARD (SREB)
592 Tenth Street, N.W.
Atlanta, GA 30318-5790

Participating Schools	Participating States
Emory University	Georgia
Meharry Medical College	Alabama, Georgia, North Carolina, Tennessee
Morehouse School of Medicine	Alabama, Georgia
Nova Southeastern University College of Osteopathic Medicine	Mississippi
Oklahoma State University College of Osteopathic Medicine	Arkansas
West Virginia School of Osteopathic Medicine	Alabama, Georgia, Mississippi

WESTERN INTERSTATE COMMISSION FOR HIGHER EDUCATION (WICHE)
P.O. Drawer P
Boulder, CO 80301-9752

Participating States: Alaska, Montana, Wyoming

Participating Schools (for residents of the above three states)

Loma Linda Univ. Sch. of Med.	Univ. CA–San Francisco Sch. of Med
Oregon Health Sciences Univ.	Univ. of Southern CA Sch. of Med.
Stanford Univ Sch. of Medicine	Univ. of Colorado Sch. of Med.
Univ. of Arizona Coll. of Medicine	Univ. of Hawaii Sch. of Med.
Univ. CA Berkeley-UCSF Med. Prog.	Univ. of Nevada Sch. of Med.
Univ. CA–Davis Sch. of Medicine	Univ. of New Mexico Sch. of Med.
Univ. CA–Irvine Sch. of Medicine	Univ. of North Dakota Sch. of Med.
Univ. CA–Los Angeles Sch. of Med.	Univ. of Utah Sch. of Med.
Univ. CA–San Diego Sch. of Med.	

Participating School (additional)	Participating States
College of Osteopathic Medicine of the Pacific (now Western University of the Health Sciences)	Alaska, Arizona, Hawaii, Montana, New Mexico, Oregon, Washington, Wyoming

"Other" Categories

Schools sometimes have intermediate categories for students, such as "state-related." These apply to students who, while not currently in-state residents, have such close ties to the state that they are given consideration after in-state residents, but before other out-of-state residents. Examples of such ties are: having lived most of one's life in the state, working and paying taxes in the state but not yet establishing residence, or preparing to move to the state because of a firm job offer or for specific personal reasons. Not all schools have this category, but if your situation is similar to these, consider investigating whether the schools that interest you do. It may mean that there are additional schools where you have a good chance of getting admitted.

Some schools also give special consideration to their alumni's children (known as "legacies"). Some state schools consider them on the same basis as in-state students, even if they live out-of-state. They generally have to pay the out-of-state tuition, however. No one will tell you about this. But if one of your parents is a physician, have her check with her alumni office to see if the school will give you special consideration.

Minorities and Medical School Admissions

Most medical schools admit a significant number of minority students. You may have a better chance of acceptance, however, if you apply to schools in areas where your minority is not well represented. This may give you a slight advantage.

There is, of course, a caveat to this advice. You must be personally strong enough to survive in a place that you have already defined as lacking cultural supports for you. And, if you plan to socialize within your religious or ethnic group, you may be short-changed without any cultural support. Think very hard and thoroughly investigate all aspects of the potential cultural life in a community before applying (or at least before committing) to its medical school.

Besides actually touring the community to observe the setting in which the school is located, contact the school's minority affairs office, the town's chamber of commerce, or look in an almanac or other reference book for statistical information about the city. Then contact any identifiable cultural organizations, such as a church of your denomination.

U.S. News & World Report March 1996 Rankings

Each March, *U.S. News & World Report* publishes its evaluation of the "top" U.S. medical schools. These are broken down into several categories. The rankings are based on: the school's reputation among medical school deans, senior faculty, and residency directors; how selective they are in taking medical students (average GPA and MCAT scores of entering students); and the ratio of the full-time basic-science and clinical faculty to the total number of medical students. When ranking the "primary-care schools," they also include the percentage of graduates entering "primary-care residencies." For the "Specialties" rankings, they use only the ratings from medical school deans and senior faculty.

By now, you should know why any list of the "best" medical schools will not do you much good. You need to choose the factors in which you have an interest and weigh them accordingly. However, since so many people have an interest in seeing how others rate medical schools, here are the 1996 *U.S. News & World Report* rankings:

Primary-Care Medical Schools

1. University of Washington
2. University of Massachusetts, Worcester
3. Oregon Health Sciences University
4. University of New Mexico
5. University of California, San Francisco
6. University of Missouri, Columbia
7. Southern Illinois University, Springfield
8. University of Iowa
9. Michigan State University
10. University of Kentucky
11. University of Minnesota, Duluth
12. Medical College of Wisconsin
13. Univ. of Colorado Health Sci. Center
14. East Carolina University
15. University of Kansas Medical Center

Specialties
(How much of any "excellence" in these areas trickles down to medical students is uncertain.)

Family Practice
1. University of Washington
2. University of Missouri, Columbia
3. University of New Mexico
4. Oregon Health Sciences University (tie)
4. East Carolina University (tie)

Internal Medicine
1. Harvard University
2. Johns Hopkins University
3. University of California, San Francisco
4. Duke University
5. Washington University

Pediatrics
1. Harvard University
2. Johns Hopkins University
3. University of Pennsylvania
4. University of California, San Francisco
5. University of Washington

Rural Medicine
1. University of Washington
2. University of New Mexico (tie)
2. University of Minnesota, Duluth (tie)
4. University of North Dakota (tie)
4. East Carolina University (tie)

Women's Health
1. Harvard University
2. Johns Hopkins University
3. University of Washington
4. Duke University
5. Yale University

Research-Oriented Medical Schools
1. Harvard University
2. Johns Hopkins University
3. Yale University
4. Washington University
5. University of Washington
6. University of California, San Francisco
7. University of Pennsylvania
8. Columbia University
9. University of Michigan, Ann Arbor
10. Stanford University
11. University of Washington
12. Cornell University
13. University of California, Los Angeles
14. Vanderbilt University
15. Baylor College of Medicine
16. University of Chicago
17. University of Pittsburgh
18. University of California, San Diego
19. Case Western Reserve University
20. University of Texas, Southwestern
21. Albert Einstein College of Medicine
22. Mayo Medical School
23. New York University
24. Emory University
25. University of Alabama, Birmingham

Gourman Reports

Another commonly used source of medical school rankings, based on criteria that are never stated (and have been described by some as "dubious" and "fictional") is *The Gourman Report*. Since these rankings can, at best, be considered rough guides, in the listings below, rather than actually ranking each school as Dr. Gourman does, I have placed the U.S. schools into three groups, and the Canadian schools into two groups, each alphabetically arranged. As you can see, some schools that the *U.S. News & World Report* rates highly do not do so well on this list.

U.S. Schools*#

Highest-Rated Schools		
Baylor	Geo. Washington	Pennsylvania, Univ. of
Boston	Georgetown	Pittsburgh
Bowman Gray	Illinois, Univ. of	Rochester
Calif.–Davis	Harvard	Stanford
Calif.–Irvine	Indiana	SUNY–Buffalo
Calif.–San Diego	Iowa	Tufts
Calif.–San Francisco	Johns Hopkins	Tulane
Calif.–UCLA	Michigan, Univ. of	Vanderbilt
Chicago–Pritzker	Minnesota–Minneap.	Virginia, Univ. of
Columbia	Mount Sinai/NYU[C2]	Washington U. (MO)
Cornell	North Carolina	Washington, Univ of
Duke	Northwestern	Wisconsin, Univ. of
Emory	Ohio State	Yale

Mid-Rank Schools		
Alabama	Kansas	Pennsylvania State
Albany	Loma Linda	Rush
Albert Einstein	LSU–New Orleans	Saint Louis
Allegheny UHS[C1]	LSU–Shreveport	South Carolina, Med U
Arizona	Louisville	SUNY–Brooklyn
Arkansas	Loyola–Stritch	SUNY–Stony Brook
Brown (prog)	Maryland	SUNY–Syracuse
Calif., Southern	Mayo	Tennessee, Univ. of
Case Western Res.	Meharry	Temple Univ.
Cincinnati	Miami	Texas, U–Galveston
Colorado	Michigan State	Texas, U–Houston
Connecticut	Mississippi	Texas, U–San Anton
Creighton	Missouri–Columbia	Texas, U–Southwest
Dartmouth	Missouri–KS City	UMDNJ-NJ Med
Florida	Nebraska	Utah
Florida, South	New York Medical	Vermont
Jefferson	Oklahoma	Wayne State
Kentucky	Oregon	West Virginia

	chools	
		Tennessee State, East
		Texas A&M
)		Texas Tech
:a		UMDNJ-RWJ
al Coll.		Uniformed Serv. Univ.
eastern		Virginia, Eastern
		Virginia, Med. Coll.
)		Wisconsin, Med Coll
lina, Univ. of		Wright State
ɔta		

ge of Pennsylvania and Hahnemann University

edical School and New York University Medical

these ratings: University of South Alabama,
teopathic Medical Schools.

	Schools	
		Queen's
Laval	McMaster	Toronto
Manitoba	Montréal	

Other Schools		
Alberta	Newfoundland	Saskatchewan
Calgary	Ontario, Western	Sherbrooke
Dalhousie	Ottawa	

* The ratings for U.S. and Canadian schools are not directly comparable.

\# These ratings are based on: *The Gourman Report: A Rating of Graduate and Professional Programs in American and International Universities,* 6th ed. Los Angeles, CA: National Education Standards, 1993, pp. 126-34.

Acceptance Rates

It would be nice to be able to compare acceptance rates for the various medical schools. However, that is difficult, if not impossible. Medical schools actually accept more students than they have room for in their first-year class. Many students receive multiple acceptances and, of course, each can go to only one school. The best you can do is to compare each school's percentage of applicants interviewed, the number of interviewees, and the size of their first-year class (figure 15.4). This will give you a rough idea of how competitive the school is.

17: Foreign Medical Schools

Misery acquaints a man with strange bed-fellows.
Shakespeare, *The Tempest*, II, 2

'Tis a lesson you should heed:
Try, try, try again.
If at first you don't succeed,
Try, try, try again.
W.E. Hickson, *Try and Try Again*

THE ADMISSIONS PROCESS THAT U.S. AND CANADIAN medical schools use is not perfect. They routinely reject individuals who would make good (or great) physicians, and accept others who do not belong anywhere near patients. This is unfortunate (for both patients and the medical profession) but not unfair—everyone knows the rules. Foreign medical schools that cater to applicants rejected by U.S. and Canadian schools see themselves as "second-chance" schools. Whether they do indeed represent a second chance, or are the last resort of desperate people, depends upon the individual applicant and on which school he or she selects.

How lucky do you feel? Or more correctly, perhaps, how desperate are you? You have to be both to succeed at a foreign medical school. My best advice, and the advice from many who are experts in this area, is: DON'T GO!

Since you are continuing to read, you aren't planning on taking this advice. So, here are the specifics; you must decide whether this path is right for you.

Approved/Non-Approved Schools

The United States (including its Territories), Canada, and Australia are the only countries which have intense, government-sanctioned licensing bodies for medical schools. In the United States, the Liaison Committee on Medical Education (LCME) and the American Osteopathic Association (AOA) accredit medical schools. In Canada, the LCME and the Committee on Accreditation of Canadian Medical Schools (CACMS) jointly accredit the schools. Australia's schools are accredited by the Australian Medical Council, which is similar to the American and Canadian agencies.

None of these bodies accredits schools outside its geographic boundaries. In this book, "foreign school" means any medical school not accredited by the U.S. and Canadian agencies, generally indicating schools outside the United States, U.S. Territories, and Canada. At least one foreign school (Ross) claims a home base in New York, although students do not attend preclinical classes there.

Note that one school in the United States, San Juan Bautista, although located in Puerto Rico, is not LCME-approved. Only Puerto Rico has approved this school. And, because it is located in a U.S. Commonwealth, students are not eligible for an Educational Commission for Foreign Medical Graduates (ECFMG) Certificate. This means that their graduates may not be licensed in the United States other than in Puerto Rico.

Who Should Consider Going To A Foreign School?

Most of the foreign medical schools that cater to U.S. students will take nearly anyone who applies. The exceptions are those few schools whose students subsequently do the best on U.S. licensing examinations. Their high standards make it relatively difficult to get into them. If you are like most students, you will either not apply to those schools or apply but not get in. Therefore, it is not the schools, but you who must be the ruthless decision maker. Do you really have what it takes to succeed *despite* going to a foreign school? Try to be honest with yourself—don't expect these schools to decide for you. Graduates of foreign medical schools are called International Medical Graduates (IMGs). Special rules exist for IMGs to get a U.S. residency training position and, in most states, to get a license to practice medicine.

Dr. Carlos Pestana, an expert on foreign medical schools that admit U.S. citizens, recommends that the only people who should go to these schools are those who are "wealthy, adaptable, a master of the multiple-choice test, very flexible in terms of specialty and location of residency training, capable of becoming an excellent physician and determined to do so, and gracious when confronted with prejudice." I would add: those who are committed to becoming physicians no matter what hurdles they may face, and those who have no other options.

Those With Money

Foreign medical schools cater to U.S. students for one reason—they want to make money. Tuition and fees at these schools are as high as those at the most expensive U.S. schools. Some are private schools that have been specifically set up as for-profit operations. Others are government-run schools that take U.S. students to generate income with which to improve the school for the country's own nationals. (Schools with very low tuition are the national medical schools that neither expect nor encourage U.S. students to apply; it is nearly impossible for U.S. applicants to get into them.)

There are other costs to consider besides tuition. Travel is one. If you want to return to the United States occasionally, there is the cost of airfare (or of a long drive from some Mexican schools). How about travel to take a board preparation course or to do clinical rotations? If you are at a Caribbean school and do some clinical rotations in Great Britain, for example, factor in at least one transatlantic airfare. Also, consider basic living expenses, which may be either higher or lower than in the United States. However, some of the amenities that Americans take for granted can be astronomically expensive. Remember, even if you are eligible for Stafford Loans, these provide a maximum of $18,500 per year—and they must be repaid. (See chapter 18, *Financial Information*.)

In the past, many U.S. students attending foreign schools were eligible for Stafford loans up to $18,500 per year through the Federal Family Educational Loan Program (FFELP). The schools, after graduating at least two classes, only had to register with the U.S. Department of Education. The actual rules set out by Congress require a school to demonstrate that at least 60% of its students are nationals of the country in which it is located, and that at least 60% of those who took the tests to qualify for ECFMG Certificates (the United States Medical Licensing Examination

[USMLE] plus the English Language Examination) in the preceding year passed or that at least one U.S. state medical board has approved their clinical training programs. (No Caribbean school currently meets these requirements.) After a very critical Government Accounting Office review (*Student Loans: Millions Loaned Inappropriately to U.S. Nationals at Foreign Medical Schools,* January 1994, GAO/HEHS-94-28), the Department of Education, through its National Committee on Foreign Education and Accreditation, has begun site-surveying some of the schools to determine if their students should continue to be eligible for U.S. loans. Even if the schools "pass," they must be recertified every four years.

Students at some schools, such as the new Baja California Medical College, are not (yet) eligible for Stafford loans. This situation, however, is fluid, so check with the schools about financial aid before accepting or declining a position.

A few foreign schools have limited funding available to assist students. Don't count on this, however, since most of these schools take U.S. students specifically to generate hard currency. It doesn't serve their purpose to give money away.

Adequate Preparation

To prepare adequately, you must have completed enough undergraduate courses to eventually be licensed and have average (or better) MCAT scores. All medical licensing boards require that you complete your medical degree and residency training, and some require completion of specific undergraduate courses. (I don't have a clue why.)

Some foreign schools accept students into the medical curriculum directly out of high school. Those schools that don't include at least premed science courses in their curricula will leave students unlicensable in many states. And medical boards are obsessively strict about their requirements. One of my residents, after getting undergraduate and medical school degrees with honors at prestigious U.S. institutions, completing a university residency program, and becoming chief resident, could not initially be licensed in California. Why? He had "tested out" of one undergraduate course rather than taking it, so he did not have the three credit-hours in this course that the state board required. He only got licensed (provisionally) after he enrolled in the undergraduate course; he got his full license only when he completed it. And *his* degrees were from U.S. schools!

The moral is: be sure you have the undergraduate credits you will need to be licensed. (The U.S. and Canadian medical schools that accept high school students and undergraduates early in their courses of study usually provide adequate course-hours. In some cases, however, such students may also have difficulties.)

The other "preparation" is an adequate MCAT score. Presumably, your ultimate goal is to be a licensed and practicing U.S. physician, and to do this you will need to pass the USMLE. Since *fewer than half of all U.S.-citizen graduates from foreign medical schools pass both Steps 1 and 2* (figure 17.1), you need a solid reason to believe that you will be among those who pass these tests. (Note that about 98% of students graduating from U.S. medical schools pass all USMLE Steps.) Your MCAT scores are the only scorecard you have with which to rate your chances. Studies show that there is a high correlation between success on the MCAT and success on the USMLE (especially Steps 1 and 2, which are required for an ECFMG Certificate).

Figure 17.1: Performance by Foreign Graduates on USMLE (% Passing)

	STEP 1		STEP 2	
	Sept. 1995	June 1996	Aug. 1995	March 1996
U.S. Citizen IMGs				
Overall average	22.9%	42.7%	39.1%	31.7%
First-time takers	38.5%	64.0%	33.8%	35.2%
Repeaters	17.9%	22.6%	39.4%	31.5%
Foreign Citizen IMGs				
Overall average	46.5%	46.8%	50.1%	46.6%
First-time takers	49.9%	51.5%	51.2%	44.9%
Repeaters	44.9%	45.2%	49.7%	47.3%
	1995		1996	
U.S. Medical Students				
First-time takers	94%		93%	
Repeaters	64%		NA	
Eventually Pass	99%		98%	

Adapted from: information supplied by the Educational Commission for Foreign Medical Graduates, Philadelphia, PA, November 1996; and *The National Board Examiner*. Winter, 1996.

Dr. Pestana recommends going to a foreign medical school only if your MCAT scores average 10 or if your total (excluding the essay) is at least 30. While students with cumulative MCAT scores of 26 or above seem to do well at LCME- and AOA-approved schools, those at foreign schools will not generally have the support, facilities, or instruction these students have. Since students with MCAT scores in the low 20s are 2 to 3 times more likely to fail the USMLE, these students are essentially wasting their time (and money) going to a foreign school. Their chances of ever practicing medicine in the United States are negligible.

Flexibility and Humor

If you go to a foreign school, your living conditions will be at least different, if not inadequate (see "Living Conditions" below); you may need to alter your residency plans to fit what is available; and throughout your career, colleagues may raise questions about your adequacy as a physician. To overcome these obstacles, you will (at the least) need flexibility and a sense of humor.

If your goal is to practice medicine in the United States, you will need to complete a residency in the United States. That means that you must first get one. Even if you succeed in obtaining an ECFMG Certificate, which allows you to apply for residency positions, most residency directors do not want IMGs—especially in the most-competitive specialties, such as general surgery, emergency medicine, and orthopaedic surgery. And you may not be welcome at the most prestigious training institutions (generally those associated with medical schools). Therefore, you may need to alter your goals to get a residency position. If you have always dreamed of being an emergency physician, for example, you may have to re-think your goal.

Just after the NRMP Match this year, several students from Caribbean schools called me to ask what they should do, since they didn't match. They were initially appalled when I suggested looking for positions in psychiatry residencies. In general, these positions were available, offered clinical training, and often closely paralleled the curriculum of Transitional Internships. This wasn't exactly what they wanted, but at least it gave them a way of entering U.S. medicine.

Some IMGs do get into very competitive residencies, but these are generally the very best students from the very best foreign schools. It's just not something that you can count on.

Lastly, the medical establishment (but usually not the patient) sneers at IMGs. Can you take the rebuffs, snide comments, and need to constantly "show your worth" as many IMGs do throughout their careers? If you can't, don't even start the process.

A Medical Career—No Matter What

Don't consider foreign medical schools until you have exhausted every option within the United States and Canada. You didn't apply to your state's schools and some private schools located in less-than-optimal locations? Why not? If you think that going to these schools will be less prestigious or more difficult than going to a foreign medical school, think again. You didn't apply to Osteopathic medical schools? Why not? If you think that many Osteopathic physicians have a difficult time in an M.D.-dominated medical profession, be assured that it is a cakewalk compared to the lot of IMGs. Re-think all your options before you leap into the difficulties posed by going to a foreign medical school.

The other consideration is whether you are so committed to becoming a physician that you are willing to suffer much more angst, turmoil, and uncertainty than medical students at LCME- or AOA-approved schools (who themselves suffer enough). Dr. Robert Marion described his own decision process in *Learning to Play God* (p. 9).

> At the end of four days of intense despondency after receiving that final rejection, I realized it was time to assess my options. I carefully examined my motivation and my staying power and, after tormenting myself and those around me for nearly a week, I reached a conclusion: I didn't want to be a dentist; I didn't want to be a graduate student in biology and end up teaching; what I most wanted to do was to be a doctor, and the longer I thought about it, the more I was convinced that I could, and would, do anything necessary to reach that goal. That's when I began looking into foreign schools.

Ask yourself: *Am I that committed?* Through a series of fortuitous circumstances, after doing a "preregistration year" at the Royal College of Surgeons in Ireland, Dr. Marion became one of the lucky few who are able to "transfer" into a U.S. medical school. (Actually, he was simply admitted, since he had not actually started the Royal College's medical curriculum.) Your luck may not be as good.

Who Attends Foreign Schools?

More than 80% of U.S. citizens who attend foreign medical schools (based on the number of those who eventually get ECFMG Certificates) come from only eleven states. Students from three of those states (New York, California, and New Jersey) make up more than half of all IMGs. The balance come from (in order): Illinois, Florida, Pennsylvania, Texas, Maryland, Michigan, Massachusetts, and Ohio.

Useful Safeguards

After reading the information provided below and reviewing materials sent by the school, there are three final safeguards to help protect your investment of time and money. The *first* is to *actually visit the school before you enroll.* "It costs a lot of money!" you say. It sure does. It will cost you even more to move, pay very high tuition and fees, and then find out that you just cannot tolerate the place. Also, as described below, you may avoid getting scammed by a school that is not well-established.

When you visit the school, talk with current students and faculty. Get a sense of how well the students like their education. Also, find out how many of their graduates succeeded in passing the USMLE, transferring to U.S. schools, or in obtaining suitable U.S. residencies. If possible, get a student newsletter to see the real "scuttlebutt."

The *second* safeguard is: *Do not enroll in any school that hasn't graduated at least one class.* Don't be a guinea pig—or worse, a roasted pig.

Finally, don't go to a medical school that won't tell you where you will do your clinical rotations. Even if they don't put the information in their brochure, if you are serious enough to visit their school (or their stateside office), they should be willing to share the information with you—in writing—at that time. If they can't or won't give you such a list, go somewhere else. If they do give you a list, call a few of the places to see if this school's students actually rotate at their hospitals or clinics.

Teaching Facilities

There are three problems with the teaching resources at many foreign medical schools: inadequate or antique facilities, and overcrowding. Many new for-profit schools, especially in the Caribbean and Mexico but occasionally elsewhere, have set up their "campuses" in a couple of rented rooms, in someone's home, or in a trailer. Even when the facilities are a little "grander," say a couple of buildings, they often have intermittent electricity (read: cooling) and water.

Many schools outside the United States lack adequate libraries or computer facilities for students' use. Both are extremely important for an adequate medical education today. Medical students must learn how to access and use information in medical libraries and on-line. In addition, many modern teaching methods (and testing methods, including the USMLE in the near future) rely on computer literacy. Those schools which do have large libraries should have modern tomes and current journal subscriptions covering the major specialties and subspecialties.

Even where schools seem to have adequate facilities, you must question whether their facilities are adequate for the number of students enrolled. One way of easily determining this is to ask, "How many students work on each cadaver?" The U.S. norm is four.

Clinical Facilities

The lack of adequate clinical teaching facilities is a major drawback at many foreign medical schools. This is primarily a problem for Caribbean schools, where the medical facilities on the islands are often inadequate for the population, let alone for teaching medical students. It also occurs at small Mexican schools. To conceal this problem, the schools often coyly say that they "allow" their students to take clinical rotations in the United States or England. What they really mean is that if students can find places to do their clinical rotations, the best of luck to them. (By the way, the schools continue to collect tuition while their students spend time elsewhere.) In addition, many institutions listed by Caribbean schools as "teaching hospitals" either do not currently allow students to do clinical rotations or are not really considered teaching hospitals (having an ACGME-approved residency program) in the specialty areas in which the students will rotate.

In 1994, the U.S. Government Accounting Office did a study to find out how accurate these listings of clinical-rotation sites are. It found that of the clinical training sites in the United States listed by (primarily) Caribbean and Mexican medical schools (plus the non-listed sites U.S.-citizen graduates from these schools claim to have used), 61% of the sites had no formal affiliation with the schools, 51% were at hospitals not associated with a U.S. medical school or at those with a very limited affiliation, 29% had no residency programs, 10% of the affiliations no longer existed, and 7% of the institutions denied that they had any relationship to the school. Some of the affiliated institutions apparently never even existed!

Adequate clinical teaching facilities are much less of a problem at established schools associated with universities (such as Mexican, Israeli, Australian, or European schools), which have their own teaching hospitals. Also, St. George's University in Grenada has current, adequate affiliations with 24 U.S. and 23 British teaching hospitals, and is working to increase these numbers.

Faculty

To mangle an old expression, there are liars, damn liars, and public relations people. Foreign medical schools seem to delight in inflating the number of their faculty. Some do this by double (or triple or quadruple) counting faculty members if they teach multiple courses. Others count faculty who are retired, who are no longer there, or who only visited the school one time. (This false advertising, of course, is also a problem at U.S. and Canadian schools where many senior faculty are in the laboratory much of the time.) When evaluating a school, ask how many faculty really teach medical students.

Of those faculty who are really on-site, are they qualified to teach their assigned subjects? If a biochemist is teaching anatomy and pharmacology, watch out! Having a professor who is only one lesson ahead of the students is not the way to really learn—or to have your questions answered.

For schools in non-English-speaking countries offering "classes in English," find out how well the professors actually speak English. While in most cases they read it quite well, speaking ability is a "whole different ball game."

Living Conditions

Students attending foreign medical schools are often astonished by their living conditions. Those at schools in major cities must learn to adjust to different (and sometimes expensive) lifestyles, customs, currencies, and diets. That, however, is a small adjustment compared to those experienced by students on some Caribbean islands, who come face-to-face with primitive, third-world conditions. Unlike the paradise of swanky island resorts they may have seen through rose-colored glasses, the students experience the reality of islands filled with deprivations and inconveniences to which they are distinctly unaccustomed. Among these are intermittent and unsafe water supplies, inconsistent electricity, unusual laws and endless bureaucracy, the lack of "normal" conveniences, erratic transportation, slow mail and often no telephone service, an inability to get almost any spare parts for broken equipment and, of course, the ever-present bugs and lizards. Such living conditions may severely interfere with a student's ability to study, and often leads medical students to quit in frustration. Not everyone is cut out for an expatriate's life.

The Schools

Citizens of the United States and Canada who attend medical schools in other countries generally pick schools that teach their classes in English. Many of these are located in the Caribbean. Some are in Europe, Israel, and other English-speaking countries (see *Appendix E*). There are, of course, excellent medical schools in non-English-speaking countries, but usually only students with special ties (dual citizenship and fluent language skills) can attend them. No matter where students go to school outside of the United States or Canada, they are considered International Medical Graduates (IMGs) and must go through all of the hoops necessary to get a residency and practice medicine in the United States.

Based on the number of U.S. citizens taking the USMLE Steps 1 and 2 through the ECFMG, it seems that most U.S. citizens study abroad (in order of diminishing frequency) in Grenada, the Dominican Republic, Mexico, Dominica, Montserrat, and the Philippines.

Track Records

Medical schools throughout the world vary widely in their admission policies—from restrictive as in the United States and Canada to "open" as in Argentina. The restrictive model selects a limited number of students expecting that all will complete their medical training. Schools in the United States, Canada, England, Israel, Ireland, Australia, and the Caribbean follow this format. The European/Latin American open model, taken from the French system, accepts nearly all applicants, but quickly (often by the second year) winnows the number of students down through a grueling course of study. Nearly all Mexican, Central and South American, and mainland European schools follow this format.

These different policies lead to disparate percentages of entering students who graduate. Figure 17.2 shows the percentage of students who enter medical school that graduate. Note that these statistics often include high school graduates (for six- and seven-year programs), so older U.S.-citizen students with good science backgrounds can expect to do much better than these numbers indicate.

Getting Information

Brochures

Virtually all the schools that cater to U.S. and Canadian students will send you glossy brochures about their institutions. These brochures show smiling students, often performing laboratory experiments, looking at radiographs, or doing clinical rounds. They generally don't show you pictures of the buildings, classrooms, wide-angle views of any laboratory facilities, or student quarters. They also don't mention that the pictures of students doing clinical rotations are rarely taken at the school itself, but rather at U.S. or British hospitals, or that, in at least one case, "their" library is not theirs, but the municipal library.

As mentioned above, they also may be very short on specifics. They generally don't include (or they misrepresent) the number of faculty members, their library and computer facilities, and the number and quality of associated teaching hospitals. Nor do they mention the number of students who transfer to LCME- or AOA-approved schools, how many recent graduates passed the USMLE and got U.S. or Canadian residency positions, and especially how many get into desirable residency programs. (Getting into a pathology residency at East Nowhere Community Hospital, for example, is not too difficult if you can first get an ECFMG Certificate.) They are also usually reluctant to divulge how many of their graduates are licensed to practice medicine in the United States and Canada, and how many, if any, have medical school appointments. Remember that anecdotal reports are much less helpful than solid information on the performance of entire recent graduating classes. Few foreign schools, however, will supply this information—it's generally too embarrassing.

World Wide Web Sites

Some schools have imitated LCME- and AOA-approved schools by establishing World Wide Web sites. Some of these have extensive information and some are still quite limited. One benefit of these on-line sites is that they usually supply e-mail addresses for potential applicants to use to ask specific questions that are not answered in their literature or on their Web site. As with brochures, however, be wary of how you interpret any school's information.

Figure 17.2: Percentage of All Entering Students Who Graduate

Country	% Who Graduate
Argentina	15 %
Canada	96
Dominican Republic	55
Finland	97
Germany	95
Iceland	100
Ireland	98
Israel	90
Mexico	54
Norway	96
Poland	85
Spain	85
Sweden	85
Switzerland	60
United States	92

Adapted from: Carlson CA. International medical education. *JAMA* 1991;266(7):921-3.

Unhelpful Public Relations Information

As with all advertisers, foreign medical schools catering to U.S. and Canadian students try to sell potential applicants on their glitz. Much of it, however, is simply "sizzle with no steak." Among the great benefits foreign schools tout (some even do it on their envelopes) are:

- *"Curricula identical to the best U.S. and Canadian medical schools."* If you are trying to attract U.S. and Canadian applicants and to suggest that graduates will be able to pass their country's medical licensing examinations, what curriculum would you use? Since all U.S. and Canadian medical schools have basically the same curricula, that is the pattern foreign schools follow.

- *"Students are permitted to do clinical rotations in the United States."* Permitted? Students at Caribbean schools *must* do rotations in the United States, Canada, or the United Kingdom. The islands do not have adequate clinical teaching facilities. (A few schools have permission to send their students to New York or New Jersey for extended clinical rotations. Those schools can rightfully make this claim, since state agencies have approved their educational quality.)

- *"The school is listed in the World Directory of Medical Schools."* The only qualification to be listed is that the school existed in 1988 when the last edition came out. (The next edition is expected in 1997.) Being around that long, however, does indicate that the school probably won't evaporate overnight as have some medical schools.

- *"Graduates are eligible for ECFMG Certification."* Graduates of only one medical school in the world (San Juan Bautista, in Puerto Rico) are *not* eligible for ECFMG Certificates. Being eligible doesn't mean that graduates can actually pass the examinations necessary to get the Certificate.

- *"Students are eligible for U.S. Government educational loans."* At the present time, all United States citizens and permanent residents are eligible for government-backed student loans to attend nearly any graduate school. This may change in the near future, however, as the U.S. Department of Education begins enforcing its rules.

- *"U.S.-based education."* Just as with many ocean-going vessels, several schools began by being incorporated "under foreign flags," but were physically located in the United States. This clever, but transient, ploy was quickly squashed by U.S. government officials. Occasionally, however, foreign schools will still try this.

Excellence Abroad

There are many excellent medical schools outside the United States and Canada. Most do not take non-citizen students, preferring to educate their own nationals. Three schools that do routinely take U.S. students stand far above the rest: Sackler School of Medicine (Tel Aviv, Israel), Touro College/Faculty of Medicine of the Technion-Israel Institute of Technology (Long Island, New York/Haifa, Israel), and the Royal College of Surgeons (Dublin, Ireland). Each of these provides a medical education good enough for nearly all of their American graduates to pass the USMLE examination required for an ECFMG Certificate, residency training, and eventual medical licensure in the United States. (Even so, graduates of these schools must still surmount the extra hurdles that residency programs and medical boards have established for IMGs.)

Sackler School of Medicine—Tel Aviv, Israel

Often rated the best foreign medical school for U.S. and Canadian students, the medical division of the well-respected Tel Aviv University is considered by many to be equivalent to any U.S. medical school.

Although the normal medical curriculum is a six-year, European-style program, there is a special four-year curriculum for the seventy U.S. students admitted each year. Because of the school's contract with New York State, most U.S. students are from New York, although the program has now been expanded to also accept other American students.

Sackler's faculty and facilities rival those of any U.S. or Canadian medical school. Its faculty-to-student ratio meets or exceeds U.S. standards, and many of its faculty are involved in world-class research valued by North American medical schools. (In many instances, these faculty members collaborate on projects with their U.S. and Canadian counterparts.) The medical school has an enormous library, with more than 1,400 medical periodical subscriptions, plus thousands of books and audiovisual programs. Each affiliated hospital also has its own medical library. Medical students use the clinical facilities at Sackler's fifteen affiliated hospitals and health centers, which have more than 6,000 beds and two million annual outpatient visits. (If only all U.S. and Canadian medical schools had these types of facilities, clinical training might be much better.)

While you need not be Jewish to go to Sackler, it helps to speak Hebrew, since you will need it on clinical rotations. Those who don't already speak Hebrew get language instruction during their first two years at the school. All class work is in English and, unlike many other non-English-speaking countries, people can get along very well speaking only English in Israel's larger cities.

Sackler's tuition is about $17,000 per year, and room and board will cost the average student about $10,000 more. (Unless noted, all costs in this book are in U.S. dollars.) Books and supplies average another $1,000 per year. The school accepts applications ($25 fee) between September and May, and conducts interviews from March through June. Acceptances are sent to students between April and July. The interviews are usually held in New York City, but regional interviews can be arranged. For more information, contact: Office of Admissions, Sackler School of Medicine, 17 East 62nd Street, New York, NY 10021; (212) 688-8811; (212) 223-0368 fax.

Touro College/Faculty of Medicine of the Technion-Israel Institute of Technology—Haifa, Israel

This five-year program, housed at the prestigious Technion Institute, has many of the same attributes as Sackler. The difference is that the program begins in the United States at Touro College on Long Island, New York, where students begin their study of Hebrew while taking their first year of basic-science courses. Students then go to Haifa, Israel, where they complete their second year of basic sciences and two years of clinical rotations at the school's large affiliated hospitals. During a fifth year of advanced clinical rotations (in Israel), students write a thesis. As at Sackler, classes are taught in English, but clinical work must be done in Hebrew.

Only twenty-five U.S. students are accepted each year, so competition is tough. Tuition is about $18,000 for the year at Touro and about $14,000 annually for years two, three and four. There is no tuition for the fifth year! Living and other expenses are about the same as those at Sackler. The school accepts applications until May 30, interviews during July, and lets students know about their acceptance within one week of the interview. (Now that's a humane approach.) For more information, contact: The Admission Office, Biomedical Sciences, Touro College, Building No. 10, 135 Carman Road, Dix Hills, NY 11746; (516) 673-3432 fax.

Royal College of Surgeons—Dublin, Ireland

Dublin's Royal College, a private institution founded in 1784 (just a wee bit of longevity?) and accredited by the University of Ireland, is the only medical school in English-speaking Europe that will consider U.S.-citizen applicants. Each class typically has one-third of its students from Ireland, one-third from industrial countries, and one-third from Third-World countries.

The normal course of study lasts six years, with the first "preregistration year" comprised of introductory science courses that most U.S. students have already completed in their premedical studies. Some students can avoid these first year classes, which one U.S. student described as "actually taught at a . . . level closer to that in an American high school, and sometimes even to junior high standards." (Request a waiver when applying.) Because English is a second language for many students, "the professors covered the material very slowly, repeating sentences over and over again."

The faculty and facilities are superb. They have a full complement of basic-science and clinical teachers. They also have a modern library to complement their superb (and carefully protected) historical collection. While the main teaching facility is the 730-bed Beaumont Hospital, there are affiliated clinical facilities throughout the surrounding area, including several hospitals specializing in oncology, obstetrics, otolaryngology/ ophthalmology, pediatrics, and rehabilitation.

Applications (fee about $125) must be received in Dublin by February 15. Tuition is about $21,500 per year plus $160 for registration and $220 for "matriculation." To this, add the appropriate travel costs and living expenses. For more information, contact: The Royal College of Surgeons in Ireland, Admission Office, 123 St. Stephen's Green, Dublin 2, Ireland; (353) 01-478-0200. However, U.S. and Canadian applicants should contact: The Atlantic Bridge Program, 1044 Adams Avenue, Suite 302, Huntington Beach, CA 92646; (800) 876-3876; (714) 723-6318 fax.

New and Interesting

There are several new programs that may be of interest to those considering foreign medical schools. Three in Australia come with proven track records, government approval, and apparently sound programs based on the newest U.S./Canadian teaching model—problem-based learning. The schools are Flinders, Sydney, and Queensland Universities. These schools, primarily for Australians, accept a relatively small number of international students. Their benefits include the use of a single application for multiple schools, being in an English-speaking country (although often with different drug and procedure names), and having excellent clinical facilities. The drawbacks, aside from still being an IMG, are that you will have to deal with dingos and roos; g'dy mites!

Flinders University—Adelaide, Australia

Flinders is a large (10,000 students) university, but it has a relatively small medical program, with 58 Australian and 20 international students per year. The course of study follows a traditional four-year curriculum, although teaching uses small-group (8-student) sessions. Special classes help prepare U.S. students for the USMLE.

The school, with its teaching and research facilities, is in the same complex as the 600-bed hospital and outpatient facility used for clinical instruction.

The school requires applicants to have a bachelor's degree (in any area of study) before they enter medical school. The school evaluates an applicant's GPA in an interesting way: They count only the last three years, weighting them progressively, as 1x, 2x, and 3x, so that the grades from the last year count three times as much as the first. International applicants must take the MCAT and are expected to score at least a 7 on each numerically scored section and an "M" on the Writing Sample.

International applications must be received by June 30, and classes begin in February. Applicants are not required to travel to Australia for interviews. Interviews are conducted in July and August in North America. Occasionally, they will do telephone interviews.

Tuition is about $22,000 per year. The cost of living is approximately equal to the lowest of that for any mainland Australian city. For more information, contact: Medical Education Unit, Flinders University of South Australia, GPO Box 210, Adelaide, Australia 5001; (800) 686-3562 (e-mail: jillian.teubner@flinders.edu.au).

Other Australian Schools—Sydney and Queensland

Beginning in 1997, Sydney and Queensland Universities will each begin four-year medical school curricula patterned after U.S. and Canadian schools. They and Flinders University will share a common application form. The three will offer a total of about 60 places for international students and about 500 places for Australians. They expect that U.S. students will compose most of the international students.

Applicants to these programs will rate the three schools in their order of preference, so that if they are accepted into more than one, they will go to the school they prefer.

Caribbean Schools

The Caribbean, or "off-shore," medical schools exist primarily to cater to applicants rejected from U.S. and Canadian medical schools. Many schools have come and gone over the past few decades, leading to their generally poor reputation. Others have been involved in lawsuits over "dirty tricks," usually for trying to lure students from one school to another, and for mailing deceptive advertising. But for candidates who carefully pick their school, the Caribbean may be a reasonable choice.

St. George's University—Grenada

Clearly the best of the lot, St. George's University once had the enviable record of being able to transfer half of each class to U.S. schools to complete their education. Nowadays, the number of transferring students has remained constant (about 50 per year or about one in eight first- and second-year students at the school), but the number of new medical students enrolled has risen to about 400 per year (200 per each enrollment period). Nevertheless, their students still have an impressive (for a foreign school) 81% first-time pass-rate for Step 1 of the USMLE. They also state that 99.8% of their "eligible graduates" (i.e., those who obtain ECFMG Certificates) obtain ACGME-approved residency positions in the United States.

Although they have called themselves a "university" since their inception in 1976, they have just recently added degree programs for subjects other than medicine. They now offer a combined M.D./M.Sc. program and a B.A. in medical technology.

The school's facilities are more than adequate, and include a reasonable faculty supplemented by a steady stream of visiting professors, laboratory facilities augmented by a new research complex, a library with computer services, a student counseling service, and a department of education. The major problem is that these facilities are located on three campuses spread over two islands, although the second island's campus is used only by students during their second year. Their clinical facilities are in the United States (including being approved for extended rotations in New York and New Jersey) and the United Kingdom. Graduation is usually held at the United Nations building in New York.

All classes are taught in English and the curriculum follows that of U.S. and Canadian medical schools. Applicants from the U.S. must already have a bachelor's degree or receive one before matriculation. Applicants must also have had one year each (with a lab) of biology or zoology, inorganic chemistry, and organic chemistry, as well as mathematics (one year), English (one semester), and physics with lab (one semester). United States citizens must take the MCAT. Those for whom English is a second language must score at least 550 on the Test of English as a Foreign Language (TOEFL) Examination.

Applications (fee $75) must be received by May 15 for an August entry and by October 15 to enter the following January. The total tuition/fee/books cost for four years is about $120,000. Students who must repeat a year do it tuition-free. Living expenses (with air conditioning) often run around $5,000 per term, excluding transportation costs. For further information, contact: St. George's University, c/o Medical School Services, Ltd., One East Main Street, Bay Shore, NY 11706-8399; (516) 665-8500; (516) 665-5590 fax.

Ross University—Dominica

Ross University is located near the tiny town of Portsmouth, Dominica (not to be confused with the Dominican Republic). The school does not have the extensive faculty and clinical-rotation sites of Grenada, its upscale island neighbor, yet it has played host to a large number of U.S. students.

The school has recently built modern classrooms and laboratories for preclinical work, including modern audiovisual capabilities. The faculty has a diverse international background. The curriculum consists of basic science for the first four semesters and physical diagnosis during the fifth semester. There are actually three "semesters" per year, so the preclinical curriculum can be completed in as little as 20 months if a student does not take any time off. The few local hospitals are used solely for physical diagnosis training in the fifth "semester."

Living conditions on the island are tenuous, with students reporting electrical, water, and health care problems. Students are particularly concerned about the planned increase in enrollment at a time when there are inadequate clinical training sites (third and fourth years) for the current students. Although it claims to have clinical training sites in the United States, the United Kingdom, and elsewhere in the Caribbean, the school will not release a list of its clinical affiliations. (Personally, I receive more calls and letters from Ross students seeking training sites or who have not matched into residency positions than from any other foreign medical school.) Many of the hospitals it uses are either not teaching hospitals or do not have residencies in the specialty areas where students rotate.

Applications (fee $40) may be submitted at any time, since three classes enter each year. Tuition and fees until graduation are about $63,000. Interviews are held in New York, Miami, California, and Michigan. For further information, contact: Ross University, c/o International

Educational Admissions, 460 W. 34th Street, 12th Floor, New York, NY 10001; (212) 279-5500; (212) 629-3147 fax.

Other Caribbean Schools

There are other schools in the Caribbean, and those listed below are fairly representative. Not even the most daring souls should spend money to attend any of these schools without first visiting them.

University of Antigua Dowhill Campus—Antigua

The University of Antigua Dowhill Campus is something of a mystery. Housed in a small building with adjacent laboratories, the school is viciously guarded against outsiders. Does this in itself suggest that they have something to hide?

The information applicants receive includes alumni newsletters and a list of some of the school's graduates with contact information. It would be wise to talk with a few of them before making a decision to go to this school.

If you are so inclined, tuition and fees are $17,500 per year for those who live on-campus (first-year students must), and about $15,000 per year subsequently.

Dominican Republic

Once a hotbed of medical training for U.S. students, it cooled off after several schools were implicated in a scam to sell fake medical degrees. That's the reputation the island now has with U.S. and Canadian medical authorities. If you are thinking about going there, be warned. One school that has been in existence since 1970, the Universidad del Este, teaches all courses in Spanish, although it does offer an intensive Spanish-language course. The Universidad Nacional Pedro Henriquez Ueña not only teaches its courses in Spanish, but all information sent to prospective applicants is also in Spanish.

American University of the Caribbean—St. Maarten

In 1996 this school relocated to the less-volcanically active Dutch/French island of St. Maarten, about 150 miles east of Puerto Rico. (They had to rapidly leave Montserrat when its volcano erupted.) There they began a building project to house their basic-science program. In the interim, they are using temporary facilities located outside the Dutch capital of Philipsburg.

Applications (fee $50) are accepted at any time, since this school accepts three classes of entering students each year: in January, May, and September. Their minimum requirements for admission are at least 90 hours of college credit, including one year of English and of biology, general chemistry, organic chemistry, and physics (with lab). Applicants must have taken the MCAT. Interviews are at the school's discretion.

The normal curriculum lasts four years, but with an accelerated program it takes 38 months. This assumes, however, that suitable clinical rotations can be arranged to fit this schedule. The school states that it has "affiliated hospitals in the United States, England, Ireland and other locations," although the list of these institutions is a carefully guarded secret. They state that their students' averaged scores "were above 200" on the June 1996 USMLE Step 1 examination.

Total tuition for eight semesters is about $55,000. Room and board ranges from about $1,500 to $2,500 per semester.

Saba University School of Medicine—Saba

This tiny island hosts one of the nascent medical schools, the Saba University School of Medicine. It is another minuscule facility with a tiny faculty, as befits an island with about 1,200 people, five square miles of (mostly vertical) volcanic land, and the tiniest international airport in the world. The local hospital has about twelve rooms, one emergency cubicle, a small laboratory, and an operating room.

Where students get clinical training is uncertain. The Dutch have apparently refused to allow Saba's students to use the larger hospitals located elsewhere in the Dutch Antilles. Tuition for the entire course of study is about $36,000.

Spartan Health Sciences University School of Medicine—St. Lucia

The only surviving school on St. Lucia is the tiny Spartan Health Sciences University School of Medicine, which began in El Paso, Texas, in 1980. Located in a two-story house, the school is smaller than its name. The library is a tiny room and the faculty is minuscule.

The curriculum lasts 36 months and student registration is three times a year. It is unclear where students do their clinical rotations. While applicants get a very nice catalog detailing the curriculum and listing basic-science faculty, the only thing said about clinical rotations is that they must be done at "acceptable" hospitals. No clinical faculty are mentioned. Tuition for the entire program is about $27,000.

Mexican Schools

Universidad Autónoma de Guadalajara

Founded in 1935, this is the largest of Mexico's private universities. Guadalajara is a large city located 260 air-miles west-northwest of Mexico City. The Universidad Autónoma de Guadalajara has more graduates (8,000+) practicing medicine in the United States than any other foreign medical school. Although for many years its reputation suffered unfairly, it is actually a solid medical school at a real university that is quite good by Mexican standards.

At Guadalajara, students must become fluent in Spanish before starting classes. Beginning in their first semester, students work at indigent-care clinics where they will need to speak Spanish—and the course examination is in Spanish. Those who are not already fluent usually learn at one of the school's accelerated Spanish courses given several times a year. While the first-semester basic-science classes are taught in English, by the fourth semester, all courses are in Spanish. All textbooks and all examinations, however, are in English (except for each semester's clinical-clerkship exam, which is in Spanish). The school recently implemented a fourth-semester, USMLE Step 1 study course run by ArcVentures, a U.S. test-review organization, and the school reports that student performance on Step 1 has dramatically improved.

Guadalajara has recently modified its third-year clinical curriculum to parallel the core rotations taught at U.S. schools. Its teaching facilities consist of the 400-bed Dr. Angel Leaño University Hospital on the campus, a 90-bed pediatric and obstetric/gynecology hospital in downtown Guadalajara, and about 10,000 teaching beds they have access to through contractual affiliations in the surrounding area. The school has applied to New York State for permission to send students there for extended clinical rotations. Clinical rotations in the United States are primarily for fourth-year students.

One major drawback of Guadalajara (and other Mexican medical schools) relates to the Mexican government's requirements to get a medical degree. After completing the first four years of medical school, during which students do not get the intense clinical experience that U.S. students get during their third and fourth years, students must do two additional years to get the "Titulo de Médico Cirujano" (M.D. equivalent). The first year is spent doing "El Internado Rotatorio de Pregrado," which is often misinterpreted as an internship; it is actually more like the third-year in-hospital rotations at U.S. medical schools. A year of "Servicio Social" must then be done at a site chosen by the Mexican government. Only then do students receive their medical degrees.

258

Guadalajara has a "rolling" admission policy, with classes entering in August and January. They recommend submitting an application (fee $25) at least six months prior to the expected entry date. Applicants generally must have a 3.0 GPA and above-average MCAT scores, although some students without these numbers may be admitted if they "have demonstrated extenuating circumstances for their less-than-competitive academic records through their work history, undergraduate record, other activities, their personal interview, and where appropriate, substantiating documentation." Interviews are held weekdays, by appointment, at Guadalajara and in San Antonio and Puerto Rico. The school indicates that only one-third of those who apply are admitted.

The paperwork required to apply to Guadalajara is extraordinary. (Do you know, for example, where your junior-high-school transcript is?) Annual tuition is $13,700. Additional fees are charged for interviewing at sites other than the medical school ($50), matriculation ($2,000), the Spanish course if you need it ($350), and other obligatory courses (Mexican government, history, and geography; $420). For students who remain enrolled in school, the annual tuition stays the same. For further information, contact: Universidad Autónoma de Guadalajara, Office in the United States, 8801 Callaghan Road, San Antonio, TX 78230-4417; (800) 531-5494, (210) 366-1611; (210) 377-2975 fax.

In Puerto Rico, contact: Universidad Autónoma de Guadalajara, Office in Puerto Rico, IBM Plaza, Suite 1124, Avenida Muñoz Rivera No. 654, Hato Rey, PR 00918; (809) 763-2457; (809) 753-0760 fax.

Universidad de Monterrey—Monterrey, Mexico

Begun in the 1970s, this private university located in Monterrey, Mexico (about six hours by car from San Antonio, TX), has flourished in recent years as private donors have contributed to their elaborate building projects. They have a substantial library, faculty, and clinical facilities.

Clinical teaching is primarily based in the two state hospitals, encompassing about 2,000 beds. Their curriculum and the post-curriculum requirements mirror those at Guadalajara, except that students need to be proficient in spoken and written Spanish *before* they go.

One of the most interesting aspects of this school is the price. In 1995, the cost was only about $1,500 per semester. Quite a bargain for a very reasonable medical school experience. For further information, contact: Dra. Margarita de Leon Esparza, Coordinadora Curricular de Medicina, Ave. I. Morones Prieto 4500 Pte., C.P. 66238, San Pedro Garza Garcia, Nuevo Leon, Mexico; (8) 338050-50; (8) 338-4452 fax.

Baja California Medical School—Mexicali, Mexico

Baja, a new school that opened in 1996, seeks to provide a way for U.S. citizens, especially for those with families, to avoid some of the cultural and financial problems usually encountered when attending foreign schools. Because it is a new school, it is uncertain whether the program will be successful. Currently, there are two major concerns for those considering this school: First, it has not yet established any clinical teaching facilities, and second, its students are not eligible for U.S. government loans.

The Baja California Medical School is located in Mexicali, Mexico, about a 90-minute drive either from San Diego or Palm Springs, California. It is affiliated with, and draws faculty from, the state university, the Universidad Autónoma de Baja California, which also has two other medical schools.

Applicants must have at least 90 college credits (in any major), including one year of biology, two years of chemistry, and one year of physics. Special consideration is given to those with medical licenses or certification, such as EMTs, laboratory and radiology technicians, pharmacists, physical therapists, P.A.'s, R.N.'s, nurse practitioners, and to those with doctoral degrees in other medical areas (including D.V.M.).

Classes, which run from 7 A.M. to 2 P.M. Monday through Friday, begin in January and September. Their materials say that they will use "innovative computer technology" for instruction. They describe this as "a $4 million proprietary software program with a presentation of all subject materials, test creation facilities for professors, and test taking by students. Each student is assigned one computer. If the student does his work, he is guaranteed to pass the USMLE. This has been tested on some students who have passed the USMLE 1 & 2. Those taking the USMLE 2 took the test while in 3rd year (not 4th), without taking some core rotations." Classes are in English and Spanish, and English-speaking students will get an intensive Spanish-language course that will be helpful in some clerkships.

At the present time, clinical teaching facilities, in conjunction with the University, consist of three county hospitals in Mexicali with a total of about 600 beds. The University plans to have its own 100-bed hospital by 1998. It is also seeking affiliations with U.S. facilities.

Applications (fee $188) are accepted anytime, since they have a rolling admission policy. Interviews are required, and can be either in person or by phone. Annual tuition is $11,000, and other fees and books are about $1,500. Individuals may reside in Mexicali, Mexico, or in the U.S. in Calexico, the border town adjacent to Mexicali. Room and board is about $4,000 per year in Mexico. Note that unlike nearly all other schools, students at BCMC are not, at this time, eligible for U.S. government loans. For further information, contact: Baja California Medical College, P.O. Box 26180, Fresno, CA 93729-6180; (800) 642-3543; (209) 434-8429 fax.

Other Mexican Schools

Many other medical schools exist in Mexico, and some accept U.S. students. In general, however, they do not have any programs to ease the transition for those who don't speak Spanish. Also, some have *very* restrictive rules that even the most conservative Americans or Canadians will have difficulty living with—such as the rules at one school (Montemorelos) against wearing any jewelry, going to movies, owning radios or TVs, wearing sleeveless shirts or blouses, and being away from campus without permission.

European Schools

Western Europe

The great traditions of Western medicine began and have flourished in Western Europe. Until at least the 1930s, it was not at all unusual for outstanding students to take their medical training in whole or in part in Europe. In the 1960s and 1970s, many Americans went to Europe, especially to Italy and Belgium, if they could not enter U.S. schools. Since then, Belgium has all but closed its doors to U.S. and Canadian students, and experience has shown that U.S. graduates of Italian schools often don't do very well when they take the tests for their ECFMG Certification.

Many great medical schools do exist in Western Europe, but the best generally don't accept applications from U.S. or Canadian students (except for Dublin's Royal College) unless the applicant has a special language or cultural connection with the country. The most obvious connection is dual citizenship. Applicants must be absolutely proficient in the country's language, since both the application materials and all instruction are in that language.

If you do apply to European schools, excluding Dublin's Royal College, experts in the field say that the best schools are those in Scandinavia, Ireland, the United Kingdom, Holland, France, and Switzerland. Those to avoid include schools in Germany (which was once the *sine qua non* of Western medical training), Spain, and Italy. One school, recently promoted to premed advisers, is the Kigezi International School of Medicine under the auspices of the Cambridge (England) Overseas Medical Training Programme. Despite its prestigious affiliation, its clinical facilities are sorely lacking.

Dealing with the applications themselves can be a burdensome process. It will usually be difficult to complete the process by mail, and will be trying, at best, in person. (Remember that Europeans have honed bureaucracy to a fine art.)

For more information, contact the individual country's consulate or the address listed in *Appendix E*. Be prepared for an immediate rejection at that level unless you *clearly state* your connection to that country and your language proficiency. (Writing your letter in their native language may help.)

Eastern Europe

Willie Sutton reportedly said he robbed banks "because that's where the money was." Short on hard currency since the political changes in Eastern Europe, many old and distinguished schools in this region have tried to copy the Israeli model by developing U.S.-style medical curricula and teaching courses in English to attract tuition dollars. Some have representatives in the United States and advertise heavily.

Students need to learn the native language before beginning their clinical studies at these schools. Although students will be immersed in the language and culture during their first two years of study, I suggest taking a look at a language book for that country before you leap into this. Some of these languages (Hungarian, for example) may be virtually impossible for most native-English-speakers to learn with any facility.

Also of concern in Eastern Europe is that many of their medical systems and technologies have fallen far behind those of Western Europe, the United States, and Canada. If your medical training does not include the techniques, medications, and equipment typically used in Western medical settings, you will not have the necessary knowledge either to pass the USMLE or to successfully compete for a residency. Also, Eastern European medical schools, including those in Russia, have been involved in scams—taking the money and then either having no school at all or not providing the agreed-upon education.

For more information, contact the schools or their representatives directly. The contact information is in *Appendix E*.

Philippines

Quite a few Americans trek to the Philippines for their medical education. Although there are many medical schools in the Philippines, U.S.-citizen graduates of three schools have had above-average results on the tests for an ECFMG Certificate: the University of the Philippines (which annually takes up to two of their alumni's children, even if they were born in the United States); the University of Santo Tomas (also called The Catholic University of the Philippines), in Manila; and the University of the East in Quezon City, Santo Thomas. All of these schools require applicants to take the National Medical Admission Test (NMAT). For information about this test, contact: The NMAT Secretariat, Center for Educational Measurement, 6th Floor Concorde Condominium, corner Salcedo and Benavidez Streets, Legaspi Village, Makati, Metro Manila, Philippines. For more information about these schools, contact: Chair, Admission Committee, College of Medicine, University of the Philippines Manila, 547 Pedro Gil Street, Ermita, P.O. Box 593, Manila, Philippines; or Office of the Registrar, University of the East, Ramon Magsaysay Memorial Medical Center, Aurora Boulevard, Quezon City 1113, Philippines; or Admission Committee, Faculty of Medicine and Surgery, University of Santo Tomas, Manila, Philippines.

Other Schools

Medical schools, of course, exist all over the world. There have, on occasion, been U.S. and Canadian students at most of these. However, the only students who should even remotely think about going to these schools are those who have definite ties to the local culture, know the language (of instruction and daily use) thoroughly, and are willing to undergo even more extraordinary difficulties to eventually get U.S. or Canadian residency training and licensure than do other IMGs. Even in industrialized nations, such as Japan, there are often medical systems, medications, and methods that are quite different from those normally used in North America. Although after you are licensed you may want to learn some special techniques at these schools (for example, acupuncture), they are not places you should attend to get your primary medical education.

Scams

Fake Schools

U.S. students who are desperate for places in medical schools are good candidates for intentional and unintentional scams. In one instance, a fake European school was widely advertised and many students applied. When they were "accepted," the school required a $1,000 deposit to "hold their spot." Only when these students arrived to begin classes did they find that no such school existed.

Temporary Schools

In the Caribbean, several entrepreneurs have quickly opened, closed, re-opened, and again closed schools, leaving hundreds of students out of money and bereft of their dreams. Sometimes these schools opened and closed under the same name on another (or even the same) island. They had great advertisements and brochures, but they weren't good enough to warrant spending the tens of thousands of dollars each student wasted on a bogus, partial medical education. Some other entrepreneurs also reportedly sold medical diplomas for cash. (These, of course, are completely worthless except to hang on the wall, as at least one of these medical school administrators supposedly did. He granted himself a medical degree several months after starting his school.)

In the 1960s and 1970s, similar episodes occurred in Mexico. A number of private medical schools sprang up in small towns. These schools often had names very similar to well-respected and established Mexican medical schools. Some of these schools were only two rooms in a private home and with one "professor" who had gotten a mail-order degree. They took students' tuition, taught for two years, and then disappeared—often reappearing in another small town under a different (or even the same) school name. These "schools" disappeared in the 1980s when medical school applications plummeted, but they may yet return with the current increase in applicants.

Somewhat less egregious, but only because they did not plan it, were the new for-profit (primarily Caribbean) medical schools that simply went broke and were forced to close their doors. This mainly happened during the 1980s when, believe it or not, few applicants needed to look outside the United States or Canada for a medical education. The foreign schools could not survive the drought and went belly up. That is why experts suggest that if you are looking at foreign schools, only consider those that have been in existence for a decade or more. They are the least likely to evaporate after you pay your money.

Agencies

A 1970s scam that is now reappearing involves agencies that "help" you get into foreign medical schools. They come in two varieties. The first type, usually with a very prestigious name and located in the United States or Canada, is nothing more than a contractor or agent for a particular medical school attempting to lure U.S. and Canadian students. These contractors' addresses are really just "fronts" for these schools' marketing services. Honest foreign schools simply say that their North American addresses are merely a convenient address for their school.

The second type of agency offers to submit applications for you to international medical schools—for a big fee. It's unclear what paying this fee accomplishes, since they don't guarantee admission to any of the schools, and many schools have open (or nearly open) admission policies. Furthermore, some of these agencies specifically encourage applicants to apply everywhere, although as discussed above, applying to Canadian, British, and Western European schools is a waste of time unless you both have a cultural "in" and are a good student. (Canadian schools are as difficult or more difficult to enter than those in the United States.) The fees you pay to these agencies don't include the individual costs for transcripts and other paperwork, nor do they include the schools' individual application fees.

Language

All mainland-U.S. medical schools and all Canadian schools outside of Quebec (and McGill within Quebec) teach all classes in English.

Some schools in other (non-English-speaking) countries also teach their courses in English or have special English tracks for English-speaking students. The following medical schools teach all their courses in English: St. George's University, American University of the Caribbean, Ross University, Spartan Health Sciences University, Iberoamerican University, Medical University at Pecs, Touro College, and Saba. Schools in England, Australia, New Zealand, and South Africa, of course, teach in English.

A number of schools around the world claim to teach courses in English. This may be true, but consider the unspoken (and often unwritten) fine print. While the classes may be taught in English, the quality of this English varies greatly, so understanding your professors may at times be difficult. Also, even though the professors speak English, the patients you will see in the clinics do not. Therefore, you need to learn the native language to work in the clinics. This is not always an easy task, especially if you are trying to learn a new language while enrolled in a very daunting medical school curriculum.

Some schools, such as the Universidad Autonoma de Guadalajara and the new Baja California Medical College, require non-Spanish-speaking students to attend their intensive Spanish-language courses before beginning school so that by the time students *van a las clínicas, ellos hablan Español.* (Other Mexican schools are not as helpful.) The medical school in Pecs (Budapest) also includes Hungarian-language lessons along with the basic sciences. Great! But when I visited Hungary, the Hungarians admitted that it is harder for a non-native speaker to learn Hungarian than to become an astronaut. If you're a whiz at languages, fine. Otherwise, watch out.

The same goes for two outstanding foreign medical schools—Sackler and Technion. At both schools, clinical work is in Hebrew (and some patients only speak Arabic or Russian). If you already know the language, fine. Otherwise, it may be difficult to learn a language not related in any way (including the alphabet) to English.

Students going to foreign schools should also consider one other, not-so-obvious language-cultural problem. While pharmacology courses may be taught using the generic drug names used throughout the world, on clinical services you will often use drugs' brand names—which vary from country to country. Also, some pharmaceuticals commonly used in other countries are not available in the United States, and vice versa. This also holds true for some medical equipment and procedures. Just because they speak English, does not mean they will use American medical terminology—they won't.

A Useful Algorithm

If you are confused about this wealth of information, perhaps the following algorithm can simplify your decision process. If you elect to go to a non-U.S./Canadian medical school, go to:

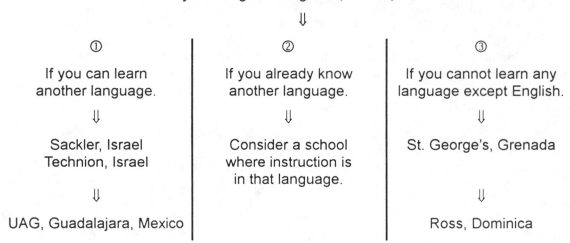

Australian four-year programs (Flinders, Sydney, and Queensland Universities)
Royal College of Surgeons, Dublin, Ireland

⇓

①	②	③
If you can learn another language.	If you already know another language.	If you cannot learn any language except English.
⇓	⇓	⇓
Sackler, Israel Technion, Israel	Consider a school where instruction is in that language.	St. George's, Grenada
⇓		⇓
UAG, Guadalajara, Mexico		Ross, Dominica

Transferring Into U.S. Medical Schools

Don't go to a foreign medical school expecting to later transfer to a U.S. school. The odds are not in your favor—and they seem to be getting worse. Nevertheless, the best way to get into a U.S. residency is to transfer into a U.S. medical school prior to graduation. To accomplish this, you will have to do *very* well in your courses during the first two or three years of medical school. You will also have to perform well on Step 1, and possibly Step 2, of the USMLE as administered through the ECFMG. Doing well on the USMLE will be an impressive accomplishment, since U.S.-citizen IMGs have consistently done worse on licensing examinations than their foreign-born counterparts.

In 1994-95, only 87 students studying at foreign medical schools were accepted for transfer into M.D.-granting schools in the United States (down from about 400 per year in the 1970s and 350 per year in the mid-1980s). Most had to repeat one or more years of medical school. Available openings only occur because a small number of students fail their classes, drop out, or take leaves of absence. About half of all schools simply leave these spots empty or offer them only to students from other LCME-approved schools who must transfer for personal reasons. The schools that do accept transfers from foreign medical schools are usually private schools seeking not only good students who can help rebuild the class size, but also students who can replace the tuition income lost when students leave.

In recent years, most medical students who successfully transferred to U.S. schools had high GPAs after completing at least two years of medical school, did very well on the USMLE, and transferred to private schools or to schools in states where they were official residents. (Note that you cannot "transfer" once you have received your medical degree.) The implicit requirement to complete two years of school before transferring plays havoc with the system, since second-year classes at many off-shore schools don't finish until mid- to late-August, when it may be too late for students to transfer to a U.S. school. This leaves students with two options: applying for a transfer while continuing at the original medical school or dropping out and hoping to be accepted as a transfer student. This latter option is not a good idea, since the odds are even less favorable for foreign medical students who are not currently enrolled in school.

Students who have tried to transfer to U.S. schools say that some medical schools, particularly in the Caribbean, are not pleased when their students transfer to U.S. schools, and they show that displeasure by delaying the transmission of transcripts to U.S. schools for months. (Some students try to bypass this problem by having their transcripts sent to them, but U.S. medical schools will usually accept only transcripts sent directly to them.) St. George's University, which encourages its students to transfer, is an exception.

Medical schools in the United States and Canada that say they accept transfers from foreign schools are listed in figure 15.5. The Deans of Students at international schools with large numbers of U.S. citizens also keep lists of U.S. medical schools that have accepted their students. U.S. schools that, in recent years, have taken from seven to ten such transfer students per year are: George Washington University, SUNY–Syracuse, Northeastern Ohio University, and the University of Miami. Those taking up to five students a year are: the Medical College of Georgia, SUNY–Buffalo, and the University of Missouri–Columbia.

Records suggest that the relatively few students who transfer to U.S. medical schools do very well. They are, however, a very select group of students.

The steps listed below may help you to locate a school willing to accept you.

1. At least a year before you expect to transfer, contact U.S. medical schools directly to inquire about their willingness to take USIMGs.

2. Mail these inquiry letters to the admission offices of all U.S. medical schools. For any school where you have any kind of "tie" (such as birthplace, undergraduate school, long residence, parents' residence, etc.), specifically mention the connection.

3. If you have to limit the number of letters sent, concentrate on non-Ivy League, private schools. State schools will often only accept students who are considered in-state residents.

4. Although Osteopathic medical schools say they don't accept transfers from foreign schools, contact them if they are located in a state where you have strong ties.

5. Do not be picky about where these schools are located, and be willing to repeat one or more years of course work.

Clerkships In The United States

Most "off-shore" (mainly Caribbean) medical schools have no local clinical-teaching facilities and, except for St. George's, will not say where their students go for clinical rotations. As one AMA spokesman said, "Most of these schools have no clinical facilities to teach medical students, so they sort of cut them loose at the end of their basic-science training and tell them to go to the mainland and find a clinical setting." This is not true for most medical schools located elsewhere in the world, which usually have substantial clinical facilities, although they are not always up to American and Canadian health-care standards.

This situation results in many U.S. students from foreign medical schools seeking sites for their third- and fourth-year clinical clerkships. This search can be long and frustrating, since some states now restrict such students from doing clerkships and the AAMC has imposed its own rules as well.

The scandal involving fake diplomas granted by some now-defunct medical schools led four jurisdictions (Maine, Montana, Pennsylvania, and Puerto Rico) to ban international medical students from taking clinical clerkships in their hospitals. Six other states (California, Florida, Massachusetts, New Jersey, New York, and Texas) regulate international medical students in clinical clerkships. New York reportedly has the toughest regulations (and highest fees) to certify the non-U.S. medical schools that send their students for clerkships; currently there are only two schools whose students may spend more than 12 weeks there doing clerkships. In addition, some U.S. medical schools prohibit "co-mingling" their students with students from non-U.S. schools during required clerkships. (Some hospitals have gotten around this with "separate-but-equal" ward teams.) These restrictions, however, attack the mechanism through which foreign-trained medical students demonstrate their clinical competence and subsequently get residency slots and get licensed. (Twenty-four licensing boards evaluate the quality of an IMG's clinical clerkships when deciding whether to grant a medical license.)

Fifth-Pathway Programs

A way to get back into the United States that still exists, but is rather moribund, is the *Fifth-Pathway Program.* The Fifth-Pathway route allows students in countries that require a year of internship or of social service before granting the M.D. degree (primarily Mexico) to take a year of supervised clinical training at a U.S. medical school. To qualify for this program, the students must have completed their undergraduate premedical studies at a U.S. college or university with grades and scores acceptable for entrance into a U.S. medical school, completed all formal requirements *except* internship/social service at a foreign medical school listed in the World Health Organization's *World Directory of Medical Schools* (last published in 1988 with the next edition due in 1997), and may have to have passed USMLE Steps 1 and 2. (Those who have completed their internship/social service requirement are not eligible.) Four U.S. medical schools list themselves as accepting Fifth-Pathway students. However, only the New York Medical College (Valhalla, NY) and Mount Sinai School of Medicine (now part of the new NYU-Mt. Sinai School of Medicine, New York, NY) actually accept students for this program. (The two others listed are the University of Puerto Rico and Brown University.) Less than 20% of those applying for Fifth-Pathway slots are accepted.

Some students in Fifth-Pathway programs complete the same rotations as do third-year students at that U.S. medical school. Others do an eclectic year, combining some third- and some fourth-year training experiences. From this springboard, USIMGs are usually able to leap into residency slots much more easily. However, seven jurisdictions (Alaska, Arkansas, Delaware, Guam, Maine, South Carolina, and Wyoming) do not accept Fifth-Pathway certificates as part of an application for licensure. Twenty-three other states and the District of Columbia currently require that the Fifth-Pathway graduates either complete the USMLE or have an ECFMG Certificate. Other jurisdictions leave acceptance of the Fifth-Pathway certificate to their licensing board's discretion, with only thirteen jurisdictions accepting it unconditionally. For more information about the Fifth-Pathway program, contact: Licensure and Certification Section, American Medical Association, 515 N. State St., Chicago, IL 60610.

USIMGs will also feel the impact of restrictions now being imposed upon all international medical graduates. Getting into a residency will become harder and harder as time passes and laws become more strict. In the future, it will take more than just excellent grades and good examination scores for you to get any position at all, let alone in the specialty that you desire.

Getting Back Into The U.S. For Residency And Practice

Before you jump into a foreign-medical-school experience, realize that completing medical school will only be the first (and usually least) of your headaches on the road to practicing medicine in the United States. Individuals who are currently citizens or permanent residents of the United States but who have received their medical degrees outside the United States, Puerto Rico, or Canada are U.S. international medical graduates (USIMGs). (A complete description of the different types of IMGs and the various processes they must go through can be found in *The International Medical Graduate's Guide to U.S. Medicine: Negotiating the Maze* by Louise B. Ball [Tucson, AZ: Galen Press, 1995]).

Here, in a nutshell, is what USIMGs have to do to practice medicine in the United States. (These will each be described below.)

- Apply for and meet the requirements for an ECFMG Certificate.

- Once the ECFMG Certificate is received, apply for a residency position. No matter what training you may have had, you must complete at least one year of residency (and often more) in the United States.

- Apply for and pass the USMLE Step 3 given by State medical-licensing boards. You must also fulfill any other requirements of the licensing boards. Once you do that, you can practice medicine.

In spite of this, by 1995, more than 155,000 (or about 23% of) physicians practicing medicine in the United States were trained outside the United States, Puerto Rico, or Canada. Their practices are generally medical rather than surgical (figure 17.3). In 1995, about 85% of IMGs worked in clinical care, with 59% in office-based practices (more than one-fifth of all office-based U.S. physicians). IMGs account for about 24% of physicians in residency training, and approximately 37% of PGY-1s. Nearly 50% of all IMGs train in Internal Medicine or a Medicine specialty.

USIMGs may have a greater image problem than do foreign nationals. While foreign-born physicians have a reason to train outside the United States, it is often assumed that USIMGs could not measure up to U.S. standards and thus had to leave the country. While this may be true for some, the fact remains that many qualified applicants are rejected from U.S. schools simply because there are not enough positions.

In 1995, 47% of IMGs in U.S. residency training programs were U.S. citizens or permanent U.S. residents. (Only 9%, however, were native U.S. citizens.) This is an increase from 1988, when USIMGs made up only 41% of the IMGs in U.S. residencies. Of the 735 USIMGs who completed the NRMP PGY-1 Match process in 1995, only 366 (50%) obtained residency positions. This is slightly lower than the rate for foreign-born IMGs (51%).

ECFMG Certification

U.S. citizens who graduate from international medical schools must get ECFMG Certification to be eligible for: (1) acceptance into an ACGME-accredited residency in the United States, (2) application to take Step 3 of the USMLE, and (3) a medical license in most states. It often also is required of Fifth-Pathway students before they can obtain positions at U. S. medical schools. The ECFMG issues about 4,500 new Certificates each year.

This is how you get that certification. First, to qualify for an ECFMG Certificate, you must be either a *student* attending a medical school listed in the current edition of the *World Directory of Medical Schools* (published by the World Health Organization) *or* a *graduate* of a medical school

Figure 17.3: IMGs Practicing Medicine in Various Specialties

	Number of IMGs	% of All Physicians in Specialty	% of All IMGs
Physical Medicine/Rehab.	1,682	32 %	1.1 %
Nuclear Medicine	474	32	0.3
Pathology	5,439	31	3.5
Pediatrics	14,352	30	9.3
Psychiatry	10,767	29	7.0
Internal Medicine	32,242	29	20.9
Anesthesiology	8,826	28	5.7
Cardiovascular Disease	5,024	27	3.3
Neurology	2,816	26	1.8
Child Psychiatry	1, 270	24	0.8
Radiation Oncology	786	23	0.5
Thoracic Surgery	524	23	0.3
Colon & Rectal Surgery	221	23	0.1
General Surgery	7,987	21	5.2
General/Family Practice	15,065	21	9.8
Obstetrics & Gynecology	7,138	19	4.6
Gen. Preventive Medicine	180	14 %	0.1 %
Emergency Medicine	2,264	13	1.5
Occupational Medicine	399	13	0.3
Otolaryngology	1,096	12	0.7
Public Health	223	12	0.1
Orthopaedic Surgery	1,874	9	1.2
Ophthalmology	1,443	9	0.9
Diagnostic Radiology	1,486	8	1.5
Dermatology	590	7	0.4
Aerospace Medicine	46	7	0.0

Adapted from: American Medical Association. *Physician Characteristics and Distribution in the U.S., 1995.* Chicago, IL: AMA, 1996, Tables A-6 and A-7.

which was listed in this directory at the time of your graduation. If you have graduated, you must also document completion of the educational requirements to practice medicine in the country in which you received your medical education. This must include at least four years of medical study for which credit was received. The specific credentials accepted for each country are listed in the *Information Booklet, ECFMG Certification and Application*, available from the ECFMG, 3624 Market Street, 4th Floor, Philadelphia, PA 19104-2685, USA.

You must submit an application to take the United States Medical Licensing Examination (USMLE) and the required documentation to the ECFMG. This documentation includes a copy (front and back) of every document (and English translations) relating to your medical education. They provide a list of what is required from schools in every country. Once they receive all the required documents, the ECFMG sends the papers back to the medical school for verification. This

Figure 17.4: Types of Applicants (Percentages) Filling PGY-1 and Advanced Positions in Specialties through NRMP Match*

Specialty	U.S. Senior Students	Osteopathic & U.S. Grad. Physicians	IMGs, Fifth-Pathway, & Can. Grads	Total Filled NRMP Positions
Anesthesiology	17 %	2 %	27 %	46 %
Emergency Medicine	82	15	2	99
Family Practice	73	9	9	91
Internal Medicine	59	4	31	94
Int. Med.-Pediatrics	80	4	5	89
Int. Med.-Preliminary	57	2	15	74
Internal Med.-Primary	60	4	25	89
Obstetrics/Gynecology	86	7	4	97
Orthopaedic Surgery	88	10	2	99
Pathology	54	4	20	78
Pediatrics	77	4	17	98
Psychiatry	49	4	31	84
Radiation Oncology**	47	NA	NA	91
Radiology, Diagnostic	55	13	11	78
Surgery, General	89	7	3	99
Surgery, Preliminary	38	2	10	51
Transitional	51	4	21	76
Total Unmatched**	7	44	49	

* Percentages may not sum exactly due to rounding errors.
** 1995 data.

Derived from: National Residency Matching Program. *NRMP Data 1996.* Washington, DC: NRMP, 1996.

---

processing may take several months (or longer), especially at European and Third-World medical schools which are not too attentive to helping with this paperwork. Schools that specifically cater to U.S. citizens usually do better.

If you receive approval to take the USMLE, you must pass both Step 1 and Step 2 to meet the medical-science-examination requirement for ECFMG certification.

In the past, individuals with *least chance of passing* the old ECFMG examination of medical knowledge (a trend that will probably continue) were U.S. citizens, over forty years of age, female, non-native English-speakers, taking the test more than ten years after medical school, and educated in countries with medium-to-high infant-mortality rates and medium per capita income.

ECFMG English Language Examinations

All IMGs must also pass an English proficiency examination for ECFMG certification, even if they are U.S. citizens or native English speakers. The test results are only good for two years (unless you get accepted into a residency). So if you pass it but don't get a residency position before it expires, you must re-take the examination.

Clinical Skills Assessment (CSA)

Because of concerns raised by residency directors, state licensing boards, and the public, the ECFMG is about to implement a new exam to test the clinical proficiency of graduates from foreign medical schools. The test, the Clinical Skills Assessment (CSA), is similar to the Objective Structured Clinical Examination (OSCE) given at many medical schools. In the near future (in late 1996 or in 1997), the CSA will be added to the requirements for an ECFMG Certificate. This test has proven to be a rather accurate indicator of a clinician's clinical abilities.

Getting A Residency Position

Even if you get an ECFMG Certificate, you have just leaped a single hurdle—more are ahead. As previously stated, IMGs have a difficult time getting residency positions, especially in the most competitive specialties and, often, any residency at the most desirable locations (nice geography or good university programs). U.S. and Canadian graduates sweat out the residency application and matching processes—and they are not IMGs. IMGs have a considerably more difficult and more stressful time obtaining training positions. As one AMA spokesman said, "The two ways they most often find [residency positions] is through family or political connections or at institutions in badly underserved areas, such as big-city public hospitals." For help with the entire process, and to see what you need to go through, check out another of my books, *Getting Into A Residency: A Guide For Medical Students*, now in its fourth edition (Tucson, AZ: Galen Press, 1996).

Aside from their reluctance to take IMGs for other reasons, residency programs, especially those that train large numbers of international medical graduates, are now concerned about changes in Medicare laws that severely restrict programs' and hospitals' reimbursement for training non-U.S.-medical school graduates. These residency programs often operate on a shoestring as it is. Threatening to restrict their funds even further has already had the desired effect of closing down many training opportunities for international medical graduates. As this book goes to press, it is expected that by 1999, Medicare funding for IMGs will be reduced by 75% and that the total number of entry-level residency positions will be capped at 126% of the number of United States M.D. and D.O. graduates. (This is reduced from the current 146%, but is well above the 110% advocated by nearly all U.S. policy makers.) This will make it much more difficult for IMGs to obtain U.S. residency positions. Discrimination? Read on.

Section 102 of the 1992 Federal Health Professions Education Extension Amendments (PL 102-408) states:

> Graduates of Foreign Medical Schools.—The Secretary [of Health and Human Services] may make an award of a grant, cooperative agreement, or contract under this title to an entity [including a medical school] that provides graduate training in the health professions only if the entity agrees that, in considering applications for admission to a program of such training, the entity will not refuse to consider an application solely on the basis that the application is submitted by a graduate of a foreign medical school.

How much sway this holds over residency directors is unknown, since most are probably not aware of it. Studies show that some residency programs discriminate against IMGs as early in the process as when they send out application materials. As residency positions tighten, however, enterprising IMGs will certainly begin making them aware of the law.

What does sway residency directors, however, is the past performance of IMGs in residency programs. IMGs, especially those that contract with programs outside a matching program, have a higher attrition rate than U.S. graduates. Also, IMGs pass some specialty board examinations, such as internal medicine's, only about two-thirds as often on their first try as do U.S. graduates.

Since residency programs are, in part, judged on their graduates' pass rates, this is important to residency directors.

At least one state medical society (New York) has developed a program to assist IMGs trying to puzzle through the maze of obtaining residency positions within the state. They hold an annual IMG Information Forum. The Forum includes informational talks, question-answer sessions, and sessions in which residency-program representatives get to meet prospective IMG applicants. For information about this program, contact Membership Support Services, Medical Society of New York, 420 Lakeville Rd., Lake Success, NY 11042.

Some international graduates are forced to take residency slots that are unfunded. In some cases they are called "externships"; in others, they actually count toward completion of a residency. It is not unusual to see offers of payment for a residency slot from either the applicants themselves or third-parties acting on their behalf. Proposals of $25,000 or more per year (plus any cost for salary, benefits, and allowances) have been offered for competitive positions. It is possible, however, that many of the individuals filling these positions are not treated as equals, do not get similar responsibilities, or do not end up with training equivalent to that of other residents in the same program.

Despite all the unfavorable press and the tough requirements, the number of IMGs in U.S. residency positions increased from 12,259 in 1989 to 23,499 in 1994. The number of IMGs in first-year residency positions increased over this same period from 2,689 to 7,044. USIMGs (U.S. natives and naturalized citizens) make up about 14% of first-year residents, but 47% of all IMG residents. In the 1995-96 NRMP Match, IMGs made up a large proportion of those entering some specialties (figure 17.4).

The American Medical Association (AMA) has formed a Department of International Medical Graduates. It is designed to tackle licensure, discrimination, and visa issues on behalf of IMGs. For information, contact the AMA International Graduate Services, 515 N. State St., Chicago, IL 60610.

Obtaining A Medical License

Each U.S. state and territory (and each Province in Canada) has its own medical licensing board. Although licensing tests have become relatively uniform, each locale has its own specific rules and paperwork required to obtain a medical license. All U.S. states require passing the USMLE Step 3. To apply to take Step 3 (which you don't have to worry about until you are in or have completed residency training), an applicant must have obtained an M.D. degree or equivalent, successfully passed the USMLE Steps 1 and 2, obtained an ECFMG Certificate or completed a Fifth-Pathway program, and met any other specific requirements imposed by the state licensing board administering the test. Information about specific state requirements is available from individual state boards, or The Federation of State Medical Boards of the United States, Inc., 400 Fuller Wiser Road, Suite 300, Euless, TX 76039, USA; (817) 735-8445.

There are thousands of IMGs in the United States who have not been able to obtain licenses to practice medicine. In many cases this is because residency programs will not accept them for training, and all jurisdictions in the United States require *at least one year of postgraduate training in the U.S. or Canada for licensure* (figure 17.5). Fifteen jurisdictions require IMGs to have at least two years of training and twenty-nine require three or more years. This exceeds what most jurisdictions require from U.S. graduates. In addition, five licensing boards (Alabama, Maryland, Ohio, Puerto Rico, Virginia) maintain lists of state-approved foreign medical schools, and will only grant medical licenses to graduates of those schools.

Even with these additional requirements, state medical boards are very wary of IMGs. They either have been snookered themselves or know of other boards which have been scammed by individuals with false medical credentials. These episodes often end up on newspapers' front pages, and states medical boards don't want egg on their faces. So, even though graduates from U.S. and Canadian schools don't have to appear in person before the medical board or submit all medical school, ECFMG, and residency paperwork (again translated by an official if not in English), you may well have to do so.

It is clear from their prior behavior that some medical boards simply don't want IMGs practicing in their states. But they can raise the postgraduate educational barriers only so high. Another ploy that some have suggested (but that no one has yet had the *cajones* to implement) is to require that most or all of a medical student's clinical training be in the country where the medical school is located. This will effectively eliminate the Caribbean schools, since none have adequate facilities to meet this requirement.

The decision to attend a foreign medical school should not be made lightly. The colossal problems include personal and academic difficulties during preclinical courses, frequent problems with acquiring adequate clinical experiences, language differences, and difficulty in obtaining U.S. residency training and getting a license to practice medicine. Take this route only if you have no other option—including waiting a year or two while you improve your credentials. You should only consider this route if you have both the fortitude to overcome all these difficulties, and the academic skills to complete the course of study and pass the USMLE.

Figure 17.5: Graduate Education Requirements for Licensure

Number of years of accredited U.S. or Canadian graduate medical
education (residency) required for a medical license.

One Year

Alabama	Kentucky[1]	Pennsylvania[1]
Alaska	Louisiana[1]	Puerto Rico
Arkansas	Maryland[1]	Rhode Island[1]
Arizona[1]	Massachusetts[1]	South Carolina[1]
California	Minnesota[1]	Tennessee[1]
Colorado[1]	Mississippi[1]	Texas[1]
Deleware[1]	Missouri[1]	Utah
District of Columbia[1]	Montana[1]	Vermont[1]
Florida[1]	Nebraska[1]	Virgin Islands
Georgia[1]	New Jersey[1]	Virginia[1]
Hawaii[1]	New York[1]	West Virginia[1]
Idaho[1]	North Carolina[1]	Wisconsin
Indiana[1]	North Dakota[1]	Wyoming[1]
Iowa	Ohio[1]	
Kansas	Oregon[1]	

Two Years

Connecticut	Massachusetts[2]	Ohio[2]
Guam[3]	Michigan	Oklahoma
Hawaii[2]	Minnesota[2]	South Dakota
Illinois	New Hampshire	Washington[4]
Indiana[2]	New Mexico	Wyoming[2]
Maine[1]		

Three Years

Arizona[2]	Maryland[2,4]	Oregon[2]
Colorado[2]	Mississippi	Pennsylvania[2]
Delaware[2]	Missouri[2]	Rhode Island[2]
District of Columbia[2]	Montana[2]	South Carolina[2]
Florida[2]	Nebraska[2]	Tennessee[2]
Georgia[2]	Nevada	Texas[2]
Idaho[2]	New Jersey[2]	Vermont[2,3]
Kentucky[2]	New York[2]	Virginia[2]
Louisiana[2]	North Carolina[2]	West Virginia[2]
Maine[2]	North Dakota[2,5]	

[1] Graduates of U.S. medical schools only.

[2] International medical graduates.

[3] Canadian training accepted only from Canadian medical school graduates.

[4] Only one year of postgraduate training required if individual graduated prior to 1 July 1992 from an international medical school approved by the Board.

[5] Second and third years of postgraduate training may be waived with proof of equivalent professional experience.

Adapted from: Bidese CM. *U.S. Medical Licensure Statistics & Current License Requirements: 1995.* Chicago, IL: AMA Publications, 1995, Tables 14 and 16.

18: Financial Information

A MEDICAL EDUCATION IS USUALLY VERY EXPENSIVE. Costs include not only tuition, which can be very high, but also living expenses and the books, special clothes (lab coats, uniforms), and equipment required for school.

Since 1960, medical school tuition has increased by 400% at private schools and 250% at public schools, even after being adjusted for inflation. The actual tuition (The University of California's schools pretend they have no tuition by calling their tuition a "fee.") ranges from less than $2,000 to $48,000 a year, depending upon whether the school is public or private and whether you are a state resident. (The Uniformed Services University is, of course, "free," but you owe them a service commitment.) State residents pay, on average, an annual tuition of $8,000 at their state's public medical schools, while out-of-staters pay about $17,500. Tuition at private schools averages more than $22,000 a year. (See figures 15.3 and figure 15.7.) Most schools also charge additional "academic fees," which can be substantial.

Medical textbooks are very expensive (up to $4,000 the first year). Lab coats and other equipment must be purchased or rented. The cost of living varies significantly across the country. In general, these costs are lowest in the deep South and in the Midwest. The farther Northeast or West you go, the higher the average living costs.

Lest you think that tuition provides the only financial support for medical schools, be aware that only 4.1% of the average medical school's budget comes from tuition and fees (3% at public schools and 6% at private schools). The balance is primarily generated from patient care revenues, research grants, and government agencies.

Paying For Medical School

You must pay for medical school with cash, scholarships, or loans, or by working for the federal or state government after you graduate. Loans constitute most of the financial aid available to pay for medical school education. However, everyone accepted to a U.S. medical school should be able to obtain all the financial assistance they need to pay their way, up to their "cost of education" as determined by the school's financial aid office, as long as they are U.S. citizens or permanent residents and *do not have a bad credit rating.*

In recent years, medical students received about $1 billion in educational loans. In 1995, 78% of the graduating medical students who borrowed money to pay for their education owed an average of more than $69,000. Forty percent of all 1996 graduates owed more than $75,000. This debt has increased 350% since 1983! (For perspective, the average graduating medical student's debt in 1971 was only $8,435.) Students at private medical schools have debts that are nearly 50% higher than those of students at public schools. The 94% of Osteopathic medical graduates who incurred debt had an average debt of $93,100. Students will face even larger debts, given that at least thirty-three medical schools now have annual tuition/fee charges of more than $20,000, and six schools now charge in excess of $25,000. In addition, nearly 16% of medical graduates' spouses have debts exceeding $50,000. Spouses and significant others of women medical graduates have significantly higher debts (>$78,000) than their male cohorts' partners (>$61,000). Also, nearly 15% of medical students take more than four years to complete medical school, which increases their debt.

A small number of students leave medical school without graduating. They may either leave for personal or academic reasons. In most cases, they will end up with a large debt for the schooling they received.

Many medical schools give an introduction to financial aid at their orientation session during the interview visit (see figure 21.2). Some who don't make their financial aid officer available to talk with applicants. If you have the chance, find out about the school's financial-aid resources during that visit.

Accrue Debt Carefully

Maintaining good credit and learning not to use credit cards indiscriminately are the two most important things premed students can do to get ready to finance their medical education.

How good is your credit? "Why does that matter?" you ask. "I'm going to medical school and will make a mint of money when I get out." Maybe. But you may not even get in if your current credit rating is poor. In 1996, one medical school *rescinded the acceptances for at least eight students* because they had dismal credit ratings and could not get the loans to pay for medical school! To avoid this situation, a small, but increasing, number of medical schools require students to submit a credit history with their application to prove that they can get the loans most students need to pay for medical school. Use the form in figure 18.1 to find out about your own credit rating.

Note that the form has TRW's address on it. You can also get your credit rating from three other national credit bureaus, although it will cost you up to $8 (depending upon the state where you reside), unless you have been denied credit through that agency within the past 60 days. The three other credit bureaus are: Equifax, P.O. Box 105873, Atlanta, GA 30348, tel. (800) 685-1111; CSC Credit Services, P.O. Box 674402, Houston, TX 77267-4402, tel. (800) 759-5979; and Trans Union Corporation, P.O. Box 390, Springfield, PA 19064-0390, tel. (610) 610-4909. TRW's telephone number is (800) 682-7654.

You've heard it before: Be careful using those credit cards! The interest rates can be astronomical. The debts seem to pile up quickly and soon can get out of control. You may want to ask yourself: Am I using my credit cards for credit or for convenience? You only use a credit card for convenience if you pay the bill in full each month. Otherwise you are using it as a very expensive form of credit—and living beyond your means—typical of more than 75% of the U.S. populace. If you have trouble with overspending, you may want to investigate using a debit card. These cards immediately withdraw money from your account when you make a purchase. If you have no money, you cannot spend the money. Think of it as the "tough (credit) love" approach. All financial aid officers recommend that you pay off all of your consumer debt before you enter medical school if you possibly can. It will save you lots of headaches in the future.

Figure 18.1: Personal Credit Rating Request Form

TRW Credit Data
P.O. Box 8030   _____ (Date) _____
Layton, UT 84041-8030

Dear Sirs:

Please mail a copy of my credit report to me. I am enclosing a copy of my valid driver's license to verify my address.

_____

Full Name (including generation: Jr., Sr., I, II)

Marital Status: ❑ Single; ❑ Married; ❑ Divorced; ❑ Separated; ❑ Widowed

_____

Spouse's First Name, if married

_____

Current Address, including Apartment Number and Zip Code

_____

_____

Prior Address (past 5 years), including Apartment Number and Zip Code

_____

_____

Prior Address (past 5 years), including Apartment Number and Zip Code

_____

Current Employer: _____   ❑ Unemployed

Social Security Number: _____

Daytime Telephone Number: (_____) _____

Year of Birth: _____

Please contact me, as soon as possible, if you need additional information.

Sincerely,

_____
Your Signature

Obtaining Financial Aid

Financial aid can come in several forms. There are federal, state, and private loans; state, military, public health service, private, and school-based scholarships; Veterans' educational benefits; and in some cases, private financial help from students' own families. Except for the last two sources, the availability of these funds may be based on a student's financial need, willingness to provide future services, background, special achievements, or interests.

More than 80% of all medical students require financial assistance to get through medical school. The only way to obtain this help (aside from family assistance and veterans' benefits) is to carefully complete the appropriate financial aid applications for each school—and return them quickly! That way, once you are accepted, the school can immediately begin to process your financial application.

Assess How Much You Will Need

The following chart (figure 18.2) is a simple guide to developing your budget for each year of medical school. When using it, remember to constantly update the information as your situation and costs change. It should give you a rough idea of how you stand financially. The amount of "expenses" that is greater than "income" determines approximately how much additional financial assistance you will need.

While in medical school, to stay out of financial trouble, you need to live within the budget the financial aid office develops when they calculate your loans and scholarships. If you elect to live like a professional when you are a medical student, you may live like a student when you are a physician (or you may not even make it through medical school to become one). Don't treat yourself to a new car to celebrate getting into medical school (unless, of course, you can afford to pay cash for that Lamborghini—in which case you're not reading this section anyway).

Note that with some loans, such as with the Unsubsidized Federal Stafford Loan, you may elect to take only part of the funds initially and wait to see whether you need the balance. For others, such as the Federal Perkins loan, if you decline the money, it will be immediately offered to another student. Check with the school's financial aid officer for specific information about the type of loans you are offered.

The Forms

In the January before you plan to enter medical school, if you haven't received a packet of financial information from each school to which you have applied, call their financial aid offices and request one. (Schools vary widely, however, on when they send out these forms. See figure 15.5.) These are big packets containing lots of information about the available financial aid, and numerous forms to complete. If you thought you saw mountains of paperwork before, you haven't seen anything until you get these packets.

It is wise to carefully complete the required application forms as soon as you can. *Students who get their financial forms back early, often before March 1, have priority in receiving assistance over others who apply later.* Since many programs quickly deplete their available funds, it's first come, first served. DO NOT WAIT TO BE ACCEPTED TO MEDICAL SCHOOL TO APPLY FOR FINANCIAL AID. Many first-time applicants make this very costly mistake.

The basic form is the Department of Education's *Free Application for Federal Student Aid*. The information requested is *very* personal and *very* detailed. Experienced counselors recommend that you complete your federal income tax forms before you complete these forms. The general guidelines are that each figure you enter on the financial aid forms must be within $200 of the

Figure 18.2: A Budgetary Guide for One Year of Medical School

Income	Fall Semester	Spring Semester
Parents/family	$	$
Spouse's earnings (net)		
Savings/other assets		
Job while in school (net)		
Financial aid (approved)		
Other		
TOTAL	$	$
Expenses		
Tuition	$	$
Other fees		
Credit card payments		
Books/supplies/instruments		
Rent/mortgage		
Utilities (phone, electric, gas)		
Household supplies/upkeep		
Food (at home/out of home)		
Recreation/entertainment*		
Travel/vacations		
Medical/insurance		
Clothing/laundry		
Car/transportation		
Parking/tolls		
Other insurance		
Dependent expenses		
Child care		
Miscellaneous		
TOTAL	$	$
RESOURCES minus EXPENSES =	$	$

* Vacation expenses and travel are not built into the calculations for financial aid.

same item on your tax form, and that the total difference for all items cannot exceed $400. If greater differences exist, you will have to amend the financial aid forms, which will take more time and possibly cost you a scholarship or a loan with favorable terms. You must include information about yourself, your spouse, and any dependents. Depending upon your status (all medical students are considered "independent students" under current federal law) and the loans or scholarships you are applying for, you may also have to provide information about your parents, including their signatures. Federal laws, for example, require parental information for applicants to the Health Professions Scholarship and Loan Programs. Type or neatly print the information on the original forms after you complete your final draft. Not only does it have to be read, but it also may be scanned into computers.

While the size of the financial packets you receive can appear quite daunting, the best way to handle them is to first remove the application from the packet and make several copies of the blank forms to use for your rough drafts. Then work through the application using the accompanying instruction booklet, one step at a time. *Keep a copy of all paperwork related to your financial aid applications, including any worksheets and your calculations!* Once you complete this paperwork, you don't want to do it again, especially if you have to justify the numbers you entered. Whenever you apply for Federal Stafford Loans, they only require some personal information and private lenders require only this plus limited credit information.

Useful Financial Terms

Although the following terms may now sound like items from a *New York Times* crossword puzzle, be assured that you will learn most of them very well—since they are necessary for your financial well-being. The sooner you become familiar with them, the better you will be able to deal with your finances.

Accrediting Agency: An agency, such as the LCME, that certifies that medical schools have met specific educational standards.

Actual Interest Rate: The annual interest rate charged by a lender, which may be equal to or less than the "applicable" (statutory) interest rate for that loan.

Applicable (Statutory) Interest Rate: The maximum annual interest rate a lender may legally charge on a loan.

Assignment: A change in ownership of the loan (i.e., a change in the lending agency).

Capitalization: An increase in the amount owed due to the lender adding accrued (but unpaid) interest to the loan principal. This occurs at varying intervals with different lenders.

Capitalized Interest: The unpaid interest added to the principal. Interest is then calculated on the new balance, which includes both the prior principal balance and the interest that has been added.

Default: The failure of a borrower to repay a loan or to fulfill other portions of the contract.

Deferment: A period during which the borrower need not make payments on the loan principal. However, interest still accrues.

Delinquency: The period after a borrower fails to make a payment.

Disability: A condition rendering an individual incapable of working, earning money, or attending school. A borrower is considered "totally and permanently disabled" if the condition is expected to continue for a long or indefinite time or to result in death.

Financial Aid Package: The total amount of financial aid a school gives a student.

Fixed Interest Rate: An interest rate that does not vary over the life of the loan.

Forbearance: A period during which the borrower need not make loan payments.

Forgiveness: Reducing the loan amount due for "Special Service," as described in the contract.

Garnishment: Intercepting a portion of an individual's wages to repay the lender for a defaulted loan.

Grace Period: The period between graduation (or ceasing to be enrolled at least half-time) and when loan repayment must begin.

Guarantee Fee: A fee charged for guaranteeing the loan. It is usually deducted from the amount the borrower receives.

Independent Student: Under current federal law, all medical students qualify for this status because they will be graduate or professional students.

Loan Transfer: A change in the identity of the loan holder or the agency that services the loans.

Need-Based Funding: Funding given to "financially needy" students, based on criteria set by the funding agency. These programs usually have the most favorable terms.

Origination Fee: Similar to the Guarantee fee, this is also deducted from the amount received. This fee covers preparation of some loan documents and other unspecified items.

Principal Balance: The amount of the loan outstanding and on which the lender charges interest. A portion of each payment reduces the principal and a portion pays the accrued interest.

Principal: The amount originally borrowed, not including any accrued interest.

Repayment Period: The time during which the loan must be repaid, excluding any period of authorized deferment or forbearance.

Repayment Start Date: The date on which the repayment period begins.

Special Service: Service to the military, medically underserved areas, or other groups or areas as described in the financial agreement. This service often counts toward repayment of all or part of the principal.

Subsidized Loan: A loan on which the federal government pays the interest that accrues during medical school, the grace period, authorized deferments, and, if applicable, post-deferment grace periods.

Unsubsidized Loan: A loan on which the borrower is responsible for paying all accrued interest.

Variable Interest Rate: Interest rates that change at set periods of time (e.g., quarterly, annually) according to the terms described in the loan agreement.

How Schools Use Financial Aid Information

Most schools DO NOT consider your financial needs when they decide whether to accept you. The admissions and financial assistance processes are separate. Most admission committees assume that every student will need financial assistance. Neither they nor the school's administration are concerned about where you get the money to pay the tuition, just that you get it. Their financial support offices are there to help you find the money you need.

Most schools first evaluate a student's eligibility for need-based funding. They match the information a student provides against criteria set by the funding programs. If a student meets the criteria for need-based programs (which have more favorable terms), he or she may receive an offer of need-based aid.

While no medical student is dismissed because of lack of funds, poor personal financial management has, in some instances, forced students to withdraw from medical school. And, since lenders are primarily concerned about an individual's credit rating, medical school financial officers are now discussing the possibility of checking the credit ratings of accepted applicants so that they can suggest to those with bad credit ratings that they work for a year to improve their credit ratings prior to entering medical school. That way, they may qualify for the loans they need to pay for school. You can get a free copy of your credit rating by contacting TRW or one of the other national credit organizations. (See "Accrue Debt Carefully" above for the addresses.)

Are You "Financially Needy"?

Since medical school is so expensive, most students are financially needy. The calculation used to determine a student's "financial need" is:

Cost of Medical Education — "Expected Family Contribution" = FINANCIAL NEED

FINANCIAL NEED — Financial Assistance = Unmet Financial Need

"Cost of Medical Education" as determined by the school includes tuition, fees, books, equipment and supplies, housing, food, transportation, personal expenses, child care, and miscellaneous expenses.

The "family" for the "Expected Family Contribution" (EFC) consists of the individual plus his spouse and any dependent children. EFC is determined by taking the family income and subtracting federal, state, and social security taxes. Financial aid officers then subtract an "employment allowance" for a working spouse, funds to support other family members, and funds for discretionary spending. The family's assets are evaluated based on their cash, savings, investments, and the net worth of any business or farm. For older students (25 years old and above), they protect a graduated percentage of their assets for retirement. Finally, they consider how many family members are in college, and estimate how much the family can contribute to the applicant's educational expenses.

Although the financial aid forms ask for parental income, since you are a health-professions student you need not include this information. However, voluntarily submitting your parents' financial information will give your school the data they need to consider you for additional federal programs administered by the Department of Health and Human Services. Parental information is also often required by schools when selecting students to receive scholarship funding.

If sufficient financial aid is available, the "Unmet Financial Need" (the money you don't have and cannot get) will be zero. If it isn't, contact the school's financial aid counselor for guidance.

The Award Letter

After your forms have been processed and you have been accepted to a medical school, the financial aid office will send you an "award letter" specifying the amount and type of aid the school can provide. Typically, it will list a combination of loans and, perhaps, a scholarship. Funding from sources you must obtain on your own, such as from the military or National Health Service Corps, will not be listed in the letter. If you enter one of these programs, you must notify the school's financial aid office so it can be part of your financial aid calculations.

You may accept some, all, or only part of the proffered funds. You may also discuss with the school's financial aid officer any data in the letter about which you are concerned. In some instances, financial aid officers have the discretion to modify the "Cost of Medical Education" or "Expected Family Contribution" used in the calculations. They might do this, for example, to include the costs of children's day care or to reflect the changes to a family's financial situation that will result when the student leaves a well-paying job to enter medical school. Requesting such changes does not endanger the awards they have already offered you. Whether your appeal will succeed depends on how well you document your case, what federal law allows, how badly they want you as a student, and how much money they have for financial aid. The amounts available for financial assistance vary widely from school to school.

Accepting a financial aid package does not obligate you to attend that medical school. If a school you would prefer to attend subsequently offers you a position or a better financial aid package, you are free to accept its offer. If you decide to decline either all the financial aid a school offers or the acceptance to that school, you must return the award letter within their deadline. Otherwise, the school assumes you accept all the offered aid. If you decline part of the financial aid, do not complete the loan forms for the full amount or make the loan applications out for less than the offered amounts. (Loan amounts are usually for the entire school year, so don't decrease the amount thinking you can get more when you begin the second semester.)

The Best Strategy

When the ton of paperwork for loans and scholarships arrives at your door, you have two options: pull out your hair in frustration, or take two aspirins (or your favorite non-steroidal anti-inflammatory agent) and get to work collecting the necessary information and filling them out. Remember all those minimum-wage jobs you had? The time you spend completing these forms will earn you far more than they paid. And the earlier you return these completed forms, the better your chance of receiving the most favorable financial aid terms. (Since some of these are renewable, if you do it right once, you're "in Fat City.")

Apply For All Types Of Aid

Go for it all—scholarships and loans. See what the school's financial aid office can find for you. Also, check with your local library for reference books listing other available financial aid. Contact organizations to which you, your spouse, your siblings, or your parents belong. They or their national bodies may offer little-known financial assistance. Because these funds usually are not well publicized or are available to only a small group, they are often not disbursed. If you don't check, you won't know about them. Don't, however, pay "application fees" to services to find loans for you. They are rarely worth the cost.

In recent years, more medical students (nearly 50,000) received Federal Stafford Loans than any other loan or scholarship. In decreasing order, students received financial aid from: Supplemental Loans to Students [Recently incorporated into the Federal Unsubsidized Stafford Loan Program] (30,000), scholarships from individual medical schools (27,000), Federal Perkins Loans (14,000), loans from individual medical schools (12,000), other scholarships (10,000), HEAL loans (10,000), Health Professions Loans (6,000), MedLoans/ALP (5,600), and other sources.

Measuring financial aid in terms of the average amount per student, however, the Armed Forces Health Professions and the National Health Service Corps Scholarships generated the largest annual amounts ($19,000), although these are considered taxable income. In decreasing order, other major sources were: Exceptional Financial Need Scholarship ($14,500), Medical Scientist Training Program ($14,400), Health Professions Students (FADHPS) Scholarship ($14,100), other scholarships with service commitments ($12,800), HEAL loans ($10,800), MedLoans/ALP ($8,300), Stafford Loans ($8,000), Supplemental Loans to Students ($7,800), state-funded scholarships ($7,000), Health Professions Loans ($6,000), and others. Federal Perkins Loans, not on this list, averaged only about $2,600 per student annually.

Understand Your Loan/Scholarship Terms And Obligations

Some financial aid programs are described below. Note that programs may change at any time, based on the whims of the funding agencies. This is particularly true for the federal government's programs.

Each loan has different rules about when, and exactly how, you must pay back what you borrowed. Consider when interest begins accruing and whether you will be able to put off repaying the loan principal or interest during your residency. Some loans and "scholarships" now also include service obligations. Read the fine print carefully and review the rules described below before obligating yourself.

Since the information about loans and scholarships changes annually, a good source to update your information is Carnegie Mellon University's Web site:

http://www.cs.cmu.edu/~FinAid/

which contains links to current information about virtually all the financial aid information you could want, as well as some nifty tools to calculate your financial need and "expected family contribution." Another Web source (http://www.studentservices.com/fastweb/) provides a free scholarship search.

Scholarships Without Payback Obligations

School-Based

Most medical schools have special scholarship funds for their students' use only. Financial aid offices will have the information about these funds.

State

Many states have scholarship programs (usually need-based) for medical students. Each school has information about what is available in its state. Many of these scholarships have service obligations attached. If you are from a state without a medical school, contact the premed adviser at the largest of your state's undergraduate schools to find out what is available.

National

Health Professions Scholarships–Scholarships for Disadvantaged Students (SDS)

This is a need-based program administered through the Department of Health and Human Services. Although the student will be the recipient of the funds, all applicants must supply information about their parents' income and finances to be eligible for this program. The amount of the scholarship varies. There is no payback obligation.

For Special Groups

Other special scholarships are available, but you may need to conduct your own search for them. Medical schools do not always have a complete list of such scholarships, since the available funds and the criteria change frequently, especially for the smaller programs. If you do get such funding, inform the school's financial aid office, since these amounts must be coordinated with other aid provided to you.

National Medical Fellowships

These scholarships are available, during the first and second years of medical school, to U.S. citizens who are African-American, Mexican-American, Native American, or mainland-Puerto Rican. Most of these scholarships are awarded based on financial need. Contact them at: 110 W. 32nd Street, New York, NY 10001-3205; (212) 714-0933.

Native Americans

Association of American Indian Physicians. This organization offers scholarships to Native American medical students. Contact them at: 1235 Sovereign Road, C-7, Oklahoma City, OK 73108; (405) 946-7072.

Association on American Indian Affairs. This organization offers several different scholarships for Native Americans. Contact them at: Box 268, Sisseton, SD 57262; (800) 895-2242.

American Indian Graduate Center. Members of federally recognized tribes may apply for scholarships. The scholarships are awarded based on financial need. For further information, contact: American Indian Graduate Center, 4520 Montgomery Boulevard, N.E., Suite 1B, Albuquerque, NM 87109; (505) 881-4584.

Tribal Funds. Many tribes have moneys for their members to attend school. The availability and amount varies with the tribe. Some of these programs may have payback obligations.

Women

American Association of University Women. This organization's Educational Foundation sponsors several awards for women in their final year of medical school. The amounts and requirements vary. They also offer Career Development Grants for women in the earlier years of medical school. For further information contact: American Association of University Women, Educational Foundation, 1111 16th Street, N.W., Washington, DC 20036.

American Medical Women's Association. The American Medical Women's Association offers one $4,000 scholarship to a student member who is in her first, second, or third year of M.D. or D.O. school. Contact them at: AMWA, 801 North Fairfax Street, Suite 400, Alexandria, VA 22314.

Scholarships With Payback Obligations

Free lunches do exist, but they are rare. More commonly, medical students mortgage their future when they accept loans and some scholarships. Some financial aid officers now say it's not "strings" that are attached to some of these programs, but "shackles." Be aware of the obligations you incur before accepting the money.

Exceptional Financial Need Scholarship Program (EFN)
Financial Assistance for Disadvantaged Health Profession Students Program (FADHPS)

These are need-based programs. The annual family contribution cannot exceed the lesser of $5,000 or one-half the cost of education. For the FADHPS program, the student must also come from a disadvantaged background. Only U.S. citizens and permanent residents are eligible. The EFN program provides tuition and other educational expenses, while the FADHPS program provides up to $10,000 annually. Although each award is only for one year, prior recipients have priority over others for getting awards in subsequent years.

Recipients must agree to complete a primary care (family practice, general internal medicine, general pediatrics, or preventive medicine/public health) residency no later than four years after graduating from medical school. They must also agree to practice in that specialty for at least five years. If the recipient breaks the agreement, all funds plus interest (at the maximum prevailing rate) from the date the recipient breaches the agreement must be repaid within the following three years. If you are thinking about this scholarship, be aware of the stiff penalties imposed if you should change your mind. Read the contract carefully!

Health Professions Scholarship Program (HPSP)

The HPSP scholarships sponsored by the uniformed services pay for students' tuition, books, fees, and other required medical school expenses. In addition, they provide a (taxable) stipend at the O-1 (entry-level officer—a second lieutenant or ensign) level. In return, participants generally owe four years of military service when they get out of school (one year for each sponsored year).

Students in the program also must do a clinical rotation at a military facility during both their junior and senior years of medical school. They will, however, be paid at a higher level during this active duty and have base privileges. Participants are also required to apply for military residencies, unless they get waivers based on the specialty they want to enter. These waivers are hard to get, and are granted only on the provision that the service needs the specialty and that there are too few military residency spots available in that specialty. With the downsizing of the military medical corps, few people qualify for this waiver.

To be eligible for any of the HPSP programs, the individual must

- be a U.S. citizen,
- be enrolled in or have an acceptance letter (not a wait-list letter) from an accredited M.D.- or D.O.-granting medical school in the United States or Puerto Rico,
- not be obligated to any other party (such as a state) after graduation, and
- meet all other requirements (including the physical examination and being "of good moral character") for a commissioned officer.

Health Professions Scholarship Programs are relatively competitive, with about half of all applicants being accepted. Military boards select applicants based on their GPAs, MCAT scores, work experiences, extracurricular activities, letters of reference, and often essays. (Sounds a lot like applying to medical school again.) The Air Force says that it offers more scholarships to those attending less-expensive schools, with the fewest scholarships going to those attending schools costing more than $20,000 per year. The other services use similar protocols.

A former military physician, who went through this program, gives this advice: "If you are thinking about taking an HPSP scholarship, don't do it for the money. There are other ways to get the money. Only do it if you really want to be a military officer first (and a physician second). Otherwise, it will be an extremely onerous experience." Having been through this program myself, I agree and have an additional warning: Don't believe everything the recruiter says or the glossy brochures illustrate. Evaluate the plusses and minuses for yourself. It's unlikely that you are going to "pull a fast one" on Uncle Sam, but he may pull one on you. Tread carefully.

There are unique aspects to each service's program.

Navy Medical Scholarships

The Navy has the worst reputation in regard to its treatment of young physicians. After completing internship, physicians are usually assigned to duty as general medical officers—and are usually at sea for at least a year or two. As the Navy's recruiting brochure says, "Medical Corps officers typically serve as general medical officers between their internships and residencies." Some of them are assigned to serve with Marine Corps units. Upon completing their tours as general medical officers, physicians may then apply for residencies.

As with the other programs, Navy HPSP students receive school-required fees and expenses (except room and board); and reimbursement for microscope rental, required books, and equipment, and a monthly stipend. Information about Navy scholarships can be obtained from: U.S. Navy Opportunity Information Center, P.O. Box 9406, Gaithersburg, MD 20898-9979; phone (800) 327-6289; World Wide Web at http://www.navyjobs.com.

U.S. Army Scholarship Program

After participants are commissioned as reserve officers, the Army pays for their tuition, required books, rental of most nonexpendable equipment, and most academic fees. Participants also receive ten and one-half months of stipend each year as reserve officers. For the other one and one-half months each year, they receive the salary and allowances of a Second Lieutenant while they are on "Active Duty for Training." During this time, participants normally work at major Army medical centers in the United States or elsewhere. If school assignments do not permit this time away, students get the same pay but are on "active duty" at school.

Participants must apply for an Army internship. If they get a position (most do), they must accept it. The Army has been better about allowing individuals to complete their training than, for example, the Navy. The active duty obligation participants generate varies, but is usually one year for each year of scholarship. For more information about Army scholarships, contact: U.S. Army

Recruiting Command—RCHS-OP, ATTN: Operations Branch, Room 2002, 1307 3rd Avenue, Fort Knox, KY 40121-2726.

USAF Scholarship Program

After being commissioned as a reserve officer, each Air Force participant receives tuition, required educational fees, approved books, supplies, small equipment and microscope rental, plus ten and one-half months of stipend each year as a reserve officer. For the other one and one-half months each year, the Air Force pays participants the salary and allowances of a second lieutenant while they are on "Active Duty Tours." During the first two active duty stints, participants must attend courses whose names alone give you a sense of the military mind: "Health Professions Officer Indoctrination Course" (taken the summer before beginning school) and "Indoctrination to the Air Force Medical Service and Aerospace Medicine" (taken between the first and second years). The third- and fourth-year stints are at Air Force medical teaching facilities. If school assignments do not permit this time away, students get the same pay while on "active duty" at school.

Participants must apply for an Air Force internship. If they get a position (most do), they must accept it. The Air Force has been better about allowing individuals to complete their training than, for example, the Navy. They are not interested, however, in those pursuing dual specialties, such as pediatrics–internal medicine. The Air Force also says that it is not interested in those students combining advanced-degree programs, such as M.D.-Ph.D. The active duty obligation varies, but it is usually one year for each year of scholarship. For more information about Air Force scholarships, contact: USAF Medical Recruiting, Medical Recruiting Division, HQ USAFRS/RSHM, 550 D Street West, Suite 1, Randolph AFB, TX 78150-4527.

National Health Service Corps (NHSC) Scholarship Programs

The NHSC is the component of the Public Health Service (PHS) Bureau of Primary Health Care that recruits physicians and other health professionals for underserved areas in the United States. Both M.D. and D.O. students are eligible for scholarships if they agree to train in and to practice general internal medicine, family practice, general pediatrics, general psychiatry, or obstetrics & gynecology in a federally (PHS) designated underserved area. For this, the NHSC pays all medical school tuition and fees, a monthly stipend, and other "reasonable educational expenses." Program participants owe one year of service for each year of support, with a two-year minimum.

Qualified applicants must agree to complete a primary care residency. They also must have the characteristics that suggest they will remain with the NHSC. These are:

- Strong motivations to practice primary care in a health-profession-shortage area after completing their commitment.

- Experience with indigent or underserved communities.

- Understanding and accepting the NHSC's mission.

- Being available during medical school to participate at rural or urban community-based health care facilities.

Individuals who meet these requirements and have documentation from their school that shows they are (or would have been) eligible to participate in the federal "Financial Assistance for Disadvantaged Health Professions Students" will be given preference over other applicants.

Only about 150 to 250 NHSC scholarships have been awarded annually to medical students in recent years. Fewer than 10% of all applicants get scholarships. In 1995-96, for example, 1,841 medical students applied, and 148 (115 M.D. and 33 D.O.) received scholarships. Although the

NHSC is under the Public Health Service, most scholarship recipients do not become commissioned PHS officers.

Information about NHSC scholarships (and their loan-repayment programs) can be obtained from: National Health Service Corps, Scholarship Program, U.S. Public Health Service, 1010 Wayne Avenue, Suite 240, Silver Spring, MD 20910; phone (800) 638-0824.

Information about additional NHSC programs can be obtained from:

- Commissioned Officer Student Training & Extern Program (COSTEP), PHS Recruitment, 8201 Greensboro Drive, Suite 600, McLean, VA 22102; phone (800) 221-9393, [VA] (703) 734-6855, (703) 821-2098.

- Advanced Educational Program in General Medicine, AMEDD Regional Office, 5111 Leesburg Pike, Room 695, Falls Church, VA 22041; phone (703) 681-6177.

- National Health Services Corps, Community Scholarship Program, Division of Scholarships & Loan Repayment, Loan Repayment Programs Branch, 4350 East-West Highway, 10th Floor, Bethesda, MD 20814; phone (301) 594-4400 or (301) 594-4981.

- National Health Service Corps, Health Promotion/Disease Prevention Project (HPDP), American Medical Student Association, 1902 Association Drive, Reston, VA 22091; phone (800) 729-6429, ext. 216.

Indian Health Service Scholarship Program

This federally funded scholarship program, only for Native Americans or Alaskan Natives from federally recognized tribes, is very similar to the National Health Service Corps Scholarship Program described above. (They also have a loan-repayment program.) Recently, this program has had funding problems. For more information, contact: Indian Health Service, Room 6A-29, 3600 Fishers Lane, Rockville, MD 20857.

State Programs

Many states have programs to assist state residents through medical school. Most require some type of service obligation, usually in primary care. Each state's programs are described in the AAMC's book, *State and Other Loan Repayment/Forgiveness and Scholarship Programs*. The book is available from: AAMC Section for Student Programs, 2450 N Street, N.W., Washington, DC 20037-1123; phone (202) 828-0681.

Loans

Getting loans to help with medical school costs makes most students feel pretty good. Don't get carried away. The following are some things to keep in mind about borrowing money:

- Every time you borrow you obligate part of your future income.

- You may wind up paying back up to $3.50 for every $1.00 you borrow.

- It is your responsibility to repay the loans, and to keep the lenders apprised of where you live, name changes, your phone number, and of any special circumstances why you shouldn't be paying them back, such as deferments, forbearance, grace periods, special service, or disability. (See "Useful Definitions," above.)

- If you don't repay your loans or meet your required obligations, both private and government lenders can get very nasty and mess up both your credit rating and your life. The federal government, for example, publishes a list of those who fail to repay student loans that is widely distributed. They also send this list to medical associations, state licensing agencies, and medical schools.

Compare Loan Costs And Lenders' Policies

All loans are not equal. If you have the option of taking either of two $15,000 loans, you need to carefully consider the costs of both and the policies of each lending agency. Don't just compare the interest rates, although these are very important. Also compare the attributes listed below for each loan.

- Does the loan have extra fees attached, such as a "loan-origination" or a "guarantee" fee?

- Does interest accrue during medical school? If it does, can this interest be added to the principal (capitalized) so you don't have to pay it while in school? If so, do they add the interest to the principal every three months, at graduation, or on another schedule? The longer it takes to add the interest to the principal the greater your savings.

- Does the lender generally sell its loans (to other lenders) on the "secondary market"? The second lender (the one who buys your loan) may change the loan's terms, for example, by not honoring the first lender's liberal policy on capitalizing interest.

- When does the repayment period begin? Is there a "grace" period during which you don't have to begin repaying the loan? Loan terms may allow students a one- to nine-month grace period following completion of medical school.

- Are there provisions for deferments, such as during residency, fellowships, military service, etc.? Are these deferments interest-free or does interest accrue?

- Once repayment begins, how often are the payments due?

- How long is the repayment period?

- Are there service obligations associated with the loan? If so, can you live with them? If you change your mind about fulfilling these obligations, how Draconian are the adjusted repayment rules?

Loan Repayment Terms

Normally, loans do not have to be repaid until at least six months after graduating from medical school. Most do not have to be paid back until after you finish your internship and begin residency training. As described above, a "grace period" is the time between completing school (while going at least half time) and beginning to repay the loan. Unsubsidized loans accrue interest during the grace period, while subsidized loans do not.

During part or all of their residencies, physicians generally have two options, depending on their overall financial situation: to avoid paying the loans while accruing interest on *some* of them (deferment), or to avoid paying the loans but still accrue interest on *all* of them (forbearance or deferment of unsubsidized loans). The requirements for implementing these options have become more strict in recent years. The rules will certainly continue to change over time, so check with your loan officer to find out the current regulations.

During forbearance and during deferments for unsubsidized loans, interest still accrues. It can either be paid as it accrues or be added to the principal, i.e., "capitalized." If the interest is capitalized on a quarterly basis (as some lenders do), the cost of the loan increases substantially, since after interest is capitalized, you then accrue interest on the original principal plus the capitalized interest payments. Some lenders capitalize the interest at the end of medical school—this practice makes these loans exceptionally attractive to borrowers.

Sometimes large portions of certain loans, or even the entire loan amount, will be "forgiven" (eliminated), if the recipient works in a particular field (usually primary care) or in a particular location (either a state or, more commonly, a designated "health-profession-shortage area" [HPSA]) for a specified amount of time. Recipients must agree to these stipulations at the time they get the loans.

Loans sponsored by the federal government (most of the loans taken by medical students) may be canceled only if the recipient dies or is "permanently and totally disabled." Very few loans are canceled. Most loans remain in effect even if the recipient drops out before completing medical school.

Sample Loan Costs

The following examples illustrate the relative amounts a typical medical student who qualifies as financially needy may have to repay. (Note that changing rules and using different lenders will alter the amounts.)

Federal Subsidized Stafford Loan: $34,000 Borrowed

Terms: $8,500 borrowed per year for four years. No interest accrues during medical school. Interest rate is 9%. (Interest rates are now capped at 8.25%, but who knows what the future may bring.)

Repayment: $430.70 per month X 120 months = $51,684.

Federal Unsubsidized Stafford Loan: $40,000 Borrowed

Terms: $10,000 borrowed per year for four years. Interest rate is 9%. Interest is calculated once a year (simple interest). Interest accrues during four years of medical school, with the interest capitalized at graduation ($9,000).

Repayment: $620.72 per month X 120 months = $74,486.40

Federal Perkins Loan: $10,000 Borrowed

Terms: $10,000 borrowed over two years with no interest accruing during medical school, and 5% interest during repayment.

Repayment: $106.00 per month X 120 months = $12,720.

Loan Management

All borrowers, including medical students and residents, need two qualities to manage their loans: organization and calmness. Residents who are currently repaying their loans (or managing to stay in deferment or forbearance) report constant hassles and rudeness from the lending institutions. (They weren't rude when you were applying, were they?) The best way to avoid hassles with lending agencies is to keep accurate records of all loan agreements, paperwork, correspondence, and telephone conversations with these agencies.

First, create a filing system for your loan and scholarship (especially any scholarships with payback obligations) paperwork. If you have more than one loan, create a file for each. This will help you avoid panic when you get a threatening letter from the lender. Keep a copy of all correspondence in your file. Also keep a log of all telephone calls, including the time, date, the subject, the names of the people with whom you spoke and what was said by whom. If you call the lender, stay calm. You will most likely be talking, at least initially, to folks with limited knowledge about loans and the specific rules governing your loan. Have your account or loan number (usually your Social Security number) and your file for that loan available.

If you mail material to the lender, send it certified, return-receipt requested. Although this costs more and you have to go to the post office, it's worth the trouble. An unbelievable amount of borrowers' correspondence gets "lost" on the way to lenders. If you request deferment or forbearance forms, inform the lender that you are in a medical residency training program, even if they don't ask for this information.

Loan Consolidation

Loan consolidation allows a borrower with several different loans to lump them together and only make one payment. Essentially, this is a new loan (for the total amount of the old ones) with new terms and a new interest rate. You may want to consider this option, because it streamlines the paperwork (and saves your sanity) to have only one loan payment per month rather than several payments on different schedules to different lenders. However, if you are considering this option, first read the fine print carefully. Be sure not to sacrifice favorable loan terms for the convenience of consolidating your loans.

The government has two consolidation programs available. The Federal Consolidation Loan Program can consolidate loans made under the following programs: Federal Stafford Loan, Federal Supplemental Loans for Students, Federal Perkins Loans, Federal Nursing Loans, and Health Professional Student Loans (HPSL). Under Sallie Mae consolidation, depending on the size of their debt, borrowers may have up to thirty years to repay their loans. The interest on these consolidated loans is a weighted-average of the original interest rates, rounded up to the nearest whole percentage point. The second government loan consolidation program is for an "administrative" consolidation of loans made through the Health Education Assistance Loan (HEAL) program. For information about these and other federal loan programs, call (800) 433-3243.

There are a number of loan consolidators you can use. Locate them through your financial aid officer or your lenders. As with any loan, shop around for the best deal you can get.

Loan Programs

These descriptions of some commonly used medical student loan programs will give you an overview of what is available. *The rules change each year.* Get the most current information from the medical schools' financial aid offices.

Federal Stafford Loans

Stafford Loans are administered under the Federal Family Education Loan Program (FFELP). For information about these loans, their eligibility requirements, explanations about how financial need is determined, help with completing the forms, and additional federal student aid publications, call (800) 4-Fed-AID (800-433-3243). Hearing-impaired individuals can contact a TDD by calling (800) 730-8913.

Subsidized

This is a need-based program, formerly called "Guaranteed Student Loans" or GSL. Citizens and permanent residents of the United States are eligible. In this program, the federal government subsidizes interest payments. The maximum annual loan amount is $8,500. Students may borrow up to a total of $65,500 for undergraduate and graduate school. The maximum loan-origination fee is 3% and the maximum loan-guarantee fee is 1%. These are taken out of the loan amount. No interest accrues while the borrower is in school, and there is a six-month grace period following graduation. The interest rate varies with a cap of 8.25%. Up to 70% of the debt can be canceled for Peace Corps or Vista service.

Most physicians will be eligible for a 3-year deferment based on economic hardship during residency. The deferment rules require that the individual have either (1) a federal education debt equal to or greater than 20% of their adjusted gross income, or (2) an adjusted gross individual income minus federal education debt burden of less than 220% of the federal poverty level for a family of two. Given current resident salaries, virtually all residents qualify.

Unsubsidized

This is not a need-based program. United States citizens and permanent residents are eligible. The maximum annual amount loaned is $18,500 (less the amount of any Subsidized Federal Stafford Loan). Students can borrow up to a total of $73,000 in the unsubsidized program for undergraduate and graduate school. The loan terms are the same as those for Subsidized loans, except that borrowers must pay interest on the loan while in school, during the six-month grace period following school, and during any authorized deferment period. If it is not paid while a student is in school, the interest will be added to the principal amount of the loan (capitalized). Since lenders' policies vary concerning when interest is capitalized, it is wise to shop among the available lenders. Up to 70% of the debt can be canceled for Peace Corps or Vista service. Physicians are automatically eligible, *but must apply*, for forbearance during residency, however they must pay (or capitalize) interest during this period.

Federal Perkins Loan

This need-based program (for the exceptionally financially needy) was formerly called the National Direct Student Loan (NDSL) program. U.S. citizens and permanent residents are eligible. The maximum annual amount is $5,000. Students may borrow up to a total of $30,000 for undergraduate and graduate school. There are no loan-origination or loan-guarantee fees. No interest accrues while in school or during the nine-month grace period following graduation. Recipients may qualify for up to three years of economic-hardship deferment. The interest rate is 5%. Loans must be repaid within ten years after beginning repayment. Because this program has relatively limited funding, it is unusual for students to get a Federal Perkins Loan every year. For more information, contact (202) 708-8242.

Health Education Assistance Loans (HEAL)

HEAL is a need-based program. U.S. citizens and permanent residents attending U.S. medical schools are eligible. (In mid-1996 it had not been funded for new recipients, although this could change.) You must have a good credit record to get these loans. A maximum of $20,000 is available annually, with a total of $80,000. These loans have variable interest rates, with a maximum being the average interest rate for 91-day Treasury Bills plus 3%. Interest accrues while in school and during the nine-month grace period following graduation (or for nine months after an approved internship or residency). Deferments of up to four years for internship, residency, and service in the armed forces, Peace Corps, or NHSC are available. Excluding deferments, borrowers have up to twenty-five years to repay the loans. If you default on your loan, the federal government (which underwrites the loans) steps in to make your life miserable. They send the list of defaulters to medical schools, professional associations, and state licensing boards. Most HEAL loans come from private lenders, such as banks and credit unions, so it is advantageous to shop for the best interest rates and terms. If the medical school's financial aid office doesn't have information about these loans, contact: HEAL, Room 8-38, 5600 Fisher's Lane, Rockville, MD 20857; (800) 848-0979.

Health Professions Loans

These are need-based programs. Although the medical student will be the official borrower, applicants must supply information about their parents' income and finances to be eligible for this program, since the program is designed for the neediest students.

Loans for Disadvantaged Students (LDS)

For this program, the applicant must be disadvantaged. (Loosely speaking, "disadvantaged" means being at or nearly at the official poverty level.) The maximum amount available is tuition plus $2,500 per year. The loans remain interest-free during medical school, residency, two years of fellowship, and three years in a uniformed service or the Peace Corps. The interest rate during repayment is 5%. The loan must be repaid within ten years after completing school. There is no service obligation.

Primary Care Loan (PCL)

While this is a need-based loan, applicants need not be "disadvantaged." The maximum amount available is tuition plus $2,500 per year. U.S. citizens and permanent residents attending accredited U.S. medical schools are eligible. The loans remain interest-free during school and residency. The interest rate during repayment is 5%. The loan must be repaid within ten years after completing school. Recipients must complete an ACGME- or AOA-approved primary care (family practice, general internal medicine, general pediatrics, combined medicine/pediatrics, or preventive medicine/public health) residency no later than four years after graduating from medical school. They must also agree to practice in that specialty until the loan is repaid. If recipients do not enter primary care, their loans are recomputed using a 12% annual interest rate starting from the dates they were issued. This total amount must then be repaid within three years from the time the borrower breaks the agreement. If you are thinking about this loan, be aware of this stiff penalty for changing your mind about your specialty choice.

Other Loans

Private Loans

There are many sources of private loans for medical education, as long as your credit is good. The interest rates and terms are not generally as favorable as those provided by the government or professional organizations. But, as long as they have good credit ratings, medical students generally do not have difficulty getting extra money if they need it and stay within their approved financial-aid budget.

MEDLOANS.

The AAMC sponsors this private loan program for full-time students who are U.S. citizens or permanent residents accepted by an AAMC-member institution (U.S. medical school). MEDLOANS allows students to access two loan programs with favorable terms and conditions. (You can also apply for these programs through the AMCAS-E computer program.) These programs are the Federal Stafford Loan and the Alternative Loan Program (ALP), which accesses private loan sources. Contact the AAMC, Division of Student Affairs/Educational Services, 2450 N Street, N.W., Washington, DC 20037-1126; phone (800) 858-5050.

AMWA

The American Medical Women's Association has a limited fund available for loans to its student members who are enrolled in M.D. or D.O. schools and are U.S. citizens or permanent residents. They award loans of $1,000 or $2,000 per student per year, up to a maximum of $4,000 during medical school. The interest rate is 10% and repayment, which must be completed within three years, begins in December following graduation. Applications are available each January from: AMWA, 801 North Fairfax Street, Suite 400, Alexandria, VA 22314.

Other Funding Sources

Veterans Benefits

Veterans who believe they are eligible for educational benefits should contact their local or regional VA offices for applications (VA Form 22-1990v).

Foreign Medical Schools And Non-U.S. Citizens

Only U.S. citizens or permanent residents are eligible for most of the financial aid, including loans, targeted at medical students. A few medical schools have some funding available for foreign students.

U.S. citizens or permanent residents attending foreign or unaccredited U.S. medical schools may be eligible for Unsubsidized Stafford Loans, although the federal government is in the process of enforcing its very restrictive rules, so many of these schools' students (especially in the Caribbean) may no longer qualify. Private loans still may be available.

Working During Medical School

Some students can successfully work during medical school to supplement their income. *Very limited* part-time work, especially if it is related to medicine, may actually be beneficial. Such jobs will allow you some time to think seriously about things other than school work. But many students with jobs have overextended themselves and subsequently had to either take a leave of absence or withdraw from school. Be careful and be warned. Any outside work must be very limited for you to succeed as a medical student—which, by itself, it is a very strenuous and time-consuming job.

Paying It Back

Some students believe that no matter how much money they borrow, they will be able to easily pay it back once they are earning a physician's salary. But completing a residency and fellowship can take up to seven years, and large loans can be burdensome, even to those who may eventually earn high wages. At this point, you may be willing "to spend whatever it takes" to go to medical school, but the choices you make in your borrowing and spending will determine how much discretionary income you will have when you graduate and begin paying off your loans. Jeffrey E. Hanson, Ph.D. at Northwestern University has come up with a nice form (figure 18.3) that you may want to use when considering how much you want to borrow and spend.

The amount at the end of figure 18.3 is what you will have left at the end of each month. If this is a negative number, you can borrow less (and spend less) now, or spend less (or continue borrowing) when you get out of medical school or residency. Note that it's much cheaper to reduce your borrowing now. Also, note box #2: "What I Have To Pay For." Unless you want to go directly to jail (in some cases), expect to pay these bills—even if paying them does not leave you much money to eat.

Why NOT To Go Into Medicine For Money

One aspect of entering medicine which is rarely, if ever, spoken about except in a humorous fashion, is the expected financial remuneration. While it may be both noble and consistent with the values that bring people into the medical field to try to ignore financial considerations completely, it is unrealistic.

Figure 18.3: How Far Will My Paycheck Go?

INCOME
    My annual salary/wages: $_____
    My spouse's salary/wages: $_____
    Other income: $_____ $_____
    Total annual income *(sum of above)*: $_____
    MONTHLY INCOME *(Total annual income ÷ 12)*: $_____**(1)**

WHAT I HAVE TO PAY FOR
    Taxes *(assume 1/3 of total monthly income)*: $_____
    Employment benefits *(e.g., your share of medical insurance)*: $_____
    My monthly student-loan payment *(assume a monthly*
       payment of $125 for every $10,000 you owe): $_____
    My spouse's monthly student-loan payment: $_____
    My total monthly credit-card payment *(assume monthly*
       payment is 2% of total credit-card balance and include all
       other personal debt payments): $_____
    My spouse's total monthly credit-card payment: $_____
    TOTAL OF WHAT I HAVE TO PAY EACH MONTH *(sum above)*: $_____

DISCRETIONARY MONTHLY INCOME
    Total monthly income *(from Box 1)*: $_____**(1)**
    Total monthly required payments *(from Box 2)*: $_____**(2)**
    TOTAL MONEY AVAILABLE FOR LIVING EXPENSES *[(1) - (2)]*: $_____**(3)**

WHAT I WANT TO PAY FOR
    Housing: *(e.g., rent, mortgage)* $_____
    Utilities/telephone: $_____
    Food: $_____
    Transportation *(e.g., car payment(s), parking fees,*
       insurance, gas, upkeep): $_____
    Clothing: $_____
    Insurance: *(e.g., home, life, medical, dental)* $_____
    Retirement investments *(financial planners recommend*
       saving 10% of gross monthly income per month): $_____
    Other personal expenses *(e.g., entertainment, vacations,*
       pet care, personal care): $_____

    TOTAL OF WHAT I WANT TO PAY EACH MONTH *(sum of above)*: $_____**(4)**

The amount of money I have left over each month *[(3) — (4)]*: $_____

This form reproduced with permission of Jeffrey E. Hanson, Ph.D., Northwestern University.

For physicians, it can be said that money is the root of all (or at least much) sadness. Certain aspects of medical practice make it extremely attractive to individuals who either have experienced or fear economic instability in their lives. Among these are the facts that:

- Medicine is one of the most consistently lucrative of all professions.

- Some specialists make extraordinary incomes.

- U.S.-trained physicians are rarely involuntarily unemployed.

Individuals who enter medicine for these reasons often are disappointed, depressed, and unhappy physicians. The additional money does not make up for having to shoulder the responsibilities, work the long hours, or bear the stresses of being a physician. Those who choose high-paying specialties solely for the income usually become very unhappy practitioners.

Physicians who remain happy in their work derive satisfaction from their work, not from the monetary rewards. Remember, being a medical professional is a lifelong commitment, not a short-term goal.

Residents'/Fellows' Salaries

Unlike nearly all other aspiring professionals, residents never negotiate salary—it is fixed in advance. Generally, institutions give the same salary to all residents in the same postgraduate year of training. Yet salaries can vary considerably from institution to institution, and from one region of the country to another. In general, interns (PGY-1 residents) receive an average salary of $34,000 in the Northeastern United States, and of $30,000 in the West. Salaries rise about 10% per year during training. Housestaff salaries have actually remained fairly constant over the last twenty-five years, if adjusted for inflation.

Residents' salaries should be compared to the cost of living in particular locales. Residents may have difficulty "making ends meet" in Washington, DC; San Francisco; Boston; New York City; and parts of Los Angeles, even with relatively high salaries. However, much lower salaries may allow for a nice lifestyle in many smaller, southern, or midwestern cities.

Practicing Physicians' Salaries

Many medical students seem to believe that their educational investment will pay off handsomely. More than one-third of graduating medical students expect to be earning more than $200,000 annually within ten years of completing their postgraduate training.

In general, the surgical specialties are the most lucrative. And the difference between the income of a surgeon and his or her non-surgical colleague can be truly amazing. This is because, at present, the (insurance) payment schemes reward *doing* (procedures) at a much higher level than *thinking* (cognition). While pediatricians have median annual incomes of $100,000, radiologists accrue twice as much (figure 18.4). Recent estimates are that new internists get only one-fourth to one-half the starting salary of those physicians trained in procedurally or technically oriented areas. This may change somewhat in the future as mechanisms for physician payment are rearranged on the federal, state, and private levels through "health-care reform."

If the past is any indicator, though, the disparity between doers and thinkers will persist. For example, a major income realignment was to have occurred in the early 1990s with the implementation of the Resource Based Relative Value Scale (RBRVS). Despite predictions from the government, American Medical Association, and other reputable sources that primary-care practitioners would benefit, they didn't. In fact, primary care physicians have been shown to have a substantially worse return on their investment in professional education than do medical or surgical subspecialists, attorneys, dentists, and those in business.

Figure 18.4: Median Physician Annual Incomes After Expenses and Before Taxes

Specialty	Income
Radiologists	$ 240,000
Surgeons	225,000
Anesthesiologists	220,000
Obstetrics/Gynecology	200,000
Pathologists	170,000
All Physicians	**156,000**
Internists	150,000
Pediatricians	120,000
Psychiatrists	120,000
Family Physicians	110,000

Adapted from: American Medical Association. *Socioeconomic Characteristics of Medical Practice*. Chicago, IL: AMA, 1995, p. 148.

The changing health care environment, however, should eventually decrease the income of and need for many specialists. So far, this has not been widespread. In general, though, managed-care organizations try to keep their patients away from medical specialists who cost more than primary care practitioners.

Other changes may also affect the incomes of certain specialties. Recent rules concerning physician reimbursement have severely reduced the income of clinical pathologists. The government unilaterally disallowed payment for a large portion of their practice. This, as is usually the case, was followed by a similar move by all other insurers. The government is now seriously looking at making similar changes in reimbursement for other hospital-based specialists, such as anesthesiologists, radiologists, and emergency physicians. How this will affect their income is uncertain.

Then there is the malpractice-insurance dilemma, cycling from a crisis level to merely being uncomfortable. It will continue to affect some specialties until broad tort reform is enacted. Obstetricians still find it difficult in some locales to deliver babies at a cost that new families can afford, while paying the ever-increasing premiums for their malpractice insurance. In many cases, family practitioners have completely stopped doing obstetrics, outpatient orthopaedics, and surgery. Radiologists have recently joined the luckless group of the most-frequently sued specialties, mainly because of the risks of inaccurately reading mammograms. Neurosurgeons, plastic surgeons, and many other specialists now face similar large increases in the already astronomical cost of malpractice insurance. While the highest-income specialties are still lucrative, even after subtracting the malpractice-premium cost, the net remuneration is not quite as attractive as it would first appear.

Overall, physicians earning the highest net income live in the west-south-central United States (Arkansas, Louisiana, Oklahoma, or Texas) and in metropolitan areas with fewer than one million people, are not in solo practice, are not linked to a managed care group, and are 46 to 55 years old.

The Importance Of Income

A final note is necessary concerning the importance of income at various career stages. For the entry-level physician, income is extremely important. This makes sense, since most new physicians have enormous debts, no money, and increasing financial responsibilities. At mid-career, however, income is of only medium importance, with job security being the most important factor keeping the physician in practice. At this stage of a physician's career, job satisfaction is equally as important as income. Job satisfaction becomes of overwhelming importance for physicians in the last third of their careers. Those who have high job satisfaction presumably keep working longer than those who do not, and have more fun while they are working.

Debt And Specialty Choice

No one has consistently shown that medical students make career choices based on their level of debt. However, some studies, such as that shown in figure 18.5, suggest a trend in that direction. Most of the highest-paying specialties, though, have also been the most difficult to enter. Perhaps many medical students simply are attracted to those specialties, or by the promise of a nice income—whether or not they have large debts.

Conclusion

The bottom line is to:

- Make certain that your credit rating is good before you apply for financial aid.
- Complete your income-tax forms early for the year before you want to enter medical school.
- Get financial aid information from the medical schools to which you are applying;
- Complete the forms and submit them as quickly as possible, but definitely before their "priority" deadline.
- Apply for any separate programs in which you are interested (such as the HPSP or NHSC scholarships).
- Search on your own for additional funding sources.
- Carefully read the fine print on all loan or scholarship papers.
- Complete the loan application forms and scholarship agreements (if any) and return them to the schools.
- Be prepared to live within the budget prescribed by the financial aid office.
- Be certain about your commitment to a medical career before signing those loan papers. Ask yourself if it is worth $100,000. (Climbing Mt. Everest only costs $65,000.)

Figure 18.5: Influence of Indebtedness as it Relates to Medical Students' Career Choices*

		Minor/Moderate	Major
Debt <$50,000			
	Gen specialty	24 %	2 %
	Med specialty	19	5
	Surg specialty	19	3
	Support specialty	24	5
Debt $50-$75,000			
	Gen specialty	18	5
	Med specialty	29	5
	Surg specialty	28	7
	Support specialty	36	12
Debt >$75,000			
	Gen specialty	33	8
	Med specialty	31	8
	Surg specialty	34	14
	Support specialty	39	20

* Each row shows the percentages of medical students, at each level of debt and for each specialty area, who felt that the amount of their debt had played a "Minor/Moderate" or "Major" role in their specialty choice. No row's total percentages equals 100% (the maximum is 59%), showing that for many students, this isn't an important consideration.

Adapted from: Kassebaum DG, Szenas PL. Relationship between indebtedness and the specialty choices of graduating medical students. *Acad Med* 1992;67:700-7.

19: Combined-Degree Programs

Whenever men attempt, they seem driven to overdo.

Bernard Baruch

As IF MEDICAL SCHOOL WEREN'T DIFFICULT enough, some hardy folks decide to combine their medical education with training for other advanced degrees. Whether you are interested in pursuing such a program or simply want to find out what the "gunners" are doing, read the following discussion of the available options. Figure 19.1 lists schools offering formal combined programs in which medical students can simultaneously earn another advanced degree.

Combined M.D./D.O.–Ph.D.

Nearly all U.S. M.D.-granting, and some D.O.-granting, medical schools offer students the option of combining their training for a medical degree with fulfilling requirements for a Ph.D. About 2% of all medical students graduate from such combined-degree programs. The hope is that they will form the core of the physician-scientist community, practicing medicine while pursuing studies that will advance medical practice. In reality, most of these individuals pursue either the practice of medicine or scientific research exclusively—in part because each really belongs to a separate and distinct world (with markedly different thought processes). Time constraints also influence most individuals' decisions to take one or the other path. A very high percentage of physician-Ph.D.'s end up on medical school faculties.

Medical schools offer Ph.D.'s in many disciplines. Some only offer them in medically related sciences, while others also offer programs in other disciplines. The AAMC's annual *Medical School Admission Requirements* contains a table showing which medically related science Ph.D.'s are offered at each M.D. school. Applicants must inquire directly to find out which non-science Ph.D.'s each medical school offers. If the school is part of or affiliated with a larger university, get the graduate school's catalog for a list of Ph.D. subject areas. In some cases, non-science Ph.D.'s are awarded through adjacent campuses or schools, and are limited only by the degrees such schools offer and their faculty's flexibility. Those interested in combined D.O.-Ph.D. programs must directly contact the individual schools for more information. (See figure 19.1 for a list of programs.)

The method of applying to combined medical degree-Ph.D. programs depends upon the individual school(s) and graduate programs involved. In some cases, applicants must take not only the MCAT, but also the General and Subject Graduate Record Examinations (GREs). In most cases, admission into both medical school and the Ph.D. program requires two different applications and two sets of interviews. Applicants may be accepted to one, both, or neither of the programs. At some institutions, after combined-degree applicants are interviewed, they are removed from consideration for the medical degree-only program.

If you apply to a combined-degree program, do not accept a position until they guarantee your funding in writing. Once you accept a position, begin searching immediately for a faculty adviser. Don't wait until you get onto the medical campus. This will markedly speed your progress through the Ph.D. portion of the program. Select someone who is well-known in the field, personable, and available.

While the campus tour is of only moderate importance to typical medical school applicants, it is extremely important to those considering a combined medical degree-Ph.D. program. Are the library facilities, including the hours they are open, adequate? Do they have extensive on-line services? Are the laboratories (or other facilities you need if pursuing a non-science Ph.D.) modern and up-to-date? While most medical students can complete their degree in any environment, Ph.D. candidates have a specific performance task (their dissertation), and must have the facilities to complete it.

Questions you should anticipate when applying to these programs are:

- What research have you done or are you doing now? (This is the number one question. If you can't answer it adequately, forget about applying to these programs. An "adequate" answer includes being specific about your contribution to the research, why the research was done, what theories supported doing it, and the (potential) implications of the results.)

- Why do you need or want both degrees?

- What are your research interests?

- How will you have enough time to pursue both careers? (No one has yet discovered a truly adequate answer to this question.)

Funding

Several methods exist for funding your medical degree-Ph.D. education. The two that usually provide the best funding are the Medical Scientist Training Program (MSTP) and the Minority Access to Research Careers (MARC)—both oriented toward earning science Ph.D.'s.

Medical Scientist Training Program (MSTP)

Formal federal support for combined M.D.-Ph.D. programs is provided through the Medical Scientist Training Program (MSTP). The National Institute of General Medical Sciences supports programs, now at 32 medical schools, that provide both basic- and clinical-science training to highly motivated students with outstanding research and academic potential. If accepted, students receive tuition and a $10,000 annual stipend for up to six years (although the course of study may be longer). There are about 150 new positions each year, and the competition for them is fierce. Applicants must be U.S. citizens or permanent residents. For further information regarding the MSTP and a current list of participating medical schools, contact: National Institutes of Health, Medical Scientist Training Program, Program Administrator, Room 905, Westwood Building, Bethesda, MD 20892; (301) 594-7744. Then contact the individual schools for their information.

Minority Access to Research Careers (MARC)

The Minority Access to Research Careers (MARC) program is similar to MTSP, except that it is for underrepresented minority students. Grants are given to schools whose students are primarily from underrepresented minorities. The schools then distribute the money so selected students can pursue studies leading to a Ph.D. and a research career. For a list of participating schools and more information, write: Director, MARC Program, NIGMS, Westwood Building, Room 9A-18, Bethesda, MD 20892.

Other Programs

Don't limit your search to just federally funded programs. Many schools (if not most) with combined programs offer participants funding similar to that from the MSTP. The money just comes from other sources. If you find a program that otherwise meets your needs, contact the school to find out about available funding.

Combined Medicine–Law

Five schools have officially combined medicine–law programs, although other schools may be willing to consider this combination. Thus, in most cases, other than applying to one of the officially combined programs, applicants will need to go through the entire and separate admission procedure at each school and then arrange to have adequate blocks of time to complete each curriculum. This can be very difficult, but it has been done. Law school normally lasts three years, with the first year being the toughest. See figure 19.1 for a list of programs. Contact the schools' admission offices (*Appendix E*) for more information.

Combined Medical Degree–Master's Degrees

About 1% of all medical students graduate from programs combining a master's and a medical degree. The two most common are medical degrees combined with either a Master of Business Administration (M.B.A.) or a Master of Public Health (M.P.H.).

Medical Degree–M.B.A.

With the marked changes in health-care-delivery systems, it has become evident that more physicians should be fluent in business terminology and techniques. Students often ask me whether it is worthwhile spending the extra time to also get an M.B.A. while going through medical school, and whether residency directors will see this as a positive or a negative factor. My advice has been that since physicians are, in general, poorly prepared to be leaders in health care systems, and these systems run on business, not medical, principles, an M.B.A. is indeed worthwhile. Forward-looking residency directors, especially those who have had significant administrative experience or have dealt frequently with managed-care organizations, will undoubtedly view this education in a very positive light.

Eleven schools offer an official program leading to a combined medical degree–M.B.A. (See figure 19.1 for a list of programs.) Each has different admission requirements and curricula. The M.B.A. curricula are very different at each school, therefore investigate M.B.A. programs very carefully before applying to schools. The normal length of study for an M.B.A. degree is two years. Contact each school's admission office (*Appendix E*) for more information.

Medical Degree–M.P.H.

Physicians often get a Master of Public Health (M.P.H.) degree to study epidemiology, to broaden their understanding of public health issues, or to fulfill the requirements of a residency in public health, aerospace medicine, or preventive medicine. Nineteen medical schools now offer the M.P.H. degree in a formally combined program often leading to a medical degree (figure 19.1).

Figure 19.1: Schools Offering Formal Combined-Degree Programs

Ph.D.

Nearly all U.S. M.D.-granting medical schools
Michigan State University College of Osteopathic Medicine
Ohio University College of Osteopathic Medicine
Texas College of Osteopathic Medicine

M.S. or M.A.

Bowman Gray	University of Illinois	New York Coll Osteo Med
Loma Linda	University of Sherbrooke	Université de Montréal
Medical College of Wisconsin	Wayne State University	UC-San Francisco
NYU–Mt. Sinai	Duke University	University of Arkansas
UC–Davis	Medical College of Ohio	Washington University

M.B.A.

Bowman Gray	Dartmouth	Jefferson Medical College
New York Coll Osteo Med	NYU–Mt. Sinai	Philadelphia Coll Osteo Med
Tufts University	UC-Davis	University of Chicago
University of Illinois	University of Pennsylvania	

Masters of Health Administration (M.H.A.)

Jefferson Medical College

Masters of Management (M.M.)

Northwestern University

J.D.

Duke University	Indiana University	Southern Illinois University
University of Chicago	University of Illinois	

M.P.H.

Arizona	Boston University	George Washington Univ.
Duke University	Emory University	Nova Southeastern Coll
Harvard University	Johns Hopkins University	Osteo Med
Oregon Health Sciences Univ.	Philadelphia Coll Osteo Med	Tufts University
Tulane University	UC–Davis	UC–San Francisco
UMDNJ–Robert Wood Johnson	University of Michigan	University of North Carolina
University of South Carolina	University of South Florida	
(in development)	Columbia University	

Engineering

George Washington University	Harvard University	Indiana University
University of Kentucky		

Tufts University offers a unique four-year combined M.D.-M.P.H. program, during which students take additional classes each year. They also must do clinical "practicums" in public health venues every summer, during one block in their third year, and during their fourth year.

Pros And Cons Of Combined-Degree Programs

If you are considering a combined-degree program, first consider the positive and negative aspects of such a program. Also determine whether you are pursuing the second degree to avoid or to enhance your medical career.

Pros

- Prepares you for a career in academia, law, or medical administration, depending upon your second degree.
- M.D.-Ph.D.'s often have an advantage when applying for grants.
- Prestige within academia.
- Affords more options and opportunities than simply having an M.D. or D.O.

Cons

- Big (long) commitment.
- No guarantee that you will be able to use the skills gained from your other degree when you finish, since there is decreasing funding for research and a surplus of lawyers.
- You will be a different person when you finish. Seven or more years is a long time, and you may not want to do research, practice/teach law, or do medical administration when you finish. Or, you may not want to practice medicine.
- An M.D. or D.O. degree by itself already provides a vast number of career options, including research and medical administration.
- You will be very poor for a long time.
- Using your combined degree often means residing in a relatively large city.

Applying To A Combined-Degree Program

"Other degree" interviews require special preparation. Do a Medline (and other similar database, such as CancerLine) search to find publications by the faculty at the other program. You can access these through the library at your local medical school or at many universities. Use *Westlaw* or *Lexis* for the J.D. programs. These databases can be accessed through a local law school, some university libraries, or a friendly lawyer.

These searches allow you to identify specific faculty members sharing your interests. It looks very good on your application to say that you are applying to that school's program because, like Professor Potatohead, you have a strong interest in investigating, for example, "the mitochondrial activity of the spud." Also, since some programs allow you to pick your interviewers for the "other" degree, you will have an idea about what the interviewers do, so you can intelligently converse with them.

This additional investigation is particularly useful for the medical degree-Ph.D. programs. They want to see that an individual has a firm commitment to a life of research, not just to the $200,000 or more in tuition and stipends they will get while in the program.

Particularly at combined-degree programs, expect to have some interviews by students in the program. They, as well as some of the other non-medical interviews, may be "blind" by design or because of their own laziness. (A "blind" interview is one in which the interviewer has not seen any of your application materials and must gather all information in the interview. It is a very poor and sloppy interview method.) You may have to answer questions that you have already answered, in detail, in your application materials.

In combined-degree interviews you may have some unique questions of your own to ask. For example, can you begin your research or any required projects before you formally begin classes? (Are you a dynamo who can't wait to start?) How much time do most students take to get both degrees? (Unlike the typical medical school program, many of these programs have more flexible timetables—although the funding is usually not too flexible.) How much leeway do you have to choose the individual who will work with you? How flexible is the schedule? How are the two programs integrated?

You will, of course, also want to ask the questions about the medical degree program listed in chapter 24, *Your Questions*.

Combined-degree programs can offer you additional career choices, but you must consider the amount of time (and income) you sacrifice to get a second degree. Before you set out on this course, ask yourself whether you are interested enough to make the necessary sacrifices.

20: Preparing For The Visit

When we are summoned from afar,
Ourselves, and not our words will count—
Not what we said, but what we are!

William Winter, *George Fawcett Rowe*

Gathering Information

BEFORE GOING TO A MEDICAL SCHOOL INTERVIEW, you must know about medicine, the school, its curriculum, and any special programs it has. If you don't, you might just as well not go to the interview, since interviewers will not believe you are a serious candidate. Two sources for this information are the "School Entries" section in the AAMC's annual *Medical School Admission Requirements* and each school's catalog, brochures, and additional papers which are sent to applicants. If you know, or have an opportunity to talk with, a school's current medical students (such as if you are staying with them) or graduates (who may be residents at a local hospital), you may obtain additional information from them. Also, if you have time the night before your interview, stop by the school's medical library and glance through some recent alumni bulletins. These can provide you with valuable insights into the workings of the medical school.

Preparing For The Interview

No matter how irrational it may seem, the ten- to thirty-minute interviews at medical schools count for at least as much, in most cases, toward your acceptance into the medical profession as do all of your accomplishments in the previous 3½ (or more) undergraduate years. That's not just my personal belief. Several recent studies have shown this to be true. When you prepare to go for interviews, put your best effort toward doing a good job. This is where it all comes together!

The Mock Interview

How well will you do when you actually sit in the "hot seat," being interviewed for that medical school slot you want above all others? Do not wait until you are sitting in that chair to find out! When you think that you are prepared to go out on the interview circuit, arrange for a mock interview. Doing this will make you calmer and more organized, and help you to appear more polished during the real thing.

What is a mock interview?

A mock interview is to an interview as near-drowning is to drowning. In both cases you think that you are going to die, but in the former, you end up out of danger. Your mock interview should closely imitate the actual interview process. You must prepare for it in exactly the same way that you prepare for your real interviews. Dress the same, carry identical materials with you, and go over your interview answers just as you will before interviews at medical schools. This interview must be as realistic as possible so that you will get the most accurate and useful feedback. If you don't feel anxiety, you're not doing it correctly.

Who should conduct the mock interview? Ideally, your mentor, if you have one, and the premed adviser. If they are not available, ask another faculty member with interviewing experience. Tell them, if they do not know, that you want the mock interview to be as realistic as possible. Tell them to ask you the "difficult" questions and to treat you in the same manner they would treat any applicant—not as someone they already know. Then ask for feedback about the way you presented yourself, your appearance and grooming, and how you handled the questions. This should yield an overall assessment of areas to be improved upon before you hit the interview trail.

Note that a premed-committee interview is *not* a mock interview—it's the real thing! This interview may count as much as the interviews at some medical schools. Schools take premed-committee evaluations very seriously. These interviews are not the place to practice.

One useful technique for self-critique is to audio- or videotape the interview. Would you select the person you hear or see? What seems wrong with the applicant (you)? How can you improve your interview performance next time? As with all other parts of the application process, this takes a little extra effort. Experience has shown that it pays off in a big way.

Besides the formal mock interview, it also helps to review interview elements in your mind during those odd times when you are commuting, awaiting others, or sitting through a really boring lecture. Review anticipated questions and situations, as well as those from previous interviews. Don't sweat over past interviews, just analyze how they could have gone better. This frequent review will keep you prepared to face the next interview without needing too much last-minute preparation.

Timing

Applicants often have little leeway when scheduling their interviews. The best way to get an early interview (and possibly an early acceptance) is to submit all your application materials as soon as possible. Then, if your schedule permits, accept the earliest interview dates that medical schools offer you. (See figure 21.2 for individual schools' interview schedules.)

When traveling to interviews, students will inevitably miss classes and, sometimes, laboratory sessions that are hard to make up. One way to avoid this is to try to carry a somewhat lighter schedule, without laboratory courses, during the time you will be interviewing. If you plan your schedule far enough in advance, this is often possible. Also, be sure to explain your absences to your instructors if your classes are small enough so that you will be missed. Although I was only going to miss one laboratory class, I told the teaching assistant. When he asked why I would be gone, I told him that I would be interviewing. He told me he would be gone also—he would be interviewing at the same medical school that day. We ended up as classmates.

Dressing The Part

Some applicants to medical school find it distasteful to "sell out" to the establishment and dress in the manner some have referred to as a "medi-clone." If you are one of those students, think of proper attire as camouflage to hide the "rebellious you" in a land of "straight arrows." This is the world you want to inhabit, so begin playing by its rules.

The key here is to do what others do—but better. Yes, there is a "uniform" to wear. It is conservative, tasteful, and neat. It looks like upper-middle-class (Yuppie) success. And it works. Of course, you wear blue jeans and sweatshirts (or less) as an undergraduate. You love to hang out in low-key duds. That's fine for weekends with your friends, but now it is time for you to shine—both literally and figuratively. While people in some areas of the country (e.g., Northwest) traditionally dress more casually than in other areas, don't assume that this applies to medical school interviews. If in doubt, before you go, ask the admission office what most applicants wear to the interview.

One interviewee, medical student Scott Fishman, described this uniform as "remarkably drab . . . a ridiculous costume . . . a rite of passage." (The well-fashioned interview. *The New Physician* March 1990, pp. 13-14.) He went on to say that "sitting there waiting for our turns outside the interviewer's office, we all look like we are going to a funeral." Perhaps. But better to wear the uniform and look as if you're going to a funeral, than to not wear it and attend your own.

No, you don't have to go out and spend lots of money you don't have on clothes you can't afford. Just do what you can to get into the uniform. Ideally, interviewers should not be aware of your clothes; you want them to remember *you*, not what you wore. The proper dress for medical school interviews is essentially identical, no matter where in the country you are applying. Appropriate dress can help you a little. The wrong outfit will destroy you.

Men

A *suit* is the standard dress for an interview. It should be solid or pinstripe, navy or gray. "The men who run America," says John T. Molloy, author of *Dress for Success*, "run it blue, gray, and dull." Do not wear a suit with bright or avant-garde colors or designs. "If you try to spruce up the look," Mr. Molloy continues, "you're in trouble." The suit need be neither expensive nor in the latest style, but it should be well-cut and well-tailored. If you either don't have or cannot afford a suit, wear a navy-blue sport jacket with matching pants. If you don't have these either, it is time you visited a clothing store. Charge the bill to your future, although don't spend money indiscriminately. Serious and solid is the image you are looking for in your outfit. And *before* you show up at your first interview, make sure that your clothes fit well. Few things distract an interviewer more than watching an applicant fidget with his tight collar.

Wear either a white or a pale-blue solid-color *shirt*. Long sleeves are in order if you plan to remove your jacket. Avoid stripes, loud colors, or any weird designs. Shirttails should be long enough to keep the shirt tucked in, even when you raise your arms. With the top button fastened, your collar should fit snugly, but not so tightly that your eyes bulge. A friend and resident, Peter Brown (Vermont, '94), talks about an interesting experience he had on the interview circuit.

Having graduated some years before, I was working full-time at an exhausting and time-consuming job with the New York City Child Protective Services. I had little time to really prepare for my medical school interviews, especially in terms of my clothes. (Being a bachelor is not always that great.) I found that I did not have a clean shirt that was ironed, and my ironing skills are, at best, rudimentary. Needing a shirt, however, I picked a clean shirt that went with my suit and simply ironed the front of the shirt. "No problem," I thought, "I'll be wearing a jacket anyway." During my first interview, the room was extremely hot and the interviewer suggested that we both remove our jackets. My eyes must have bulged at the suggestion, judging from his facial expression. Then I burst out laughing. I explained the situation to him. He began laughing too, saying that, as a bachelor himself, his shirt was probably in worse shape than mine. It was a great way to establish instant rapport.

Peter, of course, understands that he was very lucky to have pulled this one off. He says he always made sure that he had fully ironed shirts after that.

Wear a *tie*—even if you are a laid-back individual. An open-neck shirt and gold chain just won't cut it. Your tie should be solid, have repeating stripes (rep), small polka dots, or repeating small insignias (club). Avoid gaudy, bright colors, large patterns, and black. The "power colors" are red and navy. Knot the tie so its tip meets the belt and put the back of the tie through the label, so the ends stay together. Do not wear a bow tie. It gives the impression that you are (1) odd, (2) like showing the world that you're odd, and (3) out of touch with this decade.

Wear black or very dark brown conservatively designed *shoes*. Make sure that they are in good repair and shined. Dirty shoes are male applicants' most common clothing error. Wear calf-length plain *socks* that match your suit. If you wear an *undershirt,* a crew neck looks best, since it doesn't show through a shirt. A plain, dark leather *belt* with a small square buckle works well. If you wear suspenders, be sure that they button to your pants. If you carry a wallet, make sure that it does not bulge out of your pocket.

Now for the *accessories*. The key here is sedate. Limit jewelry to a watch and wedding band (only if you are married). Avoid any unusual watches, such as a dive watch or one with a picture of Mickey Mouse on the front. No lapel pins, no ID-bracelets, no tie clasps—and definitely, *NO EARRINGS!* (If you are an East Indian woman for whom a nose ring is generally accepted, still think twice about wearing it to interviews, especially in the South or Midwest. Anyone else, NO NOSE RINGS!) No matter what the protestations, that little flash of gold will cost you big points. Inappropriate, or too much, jewelry will elicit very strong negative responses. If you wear *glasses*, make sure you have standard frames. No initials on the lenses or unusual colors, please. It's best to avoid tinted or photo-gray lenses, since they tend to place a barrier between you and the interviewer. Also, keep the lenses clean. The pen and pencil you carry should look classy. They should not look like they're leftovers from your last trip to the miniature golf course. And don't stick them in a shirt-pocket protector. A serious candidate will carry a small, folding, zippered leather-covered note pad with the materials to make notes and room to store papers.

As for *personal grooming*, be neat, squeaky clean, and conservative. Your hair should be short. If it's shorter than you like it, it's probably close to the right length. Ask your mentor (if he or she is over thirty-five years old), a parent, or close (older) friend to advise you on this. Definitely no ponytails, punk, or otherwise unusual haircuts. Your hair must also be something close to a natural color. One excellent student appeared, both on paper and during the interview, to be a "shoe-in" at a fine medical school. The interviewers, however, said that they couldn't avoid concentrating on his purple hair. He did not get into any medical school. Assuming that your hair is a reasonable shade, also make sure it has been very recently trimmed and washed. Invest in a good haircut about one week before the interview; new haircuts look best after one week. If you wear facial hair, avoid goatees and handlebar mustaches which have strong negative connotations. Trim and manicure your nails. Remember, you want to be a physician, putting your hands on, and in, patients.

The *odor* the interviewer perceives should only be that of deodorant or nervousness. Avoid after-shave. You are not going on a date. If you are concerned about your breath, carry breath mints. And above all, no alcohol within twenty-four hours of the interview. There are enough perceived and anticipated problems with drug and alcohol abuse in the medical field. You do not have to show the interviewers that you could be some part of the problem.

The bottom line is that you want to look as much like a successful upper-middle-class physician as possible. That's the direction in which you wish to head. Wear the garments which symbolize the successful individual in our society. There is no need to flaunt your lifestyle in your dress. Leave your personal preferences out of this. They can only harm you.

Women

Although styles are changing in the workplace, the standard dress for a woman going to an interview is still the *suit*. In this case it is a skirted suit. A good skirted suit suggests that you are an upper-middle-class professional—just the image you want to project. Don't be led down the path to destruction by following fads or fashion. The classic suit is the uniform of success. Find out what woman accountants or lawyers who work for large firms wear. This will be the "classic" style.

When purchasing a suit, choose wool, linen, or a synthetic that simulates either. The fabric should be solid, tweed, or plaid. For solid suits, the three best colors are gray (a couple of shades lighter than charcoal), medium-range blue, and dark maroon. Stay away from bold, flashy patterns. The skirt should extend to just below the knee (no miniskirts!) and the matching jacket should be a blazer-cut with long sleeves.

Two alternatives to the suit are a tailored dress or a skirt worn with a jacket. Neither is as powerful as the suit, but if you do not feel comfortable in a suit, these are two reasonable substitutes.

Your blouse should be simply cut, neither too frilly nor with excess lace. The neckline must not be too low. If it is equivalent to a man's shirt with one button open, it will be acceptable. The blouse should be cotton, silk, or a look-alike synthetic. In general, it should be in a solid color complementary to the suit. That usually means white, cream, or pastel—not red or fuchsia.

Shoes should be simple pumps, closed at the toe and heel—and not brand new. They should be in a dark or neutral color that is compatible with your suit. The heels should not be more than 1½ inches high. Do not wear boots. Most applicants will be doing a lot of walking around the medical center; be sure that you will survive in the shoes you wear. Although a *scarf* is not as essential as a man's tie, it can be eye-catching if used properly. Wear silk or a look-alike synthetic and tie it in an ascot, necktie, or scout style. If worn, a scarf must have simple lines and no frills to detract from the center of attention, your face. Hosiery should be skin-colored.

As with men, the less *jewelry* that you wear the better. Aside from a simple watch and wedding ring, be careful about what other ornaments you wear. While a brooch or a simple necklace with very simple earrings are often suitable, multiple rings, bracelets, or anything ornate or gaudy is not. The current fad of wearing multiple earrings may be looked at with some disfavor by conservative interviewers. The appropriate watch is plain gold or silver. If you need to wear an *overcoat*, make sure that it is long enough to cover the bottom of your skirt. Many coat styles are acceptable—furs are not. If you wear gloves, make them leather. They should match your coat in color. *Do not carry a purse.* Carry a leather zippered case or attaché case for any necessities, including a small leather-covered note pad. This connotes power and authority. Put everything that you need in it. But do not overstuff it or keep it sloppy—you may have to open it during an interview.

As for the more *personal items*, such as hair, makeup, and perfume, just remember that you are going to a business interview, not on a date. (The important "business" is, of course, getting into medical school.) If the interviewer is aware that you are wearing perfume, you are wearing too much. Similarly with makeup—it works best when it is not obvious. Be especially careful to avoid obvious eye-shadow or eye-liner. Your hair should be clean and conservative in appearance. If it is long, it is often a good idea to put it up to keep it from looking sloppy. Many consultants recommend that women should not have hair styled so that it covers either eye.

The bottom line is that you dress for the interview in a uniform. Although there is considerable variation allowed, for maximum success applicants should adhere to the standard style. As one woman who did very well in her interviews said about the wardrobe, "sophistication and maturity are the keys to success."

Clothing As Camouflage

Clothes can hide real or perceived problems. For those "Doogie Howser" types who think they look too young to be taken seriously, dressing conservatively will age you a bit. Wearing glasses, even if you normally wear contacts, also helps.

Some people are self-conscious about their weight. Clothes can help disguise those extra pounds. Both men and women can wear suit jackets slightly longer than normal, and women can wear a loose jacket over a business dress or flared skirt. The key is to be certain that your clothes fit well. Even thin people look heavy if their buttons are popping out or their collar is too tight.

Wear The "Uniform" Stylishly

Now that you have acquired the uniform, make sure that you get the most out of it. Your clothes must appear neat, clean, and pressed. Do *not* travel in your clothes and show up five minutes before the interview looking like a Raggedy Anne doll that has gone through the washer. If possible, arrive at the interview city the night before, having traveled in your normal attire. You will get a good night's sleep and put on your freshly pressed uniform the next morning to go to the interview. Take the appropriate garments, such as overcoat, umbrella, etc., to protect your uniform in case of inclement weather. When you get to the interview site, slip into the restroom and give yourself a last-minute inspection.

Once you dress correctly for your interview, forget about your clothes. They should be a natural part of you. Think of these clothes like new hiking boots. You don't want to go twenty miles in a new pair without breaking them in first. If you aren't comfortable in these fancy duds, wear them a few times before you hit the interview trail.

How To Pack For The Interview Trip

When packing for interviews, your motto should be "less is more." Sophisticated travelers decrease the amount they carry by making sure that all their clothes are compatible, by packing clothes that can serve more than one function, and by avoiding the tendency to pack for every possible eventuality that could happen on the trip. Remember to include a small sewing kit for emergency repairs.

Packing lists ease pre-trip anxieties. Once you decide what to take with you on one trip, analyze your list, modify it, then use the same packing list for subsequent trips. That way you won't forget anything. Keep the list with you to serve as a record of your belongings in case your bags are lost.

How To Pack a Suitcase

Whether you use a large suitcase or a small carryon, your clothes should arrive intact and as pristine as possible. To accomplish this, place trousers, skirts, dresses, shirts, blouses, and jackets (all zipped or buttoned, and folded along their natural seams) in the suitcase, alternating side to side. Suits will stay at their best if they are first placed in a plastic dry-cleaner's bag. Lay all items partially in the suitcase, then fold the remainder inside, one garment over the other (figure 20.1). Each item will then cushion the others and help prevent creases. Pack shoes, stuffed with toiletries, socks, etc., along the hinged side of the bag. Finally, stuff rolled T-shirts, undergarments, sleepwear, and sweaters in any available space to cushion the contents and keep them from shifting. The result should be neat and clean clothing.

Figure 20.1: Packing a Suitcase

Putting It All Together

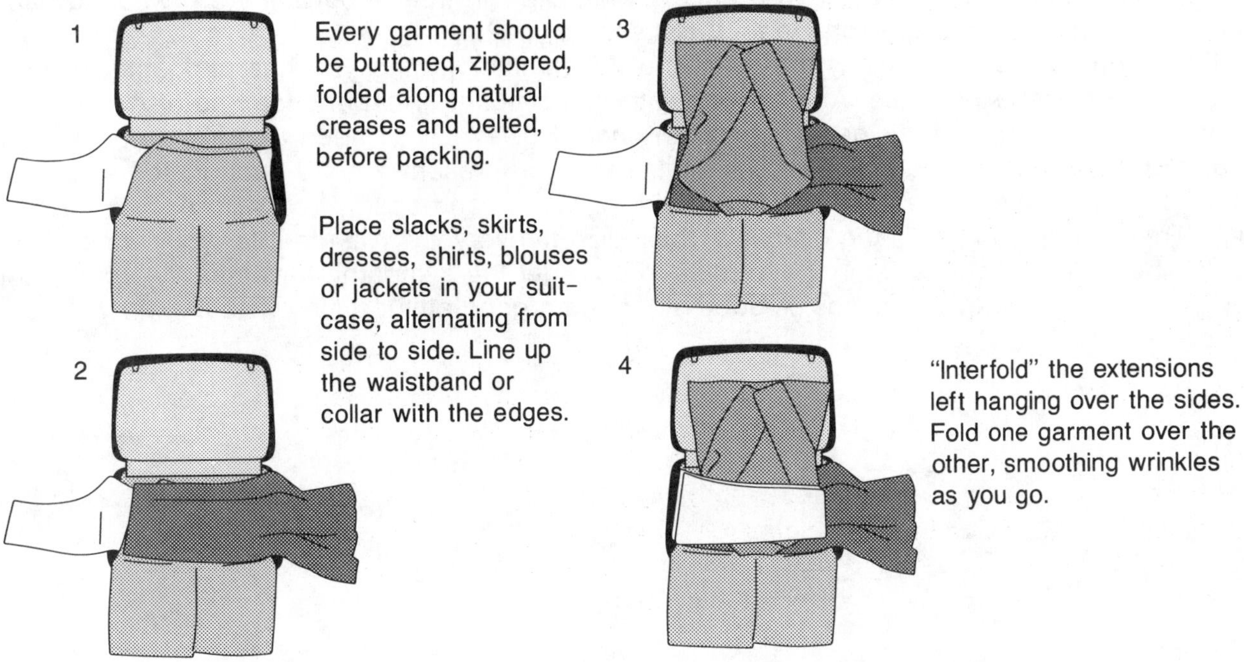

1 Every garment should be buttoned, zippered, folded along natural creases and belted, before packing.

Place slacks, skirts, dresses, shirts, blouses or jackets in your suit-case, alternating from side to side. Line up the waistband or collar with the edges.

2

3

4 "Interfold" the extensions left hanging over the sides. Fold one garment over the other, smoothing wrinkles as you go.

Each item will cushion the other, helping to prevent creases.

What To Do If Your Suitcase Is Lost

Use Carryon, If Possible

One danger of flying is that your checked baggage won't show up—at least not in time to do you any good. The fact that it appears back at your home the day after the interview is little consolation for being forced to dress in "low camp" style for the interview at your most desired school. The solution, especially if you are only going to be away from home for one or two days, is to use a carryon suit bag and an under-the-seat bag. This often suffices very well, saves you time retrieving your bags at the airport, and alleviates any worry about your uniform not showing up. It is *essential* to carry interview schedules, airline tickets, travelers' checks, credit cards, driver's license, jewelry, hotel and automobile confirmations, airline schedules, medications, and telephone numbers and addresses for your travel agent and your interviews with you. (I have seen more than one distraught applicant whose bag containing his interview materials and, of course, his clothes, had been lost.)

Be careful when choosing your carryon bags. Each airline, and even each plane or configuration of seats on a particular airline, has a different allowable space for carryons. It is wise to check with a travel agent or the airline to avoid arriving at the airport with one bag too many. Typically, airlines allow each traveler two carryons, not counting purses, umbrellas, coats, cameras and books. The typical maximum size for under-seat bags is 9" x 14" x 22", for overhead compartments it is 10" x 14" x 36", and in cabin closets, 4" x 23" x 45". If possible, get a rolling carryon and a garment bag that attaches to it. That may save some strain on your back.

Honesty Works (The Sympathy and Uniqueness Votes)

Okay, so you weren't able to use the carryon method—and now your baggage is somewhere between here and Outer Mongolia. You have an interview in three hours and are wearing hand-me-downs from a backwoods orphanage. What should you do?

First, don't panic. Any faculty member who will be interviewing you has undoubtedly had a great deal of travel experience. And anyone with that amount of experience has also had his or her bags misplaced by the airlines—more than once. However, you need to make some show of good faith. First, badger the airline representatives. If you present a good enough sob story, they might front you money for a decent shirt and tie (or blouse and scarf). You will need at least this much. Then, when you get to the interview, apologize to everyone you meet for your appearance. The "airline-lost-my-luggage" story never fails to both get the sympathy (or empathy) vote and to keep you in the interviewers' minds. A good story and a good attitude may actually win you some points.

21: The Visit

The style is the man himself.

Buffon, *Discourse*

Travel

THE EXTENSIVE TRAVELING that you undertake during the interview process may be the most that you have ever done. It may be your first real chance to see many parts of the country. It can also be a rude introduction to the frequent delays, cancellations, and sardine-can-like accommodations of our nation's air-travel system.

Simply traveling to many parts of the country, packing and unpacking in hotels, and finding your way around strange cities will be very tiring—not to mention costly. There are, however, some ways you can decrease your fatigue and make traveling the interview circuit more tolerable, if not actually pleasant.

Clustering Interviews

The first method is to cluster your interviews. This can be done either chronologically (to effectively use available blocks of time) or geographically.

It is not unusual for some applicants to fly back and forth across the country several times for interviews. Clustering interviews geographically saves both time and the considerable effort necessary to travel great distances. It also, of course, saves money. Clustering reduces your interviewing costs by lessening your time away from home (usually spent in hotels) and the amount of traveling you do. These costs can run anywhere from nothing to $5,000 or more, depending upon the geographical range in which you evaluate schools, the level of your accommodations, and your savvy in clustering interviews to use available transportation in the least-expensive manner possible.

To cluster interviews, it is essential that you have both luck and flexibility. The harder you work on the problem, the luckier you will become. Flexibility results from getting your materials to schools early. This will allow you a maximum number of interview dates to choose from. Luck is involved in being offered interviews at the right schools in time for you to arrange clusters. Work with the admission secretaries to try to arrange these clusters of interviews. Most of the time they will understand your situation and be willing to try to help you out.

Some obsessive-compulsive individuals will try to schedule multiple interviews day after day for a period of time. This is very dangerous. Not only will these individuals become stressed out, but they will also have very little flexibility if they encounter transportation delays. Remember, bad weather shuts down many of the nation's major airports during the interview season. As one medical student said, "The only problem I had doing my interviews was flight delays. For example, because of the Blizzard of '96, my interview at Harvard Medical School had to be rescheduled for a later date. I had to pay an extra $50 plus the difference in the flight costs." In addition, they will have too little time to digest the information obtained from one interview before getting involved in the next one.

One method some applicants have used to obtain additional insight into the school at which they have just interviewed is to informally drop by the hospital that evening or the next morning to talk with some students, and perhaps sit in on a class. This practice provides an opportunity to get a better perspective on the information gained in the midst of hectic interviewing. Such applicants also often take some time to get a feel for the community in which the school is located while they are there. But if you are going to do this, you need extra time. Take that time, even if you are clustering your interviews chronologically.

Special Fares

Another way to save money is by using special fares available from airlines, railroads, and bus companies. Often these allow you unlimited travel during a specified period of time. With the deregulation of the travel industry and its resultant fierce competition, the rates, rules, and special offers change with dizzying frequency. Shop around and use several travel agents, if necessary, until you are satisfied that you are getting the best possible value for your money. Don't forget to tell them that you are applying to medical school. "Medical" indicates that you may generate very good business in the future. "School" (i.e., student) may entitle you to special rates on some carriers. Remember, the only people who pay full fare for transportation, especially air travel, are those who have someone else pay for their trip. Your savings can be astronomical. Frequent-flyer programs can also save you money by supplying you with free car rentals, free airline tickets, and free or reduced-price hotel accommodations.

While getting cheap airline fares has become more complicated in the past few years, there are some specific strategies you can use. Once you know which cities you will visit for interviews, learn what the standard 21-day advance-purchase fare costs. Then, if you find a fare that is 45% to 50% less, book it immediately. These discounts are usually available only for limited times and there may be only a few seats available at that rate. You can also save up to 70% off the price charged by major airlines by flying one of the no-frills, low-cost carriers.

Although not usually any cheaper than airline travel, trains may be a more convenient transportation method on the coasts. The primary benefit of this travel mode is that train stations are located inside cities so less time and money are involved than in getting to the airport.

The National Association of Advisers for the Health Professions (to which your premed adviser probably belongs) offers some airline discounts. The discounts and conditions change each year, so check to see what is currently available.

If you must rent a car, the average daily rate in 1996 was $46. You can often pay less by checking with several different rental agencies for special rates. Local car rental agencies and those not located at the airport (but who will pick you up there) often have much lower rates than the major national companies. You can get their telephone numbers from the phone books at your library. If you do drive to your interview, check beforehand to find out where to park. At many medical schools, visitor parking is almost impossible to find.

Surviving Air Travel

Most medical school applicants fly to their interviews. As a business traveler, rather than a vacationer, you must do everything possible to save time and fly comfortably. Figure 21.1 lists suggestions gleaned from thousands of business travelers on how to do this.

Traveling By Car

Many applicants can drive to interviews, since they apply to schools within a reasonable distance from their homes. (What is a "reasonable" distance varies with the individual and his car's condition.)

While this may seem to be relatively simple, note that parking at most medical schools is a nightmare. If you drive to the interview, allow lots of time to find parking. In some cases, you may have to allow an extra hour, either to find a parking spot or to hike from the available parking to the school.

One trick that may be worth the few extra dollars, is to park in a commercial lot or garage in the general vicinity and then take a taxi to the school. It may save you lots of time and, especially in large cities, hassles.

Cheap Lodging

One source of information about inexpensive lodging is the admission office for the medical school where you will interview. If such information is not included in the material they send, call the secretary and ask about good, inexpensive, and *safe* lodging near the school. You will not be the first one to ask, and the school probably has a list of good places to stay. Some schools even offer accommodations in students' homes to applicants who request it (see figure 21.2). If this is available, use it, since this provides many benefits besides cheap lodging.

Sometimes you will need to use hotels. The average hotel room cost $69 per night in 1996. The rate is higher in major business and resort cities. Contact hotels directly to get the best rates.

Simultaneous Vacationing

As mentioned, the interview circuit is no picnic. But in some situations, you can turn it into a real vacation. If you try to chronologically cluster interviews but there is a gap in your schedule, see if there are vacation spots in the surrounding area. A vacation can be a relaxing break in the action—a needed rest period at a relatively low cost, since you are already nearby. If you have a spouse or significant other, he or she might want to meet you at this spot. A friendly face will be a very welcome sight and may help to bolster your spirits. And having someone to discuss your thoughts and to share your experiences with may add to the relief. Given the stresses of medical school and the anticipated heavy work schedule to come, you and (if you have one) your spouse or significant other probably need a vacation anyway!

Schedule

It's vital that you not only know your schedule but also arrive on time, if not early. There are many applicants and slip-ups, such as being late, will count against you. Most medical schools interview on a tight schedule. Everyone involved has a specific job to do at a specific time. If you don't arrive on time (Murphy's Law says that the only time faculty members will be on time is when you are not), you can botch the entire schedule for everyone concerned. They won't be happy about it and "if they're not happy, ..."

Figure 21.1: Air Travel Made Easier

- Take early morning or late-night flights. Delays are common late in the day. (Late-night flights may also be less expensive.)

- If you arrive at the airport early, try to get on an earlier flight.

- Arrive at the airport early enough to get through the enhanced security procedures.

- Board the plane as soon as possible. You will have a better chance of storing your carryon bags, and finding a pillow, a blanket, and a good magazine.

- Sit in the front of the plane to be one of the first off.

- Get an aisle seat. You can get to the bathroom easier and get off the plane faster. (You may, however, be disturbed by the "inside" passengers climbing over you to get out.)

- If you are right-handed, sit on the right side of the plane. That way, people passing you in the aisle won't jiggle your arm when you work or eat.

- Carry foam ear plugs if you want to sleep on the plane or if you will be flying on a small (usually commuter) plane. Also carry eyeshades if you want to sleep on the plane.

- Join the airlines' frequent-flier clubs. This may allow you to board earlier and get special perquisites. Use one airline as much as possible to maximize benefits.

- If you will fly a lot on one airline, consider joining its airport club. The relaxation between flights may be worth the cost of a one-year membership.

- Join hotel and car-rental clubs if you will be using them frequently.

- Don't check luggage, if at all possible.

- Use a carryon bag with wheels and, if necessary, a garment bag that clips onto it.

- Dress comfortably. Unless you will go directly to your interview, carry your interview clothes and dress casually for the flight. You and your suit will be better for it.

- Pack a snack. Many airlines no longer offer meals. Flight delays may shorten time spent in airports and prevent travelers from eating between flights.

- Order special meals, such as vegetarian, weight-watcher, or kosher meals (if there are meals on the flights). These are usually fresher than the other meals airlines serve.

- Keep your travel agent's telephone number handy. (Many have 800 or 888 numbers.) If your flight is canceled, call the agent to re-book you, rather than standing in line with the angry masses.

- Have a copy of the current month's *Official Airline Guide* (or a copy of the relevant pages) to help reschedule flights if necessary. You may get this at your library or from some of the more-traveled faculty.

- Use the airplane's restroom before landing. This may save up to twenty minutes on the ground if you are first to arrive at the taxis or car-rental counters.

- Use a skycap to avoid taxi lines. A small tip can save lots of time.

Once you begin your interviews, things can go wrong that are beyond your control. Interviewers run late, don't show up, or keep you longer than they should. If this happens to you and you think that these events will be detrimental to your application, report the problem to the admission office. They may not be aware that this is occurring and may make special arrangements to rectify the situation. One medical school applicant described his interview as

> . . . a disaster. I showed up early for my first interview, but the interviewer didn't show up until five minutes before it was supposed to end (for a 30-minute interview). He kept me late and the second interviewer was visibly upset that I was late. I explained, but that didn't seem to help. I guess I should have said something to the admission office staff, but I didn't. (He didn't get into that medical school.)

Information Gathering

While at the school, you have many opportunities to find out more about it. Since you may spend four or more years there, find out if it will meet your needs. You need this information to complete your Must/Want Analysis for this school.

A Typical Medical School Visit

Typically, medical school visits are divided into the orientation (and description of financial aid), tour, and interviews (figure 21.2). Some schools permit (and a few encourage) students to attend classes if they are in session. If you have the chance, this is always a great idea, since it helps you get the "flavor" of the school.

Not all schools have an orientation, even though this is an excellent way to give every applicant uniform and updated information about the school, as well as being a dynamic arena in which to "sell" the school to top-notch candidates.

Most schools provide a tour, usually led by a current medical student. You can classify medical school facilities as relatively new (or refurbished), old, or very old. That is less important than finding out whether the facilities are adequate to meet your educational needs, are relatively comfortable (you will spend many hours in the lecture halls and laboratories), and are safe (many of those hours will be late at night). Ignore the fancy multimillion dollar "cyclohexojumbodubotron" they show you. How often do you think you will even go near it? That's just for public relations. Stick to the important basics. For example, is the library open twenty-four hours a day? Your schedule won't be 9 A.M. to 5 P.M. You need access to the library nearly around-the-clock. (You also need this access to the anatomy labs.)

Many schools use more than one hospital for education. If possible, see all of the school's affiliated hospitals rather than just the primary one. They may not want to show you some institution(s) for a very good reason—you would not apply to the school if you saw them!

The interviews are the third part of the visit. This is where the "rubber meets the road"—and where you have the possibility of going flat, blowing out, or speeding your way to victory. Since they are so important, interviews are discussed in their own chapters.

Occasionally, the "typical" interview visit has a twist that can influence which medical school you select, as this story shows.

> At one school known for its research, a very good applicant, who had done research as an undergraduate, was initially interviewed by a member of the clinical faculty. While reviewing the student's résumé, the interviewer began asking about the applicant's research experiences and interest. Seeing that this was of major interest to the student, the interviewer called the admission office and arranged for the next interviewer to be changed to a researcher. This is the school the applicant eventually attended. He was impressed with their real interest in his needs and by their flexibility.

Figure 21.2: Medical Schools—Interviews and Visits

School	Months	Days	Length	No.	Open File?	Type	Meal/ Tour	Orien- tation	Housing
Alabama	Sept-Mar	Th	½ hr	3	part	U	Y/Y	Y/$	($)
Alabama, South	Sept-Mar	W	½-¾ hr	3	open	U	Y/Y	Y/$	Info
Albany	Sept-Apr	WTh②	NA	2	open	NA	Y/Y	Y/N	S & ($)
Albert Einstein	Aug-May	M-F	¾ hr	1	NA	U	Y/Y	N/N	?S
Alberta✧	Jan-Mar	M-S	¾ hr	1	part	U	N/N	N/N	No
Allegheny UHS^C	Sept-Mar	MTW	½-¾ hr	1	open	U	Y/Y	Y/$	S
Arizona	Sept-Mar	M-Th	½-1 hr	3	closed	Semi	N/Y	Y/-	?S
Arizona Osteo♣	Nov-May	M,F	½-¾ hr	1°	part	NA	Y/Y	Y/$	No
Arkansas	Aug-June	M-F	1 hr	2	closed	Semi	Y/Y	N/-	Yes
Baylor	Sept-Feb	FS②	½ hr	3-4	both	NA	Y/Y	Y/$	?S & ($)
Boston	Oct-Mar	M-F	¾ hr	1	open	U	Y/Y	N/N	($)
Bowman Gray	Oct-Mar	Not Th	¼ hr	1°	part	Semi	Y/Y	Y/$	?S
British Columbia✧	Oct-May	M-F	1 hr	1	open	U	N/N	N/N	No
Brown (prog)##	No interviews; Applicants may visit school							
Calgary✧	March	M-F	1 hr	1	open	U	N/N	N/N	?S
Calif.–Davis	Oct-Apr	M-F	1 hr	2	open	U	Y/Y	Y/-	($)
Calif.–Irvine	Oct-Apr	Th	1 hr	2	Part	Semi	Y/Y	Y/$	?S
Calif.–San Diego	Sept-May	Th	1 hr	2	Open	Semi	Y/Y	Y/$	?S & ($)
Calif.–San Fran	Sept-Mar	M-Th	¾ hr	2	Closed	U	Y/Y	Y/$	S
Calif.–UCLA	Nov-May	M-F	½-1 hr	1-2	Open	Struc	Y/Y	N/-	?S & ($)
Calif., Southern	Oct-Apr	M-F	1 hr	1	Closed	U	Y/Y	Y/-	?S & ($)
Caribe^S	Nov-Apr	M-F	½ hr	1°	Closed	Struc	N/Y	N/N	No
Case Western Res	Oct-Mar	M-F	½-1 hr	1	Open	Semi	Y/Y	Y/$	?S & ($)
Chicago–Pritzker	Oct-Apr	MTTh	¾-1 hr	2-3	Open	Semi	Y/Y	Y/$	S
Chicago Medical	Oct-May	Varies	¼-¾ hr	2	Open	Semi	Y/Y	Y/N	?S & ($)
Chicago Osteo♣	Nov-Apr	MF	NA	1°	Part	Semi	Y/Y	Y/$	($)
Cincinnati	Sept-Feb	MT	1 hr	1	Open	U	Y/N	N/$	?S & ($)
Colorado	Sept-Apr	M-F	¾ hr	2	Part	U	Y/Y	Y/-	($)
Columbia	Sept-Mar	M-F	½ hr	1	NA	U	Y/Y	N/N	S
Connecticut	Aug-Apr	M-F	½-1 hr	1-2	Choice	U	Y/Y	N/-	?S
Cornell	Oct-Mar	MTW	½-¾ hr	2	Open	U	Y/Y	Y/Y	?S
Creighton	Nov-Mar	F	½ hr	NA	Closed	U	Y/Y	Y/Y	S & ($)
Dalhousie ✧	NA	NA	NA	NA	NA	NA	NA	NA	NA
Dartmouth	Oct-Apr	NA	½ hr	2	Both	Struc	Y/Y	N/$	S
Duke	Sept-Feb	M-F	½ hr	2	Open	Semi	Y/Y	Y/$	?S & ($)
East Carolina	Aug-Apr	M-F	¾ hr	2	Part	U	N/Y	Y/$	NA
Emory	Oct-Mar	MF	NA	2#°	Part	U	Y/Y	Y/$	NA

Figure 21.2: Medical Schools—Interviews and Visits, cont'd

School	Months	Days	Length	No.	Open File?	Type	Meal/ Tour	Orien- tation	Housing
Florida	Sept-Mar	F	1 hr	2	Open	U	Y/Y	Y/$	($)
Florida, South	Oct-Apr	M	¾ hr	2	Closed	U	Y/Y	Y/$	S
Geo. Washington	Sept-Apr	TFS	20 min	2	Part	Semi	Y/Y	Y/$	?S & ($)
Georgetown	Sept-May	Not W	½ hr	1	Part	NA	Y/Y	Y/$	NA
Georgia, Med Coll	Oct-Mar	MF	1 hr	2	Closed	U	Y/Y	Y/-	?S
Harvard	Sept-Jan	Not W	¾-1 hr	2	Open	U	Y/Y	Y/$	S
Hawaii	Oct-Mar	All	1-2 hr	2	Part	U	N/N	N/-	No
Howard	Sept-Aug	TWS	NA	NA	Open	Semi	Y/Y	Y/-	No
Illinois, Southern	Aug-Mar	M-F	¼-1 hr	2-3	Both	Struc	N/Y	N/$	($)
Illinois, Univ. of	Nov-Mar	M-F[N]	¾ hr	1°	Open	NA	N/Y	N/$	($)
Indiana	Sept-Feb	W	¾ hr	1°	Open	Semi	N/Y	Y/$	($)
Iowa	NA	NA[N]	NA	NA	NA	NA	NA	NA	NA
Jefferson	Sept-Apr	W	½-¾ hr	1	Open	Semi	Y/Y	Y/$	S & ($)
Johns Hopkins	Sept-Mar	ThF	NA	1	Open	Struc	Y/Y	Y/$	S
Kansas	Jan	1st wk	1 hr	1#°	Part	NA	Y/Y	Y/$	?S
Kentucky	Aug-Apr	TS	¾ hr	2	Open	Semi	Y/Y	Y/N	?S
Kirksville Osteo ♣	NA	MThF	¾ hr	2	Open	Semi	Y/Y	Y/$	?S
Lake Erie Osteo. ♣	Nov-Mar	MThF	½ hr	2°	Open	NA	N/N	N/N	($)
Laval ✧F	May[A]	NA	NA	1#‡	NA	Semi[F]	NA	NA	NA
Loma Linda	Nov-Mar	M-F	½-1 hr	1-2	Part	U	Y/Y	Y/$	($)
Louisville	Sept-Apr	WTh	½ hr	2	Part	NA	Y/Y	Y/N	?S
Loyola–Stritch	Sept-Apr	M-F	1 hr	3	Part	Struc	Y/Y	N/N	S & ($)
LSU–New Orleans	Oct-(F)	MTW	½ hr	3	Both	Str/U	Y/Y	Y/N	($)
LSU–Shreveport	Oct-Mar	T	½-¾ hr	2	Open	Semi	N/Y	Y/$	NA
Manitoba ✧	Feb-Mar	S	1 hr	1°	Part	Struc	N/Y	Y/Y	?S
Marshall	Sept-Mar	MTW	½-¾ hr	2	Open	U	N/Y	Y/N	No
Maryland	Oct-Mar	MW	¾-1 hr	2	NA	Semi	Y/Y	Y/$	?S & ($)
Massachusetts	Oct-Mar	TW	½ hr	2	Closed	Semi	N/Y	Y/$	No
Mayo	Sept-Apr	M-F	½ hr	2	NA	NA	Y/Y	N/N	?S
McGill ✧	Apr[Q]	M-F	½ hr	2	Part	U	N/Y	Y/N	S
McMaster ✧	Mar-Apr	SSun	¾ hr	2#°	Part	Struc	N/N	Y/N	No
Meharry	Sept-May	F	½ hr	2	Open	Struc	Y/Y	Y/N	S & ($)
Mercer	Oct-Mar	TWTh	NA	2	Both	U	Y/Y	Y/$	No
Miami	Sept-Mar	MF	NA	1	Open	Struc	Y/Y	Y/$	?S & ($)
Michigan St. Osteo. ♣	Oct-Feb	M-F	¾-1 hr	2	Struc	Part	Y/Y	Y/N	S & ($)
Michigan State	Sept-Apr	Th	½ hr	2	Closed	Struc	Y/Y	Y/$	($)
Michigan, University	Sept-Mar	F	½ hr	2	Open	U	Y/Y	Y/Y	?S & ($)
Minnesota–Duluth	Oct-Apr	M-F	1 hr	2	Open	Semi	Y/Y	N/N	No

Figure 21.2: Medical Schools—Interviews and Visits, cont'd

School	Months	Days	Length	No.	Open File?	Type	Meal/ Tour	Orien- tation	Housing
Minnesota–Minneap.	Sept-May	M-F	NA	1	Part	Semi	Y/Y	N/$	No
Mississippi	Aug-Mar	M-F	½-1 hr	3	Part	Semi	Y/Y	N/N	No
Missouri–Columbia	Sept-Apr	TWF	¾ hr	2	Open	U	Y/Y	Y/N	?S
Missouri–KS City⑥	Dec-Mar	Not T	½-1 hr	2	Open	Semi	N/Y	Y/Y	($)
Montréal✛F	Mar-May	MF	2 hr	1°	Closed	Struc	N/N	N/N	No
Morehouse	Oct-Mar	F	½-¾ hr	1	Both	Struc	Y/Y	Y/$	($)
Mount Sinai&	Sept-Apr	M-F	½ hr	2	Open	U	Y/Y	Y/N	S
Nebraska	Nov-Apr	W	NA	NA	NA	NA	N/Y	Y/N	No
Nevada	Sept-Feb	M-F	¾ hr	2	Closed	Semi	NA	NA	No
New England Ost.✦	Sept-Apr	S	½-¾ hr	1°	Open	NA	Y/Y	Y/N	S & ($)
New Mexico	Jun-Mar	M-F	½-1 hr	2	Open	U	Y/Y	N/N	No
New York COM✦	Nov-May	M-F	½ hr	1	Open	U	Y/Y	Y/$	NA
New York Medical	Sept-Apr	M-Th	½ hr	1-2	Closed	U	Y/Y	Y/Y	S & ($)
New York Univ.&	Nov-Feb	M-S	½-¾ hr	NA	NA	NA	N/Y	N/N	($)
Newfoundland✛	Feb-Apr	WS	1 hr	1°	Closed	Semi	N/Y	Y/Y	($)
North Carolina	Aug-Apr	Not W	¾ hr	1	Open	U	N/N	Y/$	?S
North Dakota	Dec-Jan	ThFS	1 hr	1#°	Open	Semi	N/N	N/N	?S
Northwestern	Oct-Apr	T-F	NA	1#°	NA	Struc	Y/N	Y/$	($)
Nova Univ Osteo.✦	Sept-(F)	MWF	NA	1°	Open	U	N/Y	Y/$	($)
Ohio Osteo.✦	Oct-Apr	W	½ hr	3	Open	Both	N/N	Y	?S
Ohio State	Sept-Mar	MW	½-¾ hr	1°	Open	U	Y/Y	Y/$	S
Ohio, Medical Coll.	Oct-Apr	M-Th	1 hr	2	Open	Struc	Y/Y	Y/N	?S & ($)
Ohio, Northeast ##	Nov-Mar	M-F	¾ hr	1°	Open	Struc	Y/Y	Y/$	($)
Oklahoma	Nov-Jan	Varies	¼-¾ hr	1°	Open	Semi	Y/Y	Y/$	S
Oklahoma St. Ost✦	Oct-Feb*	M-F	½ hr	2	Open	NA	N/Y	Y/$	?S
Ontario, Western ✛	Mar-June	S	¾ hr	1°	Closed	Semi	N/N	N/N	No
Oregon	Oct-Mar	T-Th	¾ hr	2	Open	Semi	Y/Y	N/$	?S & ($)
Ottawa✛	Mar-June	NA	½ hr	1°	Part	NA	N/Y	Y/N	?S & ($)
Pacific Osteo.✦	Oct-Apr	MTTh	½ hr	1°	Open	U	Y/Y	Y/N	?S
Pennsylvania State	Sept-Mar	MWF	½ hr	1°	Open	U	Y/Y	Y/$	($)
Pennsylvania, Univ	Oct-Feb	S	¾ hr	2	Part	U	N/Y	Y/$	?S & ($)
Philadelphia Ost.✦	Sept-May	M-Th	¾ hr	1°	Open	Semi	Y/Y	N/$	?S & ($)
Pittsburgh	Sept-Apr	MTF	¾ hr	2	Part	NA	Y/Y	Y/$	?S
Ponce S	Oct-Apr	M-F	NA	1#°	NA	Semi	N/Y	Y/N	No
Puerto Rico S	Nov-Feb	M-F	1 hr	1°	Closed	Struc	N/N	N/N	No
Queen's ✛	Mar-Apr	SSun	¾ hr	1°	Part	Semi	N/N	Y/N	($)
Rochester	Oct-Mar	Not T	½-1 hr	2	Closed	U	Y/Y	N/N	S & ($)
Rush	Sept-May	M-F	¾-1 hr	2	Both	NA	Y/Y	N/N	($)
Saint Louis	Sept-May	TF	1 hr	1	Both	Semi	Y/Y	Y/Y	S
Saskatchewan✛	Mar	SSun	¾ hr	1°	Closed	Semi	N/N	N/N	No

Figure 21.2: Medical Schools—Interviews and Visits, cont'd

School	Months	Days	Length	No.	Open File?	Type	Meal/ Tour	Orien- tation	Housing
Sherbrooke◊F	May	colspan... No interviews; Applicants may visit school							($)
South Carol., Med U	Sept-Mar	F	1 hr	3	Part	Semi	Y/Y	Y/$	($)
South Carol., Univ.	Sept-Mar	W	½ hr	2	Both	U	Y/Y	Y/$	?S
South Dakota	Oct-Mar	M-F	¾-1 hr	2	Open	U	N/N	N/N	No
Stanford	Sept-Mar	M-F	1 hr	2	Open	Semi	Y/Y	N/-	?S
SUNY–Brooklyn	Sept-Apr	M-Th	¾-1 hr	1	Open	U	Y/Y	Y/N	($)
SUNY–Buffalo	Sept-Apr	W	¾ hr	2	Open	Semi	Y/Y	Y/N	?S & ($)
SUNY–Stony Brook	Aug-Apr	TThF	¾-1 hr	1	Open	Str/U	Y/Y	Y/N	?S
SUNY–Syracuse	Sept-Feb	MW	¾-1 hr	2	Part	Semi	Y/Y	Y/$	?S & ($)
Temple U.	Sept-Feb	M-Th	¾-1 hr	1	Open	U	Y/Y	N/$	?S & ($)
Tennessee State, E.	Sept-Mar	M-Th	½-1 hr	2	Part	U	Y/Y	Y/Y	?S & ($)
Tennessee, U. of	Oct-Mar	MTW	¾ hr	2	Open	U	Y/Y	Y/Y	($)
Texas A&M	Aug-Jan	ThF②	½ hr	3	NA	NA	Y/Y	Y/$	($)
Texas Coll Ost ♣	Aug-Feb	TThF	¾-1½ h	2	Closed	U	Y/Y	Y/$	S
Texas Tech	Sept-Mar	WF	¾ hr	2	Open	U	Y/Y	Y/$	?S
Texas, U–Galveston	Aug-Oct	WF	½ hr	2	Part	U	Y/Y	Y/$	S
Texas, U–Houston	Aug-Jan	F	½-1 hr	2	Part	U	Y/Y	Y/$	S
Texas, U–San Anton	Sept-Dec	M	½ hr	2	Part	U	Y/Y	Y/N	?S
Texas, U–Southwest	Sept-Dec	S	½ hr	2	Open	U	Y/Y	Y/N	($)
Toronto◊	Feb-Aug	M-S	1 hr	1°	Part	Semi	N/N	N/N	($)
Tufts	Nov-Apr	T	NA	2	Part	NA	Y/Y	Y/$	($)
Tulane	Sept-Mar	Not T	½ hr	3	Both	U	Y/Y	N/$	S
UMDNJ-Coll Ost. ♣	Aug-Apr	M-F	¼-½ hr	2-3	Open	Semi	Y/Y	Y/$	?S & ($)
UMDNJ-NJ Med	Aug-Apr	M-F	1 hr	1	Open	Semi	N/Y	N/N	No
UMDNJ-RWJ	Aug-Mar	M-F	¾-1 hr	1	Open	U	Y/Y	N/N	?S
Uniformed Serv. U.	Oct-Mar	Th	½ hr	2	Part	U	N/Y	Y/$	
Univ Health Sci Ost♣	Sept-Apr	MWF	¼-¾ hr	1°	NA	Semi	N/Y	Y/$	($)
Univ. Ost. Med/Hlth♣	Oct-May	ThF	¼-½ hr	1°	Open	Semi	Y/Y	Y/$	?S & ($)
Utah	Oct-Feb	M-F	½-¾ hr	2	NA	Semi	Y/Y	Y/N	?S
Vanderbilt	Aug-Mar	Not W	¾-1 hr	1	Part	U	Y/Y	Y/$	($)
Vermont	Sept-Mar	TTh	¾ hr	1°	Part	Semi	Y/Y	Y/$	($)
Virginia, Eastern	Sept-Mar	WF	NA	1°	Open	NA	Y/Y	Y/$	S
Virginia, Med. Coll.	Aug-Mar	M-Th	½-¾ hr	1	Both	Struc	Y/Y	Y/$	?S & ($)
Virginia, Univ. of	Sept-Mar	M-Th	½ hr	2	Open	U	Y/Y	Y/N	?S & ($)
Washington U. (MO)	Sept-Feb	M-F	1 hr	1	Both	U	Y/Y	Y/Y	S
Washington, Univ of	Oct-Mar	M-F	½ hr	2-3	Open	U	Y/Y	N/N	?S
Wayne State	Sept-Apr	M-F	1 hr	1	Open	U	N/Y	N/N	($)
West Virginia	Sept-Jan	Not T	NA	NA	Open	NA	Y/N	N/$	($)
West Virginia Ost. ♣	Aug-Mar	M-Th	½ hr	1	Open	Struc	Y/Y	Y/$	($)
Wisconsin, Med Coll	Nov-Apr	F	½ hr	2	Both	Str/U	N/Y	Y	S &($)
Wisconsin, Univ. of	Dec-May	MF	½ hr	1	Open	U	Y/Y	Y/$	?S & ($)
Wright State	Sept-Apr	TW	¾ hr	2	Open	Semi	Y/Y	Y/$	S
Yale	Oct-Mar	MWF	½-1 hr	2	Choice	U	Y/Y	Y/$	?S & ($)

Figure 21.2: Medical Schools—Interviews and Visits, cont'd

[+]: Canadian medical school

[▲]: College of Osteopathic Medicine

[●]: Non-U.S./non-Canadian medical school

[F]: Classes taught in French

[S]: Classes taught in Spanish

[C]: Formerly the Medical College of Pennsylvania/Hahnemann Medical Schools

[&]: New York University and Mt. Sinai are merging into a single medical school

##: Information is primarily for those not applying through the eight-year program

(F): Interviews until class is full

[N]: Restarting interviews for 1997 class.

[A]: Applicable only to non-Canadian citizens/landed immigrants

[Q]: Quebec residents. Non-Canadians interviewed Jan-Feb; Non-Quebec Canadians interviewed Feb-Mar

No.: The number of interviews

Open File?: Whether the interviewer has the student's entire application file available. If they have the entire file, it is "Open." If they have only a portion, it is "Part," and if they do not have any of the file, it is "Closed."

Type: The interview can be unstructured "U," structured "Struc," semi-structured "Semi," or the interviewer's choice "Choice."

$: Financial orientation is offered.

($): Inexpensive housing is available.

Info: Information about inexpensive housing is available.

S: Housing with students is available.

?S: Housing with students may be available.

[#]: Applicants interviewed in a group

[○]: Applicants interviewed by more than one person at once

[‡]: Applicants are placed in "simulated situations" to test their reactions

*: Interviews occur only in four weeks during this period

②: The interview process takes two days

⑥: Information about 6-year program interviews

Talk To Students

If you haven't talked to the current medical students, assume that you really do not know very much about a school. Be very wary of any school that does not give you the opportunity or insist that you talk to some of its students. Students see things quite differently than the faculty. And their perspectives, while not necessarily the same as you might have in the same situation, may be much closer to yours than are those of the school's administrators. Talks with students are usually informal and, because of limitations on their time, may occur in group settings. Nevertheless, the students' opinions, viewpoints, and insights about the school should strongly influence how you rate each of the factors on your Must/Want Analysis.

Many medical schools have current students give tours to the applicants (see figure 21.2). Most of these tours are rather boring. As they say, if you have seen one medical school, you have seen them all. The only exceptions are a few Eastern schools, such as the University of Maryland where students tour through the original medical school building, now a National Historic Landmark. Boring or not, when you write a thank-you letter to the Dean of Admissions after your visit, be sure to mention the student who gave you the tour, as well as any who may have housed you during your stay.

Besides giving you a view of the facilities and some general information about the school, these tours give you a chance to talk with one or more students who are attending the medical school where you might want to go. Take this opportunity to ask them some questions. (See chapter 24, *Your Questions,* for some of the questions you may want to ask.) Get their telephone numbers, "snail-mail" addresses, or e-mail addresses so that if you have additional questions, you can contact them. Some schools provide the phone numbers of current students who will answer applicants' questions. Ask for them.

If you have done your homework, you may have identified one or more of each school's students who are from your home town or your undergraduate school. Arrange in advance to meet with one of them while you are there. Even though they may be very busy, they must eat sometime, so perhaps you can join them and their colleagues for a meal. Even better, if you can arrange to stay with them while interviewing at their school, you should have lots of opportunities to talk about what is *really* going on at the school—and to see beyond the rose-colored picture the admission office paints.

Get Information So You Can Talk To Graduates Later

Another great source of information about a school is its graduates. While at the school, stop by the alumni office and get contact information for any of their recent graduates who live near your home. When you return home, contact them for additional details about the school. Be considerate of their time, however, since they are now residents with very hectic schedules. It's often best to call and ask them if they would be willing to talk with you by phone or in person at a convenient time.

Exam Schedule

When talking with students and perusing a school's curriculum, consider whether that school's examination schedule fits your learning pattern. Are tests scheduled every two weeks, or only as midterms and finals? Individuals differ markedly in the way they learn, in their comfort in taking examinations, and in their need for feedback on their performance. If you do best in courses where you get frequent feedback, your work may suffer at schools with only two examinations in each course. Does this school's examination schedule work for you?

Learning Skills Specialist

For many medical students, one of the most important faculty members will be the Learning Skills Specialist. This individual may be the school's only faculty member with training in how to assess a student's learning skills and with the ability to help students improve those skills. Find out if such a specialist exists at the school. If the student giving the tour does not know, check with the medical school's "teaching" or "learning" center.

Minority Applicants

Aside from the information discussed above, minority applicants should also use other criteria and get additional information with which to evaluate the school. How knowledgeable and helpful is the minority affairs office? Did you get a chance to talk with current minority students or faculty, especially those from your culture? (In some cases, the minority affairs office can arrange for you to stay with these students during your visit.) Also, be sensitive to the school's locale, ambiance, and attitude as you visit. How do you *feel* in these surroundings? The answer to that question alone may make or break your medical school career.

The Meal

Applicants may be asked to go to lunch (or sometimes dinner or breakfast) with students or faculty members (see figure 21.2). Several rules apply to this experience, as with any business lunch—for that is exactly what it is.

Stay away from alcohol! You need to be on your toes, not under the table. Even if you don't lose your wits after imbibing alcohol, your afternoon interviewers may be teetotalers and, thus, discount you as a viable candidate if you have been drinking.

Do not eat too much. The postprandial tide is a very effective soporific. You don't want to sleep through the afternoon's activities, do you?

Be sure to use good table manners. If you have never learned them before, it is essential to do so now. You will need to know how to eat in a reasonably civilized manner throughout your medical career. Start at the interview lunch. Common errors in table manners that cost people medical school slots include: holding your fork like a knife, talking with your mouth full, not putting the napkin in your lap, not breaking bread before you eat it, and pushing food onto the fork with your thumb. Even in the hospital cafeteria, some table manners are necessary. If you need help, ask a civilized friend. This example from an actual interview meal suggests how poor some people's social skills are:

> When one candidate went with some of us to a Chinese restaurant during her interview visit, everything seemed to go very well. But when she was served a fortune cookie, I saw her put the entire thing in her mouth, paper and all! Then she pulled the fortune out of her mouth and read it to us.

Finally, avoid foods that can cause accidents and embarrassment. Soups, creamy dressings, spaghetti, desserts, and greasy hand-held foods, such as tacos, can easily end up on your brand new clothes. Onions and garlic can make even the most stalwart interviewer want to avoid you. The best advice is to use lunch to ward off true hypoglycemia. Do your real eating after you have left the school for the day.

22: Preparing For The Interview

Once upon a midnight dreary,
while I pondered weak and weary, . . .

Poe, The Raven

Before You Go

Know About A Medical Career And The Required Training

IF EVERYTHING GOES RIGHT, you will have worked hard and gotten several medical school interviews. Ideally, before you began the entire application process you learned as much as you could about a medical career. If not, be certain you know what it means to be a physician before you arrive at the schools. This does not mean amassing medical knowledge. You will acquire that during your training. It means that you should know about medicine's culture. Find out what a real physician's life is like (not the television or movie image). Know what type of educational experiences you can expect to have in medical school, during your residency and, perhaps, during a fellowship. What do physicians really do? Of course, this will differ by specialty, but at least have some general knowledge about what a primary care physician does. (See chapter 3 for descriptions of the various medical specialties.)

Faculty members want to feel sure that you have learned about a medical career before you commit your entire professional life to it. If you do not know this, you may not have fully thought out your decision, and you could be very unhappy later. Unhappiness is bad for both students and the faculty. It leads to depression, anger, and poor performance. It can also cause a student to do inferior school-work, to drop out before graduation, or worst of all, to become a dissatisfied (and usually a bad) physician. Therefore, demonstrate that you have seriously thought about your career choice. Know about medicine. Read the medical-student medical journals (see *Annotated Bibliography*) to learn what current medical students think and about the changes occurring within the profession. The more you know about a medical career, the more committed to it you will appear. And commitment is among the most important qualities interviewers seek.

Know School-Specific Information

Just as you must know basic information about a medical career, you also need to know about each school you visit.

You initially received a lot of information in the school's packet. If you were as careful as you should have been, you also received additional written or oral information which updated the packet. Often more extensive information can be found in two annual AAMC publications: the

Medical School Admissions Requirements and the *Curriculum Guide*. (The AACOM has a similar book, *Osteopathic Medical College Information*.)

To get additional information about a school, run a Medline search for articles recently published by the school's faculty. (Medline is the National Library of Medicine's primary on-line bibliographic service. It can be accessed through some Web servers, and through many university, and all medical school, libraries. There may be a small charge however.) Look particularly for articles dealing with medical education. These may describe innovations in the school's curriculum or teaching methods. Gathering this information may help you avoid going to a school whose teaching methods (for example, small-groups) are not compatible with your learning style. They may also provide insight into questions faculty might ask you or about subjects they might like to discuss. In any case, the more you know about a specific school before going to the interview, the better the chance that you will leave well-remembered and highly regarded.

The Night Before The Interview

Review the information for the school before going into your interview. No matter whether this is the first school at which you are interviewing or the twentieth, it is a major *faux pas* to confuse basic information about the school where you are currently interviewing with that about another school. Have the relevant facts firmly in your mind before you set out in the morning. If you, like most people, have a little trouble keeping the details straight, make some notes for reference.

How do successful applicants (current medical students) prepare the night before their interviews? The following list, culled from a survey of medical students, demonstrates the wide diversity in preparation methods. But the four overwhelming responses were:

+++ Re-read all the application materials I sent to this school.

+++ Re-read all the information I had about this school.

+++ Reviewed questions to ask the interviewers.

+++ Thought some more about questions I might be asked.

Additional things these applicants did to prepare varied greatly, and depended upon each individual's personality, how stressed they felt, and how many interviews they already had done.

+ Saw a great movie.
+ Spoke to med students attending the school.
+ Prayed.
+ Thought about the ethical issues in health care.
+ Read the local newspaper and a national news magazine.
+ Went through another mock-interview session with a friend.
+ Reviewed my résumé.
+ Re-examined my motivations for why I wanted to be a physician.
+ Ate a bowl of oatmeal (with chocolate chips).
+ Drank coffee, coffee, coffee—too much coffee—and didn't sleep well.
+ Reviewed my own research papers and my past research projects.
+ Tried to relax a bit—very difficult to do.
+ Cruised the Internet.
+ Browsed through *JAMA*.

+ Read a good (non-medical) book.
+ Got eight hours of sleep.
+ Went shopping.
+ Went out to a nice restaurant with friends.
+ Watched television.
+ Listened to some great music.
+ Played video games in my hotel room.
+ Drank a couple beers while watching a basketball game.
+ Listened to National Public Radio.
+ Toured the city and had a good time.
+ Read some recent journals on health policy.
+ Exercised and jogged.
+ Talked with friends on the telephone.

Basic Interview Rules

Decisions are made in the first 30 seconds of the interview–the rest of the time is used to justify the decision.

An axiom in the personnel field

Once you actually get to the interview site, there are some very basic things that you need to do aside from answering any questions in a satisfactory manner. In fact, questions and answers may, in some cases, be merely window-dressing for the actual interview process.

The "behavioral interview" is becoming more common as laws limit to an ever greater extent the questions that interviewers can ask. Behavioral interviewers are much more interested in whether you look and act like a medical student and physician rather than whether you can answer any specific question. They evaluate communication skills, physical presence, motivation, truthfulness, and how suited each applicant is to be a medical student at their school.

All good interviewers look for small but important details. Some of these are discussed below.

Know How To Pronounce Your Interviewers' Names

How do you say "Dr. Swnolwyg"? You don't know? How could that be when he will be interviewing you in five minutes? It may seem petty, especially considering some of the difficult or unique pronunciations of names in the world, to expect you to know how to pronounce, on the first try, all the names of the people that you will meet. But it is expected. So you should know how. Remember that, above all else, a person's name is a unique part of him or her. Mispronouncing an interviewer's name can, even if subconsciously, leave a negative impression about you.

At the start of the day, ask the admission secretary how to pronounce any difficult or unusual names among those listed on your interview schedule. As he or she tells you, write each down phonetically so you will be able to repeat it correctly when necessary. If this is not possible, listen carefully when the individual introduces him- or herself to you. If it is a difficult name, repeat it and ask if you said it right. Don't slip up on this simple point of etiquette.

Enter And Depart In A Polite, Assured Manner

Look confident! Walk into the interview with your head up, shoulders squared, looking poised. Pause briefly as you enter the room to assert your strong presence. If you slink into an interview like a scared rabbit, how are you going to look to an interviewer? Certainly not like one of the people likely to get a spot at his school. Physicians are supposed to exude an air of confidence. Remember that initial impressions are very important. In the first minute, interviewers determine whether applicants meet their expectations. Send a message of confidence, calmness, and control.

Greet interviewers with a firm, but not bone-crushing, handshake. This goes for both men and women. The dainty "dead-fish" handshake once used by many women, as well as some men, connotes only meekness and a lack of authority. Avoid it like the plague. Extend your hand to the other person with the thumb up and out. Make sure that the web between your thumb and index finger meets the other person's web. Try to shake hands from the elbow, not the shoulder or wrist. It is also desirable to have reasonably dry hands. If your palms sweat when you get nervous, dry them off just before meeting each interviewer. One solution to sweaty palms is to sit before interviews with your palms exposed to the air rather than stuffed in your pockets or lying face down in your lap.

Greet the interviewer not only with a firm handshake, but also with an enthusiastic voice and manner. When you begin speaking to an individual, the actual words you say are much less important than the manner in which you say them. The first thing interviewers notice is your tone of voice. You will be judged by your enthusiasm, facial expressions, gestures, and posture. Therefore, try to act as if you are really pleased to have an opportunity to talk with the faculty and students. Practice this with some critical observers at home. You must not sound forced or pretentious. If you do, you will do yourself more harm than good. Sincere enthusiasm will greatly enhance your entire visit.

During the interview, sit comfortably straight, leaning slightly forward in the chair. This demonstrates your interest through nonverbal cues. You can prove this to yourself. Have a friend (trying to keep a neutral expression in both instances) first face you, sitting forward in a chair. Then have the individual lean back in a relaxed posture. If you were the interviewer, which applicant would interest you more?

Negative body-language includes resting your head on your hand, tilting your head to one side (the coy look), and fiddling with your beard, hair, mustache, or earrings. Keep your head upright and your hands away from your head. Likewise, don't fiddle with your clothes, pen, or anything else. Also, don't cross your arms, perhaps the most negative non-verbal signal you can give. Rest your hands in your lap or on your thighs.

Look your interviewer in the eyes. Applicants who look away when they answer questions suggest either that their answers are less than honest or that they are afraid of the situation. Those who look away when the interviewer is talking (a true kiss of death) indicate that they do not care about whatever the interviewer is saying. Obviously, neither situation is favorable. Always try to look an interviewer in the eyes. Some experienced interviewers suggest looking at a person first in one eye, then the other. That way, the speaker gets the feeling that the listener is listening intently; while the listener avoids having the glazed look some people get when they look at a person only in one eye (a common behavior). If you plan to try this, practice ahead of time; the first few times you do it you may become distracted and not hear what the speaker is saying.

Acknowledge what the interviewer is saying by nodding, or with brief verbal phrases, such as, "I see," "of course," or "yes." Try not to use expressions such as "wow," "way," or "cool," which connote something other than professionalism. Vary the expressions you use, so you don't sound wooden or monotonous.

If you are in the middle of answering a question and the interviewer cuts you off or moves the interview in another direction, don't get flustered. Often they do this so that they can ask specific questions they must ask within the allotted time. Remember, they are the interviewers; you are the interviewee.

Your exit from the interview must also be graceful and enthusiastic. As speech writers know, the last thing heard will be remembered best. Shake your interviewer's hand and say, again, how glad you are to have had a chance to talk with him or her. Offer to provide any other information he or she might desire about you. You will rarely, if ever, be taken up on this offer. State that you look forward to being associated with him or her as a medical student. This should take less than fifteen seconds and appear very smooth. Practice this one little segment ahead of time so you don't appear awkward. As you can see from some television interviews, even the best speakers and the most intelligent individuals often look like dolts when terminating an interview. Don't let this be your downfall.

Show Enthusiasm For This School

It is important to show your enthusiasm for a medical career. But showing enthusiasm about the school *at which you are currently interviewing* makes interviewers rate you even more highly. Base your interest on the strong points that you gleaned from the school's packet of information. Generally the areas of which the school is most proud are included in their packet. So basing your interest on these areas should get the best results.

An amazing number of applicants arrive at schools with the attitude that either (1) they are browsing and will not reveal that they really *want* a position at the school, or (2) they need not be concerned about the attitude they demonstrate.

Both approaches are wrong. Show enthusiasm! If you cannot work up any enthusiasm for a school, you should not be interviewing there.

You Are Not Selling A Medical Student, You Are Selling A Promise

Forget that you are not yet a medical student. During the interview visit, you are the promise of a bright future. You will be medicine's finest clinician, a noted researcher, a diligent healer of indigent patients, a solid member of the medical community. You will achieve this because you are an extremely hard worker who is compulsive, intelligent, responsive to teaching, happy in your work, and no trouble to the faculty.

That is the promise you are selling. To get into medical school, you must project the ability to make this promise a reality. You can make a contribution to this school and to the profession. You are the salesman. You are the product. Go forth and sell.

Interview Materials

Although it may seem rather silly to detail what you need to take with you to interviews, it is surprising how many applicants forget some basic materials. In addition to the basics, two forms, the *Interview Notes* and your *Must/Want Analysis* (each discussed below) should also be part of your standard interview equipment. These will aid you later when you evaluate each school and write your follow-up letters.

General Materials

The first two items that you need to bring with you are the *directions to the interview site* and the *telephone numbers* with which to contact the school if you either get lost or are delayed. Next, carry along whatever *information you have received from the school*. Not only should you review it immediately prior to setting out for the interview in the morning, but you may also want to consult it during the interview day to refresh your memory or recheck questionable points brought up in conversation. Of course, you should have a *list of questions* that you want to ask at each school (see chapter 24), as well as a *pad of paper and pens* to record the answers. Test your pens to make sure that they work. Bring a *photograph* of yourself to give to the admission secretary when you arrive if your appearance has changed noticeably since you submitted your applications. (In some cases, the schools may not yet have a photograph of you; give them one.) Finally, if you have any *additional credentials or paperwork that is vital for the school to have,* such as information about additional clinical experiences you have had, be certain that you bring them with you.

Finally, bring *something to read,* be it a textbook, news magazine, or newspaper. At most schools you will spend a lot of time waiting. If you have something to occupy your mind, it will make you more alert and less cranky.

Interview Notes Form

The Interview Notes Form (figure 22.1) is designed to give you an organized method for remembering key information obtained during interviews. It will also act as a reminder when you want to send follow-up notes or materials to individual interviewers. This form is the one to use to write out the phonetic spelling of the interviewers' names.

Must/Want Analysis As An Interview Checklist

The Must/Want Analysis you previously completed (see figure 16.1) can now act as an *Interview Checklist* (see the examples at figures 16.2 and 16.3). Its use both simplifies your evaluation of each school and helps you discriminate among them. The factors that compose your personal Must/Want Analysis and the weights you assigned to each one will remain constant for all the schools you visit. Immediately following your visit to each school, score on a 1 to 10 scale (10 is perfect) how well it does in each category. Even if you have previously given some items "Scores" based on written materials, those "Scores" should be considered tentative until confirmed during the interview visit. Then multiply the "Weights" by the "Scores" for each factor to obtain the factor "Total." Adding the values in the "Total" column will give you your personal ranking for the school ("School Evaluation Score").

This "School Evaluation Score" can later be compared to similar scores which you calculate after you visit other schools. In some cases, of course, your ratings may suffer from the same problem that interviewers face; early ratings will tend to be lower because they are compared to an ideal, whereas later ratings will tend to be higher since they are being made in comparison to schools you have visited previously. If this is taken into account, you should have no difficulty correctly interpreting the scores.

Figure 22.1: Interview Notes

School_____

Address_____

Secretary_____

Telephone_____

Interviewer   Notes

1. _____   _____

_____   _____

_____

2. _____   _____

_____   _____

_____

3. _____   _____

_____   _____

_____

4. _____   _____

_____   _____

_____

5. _____   _____

_____   _____

_____

6. _____   _____

_____   _____

_____

Other Notes:

23: The Interview

NEARLY EVERYONE WHO GETS INVITED for an interview has the "paper credentials" to get into medical school. Their GPAs are at least adequate, they did at least pretty well on their MCAT, they have some clinical or research experience, and their reference letters imply that they possess most of the qualities necessary to survive medical training and to be physicians.

So the interview is a very important determinant as to whether an individual is accepted to medical school. Applicants must demonstrate to the interviewers that they are not complete social misfits—or at least that they can hide it well enough to survive the interview. (If you can hide your lack of socialization, you have demonstrated that you have "growth potential," and may eventually acquire better social skills. Some physicians, of course, never develop these skills and their careers are usually spent far away from patient care.)

Purpose Of The Interview

Most, but not all, medical schools interview applicants. These interviews have two purposes: to assess applicants' characteristics and to "sell" students on their schools. (See figure 23.1.) In general, interviewers want to be sure that candidates fit in with their school's culture and mission, aren't "off-the-wall," and have the maturity to make a career decision and to be a physician.

Part of the purpose of assessing an applicant's *characteristics* is to predict the individual's success in medical school. Medical schools and interviewers both claim that they use interviews to assess "noncognitive" variables, such as "people skills," "friendliness," "interpersonal skills," "communication ability," and "social skills." While this may be true, studies show that the characteristics medical school interviewers most commonly assess (in order of frequency) are: motivation for and interest in attending medical school; interpersonal skills and character; maturity; evidence of extracurricular activities; communication skills; empathy and concern for others; social awareness and self-awareness; and knowledge, judgment and problem-solving abilities. At least one-third of all medical schools assess some or all of these qualities during the interview.

Characteristics less frequently assessed include: emotional stability, integrity and responsibility, academic performance and ability, learning approach and study habits, health-related clinical-research experience, coping skills and support, community service, leadership, work experience, deportment, and appearance.

Figure 23.1: Typical Interview from the Interviewer's Viewpoint

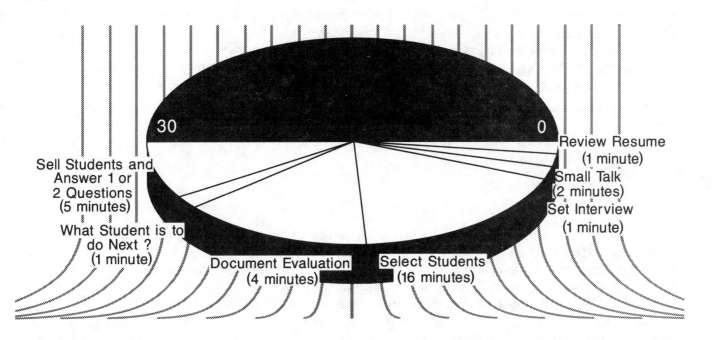

Interviewers generally assess communication and language skills informally. However, most students' interview ratings are affected by extremely good, or poor, language skills. One-fifth of schools formally evaluate language skills by keeping track of the amount of time the applicant speaks, the vocabulary used, clarity, and speech habits. (With generally untrained interviewers, however, these evaluations may not be reliable.)

Medical schools also strive to *entice individuals* whom they see as the "best" applicants to come to their school by showing off the school's best points. They do this by demonstrating their academic strengths and most-impressive facilities, and by emphasizing their community's benefits. Most urban schools emphasize their community's cultural attributes, while more suburban or rural schools describe their lifestyles. (When you get to this part of the presentation, realize that it's mostly a public-relations display.) An important part of the interview visit, however, is to allow applicants to see the reality of a particular medical school—so students aren't surprised when they arrive on their first day.

A number of studies suggest that interview scores (especially from structured interviews) seem to correlate well with the same student's subsequent Dean's letter—a summary of medical school performance sent to residency programs. Many of these letters contain an overall assessment of students compared to their classmates. Students with high interview scores most often have very favorable Dean's letters, while those with poor scores rarely have favorable letters.

How Important Is The Interview?

Very important! You may have spent four or more years achieving your GPA and several months studying for the MCAT, but most schools consider your interview evaluation to be the *most important admission factor.* Admission committees generally use the interview evaluation subjectively in their final admission decisions. On average, the interview evaluation counts 35%!

In order, the factors considered important for admission are[Johnson EK, Edwards JC. Current practices in admission interviews at U.S. medical schools. *Acad Med* 1991;66:408-12.] :

1. Interview evaluation
2. Undergraduate science GPA
3. Reference letters
4. MCAT scores
5. Undergraduate non-science GPA

According to a Cornell University study, most students not accepted to medical school but who should have been accepted based on their GPAs and MCAT scores (GPA >3.5 and MCAT >30 total) are introverts. Nearly nine out of ten of these students with GPAs >3.7 are in this category. Introversion becomes painfully obvious in the interview setting. Since faculty use interviews to assess how well applicants might interact with patients, any shyness will be a detriment.

Just so that we are clear about the differences between introverts and extroverts, the following are some typical characteristics of each, taken from Paul D. Tieger and Barbara Barron-Tieger's *Do What You Are:*

INTROVERTS

- Are energized by spending time alone.
- Avoid being the center of attention.
- Think, then act.
- Are private; prefer to share personal information with a select few.
- Think things through inside their heads.
- Listen more than talk.
- Keep their enthusiasm to themselves.
- Respond after taking the time to think things through.
- Prefer depth to breadth.

EXTROVERTS

- Are energized by being with other people.
- Like being the center of attention.
- Act, then think.
- Tend to think out loud.
- Are easier to "read" and know; share personal information freely.
- Talk more than listen.
- Communicate with enthusiasm.

- Respond quickly; enjoy a fast pace.
- Prefer breadth to depth.

Consider which group you fall into. Ask your friends, family, teachers, and premed adviser. There is no harm in having mixed traits, as many people do, as long as you don't cause an interviewer to describe you as "shy," "quiet," "private," or (horrors!) "introverted."

The mock interview, described in chapter 20, can help you overcome the most obvious flaws in your interview style, whether you are an introvert or an extrovert.

Regional Interviews

Some U.S. and Canadian schools, and many foreign schools, offer to interview applicants at regional locations convenient to the applicant. Domestic schools may employ this technique as a screening mechanism or to entice certain applicants to apply to the school, even though it is distant from where they live. Often, these interviews will be either with an admission officer who travels throughout the country or with the school's alumni who live nearby. The benefit, of course, is that applicants save time and money. The penalty is that applicants do not actually get to see the school's facilities or interact with students and faculty. If you have such an interview and think you may want to go to that school, try to visit the school itself before you "sign on." You may wait to see if you get accepted, then make a quick trip to the school.

The U.S. and Canadian schools that offer regional interviews are

• Columbia	• Johns Hopkins	• UMDNJ-New Jersey Medical
• Duke	• McGill*	• University of Michigan
• George Washington U.	• St. Louis University	• University of Puerto Rico
• Harvard	•	• University of Wisconsin

* Charges applicants $100 for a San Francisco interview.

Most foreign medical schools offer interviews in the United States or Canada. While this is very convenient, the danger of not seeing what you are getting for your tuition is greatly magnified for these schools (see chapter 17, *Foreign Medical Schools*). Except for the relatively few foreign schools with stellar reputations and great track records, *do not accept any offer until you see the school*. In some cases, students have paid their money, traveled to the school, and found that it didn't even exist! Be careful.

An Interview Day

The medical school interview has changed little over the past fifty years, except that women and minorities now participate in significant numbers. Good evidence for this is Howard Becker et al.'s description of late-1950s interviews in their book, *Boys in White* (U. Chicago Press, 1961).

> In the fall of the year, several thousand college seniors get out of their casual college clothing, put on the uniform of the young executive . . . and present themselves to be interviewed by the admission committees of medical schools. They are a picked lot. They have done well in college, and they have given good account of themselves in the standard tests taken by all students who apply to enter medical schools in this country.
>
> The interview is a serious affair. At stake is one's opportunity to enter one of the most honored and—at the present in America—most lucrative of the professions. They comport themselves on this solemn occasion not as boys but as men. The teachers of medicine who interview them look at them seriously and anxiously. They ask themselves and one another, "Will this bright boy really make a medical man?" (p. 3)

Okay, now it's your turn. You have your interviews set up and you are ready to go and "knock their socks off." Remember that it is not only your interview performance, but also your conduct throughout your entire time at a school that will determine whether the interviewers rank you highly. So here are some last-minute tips to help you smooth out any remaining rough spots in your presentation.

Timeliness

To mangle an old saying, "Timeliness is next to Godliness." You will make a major impact on all interviewers, a significantly *negative* impact, if you are late for your appointments. Excuses are fine for your mother, your spouse, and sometimes your friends and teachers. But they do not work on medical school faculty. Their time is valuable, and faculty members they have set some of it aside to interview you. Don't waste their time, or yours, by being late.

Of course, unavoidable delays do occur. Unexpected bad weather and transportation breakdowns are the two most common causes (especially during part of the interview "season"— which has some of the worst weather of the year). If you run into difficulties that will cause you to be late, have the courtesy to call ahead. Even if you only think that you might be delayed due to these or other valid factors, let the school know early. They will then be able to reschedule people and, possibly, to work you in at a later time or on a later date. Do not leave them wondering what happened to you. Even if you do not care about that school, leaving them hanging is extremely discourteous and unprofessional. *The key to success is to show up on time, ready for action!*

Confirm Your Interview

Although you are expected to be on time and at the correct location, either you or the school may have made a scheduling error. It is very embarrassing for an applicant to show up on the wrong day for a scheduled interview because of miscommunication.

Occasionally there is a disaster at the school that mandates that interviews be postponed or rescheduled. Mistakes happen, especially when there are dozens or hundreds of individuals interviewing at the same school during a short period of time. And since you may very well be on the road, there may be no way to contact you about such a situation. The professional way to avoid complications is to call ahead to confirm your interview a day or two before traveling to the school. That way you stand little chance of making a wasted trip or being embarrassed by a scheduling mistake.

Know The Schedule

If you can get your interview day's schedule for each school before you arrive, so much the better. Have them fax or E-mail it to you. You will then know how to pace yourself throughout the visit. You will also be able to plan specific activities for any "free-time" blocks. These periods can be used to visit the library, the wards, the school's other teaching hospitals and clinics if they are nearby, and the cafeteria. Since this could be the food you eat for the next several years—how bad is it?

If you cannot get your entire schedule, at least find out what time you begin. Recheck your information the afternoon before to make certain that it is correct. You cannot afford to be late. It usually helps if you are *early*. Even if you have never been early for anything in your life, this is an excellent time to start.

Once you get started on your interviews, it is up to the interviewers themselves and the admission secretary, to keep everyone on schedule. Many interviewers have a bad habit of running over their allotted times. Do not let this make you uncomfortable. However, when you get to the next appointment late, apologize immediately and explain that you just got out of your last interview with Dr. X. If it happens to you, it has happened to others—and faculty members will understand and not count it against you. They probably are already aware of their colleagues' foibles.

Leave Some Time Flexible

Now that you have gotten the interview and have worked hard to make a good impression, do not ruin it all by running out early. Would you leave a fancy dinner party before dessert? Of course not. Scheduling departing flights out of town without giving yourself enough flexibility to "eat dessert" is the same situation. If you book yourself too tightly, you will not allow yourself any leeway in case your interviews run overtime. When they do, it will usually be because one or more of the faculty has an extra interest in your candidacy. This is a golden opportunity; don't blow it.

Also, you may find you have a greater interest in a school than you initially thought you would. In that case, you may want to investigate that school's finer points while you are there. You will need some extra time to do this. Remain flexible.

Attitude

SMILE! It doesn't cost you anything. Of course you are prepared to be on your best footing with interviewers. But astute admission officers are just as interested in how you act outside the formal interview setting as in how you do in it. This indicates to them how you will act during day-to-day activities, how you will interact with your peers, and whether you will be able to get along with the faculty and the medical staff.

Be pleasant to everyone. And be pleasant at all times. This does not mean you must fawn over the students and bow down to the secretaries. It does mean, at the least, that you should not ignore them. They are real people. Treat them as the friendly individuals they probably are. Be pleasant and try to interact with them warmly. This also holds true for other applicants. If you are liked by the other applicants, this is often seen as a very positive point in your favor. When applicants are observed as a group, those who get along with others can be clearly identified. And working well with a team is a key ingredient in being a successful physician. The bottom line, then, is that input from sources other than the interviewers is often very important. You should consider yourself under observation the entire time you are at the school. The show doesn't stop when you walk out the door at the end of the day; it continues with every subsequent phone call and written communication you have with the school.

The Typical Interviewer

All schools use both physician and non-physician faculty to interview applicants. About two-thirds also use current medical students, nearly half use alumni, and one-third use admission office staff. Only about one-fifth of medical schools use residents as interviewers, and generally the residents went to that school (recent alumni). One-fifth also use community "representatives," including physicians in private practice and lay community leaders.

Some studies [Elam CL, Johnson MMS. Prediction of medical students' academic performances: does the admission interview help? *Acad Med* 1992:67:S28-S30.]suggest that ratings given by women interviewers correlate better with subsequent medical school performance than do ratings by men. Only scores from physician-interviewers significantly and consistently correlate with medical school performance. Therefore, if you think you will do well in medical school, hope for a woman physician to interview you.

Uniqueness

Interviewers, like all individuals, receive only a small portion of the information sent to them. There is a great deal of "noise" between the sender's encoded message and the receiver's decoding of that message (figure 23.2). Interviewers take your information and change it to fit their preconceived ideas. It is from this information that they make decisions. As an applicant to medical school, you battle three communication devils.

Selective Exposure

People are constantly exposed to a tremendous amount of stimuli. They really notice only exceptional deviations from normal patterns. These deviations can either be positive (beneficial to you) or negative (counterproductive to you). It is essential that you be noticed—and noticed positively.

Selective distortion

People tend to interpret data in ways that support, rather than challenge, their preconceptions. These preconceptions of you will, most likely, be based upon the written material that you have supplied to the school. It is your job to add to the positive feelings you have already worked so hard to create.

Selective Retention

People forget much of what they learn. And they forget it quickly. Your job is to make sure that they remember you.

Interviewer Training

Most medical school interviewers have little or no training for the job. While the clinicians may be gifted clinical interviewers, they are generally not prepared to interview medical school applicants (which is much more akin to a job interview than a clinical interview).

While most schools claim to train their interviewers, the instruction is usually general and consists of reading materials. (Common sense tells you that most faculty won't read them.) Some schools provide lectures on interview techniques and some show videotaped interviews, role-play, and have new interviewers sit in with more experienced interviewers (often learning their less-than-stellar techniques). Less than half of all medical schools provide interviewers with any training in questioning, recruiting, and rapport techniques. Few schools offer interviewers education about rater bias or structured interviewing.

Since they have so little training, how well do these interviewers do in selecting the best applicants to their medical school? A recent study using simulated applicants showed that interviewers pick out whether an applicant is "good," "average," or "poor" about half of the time. Experienced interviewers did better than novices, but how well an applicant interacts with the interviewer clearly plays a big role in his getting accepted at many medical schools.

That is why, at many schools, applicants have a formal opportunity to evaluate their visit, including their interviews, before they leave. If anything egregious happens during the interview, be sure to notify the Dean of Admissions. In some cases, they can offer you another interview while you are there.

In sum, most medical school interviewers are essentially untrained to do the most important single evaluation that determines whether you will get into medical school.

Figure 23.2: Elements in the Communication Process

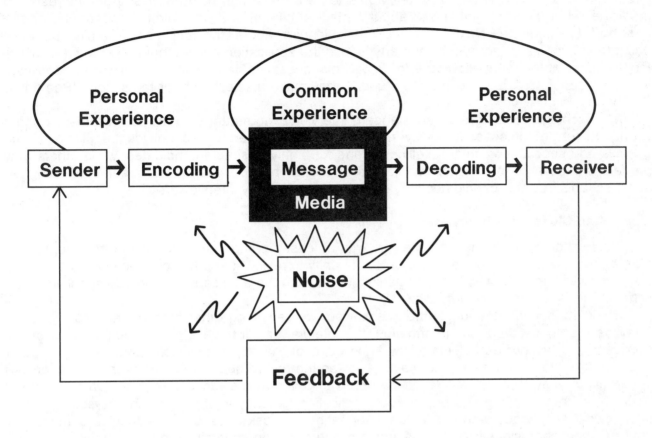

Don't Worry About The "Competition"

One applicant wrote that "One would arrive at the waiting lounge and there in the crowd of applicants *he* would be—the guy with the perfect tan, athletic build, and air of quiet perfection—he even seemed to *smell* successful. . . Speaking in dulcet tones, he would let slip that he'd already received two admission offers, including one from Harvard. And it was still only October." So what?

There are one or two Mr. or Ms. Perfects in each medical school class. Don't worry about them—and don't let them rattle you. Most of your class will be composed of people just like you, trying hard, but with obvious flaws. In other words, real people. Ignore the "Perfects" and stick to your game plan.

A Typical Interview

The most common interview is the one-on-one serial interview, in which you go from interviewer to interviewer, with each asking his or her own questions. Nearly two-thirds of medical schools have applicants do two interviews, nearly one-third require only one, and a relatively small number require three or four (see figure 21.2). The average medical school interview lasts 44 minutes.

Most experienced interviewers begin the interview, after suitable amenities, by gathering information, such as why the applicant wants to be a physician, how he or she got interested in medicine, what the applicant knows about a medical career, and what direct exposure he or she has had to medicine. Next, they will often inquire about the applicant's family, personal background, interests, education, and anything in the application packet that needs to be clarified. Finally, most interviewers allow time for applicants' questions. If interviewers believe the applicant to be a "good catch" as a prospective student, they make a sales pitch for the school. (See figure 23.1.)

Most schools conduct relatively standard interviews, no matter who the applicant is. At about twenty percent of the schools, however, interviews are modified for the individual applicant. Some schools add special recruitment (selling) efforts for highly desirable candidates, while others may probe the motivation of weaker candidates and even provide alternative-career counseling. At some schools, minority candidates may be paired with minority interviewers.

Open- And Closed-File Interviews

Most schools supply their interviewers with at least the important information from applicants' admission packets, so that they have an opportunity to review it in advance (see figure 21.2). This way, interview time is not wasted re-hashing information the applicant has already supplied to the school. This is an *"open-file" interview.*

Some schools do not supply the interviewers with anything other than the applicant's name. They believe that without this information, the interviewer will have a more objective view of the applicant and will not be influenced by knowledge of the applicant's academic record. In other cases, interviewers may simply not have reviewed the record due to their laziness or a misguided sense of fair play. These are *"closed-file" interviews.* If you are faced with this situation, you will need to recite everything you put in your application to many interviewers. In this setting, some interviewers simply abandon the factual information and ask questions designed to demonstrate your personal characteristics. In any event, smile through the adversity and be gracious.

Structured Interviews

Most interviewers simply ask their favorite questions, being careful to steer away from illegal areas. Some schools, however, now employ structured interviews in which the interviewer asks standardized questions (see figure 21.2). It has been shown that this type of interview has a higher validity and reliability than a free-floating interview.

Generally, there are four types of structured interview questions.

Situations

Interviewers ask all applicants to discuss one or more standard situations. You may, for example, be asked a hypothetical ethics question.

Knowledge

Applicants may be asked to recall specific information from classes they took or about activities listed in their application. Applicants for combined medical degree-Ph.D. programs encounter these questions most often.

Tasks

Applicants may be asked to perform simple tasks, such as tying a knot. Often this is not meant to test you specifically, but to be certain that all applicants are tested in this way so there does not seem to be discrimination against disabled applicants. In rare cases, you may be asked to take a short test, such as an abbreviated personality-profile examination.

School Requirements

You may be asked whether you can you meet the school's entry and performance requirements. Again, these questions are normally asked to meet the legal requirement so that the disabled are not asked different questions than everyone else. In some cases, however, interviewers may ask because they question your prior performance or motivation.

You may not initially be aware that an interview is structured unless the interviewer tells you, you see him or her reading questions from a form, or you have found out from other applicants or medical students. You need not do anything special during this type of interview. Just be aware that the interviewer may be a little more constrained than normal and that the conversation may not be as relaxed, since this type of interview limits his or her range of questions. Your answers will be compared to those of other applicants who have been asked the same questions.

Stressful Interviews

Stress interviews were very common at one time. Interviewers asked questions to purposely make applicants confused, fearful, and hostile. One of the apocryphal tales that continues to make its way around the interview circuit (akin to urban legends) is that of the applicant who is asked by the interviewer to open the window. No matter how much effort the applicant exerts, he can't open it. Of course, it's been nailed shut. You won't encounter anything that obvious. But some admission officers believe they can weed out applicants who can't handle stress. Others treat applicants shabbily because that is how they treat their students. The applicants they actually eliminate this way are those individuals with enough self-esteem to determine that they don't want to work with people who treat potential students like dirt. While the business world stopped using this method long ago, some schools still use it.

Panel Interviews

Occasionally, you will be faced with a rather unusual scenario—the panel or group interview, in which several individuals all interview you at the same time. There is a reason business people call this the "gang bang." It is generally considered a poor interview technique, both from an interviewer's and from an applicant's perspective. However, it is still in use, primarily because it is thought to save the interviewers' time. Some people also believe this technique is useful to assess the sophisticated communication skills that physicians need.

About ten percent of medical schools use panel interviews and most premed committees use them. Most only have two interviewers, but some schools have up to eleven people on a panel. All panel members may question an applicant. Some schools use these panels to interview more than one student at a time. (See the next section.)

These interviews will generally be conducted using either a question or a scenario format. In the question format, each panel member asks his or her own questions. In the scenario format, candidates discuss one or more cases with the entire panel. At one large medical school, each member of a seven-person panel asks applicants the same question. (This must get boring.)

Your best approach in this type of interview is to look at the individual who asked the question when you answer. In the case of the scenario, since it is a question from the entire group, look at all the members while answering. If an individual member asks you a follow-up question, address only that person when answering. Do not try to determine the most influential people on the panel and direct most of your attention to them. The others will feel slighted. When the panel members meet later to discuss the candidates, your implied insult will damage your chance of getting into that medical school.

For some reason, panel members may feel obliged to put stress on interviewees, as one candidate found to her dismay.

> One interviewer, who was sitting across from me, looked at his watch as soon as I began answering his question. He must have looked at his watch twenty times during the 30-minute interview. I completely lost my train of thought and went into a "blabber-blunder'" mode for about five minutes—complete stream-of-consciousness. By the time I left the interview, I was devastated, thinking that I had no chance of getting into that medical school. Only later did I learn that the group usually picked one person to be "rude," so they could see how the interviewee reacted under pressure. Actually, I got accepted to that school anyway.

A particularly nasty variation used at some schools is to sit the applicant between the wings of a V-shaped table facing the interviewers seated on both outside wings. They then pepper interviewees with questions, alternating sides to make candidates swivel their heads back and forth to answer each question. One applicant quickly adjusted by simply slowing down and completely turning to face each questioner when she answered. Her solution was to avoid getting flustered. You could also get up and move your chair back so the angle to view the interviewers is not so acute.

Multiple-Interviewee Panels

Even worse is another technique employed (thankfully) by only a few Gestapo-like schools. At the end of an interview day, they bring two or three students at a time into a roomful of faculty. They then rapidly ask the students the same questions at the same time. This is really an abuse of power. My suggestion, if this happens to you, is to stand up, thank them for their time, and leave without participating.

> One school had three students being interviewed at once by a panel. A woman from an excellent Midwestern school was seated with two Ivy League men. One of the men dominated the discussion. When they were asked what they did in stressful situations and she answered that she talked it over with her twin sister, this other applicant guffawed. She became rather depressed by this episode. Another applicant in a similar situation stood up, walked out, and later received a written apology from the Dean of Admissions. This second applicant ended up going to that school. The obnoxious character did not.

If you are faced with any type of panel interview, remember that it will be as unnerving an experience for everyone else as it is for you. So, keep cool and knock their socks off!

Silence

The most stressful time in any interview can be a period of silence. This is an occasion to reveal all of your twitches, nervousness, and insecurity. It is also an opportunity to show self-assurance. Be strong!

Silence occurs for several reasons. Rarely are faculty-interviewers disciplined enough, or nasty enough, to impose a period of silence simply to test an applicant. Rather, they may remain quiet while they contemplate a question or your answer. They also may suddenly have remembered that they didn't turn off their headlights when they parked their car that morning. Don't feel that a period of silence is negatively directed at you. Sometimes the interviewer doesn't even know it's happening.

> At one school, the interviewer fell asleep during the interview. He asked a simple question, and I had barely started my answer when he started snoring. I just ended with a sigh, and said "And so that's what happened." I never did answer his question, but he never realized it. I got accepted to that school in spite (or because?) of this.

Some people respond to silence during an interview by fidgeting. They brush their hair back, move around in their chairs, straighten their clothes, or mutter to themselves. Others try to break the silence by repeating (or worse, contradicting) what they just said. Don't do it. Sit still, be calm, and be quiet—it too will end. One way experienced individuals combat periods of silence in interviews is to simply begin counting the time to see how long the silence lasts. It will seem like days, but it rarely lasts more than fifteen seconds. This may be a technique you can practice during mock interviews.

You too can occasionally use silence to demonstrate your contemplative side. If an interviewer asks a particularly deep or thoughtful question, you don't have to jump in immediately with an answer, even if you are prepared for it. Wait a few seconds as you "think" it through. Rather than appearing impulsive, you will now seem to be a deep thinker.

Non-Interview Visits

There is one type of school visit, still very rare, to which you may go. This is the non-interview visit, which is essentially the same as a traditional interview visit, but without the interviews. If you are invited for a visit, it implies that the school is interested in you. In some cases, you may visit the school or not as you see fit, since a visit does not impact your acceptance. You are not rated on the basis of your performance during these visits, unless you act really obnoxious.

At present, only Brown University does not generally interview medical school applicants. (After a hiatus, the University of Iowa began interviewing applicants again in 1996.) The faculty screens applicants on the basis of their undergraduate performance, MCAT scores, and by using other written materials they feel are important. They then assume that students they admit to their school are acceptable. Their studies, based on medical school and residency performance, show that there appears to be no difference between medical school classes chosen based on interviews and those chosen without interviews.

Faculty use non-interview visits primarily to show applicants the school. During the visit, applicants see the physical plant, didactic program, and the school's social milieu. They are usually given many opportunities to interact with faculty and students, and enough time to have all their questions answered. Generally, they are given a better picture of the school than would be possible during a more traditional visit. Applicants invited for these visits get the maximum possible information; this assures that those accepting positions at the school do so with a sound knowledge of what they are getting into.

There are several principles upon which this system is based. The first is that an interview, especially when using faculty-interviewers who are untrained in personnel selection, is as likely to give erroneous information as valid facts. A second is that creating a medical school class with happy students is best assured by giving applicants as much information as possible ahead of time. The last is the assumption that if you have qualified applicants, those that want to come to a particular school for their education make the best students and, eventually, the best possible physicians.

One other medical school, Mayo, has been investigating the use of a structured telephone interview for more than two years. They have found that this predicts admission committee decisions better than undergraduate GPAs and MCAT scores. The problem, of course, is that the applicants do not visit the school. (It might come as a very nasty surprise to learn just how cold Rochester, Minnesota, gets in the winter.)

Visits without interviews are, at best, considered avant-garde. You probably will not be exposed to them. But if you are, do not be put off by them. You should still handle yourself in the same manner as described elsewhere in this book.

24: Your Questions

I keep six honest serving men
(They taught me all I know):
Their names are What and Why and When
And How and Where and Who.

Kipling, *The Elephant's Child*

Judge a person not by his answers,
but by his questions.

Voltaire

IN ADDITION TO ANSWERING QUESTIONS, you will need to ask your own questions during your interview visit. It is important to know not only what questions you want to ask, but also what you are searching for in the replies. You want to hear specific answers, e.g., the percentage of students that have passed the USMLE on the first try, and to observe the other person's attitudes toward the subjects you raise. Notice as well their attitudes toward you as a person and toward students in general. Are they friendly and open? Or haughty and cold? This could make a big difference in how you rank the school.

When you ask your own questions, do so in a courteous, diplomatic manner. More than one applicant has "gone down the tubes" by trying to cross-examine interviewers. Doing so is crass and demonstrates immaturity. Ask your questions in a way that expresses enthusiasm for a positive answer. Rather than the question, "What problems have students had adjusting to the curriculum changes?" you might inquire, "What kind of an impact have curriculum changes had on the students and faculty?" The first is accusatory, the second merely inquisitive. Get your information. But be nice about it.

Ask simple, straightforward, open-ended (requiring something other than a "yes" or "no" answer) questions. Do not ask questions with multiple parts or that are too long to follow easily. If you ask these types of questions, you may not get the information you want; and you will probably make a negative impression on the interviewer.

Know when to ask your questions. Most schools try to allow applicants the opportunity to have their questions answered fully. They gain as much, or more, information about you from your questions as they do from your answers to their questions. But wait until the proper time to ask your questions. Let the interviewers ask their questions first. Wait for them to ask if you have any questions of your own.

Finally, ask the right people the right questions. At the start of your interview day, ask the admission secretary which individuals you will meet with and what their positions are within the school. Ask full-time faculty (especially basic-science faculty) about changes in the curriculum. Ask clinical faculty about the current status of graduates. Do not ask them about the teaching quality or student esprit de corps. These are questions to ask students.

Prepare a typed list of your questions in advance so that you can easily refer to it (and read it) during your interviews. What are some of the questions you should ask, and what should you look for in the answers? The list below is divided into questions you will primarily want to ask the faculty and those that you will want to ask students. You may want to ask both groups some questions, especially Question 21, "Could you give me (show me) an example?"

The List—To Ask Faculty

1. Where are your recent graduates?

This question is actually a two-parter. The first part asks, "Where are your recent graduates geographically?" Are they only in residency programs near the school or are they spread throughout the United States? This gives you a realistic perspective about the school's orientation and its reputation among residency programs. The places where recent graduates have obtained training positions reflect how well-thought-of the school is and the quality of graduates they have produced.

The second part of the question asks, "What types of residencies do your graduates enter?" Have they primarily gone to community-based primary care residencies, or are they also at academic centers in difficult-to-match-with specialties and programs? How many have gone into practice and how many into research? Is there a balance, or are the numbers heavily weighted in one direction or another?

Ask this question in a general manner. If either part is not answered, follow it up with a more specific question designed to get the missing information. If you cannot get adequate information, simply ask, "May I see a list of residency programs where your recent graduates went?" All schools have these lists, at least for their most recent class. You then can evaluate the answer at your leisure. Also, find out (from the student records or school's alumni office) if any recent graduate lives near your home. If so, you could gain valuable insight into the school by talking with this individual.

2. For which special programs is this medical school well-known?

If you know of any special programs the medical school has, either from their brochure or from talking with students, you may want to ask for more details. You also want to know about any other special programs, some of which may be too new to list in the brochures or which have not yet started. These will be extra perquisites of attending this medical school, and the interviewers will generally be thrilled that you asked about them. This allows them to show off their school to its best advantage.

Remember, however, when evaluating the interviewers' answers, that programs in which you do not plan to participate (such as an international electives program which won't fit in with caring for your three young children) is of no benefit to you. It may, though, demonstrate the school's educational direction, which is very useful to know.

3. How many courses use problem-based learning?

Problem-based learning, or PBL, is the newest wrinkle in medical education. The concept stems from the need to teach physicians to independently solve many clinical problems and to continue to learn and stay current with medical changes throughout their careers. PBL shows students techniques for solving these clinical problems.

PBL is a logical method for introducing the physician's mindset into the teaching environment. Students are given problems (often clinical cases) to solve. They then find appropriate resources and solve the problems (often with a study group). The students use information from diverse sources, encompassing several courses. The process, of course, is similar to the method clinicians use to solve clinical problems on a daily basis. The difficulty with applying this method to basic-science courses is that it is best done in small groups. This requires more faculty. At a time when medical schools' budgets are being decreased, using more faculty for teaching becomes very difficult.

A few schools, such as Harvard, Hawaii, and Kentucky, have taken the PBL "bull" by the horns and run with it. Most of their courses, both preclinical and clinical, use this teaching method. The majority of schools, though, have lackadaisically applied the method to a few preclinical courses or to parts of courses, and have not altered most of their teaching methods. In most cases, they also still rely on using standard testing methods (paper and pencil) to evaluate students, rather than using their contributions in these small-group sessions.

If PBL-type instruction strikes you as useful and compatible with your learning style, you may want to investigate it further.

4. How much flexibility is there in the course work (number of electives) and in the timing of the courses (accelerating, decelerating, time off) during the preclinical and clinical years?

None of us can anticipate all the twists and turns our lives will take. Although you may plan to zip through medical school, family, health, or other reasons may make you slow down or take time off. How flexible is the school? If something untoward happens, do they have policies allowing students to make up lost time without harsh penalties? Will your loans and scholarships remain active even if you must take a decreased course load or a leave of absence? Will your tuition decrease if you take fewer (or no) courses for a period of time?

You may, on the other hand, wish to accelerate your medical school experience. Is that possible? Can you go straight through without breaks? Will the school give you any credit for advanced study that you completed before medical school? If so, can you take advanced classes to shorten your route to a medical degree? If you do finish early, will the school allow you to "graduate" early to start your residency training? Again, each school has its own rules, and sometimes these change over time. It's best to know them in advance.

5. What changes do you anticipate in the school's curriculum?

This is a question to ask a Dean or basic-science faculty member. Clinical faculty are often not aware of curriculum changes until long after they have been implemented.

You should expect to hear about such changes. Most U.S. and Canadian medical schools are constantly implementing curriculum changes. In some cases, these have little impact on students—either because they are relatively minor or because the school can't seem to get its act together to structure and fully implement them. In other cases, the curriculum and teaching methods undergo dramatic changes over a short period. One such change has become the current fad among medical schools, educators, and funding agencies—problem-based learning (PBL). (See Question 3 for a discussion of PBL.)

So, if you learn that the school is going to implement PBL, ask how long they have been working on introducing it into the curriculum, which courses use it, how much of each course is taught in this way, and whether they have adequate facilities and faculty to use this method. Later, ask the students the same questions. Also ask the students how well PBL is working, and how well they think they are learning using this method. You might want to ask similar questions about the use of computers for teaching and for testing in the school's courses.

6. How much of an administrative, legal, and bioethics curriculum is there?

Although academicians have been slow to recognize it, medicine is also a business—sometimes a dangerous business. How much training in the administrative and legal aspects of medical practice will you get at this school? Will you acquire at least a basic understanding of managed care and other health-care-delivery systems? Will you receive in-depth training about the legal pitfalls now so common in medicine, or will this come only after your first malpractice suit? How about the ethical issues that now pervade medicine and society? Does the school offer a formal bioethics course, or is it a hit-or-miss subject area? Although these topics are not within the "hard science" component of medicine, they fall into the two other, often-neglected components: medicine as an art and medicine as a business. Schools that neglect these components do so at their own, and their students', peril.

7. How well have students done in their class work?

Nearly all applicants want to ask this question. The answer you will get, however, is of little help in evaluating the schools. Nearly every medical school has the same percentage of students who get "Honors" and the same percentage who fail their courses. The difference, however, is that the criteria schools use to determine these rankings are based on their student bodies and the educational expectations at that school.

The question you should ask is: How do the school's students do on Step 1 and Step 2 of their licensing examinations (USMLE or NBOME)? (See *Question 14.*) This is important not only as a measure of the school itself, but also when residency directors assess applicants from many different medical schools. The licensing examination scores are the only "even playing field" on which they can compare applicants. It is also vital when assessing non-U.S./Canadian medical schools. Graduates who cannot pass Steps 1 and 2 of the USMLE cannot do a U.S. residency and cannot get licensed to practice medicine.

8. What are the clinical opportunities for students during their preclinical years?

Of course you will eventually be exposed to the clinical side of medicine, but if you are like most students, you want to have clinical experiences as soon as possible, not wait two more years to start working with patients while you vegetate in the classroom and laboratories. Are there early opportunities to work with clinicians?

The typical answer is that you begin your physical diagnosis course sometime during your first year. This means that (usually) a resident or a "standardized patient" (a patient trained to teach you specific parts of the physical examination) will instruct you, with a small cohort of your classmates, in the basics of taking a history and doing a physical examination. All well and good. But this is to clinical practice what the crust is to a pizza—it's a necessary foundation. It makes the pizza much better if it is well-done, but it lacks any zing on its own. Your real question is whether you will have an opportunity, be encouraged, or even be required to actively participate with clinicians while you learn the basic sciences.

This may be a personal bias, but if I found that there was no opportunity for early clinical exposure, I would be reluctant to go to that medical school. I have found that most medical students learn best if they can relate their classroom work to the patients they see in the hospital and clinics. Clinical work also reminds them that patient care is why they are in medical, rather than graduate, school.

9. What type of clinical sites (ambulatory, private preceptors, private hospitals, rural clinics) are used for clerkships? How many students do rotations at other institutions or internationally?

Medical schools have a variety of clinical settings available for students' work. Which ones does this school offer? Is there a wide variety of both outpatient and inpatient facilities, with a large number of electives offered at each location? Or are all the facilities generally the same, with little chance for electives? Do the types of clinical facilities mimic the medical practice you envision yourself having? (If you want to do missionary medicine, for example, get some clinical experience at remote sites.)

Since you will spend more than half of your medical school time in clinical settings, this information is very important. Be aware that many older, poorer, and badly funded medical school-associated hospitals and clinics don't have enough staff (you do the "scut" work), up-to-date working equipment (you make do using available materials), or the necessary variety of clinicians (you must refer interesting patients to other facilities) to provide you with the quality experience you need.

Medical schools in the United States and Canada have an excellent reputation specifically because of the superb clinical training they provide. Don't short-change yourself. Investigate the clinical sites that are available at each school.

10. How many students are involved in (required or voluntary) community service?

Some medical schools have outreach programs, often for the aged, the poor, or children. These programs allow students to get early and ongoing clinical experiences while working within the local community. Such programs offer students excellent clinical opportunities, so find out if they exist. The type and extent of (and support for) these programs also gives you insight into how the school regards its community—and vice versa. (Some schools allow students to begin these patient-contact experiences in the first year.)

11. How does the school deal with students who are exposed to infectious diseases? Is disability insurance provided?

Medical schools have (again), in recent years, become more aware of the dangers to medical students from infectious diseases. (Before the antibiotic era, it was not unusual for medical students or young house-officers to die from contagious diseases, such as tuberculosis.) Today, each school must have policies for dealing with students who acquire or who are exposed to serious infectious diseases. Some schools provide free immunizations, prophylactic medications, and disability insurance, while others believe that students can fend for themselves. For example, 107 M.D.-granting U.S. medical schools require students to have health insurance, and 75 require disability insurance.

Every medical student should be immunized against hepatitis B, tested for tuberculosis, and checked for a Rubella titer (necessary for obstetric work). Check to see if the school pays for these. Of course, *you* don't plan to be stuck by a possibly HIV-positive needle, or to acquire a serious infectious disease. But, for the sake of argument, what if you do? Will this school help you out? For peace of mind, find out before you need to know.

12. What research opportunities are available?

Some applicants may envision careers in academia or research. If you are one of them, look for a school that can provide you with the resources and guidance to do research.

Start with the question "What research projects are current medical students working on now?" That will give you a range of interests and the levels of activity. Are faculty mentors available? Is funding for student projects easily obtained, or will you have to scrounge for it? Is research barely tolerated or actively encouraged? How fairly have students been treated when working with faculty members on research projects in the past? (Have the students done the work and been given secondary, or no, credit?)

Also find out about the facilities and time available to do research. Are facilities provided by the institution? Can you take a leave of absence to pursue research or a research-oriented degree? In addition, if you do research and it is accepted for presentation at a national meeting, will the school pay for you to go? Will they give you the necessary time off? Ask now to avoid disappointment later.

13. What type of student evaluations are used? How often?

Frequent feedback is essential for medical students' mental health, as well as to insure their best performance. At one time, a well-known medical school had no required examinations until the end of the second year, when students took the first part of the licensing examination. The suicide rate soared. This was because many of the students, rather than being calmed by their instructor's assurances that they were learning more than enough to pass the examination, were scared witless that they couldn't possibly know enough.

Much of a medical school's curriculum is "open-ended," meaning that there is no real limit to the knowledge encompassed within a subject area. A student, for example, could study anatomy and biochemistry for his entire career without knowing all there is to learn about the subjects. Yet medical students must take a national examination covering all subject areas. They do best, therefore, if they get repeated feedback by taking examinations similar to the licensing examinations in each area. This pertains not only to the preclinical, but also to the clinical years.

Unfortunately, most medical schools have not yet caught up with the changes the USMLE has made in its examination format. Many medical students now take tests in their classes that do not follow the question formats on the USMLE. The new format contains many questions integrating diverse subject areas. Since this is really how clinicians apply the basic-science and clinical knowledge they have learned, it makes sense. These questions are, however, difficult to write—especially if it means actually having faculty from different disciplines work together to formulate them. More importantly for medical students, these types of questions can be difficult to answer if you first experience them when taking the licensing examinations. Therefore, it is useful to know if the school has changed its testing methods to mimic those used on the national exams.

You also want to know whether students get feedback during clinical rotations, or only after finishing each specialty's clinical work and taking the course's written test. The latter suggests sloppy teaching methods. As an applicant, you may ask to see a sample set of evaluations for a student's clinical rotation. Be careful, however. Evaluation and teaching methods may vary among departments within a medical school. And, although they are not supposed to vary by location, they often do.

14. How have your graduates done on the USMLE or NBOME? How does the school assist students who do not pass?

The primary goal of a medical school education is to prepare you to practice medicine. An important milepost in your career will be passing the medical licensing examination (USMLE for M.D.'s or D.O.'s, and NBOME for D.O.'s only), also often referred to as "The Boards." (At many schools, passing individual parts of this examination is also required before students can advance to their next academic year or can graduate.) Your score on "The Boards" may well determine the type and site of the residency you can obtain, so doing well is important. How have students at this school done on each part of their licensing exams? How many passed on the first try? This can be asked tactfully, as in "How many of them had to take their Boards more than once?" (Some schools have had failure rates of 10% or more above the national average on USMLE Step 1.)

Also ask if there are any special programs to prepare students for these exams, and any special programs to help those who "don't do well" (who fail) on their first attempt.

Some of the faculty members interviewing you should know this information or should be able to easily obtain it from the Dean of Students. If they don't know it, contact the Dean of Students to inquire about this. Be sure to say that you are interested because you are applying to the school. Although information on specific students is, of course, confidential, the cumulative data should be available to all applicants. If they won't tell you this information, there may be a problem.

15. What does the Student Code of Honor cover? What is the policy on parental leave? What is the policy on infections in medical students?

If you are interested in a medical school's specific policies, determine how best to ask about them. You want to know about the Honor Code? Great question! This suggests, correctly or incorrectly, not only that you are aware of the profession's ethical norms, but also that you understand how medical schools operate. Interviewers are usually impressed that anyone even thinks to ask this question. Follow it up by asking how well the code operates, and whether students are involved in its associated arbitration process.

Twenty years ago, just asking about a parental (at that time called "maternity") leave policy would have doomed an applicant's chances of getting into a medical school. Today, parental leave policies are probably among the safest policies to discuss. Nowadays, pregnancy among medical students and their partners is no longer a rare event, and most interviewers expect any married or engaged applicant to ask about these policies.

Asking about infections among medical students, however, may be near the "taboo zone." Simply asking this question suggests that you have a personal problem with which the school probably doesn't want to deal. While the Americans with Disabilities Act of 1990 supposedly prevents discrimination toward applicants with infectious diseases, few schools will accept applicants who could cost them money (increased premiums on health insurance policies), cause them adverse publicity, or subject them to legal actions from patients or other health care workers.

16. How many students dropped out of school recently?

With 400 or more students at most medical schools at any given time, some of them will inevitably leave school before graduating. This occurs for many reasons. Many take leaves of absence due to family or personal crises, expecting to return. Some transfer to other schools. A few decide that a medical career is just not for them. (For example, Michael Crichton, the well-known author, described how a faculty mentor kept encouraging him to stay in school, although he had already determined that he was not cut out to be a physician.) This information is not, however, what you are after. You are asking whether any students have left because they failed academically. This happens at every school. But how did the faculty try to help the student before he or she was forced to leave? Are there tutoring programs for those in academic "hot water"? Of course, you won't need these services. But it is nice to know that they are there if a friend of yours does.

17. How does your mentor/adviser system function? Who are the advisers—faculty members, other students, or both?

As mentioned elsewhere in this book, medical students do best if they have mentors. The definition of "adviser" varies widely among medical schools. While each medical school has a system to supply advisers and most medical students utilize these individuals (with varying intensity and success), it is useful to know in advance what the school offers. Do they assign individuals who will see you as a faceless number and "rubber stamp" your forms, or individuals who will help you over rough spots and offer career advice?

18. **What kinds of academic, personal, financial, and career counseling are available to students? What services are also offered to their spouses and dependents/children? What support services or organizations are there for ethnic minorities and women?**

If the medical school has none of these services available, it indicates that they: (1) have little regard for your future welfare and (2) have little understanding of what their mission as a school really entails. In either case, you are now forewarned.

Most students must finance their medical education with a complex arrangement of scholarships, loans, and grants. Even those who don't must balance personal and school finances. Personal financial management is not usually taught in the premed curricula, and the "school of hard knocks" is a terrible place to learn the ropes. Many medical schools offer special programs on personal financial management and provide counseling (which often includes services for the student's family) to assist students if they face personal or financial difficulties. Financial aid offices often provide assistance with personal finances. They also may have evening courses on basic financial management. If such programs are available, they may be a big bonus to you and save you many anguished hours trying to salvage your credit rating or making ends meet near the end of the month.

Schools with large numbers of minority students often have special advisers and support groups for them. Women students also may have their own faculty- or student-run support groups, although these are generally not as well-funded as those for minorities.

All schools help their students to some degree in finding residency positions. What has this school done for its recent graduates? With the increasing difficulty of locating positions in some fields (e.g., general surgery, emergency medicine, orthopaedic surgery), it is important to learn how much effort the staff expends helping its students. Some schools hold seminars to educate students about the entire process, some provide specialty-specific counseling. Some even use the faculty's contacts to advocate with residency programs for their students.

19. **How stable are the current tuition and fees? If they aren't fixed, at what rate will they increase?**

You will be paying a lot of money in tuition and fees (unless you go the Uniform School for Health Sciences). Fairness dictates that schools tell you how much they think these costs will increase over the next four years. Many schools plan tuition and fee increases that far ahead, so they can provide you with this information. Ask now so you won't have an unpleasant surprise halfway through medical school.

20. **What impact has health care reform had on this school's teaching and patient care?**

This is far from an idle question, 1996 saw the most devastating and grievous insult to medical education in this century. Medicare rules and punitive actions (fining one medical school $30 million and another $12 million) have made most university teaching hospitals seriously restrict what medical students can do clinically. For example, while third- and fourth-year medical students (on their clinical rotations) routinely wrote histories, physical findings, progress notes, and orders in the patient charts that were countersigned by their supervising physicians, they can no longer do that in most cases. Managed-care organizations have siphoned off many patients from teaching hospitals or these hospital's teaching services and clinics. How is this medical school responding to assure that their students continue to get a quality clinical education? Do they have a plan to make sure their students graduate with a good fund of clinical knowledge and skills? Or will they simply use the "European" system of waiting until medical students graduate to let them really learn clinical medicine?

21. Could you give me (show me) an example?

This is one of the most important questions you can ask during interviews. Ask it to supplement information you get from faculty and students.

While trying to ascertain whether you and a medical school are compatible, you need to have firm information, not unsubstantiated statements. "Our student on-call schedule is very benign," says the interviewer. "Could you show me the current students' night-call schedule for your service?" you ask. After you see the schedule, you will know if it really is as easy as he claims it is. Don't forget that the interviewer's interpretation of what "benign" means could be very different from your own interpretation. (If, as in some schools, the students don't stay all night, find out when they leave and when they must be back.)

Many questions lend themselves to confirmation or explanation. Asking for examples is a safe, pleasant, and enlightening way to get further information about important points.

You can never ask this question too often.

The List—To Ask Medical Students

22. Tell me about the library and extracurricular facilities (i.e., housing and athletic/recreational facilities).

The library is the bellwether of an institution's educational commitment. Is it stocked with useful and up-to-date materials, staffed with knowledgeable and helpful people, and open long (or all) hours? Many students need the library not only for its resources, but also for its quiet. Those who live in noisy surroundings need it as a place to study, and many medical libraries provide special rooms for group study. Does the library have audiovisual and computer materials to supplement printed material? How about access to on-line databases? If so, the school has done its job.

Do you plan to live on your own, or would you like the option of a school-sponsored dorm or other housing? Many schools provide low-cost housing alternatives, generally in close proximity to the school. Given the time (and financial) pressures of the first and second years, these options can look very good.

Since, despite your best intentions, you really cannot study twenty-four hours a day, you may be interested in free or low-cost recreational facilities. If they are located near the school, they can provide an enormous boost to your mental and physical well-being, as well to the camaraderie among classmates.

23. What computer facilities are available to students? Are they integrated into the curriculum/learning?

The new century will be computerized, and the medical field, although currently lagging behind other segments of society, will be no exception. Practitioners will need to be computer literate, using them as readily as their stethoscopes. Does the school provide access to computers and use them for teaching? Are computer labs or specialists available to students? How about special computer courses? It's no longer enough to know how to take a medical history and do a physical examination. You also need to know how to access computerized medical records, lab results, bedside nurses' notes, clinic schedules, library materials, databases, and eventually, billing records.

Somewhat beyond the call of duty, some schools also provide students with microcomputers to use for class work. Others require them to purchase their own. Many, especially those associated with universities, also provide e-mail addresses and World Wide Web links that will, in the future, become essential.

24. Is there a note-taking service? If so, is it University- or student-run?

Note-taking services can be a wonderful boon to many medical students. However, if you see one note-taking service, you've seen only one. Each works slightly differently, calculates its fee differently, and offers products of different quality. So, if such a service interests you, find out the details. Aside from the cost, begin by finding out how the service runs. Do faculty members provide the "notes," or at least correct those taken by students? If not, errors often creep into them—a major flaw in any such service. If taken by students, are the notes transcribed from lecture tapes or simply from class lectures? If the latter, note-takers can miss significant material. Are the notes taken by only one or two excellent note-takers, or does the job rotate among participants? As you know from viewing some fellow-students' notes, this latter method is not optimal—but is usually cheaper. Some note-taking services also provide copies of old examinations to use for studying. These can often be very helpful. One caveat, of course: Many students do much better when they take their own notes and use them for studying. If you are one of these, only use a note-taking service as a supplement.

25. Do students regularly have an opportunity to formally evaluate the faculty? What changes have been made recently as a result of this feedback?

This question really asks, "How important is the educational mission?" Feedback on the faculty's performance is an essential part of all education. If the school is serious about educating medical students, it will have a good evaluation system. Virtually all schools, however, will say that they have an evaluation system, since their licensing body requires it. What is really telling is if they can recite substantive changes that have been made based on these evaluations. That means that they not only have the system, but also value their students' opinions.

26. What contact will I have with the clinical faculty?

The material that the school sent to you said that they have hundreds (or thousands, in some cases) of clinical faculty members. Did they happen to specifically mention how often you will have contact with *any* of them? The faculty can only help you if you have direct contact with them. If faculty members hide in their offices or labs rather than attend in the clinics, wards, emergency departments, or operating rooms, they might as well not be there. Many of those listed as faculty may be on clinical services with which students have little or no contact, such as radiation oncology or nuclear medicine. Others may be located at remote sites where students don't go.

So the questions that you should ask are, "How often are the faculty members present?" and "How often do students find that faculty input is not available?" You might want to specifically ask "How available are they on nights and weekends?" Of course, as a student, you will usually be taught by residents. But you will also want input from the faculty, who are supposedly in that position because of their knowledge and experience. Do members of this school's clinical faculty teach students on a regular basis?

27. Is a car necessary to get to clinical rotations or decent housing? Is parking a problem?

Do you need or want another hassle in your life? As you already know, cars eat up money, cause unexpected difficulties when they break down and, of course, give you greater mobility than you might otherwise have. If a medical school is in a large city with excellent public transportation, you may be able to survive without a car—at least for the first two years. Your classes will generally be held on a regular schedule and any outside clinical work will generally be in the school's vicinity.

But when you get on your clinical rotations, you will work bizarre schedules and will often be "farmed out" to different hospitals (sometimes in other cities) for these clinical experiences. Will you need a car then? If you won't (as in Chicago or New York, for example), you may be able to save a lot of money and aggravation.

Finally, how about parking? Is it difficult to find (or expensive) at the medical school, hospital, and other clinical sites? If you drive to your medical school interview, you may get a taste of what the parking is like. Is this the norm for students, or just for visitors?

28. Is there an adequate support staff available?

Medical students commonly feel overworked during clinical rotations because there are too few people to perform what are typically non-physician tasks. You owe it to yourself to find out how much "scut" work the school's medical students typically perform.

Who starts routine IV lines, draws blood, and does clerical work? Who pushes patients to x-ray or to radiation oncology for treatments? Does the institution provide an adequate level of nursing and ancillary support?

The opposite situation applies at some schools, and this can be even more dangerous to a student's education. If nurses or special technicians start most of the IVs, put in most of the catheters and nasogastric tubes, or draw most blood samples, students miss out on valuable opportunities to learn procedures they will perform throughout their careers. While some students may complain that they do these procedures so often "they can do them in their sleep," that is exactly when you will have to do most procedures during residency—so you had better know how to do them very well.

While faculty may be able to tell you about some of the available clinical support, ask the students and residents for the real answers. Don't complain after the fact. Find out in advance.

29. What is the call schedule on third-year rotations?

In general, the third year is when you will have your first real contact with the clinical side of medicine—including working nights and weekends. It is a very stressful time, second only to internship. (For most students, the stress is balanced by their excitement about learning new procedures, seeing new clinical environments, and the fact that they have finally found their way to clinical medicine.) Third-year schedules can affect your learning in two ways. The first is by providing too little time for learning. Students on some services work such long hours that they do not have enough time to read and absorb new information. In good clinical settings, however, the practical knowledge and skills they obtain make up for this. Also, even though the hours may be long, most clinical rotations have "down times" during which the student's clinical duties are light or non-existent. Those are fine opportunities to read (or to waste time).

The second way third-year schedules can affect your learning is by providing too much free time. This rarely occurs, but it can have an adverse effect on your clinical proficiency. An example is when students do not spend the night with their hospital-based teams. While this may sound great, the result is that residents and faculty view students as frivolous attachments to their teams, since they are not around when their help is most needed. In addition, since students gain so much clinical experience after normal hours when fewer people are left to work, they lose valuable educational opportunities by not being there.

At most schools, your fourth-year schedule will mostly be your responsibility and the educational value will depend, almost entirely, on the rotations you select. Therefore, it is the third-year, rather than the fourth-year schedule you should ask about.

30. What is the patient population I will see?

Patients (their numbers and age distribution, the nature of their diseases, and who cares for them in what settings) are the basic element of all medical training programs. The school's hospital and clinic rotations must provide an adequate number of patient-encounters for a thorough education.

Find out about the patient population served and the distribution of disease processes. Some teaching hospitals have an overabundance of a few types of disease processes, such as penetrating trauma, tertiary oncology, or AIDS. A skewed distribution does not provide adequate training for students who will eventually serve a more diverse population having more common diseases. In addition, as more medical care is being delivered in outpatient settings, students should see patients in the clinics and outpatient surgeries.

31. On what medical school committees (e.g., curriculum, admissions) do students have representation?

You may want to ask this question even if you have no plans to become active in your medical school's politics. Student representation, especially if it includes voting and other rights of committee members, shows a school's commitment to medical student input and involvement. If students currently going through the curriculum don't have a ready conduit to the curriculum committee, for example, it demonstrates that the faculty (or at least the school's administration) wants a barrier between students and teachers. Do medical students have a significant voice in determining and changing school policy? If they do, there is probably more of collegial relationship between the faculty and the students. If not, the student body can become very frustrated banging their heads against the proverbial brick walls to get changes made in the school's education and management.

32. Do the students socialize as a group?

Group socialization demonstrates one element of esprit de corps. Social events help to relieve stress and cement personal friendships with colleagues that can last a lifetime. Are social events class-wide or institution-wide? You may also want to ask about the ratio of married to single students (in the current first-year class or in the institution), how many students have children, and how often do social events involve spouses, significant others, or children. Does there seem to be any particular area of special interest among the students and faculty, or do their interests vary?

Is socializing related to educational activities, such as journal clubs? Or are there separate events, such as volleyball games or picnics? Note that if the activities are student-organized, they may vary considerably from year to year.

Confirm Questionable Points

A number of the questions that you raise may be critical. In part, which questions these are will depend upon your own Must/Want Analysis. Even though the questions are important, you may not get straight answers to some of them. This may be because no one knows the answer at the moment. For example, in October no one may really know how many of the faculty will still be on-site next July. But you may be getting the run-around for other, more nefarious, reasons. If you ask a faculty interviewer about how much faculty interaction there is with students and he hems and haws, then you will need to search elsewhere for the real story. This is where the technique of cross-checking facts comes into play.

Whenever you have some doubt about the answer to an important question, repeat the question to another interviewer. Or better yet, if it is appropriate, ask a student. In fact, if the issue is extremely important to you, ask everyone you talk to the same question. But be sure not to do so within earshot of others you have already asked (or will ask) that same question—it will be taken as a sign that you doubt their honesty which, of course, you do. Remember that the school is trying to sell its product to you at the same time that you are selling yourself to it. Not all salesmen are honest. *Caveat emptor!*

Things Not To Ask

There are specific questions that you must not ask during an interview, even though the answers are important to you. These questions basically involve two areas: vacation and competition. Let's discuss them individually, so you will at least know what information to get from *appropriate* sources.

If you don't think that *vacation* is important, wait until you have been up most of every night for a week studying for finals or board exams. At that point, dreaming about an upcoming vacation may be all that keeps you going. Most students have 8 to 12 weeks of vacation between their first and second years, with an equivalent amount during their third and fourth years, although they have more choice as to when they schedule this time off. Usually, the school specifies the amount of vacation time and its scheduling in the material they send to applicants. If you don't have the information, either ask for a typical student's schedule (which will include vacation) or ask a non-interviewer student. Don't ask an official interviewer, since inquiring about vacation time during any interview is akin to asking whether you will actually have to do any work in medical school. While everyone understands that vacation—even a student's vacation—is important, interviewers assume that during the interview you will concentrate on the great educational experience that they offer, rather than your time off.

Who is your *competition?* It doesn't matter! Asking about other applicants will serve no good purpose and can only direct an interviewer's attention away from you. The key, as has been stressed throughout this book, is to put your own best efforts before the admission committee and let them select you based upon what they see. Forget the others. Concentrate on selling yourself.

Things Not To Do

Just as there are certain questions that you should avoid, there are certain things that you should not do during the interview. The following are attitudes or actions that will evoke negative responses from interviewers.

Show Discouragement

Be upbeat! This is your time to shine. One poor interview should not influence the rest of your visit. Remember that the interviewer may not have thought it was a poor interview at all. Looking "down in the dumps" will destroy any positive effect that your interview could possibly have made. Stand up straight. *SMILE*—it won't break your face. If you cannot find the courage to smile through some adversity now, you are really going to be in trouble when you get into medical school and residency.

Disparage Other Schools, Faculty, Or Applicants

You might very well be asked about the other schools that you have visited. The question could be phrased as, "Tell me about the poorest schools that you have visited." Although this may be tempting—you may have interviewed at some places you really didn't like—back up a minute to redirect the question. Say that you are not in a position to determine which schools are poor, but there may be some that do not seem to meet your needs. Then you can describe specific aspects of schools that you feel did not fully meet your expectations. But go easy. If you really berate a school that you have visited, the interviewer might wonder what you will say about his or her school when you go elsewhere.

Do not say anything derogatory about faculty at another institution. It should go without saying that you will not berate faculty at the institution where you are interviewing. No matter what you think, academic medicine is rather close-knit. There is a good chance that the person you are describing is well-known to the interviewer.

Falsify Background

Although it may appear that you could say almost anything about your background during the interview and get away with it, you do so only at great risk. The first danger is that you will immediately be discovered.

Not many years ago, an applicant was eloquently describing his activities in the Emergency Medical System. He stated that he frequently responded to calls even while in school. It was quite an impressive achievement. Yet as he went on with his story, it became obvious to the interviewer that he was being less than honest. For, while he was describing activities in the opposite end of the country, it just so happened that the interviewer was also from that area and picked up on major factual errors in the story. These were confirmed by a call to his adviser.

The second danger is even worse. If information that you provide when you apply for any position, including that of medical student, is later found to be false, it is grounds for immediate dismissal. Thus, giving fraudulent information puts you in jeopardy throughout medical school. Stick to the truth. Make it appear as favorable as possible, but stick to the truth.

A number of years ago, a Dean of Admissions at a U.S. medical school was discussing a student's application with the premed adviser at a large university. The premed adviser was lauding the attributes of a particular student. The Dean replied that she hoped that this student was not the same (bad) caliber as a current student they had from that school. After a moment of silence, the premed adviser said he would get back to the Dean—he had something to check. When he called back, he related that the medical student in question, now a senior in his seventh-year of medical school (having failed and repeated the first, second, and third years and who was now only weeks away from graduation) had never graduated from their school, much less gotten the glowing reference letters the student had submitted. After an investigation by officials, including the FBI, the student was dismissed, along with a number of individuals at other medical schools who had also used fraudulent credentials when applying.

Inappropriate Humor

There is a place for humor in interviews. One medical student said:

I'm always ready with a joke. So when I was asked by an interviewer if I knew any good ones, I said, "Sure. A horse walks into a bar and sits down. The bartender says to the horse, 'Hey, what's with the long face?' I'm sure that swung it for me." (After asking that question, the interviewer got what he deserved.)

However, while jokes can be stupid, they should not be offensive. Even if an interviewer laughs after you tell an off-color, sexist, or racist joke, you almost certainly will have lowered yourself in his eyes. In fact, off-color or inappropriate humor is considered by a large number of administrators to be the major breach of etiquette in the classroom and workplace. If you have an uncontrollable urge to tell these types of jokes, at least keep them out of the interview.

Drink Coffee, Smoke, Chew Gum, Or Bite Nails

Four activities that you must not indulge in during an interview are drinking coffee, smoking, chewing gum, or biting your nails. You may be offered coffee by each interviewer. They mean well.

But do they also offer you a bathroom break in the middle of the interview? No! And if you are concentrating on a full bladder instead of the interviewer's questions, you could end up in deep trouble.

There are four problems with smoking. The first is that it is unlikely that your interviewer smokes, since the habit is now relatively rare among physicians and medical students. The second is that smoking looks bad during an interview. So even if you are addicted, hold out until the interview is over—or you have left the school for the day. The smell that lingers on your clothes and breath if you smoke will not endear you to non-smoking interviewers. Third, interviewers may be biased against hiring smokers. As of yet, no medical school has gone public with an explicit ban on accepting smokers, but it is likely that it would be legal. There is no protection under current civil rights legislation for smokers. This makes it legal for an interviewer to ask whether you are a smoker. Note, of course, that if they inquire, it can only be a (un-Lucky?) strike against you. Fourth, an old ploy, used to put an applicant in an awkward position, is to suggest that you smoke and then not have an ashtray available for you. You can avoid this (rare) problem by not smoking.

Chewing gum is absolutely out. It evokes a fatuous, sophomoric image which will destroy everything that you have worked so hard to achieve. If blowing bubbles is your "thing," hold out until you leave the hospital. No one is physiologically addicted to chewing gum (except, perhaps, nicotine gums—use patches during interviews). One stick of gum at the wrong time can cancel your chance for a medical school slot.

Finally, even though you are nervous and your common response is to bite your nails (or fidget in your chair or play with things on the interviewer's desk), restrain yourself when at medical schools. It signals your neuroses to interviewers. To clinicians, it also demonstrates potentially dangerous, infection-producing behavior.

Control The Interview—Gently

As you will see in the next chapter, it is often possible to steer an interview in a direction that is beneficial to you. You can mold your answers to interviewers' questions in such a way as to bring out your most favorable points. However, this must be done subtly. Some interviewers may view your pushing an interview in a specific direction as being impudent. This, of course, would be counterproductive. So if you can, steer the interview in a beneficial direction—but do it so gently that the interviewer does not notice.

Why Interviews fail

There are six main reasons why interviews fail.

The first is due to the applicant's *arrogance or cockiness*. You may be "hot stuff," having come from a high-powered undergraduate school where you achieved stellar grades, whipped the MCAT, and acquired research and clinical experience. So what! Believe it or not, there are plenty of others just like you who are being interviewed. The interviewer won't be impressed, since he or she was probably a similar "star" when applying to medical school. Those factors got you this far. The point during interviews is to see if you are personable and have the qualities we desire (but don't necessarily achieve) in the physician population. Eat a little humble pie before you begin your interviews. Think of how exalted you will feel if you don't get accepted. Save the strutting for your friends and family (most of whom also won't be too impressed).

The second reason interviews fail is due to *inadequate preparation* on the applicant's part. This book helps you to prepare for the medical school interview. In the end, however, it is up to you to know about the medical field, the school, the faculty, your own ambitions and desires, and the questions that you will probably be asked during interviews. It takes hard work on your part to get ready for interviews, but in the end it is worth it.

The third reason that interviews fail is because the *applicant does not listen to the interviewer's questions.* This results in miscommunication, distorting the messages coming in and going out. This is what happens when you let your mind wander during an interview—and it spells disaster. Remember that an interview is a battle of wits. If your thoughts stray during this war game, you lose!

Since many medical school interviews are conducted in busy offices, clinical settings, or even hallways, you may have to concentrate very hard on the interview to avoid the ever-present distractions, sometimes justifiably called "interview blockers" (figure 23.2). This can be difficult, but your experience studying in noisy dorms and libraries should help you to concentrate on the task at hand. And don't just listen to the question, *listen to how the question is asked.* Many times an interviewer will give the astute listener clues to the answer he or she expects to hear. Figure 24.1, *Guidelines for Effective Listening,* should help you out.

Occasionally your mind may go blank during an interview. It's okay. Just apologize to the interviewer and simply ask for a moment to think about the question or, second best, ask the interviewer to repeat the question. As Sam Donaldson, the television newsman, says, "Even the pros get tongue-tied."

One caveat. If you have carefully read the questions and answers in chapter 25, you may be planning how to answer what you think will be the next question. Or, you may be analyzing how you might interact during your classes and clinical rotations with the faculty and students you have met. Stop! Turn off that mental audiotape and listen to the interviewer. By now you should be able to answer questions without rehearsing, and there will be plenty of time later to analyze your visit. Concentrate on what the interviewer is saying now.

If you really listen, and you still can't understand what an interviewer is looking for, ask for clarification. This might also work (once) if you miss a question completely—but it would be unwise to use it repeatedly. Remember that the most ego-gratifying thing you can do for interviewers is to listen to them.

Figure 24.1: Guidelines For Effective Listening

1. Demonstrate attentiveness.

2. Listen for "what" and "why" questions.

3. Listen for key issues.

4. Keep your mind from drifting to other thoughts.

5. Mirror back the interviewer's messages.

6. Do not interrupt the interviewer.

7. Ask clarifying questions.

8. Identify feelings and attitudes in the interviewer.

9. Do not let "trigger words" like "foolish," "immature," etc. provoke an emotional response.

10. Do not waste time evaluating the interviewer.

If you are asked a question you just don't know how to answer, be honest and say so. Perhaps you can say, "I'll have to think about that. Can we come back to it later?" Normally, the interviewer will oblige. It is then your responsibility to return to the question before the end of the interview. At that point, if you still cannot come up with an answer, say that you will continue to think about it and get back to the interviewer by letter. Then, in your thank-you letter, give that interviewer an answer to his or her question. In these cases, honesty (and thoughtfulness in later responding by letter), rather than bluffing your way through an answer, may be your ticket to success.

A fourth reason for interview failures is that interviewers may get annoyed by *having questions answered that were not asked*. Here, you are treading the fine line between guiding the interview and destroying it. Answering a question about your spare-time activities with a description of your undergraduate awards makes you sound like a politician; they routinely give answers that have no relation at all to the questions that were asked. Rather, talk about the rock band you organized or the Internet bulletin board you established. These both answer the question and highlight your initiative and talents.

Similar applicant behavior that interviewers detest includes answering questions with questions, telling jokes to change the subject, and answering with gibberish. Like reporters, good interviewers will simply repeat their original question until they get a straight answer. Also, because interviewers are human, answers that might work one day may not on another. Many factors can influence an interviewer's behavior (figure 24.2).

The fifth way to wreck your interview is to *ramble*, thus providing superfluous information. Interviewers are easily bored—not surprising given the number of applicants they often must see in one day. If you have a lot of information to impart in answer to a specific question, tell the interviewer the main points, and then ask if he or she would like you to continue. For example, if you are asked to describe your most interesting volunteer experience, give the highlights in several sentences and then ask if the interviewer would like to know more. Since you are watching the interviewer while you answer, you may note nonverbal cues indicating that you have said enough. In general, keep your answers brief, to the point, and interesting.

Figure 24.2: Factors Influencing an Interviewer's Behavior

1. Age & Stage In Life Cycle
2. Cultural Background
3. Interests
4. Prior Experiences
5. Goals/Aspirations
6. Successes/Failures
7. Mood
8. Personality

The sixth reason interviews fail is that the applicant inadvertently gives *warning signals* to the interviewer that there may be an unstable personality lurking behind a deceptive smile. Trained interviewers seek specific warning signs (figure 24.3). Very few faculty interviewers are sophisticated enough in the techniques of employment interviewing to consciously recognize these signs. Being good clinicians, though, they unconsciously assimilate clues and will give the applicant a poor rating. It would be a good idea to review the warning signs and make certain that you do not demonstrate any unintentionally.

Interview Disasters

Interviewers see some pretty strange behavior during medical school interviews. (They understand that premeds are strange, but there are limits.) In general, what interviewers look for to eliminate applicants from consideration are arrogance, superficiality, egocentrism, over- or under-confidence, and incompetence.

Life, however, is often stranger than fiction, and so are some interviews. An applicant's behavior often reveals his or her true nature. Below are some unusual, but real, things that have happened during interviews.

- One applicant remained standing when offered a chair, to maintain his superior position.
- On her arrival, one applicant put her over-stuffed briefcase on the interviewer's already-full desk.
- Another left the dry-cleaning tag on his jacket, saying that he wanted to demonstrate just how neat and clean he was.
- One applicant tucked his long hair under his collar, thinking that no one would notice.
- When told to take his time answering questions, an applicant began writing out the answers before speaking.
- One applicant described his recent divorce—blow-by-blow.
- Another contradicted everything the interviewer said.
- After sneezing, one applicant asked for a Kleenex, and then another. She had neglected to bring any, although she had a cold.
- One applicant finished all of the interviewer's sentences for her.
- Another suggested that he had friends in the administration who would get him in.
- As the interviewer described the school's important features, one applicant yawned widely and stared at his watch.
- When an interviewer received a telephone call, the applicant sulked, taking it as a personal affront.
- In one instance, however, the call was from an applicant's mother, asking that her son be strongly considered.
- Another brought his five children and the family cat to the interview.
- At the end of the interview, one applicant simply asked, "How did I do, coach?"

Hopefully, you won't make any of these errors. Just think, if this is how other applicants behave, you don't have much to worry about. Of course, most applicants to medical school are smart enough to avoid such crass behavior.

Figure 24.3: Warning Signs for Interviewers

- Inconsistent answers during the interview.
- Inconsistencies between what is said in the interview and past performance.
- Abrasiveness or any other personality quirk that makes the interviewer uncomfortable.
- Evasiveness.
- A pattern of unhappiness in former jobs.
- Blaming others for all the applicant's problems.
- Dullness when responding to questions.
- A pattern of taking advantage of, or of deceiving, other people.

Adapted from: Perham JC. Spotting bad apples: the warning signals. *Dun's Business Month.* October 1986, pp. 54-56.

Interviewer's Evaluation of Applicants

Nearly half of all medical schools simply have the interviewer rate the applicant using a narrative statement, without any formal rating scale. The balance use Likert-type scales with numbers or adjectives (from 1=poor to 5=excellent) to describe either end of the scale. A few schools have behavioral descriptions (e.g., works in medical area 20 hours per week) as their guide. Although every school has a different rating form for interviewers to complete, the essential items will always be the same. Figure 24.4 is a typical interviewer's rating form.

When, as is usual, there is more than one interviewer, the admission committee gives a final "interview score" at nearly half the schools. At another one-third, there is an automatic arithmetic addition or averaging of the scores. At the remaining schools, the interviewers reach a consensus by discussing the applicant interviews with each other.

Figure 24.4: Interviewer's Rating Form

Applicant Name_____ Date_____

1. General: Physical Appearance (dress, grooming), Character (reliability, honesty, integrity), Timeliness, Energy

1 (Poor)	2	3 (Average)	4	5 (Excellent)

2. Knowledge: About medicine, About this school, Computer literacy

1 (Poor)	2	3 (Average)	4	5 (Excellent)

3. Intellect: Mental Ability, Judgment, Flexibility, Communication Ability

1 (Poor)	2	3 (Average)	4	5 (Excellent)

4. Emotions: Work Ethic, Personality, Motivation, Teachable, Attitude, Sense of Humor, Stability, Outside Interests, Self-Confidence

1 (Poor)	2	3 (Average)	4	5 (Excellent)

5. Record: MCAT Score, Class Rank, Undergraduate School, Quality of Reference Letters, Clinical Experience, Extracurricular Activities, Honors/Awards, Research

1 (Poor)	2	3 (Average)	4	5 (Excellent)

_____ **Average of Scored Items**

Narrative Summary:

Recommendation: (circle one)

Reject   *Conditional*   *Accept*

Sell Yourself

The bottom line during an interview is that you *must sell yourself.* At the same time, you also need to elicit information. To have the best chance of being accepted by the schools which interest you, you must do a good job of showing your own wares. Interviewers look for specific attributes in applicants (figure 24.5). When talking with individuals at each school, keep these attributes in mind. Remember that interviewers rate these elements in all the applicants they interview. It is your job to demonstrate how closely you resemble the interviewer's ideal candidate by exhibiting the sought-after traits.

If you don't sell yourself, no one else will do it for you!

Figure 24.5: Key Personality Traits Interviewers Seek

PERSONAL

Enthusiasm
Motivation/Initiative
Communication Skills
Chemistry
Energy
Determination
Confidence
Humility

PROFESSIONAL

Reliability
Honesty/Integrity
Pride
Dedication
Analytical Skills
Listening Skills

25: The Questions—The Answers

Silence is the only good substitute
for intelligence.

Folk saying

As I walk'd by myself, I talk'd to myself,
And myself replied to me;
And the questions myself then put to myself,
With their answers, I give to thee.

Bernard Barton, *Colloquy With Myself*

WHAT MUST YOU REMEMBER in the process of preparing for, and participating in, the interview? Only two things: *sell yourself by showing your best qualities and prepare in advance.*

Interviews generally start with some simple pleasantries and then move on to the skills/attitude evaluation (figure 23.1). In this part of the interview, no matter what the format or the type of questions they use, most admission officers look for three qualities in applicants: *intellectual strength, energy, and personal compatibility* with faculty, staff, and current students. Interviewers don't really want "the truth." They want "correct" answers. If you believe there is no such thing as the correct answer to a typical interview question, you are sadly mistaken. Good interviewers know exactly what they are looking for in a medical student. They know how to extract the needed information in a way that is disarmingly benign. Their questions are simply tools with which to hammer out an impression of the applicant. (Many interviewers, of course, are not that good and have no clue what to expect from a question.)

Intellectual Strength

Admission officers already know a great deal about your intellectual strength. Reference letters, MCAT scores, transcripts, and narratives of your undergraduate performance have preceded you. That is what got you in the door for the interview. Now it is time to see if you can think on your feet. Can you apply what you know to new situations? Are you really interested in learning, or just in getting through school so you can practice medicine? Do you know about anything other than your school work? Was it your quick smile rather than a solid intellect that got you your good grades? Do you believe that you have very little left to learn? Basically, the interviewer tries to determine what you know, how well you are able to apply what you have learned, and if you really want to learn any more.

Energy

Medical students spend the majority of their time attending to their studies and memorizing vast amounts of information. No matter where a school is located or how well the curriculum is arranged, fatigue, stress, and depression can result. The less these afflict a school's students, the fewer are the problems with which the faculty must deal and, consequently, the happier they are. Make them happy. Demonstrate that you have the good humor, self-confidence, and stamina to go the distance. But don't just say the words—show them by your actions during your entire interview visit.

Personal Compatibility

A "personality" already exists for the school. Will you fit in? Will they be comfortable with you? A little thought and a lot of care are necessary here. A hyper-aggressive image may work at some schools, but fail at others. Modify the image you project to meet the situation. But don't fool yourself. If you will not fit in with a group, it is better to find that out during the interview, rather than after you arrive for a four-year (or longer) stint as a student.

Presenting Yourself

Show Your Best Qualities

As you answer the interviewers' questions, remember to highlight your best qualities to *sell yourself!*

And do not sell yourself short! Know what your strengths are. Know what the school is looking for. And if you don't have an obvious opportunity to let the interviewers know how well you meet their needs, make one. This may come through answering questions—all questions—with different strengths you want to emphasize. Or it may come in the form of a "question" at the termination of the interview, e.g., "Is it true that students have an opportunity to get involved clinically during their first year? I'm really excited about that possibility."

Prepare

When getting ready for the interview it is absolutely essential to *prepare, prepare, prepare!* How many hours have you spent studying, preparing for exams? One thousand? Five thousand? The interview is, perhaps, the single toughest exam of your life. Make sure that you spend enough time studying for it. The steps to preparing for an interview are very straightforward; learn to talk about yourself easily, and learn the types of questions interviewers ask and what they hope to learn from your answers. Then combine these and formulate your answers in advance.

Talking About Yourself

Talking about yourself can be very difficult. Most people are loath to extol their own virtues. However, you must be ready to tell the interviewers about your positive qualities so that they hear them loud and clear.

First, put yourself in the position of the faculty and students where you will be interviewing. What job skills and personal characteristics would you want in an individual applying to *your* school? You should be able to get a good idea of what they are looking for from the material you have collected from medical student organizations, from the school's own information, and from conversations with medical students and physicians. Write these characteristics down. Then write out questions you would ask to discover if an applicant has those characteristics.

Next, list your strengths that match these characteristics. This step requires a good bit of objectivity. You may need some help from your adviser or a close friend. The following exercise will help you get into the habit of thinking and talking positively about yourself.

Exercise 1:

List *three accomplishments* of which you are proud and what each indicates about you.

1. _____

2. _____

3. _____

List *three attributes* which you have that will make you an excellent medical student.

1. _____

2. _____

3. _____

Then, list *three abilities* you have that will make you an excellent physician.

1. _____

2. _____

3. _____

Now, can you use these accomplishments and abilities in a short narrative that describes you? If you can, you have made a good start toward a successful interview.

Finally, write some great answers to the questions you developed. Be sure to incorporate your accomplishments and abilities into your answers. But do not memorize them word for word—they will sound forced. Guests on television talk shows prepare by making a list of the ten questions they *don't* want to be asked—and then developing answers for each of them. Note that this process may change a bit as you gain interview experience. But it gets easier and easier each time you do it. And it is worth the effort.

It's said that the famous lawyer, F. Lee Bailey, doesn't believe that he has won so many difficult cases because he is smarter than his opponents—he is just more obsessive-compulsive. Preparation is his key to success. Your preparation will also be your key to getting into a medical school.

Types of Questions

Typical interviewers use only five types of interview questions, although they can be phrased in many different ways. Recognizing the type of question the interviewer is asking will help you determine what information he or she is seeking.

Closed Question

These questions ask for specific information and simple, definitive answers. "How many years did you go to undergraduate school?" for example, deserves merely a simple answer, such as "four years." Nothing deep here. Interviewers use closed questions to elicit information seemingly absent from the application materials.

Open-Ended, Informal Question

These questions also ask for specific information, but require more in-depth answers. Such a question might be, "What clinical experiences have you had so far?" While the question requires specific information, it allows the applicant a chance to speak and become relaxed.

Open-Ended, Attitudinal Question

These questions determine how well an applicant organizes his or her thoughts before speaking. An example is "What do you think of physician advertising?" Most interviewers want to see if the answer is concise and to the point.

Probing Question

Interviewers ask probing questions as follow-ups to open-ended questions. They are especially useful after the applicant has given an answer expressing an opinion. An example of this type of question is "Why do you feel that way?" This forces applicants to defend and further explain their previous answers. It also allows an interviewer to control the direction of the interview.

Sometimes an interviewer will go back to an earlier answer, quote the applicant, and ask a probing question, such as "You said you felt this area of the country was more progressive medically than your undergraduate school's area. Why is that?"

Leading Question

Interviewers use leading questions to direct applicants' answers or to see if they have the gumption to express their own opinions. Unfortunately, it is not always easy to tell what is expected. Such a question might begin, "Medical students should do night call just like residents." And be followed by, "Don't you agree?" The interviewer may be serious or merely prodding the interviewee into an untenable position. If the intent is unclear, a way to find out *before answering* is simply to ask, "What makes you think that?" (In this case, interviewers often welcome a question in response to their own.)

Impossible Questions

Applicants to medical school often encounter questions which they can't answer—either because they lack the experience to answer them or because there simply is no answer to that particular question. Interviewers may ask, for example, about specific clinical scenarios or about how to solve the problems with health care delivery in the state. It's not only okay, but also prudent to say "I don't know." Add, of course, that in the first case you don't (yet) have the knowledge and experience to answer the question, and in the second, that you would love to hear the interviewer's thoughts on the matter. (You would, wouldn't you?) The key is to admit that you don't have a clue when you are asked questions that you really shouldn't be able to answer.

Helpful Sources

Many premed offices keep files containing the questions that applicants from your school have been asked at specific medical schools. They also often have information about the interview formats different schools use. You may want to check with your adviser, since having some advance warning can be very helpful. Information about medical school applicants' interview experiences also shows up at various sites on the World Wide Web. Contact your premed advisor or club for the current Web addresses for this information.

Questions And Answers

The following questions are those that applicants to medical school have been asked over the past several years. Following the prototypical question and a discussion of possible answers, I have listed similar questions that applicants have been asked. Some are much more thoughtful or original than the classic questions—such as "Why do you want to be a physician?"—to which nearly all applicants tire of responding. Perhaps some interviewers will read this list and buff up their interviewing "act." While these are the questions for which you should be prepared, it is impossible to prepare for or to predict every possible question. If you prepare for the questions listed below, you will have the confidence to answer anything an interviewer asks.

1. How are you today?

What a pleasant way for an interviewer to begin. A simple ice-breaker, you think. Wrong! Sophisticated interviewers use this and similar questions as rapid and effective screening tools. "Gee, it's raining outside and I got soaked coming here," said one applicant. "I'm really frustrated that my plane was late and that I had trouble getting a cab," whined another.

Interviewers look for individuals whose demeanor stays upbeat even under adversity. The travails on the interview circuit are insignificant when compared to those of medical school, residency, and medical practice. Simple opening questions delivered in an off-hand manner often expose an applicant's true personality far better than the well-rehearsed "deep" questions that most applicants have come to expect.

The point is, there are no innocent questions!

- Did you have any trouble finding us or getting here?
- You're looking a little flustered. What's wrong?

2. Do you have any questions?

This is the "behavioral" interviewer's classic opening. The interviewee is expected to take the initiative right from the start. Many applicants ask standard questions and, therefore, waste this opportunity.

When the "any questions" opportunity begins an interview, use it to show that you are achievement oriented, and really do know about medical school and the medical career on which you are embarking. An example might be, "I recently read in *American Medical News* that many schools now use computer-based teaching and examinations—especially in anatomy and pathology. Is that true here? I have a particular interest in computer programming. Would the instructors be interested in helping me to develop programs for their use?"

Get such information from reading recent issues of American Medical Student's Association's, *The New Physician* or from the American Medical Association's, *American Medical News (AMNews)*. Both publications contain a wealth of information about the current state of medical education and medical practice. Most college libraries subscribe to both. You can also get copies of *AMNews* from many physicians.

Faculty members most commonly ask this question because they are poor admissions interviewers. They often do not know what other questions to ask. Since many applicants find this is the most common question they are asked, you may want to make a long list of your own questions to use as answers. Never answer "No," since, no matter what the situation, a negative answer indicates that you do not have a serious interest in that school.

- Do you know much about our medical school?

- If you were in my (the interviewer's) seat, what you would ask? . . . Okay, now answer those questions.

3. Tell me about yourself.

This is the granddaddy of open-ended queries. You have the opportunity to say almost anything you want. You can put your best foot forward or stick it right in your mouth. This question gives you, by design, no hint of how to answer it. You can go off on almost any tangent. And if the interviewer is any good, you will be able to talk for as long as you want. The longer you talk, however, the less chance you have of scoring high on that interviewer's list of candidates.

To answer this and similar open-ended questions, first respond briefly and succinctly to the single question, "What motivates you?" For example, you might cite your most applicable qualities by stating, "I am a hard worker with a longtime interest in medicine. My role models and my reading first got me interested, and my volunteer clinical experiences only solidified my desire to be a physician." Then stop. Ask the interviewer if you should continue. This demonstrates that you understand the interactive nature of interviews and that you have consideration for the other person's role. When you ask whether you should continue, many interviewers will direct you to other areas for further discussion. This will help both you and the interviewer a great deal by allowing you to answer the questions that the interviewer really wants to ask.

One student, anticipating this question, went into his interviews with confidence. He thought he had discovered the secret to successful medical school interviews—"a story" that would intrigue interviewers and make him a memorable applicant (in a positive way). The student had had an adventurous year off after undergraduate school, and he was prepared to talk about it in a way that emphasized his strengths. As he said, "I know lots of folks with great grades and solid MCAT scores who never got in. Perhaps they just didn't have a good story to tell." This student understood that he should be prepared for the questions and be interesting to the interviewer.

- What three adjectives best describe you?

- What are your team-player/leadership qualities?

- What might give me a better picture of you than I can get from your résumé?

- Tell me a story about yourself that best describes you.

- If you were going to die in five minutes, what would you tell someone about yourself?

- Of which accomplishments are you most proud?

- Do you have any hidden achievements or qualities of which you are secretly proud?

- Tell me about your elementary school years.

- Tell me about your adolescence.

- How have you changed since high school?

- What was the most important event in your life?

- What shaped you and got you to where you are today?

- What was the most difficult thing you have ever done?

- What do you like to cook?

- If you died right now, what would you want on your tombstone?

- How would your best-friend/roommates/relatives describe you? What negative things would they say?

- Why did you write . . . in your personal statement/essay?

- What one thing do you want conveyed to the admission committee?

4. What are your strengths and weaknesses?

This is the "Tell me about yourself" question phrased negatively. It asks, "Tell me what's wrong with you."

Do you want to answer that question? Of course not. And it is extremely unlikely that you will ever come up against it. But a very common inquiry, about your strengths and weaknesses, is essentially the same question. Basically, the interviewer asks you to jump off a cliff of your own design. All you need to do is to redesign the cliff so you can climb rather than jump.

First, answer the question about your strengths concisely. Beware of talking too much. Then work on the other half of the question—the dangerous part.

At this point, you must turn your "weaknesses" into more strengths. Of which character flaws would the interviewers at a medical school approve? Is your weakness that you are obsessive about completing your work in an exacting manner? Or is it intolerance for your compatriots who do not perform their assigned tasks with a professional attitude? Maybe it is an inability to go home at night until all your work is completed. These are, undoubtedly, the types of "failings" that the faculty will be interested in encouraging rather than disparaging. But in relating these faults, show at least a little remorse about having them. Don't be glib.

Nearly all medical schools report that their interviewers ask about strengths and weaknesses. How boring!

- Tell me about your "secret identity," the part of your personality that you don't ordinarily share with strangers.

- Are there any skeletons in your closet that you want to tell me about?

- How well do you take criticism?

- What is your pet peeve?

- If you could change one thing about your personality, what would it be?

- What are your three strongest qualities?

- What are your two worst qualities?

- Have you demonstrated leadership in any extracurricular activities?

5. If you could be any cell in the human body, which would you choose to be, and why?

This is not much different from the directive to "Tell me about yourself." It is, however, a bit more inventive and has been used by many interviewers, especially for biology/zoology majors, ever since it found its way into *The New England Journal of Medicine* (1990;323:838).

Unfortunately, you may have a hard time not being reminded of *Saturday Night Live*'s Baba WaWa's similar question, "If you could be any kind of twee . . . ?" (Don't laugh when you're asked this question!)

Many applicants say that they would want to be neurons "to be in control, to be stimulated and stimulating, and to be the center of all things." Since you are now prepared in advance for this question, try to be original. Don't be surprised if this question pops up along the interview route.

- Do you see yourself as more relaxed/casual/informal or as more serious/dedicated /committed?

- Which is more important, the ability to organize, structure and prioritize, or the ability to be flexible, modify, change, and make do as needed?

- Which is more important, knowledge or imagination?

- If you could be any kitchen object, what would you be?

- What is the strangest Halloween costume you ever wore?

- What was your favorite book when you were eleven years old?

6. If your house were burning, what three objects would you save?

Some interviewers really believe Freudian analysis will help them choose the best medical students. While this may seem to be essentially the same type of question as above, think again. This question narrows the scope to a very concrete and personal level by asking, "What do you value in your own life?" How important are material objects to you? Are you "sensitive" enough to reach for your beloved's picture, or are you "sensible" enough to grab the car keys and credit cards?

There is no one correct answer to this question; the best answer depends upon the nature of the person asking the question. Sometimes the questioner actually wants to know whether you have planned ahead or can think quickly, since a fire is a real possibility in our lives—unlike turning into a tree or a cell.

An alternative form of this question is "If you had to repack your belongings, what would you have left behind?" This question is even more concrete, at least for the majority of students traveling to interviews. The follow-up questions will certainly be "Why leave that behind?" and "Why did you bring it?" Pack carefully.

- If you had unlimited money and two free hours (one day, one week, one month), what would you do?

- If you had three wishes, what would they be? (Shades of *Aladdin*.)

7. What kinds of people are your friends?

"Know my friends, know me," goes an old expression. People attract similar folks as friends. Applicants' descriptions of their friends often give interviewers deep insights into their personalities. This question essentially asks you to talk about yourself in the third person.

Answer this question as if you were describing yourself. Interviewers often respond favorably when married applicants state that their spouses are their best friends. Describing a spouse's glowing personal attributes only serves to enhance the applicant, as long as these attributes are not used as a contrast to the candidate's own qualities.

- Describe your best-friend/roommate/spouse and his life.

- How are you similar and dissimilar to your best friend?

- How would your friends or coworkers describe you?

- If you could dine with anyone from the past, present, or future, who would it be?

8. Who are your heroes?

Related to the question "Tell me about yourself," this is a deep probe into your psyche. It evaluates your self-image, direction, and goals. How the interviewer interprets your answer may, to some degree, reflect his or her own personality, age, and background. This is perhaps the most difficult interview question to answer. In an age without obvious heroes, your choice will, by necessity, be very personal.

There are several possible responses to this question.

One answer you may have already thought of is that you have no heroes. You have, however, just completed many years of schooling, during which you had many new experiences and met countless interesting people as teachers, friends, and coworkers. Viewed from that perspective, it would be an unusual, and perhaps very narrow-minded, individual who could not find someone to look up to as a role model.

Another possible answer is to cite a family member, friend, or personal acquaintance. The follow-up question, of course, will be "Why?" There should be some identifiable attribute this person demonstrates that justifies your distinguishing him or her as your hero. A parent, sibling, or spouse is usually a very good choice. It shows respect for your family and a firm commitment to your roots. If you choose a physician as your hero, be prepared to explain how you are trying, or will try, to emulate that person's attributes in your personal and professional life, as well as how you interacted with him or her. This can get somewhat sticky since, if you only had a superficial interaction, it might suggest you only have a superficial idea about what medicine is and what physicians do.

Historic or public figures are perfectly acceptable answers. These heroes can be drawn from science, education, or many other fields. Discussing the attributes of a lesser-known historical figure may lead the interview into new and interesting areas. You must be prepared to discuss the individual's attributes in depth. Tread lightly, however, if your hero is a contemporary religious or political figure. An interviewer's bias may affect her evaluation of you if your hero exemplifies major philosophical differences between the two of you.

The worst answer is to name a contemporary star of television, the movies, or popular music. In that case, both you and your answer will probably be seen as very superficial.

- What is your favorite movie? Why?
- What is the last book you read?
- What do "success" and "failure" mean to you?
- What do you believe?
- Do you have any Black, Hispanic, etc. role models in medicine?
- What physician characteristics do you admire most? least?
- Tell me about your father/mother.

9. What do you do in your spare time?

The primary danger here is to give too long an answer. Everyone likes to talk about him- or herself and this is an invitation to do just that. But keep it brief. If you collect rocks, for example, you might say, "I am an avid rock collector and have been for about five years. I have had the opportunity to travel across the United States and Canada pursuing my hobby." Then stop. If the interviewer wants to know any more, he or she will ask.

Your answer should show that you are not a couch potato (although a computer aficionado is okay). Do not describe activities that may cause you injuries resulting in prolonged leaves of absence from school. Also, pick a non-controversial activity; avoid discussing hunting, guns, or religion unless you are certain that you will not raise the interviewer's hackles. In general, speak about community-oriented and people-centered activities. The focus of the rock collector's description might be the people she meets at collector's conventions.

The questioner usually wants to learn three things from this query.

First, does the applicant have any interests outside of school and work? An interviewee with no outside interests sends a serious danger signal. Medical students and residents who have no outlet for their anxieties, stresses, and frustrations may decompensate—and become a problem for the faculty. If you have no overriding outside interests, simply mention what you do in your spare time. Yes, spending lots of time with your family, spouse, children, and friends is certainly an outside interest.

Second, is the applicant more enthusiastic about his or her avocation than about the prospect of going to medical school and practicing medicine? Show equal enthusiasm for both.

Third, the interviewer is screening out those applicants who are so wrapped up in themselves that they will not be able to pay any attention to their patients, peers, and faculty. How do they spot these individuals? They are the ones who go on and on and on about their other activities with no prompting—even after the interviewer gives negative cues, such as turning away from the applicant, coughing, or even standing up. Answer questions about your outside activities as you have answered the other questions—fully, briefly, and with enthusiasm.

- What are your favorite games and sports? Why?

- What do you do for fun?

- How and why did you choose your outside activities?

- If you had a completely free day, what would you do?

- What is the most bizarre thing you have ever done (or did in high school or in college)?

- What was the most unusual occurrence in your life? in the past month?

- Do you think you can remain intensely focused on medicine for the next four years—or more?

- Besides your future medical accomplishments, what do you wish to be known for by your peers, friends, and family?

- Where have you traveled? Why?

- What non-medical magazines do you regularly read?

- What have you contributed to groups and activities in which you participated?

- What have you learned from your volunteer work?

10. What clinical experiences have you had?

At most medical schools, interviewers won't ask whether you have had clinical experiences, but rather what these experiences were. They do not expect applicants to appear for interviews without having had medical experiences. With the current glut of excellent applicants, most medical school admission committees view it as an extraordinary, and unacceptable, risk to train future physicians who do not know what they are getting themselves into.

Whether your clinical experiences were paid or not, whether you mainly observed or actually participated in patient care, and whether they lasted over a period of years or were a concentrated experience, you should have gained some valuable insights from them. What did you learn? What did you see? Which of these experiences did you like? Which didn't you like? Why? Did they reinforce your desire to be a physician or tend to dissuade you? These are the details that interviewers seek. Describe your experiences with one or two illustrative stories. Think about them before your interviews.

Nearly all medical schools report that their interviewers ask applicants about their experiences in health care, and about what they are proud of having done in the field.

- How long have you stood on your feet at one time?

- Has someone ever come to you for help with a major personal crisis? What have you done to alleviate their emotional pain?

- What are patients most afraid of when they visit a doctor?

- What would you find most difficult to deal with if you were a patient?

11. To which organizations do you belong?

People join organizations that further their own agendas, be they recreational, spiritual, political, or professional. The organizations you belong to reflect your goals, background, and interests. The relevant question here is, how much do you want to reveal?

The groups you join often loudly signal your religion, political or sexual orientation, and cultural heritage. Since prejudice exists in many guises, it may be best to simply discuss the school-based (and if applicable, the professional) organizations to which you belong. These should include the premedical club/honorary, any special organization associated with your major subject area, organizations associated with your volunteer activities or work (e.g., Boy Scouts, National Association of EMTs), or if you are out of school and working, any related societies.

Most interviewers now understand that pressing you for information about other organizations might violate state and federal laws. Note, however, that anything you included in your application materials is fair game during interviews. If you list an organization on your application or résumé, or in your personal statement, the interviewer may ask you about it. Although the following questions are all illegal, you'll probably hear some variation of them anyway.

- Your name sounds Hispanic (Arabic, Italian, Vietnamese, etc.). Is it?

- How did you learn to speak (non-English language)?

- Would you have any trouble working with our predominantly Catholic (LDS, Jewish, etc.) patients?

- When was the last time you went back to (country of origin or family's origin)?

- Why do you think you are a minority?

12. What are your plans for a family?

You probably will be asked a variety of questions that are not only uncomfortable to answer, but also patently illegal under state or federal statutes. These questions also provide ammunition for discrimination-in-admission lawsuits. (These suits are rarely brought, however, because discrimination is hard to prove in court.)

To determine whether a question is legal, ask yourself, "Is it important to my performing as a medical student?" If it is relevant, then the question is probably legitimate. (The law, however, can be convoluted. See figure 25.2.)

Questions about family, child care, and birth control are most often directed at women applicants. Other candidates may hear inquiries about race, nationality, physical infirmities, religion, and other subjects which are illegal for interviewers to raise. (See also chapter 10, *Unconventional Premed Students,* and "Illegal Questions" below.)

A legal way to ask such questions is "Is there anything about your personal life that may affect your performance in this demanding school and profession?" Your answer is "No." The following are some additional illegal questions you may hear.

- How important is your family to you?

- How do you propose to juggle marriage (relationship) and medical practice?

- What do your parents do for a living?

13. If you could not be a physician, what career would you choose?

Once again, let's see who is really hiding beneath the polished applicant veneer. How deeply are you committed to medicine? Is it a whimsical interest, or is it a burning desire that forms the core of your existence? How easily can you come up with an answer that you find acceptable? How upset do you seem by such a prospect?

Very few people can fake a response to something this important. Interviewers, especially those who live and breathe medicine, use this question to find people who have their same level of commitment. Older interviewers use this question frequently, since many distrust the resolution of younger generations.

This question is also used because some studies suggest that there is a high correlation between alternate career interests and certain medical specialties. Applicants ultimately going into anesthesiology or radiology, for example, usually cite highly technical professional fields, such as engineering, research, the "hard" sciences, law, architecture, or finance-related businesses as alternative choices. Those entering pediatrics tend to view teaching, other health-related professions, the humanities, the arts, or non-professional careers as acceptable alternatives.

Variations of this question may also be used to test an applicant's grasp of reality. The interviewer may ask "What do you think you will do when you stop practicing medicine (at the end of a career)?" Others will probe even a strong answer to see whether applicants have considered any alternatives if they do not get into medical school (at least this time) or suddenly could not practice medicine.

- Why did you choose to be a physician?

- If your brain was the only part of your body that worked, what would you do with your life?

- What will happen if you develop a debilitating disease while in medical school? residency?

14. You seem really interested in research. Why do you want a medical degree?

Well, what do you *really* want to do with your life? The clinician-interviewer may be asking, "Are you going to medical school simply for another credential to use as a stepping-stone into research?" The Ph.D.-interviewer may be asking, "Why are you bothering with a medical degree when you can be a researcher?" Obviously, the answers to these two questions will be different—and will depend in large measure upon your background and interests. At this stage, however, a "safe" answer is that you plan on having a career in clinical research, and you will vary the percentage of time spent in each area based on your funding and interests. A rather negative corollary to this question is "Are you another Michael Crichton?" This reference is to the well-known, high-profile author of *Jurassic Park* and other works, who has said he only went to medical school to gain a solid background for his writing. Medical faculty don't consider this a good use of their time or of valuable medical school spots. If you have this type of aspiration, keep it to yourself.

- If you have such an interest in research, why aren't you applying to our M.D./Ph.D. program?
- If you had to choose between getting an M.D. and a Ph.D., which would you select and why?
- How might acupuncture work? Do we know enough about physiology and biophysics to determine that?
- What are the most important traits for a clinician/researcher?
- How will the research you have done alter scientific thought? Help mankind?
- Let's discuss the details of the research you have done.
- How did the idea come to you for any research you initiated?

15. In what specialty would you like to practice?

With medical schools' and legislatures' emphasis on primary care (general internal medicine, general pediatrics, family practice, obstetrics/gynecology), applicants who already think they would like to specialize in another area have a tough decision to make. Should they tell "the truth" or fudge their answers? Consider two things. First, most medical students change their minds about which specialty to enter, as do many residents. Therefore, it is perfectly reasonable to say, "I'm really not sure where my talents or interests lie. I simply want to help people by practicing medicine." Second, telling the truth during interviews is essential, because lying (and remembering to whom you told which lie) is very hard work, is difficult for most folks to pull off, demonstrates poor character, will make you feel badly about yourself, and is not necessary. Even if your past experience strongly suggests that you will enter a particular field (e.g., a decade of experience as a psychiatric social worker), you can honestly say that you are leaving your options open. In my experience, many students who are "sure" that they will enter one specialty because of their past experiences often unexpectedly find their niche in a totally different area. Note that most students who think that they want to enter a primary care specialty do so, while few students who enter medical school believing they will enter a subspecialty end up in primary care.

- In light of the bleak future for subspecialists, why would anyone go into cardiology or gastroenterology today?

16. How do you make important decisions?

As you discuss some very important life decisions you have made, the interviewer may wonder how you came to these decisions. Individuals vary in how they make important decisions. Their methods reflect their personalities and thought processes. Are they thoughtful, deliberate, and slow, or are they inattentive, impulsive, and quick? Or, does their decision-making method vary appropriately with the situation?

Be prepared to discuss your own decision-making strategies with interviewers. Think carefully before you respond to this question, however. Interviewers may ask you if you used those strategies when you decided to enter medicine or to apply to their school. Or they may ask how your method affected your ability to perform in specific situations, such as when making other obvious life-decisions revealed by your application materials.

If you use the Must/Want Analysis to help decide on the qualities you want in a medical school, take a copy (without the school's ratings) to your interview and show it to any interviewers who asks you this question. They will probably be impressed with your logical and deliberate decision-making process.

- Are you a "risk-taker" or "safety-minded"?
- What made you choose your undergraduate major/minor?
- How did you select your undergraduate school?
- What was the most difficult decision you have had to make in your life? How did you make it?

17. What were the major deficiencies in your premed training?

This is an opportunity to demonstrate some realistic insight into the past 3½ years (or more) of your life. How well has your undergraduate experience prepared you for medical school? What were the strongest educational elements? Which were the weakest? If you could retake your undergraduate education, what would you change? No interviewer believes that any undergraduate school is perfect. (Sorry to disillusion you Ivy Leaguers). Avoid taking major swipes at your school. You will be an alumnus of your undergraduate school no less than you will be an alumnus of the medical school at which you train. While a rah-rah response is not appropriate, neither is downgrading the training that you have received. Remember, your undergraduate education has gotten you as far as this interview.

While mentioning any deficiencies in your training you have the perfect opportunity to talk about your plans to remedy the deficit. These may include taking extra work or courses during the balance of your senior year, your independent-study plans, or clinical experiences you have arranged during the balance of the year or during the summer before medical school.

- Why did you choose your undergraduate institution and major? How satisfied are you with your decision?
- What non-science college courses interested you the most?
- What does your major (science or non-science) have to do with being a physician?
- Which undergraduate course would you recommend that all students take (regardless of the grade you got in the course)?
- Did you enjoy your college classes? Why?

18. How do you explain your low grades? leaves of absence? poor MCAT scores?

Not everyone who reads this book has an unblemished, outstanding record. In fact, very few applicants to medical school do. Most have some area of their records that requires an explanation. Perhaps you did poorly in a science course or on the MCAT, and had to repeat it. Or maybe you had to take a semester off at some point in your schooling. You should expect to be asked about these deficiencies or variations from the norm if the faculty members interviewing you are at all on the ball.

You already know what these issues are, and you need to be prepared to explain them. If there is a good justification for a questionable action, such as having to take time off due to a death in the family or a personal illness, explain. But if the poor grade or poor MCAT performance was, as is usual, due to your failure to put forth your best effort, just say so. Do not give excuses; they will sound lame to almost everyone except you. Your answer should be a variation of the terse military response, "No excuse, sir!" Say that you did not give the course, test, etc. your best effort. If you think you can get away with it, blame it on immaturity, ignorance, or youth. This works best if the problem occurred during your first year in school, especially if you can demonstrate that you have expended more effort in subsequent years. For applicants in graduate school or postbaccalaureate programs, you must demonstrate that you have done significantly better in your recent schooling than in undergraduate school. If you have any questionable areas hanging over your application, be prepared in advance to answer for your aberrant behavior.

- If you could begin your schooling again, what would you change?
- Have you ever dropped a class? Why?
- Have you ever quit or been fired from a job? Why?
- With your undergraduate grades in (college subject), how did you even get an interview here?
- Do you use drugs?
- Do you like to study? How do you study best? What motivates you to keep studying?
- What did you do during this (specified) period of time?

19. Have you always done the best work of which you are capable?

If you imagine that you can just answer yes or no to this question, you haven't gotten the drift of the interviewing business yet. The correct response to this question must not only show that you have put in a tremendous effort, but also demonstrate humility—by acknowledging that you could often have done a better job.

How to do this? Simply say that you have always striven to do the best possible job that you could, but the results did not always match your effort. This again stresses that you are a hard worker, you are humble, and you understand your limitations—all positive attributes. And this is all nicely wrapped up in that one-sentence answer. Very elegant.

- What have been your biggest failures in life?
- What have you done to ensure that these failures won't happen again?

20. With which types of people do you have trouble working?

This question really asks, "Why won't you fit in well with your medical school class or with the clinical team that exists at our hospitals and clinics?" In essence, what personality problems do you have? Will Rogers said, "I never met a man I didn't like." Maybe so, but most people have some difficulties dealing with arbitrary, obnoxious, and loud individuals. This is not, however, what you want to say. The correct answer, if you cannot honestly state that you usually get along with everyone, is that you generally have problems with those individuals who do not pull their own weight. This is also the answer to the parallel question, "What qualities drive you crazy in colleagues?" Again, this emphasizes your interest in, and ability to do, hard work. At the same time, it will normally hit a responsive chord in the interviewer, who probably also dislikes picking up the workload for slack colleagues. No one, of course, ever recognizes this problem in him- or herself.

Are there certain types of people that you consistently prefer not to deal with? No one will expect you to be thrilled to deal with whining, abusive, demanding, alcoholic, or drug-seeking patients. Most physicians do not like to treat such patients. If, however, you really dislike dealing with certain racial, ethnic, or age groups, or with people in general, you should probably reconsider your decision to pursue a medical career.

Some interviewers will attempt to get the names of negative references by asking, "Who didn't you get along with in undergraduate school, in the clubs or organizations to which you belonged, or in past jobs?" Luckily, this is an unusual request, if only because programs are besieged with too many applicants to follow up on the information. If you are asked for such references, your willingness to provide them and your ability to explain why you didn't get along with certain individuals will say a lot about your self-confidence, honesty, and insight.

- Describe the best/worst teacher you ever had.

- Do you prefer to work under supervision or on your own?

- As a physician, how will you deal with non-compliant patients?

21. How do you normally handle conflict?

Hopefully, you can answer that your interactions with people rarely lead to conflict but, when there is a problem, you try to work it through to a reasonable and amicable settlement.

You may want to prepare an example of just such a situation that you faced and how it was resolved. Optimally, this example will demonstrate that the conflict was handled in a thoughtful and good-natured manner, with goodwill restored at the end. Your attitude, facial expressions, and body language when telling such a story will reveal much about your personality and your real ability to harmoniously work with others.

- How do you respond when you are having problems with a parent, peer, coworker, or teacher?

- Have you ever challenged a teacher in class or a supervisor at work? What were the circumstances?

- How do you handle criticism, whether it's fair or unfair, from a superior, a subordinate, a peer, or a family member?

- What was the most useful criticism you ever received? Why?

- What would you do if your boss told you to do something you know is absolutely wrong (medically or morally)?

- What was your most difficult/stressful life experience? How did you handle it?

- What frustrates you the most?

22. With what subject did you have the most difficulty?

Similar to the question concerning your strengths and weaknesses, this one asks you to incriminate yourself. You cannot plead the Fifth Amendment, so you need to know how to work through it. If you obviously had problems with a course, as evidenced by a poor grade or dismal narrative evaluations, you will have to address this. Do so in a direct manner. Otherwise, use the same strategy you used for the strength and weakness question. Pick "difficulties" that will exhibit some of the strengths that you want the interviewer to see.

For example, by stating that you found organic chemistry very difficult because of the vast amount of seemingly pointless information you spent countless hours memorizing by rote, you will impress the interviewer with both your insight and your hard work. (You will also strike a responsive chord in most clinician-interviewers who detested organic chemistry and cannot understand why it is still part of the premed curriculum.) In general, emphasize that any trouble that you have had was the result of the long hours you spent (explanation, not a complaint) in the learning process. However, if you really did poorly in a course, you are probably being asked to explain why you did so poorly (Question 18).

Commonly, the interviewer will have already spotted your problem area and will also ask, "How will that affect your performance as a medical student?" Of course, your answer is that it won't affect your performance, since you already have (or have a plan to) overcome any problems through hard work or extra training.

- Tell me about the (subject) class you took as a college freshman.
- What has been your greatest challenge?

23. Why do you want to be a physician?

This is probably the question most often asked of medical school applicants. The question poses two dangers. The first lies in not having a good answer. If you have gone through the steps in this book, you will have no trouble answering it. You initially matched your personal goals to those that can be fulfilled through medical practice. Then, you talked with multiple physicians, read as much as you could about medicine, and tested whether medicine really interested you by spending time working in a clinical area. With this background to support your answer, you should have little trouble convincing the interviewer that you have firm and valid reasons for becoming a physician.

The second danger is that you will be asked this question so often—sometimes two or three times at each school—that you will become bored with your own answer. This will be obvious in your response and will reflect poorly upon your candidacy. Since each interviewer tends to ask applicants similar questions, your response will be compared with the answers from other candidates. Be enthusiastic when replying to this question—every time. Try to take a new tack when answering the question with different interviewers. This way you will avoid repeating the same phrases, which will sound stale and trite not only to you but also to them. You have an excellent answer to this question; make certain that your delivery matches it.

- What do you think you will contribute to the medical profession or to your community as a physician?
- How can you be sure that medicine is the right career for you?
- You said (a statement) in your application essay. What did you mean?
- What would you want your patients to say about you?
- What can be done to ensure that medical students are in medicine for the "right" reasons?
- With all the computer skills you have, why do you want to be a physician?
- The future of medicine looks bleak. Why do you think so many people are still pursuing a medical career?
- How did your family life contribute to your decision to become a physician?
- Do you know what you are getting into? Have you talked with physicians about what a medical career is really like?

24. Why did you apply to our medical school?

There are lots of medical schools: public and private, M.D.- and D.O.-granting, research- and clinically oriented. So why this school? Since this question is so basic, it is not surprising that interviewers ask it quite often. Since you based your medical school selections on your personal Must/Want Analysis, you have some excellent answers to this question. Maybe the school is particularly strong in research, which is an area you value highly. Or perhaps the faculty is outstanding, especially in particular areas that interest you. How about their reputation for primary care or for turning out great clinicians? Your answer to this question should include whatever attracted you to the school. In addition, it never hurts to say that the school also got a strong recommendation from your premed adviser or from clinicians you know.

Review all material you have about the school, as well as your personal evaluation of it, before beginning the day's interviews. If you remember to individualize your answer for each school, you should have no problem. Your knowledge of the school should include

- Class size
- Academic mission
- Teaching methods (PBL, etc.)
- Research opportunities
- Grading system
- Student services
- Academic support services

- Early clinical exposure
- Sites for clinical clerkships
- Elective opportunities
- Community outreach programs
- USMLE or OSCE for promotion/graduation
- Quarter/semester program
- Percent of women and minorities admitted

If you lack some of this information, that's okay. Make sure you ask for it at your first opportunity.

A more personal way to ask this question is, "Why are you willing to leave the West (or Northeast, Midwest, etc.) to come here for your medical education?" Rather than obviously directing the question toward the school's educational elements, the interviewer appears to be asking a more personal question. Without thinking, you may answer, "Well, I don't really want to live anywhere but the Boston area, but I heard this was a good school and I thought I'd take a look." Bad move! You have fallen into the interviewer's trap. It is not even worthwhile considering you as a serious applicant now, since you just said you would be unhappy away from Boston. The better answer is to say (hopefully with some truth) that you are willing to move anywhere to get an excellent medical education. Then tell the interviewer what you consider to be the school's finest qualities.

- What qualities are you looking for in a medical school?

- What interests you most about this medical school?

- What have you heard about our medical school that you don't like?

- Are you applying here because it is a familiar environment?

- Why do you want to leave (city or state where you live)?

- What do you think will be the most difficult aspect of living in this city, coming as you do from (city or state where you live)?

25. What will be the toughest aspect of medical education/practice for you?

This is another way of asking you about your strengths and weaknesses. Only the most skilled interviewers ask this form of the question.

Medicine clearly has complex areas to master as well as onerous aspects. What do you foresee as difficult areas for you? You may discuss your learning to master certain skills or dealing with the vexing areas of medical practice.

It would be unrealistic for you not to recognize some of the difficult personal or professional aspects of medical training and practice. Failure to cite any indicates that you know little about medical school, a physician's life, yourself, or all three. A good way to answer this question is to note one or more of the small or commonly recognized difficulties (such as the large amount of material students must memorize) and describe how you intend to overcome each one. The fact that you visualize only small or common problems will either placate the interviewer or lead to other questions, so he can be certain that you haven't missed the big picture.

If you are questioned about the "most enjoyable" part of medicine for you, answer with the most specific terms you can. Cite examples of experiences that excited you while doing clinical work, stimulated you to read further, or suggested interesting research opportunities. The more specific you can be, the better your answer will be received, and the better the interviewer will remember you.

Two-thirds of medical schools report that their interviewers ask applicants about their willingness to live a medical student's, resident's, and physician's life.

- What would you be willing to sacrifice to become a physician?
- What is the greatest sacrifice you have already made to get where you are?
- Are you willing to work graveyard shifts and all weekends for a month or more at a time?
- How will you handle the least interesting or least pleasant parts of medical school/residency/medical practice?
- What qualities are most important in a physician?
- What makes you think you can memorize the mass of information needed to complete medical school?
- Have you ever noticed negative aspects of doctors with whom you have come in contact?
- What negative aspects do you see to pursuing a medical career?

26. How will you finance your medical education?

This question is one most prospective medical students must carefully consider. The only people exempt from this concern are the approximately twenty percent of medical students who can finance their education without loans, grants, scholarships, or otherwise mortgaging their future by obligating themselves to working in specific locations or specialties. (See chapter 18, *Financial Information,* for additional advice.) Unless you are one of these fortunate few, your medical education will be one of the biggest expenses you ever incur—for most students, it will certainly be the biggest so far in their lives. Medical school faculty are well aware of this and want to be sure that you have carefully considered the amount and type of debt you may incur. *Note, however, that admission decisions are not made on the basis of financial need, but rather on merit.* Interviewers may also be interested in how savvy you are about the complicated financial system, and may even want to give you a few tips—especially if they see you as an excellent candidate.

- Did you know that you'll be over $150,000 in debt when you begin residency?
- What income do physicians have? Is that appropriate?

27. Why should we take you in preference to the other applicants?

Danger! This is one of those questions designed to quickly lead you down the garden path to disaster.

What is your first response? Most students would attempt to defend themselves against attack by trying to compare themselves favorably with other applicants they either know or imagine. Wrong move!

Start by acknowledging that you do not make the decision about who gets into medical school. State that you are not qualified to make that type of decision. In addition, acknowledge that there are, undoubtedly, many good applicants applying to the school. Then, state that you can really only describe your own qualities and ask the interviewer if he or she would like you to do just that. If the answer is yes, you have an excellent opportunity to tout your best qualities and finest achievements. Obviously, to answer the interviewer's initial question, you should stress those qualities that distinguish you from other applicants. Concentrate on some of the areas mentioned previously—your *energy level*, your *desire to do and to learn*, and your *ability to get along with others* under all circumstances. Never disparage other applicants. Only stress your own excellence.

- What can you add to a medical school class?
- What computer experience do you have?
- What are some of the qualities a good physician should possess? Do you possess them?
- How will your background in (major or career) be of any use in medicine?
- If you were on our admission committee, what would you look for in a candidate?
- Why should I tell the admission committee to pick you?
- If we had one spot left in the class, what one of your attributes qualifies you more than any other candidate?
- What makes you unique?
- Give me your sales pitch.

28. I don't think you'd be right for this medical school/a medical career.

Medicine has some pretty crass folks populating its ranks, but very few would actually invite you for an interview and really mean it when they tell you that you would not be right for their school, much less a medical career.

If you are told this, recognize it for the ploy that it is. It is meant to fluster and confuse an applicant. A rather nasty maneuver, used only by cruel interviewers, it can easily be sidestepped if you recognize it and remain calm. This is a statement that can only be answered successfully with a question. That question is, "Why do you say that?"

If you come out swinging to defend yourself, you lose. Put the interviewer on the defensive by asking your question in your nicest, most polite manner. This will throw him or her off guard, and you might even receive an apology.

- Describe the ideal medical school curriculum.
- With your obvious (musical, artistic, literary, etc.) talents, why are you pursuing a medical career?
- Montana . . . Hmm . . . Isn't that where the Unabomber lived?
- I see that neither of your parents graduated from high school. What does that say about your genetic background?
- How would you contribute to this school's glorification?

29. What is your energy level like?

Although this may be an interviewer's standard question, watch out. Some only ask it of applicants who demonstrate diminished energy levels during their interviews. This is the time to appear animated. If you feel yourself fading, pump out a little more adrenaline and beef up your act. If you can't do it now, what will your performance be like at 3 A.M. while you are on call with a ward team?

A question about your energy level must be answered with an enthusiastic "Very high." A very brief anecdote of just how high it is would be appropriate. An example might be, "I was able to work thirty hours a week while maintaining a full course load—including labs." Try to make your anecdote relate to work, school, volunteer activities, or all three.

- How many hours of sleep do you require each night?
- How well do you function without adequate sleep?

30. How well do you function under pressure?

Every physician, at one time or another, has practiced medicine under pressure. Some specialties have frequent stressors, and the physicians in them seem to thrive under this stress. Asking you about your performance under stress is, therefore, a natural question. The interviewer wants to know two things. First, have you thought about the pressures inherent in medical school education, residency training, and medical practice? And second, are you up to them?

The best way to answer is to cite specific examples of your past performance under stress. Personal (and poignant?) stories work well here. Be sure that the examples, however, do not show that the stress resulted from your negligence, procrastination, or obstinacy. Assure the interviewer that you are up to medicine's challenges.

A potential curve ball here may be a secondary question dealing with the administrative stressors brought on by government and third-party payer interference with medical practice. This question may be raised because it is constantly, and annoyingly, on many practitioners' minds. If this topic is introduced, either state that you are certain that you will learn to handle these problems during your training, or respond by simply asking the interviewer "What are the biggest problems you are facing in this area?" In all likelihood, the interviewer will be pleased to speak about the subject at length. Be a good listener.

- How do you handle stress?
- Can you handle stress without the resources you are accustomed to relying on?
- When was the last time you cried?
- Have you ever faced death? How did you handle it?

31. Tell me about the patient from whom you learned the most.

If you have had any patient-contact clinical experience, whether it was volunteer or paid, you can expect this question. This question is a favorite of elderly professors, as well as smarter young interviewers. It examines your medical knowledge, your insight into the patient's condition, your ability to think quickly, your attitude toward medicine and learning, and your compassion. If an interviewer asks this question, the balance of the interview will remain on the same topic. How, then, should you approach it?

To be able to answer this question satisfactorily, you must prepare at least two patients' cases in advance. Try to choose examples in which you understood at least some of the issues, such as with a patient in a great deal of pain or one at the end of his life. Select patients you cared for or with whom you spoke at length (or spoke with the family). If they had specific diseases or injuries, read about them in depth. If they presented specific issues, such as using an advance directive or refusing care, read something about that, too.

What did you learn from these patients? Was it just the nature of the disease? Normally, this will not be enough. Did you learn something about physicians' limitations, the patient's fears and perceptions of the medical system, or the workings of the health care system itself? If you did, be prepared to say so. Also, if you have an opportunity to get follow-up information on the patient, so much the better. Following up on interesting patients demonstrates both a concern for them and your excitement in learning.

If you have prepared for this question and have begun to answer it appropriately, the interviewer may interrupt you with a "war story" of his or her own. Sit back, listen, and enjoy. You did just fine.

- What were your most memorable experiences in college?

- Tell me about the non-physician health care provider who most influenced you.

32. What is your greatest fear about practicing medicine?

If you don't have some fears about eventually taking responsibility for your patients' welfare and sometimes their lives, you're a fool and no one wants you practicing medicine. But, of course, you do have trepidation. Is four years (or in some cases less) of medical schooling enough? Will you be good enough to take on this responsibility and do a great job? Will you be able to fulfill your role as a physician and a spouse/parent?

All physicians have some of these fears. Expressing them only shows that you know something about a medical career and are exploring your role within the profession. It may be difficult to fill the shoes of the great clinicians about whom you have read, and those you know and will get to know while in medical school and residency. Tell the interviewer your fears, and explain that you know every physician has questioned him- or herself the same way. Then state that you are up to the challenge.

- How do you feel about treating AIDS patients? Patients with Ebola virus?

33. Where do you see yourself in five (ten) years?

Some realism, in addition to reviewing the medical school's mission (in their catalog and other documents), is required to answer this question. The questioner is attempting to find out if you have some life goals—and if these are consistent with the training that the school offers.

Have you looked beyond your existence as a student? Do you envision a high-powered career in clinical research? Or a family practice at a rural or remote location? Are you equipped intellectually and emotionally to do either of these? Is this medical school designed to prepare you for the career you desire?

Incongruent goals stem from your evaluation of either your own abilities or the medical school's goals and mission. Medical school deans (including the Dean of Admissions) and most of the faculty usually have at least a general vision of what they would like most of their graduates to do with their careers. They want your goals to be consistent with those of the school. This is beneficial to both you and them. If a school's curriculum has been designed primarily to produce primary care physicians, students who hope to become academic or research gurus will be very disappointed, and so will the school's faculty.

You should have previously analyzed the school's written materials. Do they promote goals consistent with your personal goals? If the two widely diverge, perhaps you should consider looking elsewhere. Do not, however, be too certain about your final career direction. Many, if not most, students significantly change their career orientation during or shortly after training. This should not upset you. It is a normal part of learning and maturation. So answer this question by giving a general response while listening to the interviewer. Try to understand the diversity of learning experiences that exist within the school's curriculum. Leave enough latitude in your reply, however, to allow for other possibilities in your future. Also, always phrase your answer so that it illustrates that your decision may change with training, experience, and age.

- In ten years, in what specialty and under what circumstances will you be practicing? Who will be paying for your services?

- Draw a picture of yourself in ten years.

34. How do you see the delivery of health care evolving in the twenty-first century?

This can be a very tricky question. It tests your knowledge of current events and politics, as well as your humility in recognizing that you do not have the ultimate answer. The interviewer, though, may think that he or she does. Only people who already have definite opinions about the trends in health care will ask this question. They actually may want to use it as a jumping-off point from which to expostulate on their pet theories. People like to hear themselves talk. If you give an interviewer a chance to say what is on his or her mind while you appear interested, you will do just fine.

The strategy for you is to give a broad answer to the initial question, such as "I expect that there will be numerous changes, not only in the way medicine is practiced, but also in the way it is paid for." You can go on to add that you do not have any definitive answers. This will give the interviewer a chance to jump in and give you either the lecture that was lying in wait, or at least some definite hints as to what he or she is thinking. You do not want to stick your neck out without some guidance.

This question is probably the closest that you will get to a direct inquiry about your political views, which is illegal to ask of medical school applicants (and in pre-employment questioning). Listen closely, nod your head a lot, and do not go out on a limb without some support. If you want some solid background, read *Physicians for the Twenty-First Century*, published by the AAMC. (See the *Annotated Bibliography*.)

- Is health care a right or a privilege?

- What are your thoughts on Naturopaths and herbal medicine?

- How do you think a socialized medical system will affect medical progress?

- If you were made King of the United States, what one thing would you change about health care delivery? Why?

- What is managed care? HMOs? PPOs? Capitation?

- What is the biggest challenge facing health care delivery?

- What does "a cross-cultural approach to healing" mean?

- What will you do as a physician to curb the rising costs of medicine?

- What is the nurse's role and how much responsibility should a nurse be given for patient care?

- Where does the money go in a prepaid medical system?

- What recent newsworthy medical event or announcement would you like to discuss?

- What is your least healthy personal habit?

- What is the solution to the health care crisis?

- What do you think is the number one issue in medicine today?

35. If a patient just stabbed your best friend . . . ?

A favorite question of many interviewers is the ethics scenario. In virtually all cases, it involves a situation in which there is no "correct" answer. However, as with all ethics questions, there are wrong answers.

The key to answering this question appropriately (the question itself is usually, "What would you do?") is to tell the interviewer that you need a moment to think about it. Then formulate at least one answer that does not violate your personal values. Relate this to the interviewer. It is best if you do not give responses based upon your religion. Generalities, such as protecting patient autonomy or avoiding paternalism, work best. (If you don't understand these concepts, you may want to check out *Ethics in Emergency Medicine*, which has both general discussions of these concepts and discussions of interesting illustrative cases. See *Annotated Bibliography*.)

Do not appear dogmatic; state that you are sure that there are other possible options. The interviewer may want to discuss the problem. If so, listen to the options presented and discuss them. Do not argue! Try to see the interviewer's point of view, but do not escalate the discussion into a religious debate or a shouting match. There's an old saying which suggests that one should never discuss religion or politics with friends, or you are bound to lose them. That applies just as well to medical school interviewers.

Nearly all medical schools report that their interviewers ask applicants "opinion-type" questions.

- What would you do if the housestaff at the medical school's hospital had a "job action" (strike)?

- What would you do if you saw another medical student, a resident, or a physician snorting cocaine at a nightclub? While doing clinical work?

- What do you think about using animals in medical research and teaching?

- Should physicians be involved in assisted suicide or active euthanasia?

- What ethical questions will the health-care-delivery system face in the future?

- Should applicants who say they don't want to treat (AIDS, hepatitis B, life-threatening plague, etc.) patients be admitted to medical school?

- What would you do if you knew that someone in your class was cheating on an exam?

- Is health care rationing ethical?

- Would you treat a colleague and a patient, each coming to you with an unwanted pregnancy, differently?

- How would you respond if a resident or a colleague wanted to keep a therapeutic error a secret from a patient and the patient's family?

- What do you think of hospitals that refuse admission to patients without insurance?

36. What do you think of what is happening in the (economy, Middle East, Congress)?

This question examines whether you have pulled your head out of your textbooks in the past several years. It's wise to prepare for it by reading weekly news magazines for a month or two prior to the interview season. It is also prudent to read the newspaper and, if possible, watch the morning news on the day of your interview. As for the question itself, hope that it is on a relatively innocuous subject. If not, don't antagonize the interviewer by giving a polarized viewpoint. Try to take a balanced view—looking at both sides of the issue, e.g., "on the one hand . . . , but on the other hand . . ." This shows that you do not have your head in the sand and that you are a diplomat—both desirable qualities.

- What was the last non-textbook you read?

- Are physicians doing enough to improve public health policies?

- Are physicians doing enough for women's issues?

- What do you think is the largest problem facing American society on a state-wide or a national basis?

37. Teach me something not related to your school work in five minutes.

This is now the "question" I use most often. It shows me a great deal about applicants, including how well many of them think on their feet. It is also more fun to start off an interview this way rather than with many of the routine questions most interviewers ask.

With this directive, applicants have a marvelous opportunity to discuss something in which they are an expert—and the interviewer has guaranteed that he or she will pay rapt attention. Pick a topic that you know really well and that you can explain a small piece of to a novice in five minutes.

But which topic is best? Is it something about your hobby, something unique you learned in childhood, something from a previous job, or something truly different, such as a lesson you learned through a difficult experience? The solution here is to pick a topic that will interest listeners, that fascinates you, and that can be successfully taught in the allotted time. Among the topics applicants have discussed are how to tie fishing lures, how to write a simple computer program, how to select a ripe melon, and how to load a pack horse. I didn't always understand them, but they were always interesting. Often this directive leads naturally to further questions about the topic, the circumstances in which the subject was learned, and about the applicant.

Many applicants and interviewers find this the best, and most productive, interview question.

- Without using your hands, tell me how to tie a shoelace.
- How are art and medicine similar?
- What is "beauty"?
- Why are manhole covers round?
- Give an example of a problem you solved and describe how you went about solving it.

38. Where else have you interviewed?

This is many interviewers' favorite question. Don't become paranoid when you hear it. In most cases, they are not trying to test your interview choices. They are doing two things.

First, they are determining whether you have selected enough medical schools to have a reasonable shot at getting into one of them. (If you are an outstanding applicant and only apply to one or two state schools, this might be acceptable.)

And second, they may want to find out current information about other medical schools and their interview/application procedures. Often, you are the best available source of information about other medical schools. Interviewers will be interested in pumping you for facts. Give them what they want. Tell them about what is going on in the places you visited. If you just do not remember some of the specifics about these schools, be honest enough to say so. The interviewer will appreciate this. Be enthusiastic. But, as mentioned before, under no circumstances should you say anything derogatory about another school. If you say negative things about other schools to this interviewer, what will you say about his school when you go elsewhere? Negative comments are a sign of immaturity. Avoid them.

39. What if you don't get into medical school?

Okay. Now let's see you sweat a little. This question has become more frequent as the number of applicants has increased. If you are not prepared for it, you may internalize it and consider that it is a backhanded way of suggesting that you had better make other plans, since you won't be getting into (at least this) medical school. Keep cool. That is not usually why interviewers ask applicants this question.

The interviewer is trying to determine whether you have had the foresight to plan for contingencies. Planning ahead says something about your personality. These days, not making alternative plans when applying to medical school is just plain foolish. And people who do foolish things with their lives are not the people these schools look for as students. Interviewers would like you to mention alternative plans that include what you will do for the next year if you don't get in this year.

40. Can you think of anything else you would like to add?

The answer to this question should always be "Yes." If the interviewer has neglected any critical area that further explains your qualifications for medical school, mention it now. Even if everything was covered, use this opportunity to give a summary of your sales pitch.

This is an alternate form of the frequent query, "Do you have any (other) questions?" that can be positioned at either the beginning or the end of the interview. It can also be a disaster at the end of a long interview day when you are tired, hungry, and sleepy. The wimpy response, "No, I think all of my questions have been answered," is not likely to score very many points with an interviewer.

Even if prior interviewers have already answered all your questions, ask one of them again. It is very useful to take this opportunity to confirm or clarify information that you consider important. You might also raise a point that demonstrates your knowledge about the school. For example, ask "How will the school's new problem-based-learning curriculum affect medical students' clinical abilities?" In any event, do not leave the interviewer in the lurch when you are given an opportunity to ask a final question.

- Is there anything else I should know about you?

Illegal Questions

Interviewers continue to ask many applicants, especially women, blatantly illegal questions (figures 25.1 and 25.2). In a recent survey, one-third of all medical school students reported being asked illegal questions during their medical school interviews. One applicant reports receiving a letter from a large medical school *before* she interviewed "apologizing for anything said in the interview" and stressing that it did "not reflect the school's beliefs." Those most commonly asked are about marriage and family plans. Indeed, asking women about childbearing and child care is the most common gaffe interviewers make. Besides implicitly asking whether a woman has children, this assumes that she must be the sole person responsible for making child care arrangements. (Also, a few "dinosaur" interviewers still exist who think that if a female applicant inquires about the provisions for maternity leave, she should be written off as not being a serious candidate.)

The physically disabled are also frequently asked illegal questions. While applicants may be asked about their ability to satisfy essential requirements (as determined by the school and published), the Americans with Disabilities Act allows interviewers to ask these questions of the disabled only if all applicants are asked the same questions. Also, even if an applicant has a visible disability, such as using a wheelchair, a cane, or a guide dog, or has voluntarily disclosed his or her disability, interviewers may not ask about its nature or severity, the condition causing the disability, the prognosis, or treatments. An increasing number of lawsuits are being filed by disabled medical school applicants so, hopefully, interviewers will become better-informed about what constitutes illegal questions.

The same rules apply to both privately and publicly funded medical schools.

Since applicants are apparently still being asked illegal questions (why this is allowed to continue is uncertain), it is important for you to be prepared for these questions.

Figure 25.1: Illegal Questions—Sex Discrimination

1. What was your maiden name?

2. Do you wish to be addressed as Miss? Mrs.? or Ms.?

3. Are you married? Single? Divorced? Separated? A single parent?

4. I notice that you are wearing an engagement ring. When are you going to be married?

5. What is your spouse's name? What does (s)he do for a living?

6. How does your spouse feel about your having a medical career?

7. Do you believe medical students should have to use birth control?

8. Are you planning to have children? Anytime soon?

9. How will you take care of your children while you are at school?

How Should You React To Illegal Questions?

How *should* you respond to illegal questions? This can be very tricky. There are several possible ways to respond.

First, *answer* the question in the most favorable manner possible. This is the most politic thing to do and will not eliminate you from the pool of potential applicants to that school. Most applicants take this tack, both in the medical field and in other situations. You can use either direct or indirect answers. For example, when asked about plans for a family and children, a candidate may answer "I plan to have children near the end of my residency." Since you might find this option distasteful, you could use an indirect answer, such as "My training comes first." If you already have children, you might directly address the interviewer's concerns by stating that your past performance demonstrates that your family responsibilities do not detract from your work. These answers will not usually jeopardize your chance of obtaining a medical school slot. Directly answering such questions may be preferable to saying "I prefer not to answer," since, just as they do when someone invokes his Fifth Amendment rights, listeners will often infer the most negative response. Also, the interviewer probably does not even realize that he (or she) is being sexist and is violating both federal and state civil rights codes.

You may not, however, want to answer such questions, either because of the nature of your response or because your principles just will not allow it. You then have three choices. The first, which will still permit you to remain a viable applicant, is to *finesse* the question. One way to do this is to laughingly ask whether the answer to the question, or the question itself, is relevant to being a medical student. If you do this lightly, the interviewer, who has probably been poorly prepared to do this type of interviewing, will be able to back off and save face at the same time. However, finessing a question must be handled with skill. Smile and be very pleasant while you parry pointed questions. If you handle it correctly, you will still be a viable candidate for the school. But if you derisively ask whether the question is relevant, or simply state that the question is illegal (your second choice), you will be on the interviewer's black list. Don't plan on getting into that medical school—feistiness is fine, impertinence is not.

Figure 25.2: Other Questions—Legal and Illegal Forms

Legal Form	**Illegal Form**
1. How well can you handle stress?	1. Does stress ever affect your ability to be productive?
2. Are you currently using illegal drugs?	2. What medications do you currently use?
3. Do you drink alcohol?	3. How much alcohol do you drink per week?
4. Do you have 20/20 corrected vision?	4. What is your corrected vision?
5. Can you perform as a student with or without reasonable accommodations?	5. Would you need reasonable accommodations to perform as a student or physician?
6. How many days were you absent from school last year?	6. How many days were you sick last year?

Adapted from: Equal Employment Opportunity Commission. *Enforcement Guidance on Pre-Employment Disability-Related Inquiries.* Washington, DC: GPO, May 1994.

Another option is to *refuse* to answer the query, perhaps stating that it is illegal to ask it or that it is none of the interviewer's business. Such an answer, however, while it is perfectly correct and legitimate, may ensure that you will not be admitted to that medical school. You may also report such illegal questions to the admission office (while you are still at the school) and ask for an alternate interviewer. Nearly all schools have a provision for this.

But if, as a result of answering such questions, you do not get in and you still want to go to that school, you have the option of taking legal action against it for violating your civil rights (your third choice). Such action has been successful in the business world many times. It is only a matter of (a short) time until these suits become frequent in the medical community. In fact, they may become commonplace enough that there will be much tighter control over the entire interview process in order to avoid legal entanglements.

Still, you should relax when confronted with these illegal and uncomfortable questions. This will yield the best results.

26: Waiting For, Choosing Among, And Accepting Offers

When the gods wish to punish us
they answer our prayers.

Oscar Wilde, *An Ideal Husband*

Waiting—The Hardest Part

NOW YOU MUST WAIT. Make sure that the medical schools you have applied to can contact you. If you must be away from the address and phone numbers you gave them, arrange for someone who knows how to reach you to pick up your mail and listen to your messages. If this is impossible, contact the schools by telephone and in writing to give them your new contact information. I don't know of any students who have actually lost regular acceptances to a medical school because they couldn't be contacted, but some came awfully close. (I do, however, know of students who missed getting first-week-of-medical-school-replacement positions because the school could not find them.)

If you are put on a school's waiting list, continue to communicate with their admission office so that they know you are interested. Carefully look through all their materials to find out how interested they are in receiving additional information, calls, and letters about current activities from students on their waiting list. Some schools are quite interested, but a minority say that they don't want to hear from these applicants. In some cases, your premed adviser can find out for you. Many schools keep track of these contacts. Even if you don't get accepted this time around, they may place you high on their list next year when you re-apply.

Most medical students, and of course all applicants who were not accepted, have experienced the anguish of receiving rejection letters. Dr. Robert Marion eloquently described his own experience in *Learning to Play God* (p. 8):

> Rejection letters are easy to spot in the mail. Painfully thin, the envelopes contain just a single sheet of stationery: "After careful consideration of your application," the letters all read, "we regret to inform you that we cannot offer you a place in our medical school class." Regardless of the reasons listed for the rejection, my reaction to these letters was always the same: first a queasiness would develop in the pit of my stomach, then an ache would begin in the front of my head, followed finally by the feeling that I'd had the wind knocked out of me. It got so bad that by February the queasiness began almost as soon as I saw the mailman coming down the street.

Another student said of the mailman, "I think the he got sick of my asking him to be sure there weren't College of Medicine letters for me that had fallen on the floor of his truck."

While you wait to hear if you have been chosen, be sure that you also investigate alternative activities you can do during the next year—if you don't get accepted this time around.

A few students on the waiting list won't hear that they have been accepted until the first week of medical school. If a student just doesn't show up, they may contact the next person still on their list and offer them the position. This happens to probably only twenty or thirty students a year—but if they can be flexible and quickly join their classes, it's like striking gold.

Early-Decision Programs (EDP)

Some students don't have to go through the agonizing spring ritual of waiting to hear from medical schools—they already have their acceptance letters. Most medical schools have programs to accept well-qualified applicants by October 1. These are called Early-Decision Programs (EDP). In the 1996-97 academic cycle, 93 schools had such programs (see figure 15.2). Each school's listing in the AAMC *Medical School Admission Requirements* or the AACOM's *Osteopathic Medical College Information* states whether it offers an EDP.

Since participating medical schools accept only a small percentage of their students through EDP, only the most highly qualified students should use this mechanism. If you fall into this category and are willing to accept the rules that govern the program, however, it can markedly reduce the anxiety of waiting through many more months to hear from medical schools.

The rules for participating in an EDP are straightforward.

- The applicant may apply to only one U.S. medical school (AMCAS- or non-AMCAS-participating).

- The EDP deadline for AMCAS-participating schools to receive all application materials and transcripts is August 1. Dates for non-AMCAS schools are listed in the AAMC *Medical School Admission Requirements*. For Osteopathic medical schools, contact the school for the information.

- The school notifies applicants whether they have been accepted by October 1.

- If accepted into a school through the EDP, students agree to attend that school.

- Students may apply to other medical schools if:

    they receive an EDP rejection,
    they receive a formal (written) release from their EDP commitment, or
    the October 1 deadline for notification has passed.

About half of all students who apply through EDP get accepted into medical school through the program. If an EDP applicant fails to get accepted to the medical school to which he or she has applied, that applicant is automatically placed in the school's regular applicant pool and may then apply to other schools as well. Such applicants will still have time to apply to other schools; medical schools intentionally set their regular admission deadlines after October 1 to attract these very desirable applicants.

Acceptance Letters

Dates Schools Accept Applicants

Medical schools accept applicants on a variety of schedules. Some send out initial acceptances following each batch of applicant interviews. Others have fixed dates when they send acceptances. Keep a log in the file with your Must/Want Analyses of information about the various school's acceptance schedules. You can find these dates in the AAMC's and AACOM's books, as well as on AMCAS-E and AACOMAS By Computer.

The only constant is that May 15 is, for virtually all applicants, the "day of reckoning." All medical schools have agreed to have a final list of students on this date. Most conform to this schedule. Many schools use this date to send out rejection letters and to notify students who are on their waiting lists that they still have a chance.

Prior to this, admission offices normally send out letters only to students who have been offered admission but who have not yet made up their minds about either where to go or whether to go to medical school at all. Called the "fish-or-cut-bait" letter by some Deans, it informs the applicants that unless they notify the school that they accept the proffered position by a certain date, the slot will be given to someone else. (Many applicants don't realize that each M.D. school's admission office has a list of all the students the other schools have accepted. So they know what choices you have to make.)

The Letter

Acceptance letters are nearly always sent with the U.S. Post Office's "return-requested" notice attached. If you see a letter from one of "your" medical schools in the mailbox before mid-May, it probably contains good news. Congratulations! Rejoice!

Occasionally, the postal service fails to deliver (literally). This can lead to some interesting interactions when an admission officer finally does contact the applicant.

One student, who was applying for her second time, didn't respond to a letter of acceptance. The admission office knew this applicant well, since she had badgered them with questions about whether her material had arrived, when she would show up for interviews, and where she was on the waiting list. Yet when they finally sent an acceptance letter, there was only silence. Rather than sending another letter, the staff did something they rarely do. They called the student's home. She answered the phone. When they asked why she hadn't responded to the acceptance letter, the staff members only heard five minutes of screaming. When she finally calmed down, she gasped that she had never received it, but would be at the office within thirty minutes to get a copy and to personally respond. The staff thanked her, but said that her acceptance had to be in writing. Less than twenty minutes later, she appeared with a signed letter accepting the position.

Another student, who did not receive his acceptance letter either, was so overjoyed when he heard (by phone) that he had been accepted that he rushed right down to the admission office with his entire family and had everyone pose with him and his family for some "candid" pictures.

You're Accepted. What Now?

You are overjoyed by your acceptance to medical school and you want to call the school. Fine, they'll appreciate basking in your bliss. Just calling, however, won't suffice. Sit down and write an acceptance letter to the Dean of Admissions. Specify not only that you accept the position, but also include contact addresses and phone numbers for the time remaining until you begin medical school. If they have asked for any additional information, send it with this letter or tell them when you will send it.

This is an important letter, but you *don't* have to send it overnight mail; the school can wait a few days to hear from you. If you are accepted before April 15, you generally have at least two weeks in which to notify the medical school whether or not you accept their offer. After April 15, they may ask you to respond to them more quickly. Do, however, send you response by certified mail, with a receipt-requested card. That way you'll know that they have received it. If you don't get the receipt card back in ten days, call them to find out if they got your letter.

They may require a deposit to hold your place. According to the rules U.S. M.D.-granting schools have agreed to, this should not be more than $100, and generally it is far less. This deposit should be fully refundable, in case you change your mind about going to that school, until May 15, although some schools use cutoffs as early as March 1. Some schools, including those in Canada, generally refund the deposit even later. Schools requiring a nonrefundable payment before May 1 to hold a place include: Howard ($150), Wayne State ($50), Ponce ($1,000), Medical University of South Carolina ($50). A number of others require large payments by May 15. Osteopathic medical schools require a deposit up to $1,000 to hold a spot. Often, most or all of this is nonrefundable.

After you have written your letter to the school, take another look at the letter they sent to you. Now, read the fine print. *Most acceptance letters say that you are admitted as long as you continue to perform as well as you have in the past.* Unfortunately, each year some students, once they get accepted to medical school, "blow off" the rest of their courses. They're in, right? Wrong! If you fail a course or otherwise show that you have done poorly in this last school term, the medical school can and will withdraw the acceptance. They don't like to do it and students don't like to receive this news. As one student who didn't understand this said,

> I applied and was accepted the spring before medical school started. I had previously gotten my degree, but to remain intellectually stimulated, I had enrolled in a class as a non-degree graduate student. After I got accepted, I was no longer interested in going to school for the next few months, so I failed the class. As required, I had to report my grade to the medical school's admission office. The committee re-reviewed my application packet and withdrew my acceptance. I was appalled that I could have such a short medical school career—accepted in February and kicked out in April— before I ever started class! This was amazingly stressful, disconcerting, and a very hard way to learn that admission committees are serious about passing *all* courses. [This student applied again several years later, was accepted, and actually matriculated into medical school.]

The key is to keep on plugging along—in an acceptable manner—until you finish school.

How To Deal With Multiple Acceptances

Some applicants are in the enviable positions of having to choose among several schools to which they have been accepted. If you have used the Must/Want Analysis to select schools, you have a good basis for choosing the school that's best for you. Additionally, you may want to consider the availability of financial assistance at each school. (Each school will probably offer you a different amount and selection of financial aid, depending upon their resources and the class composition.)

Schools must give you at least two weeks to decide whether you will accept their offer. You are not obligated to accept a medical school slot just because it is offered to you (unless you are accepted in an early-decision program). Under AAMC rules, after May 15 medical schools may require applicants to decide whether they accept the school's offer of acceptance within less than two weeks.

Since medical schools have different schedules, you may get your first acceptances from schools you find less appealing rather than from the one where you would prefer to go. (Some well-known schools were, at least for a time, notorious for sending out acceptance letters very late, causing a flurry of withdrawals from other schools. Hopefully, this crass behavior is a thing of the past.)

It's always best to accept the "bird in the hand." *Accept the first offer you get, no matter how the school ranked on your list.* If you later also get accepted by a school higher on your list, quickly send polite and professional letters (1) withdrawing your acceptance to the first school, (2) withdrawing your application from schools lower on your list, and, of course, (3) accepting the second (higher-rated) school's offer. Continue this process until either you don't get any further acceptances or your first-choice school offers you a position. Don't procrastinate about making a decision while holding two or more acceptances. This isn't fair to the schools or to the other applicants hoping to get a position. Anyway, if you have used the Must/Want Analysis, it won't be necessary.

Deferred Acceptances

Some medical schools allow students are who are accepted to postpone their medical education. This is called a "deferred acceptance." Although students give a variety of reasons for postponing medical school, most admission officers believe that the primary reason is usually that the students are not sure they want to make the commitment. This is borne out by the relatively high percentage of these students who never do go to medical school.

Figure 15.3 lists the U.S. and Canadian medical schools that will consider requests for deferred admission. There is no uniform policy among schools regarding deferred acceptance; deferrals are generally granted on a case-by-case basis. Some schools, for example, will not allow deferrals for students who were accepted from their waiting list. Most schools that accept deferrals will defer matriculation for only one year. Some schools, however, such as Yale, Johns Hopkins, New York Medical College, and the University of Pennsylvania, have occasionally granted longer deferrals.

If you are accepted to a medical school that allows individuals to defer their starting date, find out the specific rules involved. There are two types of deferrals granted, and students usually must specify, in writing, which method they intend to use. The first type is a deferral granted with the understanding that you will "re-apply" only to that school and that you will automatically be accepted. "Re-applying" usually means resubmitting only the basic uniform application the school uses so that you are in the national computer system for that year. The schools may also want a summary of what you have done since you last applied. In general, however, this type of deferral allows you to be admitted to the school with only a pro forma application procedure.

With the second type of deferral, you specify that you intend to repeat the entire application process at multiple schools, taking your chances as you did the first time you applied. Essentially, you decline the school's offer to accept you as a student. Only choose this method if you are sure you don't want to be a physician or if you have a solid reason to believe that you can be admitted to a "better" medical school the next time around. This is a very risky game to play if you want to go to medical school, although as the following story from a current medical student shows, it sometimes succeeds.

I was accepted to a medical school during my senior year of college. But my boyfriend of four years had been at the U of W as an undergraduate the whole time I was at Notre Dame. He wasn't' graduating until a semester after me. So when I didn't get into U of W as a senior, I had to decide if I would go to the school that accepted me or risk re-applying to the U of W. I followed my heart and moved to be with him, worked for a year, and had to re-apply to both schools. (I couldn't defer at the other one). It was a little scary, and people doubted me. But I was accepted at both schools the next year, and now we are engaged and get to stay together. Anyway, my adviser said that the school that let me in wouldn't let me in a second time. But, because I was honest and had really benefited from the year off, I was only a better candidate the next year and they realized that. So don't always trust the advice of those who say they know what they are doing. (I am sure you don't want to put that in the book.)

In 1996, Cornell University Medical College made headlines when they "bumped" students because they had accepted too many. Of the 249 applicants they accepted into their first-year class, 119 said they would enter Cornell. This was a far higher percentage than in prior years. Unfortunately, they could only accommodate 104 students. Cornell began offering incentives to any 15 applicants who accepted their offer of admission, but for whom they did not have room in their first-year class. Those students willing to wait a year to enter were offered one year's tuition, a guaranteed spot in the 1997 class, and inexpensive (for New York City) student housing immediately. Most students didn't think Cornell's offer was worth the delay. (Financially, it certainly wasn't.)

Changing Your Mind

It may be hard for those who are struggling to get into medical school to believe, but every year, more than 1,000 students who have been accepted to U.S. M.D.-granting medical schools never enter them. Some of these students go to Osteopathic medical schools, and a few have personal or medical tragedies that preclude their ever going to medical school. Most, however, after pursuing what they thought was their dream, simply realize that they do not want a medical career.

Although these students may get grief from their families and friends, they have undoubtedly saved themselves a great deal of anguish by not pursuing a career in which they were not interested. They also have saved many patients the heartache of having a physician who simply "goes through the motions." Although these individuals might have second thoughts about this decision, if they are not firmly and fully committed to a medical career and a physician's life, then the best time to jump ship is before they set out on the very long journey.

Their spots then become available for applicants who are committed to medicine and who desperately want to become physicians. This is truly a win-win situation for all parties.

What Else Do You Need To Do?

Your first responsibility is to keep the school informed about your telephone numbers and your contact address(es)—"snail mail" and e-mail. They will need to send you information about your class's orientation, special summer programs, and curriculum changes. Make sure they can find you.

In addition, you must do two more things so that your school is ready for you: complete various forms and paperwork and arrange to pay for your tuition and other expenses. It is important to complete any forms the school sends you immediately. Imagine, if you will, sitting in class your first day, nervous and hoping that you will do okay, when you are called to the front of the lecture hall to receive papers you didn't complete when they were first sent to you. Embarrassing? You bet! And it doesn't make a great first impression on your teachers.

Now that you have been accepted to medical school, the time has come for you to find out about loans, scholarships, and grants. Shouldn't you have done this before? Of course. But history shows that applicants, especially when applying for the second or third time, neglect the financial forms, believing that it will be okay to complete them after they get accepted into medical school. Usually, they completed all these forms, for naught, the first time they applied, and they aren't that interested in doing it again. Unfortunately, by the time they get accepted and then complete the financial forms, there may be only a few funding options still available to them at many medical schools. And the ones that are left will certainly not be the cheapest. If you are in this position, proceed to the school's financial aid counselor immediately, without passing "Go," to get the best help available.

Have An Alternate Plan

What are you going to do if you don't get into medical school? Every year, nearly two out of three applicants to medical school are rejected. Many of these individuals re-apply in subsequent years and many of them are successful, having "learned the ropes" the first time around (see chapter 10, *Unconventional Premed Students*). Others decide to apply to foreign medical schools, some of which have "rolling" admission policies, so students can be admitted at various times during the year. Most will eventually abandon the effort, however, and go on to other careers within or outside of medicine. (See chapter 28, *Alternatives to Medical School,* for some options you might want to consider.)

You should think hard about the alternatives you have so that you are not "left in the lurch" if you don't get admitted. Several options you may want to consider are

Go To Graduate School

- Do you know what it takes to get in?
- Are you interested in any particular area?
- If you do not subsequently get accepted to medical school (or don't want to re-apply), is this a field that interests you as a career?
- Can you afford to go to graduate school?

Get A Job

- Are you qualified for a job, especially one you would like?
- Are jobs available in your local area or would you have to move?
- Can you get a job in a health-related field if you plan to re-apply?
- Can you afford (financially) to take the job you want?
- Will the job allow you enough time to re-apply if you want to?
- Could this job be a steppingstone to permanent employment if you don't eventually go to medical school?

Other (For The Independently Wealthy Few)

- Travel (especially while volunteering at a remote medical facility)
- Research ("Volunteer" research positions abound at medical centers, especially for those with science degrees. Most people are paid for this, but the pay is usually only the minimum wage unless you have special qualifications.)

A Unique Opportunity

Applicants who fail to get accepted to a medical school and who want to improve their credentials before re-applying should consider The Finch University of Health Sciences'/Chicago Medical School's special one-year program, leading to a Master of Science. This rigorous program includes many of the courses that first-year medical students take. About 70% of this program's students are subsequently accepted into medical school, with about 40% of those entering Chicago Medical School. A few of the best students enter Chicago Medical School with advanced standing, while the others enter at the first-year level.

Rejections And Reapplications

It is said that defeat is a temporary condition. Quitting is the only thing that makes it permanent. Rejection is a part of most medical school applicants' admission process.

Rejections

Two out of every three medical school applicants fail to get into medical school, and nearly all applicants receive at least one rejection letter, even if they do eventually get accepted. (One applicant, who was later accepted somewhere else, was distraught when a medical school sent her two rejection letters—in one month! That's overkill.) Some applicants who are on waiting lists keep their hopes alive. But they finally realize, as the summer drags on, that they will not get in. How does that make them feel? Depressed, anxious about the future, and less confident about themselves. They often go through five stages of "grieving": initial shock, anger and blaming, rationalization, depression, and resolution.

When they experience the initial shock of rejection, it comes like "a hammer blow to the head." For years they have dreamed of entering medical school, and for the past year they have spent lots of time completing forms, taking tests, interviewing, and planning to enter medical school. Now, that dream is gone and they must seek another (at least temporary) path. Often, however, they fail to seek out the help and guidance they need, because they are immobilized by shock, shame, and fear. In the second stage, applicants direct their anger at others, such as the medical schools' admission committees, their premed advisers, or indeterminate "others" who were "unfair," "out to get them," or "prejudiced against [ethnic/religious/racial/geographic group or males/females]." Unfortunately, focusing blame on outside forces only delays the student's assessment of the personal reasons for rejection and their decision to make changes to try again.

Next, applicants rationalize, comparing their traits to those of peers who were accepted. These comparisons are often superficial and focus on only one or two traits in which the rejected applicant is clearly superior. Again, this only delays the day of reckoning that comes with the next stage, depression. In this stage, applicants feel worthless, often wondering why they thought *they* could get into medical school. It's at this stage that many promising applicants give up the dream. If, however, they work through their self-doubts, they (with the help of a good premed adviser, if one is available, or with the support of family and friends) can reassess their strengths and weaknesses, develop an action plan to correct any deficiencies in their applications, and formulate a timeline for reapplication. Whether they give up their dream or re-apply, they have come to resolution. (The personal statements in chapter 13 show that, while some initially "give up" their dream, it sometimes returns later in life.)

Reapplications

If you are not accepted into medical school the first time you apply, you may want to apply again. What makes you think, however, that you will be any more successful the second time around? The answer is that you will know the system a little better, have feedback from some of the schools from which you were rejected to help strengthen your application, and demonstrate commitment to a medical career by re-applying.

Many students who have been accepted to medical school on their second try have commented that they only learned the system during their first application process. Often they did not seek out the necessary information or the people who could have helped guide them successfully through the process on their first try.

If medical schools reject your application the first time you apply, ask them for feedback about your deficiencies and, about how to improve your application. Some medical school admission committees specifically record this information to pass on to rejected applicants if they ask for it. Some medical school admission officers will even counsel rejected students after they complete that year's hectic admissions process. They may suggest improving grades and knowledge in certain areas (perhaps by taking graduate-level courses) or updating information from courses that were taken many years before (normally for older applicants). They often suggest getting more recent or more intense clinical exposure. Occasionally, they may also counsel applicants to improve their interviewing skills and image. (If you got your application in late, you need time-management skills, whether they say so or not.) Occasionally, rejected applicants will be offered a "deal"—acceptance if they fulfill specific criteria, such as passing one or more specific science courses with an "A".

While some medical schools will counsel rejected applicants, the increasing number of applicants has overwhelmed some schools that previously offered this service. If their counsel is not available, seek out a premed adviser who is willing to help you. Since you want to show schools that you have changed (improved) one or more key aspects of your application, get assistance in assessing what factors they may have considered weak. Go through the entire checklist: reasons to be a physician, motivation, MCAT scores, GPA, application process, knowledge about a medical career, and interview style (especially any tendency towards introversion). Examine each aspect for weaknesses, strengths, and areas where you can improve. Simply taking graduate-level courses without a specific plan of action has little value.

Many "second-timers" get accepted to medical schools, as do a few who are applying for the third time or more. This is, in part, not only because they have improved previously cited deficiencies, but also because they have shown commitment to a medical career by sitting out a year or more and still re-applying. This can be both a financial and personal hardship. Committees understand this and often think that if you are still willing to re-apply after a year or more delay, you must be serious about getting in. One older applicant epitomized this attitude when she said, "I was bullheaded and stubborn. I wouldn't go away, so they finally let me in." As another applicant, who (barely) got in on his second attempt, said

> It takes persistence, tenacity, and an uncompromising desire to become a physician. It took me two tries to get in. The second time the door hit me in the butt on the way in—I was number 31 on the waiting list, and they only took 31 students from the list. Once you've decided that medicine is what you want, never give up regardless of how hopeless it seems. The higher the fruit, the sweeter the taste."

If you decide to re-apply and have used a premed office to handle your file, be sure to tell them you are re-applying so that they move your packet to the file for active applicants. Otherwise, it may end up in storage, where it doesn't do you any good.

The large rise in medical school applications seems now to be due to the increased number of individuals who, rejected on their prior attempts, continue to apply to medical schools. Whether or not an applicant reapplies relates directly to the post-rejection support received from family and friends. With this support, applicants will generally re-apply. Since nearly two out of every three applicants is rejected, this is a large group of people. So, how do these folks do if they are accepted?

Studies show that there is no significant difference in the performance in medical school between those who are accepted on their first attempt and those who were initially rejected but eventually got into medical school. Differences between these accepted and initially rejected applicants seemed to rest primarily on admission committee preferences. This reinforces many applicants claim that, at least for those marginal applicants, getting in seems to be a "crap shoot."

Applicants who don't get into medical school seem, for the most part, to go into other non-medical, high-status careers.

27: Getting Ready For Medical School

Thy word is a lamp unto my feet,
and a light unto my path.

Psalms, 119:105

Completing Prerequisites

SOME APPLICANTS, ONCE THEY HAVE BEEN ACCEPTED, still must complete specific prerequisites. This often means successfully completing the current year's course work or degree program. In some cases, it may also mean completing the school's special requirements. Many Canadian schools, for example, require admitted students to complete courses in first aid or cardiopulmonary resuscitation before starting.

Check your acceptance letter and additional materials the school sends you to see if you have any special requirements to fulfill before starting classes.

Preparing Yourself

Time Management

To get as far as you have, you had to learn some good time-management skills. Now you must hone them to a fine point. Medical students cite their lack of time-management skills as one of their biggest, most keenly felt deficiencies. To use your time effectively in medical school, you must learn to:

- Study effectively
- Do multiple activities simultaneously
- Delegate
- Use "to do" lists
- Realistically prioritize your life activities

Study Effectively

You certainly have done well in school and on tests. But do you really use your study time to maximum advantage? How often do you let yourself be interrupted by "little things"? While you are studying, do you suddenly think of that letter you have to write, the phone call you have to make, or a friend you have to visit? You may have gotten away with that behavior as an undergraduate, because the workload is much lighter. Not so in medical school. If you have not learned to concentrate on the task at hand without being interrupted, you will spend many wasted hours at the books—not learning, not relaxing, and not doing anything else that is useful.

To study effectively, find a place where you will have few interruptions Stick to a study schedule (a set amount of time or material to cover) and, most of all, don't allow extraneous thoughts to interrupt your studies (don't daydream or worry).

One common interruption is the telephone. Turn it off while you are studying (or sleeping). One medical student finally realized that it was okay to turn the telephone off for a while, "Since you are not God and She is not likely to call."

Learn To Do Multiple Activities Simultaneously

"Type-A" people often claim that they accomplish so much because they can do several things simultaneously. Often they say that they *must* perform multiple tasks simultaneously to keep from getting bored. Yet these individuals don't actually perform two activities that require concentration at the same time. Instead, they usually skip back and forth between them. A typical example is reading and watching television (not recommended for medical students while studying). What people really do is to read during commercials or when shows run through predictable plot segments. These are people who become easily bored, and they use these "slow" times in one activity to do another.

Another way people do multiple things simultaneously is to consciously interdigitate two or more activities. If you need to go to the laundromat, bring along other things you can accomplish in a noisy, uncomfortable setting with frequent interruptions. Studying won't normally be one of these activities. Rather, this time could be used to write letters, pay bills, and read newspapers or journals. This means that you must think about how much time you will spend at the one activity (washing clothes) and what tasks you need to do that can effectively be done during that time. Sometimes it means putting off some things until they can be done together. People who use time effectively would never just sit and watch their clothes "go through the spin cycle."

Learn To Delegate

Do you have to do everything yourself? No!

You may often feel that if you don't do it yourself, it won't be done right. Being a "control freak," in part, defines the obsessive-compulsive personality of many medical students. The truth is that if you don't do a task yourself it may not be done exactly as you would have done it, but it usually gets done in an acceptable way. Lighten up and learn to let go a little!

Your spouse, significant other, friends, peers, and others are perfectly capable of doing many of the activities you often do. Share the responsibility and let them help. This not only frees up some of your time, but also fosters a sense of community and solidifies relationships.

One caveat about delegating. Some people try to delegate too much. When you need something done only once, you should do it yourself if someone else's doing it will result in an unacceptable delay before it is finished. Also, do it yourself if it will take you at least as much time to explain what you want done as to do the job itself. Examples include typing short letters, faxing documents, or completing forms. However, even if a job takes longer to explain than it takes to do, if it needs to be done frequently, it is worthwhile spending the time to instruct someone else how to do it. Examples of this are balancing the checkbook and buying groceries.

However, be sensitive to the time-pressures and hectic schedules of those around you. Spouses and significant others have their own responsibilities and may not appreciate having all your chores "dumped" on them. Ask gently; don't assume their compliance.

Use "To Do" Lists

People are most often distracted by all the little things that they must do in life but frequently forget. Although it may seem trite, keeping a "to do" list helps you remember, sort, and prioritize these activities. When you suddenly remember (while studying, of course), that you must do something the next day, rather than let it interrupt you or cause you to start obsessing about remembering it tomorrow, simply write it down and continue your present task.

The "to do" list also helps you to effectively use your time when performing multiple activities. By reviewing which activities you have to do and the places you must go, determine how to do them with the least amount of backtracking (even if they are all within a single complex like the medical school). This allows you to maximize the activities you can interdigitate with others. This works especially well when running errands.

Lastly, to avoid worrying about losing all your "to-do" lists, buy a pocket-sized spiral notebook in which to write them all. Cross out items as you do them, discard pages when completed, and occasionally consolidate your lists to a fresh page. This will save you a lot of time, not only by optimizing your schedule, but also by pointing out which activities you didn't have to do in the first place. (These are the items that you have successfully avoided so long that you have "consolidated" them onto your new lists several times.)

Realistically Prioritize Your Life

You only have 24 hours each day. (Even medical students suffer under this natural law.) You cannot, therefore, do everything you want to do. You must decide which activities are most important to you. Prioritizing your life activities is the hardest part of time management. *Realistically, you will have to give up some things to succeed in medical school.* What will they be?

First, make a list of the things you do now and expect to continue doing while in medical school. Also list the things you expect to begin doing. An example of one student's list is shown (alphabetically) in figure 27.1.

Figure 27.1: Life Activities During Medical School—Example

Attend class
Attend religious services
Exercise
Go to parties
Read magazines
Read novels
Read the newspaper
Spend time with my children
Spend time with my friends
Spend time with my spouse/significant other
Study
Travel
Volunteer clinically
Watch television
Work, part-time

Figure 27.2: Prioritized Life Activities During Medical School—Example

1. Attend class
2. Study
3. Volunteer clinically   **HIGH**
4. Spend time with my spouse/significant other
5. Spend time with my children

6. Work, part-time
7. Spend time with my friends
8. Read the newspaper   **LOWER**
9. Attend religious services
10. Exercise

11. Go to parties.
12. Read magazines.
13. Read novels.   **ELIMINATE**
14. Travel.
15. Watch television.

Next, prioritize the items on your list, as our example student has done (figure 27.2). One excellent rule for prioritization, which this student used, is to highly rank anything that cannot easily be replaced, such as friends and family relationships.

The student in our example eliminated some activities she enjoyed and had commonly done in the past. She loved to read novels and to travel. In high school, she described herself as a "party animal." But medical school takes its toll on personal activities. She had the foresight to make a rational, proactive decision about what was most important to her. This helped her to effectively use her available time. (Yes, she attended a few parties with her class and family during medical school, but these were exceptions, rather than the rule.)

Learning Disabilities

If you have any reason to suspect that you have a reading or test-taking deficiency, get a professional evaluation. There often are resources available at colleges' learning centers.

How do you recognize such a problem? A key signal is that you do markedly worse on standardized tests (such as the MCAT) than would be expected considering your normal course performance. Not that you failed (or you wouldn't have been accepted into medical school). You just didn't score as high as you should have—and there was no reasonable explanation why you did so poorly. (Not studying, being ill, or partying the night before the exam are all good explanations for poor performance.) If you couldn't finish most sections of the MCAT and had to leave many questions blank, you may have a reading problem.

The point is that if you have a learning disability (usually a problem with reading or test-taking—they are often interrelated), the problem won't fix itself. But you can learn how to improve your performance by getting professional assistance.

Even if you have dyslexia, you can be helped to read (and write) better and you won't have much time for this once you are in medical school. Do it now! The most important reason to get help, however, is that you may be required to get it to obtain a medical license. This is because if you have a disability that necessitates your asking for special accommodations to take the USMLE or NBOME licensing exams, the testing agencies will require you to submit documentation of your disability and a personal statement describing the history of your disability. For example, if you have a reading problem, you must have a psychologist's evaluation and letter.

Children

If you have small children while you are in medical school, they will invariably get ill at exam time. Before you start school, it is essential to arrange for baby sitters, qualified and able to care for sick children, who are available on short notice. (Always have back-ups on your list.) Also, find a family physician or pediatrician who can quickly work you into his or her schedule. As a medical student, you will not have time to wait in a doctor's office. (Remember that when you go into practice.) Single mothers have to personally deal with these problems most frequently, but even couples have the same difficulties, since working spouses (and they probably will be working so you can eat) often have less flexibility than medical students do.

Locating Special Resources At School

Dean of Students

The Dean of Students is your contact with the faculty and the medical school's administration. He or she "knows the rules" and will have the most up-to-date information about new school policies, changes in national policies affecting medical students, your professional licensing examinations, and residency matching programs. If you get into academic or other difficulties, this is also the person you will need to see. Find out where the Dean of Students' office is, and if possible, introduce yourself to him or her.

Medical Library

Find out where the school's library is, and what resources they have. Nowadays, they function as learning resource centers and provide not only books and journals, but also videotapes, audiotapes, CD-ROMs, computer programs, and on-line services (including medical database searches). If you don't know how to use these services, ask. The reference librarians will guide you through the learning process and the school's computer gurus will help you learn the vital computer (research and word-processing) skills you will need as a medical student, resident, and practicing physician.

Student Organizations

Every medical school has student organizations. Even though your time is limited, there are several good reasons, including those listed below, for you to participate in at least one of these groups. For a list of medical student organizations, see *Appendix B.*

- *Make a difference in your community.* Many groups do community outreach, run clinics, or assist other agencies in their charity work.

- *Network.* Most organizations provide an opportunity to meet other students, residents, and practicing physicians on both local and national levels. These are ties that can last your entire career.

- *Political action.* Students do have a strong voice on the national medical scene—including at the American Medical Association. See your ideas become national policy and your programs expand far beyond their local areas.

- *Fun.* Working with other professionals can be fun. You will need some "down time," and this is a great opportunity to get it.

Getting Organized At School

Finding A Place To Live

Some schools have dormitories or student housing. Most don't. If you ask, and usually even if you don't, your medical school will send you information about available housing. Schools will also normally include other information about their cities and the surrounding communities. If you want to supplement this information, simply contact that city's Chamber of Commerce or Visitors' Bureau.

Moving To A New City

If you have been accepted at a school far from where you now live, you need to move. Since this may be a new experience for you, and because many students have told me that they got "burned" when using movers, here are some helpful tips for hiring professional movers.

- Before contacting any mover, call your local Better Business Bureau to find out if they have had any complaints lodged against the company you are considering. Beware of fly-by-night movers. The larger national movers have local branches that can help with long-distance moves, and sometimes even local moves. You can contact their national office if things go wrong.

- Get a written estimate from at least three movers. Understand that these estimates come in three forms: *Binding,* in which the price remains fixed once the estimate is signed by both parties; *Non-binding,* in which you can be charged almost any price, and *Not-to-exceed $X,* which sets an upper limit on how much the move will cost. Remember that cheaper doesn't always mean better.

- Get details about any charges not covered by the estimate. These may include packing and unpacking, extra distances from the house or apartment to the truck (on either end of the trip), packing materials, stairs at either end of the move, and insurance.

- Carry any irreplaceable items with you. Do not entrust diplomas and other legal documents, heirlooms, family photographs, jewelry, safe-deposit-box contents, or other highly valued or easily broken items to the movers.

- Get adequate insurance for the possessions you will move. If you have a homeowners' insurance policy, check to see if it covers your possessions while the mover has them. *Basic (interstate) moving insurance* only covers about 50 cents for each pound of material lost. The other options are *full-replacement-value insurance,* which costs about 85 cents per $100 of declared value of your goods; *depreciated-value-of-goods insurance* (what the goods are worth today), which costs about 25 cents per $100 of declared value of your goods; or a *full-*

replacement less-a-deductible insurance policy. This latter is relatively inexpensive, but you must cover the deductible.

- Make a detailed list of all goods moved, including a list of everything in each box. The mover will make his own list of items and note whether furniture is "scratched," "dented," etc. Go over this list with the mover and be certain the items' conditions are correctly stated on his list. Number the boxes so you can see quickly if any are missing. (While it may be a pain, be sure to account for each box or item at the end of the move—before the movers leave.)

- Take photographs of any large or expensive items you must entrust to the movers, such as electronic equipment. Carry these photographs with you.

- Carry contact numbers for your mover's dispatcher so you can locate your truck when it is delayed. (The frequent-mover's law: Never expect the moving truck to arrive when scheduled.)

In The New City

Once you are in a new city, here are some things you should do:

- Notify the Department of Motor Vehicles of your new address or get the information to obtain a driver's license and to register your car in the new state.

- Register to vote.

- Call the Sanitation Department to find out when the trash will be picked up.

- Transfer any insurance policies to agents in your new community.

- Find a new bank and open an account.

- Find baby-sitters and day care for children.

- Check out nearby grocery stores, dry cleaners, gas stations, and drug stores now. You probably won't have a lot of time after you start school. Check with the Dean of Students' office for information about local stores, schools, and services. Some may have special discounts for medical students.

- Find out where to park for school, or how to get there using public transportation.

- Transfer your medical and dental records to providers in your new community. Check first with the medical school to see if they have a medical or dental plan for students.

28: Alternatives To Medical School

If you can't do what you want, do what you can.

Jewish Proverb

ABOUT HALF OF ALL UNSUCCESSFUL APPLICANTS to medical school eventually work in health-related occupations. Most of these fields demand additional training to be eligible, while some may require only bachelor's degrees and provide on-the-job training. While there are many positions in the health care fields (figure 28.1), some occupations that provide primary health care are discussed in detail below.

Many "premed" advisers also counsel individuals about other health-related professions. In some cases, they do it themselves, or have others in their office or on campus to whom they refer students. If you are set on a health-care career but find that you either do not want to go to or cannot get into medical school, contact the premed adviser to obtain the information you need

Physician Assistant Programs

Physician Assistants (P.A.'s) practice medicine under the supervision (often remote) of a licensed physician. More than 25,000 P.A.'s currently practice in the United States and more than 2,000 new P.A.'s graduate annually. They, like nurse practitioners, are considered "mid-level practitioners." In rural areas, they may be the only practitioners, with their supervising physicians many miles away. After their initial training, some P.A.'s, especially those at major medical centers, may concentrate (specialize) in specific areas, such as emergency medicine or a surgical subspecialty. The scope of P.A.'s' responsibilities are generally limited only by the physicians for whom they work. Some areas of the country are more hospitable to P.A.'s than are others, although P.A.'s work everywhere in the United States. They have prescribing privileges in forty-seven states. The average P.A. is thirty-one years old and 61% of them are women.

As of mid-1996, there were 68 Physician Assistant programs in the United States accredited by the Commission on Accreditation of Allied Health Education Programs. Another 14 existing programs have applied for accreditation, and 30 more are about to open. They are located at medical schools, universities, teaching hospitals, and within the armed forces. Most programs last about two years (without breaks), and include both didactics and labs (essentially the same curricula as medical students take, although abbreviated). In addition, P.A.'s do clinical rotations through the same services that most third-year medical students do (sometimes with these students) and in emergency medicine, ambulatory clinics, long-term health facilities, and physicians' offices. The focus is on primary care. Some programs give their graduates not only a certificate of completion, but also a master's degree in Health Science. The average tuition for the entire course of study is $18,000.

The average student admitted to P.A. programs already has a bachelor's degree and at least four years of health care experience, usually as a nurse, EMT, or other allied-health professional. Between 1992 and 1996, there was a 400% increase in applications to P.A. programs. Students are usually expected to complete the following courses before applying: biology, chemistry, English, humanities/social sciences, mathematics, and psychology. In nearly all states, a P.A. must pass the National Physician Assistant Certification Exam. Like the physician licensing exam (the USMLE), it is a product of the National Board of Medical Examiners. To remain certified, a P.A. must complete 100 hours of continuing medical education every two years and pass a recertification exam every six years.

The mean annual income for Physician Assistants is over $60,000, with new graduates having a mean income of about $50,000. Most work for individual physicians, group practices, HMOs, and outpatient clinics. The job market for P.A.'s is excellent, with an estimated six jobs for every new graduate. Nationally, P.A.'s work in family/general practice (37%), surgery (22%), other (19%), emergency medicine (8%), internal medicine (8%), obstetrics & gynecology (3%), and pediatrics (3%).

For more information, contact: the American Academy of Physician Assistants (AAPA), 950 North Washington Street, Alexandria, VA 22314-1534; (703) 836-2272.

Advance-Practice Nursing

Advance-practice nursing includes certified registered nurse anesthetists (CRNA), certified nurse midwives (CNM), and nurse practitioners (NP). All have independent patient-care responsibilities and begin with a nursing degree.

CRNAs give anesthesia. They must be under a physician's (although not necessarily an anesthesiologist's) direct supervision. The more than 25,000 CRNAs who currently practice in the United States provide more than half of all anesthesia. Training, often quite intense, lasts between 24 and 36 months. To be certified, graduates must pass a national examination. The average annual CRNA salary is about $88,000.

CNMs provide prenatal, delivery, and postnatal care. There are only about 4,000 CNMs in the United States, since many states restrict their practices. CNM programs last about two years. Of the 41 accredited programs, 29 offer master's degrees. Their annual salary averages about $54,000.

Similar to P.A.'s, nurse practitioners (NPs) are considered "mid-level" medical caregivers. They often work independently to provide health care services. All hold at least a bachelor's degree in Nursing and are licensed as R.N.'s. Unlike P.A.'s, who train using a medical model, NPs train using a nursing model. All NPs may prescribe medications, although in some states they must first consult with a physician. State laws define the nurse practitioner's scope of practice. Their annual salary averages about $50,000.

Most NP programs last two years (if students go full-time) and grant master's degrees. The programs include both didactics and clinical practice. Special programs exist for training nurse practitioners in family practice, pediatrics, neonatology, geriatrics, and adult medicine.

Four different bodies credential NPs: the American Nurses Credentialing Center; the National Certification Board of Pediatric Nurse Practitioners and Nurses; the American Academy of Nurse Practitioners; and the National Certification Corporation for the Obstetric, Gynecologic and Neonatal Nursing Specialties. Not all states require that NPs have national certification to practice.

Unlike P.A.'s, nurse practitioners are independent practitioners who are licensed and who can independently diagnose and treat patients. Many, however, work with physicians in offices and hospitals. Eleven jurisdictions allow them to practice completely independently or with only a minimal relationship with physicians. These are Alaska, Arizona, Iowa, Maine, Montana, New Hampshire, New Mexico, Oregon, Vermont, Washington, and Washington, DC.

Many nurses struggle with the decision about whether to enter an NP or a P.A. program. Especially in the more generalist-oriented NP programs, some nurses have been "turned off" by the rehashing of care plans and similar debris from their undergraduate nursing curricula. The programs, however, vary tremendously in their admission criteria, curricula, and the quality of their graduates. *Caveat emptor.*

For more information, contact: the American Academy of Nurse Practitioners, Capitol Station, LBJ Building, P.O. Box 12846, Austin, TX 78711, tel. (512) 442-4262; the American College of Nurse Practitioners, 2401 Pennsylvania Avenue, N.W., Suite 350, Washington, DC 20037-1718, tel. (202) 466-4825; the American College of Nurse Midwives, 818 Connecticut Avenue, N.W., Suite 900, Washington, DC 20006, tel. (202) 728-9860; or the American Association of Nurse Anesthetists, 222 South Prospect Avenue, Park Ridge, IL 60068-4001, tel. (708) 692-7050.

Dentistry

Unlike medicine, dentistry is still primarily comprised of private practitioners. Of the 150,000+ active dentists in the United States, more than 90% are in private practice, and about 79% practice general dentistry. The balance are in dental specialties. Dentistry remains one of the most-respected professions, and dentists have flexible working hours, a variety of work settings, and many opportunities to be creative in their work. A study published in the *New England Journal of Medicine* (May 5, 1994) suggests that dentists have a higher return on their educational investment than do primary care physicians.

Applicants must take the Dental Admission Test (DAT). The test is offered in the spring and the fall. It consists of four sections:

1. Survey of the Natural Sciences
   Biology
   General Chemistry
   Organic Chemistry

2. Perceptual Ability
   Angle discrimination
   Form development
   Cubes
   Orthographic projections
   Apertures
   Paper folding

3. Reading Comprehension
   Ability to read, organize, analyze, and remember new information

4. Quantitative Reasoning

Preparation materials for the DAT include the *Dental Admission Test Preparation Materials* and copies of old tests, available through the American Dental Association's Dental Admission Testing Program.

Nearly all U.S. dental schools require one year each of: English or English literature, introductory chemistry, organic chemistry, physics, and general biology. About one-third of all dental schools require college-level mathematics (and half of those specify one year of calculus).

The specific requirements are listed in the *Admission Requirements of U.S. and Canadian Dental Schools,* published annually by the American Association of Dental Schools. Many U.S. dental schools participate in the Dental Schools Application Service (AADAS).

Slightly more than half of all applicants to U.S. dental schools get accepted. More than 80% of those accepted have at least four years of undergraduate education, and nearly 70% obtained undergraduate degrees before entering dental school.

Following four years in dental school, many graduates (with a D.D.S. or D.M.D.) take specialty training in endodontics, orthodontics, pediatric dentistry, prosthodontics, oral surgery, periodontics, and other areas. These programs have very stiff entry requirements and only the best students get into them (often after a required minimum time practicing general dentistry).

For more information, contact: the American Dental Association, SELECT Program, 211 East Chicago Avenue, Suite 1840, Chicago, IL 60611-2678, tel. (312) 440-2689; or the American Association of Dental Schools, SELECT Program, 1625 Massachusetts Avenue, N.W., Washington, DC 20036. (The Dental Admission Testing Program uses the Washington, DC address.)

Podiatric Medicine

Podiatric Medicine, more commonly known as Podiatry, is a separate medical area devoted to the care of the foot and ankle. Podiatrists use surgery, medications, and orthotic devices to treat foot ailments. Depending upon the state's regulations and the practitioner's training, podiatrists may be able to do surgery anywhere on the lower extremity. About 29% of all podiatrists are women and 31% are minorities. Podiatrist's annual salary averages $100,000.

Applicants to a college of podiatric medicine must take the MCAT, and complete at least three years or ninety semester-hours of college credit, including English and the following laboratory courses: biology, general/inorganic chemistry, organic chemistry, and physics. In general, the average GPA and MCAT scores for those entering podiatry school (GPA about 3.1; MCAT scores about 6.9) are lower than those required for medical school. MCAT scores have been shown to correlate better with performance during the first two years of podiatry school than do an applicant's undergraduate GPA or science GPA. Slightly more than half of all applicants to podiatry schools are accepted.

More than 1,000 individuals apply for approximately 525 positions in podiatry schools annually. The annual application deadline is June 1, although applications received prior to April 1 get priority consideration. Six of the seven podiatric schools participate in a centralized application service. These applications can be obtained from the American Association of Colleges of Podiatric Medicine, Application Service (AACPM), 1350 Piccard Drive, Suite 322, Rockville, MD 20850-4307; phone (800) 922-9266.

After four years of podiatry school, graduates (with a D.P.M.) must usually take at least one year of postgraduate residency training to become licensed. Residencies must be in institutions that also have physicians-in-training so that residents can get an interdisciplinary experience. These residencies can either be surgical or non-surgical. Non-surgical residencies include the interdisciplinary rotating podiatric residency (RPR), the primary care-oriented primary podiatric medical residency (PPMR), and the podiatric orthopedic residency (POR) which concentrates on preserving and restoring leg and foot function. These generally last one to two years. Podiatric surgical residencies (PSR), which give additional training in operative techniques, can vary from one to three years in length, depending upon the degree of surgical expertise the individual wishes to obtain. Students use a centralized matching service to obtain residency positions.

For more information, contact: the American Podiatric Medical Association, 9312 Old Georgetown Road, Bethesda, MD 20814-1621.

Optometry

Optometrists examine eyes, test for visual acuity, and prescribe eyeglasses, contact lenses, vision therapy, and, in most states, medications. Unlike ophthalmologists (physicians), they do not do surgery. They work with both ophthalmologists and the opticians who fit, supply, and adjust glasses and contact lenses. Optometrists have a mean net-annual-income of more than $80,000, and most are self-employed.

Optometry schools require that applicants take the Optometry Admission Test (OAT), which is offered in February and October. The OAT has four sections. The mean scores of first-year optometry students have recently been: Quantitative Reasoning (321), Natural Sciences [biology (321), chemistry (315), organic chemistry (324)], Reading Comprehension (311) and Physics (314). Applications for the OAT can be obtained from the Optometry Admission Testing Program, Suite 1840, 211 East Chicago Avenue, Chicago, IL 60611-2678.

There are sixteen optometry schools in the mainland United States, one in Puerto Rico, and two in Canada. Annual tuition and fees range from under $4,000 to more than $21,000.

Applicants to schools of optometry must also fulfill the standard premed requirements, plus calculus, microbiology, statistics, and psychology. Each school has somewhat different requirements, so it is important to check with the schools. Most successful applicants have undergraduate degrees. About two-thirds of all applicants are accepted into optometry schools. The average GPA of accepted students ranges from 3.0 to 3.5, depending upon the school.

Students graduate with an O.D. degree after four years of study. For more information, contact: the American Optometric Association (AOA). 243 N. Lindbergh Blvd., St. Louis, MO 63141-7881; or the Association of Schools and Colleges of Optometry, 6110 Executive Boulevard, Suite 690, Rockville, MD 20852.

Naturopathic Medicine

Naturopaths (N.D.'s) treat diseases using "alternative therapies," including nutrition, herbal medicine, homeopathy, exercise therapy, counseling, acupuncture and acupressure, physical medicine, and hydrotherapy. There are currently two accredited schools of Naturopathy in North America and two more seeking accreditation. N.D.'s are licensed in nine states (Washington, Oregon, Montana, Utah, Arizona, Maine, New Hampshire, Vermont, and Connecticut). Washington, with the most liberal licensing laws for Naturopaths, considers them "general care providers," and allows students to get state-supported scholarships.

Most students have bachelor's degrees and have completed the standard premed courses before entering Naturopathic school. Nearly 75% of the 365 students entering in 1996 were women. Most were pursuing their second career. Their average GPA was about 3.1. Most of the school's admission deadlines are February 1. The course of study lasts four years and tuition ranges from $11,000 (Canadian) to $13,500 (U.S.) per year.

For more information, contact: the American Association of Naturopathic Physicians, 2366 Eastlake Avenue East, Suite 322, Seattle, WA 98102, tel. (206) 328-8510; or the Council on Naturopathic Medical Education, tel. (503) 328-6028.

Chiropractic

Chiropractors (D.C.'s) manipulate the spine to relieve pain. Some also claim to be able to cure systemic diseases using this manipulation. Applicants to chiropractic school must have at least two years of college including the usual prehealth courses. The average GPA of entering students is about 3.0. Of about 6,000 annual applicants, the schools accept more than half, and about 80% of accepted applicants actually enroll. The course of study is five years. Some schools now offer postgraduate residencies in various areas, including sports medicine, neurology, and radiology. There are also some programs available for Chiropractic Assistants. For more information, contact: the American Chiropractic Association, 1701 Clarendon Boulevard, Arlington, VA, 22209; tel. (703) 528-8800.

Other Careers In Medicine

Figure 28.1 contains an abbreviated list of some of the other opportunities within the health care professions. Note, however, that this is not a complete list.

You can find out more about these careers, including sources for more in-depth information, in *200 Ways to Put Your Talent to Work in the Health Field.* Copies are available from your health-professions adviser or directly from the National Health Council, 1730 M Street, N.W., Suite 500, Washington, DC 20036-4505; tel. (202) 785-3910.

Graduate School

Graduate school can be either an alternative to a health care career or preparation for another attempt at entering a health professions school. Entering graduate school simply for "something to do" until re-applying to medical school is generally pointless. Medical schools don't often see that course of action as beneficial or as "substantially improving credentials," which is what most schools look for in reapplicants. Have a clear reason for entering graduate school.

If you have an interest in a particular area and want to pursue those studies, now is a good time to do it. In some cases, individuals who took this route found a career they really enjoyed and stayed with it. Another reason to enter graduate school is to take graduate work for a degree you planned to get in the future anyway, such as a Masters of Public Health, or a Masters of Health Administration. If the degree pertains to medicine, so much the better. Finally, you may want to do graduate-level studies if your GPA was not up to medical school standards. This gives you an opportunity to improve your grades while continuing to hone your study skills. For this to be of significance to medical schools, however, the courses you take must be science-related and "rigorous" (not underwater basket-weaving).

Summary

Many career opportunities exist within the health care field. Some may fulfill your needs as well as, or better than, being a physician. Consider these options before you decide on entering medical school. If you have been rejected from medical schools, consider these options before completely abandoning any thought of entering the healing professions.

Figure 28.1: Other Health Care-Related Careers

Anatomist
Art Therapist
Athletic Trainer
Audiologist
Biomedical Engineer
Biophotographer
Biostatistician
Clinical Chemist
Clinical Microbiologist
Coding Specialist
Cytotechnologist
Dance Therapist
Dental Assistant
Dental Hygienist
Dental Technician
Dietitian
EEG Technologist
Emergency Med. Tech.

Epidemiologist
Exercise Physiologist
Genetic Counselor
Health Educator
Health Sci. Librarian
Histology Technician
Lic. Practical Nurse
Med. Records Admin.
Medical Assistant
Medical Illustrator
Medical Sonographer
Medical Technologist
Medical Writer
Music Therapist
Nuclear Med. Tech.
Nutritionist
Occupational Therapy
Optician

Orthoptist
Orthotist
Paramedic
Pharmacist
Pharmacologist
Physical Therapist
Prosthetist
Psychologist
Public Health
Radiology Technologist
Registered Nurse
Respiratory Therapist
Science Writer
Social Worker
Speech Pathologist
Surgical Technologist
Technical Writer
Toxicologist

29: Now You Are A Medical Student

The master word in medicine is work . . . Though a little one, it looms large in meaning. It is the open sesame to every portal, the great equalizer in the world, the true philosopher's stone which transmutes all the base metal of humanity into gold.

Sir William Osler

NOW THAT YOU HAVE STARTED medical school, you have essentially received the "secret handshake" for the profession. You are one of "us," physicians (albeit a neophyte), rather than one of "them," the uninitiated. Make the most of this. Assertively seek out educational opportunities, especially clinical opportunities. While these may have been difficult to obtain before, your only problem now will be to not put too much on your proverbial plate. Go forth—experience and learn!

Eleven Rules For Success In Medical School

1. Your Initial Goal: *Do well on the first set of exams.* This will give you confidence. It also helps develop the study/work habits necessary to succeed throughout medical school. In addition, the first material taught is the foundation on which the balance of the course (and often other courses) rests. If you think of the first six weeks of school as a very tough survival course, you will have the right mindset. Study as you have never studied before. Take self-assessment tests and review old exams (previously used by current professors).

2. By the third or fourth day of school, begin spending between ten and fifteen minutes each day reviewing your notes from previous days. The more repetition, the better (and easier) you will learn the material for the exams and the longer you will retain it after the exams.

3. Consciously try to process new information on three levels:

   Rote learning. You have to memorize a lot of material. You proved you could memorize large amounts of information by passing organic chemistry. Just suck it in (literally and figuratively).

   Understanding. Okay, so you memorized how the drug works. Can you figure out what the side effects might be?

   Application. If you have a patient with hypertension, which of the drugs you learned about would you dispense? Why would they be different for different patients? What side effects might make a patient stop using the medication? What are your alternatives?

   Remember that the examinations medical students take have changed. They used to require mainly regurgitating memorized material (rote learning), but now the questions test your understanding and ability to apply information. This is true for all exams you take at school, as well as the licensing exams (USMLE, NBOME).

4. Join a study group early. Study groups are essential, not only to help you study, but also to provide support and encouragement when things get rough.

5. Decide early which classes you should attend. If you spend five minutes in a class and are completely lost, leave. Read the material on your own and, if you have problems, go to your study group or to the professor for extra help. Go back to the class for the next several sessions. If your experience is repeated and you seem to be doing well with self-study, keep with it. Just be sure that you follow the course syllabus and attend any lab sessions that are part of the class.

6. Get the right books. Books are expensive and you will have limited funds to spend, so be careful what you buy. *Gray's Anatomy* and Goodman and Gilman's pharmacology text are expensive and of little use to most medical students. They have so many details that they often obscure the "big picture." Instead, begin using "review books" for various subjects early in your schooling. Condensed as they are, they bring out the important details, have questions and answers that you can use for self-assessment, and are excellent for reviewing the subject area before the USMLE or NBOME examinations. Some medical educators recommend the *Board Review Series* or the review books published by Lippincott. You also might want to look at the *First Aid for the USMLE* books, since they include students' ratings of various texts.

7. Forget about "everyone for himself (herself)." Medical school is a team effort. Think of it as being in a lifeboat. In general, the better each person in the lifeboat does, the better everyone does. The same goes for a medical school class.

8. Learn to ask for help. It doesn't matter what undergraduate school you went to, how high your grades or MCAT scores were, or what your major was. Everyone starts medical school on an even footing—and nearly everyone needs some help somewhere along the way. Ask for it early so that you don't "go under" so deep that no one can pull you out. Problems that medical students encounter include sudden financial crises (or longer-term problems), personal and family problems, and difficult course work. Studies have shown that if you do poorly on the major tests in November of your first year, you will probably have difficulty for the balance of your first two years. Get help. Medical schools have qualified professionals ready to help you work through any or all of these problems. However, you have to tell them that you are having these problems—and the sooner, the better. Asking for help does not mean that you are shirking your responsibilities. Rather, it demonstrates the level of maturity expected of a professional.

9. Read every course syllabus (the page on the front of the notes or a separate page handed out the first day of class). It describes how the class is graded. One student nearly failed pathology simply because he "blew off" watching a pathologist stain slides in the laboratory. He lost the "gimme" points the pathology faculty "donated" to the students—simply by not paying attention to the rules. (He passed, but barely. If he hadn't, it would have cost him an extra year while he repeated this major course.)

10. Keep everything from your classes. That includes syllabi, flash-cards, textbooks, review books, lecture notes, tests, sample cases, other handouts, and bibliographies. These will be invaluable when taking other courses (since, unlike undergraduate school, most medical school courses build on information from other courses) and when preparing for the Boards. It is best to organize these materials in binders, expandable files, or banker's boxes—all clearly marked for easy retrieval.

11. ***The very basic rules:*** Listen carefully and accept all the help and support offered to you. Those medical students with good attitudes who are willing to be taught eventually succeed—no matter what.

Find A Mentor Early

Mentors were discussed earlier for undergraduate school. It is very important to find a mentor during medical school. Use the same technique of asking students in their junior and senior (clinical) years about who are the best clinical teachers. You can locate these students in the hospital cafeteria or emergency department any night. Once you have the names, contact these folks to see if they are interested, compatible, and have the time to help you. It will be well worth your effort.

Recommended Texts And Study Aids

Your school will recommend texts and study aids for your regular courses. For recommendations on special texts to use to study for the USMLE (or NBOME), see the *Annotated Bibliography.*

Go Be A Clinician—Start Clinical Work Early

Why are you in medical school? It's certainly not to sit in the same (albeit tougher) classes you took as an undergraduate or graduate student. It's to practice medicine. In that case, go forth and do some clinical work!

Did you say that your school doesn't offer any clinical experiences until the second, third, or fourth semesters? Then don't rely on it to get these experiences. You're a medical student now. You are a member of the profession. Use this fact to get some clinical experience in the emergency department, with a member of the clinical faculty (your mentor, perhaps?), or with a clinician in the local community.

A medical student who knew that he wanted early clinical experience strolled into the brand-new Family Practice Clinic the week he started school. He said that he wanted to get as much clinical experience as possible and asked if they could accommodate him. The staff was astonished, and somewhat bewildered by the request. Nevertheless, they quickly conferred and agreed to the request. Minutes later, with the patient's laughing consent (she thought it was funny that she would be the first real patient for a new doctor-to-be), he participated in his first pelvic examination. Subsequently, he worked during the remainder of his medical schooling with a local family practitioner he met at the clinic. These are the clinical experiences he (actually, I) values most highly from medical school.

Get your priorities straight. Early clinical experience enhances your classroom work, keeps you focused on why you are in medical school, and makes you that much more proficient when you begin your official clinical rotations. But at most schools, it is up to you to seek out such experiences.

The Next Step—Prepare For Residency/Fellowship

Now that you are a medical student, you need to think about the next step. "The next step?" you ask. You've just been through the trying and often frustrating process of getting into medical school. Is there more? Yes, there is!

Making the decision to go into medicine was the easy part. ("Now you tell me!") It's like deciding to go out to eat. You know that you're hungry, but now you have to pick a restaurant. Medicine offers practitioners a myriad of opportunities, some well-known and some quite obscure.

You need to begin investigating these early, so that you can make a reasonable career choice based on solid information and your own wants and needs.

For the basic information, review chapter 3, *The Specialties*. Then look in the *Annotated Bibliography* for more information. Finally, go talk with practitioners in the various specialties to get a better idea of what they do and how each feels about the specialty.

30: So You Want To Go To A Different Medical School?

There are two tragedies in life. One is not to get your heart's desire. The other is to get it.

Bernard Shaw, *Man and Superman*, IV

Transferring Between Medical Schools

ONCE YOU ARE A MEDICAL STUDENT, you may be able to transfer between schools. Usually, students need to transfer for personal reasons. In recent years, students have found it increasingly difficult to transfer between schools, since they must find a school with a similar curriculum that has space to accommodate them. In some cases, for example when they wish to transfer to be near their fiancé(e) or family, the limited options available at area medical schools may force them to repeat a school year. In some cases, however, schools will try to work with a student who marries a student already in their school. Schools do not generally accept transfers into the final (usually fourth) year (see figure 15.5). Special accommodations can often be made, however, to allow students to spend most or all of their senior year at another school, while not officially "transferring."

If you want or need to transfer between schools, contact the Dean's office at the school where you want to transfer as soon as you can. Also, be certain to contact your own Dean's office, since they will have to certify that you are a student in good standing at their school, that you have successfully completed the specified academic work, and that there are no other reasons for the new school not to accept you (e.g., the Feds don't have a warrant for your arrest).

In 1994-95, for example, 367 students transferred from one U.S. M.D.-granting institution to another, and 3 transferred from Canadian schools into U.S. schools. An additional 13 students transferred from Osteopathic medical schools into M.D.-granting schools.

A more difficult feat is to transfer from a non-LCME-accredited medical school (foreign medical school) into a U.S. M.D.-granting school. This requires jumping through quite a few hoops and having more than a bit of luck. (See chapter 17 for details of the process.) Nevertheless, in 1994-95, 87 students successfully made this leap.

"Away" Electives

The most common method medical students use to get experience at other medical schools is to do clinical (and sometimes research) clerkships there, usually in their final year of medical school. These clerkships vary in how easily they can be arranged, depending upon the specialty and program involved. Because of family, financial, or educational reasons, some students arrange to spend most of or all their senior year at another medical school. Although their final degree will come from their original medical school, these students get to see how medicine is practiced at two, often completely different, sites. There is no central registry or clearinghouse for "away" clerkships. Students must contact the programs where they wish to go for specific information. The best advice is to do this as far in advance as you can, since many schools have only limited positions for "visiting" students.

Students at many non-U.S./Canadian medical schools either choose to (or must because of a lack of clinical facilities) do U.S.-based clerkships. This allows them to have clinical training similar to that of their U.S. medical school compatriots. Still, they must go through the ECFMG certification process before they can apply to U.S. residency programs.

Merged Medical Schools

Some students enter one medical school but graduate from another—without ever transferring—when medical schools merge. Two Philadelphia medical schools recently merged, as did two in New York City. More might do so in the future if the financial pressures on medical education keep mounting. The Medical College of Pennsylvania and Hahnemann University School of Medicine, both founded around 1850, now operate as one very large medical school, the Allegheny University of Health Sciences. The result has been the nation's largest medical school class on one campus, with more than 300 students. New York University and Mt. Sinai Medical Schools began merging into the NYU-Mt. Sinai School of Medicine in mid-1996. The new school is projected to have 1,177 M.D. and M.D./Ph.D. students, 1,775 residents and fellows, and 2,814 clinical faculty (although all of these numbers will probably decrease). The message is, if you are not interested in large classes, avoid schools that plan to merge.

In August 1996, Cornell and Columbia Universities announced "an alliance" between the physicians at their medical schools. They will now jointly negotiate contracts with managed-care organizations and insurance companies. Simultaneously, The New York Hospital and Presbyterian Hospital, each school's primary teaching hospital announced they will merge. Although they deny it will happen, don't be surprised to see these two schools formally merge in the near future.

Closed Medical Schools

Accredited U.S. medical schools rarely close these days. In the past decade, only the privately run Oral Roberts University Medical School ceased to exist. Students at the school were not, however, left to fend for themselves. They were either allowed to graduate (those in their clinical years) or allowed to transfer to other U.S. medical schools. National rules and agreements exist that allow medical students at accredited schools to complete their education if their schools should close.

Once you get into a U.S. medical school you are considered part of the team. And the profession looks out for its team members.

Appendix A: Abbreviations & Acronyms

AACOM: American Association of Colleges of Osteopathic Medicine

AACOMAS: American Association of Colleges of Osteopathic Medicine Application Service

AADSAS: American Association of Dental Schools Application Service

AAMC: Association of American Medical Colleges

ACGME: Accreditation Council for Graduate Medical Education

ALP: Alternative Loan Program

AMA: American Medical Association

AMCAS-E: American Medical College Application Service—Electronic

AMCAS: American Medical College Application Service

AMEA: Association for Multi-Ethnic Americans

AMSA: American Medical Student Association

AMWA: American Medical Women's Association

AOA: American Optometric Association

AOA: American Osteopathic Association

AP: Advanced Placement credit

ASR: Additional Score Report

CACMS: Committee on Accreditation of Canadian Medical Schools

CNM: Certified Nurse Midwife

CRNA: Certified Registered Nurse Anesthetist

CSA: Clinical Skills Assessment

D.C.: Doctor of Chiropractic (Chiropractor)

D.D.S.: Doctor of Dental Surgery (Dentist)

D.M.D.: Doctor of Medical Dentistry (Dentist)

D.O.: Doctor of Osteopathic Medicine

D.P.M.: Doctor of Podiatric Medicine (Podiatrist)

D.V.M.: Doctor of Veterinary Medicine

DAT: Dental Admission Test

DCAT: Developing Cognitive Abilities Test

ECFMG: Educational Commission for Foreign Medical Graduates

EDP: Early-Decision Program

EFC: Expected Family (financial) Contribution

EFN: Exceptional Financial Need Scholarship

EMAE: Expanded Minority Admissions Exercise

EMS: Emergency Medical System

EMT: Emergency Medical Technician

ENT: Ear, Nose, and Throat (Otolaryngology)

FADHPS: Financial Assistance for Disadvantaged Health Professions Students
FFELP: Federal Family Education Loan Program
FMG: Foreign Medical Graduates
FSLS: Federal Supplemental Loans for Students
GAPSFAS: Graduate and Professional School Financial Aid Services
GPA: Grade Point Average
GRE: Graduate Record Examination
HEAL: Health Education Assistance Loan
HMO: Health Maintenance Organization
HPSA: Health-Professions-Shortage Area
HPSL: Health Professional Student Loans
HPSP: Health Professions Scholarship Program
IMG: International Medical Graduate
INMED: Indians Into Medicine program
IPA: Independent Practice Association
JAMA: *Journal of the American Medical Association*
JAOA: *Journal of the American Osteopathic Association*
J.D.: Juris doctor (Law degree)
LCME: Liaison Committee on Medical Education
LDS: Loans for Disadvantaged Students
M.D.: Medical Doctor
MARC: Minority Access to Research Careers
M.B.A.: Masters of Business Administration
MCAT: Medical College Admission Test
Med-MAR: Medical Minority Applicant Registry
M.H.A.: Masters of Health Administration
MHSSRAP: Minority High School Summer Research Apprentice Program
M.M.: Masters of Management
MMEP: Minority Medical Education Program
MMRN: Minority Mentor Recruitment Network
MPDB: Minority Physicians Database
M.P.H.: Masters of Public Health
MSAR: *AAMC Medical School Admission Requirements*
MSTP: Medical Scientist Training Program
N.D.: Doctor of Naturopathy (Naturopath)
NAAHP: National Association of Advisors for the Health Professions
NBOME: National Board of Osteopathic Medical Examiners
NHMRN: National Hispanic Mentor Recruitment Network
NHSC: National Health Service Corps
NIH: National Institutes of Health
NP: Nurse Practitioner
NPSA: National Prehealth Student Association
O.D.: Doctor of Optometry
OAT: Optometry Admission Test
OMM: Osteopathic Manipulative Medicine
OMSAS: Ontario Medical School Application Service
OSCE: Objective Structured Clinical Examination

P.A.: Physician Assistant
PBL: Problem-based learning
PCL: Primary Care Loans
PGY: Postgraduate year (of residency)
Ph.D.: Doctor of Philosophy
PHS: Public Health Service
PM & R: Physical Medicine and Rehabilitation
PPO: Preferred Provider Organization
R.N.: Registered Nurse
Sallie Mae: Student Loan Marketing Association
SAT: Scholastic Aptitude Test
SDS: Scholarship for Disadvantaged Students
TOEFL: Test of English as a Foreign Language Examination
USIMG: U.S.-citizen International Medical Graduate
USMLE: United States Medical Licensing Examination
UTSMDAC: University of Texas System Medical and Dental Application Center
WAMI: Alaska, Montana, Idaho educational cooperative agreements
WICHE: Western Interstate Commission for Higher Education

Appendix B: Contact Information For Premeds

Canadian Medical Schools
Association of Canadian Medical Colleges
774 Echo Drive
Ottawa, Ontario CANADA K1S 5P2
(613) 730-0687; (613) 730-1196 (fax)

International Medical Graduates:
  ECFMG Certificate & USMLE
Educational Commission for Foreign Medical
  Graduates (ECFMG)
3624 Market Street
Philadelphia, PA 19104-2685
(215) 386-5900

International Medical Schools
World Health Organization
525 23rd Street, N.W.
Washington, DC 20037
(202) 861-3200
http://www.who.ch

MCAT Information and Application
MCAT Program Office
2255 North Dubuque Road
P.O. Box 4056
Iowa City, IA 52243
(319) 337-1357

M.D. Medical School Applications (Ontario)
Medical School Application Service (OMSAS)
Ontario Universities' Application Centre
P.O. Box 1328
Guelph, Ontario CANADA N1H 7P4
(519) 823-1940
http://ouacinfo.ouac.on.ca/

M.D. Medical School Applications (U.S.)
American Medical College Application
  Service (AMCAS)
Association of American Medical Colleges
Section for Student Services
2501 M Street, N.W., Lbby-26
Washington, DC 20037-1300
(202) 828-0600
http://www.aamc.org/

M.D. Medicine
American Medical Association (AMA)
515 N. State Street
Chicago, IL 60610
(312) 464-5000
http://www.ama-assn.org/

Medical Student Organizations
AMA, Medical Student Section
515 N. State Street
Chicago, IL 60610
(312) 464-4742
http://www.ama-assn.org/mem-datat/special/ama-
  mss/ama-mss.htm

American Medical Student Association (AMSA)
1902 Association Drive
Reston, VA 22901-1502
(703) 620-6600
http://www.amsa.org/

AAMC–Organization of Student Representatives
2450 N Street, N.W.
Washington, DC 20037-1127
(202) 828-0400
http://www.aamc.org

Association of Native American Medical Students
1235 Sovereign Row, Suite C-7
Oklahoma City, OK 73108
(405) 946-7072

California Chicano–Latino Medical Stud. Assoc.
200 Atrium Way, #210
Davis, CA 95616
(916)756-8205

Latino Midwest Medical Student Association
Univ. of IL at Chicago College of Medicine
1819 W. Polk Street, Room 145 (MC 786)
Chicago, IL 60612
(312) 996-6491

Military Medical Students' Association
Uniformed Services Univ. of the Health Sciences
F. Edward Hebert School of Medicine
4301 Jones Bridge Road
Bethesda, MD 20814-4799
(301) 295-3101

National Network of Latin American Med. Stud.
Office of Minority Affairs, P.O. Box 24-5140
Arizona Health Sciences Center
1501 N. Campbell Avenue
Tucson, AZ 85724
(520) 621-5531

Student National Medical Association (SNMA)
1012 Tenth Street, N.W.
Washington, DC 20001
(202) 371-1616

Student Osteopathic Medical Association (SOMA)
8200 Henry Avenue, Apt. F29
Philadelphia, PA 19128
(215) 483-6954
http://members.aol.com/studdoctor/

Texas Assoc.of Mexican-American Med. Stud.
8525 Floyd Curl Drive, #1005
San Antonio, TX 78240
(512) 590-4675

Osteopathic Medical School Applications
American Association of Colleges of
   Osteopathic Medicine
AACOMAS
6110 Executive Boulevard, Suite 405
Rockville, MD 20852-3991
(301) 468-0990
http://www.aacom.org/

Osteopathic Medicine
American Osteopathic Association (AOA)
142 E. Ontario Street
Chicago, IL 60611
(800) 621-1773

Premed Student Organization
National Prehealth Student Association
P.O. Box 1518
Champaign, IL 61824-1518
(217) 355-0063

Residency Programs
Accreditation Council for Graduate Medical
   Education(ACGME)
515 North State Street
Chicago, IL 60611
(312) 464-4290
http://www.acgme.org/

American Board of Medical Specialties
1 American Plaza, Suite 805
Evanston, IL 60201
http://www.abms.org/abms/

Council of Medical Specialty Societies
51 Sherwood Terrace, Suite Y
Lake Bluff, IL 60044
(847) 295-3456

State Licensing Requirements
Federation of State Medical Boards of the U.S.
400 Fuller Wiser Road, Suite 300
Euless, TX 76039
(817) 735-0722

United States Medical Schools
Assoc. of Amercian Medical Colleges (AAMC)
2450 N Street, N.W.
Washington, DC 20037-1126
(202) 828-0416

University of Texas System Medical and
   Dental Application Center (UTSMDAC)
702 Colorado, Suite 620
Austin, TX 78701

USMLE Information (U.S. Medical Students)
National Board of Medical Examiners
Department of Licensing Examination Services
3750 Market Street
Philadelphia, PA 19104-3190
(215) 590-9700

Women in Medicine
American Association of University Women
1111 16th Street, N.W.
Washington, DC 20036
(202) 728-7603
http://www.aauw.org/index.html

American Medical Association
Dept. of Women in Medicine
515 North State Street
Chicago, IL 60610
(312) 464-4392

American Medical Women's Association
801 North Fairfax Street, #400
Alexandria, VA 22314
(703) 838-0500

Appendix C: Postbaccalaureate Premed Programs

ARIZONA

Arizona State University
Brice W. Corder, Assistant Dean
College of Liberal Arts and Sciences
Tempe, AZ 85287-1701
(602) 965-2365

CALIFORNIA

California State University-Dominguez Hills
James Lyle, Premedical Adviser
Department of Chemistry
Carson, CA 90747
(310) 516-3376

California State University-Fullerton
Health Professions Coordinator
800 North State College Boulevard
Mail Stop KH203
Fullerton, CA 92634
(714) 773-3980
http://www.fullerton.edu
Open to students who lack prerequisites basic to medicine.

California State University-Hayward
Dr. John Giles
Department of Physics
Hayward, CA 94542
(415) 881-3488

California State University-Long Beach
John J. Baird, Professor Emeritus
Department of Biology
1250 Bellflower Boulevard
Long Beach, CA 90840
(213) 985-4693
http://www.acs.sculb.edu

Chapman University
Premedical Adviser
Postbaccalaureate Pre-Professional Health
Science Program
Orange, CA 92666
(714) 997-6696
http://www.chapman.edu
Open to students who lack prerequisites basic to medicine.

El Camino College
Madeline Carteron, Counselor
16007 Crenshaw Boulevard
Torrance, CA 90506
(310) 715-3551
Open to students who lack prerequisites basic to medicine.

Loyola Marymount University
Dr. Anthony P. Smulders
Loyola Boulevard at West 80th Street
Los Angeles, CA 90045-2699
(310) 338-5954
http://www.lmu.edu
Open to students who lack prerequisites basic to medicine, but who have completed bachelor's degrees with a minimum GPA of 3.40; most undergraduate courses are offered in the daytime only on a space available basis; students may take a maximum of 18 semester-hours as non-degree students.

Mills College
Coordinator, Graduate Admissions
Postbaccalaureate Premedical Program
500 MacArthur Boulevard
Oakland, CA 94613
(510) 430-3309; (510) 430-3314 (fax)
e-mail: margaret@mills.edu
Open to non-science graduates only.

San Francisco State University
Health Professions Programs
School of Science, TH323
1600 Holloway Avenue
San Francisco, CA 94132
(415) 338-2410
http://www.sfsu.edu
Open to students who lack prerequisites basic to medicine or who have been previously unsuccessful in gaining admission to medical school.

San Jose University
Chair, Biological Sciences
1 Washington Square
San Jose, CA 95192-0100
(408) 924-2429; (408) 924-4900 (fax)
http://www.sjsu.edu
Open to students who lack prerequisites basic to medicine; CA residents preferred; special counseling available.

Scripps College
Program Administrator
W. M. Keck Science Center
925 North Mills Avenue
Claremont, CA 91711
(909) 621-8764
http://www.scrippscol.edu
Open to students who lack prerequisites basic to medicine; 3.0 GPA; interview required; previous health experience desirable.

University of California-Davis
Postbaccalaureate Program
Office of Minority Affairs
UC-Davis School of Medicine
Davis, CA 95616
(916) 752-8119
http://medsponsoredprograms.ucdavis.edu
Open to underrepresented minorities or economically disadvantaged students who have been previously unsuccessful in gaining admission to medical school; CA residents only.

University of California-Irvine
Eileen Munoz, Program Coordinator
E108A, Medical Science I
UC-Irvine College of Medicine
Irvine, CA 92717
(714) 856-4603
http://meded.com.uci.edu
Open to underrepresented minorities or economically disadvantaged students who have been previously unsuccessful in gaining admission to medical school.

Univ. of California-San Diego School of Medicine
Assistant Director, Special Admissions Support
 Recruitment Program
Medical Teaching Facility (0621)
9500 Gilman Drive
La Jolla, CA 92093-0621
(619) 534-4170
http://cybermed.ucsd.edu
For ethnic minorities who have applied and been interviewed, but have not yet been accepted.

CONNECTICUT

University of Connecticut
Director, Student Services/Admissions
263 Farmington Avenue
Farmington, CT 06032
(203) 679-2152/3971
http://www.uconn.edu
One program for those changing careers; one for science majors. Both require bachelor's degrees.

DISTRICT OF COLUMBIA

Georgetown University School of Medicine
Office of Programs for Student Development
3900 Reservoir Road, N.W.
Washington, DC 20057
(202) 687-1406
http://www.georgetown.edu
Open to students who lack prerequisites basic to medicine.

Howard University
Premedical Adviser and Director
Center for Professional Education
P.O. Box 473, Administration Building
Washington, DC 20059
(202) 806-7231
http://www.howard.edu
Open to students who lack prerequisites basic to medicine or who have been previously unsuccessful in gaining admission to medical school.

Trinity College
Dr. Saundra Herndon Oyewole
Division of Natural Sciences and Mathematics
125 Michigan Avenue, N.E.
Washington, DC 20017
(202) 939-5000
Open to students who lack prerequisites basic to medicine; women only.

FLORIDA

Barry University
Dr. Elizabeth Hays
Biology Department
Miami Shores, FL 33161
(305) 899-3204
http://www.barry.edu

Florida State University
Program in Medical Sciences
R-115, 34 Montgomery
Tallahassee, FL 32306
(904) 644-1855
http://www.fsu.edu
Open to FL residents who lack prerequisites basic to medicine or who have been previously unsuccessful in gaining admission to medical school; individualized program; advising available.

University of Florida
Dean of the Graduate School
Box 115515
Gainesville, FL 32611-5515
(904) 392-4646

University of Miami
Co-Chair, Committee on Premedical Studies
P.O. Box 248004
Coral Gables, FL 33124
(305) 284-5176
http://www.miami.edu
One program for those changing careers; one for those not successful when applying to medical school. Applicants must have bachelor's degree and a 3.3 GPA in junior/senior years. Must register for at least 12 semester-hours each term.

University of West Florida
Dr. Jerome Gurst, Professor
Department of Chemistry
11000 University Parkway
Pensacola, FL 32514
(904) 474-2744
http://www.uwf.edu
Fees based on state residency.

GEORGIA

Agnes Scott College
Postbaccalaureate Premedical Prog. for Women
Office of Graduate Studies
141 East College Avenue
Decatur, GA 30030-3797
(404) 638-6252
For women with non-science bachelor's degrees

Armstrong State College
Dr. Henry E. Harris
Department of Chemistry/Physics
Savannah, GA 31419-1997
(912) 927-5304
http://www.armstrong.edu
Open to students who lack prerequisites basic to medicine.

Augusta College
John B. Black, Ph.D.
Professor, Department of Biology
2500 Walton Way
Augusta, GA 30910
(404) 737-1539
Open to students who lack prerequisites basic to medicine; fees based on state residency.

ILLINOIS

Chicago Area Health & Medical Careers Program
Illinois Institute of Technology
3200 South Wabash Avenue
Chicago, IL 60616-3793
(312) 567-8865
Open to students who have completed all course prerequisites for medical school.

Illinois Institute of Technology
Chair and Chief Health Professions Adviser
Department of Biology
Chicago, IL 60616
(312) 567-3480
http://www.iit.edu
Open to students who lack prerequisites basic to medicine; or who have been previously unsuccessful in gaining admission to medical school.

Loyola University of Chicago
Prehealth Adviser, Postbaccalaureate Pre-
  Professional Health Sciences Program
6525 North Sheridan Road
Chicago, IL 60626
(312) 508-6054
http://www.luc.edu
Open to students who lack prerequisites basic to medicine; day and evening classes available; financial aid (Stafford Loan); open admissions.

Olivet Nazarene University
Larry G. Ferren
Chemistry Box 6047
Kankakee, IL 60901
http://www.olivet.edu
Open to students who lack prerequisites basic to medicine.

Roosevelt University
Dr. Johnathan Green, Chair
Biology Department
430 South Michigan
Chicago, IL 60605
(312) 341-3676/3683

Rosary College
Sister Mary Woods
7900 West Division Street
River Forest, IL 60305
(708) 366-2490

Saint Xavier University
Chair, Premedical Committee/Science Dept.
3700 West 103rd Street
Chicago, IL 60655
(312) 298-3521
http://www.sxu.edu

Southern Illinois University
Minority Affairs and Counseling
Director, MEDPREP Program
Wheeler Hall 0202A
Carbondale, IL 62901-4323
(618) 453-6671
http://www.siu.edu
*Restricted to minorities and educationally
disadvantaged students. Illinois residents
preferred.*

Western Illinois University
Premedical Adviser
Department of Biology
Macomb, IL 61455
(309) 298-1483
http://www.wiu.edu
*Open to IL residents who lack prerequisites basic
to medicine or who have been previously
unsuccessful gaining admission to medical school.*

INDIANA

Indiana University-Purdue Univ. at Indianapolis
Premedical Adviser
Biology Department
723 West Michigan Street
Indianapolis, IN 46202-5132
(317) 274-0586
http://www.iupui.edu
*Open to students who lack prerequisites basic to
medicine or who have been previously
unsuccessful in gaining admission to medical
school.*

Valparaiso University
Dr. A. Gilbert Cook
Department of Chemistry
Valparaiso, IN 46383
(219) 464-5389
http://www.valpo.edu
*Open to students who lack prerequisites basic to
medicine.*

IOWA

Drake University
Dr. Rodney A. Rogers
Department of Biology
2507 University Avenue
Des Moines, IA 50311
(515) 271-3925
http://www.drake.edu

Iowa State University
Coordinator, Premedical & Preprofessional
  Health Prog.
204 Carver Hall
Ames, IA 50011
(515) 294-4841
http://www.iastate.edu
*Open to students who lack prerequisites basic to
medicine.*

Luther College
Dr. Russell Rulon
Biology Department
700 College Drive
Decorah, IA 52101
(319) 387-1552
*Open to students who lack prerequisites basic to
medicine.*

KANSAS

Johnson County Community College
Darwin Lawyer, Counselor
GED 155
12345 College at Quivira
Overland Park, KS 66210-1299
(913) 469-3809
http://www.johnoco.cc.ks.us/

KENTUCKY

Brescia College
Chief, Preprofessional Adviser
Biology/Medical Technology
717 Frederica Street
Owensboro, KY 42301
(502) 686-4276
*Open to students who lack prerequisites basic to
medicine; ACT scores 25+; students must hold
degree related to premedical studies; entitled to all
services extended to premed majors.*

Spalding University
B. Juanelle Pearson
Math/Science Department
851 South 4th Street
Louisville, KY 40203
(502) 585-9911

LOUISIANA

University of Southwestern Louisiana
Administrator, Department of Biology
P.O. Box 42451
Lafayette, LA 70504
(318) 231-6748
http://www.usl.edu
Open to students who lack prerequisites basic to medicine or who have been previously unsuccessful in gaining admission to medical school.

MARYLAND

Goucher College
Director, Postbaccalaureate Premedical Program
1201 Dulaney Valley Road
Baltimore, MD 21204-2794
(800) 697-4646
http://www.goucher.edu
Open to students who lack prerequisites basic to medicine, have not taken the MCAT, and have not applied to medical school.

Towson State University
Dr. Caryl E. Peterson
Department of Biological Sciences
Towson, MD 21204
(410) 830-3042
http://www.towson.edu
Requires minimum undergraduate GPA of 3.4

MASSACHUSETTS

American International College
Chief Health Professions Adviser
1000 State Street
Springfield, MA 01109
(413) 737-7000, ext. 379
Must register for minimum of 8 credits per semester.

Assumption College
Dr. Allan Barnitt, Jr.
Division of Natural Sciences
Worcester, MA 01615-0005
(508) 752-5616, ext. 293
http://www.assumption.edu
Evidence of strong academic potential required; must complete minimum of 4 different science courses; financial aid available.

Boston University
Health Science Program Office
College of Liberal Arts
725 Commonwealth Avenue, Room B-2
Boston, MA 02215
(617) 353-4866
http://www.bu.edu
Open to students who lack prerequisites basic to medicine; day and evening classes available.

Brandeis University
Assistant Dean, Academic Affairs
Kutz 108
Waltham, MA 02254
(617) 736-3460
http://www.brandeis.edu
Open to students who lack prerequisites basic to medicine.

Harvard University Extension School
Health Careers Program
51 Brattle Street
Cambridge, MA 02138
(617) 495-2926

Mount Holyoke College
The Frances Perkins Program
South Hadley, MA 01075-1435
(413) 538-2077

Simmons College
Director, Continuing Education
300 The Fenway
Boston, MA 02115
(617) 738-2141
http://www.simmons.edu
Open to students who lack prerequisites basic to medicine.

Tufts University
Carol Baffi Dugan
226 College Avenue
Medford, MA 02155
(617) 627-3299
http://www.tufts.edu
Open to students who lack prerequisites basic to medicine; small, selective program for non-traditional students.

University of Massachusetts-Amherst
Chair, Premedical Advisory Committee
c/o Department of Biology
Amherst, MA 01003
(413) 545-3674
http://wwww.umass.edu
Open to students who lack prerequisites basic to medicine.

University of Massachusetts-Boston
Premedical Adviser, Career Services
Harbor Campus
Boston, MA 02125
(617) 287-5511
http://www.umb.edu

Wellesley College
Coordinator, Continuing Education
106 Central Street
Wellesley, MA 02181
(617) 235-0320, ext. 2660
http://www.wellesley.edu
Health Professions Advisory Committee can only support applicants who complete at least four courses at Wellesley.

Worcester State College
Premedical Adviser
486 Chandler Street
Worcester, MA 01602
(508) 793-8000, ext. 8600

MICHIGAN

Madonna College
Florence Scholdenbrand
36600 Schoolcroft Road
Livonia, MI 48150-1173
(313) 591-5100
U.S. citizens and Permanent Residents only.

Michigan State Univ., College of Human Medicine
Advanced Baccalaureate Learning Experience
Prematriculation Programs
A254 Life Sciences Building
East Lansing, MI 44824-1317
(517) 355-2404
Admits only 7 to 12 students annually. Must be approved by the medical school's admission committee, and be from an underrepresented minority. Upon successful completion of the program, they are guaranteed admission to Michigan State University's medical school.

University of Michigan
Assistant Dean, Office of Student Programs
5109 Medical Science Building I, C-Wing
1301 Catherine Street
Ann Arbor, MI 48109-0611
(313) 764-8185
http://www.umich.edu
Open to underrepresented minorities, economically disadvantaged, or educationally disadvantaged students who have been previously unsuccessful in gaining admission to medical school.

Wayne State University School of Medicine
Director, Minority Recruitment
Gordon H. Scott Hall of Basic Medical Sciences
540 East Canfield Avenue
Detroit, MI 48201
(313) 577-1598

MINNESOTA

Mankato State University
Premedical Adviser
Box 34, Department of Biological Sciences
Mankato, MN 56002-8400
(507) 389-5732
http://www.mankato.msus.edu
GRE composite score of 1350; TOEFL required for foreign students.

MISSOURI

Avila College
Premedical Adviser
11901 Wornall Road
Kansas City, MO 64145
(816) 942-8400, ext. 225
Open to underrepresented minorities, economically disadvantaged students, or educationally disadvantaged students who have been previously unsuccessful in gaining admission to medical school.

MONTANA

University of Montana
Director, Premedical Sciences
Division of Biological Sciences
Missoula, MT 59812
(406) 243-6333
http://www.umt.edu

NEBRASKA

Chadron State College
Health Professions Adviser
10th and Main
Chadron, NE 69337
(308) 432-6278
http://www.csc.edu

Creighton University School of Medicine
John T. Elder, Ph.D.
Pharmacology Department
24th and California
Omaha, NE 68178
(402) 280-3185
http://www.creighton.edu
Minority students only.

Wayne State
Dr. J.S. Johar, Head
Mathematics-Science Division
Wayne, NE 68787
(402) 375-7329
http://www.wayne.edu
Open to students who lack prerequisites basic to medicine or who have been previously unsuccessful in gaining admission to medical school.

NEW JERSEY

Livingston College-Rutgers University
Livingston Advising Center, 214 Beck Hall
P.O. Box 5062
New Brunswick, NJ 08903-5062
(908) 932-5668
http://www.rutgers.edu/nbcampus/livingston
New Jersey residents only; minimum 3.0 GPA.

Ramapo College
T. Sall, Professor of Life Science
Mahwah, NJ 07430-1680
(201) 529-7731
http://www.ramapo.edu

Rutgers University-Newark
Chair, Prehealth Advisory Committee
Biological Sciences Dept., Smith Hall Rm 135
101 Warren Street
Newark, NJ 07102
(201) 648-5705
http://www.rutgers.edu/newark/N3INFOa.html
Open to students who lack prerequisites basic to medicine and/or who have been previously unsuccessful in gaining admission to medical school.

William Paterson College
Chairman, Pre-Professional Committee
300 Pompton Road
Wayne, NJ 07470
(201) 595-3453/2245
http://pioneer.wilpaterson.edu
Open to students who lack prerequisites basic to medicine.

NEW YORK

Associated Medical Schools of New York
Coordinator, Postbac Program
SUNY-Buffalo
School of Medicine & Biomedical Sciences
3435 Main Street, 40 CFS Building
Buffalo, NY 14214
(716) 829-2811
For educationally or economically disadvantaged individuals with bachelor's degrees. Stipends available.

Barnard College
Associate Dean of Students & Chief
 Premedical Adviser
3009 Broadway
New York, NY 10027-6598
(212) 854-2024
http://www.barnard.columbia.edu
Limited to Barnard alumnae or female graduates of Bryn Mawr, Mount Holyoke, Radcliffe-Harvard, Smith, Vassar, or Wellesley.

Columbia University
Director, Preprofessional Programs
405 Lewishon
New York, NY 10027
(212) 854-3776
http://www.columbia.edu
Non-science graduates who have not previously applied to medical school. Prefer 2 to 3 years of other professional experience.

CUNY-City College
Director, Program in Premedical Studies; J-529
Convent at 138th Street
New York, NY 10031
(212) 650-6622
http://www.cuny.edu.about_cuny/city.html

CUNY-Herbert Lehman College
Premedical Adviser
Bedford Park Boulevard West
Bronx, NY 10468
(212) 960-8757
http://www.cuny.edu/about_cuny/lehman.html

CUNY-Hunter
Preprofessional Office
695 Park Ave
New York, NY 10021
(212) 772-5244
http:/www.cuny.edu/about_cuny/hunter.html
Open to students who lack prerequisites basic to medicine or who have been previously unsuccessful in gaining admission to medical school.

CUNY-Queens College
Chair, Health Professions Advisory Committee
Department of Biology
Flushing, NY 11367
(718) 997-3740
http://www.cuny.edu

CUNY-York College
Dr. Jack Schlein
9420 Guy Brewer Boulevard
Jamaica, NY 11451
(718) 262-2716
http://www.cuny.edu

Dowling College
Chief Health Professions Adviser
Department of Biology
Oakdale, NY 11769
(516) 244-3185
http://www.dowling.edu
Open to students who lack prerequisites basic to medicine.

Long Island University-Brooklyn Campus
Preprofessional Adviser, Science Division
University Plaza
Brooklyn, NY 11201
(718) 488-1209
http://www.liunet.edu
Open to students who lack prerequisites basic to medicine.

Manhattanville College
Chairman, Premed Committee
Department of Chemistry Box 76
Purchase, NY 10577
(914) 694-2200 Ext. 401/320
Open to students who lack prerequisites basic to medicine.

New York University
Prehealth Adviser, College of Arts & Science
Room 904, Main Building
100 Washington Square East
New York, NY 10003
(212) 998-8160
http://www.nyu.edu
Designed for non-science majors.

SUNY–Albany
Dept. of Health Policy & Management
School of Public Health, 201 Husted Hall
135 Western Avenue
Albany, NY 12222
(518) 442-4025
Offers a Master of Health Policy and Management degree.

SUNY-Stony Brook
Faculty Committee on Health Professions
Undergraduate Academic Affairs
Melville Library E3320
Stony Brook, NY 11794-3351
(516) 632-7080
http://sunysb.edu
Open to students who lack prerequisites basic to medicine.

Union College
Associate Dean, Graduate & Continuing Studies
Lamont House
Schenectady, NY 12308
(518) 388-6011
Open to students who lack prerequisites basic to medicine. Full- or part-time students.

NORTH CAROLINA

Bowman Gray School of Medicine
Office of Minority Affairs
Medical Center Boulevard
Winston-Salem, NC 27157-1037
(910) 716-4201
For underrepresented and disadvantaged individuals with bachelor's degrees. No cost to student. Stipend.

Fayetteville State University
Chair and Premedical Adviser
Department of Natural Sciences
1200 Murchison Road
Fayetteville, NC 28301-4298
(919) 486-1691
http://www.fsufay.edu
Open to students who lack prerequisites basic to medicine or who have been previously unsuccessful in gaining admission to medical school; financial aid available if student enters as a degree candidate; must register for a minimum of 12 hours per semester.

University of North Carolina-Greensboro
Chair, Premedical Advisory Committee
Department of Biology
Greensboro, NC 27412
(919) 334-5391
http://www.uncg.edu
Open to students who lack prerequisites basic to medicine.

Wake Forest University
Dr. Robert Shorter
Box 6103 Reynolds Station
Winston-Salem, NC 27109
(919) 759-5410
http://www.wfu.edu/start.html
Open to minority students who have applied to, but been rejected by, medical schools.

OHIO

Akron University
Richard Mostardi, Ph.D.
Department of Biology
Akron, OH 44325
(216) 972-7152

Cleveland State University
Madeline Hall, Ph.D.
Associate Professor, Dept. of Biology
24th and Euclid
Cleveland, OH 44115
http://www.csuohio.edu
Open to students who lack prerequisites basic to medicine or who have been previously unsuccessful in gaining admission to medical school.

Ohio State University
MEDPATH Office, College of Medicine
1178 Graves Hall
333 West 10th Avenue
Columbus, OH 43210-1239
(614) 292-3161
e-mail: mailto:biagi.1@osu.edu>biagi.1@osu.edu
http://www.osu.edu
Open to students with bachelor's degrees and a minimum 2.5 GPA. Stipends and conditional medical school acceptances for underrepresented minorities.

Ohio University College of Osteopathic Medicine
Dr. Harold C. Thompson III, D.O.
Director, Center of Excellence
Grosvenor Hall
Athens, OH 45701
(614) 593-2365
(614) 593-0892 Fax
Open only to students who have taken the MCAT, applied to the school, been interviewed, and have bachelor's degrees. Tuition waivers and stipends available.

Wright State University, College of Liberal Arts
Office of Preprofessional Advising
445 Millett Hall
Dayton, OH 45435
(513) 873-3181
http://www.wright.edu
Open to students who lack prerequisites basic to medicine or who have been previously unsuccessful in gaining admission to medical school; U.S. citizens and Permanent Residents only.

OREGON

University of Oregon
Academic Advising and Student Services
164 Oregon Hall
Eugene, OR 97407
http://www.uoregon.edu
Open to students who lack prerequisites basic to medicine. Requires a mathematics background.

PENNSYLVANIA

Albright College
Chief Health Professions Adviser
Department of Biology
P.O. Box 19612
Reading, PA 19612-5234
Open to students who lack prerequisites basic to medicine.

Beaver College
Chief Medical Professions Adviser
Glenside, PA 19038
(215) 572-2129
http://www.beaver.edu

Bryn Mawr College
Health Professions Advising Office
Canwyll Hall
101 North Merion Avenue
Bryn Mawr, PA 19010-2899
(215) 526-7350
gopher://gopher.brynmawr.edu
Open to students who have neither previously applied to medical school nor taken premed courses.

Duquesne University
Director, Undergraduate Health Programs
Room 241, Mellon Hall
Pittsburgh, PA 15282-1502
(412) 396-6335
(412) 396-5587 Fax
http://www.duq.edu
Open to students who lack prerequisites basic to medicine or who have been previously unsuccessful in gaining admission to medical school. Non-science majors who were not premeds may get provisional acceptance to Allegheny University School of Medicine and to Temple University.

Hahnemann University Graduate School
Health Professions Peparatory Program
Broad and Vine, Mail Stop 344
Philadelphia, PA 19102-1192
(215) 762-7864
Requires a bachelor's degree, including completion of premedical requirements and MCAT.

Immaculata College
Dr. Barbara Piatka
Biology Department
Immaculata, PA 19345
(215) 647-4400

Pennsylvania State University
Health Professions Office
224 Pond Lab
University Park, PA 16802
(814) 865-7620
http://www.psu.edu

Philadelphia College of Pharmacy and Science
Postbaccalaureate Program
600 South 43rd Street
Philadelphia, PA 19104
(215) 596-8508
Open to students who lack prerequisites basic to medicine.

Temple University
Health Professions Adviser
Academic Advising Center, Sullivan Hall
Philadelphia, PA 19122
(215) 787-7971/8115

University of Pennsylvania
Coordinator, Prehealth Programs
College of General Studies
3440 Market Street, Suite 100
Philadelphia, PA 19104-6384
(215) 898-4847
One program for science majors and one for non-science majors with bachelor's degrees.

West Chester University
Director, Premedical Program
West Chester, PA 19383
(610) 436-2978
http://www.wcupa.edu
GPA 3.2 and no previous MCAT.

PUERTO RICO

InterAmerican Univ. of Puerto Rico-Metro Campus
Director of NIOMS-MARC/MBRS Programs
P.O. Box 191293
San Juan, PR 00919-1293
(809) 250-0169
(809) 250-1912, ext. 2333
Open to applicants in need of academic strengthening; PR residents only.

RHODE ISLAND

Brown University
Dean Mark Curran
Box 1959
Providence, RI 02906
(401) 863-3452
http://www.brown.edu
Open to students who lack prerequisites basic to medicine; Brown alumni or RI residents only.

University of Rhode Island
Chair, Premedical Advising Committee
Biological Science Center, B-106
Kingston, RI 02881
(401) 792-2670
http://www.uri.edu

TENNESSEE

Christian Brothers University
Dr. Stan Eisen, Head
Biology Department
650 East Parkway South
Memphis, TN 38104
(901) 722-0447
http://www.cbu.edu
Must be accepted as special student.

David Lipscomb University
Chair, Premedical Committee
3901 Grannywhite Pike
Nashville, TN 37204-3951
Open to students who lack prerequisites basic to medicine or who have been previously unsuccessful in gaining admission to medical school.

Fisk University
Director, UNCF Premedical Summer Institute
Nashville, TN 37208-3051
(615) 329-8796
http://www.fisk.edu
Minorities; TN residents only.

TEXAS

Lamar University
Chair, Preprofessional Advisory Committee
Department of Chemistry
Beaumont, TX 77710
(409) 880-8275
http://www.lamar.edu

Texas Christian University
Dr. Phil Hartman
Department of Biology
Fort Worth, TX 76129
(817) 921-7196
http://www.tcu.edu
Open to students who lack prerequisites basic to medicine.

University of Houston
Health Professions Adviser
University Studies Division
Houston, TX 77204-3243
(713) 743-8586
http://www.uh.edu
Open to minority students (African-American and Mexican-American) who have previously applied to the College of Medicine at the University of Texas Medical Branch at Galveston. Seven students are selected each year.

University of Texas-Arlington
Assistant Dean of Science for Student Affairs
College of Science
P.O. Box 19047
Arlington, TX 76019
(817) 273-2310
http://www.uta.edu

University of Texas Medical Branch
Director for Medical Student Recruitment
Ashbel Smith, G120
Galveston, TX 77555-1317
(409) 772-3256
Program for underrepresented minorities. Applicants must have applied to, but not been accepted at, this medical school. Offers conditional acceptance to medical school.

University of Texas-Permian Basin
Donald Allan, Ph. D.
Professor and Chair, Life Sciences
Box 8397
Odessa, TX 79762-8301
(915) 367-2242

VERMONT

Bennington College
Chief Health Sciences Adviser
Bennington, VT 05201
(802) 442-5401, ext. 319

Trinity College
Health Professions Adviser
208 Colchester Avenue
Burlington, VT 05401
(802) 658-0337

VIRGINIA

Old Dominion University
Prehealth Adviser
Department of Biological Sciences
Mills Goodwin Room 110
Norfolk, VA 23529-0266
(804) 683-3595
http://www.odu.edu

Virginia Commonwealth University/Medical
College of Virginia
Dean of Graduate School
Founders Hall, Room 103
827 West Franklin Street
P.O. Box 843051
Richmond, VA 23284-3051
(804) 828-6916
For those with a baccalaureate degree, a minimum 2.8 GPA, and completion of organic chemistry.

WASHINGTON

Seattle University
Chief Premedical/Predental Adviser
Department of Biology
Seattle, WA 98122
(206) 296-5399
http://www.seattleu.edu

WEST VIRGINIA

Glenville State College
Dr. Mary Jo Pribble
Glenville, WV 26351
(304) 462-7361

Appendix D: Medical School-Sponsored Summer Programs

Albany Medical College
Office of Minority Affairs
47 New Scotland Avenue
Albany, NY 12208
(518) 262-5824
Two programs for minority high school students: research and clinically oriented.

Baylor College of Medicine/Rice University
Honors Premedical Academy
Project Coordinator, School-Based Programs
Baylor College of Medicine
1709 Dryden, Suite 545
Houston, TX 77030
(800) 798-8244
Six weeks long. Requires at least one year of college with a GPA 2.75 and 3.0 in major.

Bowman Gray School of Medicine
College Phase Summer Program
Office of Minority Affairs
Medical Center Boulevard
Winston-Salem, NC 27157-1037
(910) 716-4201
Six weeks long. Underrepresented minority college students with minimum science GPA 2.5. Two tiers: one for freshmen and sophomores, another for juniors and seniors.

Case Western Reserve Univ. School of Medicine
Health Careers Enhancement Prog. for Minorities
Associate Dean for Academic Affairs
10900 Euclid Avenue
Cleveland, OH 44106-4920
(216) 368-2212
Six weeks long. Underrepresented minority college students.

Charles R. Drew University of Medical Science
Summer MCAT Preparation Program
Center for Educational Achievement
1621 East 120th Street
Los Angeles, CA 90059
(213) 563-4926
Seven weeks long. Min. science/math GPA 2.1.

Howard University
Summer Health Careers Advanced Enrichment
  Program
Director, Center for Preprofessional Education
Box 473, Administrative Building
Washington, DC 20059
Six weeks long. Disadvantaged students who completed all premed requirements and have an overall GPA of at least 2.7.

Ohio University College of Osteopathic Medicine
Summer Scholars Program
Premedical Education Coordinator
Center of Excellence, 030 Grosvenor Hall
Athens, OH 45701
(614) 593-0917
Six weeks long. Underrepresented minority students with at least one year of college-level chemistry and biology. Preference for incoming seniors and postbaccalaureate students.

Texas A&M University College of Medicine
Bridge to Medicine Summer Prog. for
  Minority/Disadvantaged College Students
Office of Student Affairs and Admissions
106 Reynolds Medical Building
College Station, TX 77843-1114
(409) 862-4065
Six weeks long. Underrepresented minority students who completed all premed requirements and have at least a 2.8 GPA.

Tulane University Medical Center
Summer Reinforcement & Enrichment Program
Associate Dean for Student Services
Office of MEDREP & Student Services
1430 Tulane Avenue, LS40
New Orleans, LA 70112
(504) 588-5327
Eight weeks long. Disadvantaged students with at least two years of undergraduate or postbaccalaureate science education.

UC–Davis School of Medicine
Summer Academic Study Program
Office of Minority Affairs
Davis, CA 95616
(916) 752-4808
Six weeks long. For underrepresented minority students at northern California colleges entering their sophomore or junior years.

UC–Irvine School of Medicine
Summer Premedical Program
Office of Educational & Community Programs
PO Box 4089, College of Medicine
University of California
Irvine, CA 92717-4089
(714) 824-4603
Six weeks long. For underrepresented minority students entering sophomore or junior years.

UCLA School of Medicine
Premedical Enrichment Program
Office of Student Support Services, 13-154
CHS
Los Angeles, CA 90024-1720
(310) 825-3575
Eight weeks long. For underrepresented minority students with a minimum of one year of college chemistry. Two tiers, depending upon amount of biology, chemistry, math, and physics. Minimum GPA 2.5.

University of Cincinnati College of Medicine
Summer Premedical Enrichment Program
Office of Student Affairs & Admissions
231 Bethesda Avenue
Cincinnati, OH 45267-0552
(513) 558-7212
Eight weeks long. Disadvantaged students with at least two years of undergraduate work.

University of Connecticut Health Center
Pre-College/College Enrichment Program, and
  Medical/Dental Preparatory Program
Office of Minority Student Affairs
Farmington, CT 06030-3920
(203) 679-3483
Two tiers for underrepresented minorities or disadvantaged students. Enrichment program, eight weeks long, is for high school seniors and college freshmen and sophomores. Preparatory Program, six weeks long, is for college juniors and seniors and postbaccalaureates.

University of Massachusetts Medical Center
Program Director, Summer Enrichment Program
Office of Outreach Programs
55 Lake Avenue, North
Worcester, MA 01655
(508) 856-5541
Four weeks long. Underrepresented minority or disadvantaged students with 30 hours of college, including 8 hours of organic chemistry.

University of Michigan School of Public Health
Summer Enrichment Prog. in Health Admin-
  istration for Undergraduate Minority Students
Dept. of Health Management & Policy
M3031 School of Public Health
Ann Arbor, MI 48109-2029
(313) 763-9900
Eight weeks long. Underrepresented minority college students entering junior or senior year, interested in health administration or health policy. Minimum GPA 2.8.

University of Minnesota
  Gen. Chemistry & Precalculus or Calculus Prog.
  Organic Chemistry & Precalculus or Calculus
    Program
  Summer Biology Program
  Summer Physics Program
Michael Michlin, Ph.D.
515 Delaware Street, S.E.
1-125 Moos Tower
Minneapolis, MN 55455
(612) 624-5904
Six weeks long (each program). Underrepresented minority students planning to take the named courses the following year.

University of Oklahoma Health Sciences Center
Headlands Indian Health Careers Summer Prog.
BSEB, Room 200
P.O. Box 26901
Oklahoma City, OK 73126-9968
(405) 271-2250
*Eight weeks long. Native Americans who are high
school seniors or in first year of college. Must
have two years of algebra and two science
courses. Minimum GPA 2.5.*

University of Pittsburgh School of Medicine
Summer Premed. Academic Enrichment Program
Director of Minority Programs
M-247 Scaife Hall, School of Medicine
Pittsburgh, PA 15261
(412) 648-8987
*Eight weeks long. Underrepresented minority
students who are either incoming college
freshmen (level 1) or college sophomores, juniors,
or seniors (level 2).*

Univ. of Rochester School of Medicine &Dentistry
Summer Research Fellowship Program (SURF)
Director, Ethnic & Multicultural Affairs
601 Elmwood Avenue, Box 601
Rochester, NY 14642
(716) 275-2175
*Nine weeks long. Underrepresented minority
students with at least two years of college and at
least six months of premed education yet to
complete.*

USC School of Medicine
HePP-Consortium for Health Professional
  Preparation
Dean, Minority Affairs
1333 San Pablo Street, MCH 51-C
Los Angeles, CA 90033
(213) 342-1050
*Six weeks long. Three tiers, beginning with high
school graduates.*

Appendix E: Medical Schools

Note about Web addresses: If the listed Web address does not work, use an abbreviated form of the address. For example: UCLA's Web address is listed as

http://www.mednet.ucla.edu/dept/som/mnsom_default.htm

If this doesn't work for you, try the shorter form: http://www.mednet.ucla.edu/

Note that many medical schools fill their classes well before their "official" application deadlines. This is particularly true for those schools who have "rolling admissions" policies and deadlines after January 1 (such as all of the Osteopathic medical schools).

United States

ALABAMA

University of Alabama School of Medicine
Office of Medical Student Services/Admissions
VH100
Birmingham, AL 35294-0019
(205) 934-2330; (205) 934-8724 (fax)
http://lhl.uab.edu/uasom/
Application Deadline: Nov 1

University of South Alabama College of Medicine
Office of Admissions, 2015 MSB
Mobile, AL 36688-0002
(334) 460-7176; (334) 460-6278 (fax)
http://southmed.usouthal.edu/com/index.html
Application Deadline: Nov 15

ARIZONA

University of Arizona College of Medicine
Admission Office, Room 2209
P.O. Box 245075
Tucson, AZ 85724
(520) 626-6214; (520) 626-4884 (fax)
http://www.AHSC.Arizona.edu/com.shtml
Application Deadline: Nov 1

ARKANSAS

University of Arkansas College of Medicine
Office of Student Admissions
4301 West Markham Street, Slot 551
Little Rock, AR 72205-7199
(501) 686-5354; (501) 686-5873 (fax)
E-mail: LWilliams@comdean1.uams.edu
http://amanda.uams.edu/uams.html
Application Deadline: Nov 15

CALIFORNIA

Univ. of California–Davis School of Medicine
Admission Office
Davis, CA 95616
(916) 752-2717
http://edison.ucdmc.ucdavis.edu
Application Deadline: Nov 1

Univ. of California–Irvine College of Medicine
118 Med Surg 1
Office of Admissions
Irvine, CA 92717-4089
(800) 824-5388; (714) 824-5388
(714) 824-2485 (fax)
http://meded.com.uci.edu
Application Deadline: Nov 1

Univ. of California–Los Angeles
School of Medicine
Office of Student Affairs, Division of Admissions
Center for Health Sciences
Los Angeles, CA 90095–1720
(310) 825-6081
http://www.mednet.ucla.edu/som/
Application Deadline: Nov 1

Drew/UCLA Joint Medical Program
Drew University of Medicine and Science
1621 East 120th Street
Los Angeles, CA 90059
(213) 563-4960
http://www.cdrewu.edu/
Application Deadline: Nov 15

Univ.of California–San Diego, School of Medicine
Office of Admissions, 0621
Medical Teaching Facility
9500 Gilman Drive
La Jolla, CA 92093–0621
(619) 534-3880; (619) 534-5282 (fax)
http://cybermed.ucsd.edu
Application Deadline: Nov 1

University of California–San Francisco
School of Medicine,
Admissions, C–200, Box 0408
San Francisco, CA 94143
(415) 476-4044
http://www.ucsf.edu/campus/schmed/SchMed.html
Application Deadline: Nov 1

Loma Linda University School of Medicine
Associate Dean for Admissions
Loma Linda, CA 92350
(909) 824-4467; (909) 824-4846 (fax)
http://www.llu.edu/LLU/Medicine/
Application Deadline: Nov 15

Univ. of Southern California School of Medicine
Office of Admissions
1975 Zonal Avenue
Los Angeles, CA 90033
(213) 342–1607
E-mail: medadmit@hsc.usc.edu
http://www.usc.edu/hsc/med-sch/med-home.html
Application Deadline: Nov 1

Stanford University School of Medicine
Office of Admissions
851 Welch Road, Room 154
Palo Alto, CA 94304–1677
(415) 723-6861; (415) 723-4599 (fax)
http://med-www.stanford.edu/school/
Application Deadline: Nov 1

COLORADO

University of Colorado School of Medicine
Medical School Admissions
4200 East 9th Avenue, C–297
Denver, CO 80262
(303) 270-7361
http://www.hsc.edu
Application Deadline: Nov 15

CONNECTICUT

Univ. of Connecticut School of Medicine
Office of Admissions and Student Affairs
263 Farmington Avenue, Rm. AG–062
Farmington, CT 06030–1905
(860) 679-2152; (860) 679-1282 (fax)
E-mail: sanford@nso1.uchc.edu
http://www9.uchc.edu/index.html
Application Deadline: Dec 15

Yale University School of Medicine
Office of Admissions
367 Cedar Street
New Haven, CT 06510
(203) 785-2643; (203) 785-3234 (fax)
http://info.med.yale.edu/medical/
Application Deadline: Oct 15

DISTRICT OF COLUMBIA

George Washington University
School of Medicine & Health Sciences
Office of Admissions
2300 Eye Street, N.W.
Washington, DC 20037
(202) 994-3506
http://www.gwu.edu/~gwumc/
Application Deadline: Dec 1

Georgetown University School of Medicine
Office of Admissions
3900 Reservoir Road, N.W.
Washington, DC 20007
(202) 687-1154
http://www.dml.georgetown.edu/schmed/
Application Deadline: Nov 1

Howard University College of Medicine
Admission Office
520 W Street, N.W.
Washington, DC 20059
(202) 806-6270; (202) 806-7934 (fax)
http://www.cldc.howard.edu/~bhlogan/hucm–
    cat.html
Application Deadline: Dec 15

FLORIDA

University of Florida College of Medicine
Chair, Medical Selection Committee
J. Hillis Miller Health Center, Box 100216
Gainesville, FL 32610
(904) 392-4569; (904) 846-0622 (fax)
http://www.med.ufl.edu/
Application Deadline: Dec 1

Florida State Univ./Univ. of Florida COM
Program in Medical Sciences
Tallahassee, FL 32306–4051
(904) 644-1855
http://www.fsu.edu/~pims/pims.html
Application Deadline: Dec 15

University of Miami School of Medicine
Office of Admissions
P.O. Box 016159
Miami, FL 33101
(305) 243-6791; (305) 243-6548 (fax)
E-mail: miamimd@mednet.med.miami.edu
http://www.med.miami.edu/UMSM/
Application Deadline: Dec 1

University of South Florida College of Medicine
Office of Admissions, Box 3
12901 Bruce B. Downs Blvd.
Tampa, FL 33612–4799
(813) 974-2229; (813) 974-4990 (fax)
http://www.med.usf.edu/
Application Deadline: Dec 1

GEORGIA

Emory University School of Medicine
Woodruff Health Sciences Center
Administration Building, Admissions, Room 303
Atlanta, GA 30322–4510
(404) 727-5660; (404) 727-0045 (fax)
E-mail: medschadmiss@medadm.emory.edu
http://www.emory.edu/WHSC/MED/med.html
Application Deadline: Oct 15

Medical College of Georgia
School of Medicine
Associate Dean for Admissions
Augusta, GA 30912–4760
(706) 721-3186; (706) 721-0959 (fax)
http://www.mcg.edu
Application Deadline: Nov 1

Mercer University School of Medicine
Office of Admissions and Student Affairs
Macon, GA 31207
(912) 752-2542
E-mail: kothanek.j@gain.mercer.edu
Application Deadline: Dec 1

Morehouse School of Medicine
Admissions and Student Affairs
720 Westview Drive, S.W.
Atlanta, GA 30310–1495
(404) 752-1650; (404) 752-1512 (fax)
http://www.msm.edu
Application Deadline: Dec 1

HAWAII

University of Hawaii
John A. Burns School of Medicine
Office of Admissions
1960 East–West Road
Honolulu, HI 96822
(808) 956-5446; (808) 956-9547 (fax)
E-mail: nishikim@jabsom.biomed.hawaii.edu
http://medworld.biomed.hawaii.edu/
Application Deadline: Dec 1

ILLINOIS

University of Chicago
Pritzker School of Medicine
Office of the Dean of Students
924 East 57th Street
Chicago, IL 60637-5416
(312) 702-1939; (312) 702-2598 (fax)
http://www.uchicago.edu/u.acadunits/BSD.html
Application Deadline: Nov 15

FUHS/Chicago Medical School
Office of Admissions
3333 Green Bay Road
Chicago, IL 60064
(708) 578-3206/3207; (708) 578-3284 (fax)
Application Deadline: Dec 15

University of Illinois College of Medicine
Medical College Admissions
Room 165 CME M/C 783
808 South Wood Street
Chicago, IL 60612–7302
(312) 996-5635; (312) 996-6693 (fax)
http://www.med.uiuc.edu/
Application Deadline: Dec 1

Loyola University of Chicago
Stritch School of Medicine
Office of Admissions, Room 1752
2160 South First Avenue
Maywood, IL 60153
(708) 216-3229
http://www.lumc.edu/
Application Deadline: Nov 15

Northwestern University Medical School
Associate Dean for Admissions
303 East Chicago Avenue
Chicago, IL 60611
(312) 503-8206
http://www.numc.nwu.edu/
Application Deadline: Oct 15

Rush Medical College
Office of Admissions
524 Academic Facility
600 South Paulina Street
Chicago, IL 60612
(312) 942-6913; (312) 942-2333 (fax)
http://www.rpslmc.edu/index.html
Application Deadline: Nov 15

Southern Illinois Univ. School of Medicine
Office of Student and Alumni Affairs
P.O. Box 19230
Springfield, IL 62794–9230
(217) 524-0326; (217) 785-5538 (fax)
http://www.siumed.edu
Application Deadline: Nov 15

INDIANA

Indiana University School of Medicine
Medical School Admissions Office
Fesler Hall 213
1120 South Drive
Indianapolis, IN 46202–5113
(317) 274-3772
http://www.iupui.edu/it/medschl/home.html
Application Deadline: Dec 15

IOWA

University of Iowa College of Medicine
Director of Admissions
100 Medicine Administration Building
Iowa City, IA 52242–1101
(319) 335-8052; (319) 335-8049 (fax)
E-mail: medical-admission@uiowa.edu
http://www.medadmin.uiowa.edu/
Application Deadline: Nov 1

KANSAS

University of Kansas School of Medicine
Associate Dean for Admissions
3901 Rainbow Boulevard
Kansas City, KS 66160–7301
(913) 588-5245; (913) 588-5259 (fax)
http://www.kumc.edu/
Application Deadline: Nov 1

KENTUCKY

University of Kentucky College of Medicine
Admissions, Room MN–102, Office of Education
Chandler Medical Center
800 Rose Street
Lexington, KY 40536–0084
(606) 323-6161; (606) 323-2076 (fax)
http://www.uky.edu/CollegeofMedicine/
Application Deadline: Nov 1

University of Louisville School of Medicine
Office of Admissions
Health Sciences Center
Louisville, KY 40292
(502) 852-5193
http://www.louisville.edu/medschool/
Application Deadline: Nov 1

LOUISIANA

LSU–New Orleans School of Medicine
Admissions Office
1901 Perdido Street, Box P3-4
New Orleans, LA 70112–1393
(504) 568-6262; (504) 568-7701 (fax)
http://www.lsumc.edu
Application Deadline: Nov 15

LSU–Shreveport School of Medicine
Office of Student Admissions
P.O. Box 33932
Shreveport, LA 71130–3932
(318) 675-5190; (318) 675-5244 (fax)
e-mail: shuadm@lsumc.edu
http://lib-sh.lsumc.edu/
Application Deadline: Nov 15

Tulane University School of Medicine
Office of Admissions
1430 Tulane Ave, SL67
New Orleans, LA 70112–2699
(504) 588-5187; (504) 588-6462 (fax)
E-mail: medsch@tmcpop.tmc.tulane.edu
http://www1.omi.tulane.edu/departments/
    admissions/admissions.html
Application Deadline: Dec 15

MARYLAND

Johns Hopkins University School of Medicine
Committee on Admission
720 Rutland Avenue
Baltimore, MD 21205–2196
(410) 955-3182
http://infonet.welch.jhu.edu/education/
Application Deadline: Nov 1

University of Maryland School of Medicine
Committee on Admissions, Room 1–005
655 West Baltimore Street
Baltimore, MD 21201
(410) 706-7478
http://som1.ab.umd.edu/som.html
Application Deadline: Nov 1

Uniformed Services Univ. of the Health Sciences
F. Edward Hébert School of Medicine
Admission Office, Room A–1041
4301 Jones Bridge Road
Bethesda, MD 20814–4799
(800) 772-1743; (301) 295-3101
(301) 295-3545 (fax)
http://www.usuhs.mil/
Application Deadline: Nov 1

MASSACHUSETTS

Boston University School of Medicine
Admissions Office
Building L, Room 124
80 East Concord Street
Boston, MA 02118
(617) 638-4630
http://med–amsa.bu.edu/BUSM/
Application Deadline: Nov 15

Harvard Medical School
Office of Admissions
25 Shattuck Street
Boston, MA 02115–6092
(617) 432-1550; (617) 432-3307 (fax)
E-mail: HMSADM@warren.med.harvard.edu
http://www.med.harvard.edu
Application Deadline: Oct 16

University of Massachusetts Medical School
Associate Dean for Admissions
55 Lake Avenue, North
Worcester, MA 01655
(508) 856-2323
E-mail: Admissions@banyan.ummed.edu
http://www.ummed.edu
Application Deadline: Nov 1

Tufts University School of Medicine
Office of Admissions
136 Harrison Avenue, Stearns 1
Boston, MA 02111
(617) 636-6571
http://polaris.nemc.org/tusm/
Application Deadline: Nov 1

MICHIGAN

Michigan State Univ. College of Human Medicine
Office of Admissions
A–239 Life Sciences
East Lansing, MI 48824–1317
(517) 353-9620; (517) 432-0021 (fax)
E-mail: MDAdmissions@msu.edu
http://35.8.145.179/
Application Deadline: Nov 15

University of Michigan Medical School
Admissions Office
M4130 Medical Sciences I Building
Ann Arbor, MI 48109–0611
(313) 764-6317; (313) 764-4542 (fax)
http://www.med.umich.edu/medschool/
Application Deadline: Nov 15

Wayne State University School of Medicine
Director of Admissions
540 East Canfield
Detroit, MI 48201
(313) 577-1466; (313) 577-1330 (fax)
http://med.wayne.edu:82/admiss/admiss.htm
Application Deadline: Dec 15

MINNESOTA

Mayo Medical School
Admissions Committee
200 First Street, S.W.
Rochester, MN 55905
(507) 284-3671; (507) 284-2634 (fax)
http://www.mayo.edu/education/mms/MMS_Home
    _Page.html
Application Deadline: Nov 1

Univ. of Minnesota–Duluth School of Medicine
Office of Admissions, Room 107
10 University Drive
Duluth, MN 55812
(218) 726-8511; (218) 726-6235 (fax)
E-mail: jcarlsio@ub.d.umn.edu
http://www.d.umn.edu/medweb/
Application Deadline: Nov 15

University of Minnesota Medical School
Office of Admissions and Student Affairs
Box 293–UMHC
420 Delaware Street, S.E.
Minneapolis, MN 55455–0310
(612) 624-1122; (612) 626-6800 (fax)
http://www.med.umn.edu/
Application Deadline: Nov 15

MISSISSIPPI

University of Mississippi School of Medicine
Chair, Admission Committee
2500 North State Street
Jackson, MS 39216–4505
(601) 984-5010; (601) 984-5008 (fax)
http://fiona.umsmed.edu
Application Deadline: Nov 1

MISSOURI

Univ. of Missouri–Columbia School of Medicine
Office of Admissions
MA202 Medical Sciences Bldg.
One Hospital Drive
Columbia, MO 65212
(314) 882-2923; (314) 882-4808 (fax)
E-mail: shari_l._swindell@muccmail.missouri.edu
http://www.miaims.missouri.edu/som
Application Deadline: Nov 1

Univ. of Missouri–Kansas City School of Medicine
Council on Selection
2411 Holmes
Kansas City, MO 64108
(816) 235-1870; (816) 235-5277 (fax)
http://research.med.umkc.edu
Application Deadline: Nov 15

St. Louis University School of Medicine
Admissions Committee
1402 South Grand Boulevard
St. Louis, MO 63104
(314) 577-8205; (314) 577-8214 (fax)
http://www.slu.edu/colleges/med/
Application Deadline: Dec 15

Washington University School of Medicine
Office of Admissions
660 South Euclid Avenue, #8107
St. Louis, MO 63110
(314) 362-6857; (314) 362-4658 (fax)
http://medschool.wustl.edu/admissions/
Application Deadline: Nov 15

NEBRASKA

Creighton University School of Medicine
Office of Admissions
2500 California Plaza
Omaha, NE 68178
(402) 280-2798; (402) 280-1241 (fax)
http://medicine.creighton.edu
Application Deadline: Dec 1

University of Nebraska College of Medicine
Office of Academic Affairs, Room 4004
600 South 42nd Street
Omaha, NE 68198–4430
(402) 559-4205; (402) 559-6840 (fax)
http://www.unmc.edu/
Application Deadline: Nov 15

NEVADA

University of Nevada School of Medicine
Mail Stop 357
Office of Admissions and Student Affairs
Reno, NV 89557
(702) 784-6063; (702) 784-6096 (fax)
E-mail: ekirk@scs.unr.edu
http://www.med.unr.edu
Application Deadline: Nov 1

NEW HAMPSHIRE

Dartmouth Medical School
Admissions
7020 Remsen, Room 306
Hanover, NH 03755–3833
(603) 650-1505; (603) 650-1614 (fax)
http://www.hitchcock.org
Application Deadline: Nov 1

NEW JERSEY

UMDNJ–New Jersey Medical School
Director of Admissions
185 South Orange Avenue
Newark, NJ 07103
(201) 982-4631; (201) 982-7986 (fax)
http://njmsa.umdnj.edu/umdnj.html
Application Deadline: Dec 15

UMDNJ–Robert Wood Johnson Medical School
Office of Admissions
675 Hoes Lane
Piscataway, NJ 08854–5635
(908) 235-4576; (908) 235-5078 (fax)
http://www2.umdnj.edu/rwjms.html
Application Deadline: Dec 15

NEW MEXICO

University of New Mexico School of Medicine
Office of Admissions and Student Affairs
Basic Medical Sciences Building, Room 107
Albuquerque, NM 87131–5166
(505) 277-4766; (505) 277-2755 (fax)
Application Deadline: Nov 15

NEW YORK

Albany Medical College
Office of Admissions, A–3
47 New Scotland Avenue
Albany, NY 12208
(518) 262-5521; (518) 262-5887 (fax)
Application Deadline: Nov 15

Albert Einstein College of Medicine
Office of Admissions
Jack and Pearl Resnick Campus
1300 Morris Park Avenue
Bronx, NY 10461
(718) 430-2106; (718) 430-8825 (fax)
E-mail: admissions@aecom.yu.edu
http://www.aecom.yu.edu/
Application Deadline: Nov 15

Columbia Univ. College of Physicians & Surgeons
Admissions Office, Room 1–416
630 West 168th Street
New York, NY 10032
(212) 305-3595
http://cpmcnet.columbia.edu/dept/ps
Application Deadline: Oct 15

Cornell University Medical College
Office of Admissions
445 East 69th Street
New York, NY 10021
(212) 746-1067
http://www.med.cornell.edu
Application Deadline: Oct 15

Mount Sinai School of Medicine
(Now part of NYU–Mt. Sinai School of Medicine)
Director of Admissions
Annenberg Bldg., Room 5–04
One Gustave L. Levy Place, Box 1002
New York, NY 10029–6574
(212) 241-6696
http://www.mssm.edu/index.html
Application Deadline: Nov 1

New York Medical College
Office of Admissions
Sunshine Cottage, Room 127
Valhalla, NY 10595
(914) 993-4507; (914) 993-4976 (fax)
http://www.nymc.edu
Application Deadline: Dec 1

New York University School of Medicine
(Now part of NYU–Mt. Sinai School of Medicine)
Office of Admissions
P.O. Box 1924
New York, NY 10016
(212) 263-5290
http://www.med.nyu.edu/training.html
Application Deadline: Dec 1

Univ. of Rochester School of Medicine & Dentistry
Director of Admissions
Medical Center Box 601
Rochester, NY 14642
(617) 275-4539; (617) 273-1016 (fax)
E-mail: admish@urmc.rochester.edu
http://www.rochester.edu/SMD/
Application Deadline: Oct 15

SUNY–Brooklyn College of Medicine
Director of Admissions
450 Clarkson Avenue, Box 60M
Brooklyn, NY 11203
(718) 270-2446
http://www.hscbklyn.edu/com/
Application Deadline: Dec 15

SUNY–Buffalo School of Medicine & Biomedical
  Sciences
Office of Medical Admissions
35 CFS Building
Buffalo, NY 14214–3013
(716) 829-3465; (716) 829-2798 (fax)
E-mail: jrosso@ubmedc.buffalo.edu
http://wings.buffalo.edu/medicine/
Application Deadline: Nov 15

SUNY–Stony Brook School of Medicine
Committee on Admissions
Health Sciences Center
Level 4, Room 147
Stony Brook, NY 11794–8434
(516) 444-2113; (516) 444-2202 (fax)
E-mail: admissions@dean.som.sunysb.edu
http://www.informatics.sunysb.edu:80/som
Application Deadline: Nov 15

SUNY–Syracuse College of Medicine
Admissions Committee
155 Elizabeth Blackwell Street
Syracuse, NY 13210
(315) 464-4570; (315) 464-8867
http://www.hscsyr.edu/~wwwserv/homepage.html
Application Deadline: Dec 1

NORTH CAROLINA

Bowman Gray School of Medicine
Office of Medical School Admissions
Medical Center Blvd.
Winston–Salem, NC 27157–1090
(910) 716-4264; (910) 716-5807 (fax)
http://isnet.is.wfu.edu
Application Deadline: Nov 1

Duke University School of Medicine
Committee on Admissions
P.O. Box 3710
Durham, NC 27710
(919) 684-2985; (919) 684-28893 (fax)
http://www.mc.duke.edu/depts/som/
Application Deadline: Oct 15

East Carolina University School of Medicine
Associate Dean, Office of Admissions
Greenville, NC 27858–4354
(919) 816-2202
http://www.med.ecu.edu
Application Deadline: Nov 15

University of North Carolina at Chapel Hill
School of Medicine
Admissions Office
CB# 7000 MacNider Hall
Chapel Hill, NC 27599–7000
(919) 962-8331
http://www.med.unc.edu
Application Deadline: Nov 15

NORTH DAKOTA

University of North Dakota School of Medicine
Secretary, Committee on Admissions
501 North Columbia Road, Box 9037
Grand Forks, ND 58202–9037
(701) 777-4221; (701) 777-4942 (fax)
http://www.med.und.nodak.edu
Application Deadline: Nov 1

OHIO

Case Western Reserve Univ. School of Medicine
Associate Dean for Admissions & Student Affairs
10900 Euclid Avenue
Cleveland, OH 44106–4920
(216) 368-3450; (216) 368-4621 (fax)
http://mediswww.meds.cwru.edu
Application Deadline: Oct 15

University of Cincinnati College of Medicine
Office of Student Affairs/Admissions
P.O. Box 670552
Cincinnati, OH 45267–0552
(513) 558-7314; (513) 558-1165 (fax)
http://www.med.uc.edu/htdocs/medicine/
    uccom.htm
Application Deadline: Nov 15

Medical College of Ohio
Admissions Office
P.O. Box 10008
Toledo, OH 43699
(419) 381-4229; (419) 381-4005 (fax)
http://www.mco.edu
Application Deadline: Nov 1

Northeastern Ohio Univ. College of Medicine
Office of Admissions & Educational Research
P.O. Box 95
Rootstown, OH 44272–0095
(216) 325-2511; (216) 325-8372 (fax)
E-mail: admit@neoucom.edu
http://www.neoucom.edu/
Application Deadline: Nov 1

Ohio State University College of Medicine
Admission Committee, 270–A Meiling Hall
370 West Ninth Avenue
Columbus, OH 43210–1238
(614) 292-7137; (614) 292-1544 (fax)
E-mail: admiss-med@osu.edu
http://www.med.ohio-state.edu
Application Deadline: Nov 1

Wright State University School of Medicine
Office of Student Affairs/Admissions
P.O. Box 1751
Dayton, OH 45401
(513) 873-2934; (513) 873-3322 (fax)
http://www.med.wright.edu
Application Deadline: Nov 15

OKLAHOMA

University of Oklahoma
Dotty Shaw Killam
College of Medicine
P.O. Box 26901
Oklahoma City, OK 73190
(405) 271-2331; (405) 271-3032 (fax)
E-mail: Dotty-Shaw@uokhsc.edu
http://www.uokhsc.edu
Application Deadline: Oct 15

OREGON

Oregon Health Sciences University
School of Medicine
Office of Education Student Affairs, L102
3181 S.W. Sam Jackson Park Road
Portland, OR 97201
(503) 494-2998; (503) 494-3400 (fax)
http://www.ohsu.edu
Application Deadline: Oct 15

PENNSYLVANIA

Allegheny University of the Health Sciences
  (Formerly Medical College of Pennsylvania–
  Hahnemann Univ. School of Medicine)
MCP<>Hahnemann School of Medicine
Admission Office
2900 Queen Lane Avenue
Philadelphia, PA 19129
(215) 991-8202; (215) 843-1766 (fax)
http://www.allegheny.edu/homepage.html
Application Deadline: Dec 1

Jefferson Medical College
Associate Dean for Admissions
1025 Walnut Street
Philadelphia, PA 19107
(215) 955-6983; (215) 955-6939 (fax)
http://www.tju.edu
Application Deadline: Nov 15

Pennsylvania State Univ. College of Medicine
Office of Student Affairs
P.O. Box 850
Hershey, PA 17033
(717) 531-8755; (717) 531-6225 (fax)
http://www.hmc.psu.edu/hmc/colmed.htm
Application Deadline: Nov 15

University of Pennsylvania School of Medicine
Director of Admissions and Financial Aid
Edward J. Stemmler Hall, Suite 100
Philadelphia, PA 19104–6056
(215) 898-8001; (215) 573-6645 (fax)
http://www.med.upenn.edu
Application Deadline: Nov 1

University of Pittsburgh School of Medicine
Office of Admissions
518 Scaife Hall
Pittsburgh, PA 15261
(412) 648-9891; (412) 648-8768 (fax)
E-mail: admissions@fs1.dean-med.pitt.edu
http://www.omed.pitt.edu/~omed/
Application Deadline: Nov 1

Temple University School of Medicine
Admission Office
Suite 305, Student Faculty Center
Broad and Ontario Streets
Philadelphia, PA 19140
(215) 707-3656; (215) 707-6932 (fax)
Application Deadline: Dec 1

PUERTO RICO

Universidad Central Del Caribe
School of Medicine
Office of Admissions
Ramón Ruíz Arnau University Hospital
Call Box 60–327
Bayamón, PR 00960–6032
(809) 740-1611, ext 210; (809) 269-6032 (fax)
Application Deadline: Dec 15

Ponce School of Medicine
Admissions Office
P.O. Box 7004
Ponce, PR 00732
(809) 840-2511; (809) 844-3685 (fax)
Application Deadline: Dec 15

Univ. of Puerto Rico School of Medicine
Central Admissions Office
Medical Sciences Campus
P.O. Box 365067
San Juan, PR 00936–5067
(809) 758-2525, ext 5213
(809) 282-7117 (fax)
E-mail: R_Aponte@rcmad.upr.clu.edu
http://wwwrcm.upr.clu.edu/school.htm
Application Deadline: Dec 1

RHODE ISLAND

Brown University School of Medicine
Office of Admissions and Financial Aid
97 Waterman Street, Box GA 212
Providence, RI 02912–9706
(401) 863-2149; (401) 863-2660 (fax)
E-mail: MedSchool_Admissions@brown.edu
http://www.brown.edu
Application Deadline: Mar 18 (for B.S.-M.D. program)

SOUTH CAROLINA

Medical University of South Carolina
College of Medicine
Office of Enrollment Services
171 Ashley Avenue
Charleston, SC 29425
(803) 792-3281; (803) 792-3764 (fax)
E-mail: marinst@musc.edu
http://www2.musc.edu/medicine.html
Application Deadline: Dec 1

Univ. of South Carolina School of Medicine
Associate Dean for Student Programs
Columbia, SC 29208
(803) 733-3325; (803) 733-3328 (fax)
http://www.med.sc.edu
Application Deadline: Dec 1

SOUTH DAKOTA

University of South Dakota School of Medicine
Office of Student Affairs, Room 105
414 East Clark Street
Vermillion, SD 57069–2390
(605) 677-5233; (605) 677-5109 (fax)
http://www.usd.edu/med
Application Deadline: Nov 15

TENNESSEE

East Tennessee State University
James H. Quillen College of Medicine
Assistant Dean for Admissions and Records
P.O. Box 70580
Johnson City, TN 37614–0580
(615) 929-6221; (615) 929-6616 (fax)
http://etsu.east-tenn-st.edu:80/~medcom/
Application Deadline: Dec 1

Meharry Medical College
School of Medicine
Director, Admissions and Records
1005 D. B. Todd Boulevard
Nashville, TN 37208
(615) 327-6223; (615) 327-6228 (fax)
http://web.fie.com/htbin/Molis/MolisSummary?FIC
  E=003506
Application Deadline: Dec 15

University of Tennessee College of Medicine
790 Madison Avenue
Memphis, TN 38163–2166
(901) 448-5559
http://planetree1.utmem.edu/
Application Deadline: Nov 15

Vanderbilt School of Medicine
Office of Admissions
209 Light Hall
Nashville, TN 37232–0685
(615) 322-2145; (615) 343-8397 (fax)
E-mail: medsch.admis@mcmail.vanderbilt.edu
http://www.mc.vanderbilt.edu/medschool/
Application Deadline: Oct 15

TEXAS

Baylor College of Medicine
Office of Admissions
One Baylor Plaza
Houston, TX 77030
(713) 798-4841
E-mail: melody@bcm.tmc.edu
http://www.bcm.tmc.edu/
Application Deadline: Nov 1

Texas A & M University College of Medicine
Associate Dean for Student Affairs & Admissions
College Station, TX 77843–1114
(409) 845-7744; (409) 847-8663 (fax)
E-mail: Med-Stu-Aff@tamu.edu
http://thunder.tamu.edu
Application Deadline: Nov 1

Texas Tech University School of Medicine
Health Sciences Center
Office of Admissions
Lubbock, TX 79430
(806) 743-2297
http://www.ttuhsc.edu
Application Deadline: Nov 1

University of Texas, Southwestern
Southwestern Medical Center at Dallas
Office of the Registrar
5323 Harry Hines Boulevard
Dallas, TX 75235–9096
(214) 648-2670; (214) 648-3289 (fax)
http://www.swmed.edu
Application Deadline: Oct 15

University of Texas Medical School at Galveston
Office of Admissions
G-210, Ashbel Smith Building
Galveston, TX 77555–1317
(409) 772-3517; (409) 772-5753 (fax)
E-mail: pow.vpaa.utmb.edu
http://www.utmb.edu
Application Deadline: Oct 15

University of Texas Houston Medical School
Office of Admissions, Room G-024
P.O. Box 20708
Houston, TX 77225
(713) 792-4711; (713) 792-4238 (fax)
http://www.med.uth.tmc.edu
Application Deadline: Oct 15

Univ. of Texas Medical School at San Antonio
Medical School Admissions/Registrar's Office
Health Science Center
7703 Floyd Curl Drive
San Antonio, TX 78284–7701
(210) 567-2665; (210) 567-2685 (fax)
http://www.uthscsa.edu
Application Deadline: Oct 15

UTAH

University of Utah School of Medicine
Director, Medical School Admissions
50 North Medical Drive
Salt Lake City, UT 84132
(801) 581-7498; (801) 585-3300 (fax)
E-mail: Mylonakis@deans.med.utah.edu
http://www.med.utah.edu
Application Deadline: Oct 15

VERMONT

University of Vermont College of Medicine
Admissions Office
E-109 Given Bldg.
Burlington, VT 05405
(802) 656-2154
http://salus.med.uvm.edu
Application Deadline: Nov 1

VIRGINIA

Eastern Virginia Medical School
Office of Admissions
721 Fairfax Avenue
Norfolk, VA 23507–2000
(804) 446-5812; (804) 446-5817 (fax)
gopher://picard.evms.edu/1
Application Deadline: Nov 15

Medical College of Virginia
Medical School Admissions
MCV Station Box 980565
Richmond, VA 23298–0565
(804) 828-9629; (804) 828-7628 (fax)
http://griffin.vcu.edu/html/schofmed.html
Application Deadline: Nov 15

University of Virginia School of Medicine
Medical School Admissions Office
Box 235
Charlottesville, VA 22908
(804) 924-5571; (804) 982-2586 (fax)
http://www.med.virginia.edu/MedSchool.html
Application Deadline: Nov 1

WASHINGTON

University of Washington School of Medicine
Admissions Office (SC-64)
Health Sciences Center, A–300
Seattle, WA 98195–6340
(206) 543-7212
E-mail: patf@u.washington.edu
http://www.hslib.washington.edu/hsc/som.html
Application Deadline: Nov 1

WEST VIRGINIA

Marshall University School of Medicine
Admissions Office
1542 Spring Valley Drive
Huntington, WV 25704
(800) 544-8514; (304) 696-7312
http://musom.marshall.edu
Application Deadline: Nov 15

West Virginia University School of Medicine
Office of Admissions and Records
Health Sciences Center
P.O. Box 9815
Morgantown, WV 26506
(304) 293-3521; (304) 293-7968 (fax)
E-mail: dhall@wvuhsc.wvu.edu
http://www.hsc.wvu.edu/som/
Application Deadline: Nov 15

WISCONSIN

Medical College of Wisconsin
Office of Admissions and Registrar
8701 Watertown Plank Road
Milwaukee, WI 53226
(414) 456-8246
http://www.mcw.edu
Application Deadline: Nov 1

University of Wisconsin Medical School
Admission Committee
Medical Sciences Center, Room 1250
1300 University Avenue
Madison, WI 53706
(608) 263-4925; (608) 262-2327 (fax)
E-mail: Janice.Waisman@mail.admin.wisc.edu
http://www.biostat.wisc.edu
Application Deadline: Nov 1

Canada

ALBERTA

University of Alberta
Faculty of Medicine
Admissions Officer
2–45 Medical Sciences Building
Edmonton, Alberta
Canada T6G 2H7
(403) 492-6350; (403) 492-9531 (fax)
http://web.cs.ualberta.ca/UAlberta/Faculties/html/
   Medicine.html
Application Deadline: Nov 1

University of Calgary Faculty of Medicine
Office of Admissions
3330 Hospital Drive, N.W.
Calgary, Alberta
Canada T2N 4N1
(403) 220-6849
e-mail: meyers@asc.ucalgary.ca
http://www.med.ucalgary.ca/ume/infoda.html
Application Deadline: Nov 30

BRITISH COLUMBIA

University of British Columbia Faculty of Medicine
Office of the Dean, Admissions Office
317–2194 Health Sciences Mall
Vancouver, British Columbia
Canada V6T 1Z3
(604) 822-4482; (604) 822-6061 (fax)
http://www.med.ubc.ca/
Application Deadline: Dec 15

MANITOBA

University of Manitoba Faculty of Medicine
Chair, Admissions Committee
753 McDermot Avenue
Winnipeg, Manitoba
Canada R3E 0W3
(204) 789-3569; (204) 774-8941 (fax)
E-mail: paragg@bldghsc.1an1.umanitoba.ca
http://www.umanitoba.ca/
Application Deadline: Nov 15

NEWFOUNDLAND

Memorial University of Newfoundland
Faculty of Medicine
Chair, Committee on Admissions
St. John's, Newfoundland
Canada A1B 3V6
(709) 737-6615; (709) 737-5186 (fax)
E-mail: munmed@kean.ucs.mun.ca
http://www.aorta.library.mun.ca/med/
Application Deadline: Dec 15

NOVA SCOTIA

Dalhousie University Faculty of Medicine
Admissions Coordinator
Rm C–23, Lower Level, Clinical Research Centre
5849 University Avenue
Halifax, Nova Scotia
Canada B3H 4H7
(902) 494-1874; (902) 494-8884 (fax)
http://www.dal.ca/
Application Deadline: Nov 15

ONTARIO

McMaster University School of Medicine
Admissions and Records
HSC Room 1B7–Health Sciences Center
1200 Main Street West
Hamilton, Ontario
Canada L8N 3Z5
(905) 525-9140, ext 22114
http://www-fhs.mcmaster.ca/
Application Deadline: Nov 1

University of Ottawa Faculty of Medicine
Admissions
451 Smyth Road
Ottawa, Ontario
Canada K1H 8M5
(613) 787-6463; (613) 562-5457 (fax)
http://www.uottawa.ca/academic/med/
Application Deadline: Nov 1

Queen's University Faculty of Medicine
Admission Office
Kingston, Ontario
Canada K7L 3N6
(613) 545-2542; (613) 545-6884 (fax)
http://meds-ss10.meds.queensu.ca/medicine/
Application Deadline: Nov 1

University of Toronto Faculty of Medicine
1 King's College Circle
Toronto, Ontario
Canada M5S 1A8
(416) 978-2717; (416) 971-2163 (fax)
http://utl1.library.utoronto.ca/www/medicine/
Application Deadline: Nov 1

University of Western Ontario
Undergraduate Medical Education Office
Medical Sciences Bldg., Room 100
London, Ontario
Canada N6A 5C1
(519) 661-3744; (519) 661-3797 (fax)
E-mail: Admissions@do.med.uwo.ca
http://www.med.uwo.ca/
Application Deadline: Nov 1

QUEBEC

Université Laval Faculty of Medicine
Secretary, Admission Committee
Ste–Foy, Quebec
Canada G1K 7P4
(418) 646-2492; (418) 646-2733 (fax)
E-mail: admission@fmed.ulaval.ca
http://www.fmed.ulaval.ca/fmed/fmed.html
Application Deadlines: Mar 1 (Canadians),
   Feb 1 (non–Canadians)

McGill University Faculty of Medicine
Admissions Office
3655 Drummond Street
Montreal, Quebec
Canada H3G 1Y6
(514) 398-3517; (514) 398-3595 (fax)
http://www.medcor.mcgill.ca/
Application Deadlines: Nov 15 (out of province),
   Feb 1 (Quebec-resident applicants to 4 year
      program),
   Mar 1 (Quebec-resident applicants to 5 year
      program)

Université of Montréal Faculty of Medicine
Committee on Admission
P.O. Box 6128, Station Centre–Ville
Montreal, Quebec
Canada H3C 3J7
(514) 343-6265; (514) 343-6629 (fax)
E-mail: admmed@ere.umontreal.ca
http://medes3.med.umontreal.ca/
Application Deadline: Mar 1

University of Sherbrooke Faculty of Medicine
Admission Office
Sherbrooke, Quebec
Canada J1H 5N4
(819) 564-5208; (819) 564-5378 (fax)
E-mail: mmoreau@courrier.usherb.ca
http://www.usherb.ca
Application Deadline: Mar 1

SASKATCHEWAN

University of Saskatchewan College of Medicine
Secretary, Admissions
B103 Health Sciences Building
Saskatoon, Saskatchewan
Canada S7N 0W0
(306) 966-8554; (306) 966-6164 (fax)
http://usask.ca/medicine/index.html
Application Deadlines: Dec 1 (out of province),
    Jan 15 (in province)

U.S. Osteopathic Medical Schools

Arizona College of Osteopathic Medicine
Office of Admissions
19555 N. 59th Avenue
Glendale, AZ 85308
(602) 362-4015
http://www.aacom.org/acom.htm
Application Deadline: Feb 1

Chicago College of Osteopathic Medicine
Office of Admissions
555 Thirty-First Street
Downers Grove, IL 60515
(800) 458-6253; (708) 515-4400
http://www.aacom.org/ccom.htm
Application Deadline: Feb 1

College of Osteopathic Medicine of the Pacific
  (now Western University of the Health Sciences)
Office of Admissions
College Plaza
Pomona, CA 91766-1889
(909) 623-6116
http://www.aacom.org/comp.htm
Application Deadline: Feb 1

Kirksville College of Osteopathic Medicine
Office of Admissions
800 West Jefferson Street
Kirksville, MO 63501
Outside-of-Missouri: (800) 626-5266, ext. 2237;
    (816) 626-2237
Inside Missouri: (800) 428-3376, ext 2237
    (816) 626-2926 (fax)
http://www.aacom.org/kcom.htm
Application Deadline: Feb 1

Lake Erie College of Osteopathic Medicine
Office of Admissions
1858 West Grandview Boulevard
Erie, PA 16509-1025
(814) 866-6641; (814) 866-8123 fax
http://www.aacom.org/lecom.htm
Application Deadline: Feb 1

Michigan State University
College of Osteopathic Medicine
Director of Admissions
C110 East Fee Hall
East Lansing, MI 48824-1316
(517) 353-7740
http://www.aacom.org/msucom.htm
Application Deadline: Dec 1

New York College of Osteopathic Medicine/NYIT
Director of Admissions
Old Westbury, NY 11568
(516) 626-6947
http://www.aacom.org/nycom.htm
Application Deadline: Feb 1

Nova Southeastern University
College of Osteopathic Medicine
Admissions Office
3200 S. University Drive
Ft. Lauderdale, FL 33328
(954) 723-1000
http://www.aacom.org/nova.htm
Application Deadline: Jan 15

Ohio University College of Osteopathic Medicine
Office of Admissions
102 Grosvenor Hall
Athens, OH 45701-2979
(614) 593-4313
http://www.aacom.org/oucom.htm
Application Deadline: Jan 2

Oklahoma State University
College of Osteopathic Medicine
Admissions Office
1111 West 17th Street
Tulsa, OK 74107
(800) 677-1972; (918) 582-1972
http://www.aacom.org/osucom.htm
Application Deadline: Dec 1

Philadelphia College of Osteopathic Medicine
Assistant Dean, Admissions & Enrollment Mgmt
4170 City Avenue
Philadelphia, PA 19131
(800) 999-6998; (215) 871-6719 (fax)
http://www.pcom.edu/
Application Deadline: Feb 1

University of Health Sciences
College of Osteopathic Medicine
Office of Admissions
2105 Independence Boulevard
Kansas City, MO 64124-2395
(800) 234-4847
http://www.aacom.org/uhscom.htm
Application Deadline: Feb 1

UMDNJ-School of Osteopathic Medicine
Admissions Office
One Medical Center Drive, Suite 162A
Stratford, NJ 08084
(609) 566-7050; (609) 566-6222 (fax)
http://www.aacom.org/umdnjsom.htm
Application Deadline: Feb 1

University of New England
College of Osteopathic Medicine
Admissions Office
Hills Beach Road
Biddeford, ME 04005
(800) 477-4863
http://www.aacom.org/unecom.htm
Application Deadline: Jan 2

University of North Texas Health Science Center
Texas College of Osteopathic Medicine
Office of Medical Student Admissions
3500 Camp Bowie Boulevard
Fort Worth, TX 76107-2699
(800) 535-8266; (817) 735-2204
(817) 735-2225 (fax)
http://www.hsc.unt.edu/schools/tcom/index.html
Application Deadline: Dec 1

Univ. of Osteopathic Medicine & Health Sciences
College of Osteopathic Medicine and Surgery
Director of Admissions and Financial Aid
3200 Grand Avenue
Des Moines, Iowa 50312
(800) 240-2767, ext. 1450; (515) 271-1450
(515) 271-1578 (fax)
E-mail: doadmit@uomhs.edu
http://www.aacom.org/uomhs.htm
Application Deadline: Feb 1

West Virginia School of Osteopathic Medicine
Director of Admissions
400 North Lee Street
Lewisburg, WV 24901
Inside West Virginia: (800) 356-7836
Outside of West Virginia: (800) 537-7077
http://www.aacom.org/wvsom.htm
Application Deadline: Feb 1

Some Non-U.S./Canadian Medical Schools

American University of the Caribbean
School of Medicine
Montserrat, British West Indies
Medical Education Information Office
901 Ponce de Leon Blvd., Suite 201
Coral Gables, FL 33134
(305) 446–0600
Two-year program in Montserrat (recently relocated to St. Maarten due to a volcano eruption.) Clinical Rotations elsewhere, often in Belize.

Flinders University of South Australia
Dr. Jillian Teubner, Medical Education Unit
Flinders University of South Australia
GPO Box 2100
Adelaide 5001 AUSTRALIA
(08) 204-4631; (08) 277-0085 (fax)
E-mail: mbjkt@gamgee.cc.flinders.edu.au
http://som.flinders.edu.au/
This is a new medical school.

Iboamerican University School of Medicine
Admission Office
UNIBE; ID #10459
P.O. Box 025577
Miami, FL 33102-5577
(800) 203-3562 (from U.S.)
(800) 265-33266 (from Canada)
Located in the Dominican Republic. The school begins three new classes each year in January, May, and September.

Jagiellonian University
Collegium Medicum, Faculty of Medicine
School of Medicine for Foreigners
12 St. Anna str.
31-008 Kraków, POLAND
(48 12)22-80-42, ext. 267
E-mail: mxstepni@kinga-kr.edu.pl
They state that their entire four-year program is in English.

Karol Marcinkowski University of Medical
Sciences–Poznan, Poland
c/o Corvestor Services Corporation
11 Market Street, Suite 204
Poughkeepsie, NY 12601–3215
(914) 454-5151; (914) 454-6612 (fax)
http://premed.edu/poznan.html
They state that their entire four-year program is in English. Poznan is in western Poland. The University has existed for over 400 years.

Kigezi International School of Medicine
c/o Cambridge Overseas Medical Training
    Programme
Cambridge Research Laboratories
181a Huntingdon Road
Cambridge CB3 0DJ GREAT BRITAIN
(+44) 1223-327282; (+44) 1223-327292 (fax)
e-mail: rv204@hermes.cam.ac.uk

Medical College of Baja California
    (U.S.A. address)
P.O. Box 26180
Fresno, CA 93729-6180
(800) 642-3543; (209) 434-8429 (fax)
http://www.valleynet.com/~bcmedical
BCMC is located in the border town of Mexicali, Baja California, Mexico. Directly across the border is Calexico, California. Mexicali is 90 minutes away from San Diego, CA and Palm Springs, CA. A student can live in CA and cross the border each day.

Medical University at Pécs
c/o Worldwide Medical Education Institute
318 Fourth Street
Union City, NJ 07087
A six-year medical school located in Budapest, Hungary. Classes are taught in English.

Ross University School of Medicine
Application Processing Center
460 West 34th Street
New York, NY 10001
(212) 279–5500
http://rossmed.edu
Located on the island of Dominica. Many students transfer from Ross to other Caribbean schools.

The Royal College of Surgeons—Dublin, Ireland
Admission Office
123 St. Stephen's Green
Dublin 2 IRELAND
(353) 1-478-0200; (353) 1-478-2100 (fax)
  For U.S. applicants:
c/o The Atlantic Bridge Program
1044 Adams Avenue, Suite 302
Huntington Beach, CA 92646
(800) 876-3876; (714) 723-6318 (fax)
This is the #3-rated foreign school and the only one of the top three where you need not learn another language to do your clinical work. Although it is a six-year program, most U.S. students can skip the first year, since it repeats U.S. undergraduate premed education.

Saba School of Medicine
c/o Education Information Consultants
P.O. Box 386
Gardner, MA 01440
(508) 630-5122
Located on the island of Saba in the Dutch Antilles. The school has three incoming classes each year in January, May, and September.

Sackler School of Medicine
17 East 62nd Street
New York, NY 10021
(212)–688–8811
http://www.tau.ac.il/~ori/sackler.html
The school is in Tel Aviv, Israel, but the admission office for U.S. residents is in NY. Sackler is often rated the top-rated Foreign Medical School for U.S. residents.

St. George's Univ. School of Medicine Grenada
Application Office
Medical School Services, Ltd.
One E. Main Street
Bayshore, NY 11706-9990
(800) 899-6337
http://www.stgeorgesuniv.edu/
Located on the island of Grenada. Encourages its students to transfer to U.S. schools, if possible, after their basic science years.

Spartan Health Sciences Univ. School of Medicine
U.S. Information Office
Skypark II
6500 Boeing Drive, Suite L-201
El Paso, TX 79925
(915) 778-5309
Located on St. Lucia. No known clinical affiliations.

Third Medical Faculty of Charles University–
  Prague, Czechoslovakia
c/o International Education Centre
29 Arthur Road, Box 228
Heidelberg, Ontario N0B 1Y0 CANADA
This six-year English-language program requires a written test and interview in Toronto, Canada. For clinical work, students must learn Czech.

Touro College School of Health Sciences/
Faculty of Medicine of the Technion-Israel
  Institute of Technology
Biomedical Program, Building #10
135 Carman Road
Dix Hills, NY 11746
(516) 673-3200
A five-year joint M.A.-M.D. program. One year is spent at Touro College in New York and four years at the Technion University in Haifa, Israel. All classes are in English. The #2-rated school for U.S. medical students applying to international medical schools.

Universidad Autónoma de Guadalajara (UAG)
Office in the United States
8801 Callaghan Road
San Antonio, TX 78230-4417
(800) 531-5494; (210) 366-1611
(210) 377-2975 (fax)
E-mail: iep@txdirect.net

 UAG Office in Puerto Rico
 IBM Plaza, Suite 1124
 Avenida Muñoz Rivera No. 654
 Hato Rey, PR 00918
 (809) 763-2457; (809) 753-0760 fax
Located in Guadalajara, Mexico. Classes are in English and Spanish. English-speaking students take intensive Spanish-language classes.

Universidad Central del Este
c/o Educational Management Services, Inc.
2350 Coral Way, Suite 301
Miami, FL 33145
(305) 860-0780
Located in San Pedro de Macoris, Dominican Republic. All classes and tests are in Spanish. The school has an intensive Spanish course. It has its own teaching hospital.

University of Health Sciences–Antigua
Dowhill Campus
Box 510
St. Johns, Antigua   WEST INDIES
(809) 460-1391; (809) 460-1477 Fax
Located on the island of Antigua. The school has a
reputation for secrecy.

Universidad Nacional Pedro Henriquez Ureña
Av. J. F. Kennedy Km 5½
Santo Domino, D.N.   REPUBLICA DOMINICA
Primarily for Dominicans, all courses are in
Spanish, as are all information and application
materials.

For General Information About Other Medical Schools, Contact The Following:

Australia
This is for schools other than Flinders.

Australian Medical Association (AMA)
42 Macquarie Street
Barton, ACT 2601   AUSTRALIA
61-6-270-5400; 61-6-270-5499 (fax)

France
If you do not speak and read French, don't even
bother asking for information from the office listed
below. (It's in French.)

Services du Conseiller Culturel
972 Fifth Avenue
New York, NY 10021
(212) 439-1455

Germany
Proficiency in German is required. Students can
enter, if they pass a test, after high school.

German Academic Exchange Service
950 Third Avenue
New York, NY 10022
(212) 758-3223
E-mail: daadny@daad.org
http://www.daad.org

Hungary
For schools other than the University at Pécs.

Consulate General of the Republic of Hungary
11766 Wilshire Boulevard, Suite 410
Los Angeles, CA 90025

Italy
You must have completed two years of college
and have a good knowledge of Italian.

Instituto Italiano di Cultura
686 Park Avenue
New York, NY 10021
(212) 879-4242; (212) 861-4018 (fax)

Norway
You must speak or be willing to learn Norwegian
before entry into medical school. You also must
complete at least one year of college.

Norwegian Information Service
825 Third Avenue
New York, NY 10022

Portugal
You must speak Portuguese to enter any
Portuguese medical school.

Faculdade de Medicina
Avenida Prof. Egas Moniz
1600 Lisboa   PORTUGAL
                 or
Faculdade de Ciencias Medicas
130 Campo dos Martires da Patria
1000 Lisboa   PORTUGAL

Annotated Bibliography

Some books are to be tasted, others to be swallowed,
and some few to be chewed and digested . . .

Sir Francis Bacon, *Essays: Of Studies*

- ✔ Books about medicine (non-fiction)
- ✔ Books about medicine (fiction)
- ✔ Periodicals and Journals
- ✔ For high school students
- ✔ The specialties
- ✔ Selecting a specialty
- ✔ MCAT preparation
- ✔ The paperwork
- ✔ Medical school
- ✔ Financial aid
- ✔ Osteopathic medicine
- ✔ Minorities
- ✔ Disabled students

- ✔ International medical students/grads
- ✔ Women in medicine
- ✔ Marriage and relationships
- ✔ Pregnancy and parenting
- ✔ Admissions and applications
- ✔ The lighter side; a little humor
- ✔ Interviewing
- ✔ Medical ethics
- ✔ Licensing examinations
- ✔ Internship and residency
- ✔ Other health-related careers
- ✔ Survival: thinking, eating, doing

References marked with a plus **(+)** can be obtained through *The Galen Press Catalog*, P.O. Box 64400, Tucson, AZ 85728-4400; phone (800) 442-5369.

Books About Medicine (Non-Fiction)

Conrad LI, Neve M, Nutton V, et al. *The Western Medical Tradition: 800 BC to AD 1800.* Cambridge, England: Cambridge Univ. Press, 1995, 556 pp. The quintessential medical history, this book surveys the Western medical tradition in all its aspects from the Greeks until 1800. In addition to describing the diseases, medical theories and medical therapies, it places them in a wide social context. Discussions of religious and alternative healing are interspersed with the major scientific advances in medicine, surgery, and pharmacology. **(+)**

Hellerstein D. *A Family of Doctors.* New York: Ivy Books, 1994, 309 pp. A saga tracing one family of physicians over more than a century of medical practice and research—from the Civil War to the present day. This book describes the triumphs and tragedies that paralleled the profound changes in medical technology and the physician's role. Heroes in medicine come in all forms—and this book introduces you to some of them. **(+)**

Iserson KV. *Getting Into A Residency: A Guide for Medical Students, 4th ed.* Tucson, AZ: Galen Press, 1996, 500 pp. Medical students suggest that this book be called, "Getting the Most Out of Medical School," since it contains invaluable tips on how to succeed not only in medical school, but also throughout your entire medical career. It guides students, step-by-step, through the process of selecting a medical specialty and obtaining a residency position. **(+)**

Lyons AS, Petrucelli RJ, II. *Medicine: An Illustrated History.* New York: Abrams, 1987, 616 pp. An extraordinary pictorial survey of medicine from ancient to modern times. The book draws on the social, political, and historical background of each advance in medical science. Every page has stunning artwork, medical illustrations, and photographs that depict medicine's history. More than 1,000 illustrations, including 266 full-color prints. **(+)**

Nash DB (ed.). *Future Practice Alternatives in Medicine, 2nd ed.* 1993. Igaku-Shoin Medical Pub., 1140 Avenue of the Americas, New York, NY 10036. A fascinating look at the changes in medical practice that have occurred, are occurring, and will take place in your lifetime. Included are sections on the role of doctors' unions, new developments in medical education, the changing roles of women in medicine, and the role of the public-spirited physician. It also reviews emerging career trends including the growing fields of Geriatrics and Occupational Medicine, as well as discussing Health Maintenance Organizations, computers in medicine, and the physician-executive. Very readable.

Gevitz N. *Other Healers: Unorthodox Medicine in America.* Baltimore, MD: Johns Hopkins Univ Press, 1988, 302 pp. Who, besides physicians, practices medicine? Botanists, chiropractors, Christian Scientists, folk healers, homeopaths, divine healers, and Naturopaths, among others—that's who. This book describes what they do and how they affect patient care. This book opens the door to the "other side" of medicine. (+)

Nuland SB. *Doctors: The Biography of Medicine.* New York: Vintage, 1989, 519 pp. Medicine's great men were neither all perfect nor all men. This "warts and all" account of medicine's pioneers demonstrates their insightfulness and leadership as well as their fears and failings. Who were members of the Hippocratic school of medicine and did they really represent our ideal? Was Semmelweis a genius or an egomaniac? And how did Taussig beat down resistance to her findings? This book rubs the patina off the schoolbook histories, demonstrating that real people were behind medicine's most important advances. (+)

Rothman DJ, Marcus S, Kiceluk SA, eds. *Medicine and Western Civilization.* New Brunswick, NJ: Rutgers Univ. Press, 1995, 443 pp. This is a comprehensive anthology depicting medicine's effect on society. Among the selections are excerpts from the Old Testament, classical Greek texts, eyewitness accounts of public anatomies (dissections), medieval treatises on witchcraft, and modern debates over brain death. Authors include Hippocrates, Galen, Vesalius, Pasteur, Koch, Freud, Plato, Augustine, Frances Burney, George Orwell, Jean Stafford, Pius XII, and others. (+)

Skolnik NS. *On the Ledge: A Doctor's Stories from the Inner City.* Boston: Faber & Faber, 1996, 157 pp. What is medicine like in the "real world"? Dr. Skolnik was idealistic when he started his first job at a family medicine clinic next to a Philadelphia housing project. He describes the triumphs and tragedies he witnessed, and the bureaucratic nightmare when the practice closed due to funding problems. In an age of health care reform, *On the Ledge* is a primer for physicians who find themselves in urban clinics and a plea to remember the medical needs of our nation's poor. (+)

Thomas L. *The Youngest Science: Notes of a Medicine-Watcher.* New York: Bantam, 1984, 270 pp. A second generation physician and former director of the Sloan Kettering Cancer Institute, Dr. Thomas poetically describes the basis for the changes in medicine from the time when his father made house calls, but had little to offer in the way of cures or effective therapy, to the technological present.

Weisse AB. *Medical Odysseys: The Different & Sometimes Unexpected Pathways to Twentieth-Century Medical Discoveries.* New Brunswick, NJ: Rutgers Univ. Press, 1991, 250 pp. This intriguing book looks at the stories and personalities of the researchers and patients who stumbled upon some of modern medicine's miraculous cures (antibiotics, chemotherapy, pacemakers, etc.). For example, learn how a sausage manufacturer and a Ford dealer helped create the first successful artificial kidney machine. How did a Renaissance alchemist's fascination with mercury and a physician's concern with syphilis point to the first effective treatment for congestive heart failure? (+)

Books About Medicine (Fiction)

Lewis S. *Arrowsmith.* New York: Penguin Books, 1924, 438 pp. An inspiring classic that led many people to medicine as a career. The tale of Martin Arrowsmith illustrates how a young doctor's devotion to science can allow medicine to become his life. Forced to give up successive sinecures—instructor in medicine, small-town doctor, research pathologist—by obstacles ranging from public ignorance to the publicity-mindedness of a great foundation, Arrowsmith becomes virtually isolated as a seeker-after-truth. Although written in the pre-antibiotic era, the issues remain as current today as they were then. (+)

Reynolds R, Stone J, eds. *On Doctoring: Stories, Poems, Essays.* New York: Simon & Schuster, 1995, 448 pp. Classic and pithy descriptions of physicians, medical practice, diseases and patients. Contributors include physicians (Sir Arthur Conan Doyle, William Carlos Williams, Richard Selzer, and others) and noted writers (Anton Chekhov, Ernest Hemmingway, Kurt Vonnegut, and Alice Walker). A book to be repeatedly read through an entire medical career. **(+)**

Schiedermayer D. *House Calls, Rounds, and Healings: A Poetry Casebook.* Tucson, AZ: Galen Press, 1996, 100 pp. A poignant look at how physicians treat patients in many settings. Written by a practicing internist with world-wide experiences, each poem is a case study of a patient or colleague. This book captures the feelings that many physicians experience but cannot express. **(+)**

Selzer R. *Letters to a Young Doctor.* New York: Touchstone Books, 1982, 205 pp. Written by modern medicine's principal essayist, this book leads the reader on an amazing journey through the world of patients, physicians, and families, with an insight and sensitivity rarely found in medical literature. Contains *Imelda,* the best medical essay by any current writer.

Shem S. *The House of God.* New York: Dell, 1978, 429 pp. This is the classic book spoken about on hospital wards, often in the dead of night while working on dying patients in the ICU. Medical students, residents, and faculty can be heard quoting the book's "rules," such as "They can always hurt you more." A tongue-in-cheek, brutally honest, and hilarious (but only for physicians) book. The inside scoop on how many physicians really feel about their patients, and a thinly disguised description of the author's real experiences. **(+)**

Periodicals And Journals

Academic Medicine. The Association of American Medical Colleges' journal, it contains articles about medical education, including entry into medical school, MCAT examinations, medical school curricular changes, and residency training. This journal will often contain some of the most up-to-date information available. Available at all medical school libraries.

JAMA (Journal of the American Medical Association). The most widely read of all medical journals, this magazine contains not only research articles, but also information on medical student and resident education, on government interactions with medical practice, and other information that will give you an insight into how physicians think and feel. Available at most public libraries, all medical libraries, and from many physicians.

Journal of the American Osteopathic Association. Similar to *JAMA*, it is produced by the Osteopathic side of the profession. A little more difficult to obtain, it is often easier to understand than some of the other medical journals. Available in libraries in areas where many Osteopathic physicians practice and in all medical libraries.

New England Journal of Medicine. The *New York Times* of clinical medicine, it contains "everything that's fit to print" for the clinician. Other clinical journals get the leftovers. Many of the research articles will be beyond most people's understanding or interest, but the case discussions are often fascinating. Reading the topic reviews is great practice for the Verbal Reasoning section of the MCAT. Available in nearly every library.

The New Physician. American Medical Student Association, 1902 Association Drive, Reston, VA 22901-1502. Published monthly and free with membership in AMSA. Has frequent articles about medical specialties, interviewing, the Match, international medical graduates, medical practice, and other topics of vital interest to medical students.

For High School Students

Birnbaum M, Cass-Lipmann J, eds. *Cass & Birnbaum Guide to American Colleges,* 16th ed. Harper/Collins, Keystone Industrial Park, Scranton, PA 18512.

Comparative Guide to American Colleges. Harper Collins, Keystone Industrial Park, Scranton, PA 18512.

Kesslar O. *Financial Aids for Higher Education, 1995.* 16th ed. Brown & Benchmart Publishers, 2460 Kerper Blvd., Dubuque, IA 52004-0539.

National Association of Advisors of the Health Professions. *Strategies for Success: A Handbook for Prehealth Students.* NAAHP, P.O. Box 5017, Station A, Champaign, IL 61825.

The College Board Guide to 150 Popular Majors. (Annual in September) College Board Publications, Box 886, New York, NY 10101-0886.

Time Management for Students. An excellent source of ideas to maximize your usable time. Useful for students at any level—but you might as well begin learning these habits while in high school. Office of Statewide Health Planning and Development, Health Professions Career Opportunity Program, 1600 Ninth Street, Rm. 441, Sacramento, CA 95814. (Free) 44 pp.

The Specialties

American Academy of Pediatrics. *Pediatrics: What's It Really Like?* Elk Grove Village, IL: AAP. A compilation of eleven articles from several sources, with various publication dates, detailing the various aspects of Pediatrics. urban, rural, small-town, academic, and alternative Pediatric practices are discussed in a positive way by practicing Pediatricians.

American Medical Association. *"The future of . . ."* series, developed by experts in each field, ran in *JAMA* in the late 1980s and in 1990. The articles still contain valuable information about some of the anticipated changes in the specialties. The citation for each specialty is listed below.

Adult Cardiology. *JAMA* 1989;262(20):2874-8.
Family Practice. *JAMA* 1988;260(9):1272-9.
General Internal Medicine. *JAMA* 1989;262(15):2119-24.
General Surgery. *JAMA* 1989;262(22):3178-83.
Obstetrics & Gynecology. *JAMA* 1987;258(24):3547-53.
Pathology. *JAMA* 1987;258(3):370-7.
Pediatrics. *JAMA* 1987;258(2):240-5.
Psychiatry. *JAMA* 1990;264(19):2542-8.

Biro FM, Siegel DM, Parker RM, Gillman MW. A comparison of self-perceived clinical competencies in primary care residency graduates. *Pediatr Res* 1993;34(5):555-9. This paper describes how comfortable Family Practice, Pediatric, Internal Medicine, and Internal Medicine-Pediatric residency graduates feel when caring for different types of primary care patients. This may be something to consider when deciding among various primary care specialties.

Bosk CL. *Forgive and Remember: Managing Medical Failure.* Chicago: Univ. Chicago Press, 1979, 236 pp. Students and residents make mistakes; sometimes serious or even fatal mistakes. How do their teachers deal with these errors and with their trainees? Which mistakes do professors "forgive" but remember? This classic book about surgical education is still the most important description available of surgical education. Bosk, after following two surgical teams at one of the nation's leading medical schools, describes the surgical culture and mores that students and residents must understand to succeed. **(+)**

Colen BD. *O.R.: The True Story of 24 Hours in a Hospital Operating Room.* New York: Signet (Penguin), 1994, 269 pp. So, what is the OR really like? A Pulitzer Prize-winning author's gripping, minute-by-minute true account of 24 hours in an operating room, as seen from multiple perspectives. A vivid look at the mysterious world of the OR, from the routine to the extraordinary surgical feats. Read this book if you are considering a career in the OR. **(+)**

Delbridge TR. *Emergency Medicine in Focus: A Handbook for Medical Students & Prospective Residents.* Emergency Medicine Residents Association, P.O. Box 619911, Dallas, TX 75261-9911. 1991, 173 pp. Everything you wanted to know about Emergency Medicine, albeit with a very personal and sometimes biased slant. Topics include the history of the specialty, career options within Emergency Medicine, the future of the specialty, how Emergency Medicine residencies and fellowships function, and how to apply.

DeLisa JA, Leonard JA Jr, Smith BS, Kirshblum S. Common questions asked by medical students about physiatry. *Am J Phys Med Rehabil* 1995;74(2):145-54. The authors answer all common questions and correct the misunderstandings about Physical Medicine and Rehabilitation. Well worth reading.

Gabram SG, Allen LW, Deckers PJ. Surgical residents in the 1990s: issues and concerns for men and women. *Arch Surg* 1995;130(1):24-8. Read this if you have any ideas about entering a Surgical residency. It details the frustrations and concerns you will face.

Gessert C, Blossom J, Sommers P, et al. Family physicians for underserved areas: the role of residency training. *West J Med* 1989;150(2):226-30. A good discussion of the influence on medical students of Family Practice programs that are specifically designed and equipped to train physicians to practice in rural areas.

Goldenberg K, Barnes HV, Kogut MD, et al. A combined primary care residency in internal medicine and pediatrics. *Acad Med* 1989;64 (9):519-24. An in-depth description of one of the combined medicine-pediatric residency training programs. Although the number of programs is growing, there is still very little information available about them. This paper provides enough specifics to be of help to anyone considering a combined program.

Hendren WH, Lillehei CW. Pediatric surgery. *N Engl J Med* 1988;319(2):86-96. A survey of the specialty and the range of current and future practice. Written by two well-known Pediatric Surgeons.

International Medicine Centre to Advance Research and Education. *Internal Medicine Data Book.* IMCARE, 2011 Pennsylvania Ave., N.W., #800, Washington, DC 20006-1808. First published in December 1992, this booklet contains nearly every statistic anyone could want to know about internists and Internal Medicine. Much of the data is drawn from the AMA's data, but here it compares Internal Medicine with other specialties. The booklet's information is divided into sections on medical education, specialty distribution and characteristics, patient information, practice characteristics, and medical economics. Definitely worth looking over if you are considering Internal Medicine or one of its subspecialties.

JAMA, Contempo Issue. This annual issue, usually available in July, contains articles describing the latest issues and developments in many medical specialties. These articles, each written by a leader in the field, provide insights into changes that will occur within the specialties and within the entire medical profession. Individual copies can be purchased from Customer Services at the American Medical Association.

Scherger JE, Beasley JW, Rodney WM, et al. Responses to questions by medical students about family practice. *J Fam Prac* 1988;26(2):169-76. A list of the most commonly asked questions about the specialty of Family Practice, but the authors give somewhat optimistic answers. The list of questions, which by itself should stimulate a lot of thought, is enough to recommend the article to anyone with an interest in this field.

Sunshine J. The job market for radiology residents and fellows graduating in 1994. *Am J Roentgenol* 1994;163(6):1305-8. Not a glowing outlook for the specialty. (No pun intended.) Read this article to find out the grim reality from one who really knows.

Weissman S. American psychiatry in the 21st century: the discipline, its practice, and its work force. *Bull Menninger Clin* 1994;58(4):502-18. A review of the current state of Psychiatry and how it may develop in the early part of the next millennium.

Wilcox BR, Stritter FT, Anderson RP, et al. Systematic survey of opinion regarding the thoracic surgery residency. *Ann Thorac Surg* 1993;55(5):1296-1302. In this relatively short article, the authors describe the practice, residency programs, and future of Thoracic Surgery in words and tables.

Selecting a Specialty

American Medical Association. *Specialty Profiles.* (annual). Chicago, IL: AMA. A weighty volume containing all the recognized specialties plus a few more, such as Legal Medicine and Clinical Pharmacology. Each chapter has a brief history and a current perspective on the specialty. A large section is devoted to the demographics of the current practitioners in the specialty, with lots of charts, graphs, and tables.

Colquitt WL: Medical specialty choice: a selected bibliography with abstracts. *Acad Med* 1993;68(5):391-436. An extensive annotated bibliography covering both published and unpublished material. The material it lists is well organized and easily accessed. The abstracts themselves provide a wealth of information, and citations are provided if you want to read the full articles.

Glaxo Welcome Medical Specialties Survey. Glaxo Welcome Pharmaceuticals, Inc. Contains descriptions of most of the medical specialties and major subspecialties. For each specialty, it includes a background, profiles of individual practitioners, and anecdotes about why individuals entered the fields. This book can be found in most medical libraries. 1996.

Iserson KV. *Getting Into a Residency: A Guide for Medical Students, 4th ed.* Tucson, AZ: Galen Press, 1996, 526 pp. This book is the standard for selecting a specialty, picking your ideal residency programs, going through the residency matching process, and having the best chance of getting the residency position you want. It includes everything you need to know about the process, beginning with entry into medical school through the preclinical and clinical years, and culminating with the all-important interviews and matching programs. (+)

Companion Disk for *Getting Into a Residency.* Tucson, AZ: Galen Press, 1996. This software makes *Getting Into A Residency* easier to use. The program customizes, prints, and does the necessary calculations for the "Personal Trait Analysis, Synthesis, and Correlation of Traits," "must/want" analysis, "Requirements for Application to Programs," and "Interview Notes." It comes in DOS and Windows™ versions. (+)

MCAT Preparation

Association of American Medical Colleges. *MCAT Student Manual.* Washington, DC: AAMC, 1995, 126 pp. This is the basic study guide for the MCAT. It contains outlines of each section's topics, hints on how to prepare, and sample questions. Buy this book as soon as you can. It comes packaged with *MCAT Practice Test I.* 1995, 97 pp.

Association of American Medical Colleges. *MCAT Practice Tests II* (1995, 99 pp.) and *III* (1995, 134 pp.). Washington, DC: AAMC. Invaluable study aids for the MCAT. *Test III* has a method for you to evaluate your strengths and weaknesses in the test's different subtopic areas.

Association of American Medical Colleges. *Preparing for the MCAT.* Washington, DC: AAMC. This 24-minute videotape provides a useful review of the ways to prepare for the various test sections and a visual demonstration of an MCAT administration.

Association of American Medical Colleges. *Scoring the MCAT Writing Sample: Examples of MCAT Writing Sample Responses and Explanations of Their Scores.* Washington, DC: AAMC, 1995, 28 pp. This booklet is an excellent resource to use to begin preparing for the MCAT Writing Sample. It contains both good and bad essays, and explains why each was graded as it was.

Flowers JL, Silver T. *The Princeton Review: Annotated Practice MCAT, 1997 ed.* New York: Random House, 1996, 231 pp. In what areas are you weak? Where do you need to put more effort? This book has an extensive diagnostic MCAT exam with explanations of the answers, and description of why each answer is correct. This book, the renamed, but highly acclaimed *Cracking the MCAT,* focuses on teaching you effective techniques to raise your MCAT scores. If you still have questions, the Princeton Review offers on-line and telephone assistance for those who buy this book. (+)

Flowers JL, Silver T. *The Princeton Review Flowers & Silver MCAT, 1997 ed.* New York: Random House, 1044 pp. This is the most-trusted MCAT prep book available. It shows you how to review for all MCAT sections thoroughly and accurately, to prepare strategically using a step-by-step study system, to analyze MCAT passages and questions, and to test yourself after every chapter with custom-tailored MCAT simulations. The Princeton Review also has a support staff to help those who buy this book. (+)

Seibel HR, et al. *Barron's How to Prepare for the MCAT, 7th ed.* Hauppaugh, NY: Barron, 1991, 471 pp. This book includes a summary of how to study and review science subjects, and includes detailed reviews of biology, chemistry, physics, and mathematics. It also contains test-taking strategies for the verbal reasoning section, hints on essay writing, and four model examinations—with the answer keys and detailed explanations of the answers. **(+)**

Schaffzin NR. *The Princeton Review Reading Smart: Advanced Techniques for Improved Reading.* New York: Random House, 1994, 270 pp. The key to doing well on the MCAT examinations (as well as in medical school and on the licensing examinations) is to read quickly and understand what you read. This book takes you through all the steps necessary to read faster with better comprehension. You learn techniques such as prereading, pen-marking, mapping, and clustering. Multiple diagnostic exercises let you measure your progress as you speed (hopefully) through the book. An excellent preparation for the MCAT Verbal Reasoning section. **(+)**

The Paperwork

Jablonski S, ed. *Dictionary of Medical Acronyms & Abbreviations, 2nd ed.* New York: Hanley Belfus, 1993, 330 pp. From A (alveolar, Angstrom, or the start of anesthesia, for example) to Z (Z.Z.'Z.", increasing degrees of obstetric contraction), this book is the complete desk-top source to decipher medical abbreviations. The pocket-sized book becomes invaluable when misreading an abbreviation might be embarrassing or even dangerous. If you don't know your MDF from your MDE, you need this book. **(+)**

Tysinger JW. *Résumés and Personal Statements for Health Professionals.* Tucson, AZ: Galen Press, 1994, 200 pp. An in-depth guide to developing résumés and personal statements that reflect who you really are. Provides step-by-step, foolproof instructions to identify and describe your accomplishments to emphasize your strengths. It describes how to develop a personal inventory, and then how to apply the inventory items to a professional-looking document that will impress admission officers. It includes numerous examples of actual résumés and personal statements. Also details how to write cover and thank-you letters. **(+)**

Venolia J. *Write Right! A Desktop Digest of Punctuation, Grammar, and Style. 3rd ed.* Berkeley, CA: Ten Speed Press, 1995, 153 pp. Do you appear as smart as you really are in your written communications? This book addresses such perennial questions as: Who or whom? That or which? Colon or semicolon? An easy-to-understand review of punctuation and grammar (with cartoons that help you understand why a sentence is wrong), and tips for improving your writing style. **(+)**

Medical School

JAMA. Education Issue. This annual issue, usually available in early September, contains the latest information and statistics on medical school and residency education. Besides the statistics, there are many valuable articles describing the latest trends in medical education. Individual copies can be purchased from Customer Services at the American Medical Association.

Klass P. *A Not Entirely Benign Procedure: Four Years as a Medical Student.* New York: Plume, 1987, 286 pp. Perri Klass not only graduated from Harvard Medical School, she lived to write about it. This provocative book shows how doctors are really trained. Written from the perspective of a woman and mother in a field dominated by men and masculine sensibilities, Klass describes how she learned to deal with patients, blood, and hospital politics during her grueling clinical years. She depicts the fears, neuroses, and commitment to medicine that medical students feel, yet may be afraid to admit. **(+)**

Konner M. *Becoming a Doctor: A Journey of Initiation in Medical School.* New York: Penguin, 1987, 390 pp. Not sure what to expect during required clinical rotations? While taking the reader on his "rounds," Dr. Konner candidly and eloquently portrays his hectic, life-changing third-year of medical school, when book knowledge comes face-to-face with the personalities of disease. He asks, "Does this experience adequately train doctors to address medicine's human side?" **(+)**

Meador CK. *A Little Book of Doctors' Rules.* New York: Hanley Belfus, 1992, 63 pp. Medical school doesn't teach you everything you need to know to be a great doctor. Real life is a better instructor. Dr. Meador's sound advice, and truisms such as "Never tell a patient 'Don't worry'," and "The higher the technology, the greater the need for human contact," apply to medical students (and physicians) throughout their careers. (+)

Polk SR. *The Medical Student's Survival Guide, 4th ed.* Denver, CO: Medencom, 1995, 411 pp. The book tells it straight by condensing the hard lessons of medical school, residency, and private practice into an eye-opening profile of what you need to know to succeed during medical training and in the real world. An excellent head-start on navigating through the dangers inherent in medical education. (+)

Financial Aid

Association of American Medical Colleges. *State and Other Loan Repayment/Forgiveness and Scholarship Programs, 2nd ed.* Washington, DC: AAMC, 1995, 137 pp. A state-by-state listing of programs that allow you to perform service to repay your student loans or to have them "forgiven." Also includes programs offered by some national organizations and the federal government.

Dennis MJ. *Barron's Guide to Financing a Medical School Education, 2nd ed.* Hauppaugh, NY: Barron, 1994, 360 pp. After explaining the general rules and terms, this book lists the available federal, state, minority, and school-specific aid programs for medical school tuition and expenses—including loans and scholarships. Nearly every medical student needs financial help, and this is a great resource to use to find it. (+)

Financial Advice for Minority Students Seeking an Education in the Health Professions. Office of Statewide Health Planning and Development, Health Professions Career Opportunity Program, 1600 Ninth Street, Room 441, Sacramento, CA 95814. (Free) A short booklet with sound financial advice directed towards minority students.

Financial Planning and Management Manual for U.S. Medical Students. Washington, DC: AAMC, 43 pp. This easy-to-read booklet explains how to plan a budget for your medical school expenses. It does not, however, contain information about specific loan or scholarship programs.

The Student Guide: Five Federal Financial Aid Programs. U.S. Department of Education, Federal Student Aid Programs, Dept. M-11, Pueblo, CO 81009-0015. (Free) While not all the listed programs apply to medical students, the booklet does contain up-to-date information about some federal programs.

Osteopathic Medicine

American Association of Colleges of Osteopathic Medicine. *Debts and Career Plans of Osteopathic Medical Students in 1994.* Rockville, MD: AACOM, 1995, 25 pp. One of the few sources for this type of hard data on Osteopathic medical schools, students, and finances. Well worth a look.

American Osteopathic Association, Division of Postdoctoral Training. Osteopathic graduate medical education. *J Am Osteopath Assoc,* (each November). This annual article provides an overview of the number of available AOA-approved and funded residency positions, the number of graduates, how many D.O.'s are taking ACGME-approved training, and new rules for specialty certification.

Gevitz N. *The D.O.'s: Osteopathic Medicine in America.* Baltimore, MD: Johns Hopkins Univ. Press, 1982, 183 pp. Where did Osteopathic medicine, the "other" medical degree, come from? Who are Osteopathic physicians? What is their training, history, and culture? This book must be read by anyone considering this field. (+)

Meyer CT, Price A. Osteopathic medicine: a call for reform. *J Am Osteopath Assoc* 1993;93(4):473-85. A plea to move away from conflict with M.D.'s and to further integrate Osteopathic and M.D. graduate medical education. It also suggests that the two branches of medicine should work together to help forge a national health policy.

Ross-Lee B, Weiser MA, Kiss L. The outlook for Osteopathic medical specialists within a reformed healthcare system. *J Am Osteopath Assoc* 1994;94(7):564-5. An excellent overview of what changes may occur within Osteopathic medicine due to the changing healthcare environment.

Minorities

Association of American Medical Colleges. *Minority Students in Medical Education: Facts and Figures IX.* Washington, DC: AAMC, 1996, 115 pp. Virtually all of the "hard data" you could want about how well underrepresented minorities are doing as medical school applicants, students, practitioners, and academicians. This book is updated more or less annually.

Career Choices: Health Professions Opportunities for Minorities. Office of Statewide Health Planning and Development, Health Professions Career Opportunity Program, 1600 Ninth Street, Room 441, Sacramento, CA 95814. (Free). This booklet gives a brief overview of the various careers open in the health care field.

Journal for Minority Medical Students. This journal focuses on the needs and concerns of minority medical students. Its annual *Keepsake* edition (see below) is a distillation of great information for minority premeds. Copies of the *Journal* can be obtained from medical school minority affairs offices and some premed offices.

Journal of the National Medical Association. Focusing on topics vital to Black physicians and those serving Black patients, this monthly journal has a wide variety of articles that should be interesting to Black premed and medical students. The articles dealing with the Association's activities and the news relating to minority practitioners will be of particular interest. A free copy can be obtained on-line (http://www.slackinc.com/general/jnma/jnmahome.htm).

Keepsake: A Guide for Minority Premed Students (annual). Produced by the *Journal for Minority Medical Students,* it provides a good overview of the premed and medical school experience from the minority student's viewpoint. It also contains up-to-date addresses for summer and other special programs. Obtain a copy from your premed or minority-affairs adviser.

Minorities in Medicine: A Guide for Premedical Students. Office of Statewide Health Planning and Development, Health Professions Career Opportunity Program, 1600 Ninth Street, Rm. 441, Sacramento, CA 95814, (Free) 34 pp. A quick overview of the entire process of becoming a physician. While the booklet is not too comprehensive, it's a good place to start.

Minority Student Opportunities in United States Medical Schools. Washington, DC: AAMC, (Annual), 287 pp. This book, revised each April, lists the minority affairs contact person at each U.S. medical school, and information about each school's programs for minority students, including recruitment, admission requirements, academic and financial aid, and summer enrichment programs. It also contains detailed, school-specific figures of the numbers of underrepresented minority students who applied, were accepted, began classes, and are in each class. These numbers are further broken down by gender and state of residence.

Project 3000 by 2000: Progress to Date. Washington, DC: AAMC (Annual), 47 pp. This report is an annual update on the AAMC's project to enroll 3,000 underrepresented minority students by the year 2000. It includes relevant facts concerning minority enrollment in U.S. medical schools.

Disabled Students

Association of Academic Physiatrists. Recommended guidelines for admission of candidates with disabilities to medical school. *Am J of Phy Med Rehabil* 1993;72(1):45-47. This association acts as an advocate within the medical profession for disabled applicants and practitioners. This article presents guidelines for schools to use to determine if otherwise-qualified medical school applicants can perform a physician's functions.

Association of American Medical Colleges. *The Disabled Student in Medical School: An Overview of Legal Requirements.* Washington, DC: AAMC, 1995, 60 pp. Medical schools use this compendium in developing their own admission and retention policies for disabled students and applicants.

Essex-Sorlie D. The Americans with Disabilities Act: I. History, summary, and key components. *Acad Med* 1994;69(7):519-24. An excellent overview of the Americans with Disabilities Act and how it relates to medical schools. While it does not address the specific question of application to medical school directly, the article gives enough information from which to extrapolate. Clear, concise, and not filled with legal mumbo-jumbo.

Helms LB, Helms CM. Medical education and disability discrimination: the law and future implications. *Acad Med* 1994;69(7):535-43. A bit more about the legal background, relevant court findings, and possible future interpretations of the Americans with Disabilities Act.

International Medical Students and Graduates

Ball LB. *The International Medical Graduates' Guide to U.S. Medicine: Negotiating the Maze.* Tucson, AZ: Galen Press, 1995, 225 pp. This book explains how to return to the United States for residency and to practice medicine. It details the steps to take, the resources to use, and the mistakes to avoid when dealing with the ECFMG, residency programs, and state medical boards. This book may save you years of turmoil. (+)

Pestana C. *Foreign Medical Schools for U.S. Citizens.* 1995, 134 pp. Personal insights into some foreign medical schools that U.S. citizens attend. The author has visited several of the schools, and has interesting things to say about them. This book is available from the author at: P.O. Box 790617, San Antonio, TX 78279-0617.

Spears RA. *Essential American Idioms.* Lincolnwood, IL: National Textbook, 1992, 247 pp. If you think that "a fine kettle of fish" is a gourmet meal, you need this book. A complete guide to the common idioms found in American English, this book will help both those for whom English is a second language and those for whom American "lingo" is an impossible corruption of the Queen's English. If you need skill in "Americanese" for the MCAT or for your interviews, use this resource to use to avoid "going up in flames." (+)

World Health Organization. *World Directory of Medical Schools.* (Published intermittently.) WHO, 49 Sheridan Avenue, Albany, NY 12210. Graduates of the listed medical schools are allowed to obtain ECFMG certification. If you are considering going to a foreign medical school, check to make sure it is listed. Unless the foreign school is still listed when you graduate, you cannot apply to practice medicine in the United States.

Women In Medicine

American Medical Association. *Women in Medicine in America.* Chicago, IL: AMA, 1991, 45 pp. This booklet is filled with statistics and information about the status of women in medicine, from medical school through residency and into practice.

Asta LM. Halting harassment. *New Physician* 1995;44:30-8. A nice review of the current situation regarding sexual harassment in the medical education environment, including some valuable resources to use if necessary.

Bickel J, Ruffin A. Gender-associated differences in matriculating and graduating medical students. *Acad Med* 1995;70(6):552-9. An overview of the differences in how men and women medical students envision their career paths at the time of graduation.

Davis C. Called by God, led by men: women face the masculinization of American medicine at the College of Medical Evangelists, 1909-1922. *Bull Hist Med* 1993;67(1):119-148. A detailed description of the tribulations women faculty members endured at the precursor to the Loma Linda School of Medicine. The experience was typical of all co-educational medical schools at that time.

Dobkin R, Sippy S. *The College Woman's Handbook.* New York: Workman, 1995, 640 pp. A peer-to-peer guide to everything a woman wants to know, ought to know, and didn't-know-she-needed-to-know about college. From eleventh-hour cramming tips to dealing with racism, from safer partying to getting into grad school, this book is packed with tips, and the sidebar format allows for skimming and light reading. Subjects include classes, housing, relationships, studying, nutrition, health, and much more. (+)

Durso C. The long and winding road. *New Physician* 1995;44:24-9. An excellent review of the tortuous path women's medical training has taken in the United States. A sidebar to the article looks at how women are faring in medicine around the globe.

Fiorentine R, Cole S. Why fewer women become physicians: explaining the premed persistence gap. *Sociological Forum* 1992;7(3):469-96. A fascinating study of the various reasons given to explain why women have supposedly not pursued their premed studies. This paper shows that most of these reasons are bogus and offers a more logical explanation.

Harrison M. *A Woman in Residence.* New York: Fawcett Crest, 1982, 266 pp. After a psychiatry residency, Dr. Harrison entered family practice. In middle age, she began a rigorous obstetric/gynecology residency at a major U.S. hospital, but quickly became disillusioned after realizing that hospitals and medical staffs often compromise the care women need, want, and deserve, for their own convenience. In this book, based on her diaries, she writes about her patients, for whom she never seemed to have enough time; about her colleagues, with whom she did not always agree; about the excitement of learning new procedures; and about the pressures that never let up. (+)

Langelan MJ. *Back Off! How to Confront and Stop Sexual Harassment and Harassers.* New York: Simon & Schuster, 1993, 380 pp. This book examines the dynamics of sex and power in sexual harassment, the motives behind harassers' actions, and why traditional responses, such as appeasement or aggression, don't work. The author also describes successful, nonviolent resistance strategies—including personal and group confrontation techniques, administrative remedies, and formal lawsuits. (+)

Nora LM. Sexual harassment in medical education: a review of the literature with comments from the law. *Acad Med* 1996;71(1):S113-8. An excellent comprehensive review of the prevalence of sexual harassment in medical education, including a balanced and insightful look at the legal status of harassment claims.

Philibert I, Bickel J. Maternity and parental leave policies at COTH hospitals: an update. *Acad Med* 1995;70(11):1055-8. A survey of the current parental- and adoption-leave policies at U.S. teaching hospitals. Somewhat depressing.

Shrager JB. Three women at Johns Hopkins: private perspectives on medical coeducation in the 1890s. *Ann Int Med* 1991;115(7):564-9. A fascinating and detailed look at the lives of three women who successfully faced the onslaught of a male-dominated profession by entering a co-educational medical school and graduating.

Western Journal of Medicine December 1988;149(6). This issue of the Journal is devoted to women in medicine. Several excellent articles highlight the unique role of and the problems faced by women having medical careers. The articles include "Careers of Women Physicians: Choices and Constraints," and "Women and Medicine: Surviving and Thriving."

Marriage and Relationships

Carter J, Carter JD. *He Works/She Works: Successful Strategies for Working Couples.* New York: AMACOM, 1995, 226 pp. Marriage isn't easy, and it becomes much more difficult when both partners work at difficult, time-consuming jobs with hectic schedules. Both partners want to make it work; both harbor unspoken anger at themselves and their mates. Some criticisms are valid, some are not. This book helps you identify the problems, and also suggests very workable solutions. (+)

Myers MF. *Doctors' Marriages: A Look at the Problems and Their Solutions, 2nd ed.* New York: Plenum, 1994, 257 pp. You don't have to sacrifice a loving marriage to complete your medical training. Dr. Myers has 21 years of experience in assessing and treating physicians, medical students, and their spouses. He discusses the issues affecting doctors' relationships and provides numerous case vignettes that demonstrate common problems in medical marriages. Topics include medical students' and residents' interpersonal relationships, men and women physicians, gay and lesbian physicians, divorce and remarriage among doctors, and older physicians. (+)

Pregnancy and Parenting

American Academy of Pediatrics. *Day Care: Finding the Best Child Care for Your Family.* 1990. A straightforward guide to the difficult process of locating good child care. AAP, Dept. C/IH, 141 N.W. Point Boulevard, Elk Grove, IL 60007.

Bickel J, ed. *Medicine and Parenting.* An excellent source of information about the problems of physicians as parents—with some excellent solutions. Washington, DC: Association of American Medical Colleges, 1991.

Eisenberg A, Murkoff HE, Hathaway SE. *What to Expect When You're Expecting.* New York: Workman, 1991, 479 pp. This is the bible of pregnancy—the book that answers the concerns of mothers- and fathers-to-be, from the planning stage through postpartum. The comprehensive month-by-month guide is filled with information on choosing a caregiver, prenatal diagnosis, exercise, childbirth options, second pregnancies, making love during pregnancy, having a cesarean section, and coping with common and not-so-common pregnancy symptoms. It also has a section specifically for new fathers. This book answers virtually every pregnancy-related question or fear. (+)

———— *What to Expect When You're Expecting: Pregnancy Organizer.* New York: Workman, 1984, 224 pp. This journal is the perfect place to record your medical information so it's handy for conversations with your doctor. This pocket-sized journal has pages for doctor's appointments, recording test results, a diary, diet checklists. (+)

———— *What to Eat When You're Expecting.* New York: Workman, 1986, 349 pp. If you are searching for foods to satisfy cravings or just wondering what to you should be eating while pregnant (when you can keep anything down, that is), the authors of the *Expecting* series have the answers. The book includes tips for maintaining proper weight gain; recipes for high-protein meatless entrees, non-alcoholic cocktails, naturally sweetened cakes and desserts; vitamin information; and nutrition charts. (+)

———— *What to Expect the First Year.* New York: Workman, 1989, 671 pp. This comprehensive month-by-month guide clearly explains everything new parents need to know about the first year with their baby. It includes information on the infant's growth and development, feeding, sleeping habits, illnesses, child safety and first aid, traveling with your baby, and handling older siblings. Also included are Best-Odds recipes and an illustrated baby-care primer. Prospective parents might want to check this out to see just what they are getting themselves into. (+)

———— *What to Expect: The Toddler Years.* New York: Workman, 1994, 904 pp. A continuation of the *What to Expect* series, this is an all-inclusive guide for the parents of toddlers. Complete with information on self-esteem, effective toilet training, tantrums, sleeping and feeding problems, selecting a preschool, sibling relations, growth and social development, discipline, and eccentric behaviors. Also advice on mixing careers and parenthood and making time for yourself in the midst of it all. (+)

Sale JS, Kollengberg K. *The Working Parents' Handbook.* New York: Simon & Schuster, 1996, 317 pp. All working parents struggle with the same anxiety, guilt, and questions. How do you: Deal with separation anxiety? Find good child care? Simplify meal preparation and bedtime? Set up a baby-sitting co-op? Preserve quality time with your child? This book presents workable solutions to help you avoid mistakes. (+)

Wiebe C. From here to maternity. *New Physician* 1995;44:40-4. A good description of some problems pregnant women physicians faced during medical school and residency. They also have some helpful suggestions.

Admissions and Applications

American Association of Colleges of Osteopathic Medicine. *Osteopathic Medical College Information (Annual) Entering Class.* Rockville, MD: AACOM, 33 pp. (Free) The official list of approved U.S. Osteopathic (D.O.-granting) medical schools. It describes each school's facilities, affiliations, entrance requirements, curriculum and special programs, admission procedures, class size, tuition and fees, and contact information. The same information is available on the World Wide Web (http://www.aacom.org) and on the AACOMAS By Computer program.

Association of American Medical Colleges. *Curriculum Directory (annual).* Washington DC: AAMC. This book has up-to-date information about the curricula at all the U.S. M.D.-granting medical schools.

Association of American Medical Colleges. *Medical School Admission Requirements (annual).* Washington DC: AAMC, 291 pp. This book is absolutely essential for anyone considering applying to an M.D.-granting medical school in the United States. It has up-to-date information about each school, including the specifics about application procedures, deadlines, and the types of applicants they are currently accepting.

The Lighter Side: A Little Humor

Bennett H, ed. *The Best of Medical Humor.* New York: Hanley Belfus, 1991, 228 pp. This is a fabulous anthology of humorous articles, quotes, and poems that will make you laugh out loud at medicine's funny side. Selections include, "Real Interns Don't Have Time to Eat Quiche," "The Fine Art of Disappearing from Meetings," and "How to Write Nifty Titles for Your Papers." (+)

Brilliant A. *I May Not Be Totally Perfect, But Parts of Me Are Excellent.* Santa Barbara, CA: Woodbridge, 1979, 160 pp. Once you are introduced to Mr. Brilliant's wonderfully zany world-view, you may never want to return to your own again. This book contains nearly 300 illustrated Brilliant Thoughts® to provoke, amuse, energize, tranquilize, captivate, and liberate you. (+)

Brilliant A. *I Want to Reach Your Mind ... Where Is It Currently Located?* Santa Barbara, CA: Woodbridge, 1994, 167 pp. A dazzling new collection of witty and wise messages to satisfy your personal quest for telling communication. Fresh, funny, wistful, bright—they may well reflect some of your own deep or whimsical thoughts. Brilliant's illustrated epigrams speak to everyone. (+)

London O. *Kill as Few Patients as Possible, and Fifty-six Other Essays on How to be the World's Best Doctor.* Berkeley, CA: Ten Speed Press, 1987. Funny short essays illustrate this practicing physician's rules about how to be a successful (and humane and compassionate) physician. While the essays are tongue-in-cheek (such as, "If you think you're indispensable, check your appointment book a week after you drop dead."), much of the underlying advice really will make you an excellent physician. **(+)**

Interviewing

Biegeleisen JI. *Make Your Job Interview a Success, 4th ed.* New York: Macmillan, 1994, 223 pp. This authoritative, advice-packed guide provides inside information and easy-to-use techniques to help you project your best image, respond with the right answers, and get the position you want. Contents include: Interview checklist, job-interview scenarios, "63 Guaranteed Ways to Muff a Job Interview," suggestions for improving your appearance and speech, and your rights under the Americans with Disabilities Act. (+)

Gabor D. *Speaking Your Mind in 101 Difficult Situations.* 1994, 239 pp. Do you always say the wrong thing at the wrong time? If you're tired of the taste of your foot, read this book for techniques to deal with specific situations, including the right words to use to say tough things—while still being tactful. (+)

Medical Ethics

Beauchamp TL, Childress JF. *Principles of Biomedical Ethics 4th ed.* New York: Oxford Univ. Press, 1994, 546 pp. If you have ever felt daunted by philosophical jargon while reading about or discussing medical ethics, this book is for you. As an introduction to the basics of medical ethics, this book begins with a discussion of terms and philosophical principles (definitions of morality, Utilitarianism, Kantianism, etc.). The authors also discuss issues particular to biomedical ethics, such as autonomy, nonmaleficence, and beneficence. This classic of bioethical writing will help you to better understand some of medicine's most important debates—and maybe answer some of those sticky interview questions. (+)

Belkin L. *First, Do No Harm.* New York: Fawcett Crest, 1993, 353 pp. This book examines real patients and real ethical decisions, with all of their pathos and uncertainty, in a big city hospital. From the very old to the impossibly young and fragile, the traumatized and those whose bodies have succumbed to disease, those with agony of the soul and of the body—who should live and who should be allowed to die? These are not the idealistic ruminations of a distant philosopher, but rather the struggles of physicians, families, patients, and ethics committees as they make terrible and agonizing decisions. A microcosm of the dilemmas facing all the players in America's health care system. (+)

Iserson KV. *Death to Dust: What Happens to Dead Bodies?* Tucson, AZ: Galen Press, 1994, 705 pp. You plan to dissect a human body in medical school? Maybe you should know a little bit about corpses in advance. Promoting organ and tissue donation, this book describes, in a question-and-answer format, everything that happens, has happened, or may happen to corpses. Interesting stories and humor pepper the very readable text. Included are detailed explanations of organ and tissue donation, brain death, embalming, cremation, cryogenics, cannibalism, forensic investigations, autopsies, burials, funeral practices and, of course, anatomical dissection. (+)

Iserson KV, Sanders AB, Mathieu D. *Ethics in Emergency Medicine, 2nd ed.* Tucson, AZ: Galen Press, 1995, 570 pp. How do clinicians make ethical decisions in the stickiest situations? How do they decide whether a patient is "competent"? What do they do when a patient refuses necessary care? This book has the answers. Discussions of actual cases from emergency medicine and prehospital care provide a straightforward approach to a wide range of ethical matters, with each focusing on a specific area of ethical decision making. Contributors include the country's best-known emergency clinicians and medical ethicists. It also has a great legal introduction. (+)

La Puma J, Schiedermayer D. *Ethics Consultation: A Practical Guide.* Boston: Jones & Bartlett, 1994, 234 pp. What is an "ethics consultation"? How is it done? When do clinicians ask for one? Whether you have an interest in medical ethics or simply want to know some of clinical medicine's inner workings, this book provides information in simple, direct, and very practical terms. (+)

Pence GE. *Classic Cases in Medical Ethics: Accounts of Cases that have Shaped Medical Ethics, with Philosophical, Legal, and Historical Backgrounds, 2nd ed.* New York: McGraw Hill, 1995, 504 pp. Quinlan, Clark, Cruzan, Baby Doe, Kevorkian. You have probably heard their names, but you may not know their importance. Focusing on the cases that have shaped and defined the field of medical ethics, this book uses in-depth descriptions to present the ethical issues, legal decisions, and historical backgrounds you need to know to understand this evolving field. These landmark cases concern coma, physician-assisted suicide, in vitro fertilization, surrogacy, abortion, animal subjects, organ transplants and artificial organs, fetal tissue research, genetic testing, mandatory HIV testing, and health care reform. (+)

Zussman R. *Intensive Care: Medical Ethics and the Medical Profession.* Chicago: Univ. Chicago Press, 1992, 252 pp. How are medical and ethical decisions made in the real world? In riveting case studies, Dr. Zussman describes how medical decisions in ICUs are considered and reconsidered, made and unmade, negotiated and renegotiated. He concentrates on the practice of medical ethics, on the ways in which right and wrong are interpreted and used in the ICU by physicians, nurses, patients, and families. This is a strong, often moving portrait of how careful planning is undermined by the unpredictability of illness, persistent self-interest, high principles, and curious compromises. A fascinating resource for anyone who anticipates working in an ICU. (+)

Licensing Examinations

American Medical Association. *U.S. Medical Licensure Statistics and Current Licensure Requirements.* (published annually) Chicago, IL: AMA. The basic information about licensure requirements in every state and territory of the United States. All the permutations and combinations of licensing are included in easy-to-read charts. It includes contact information for individual state boards, as well as hard-to-get information on IMG licensure requirements.

Asta LM. Board games: a no-nonsense guide to acing the national medical licensing exams. *New Physician* 1995;44(9):15-8. A short, excellent summary on how to prepare for the USMLE. It includes specifics about some of the review courses and materials, as well as some good hints about how to prepare for and take the examinations.

Breaden RS, et al. *Prescription for the Boards: USMLE Step 2.* Boston: Little Brown, 1996, 487 pp. Written by students for students, this is a complete review of what you need to know to pass the USMLE Step 2 examination. Addressing every subject listed in the USMLE test content outline, this book is the bible for Step 2 preparation. It includes an overview of the exam, study tips, evaluations of other review materials, a summary of medical facts, and "cram pages" to provide you with word associations to help you review large amounts of information. (+)

The Federation of State Medical Boards of the U.S., Inc. *Exchange—Section 1: USMLE and M.D. Licensing Requirements.* Euless, TX: FSMB. (published biannually) Contains the USMLE Step 3 eligibility requirements and administrative rules. Also has the requirements for initial licensure, licensure by endorsement, reregistration of one's license, licenses for postgraduate education, and other special licenses.

The Federation of State Medical Boards of the U.S., Inc. *Exchange—Section 2: USMLE and D.O. Licensing Requirements.* Euless, TX: FSMB. (published biannually) Contains the USMLE Step 3 eligibility requirements and administrative rules. Also has the requirements for initial licensure, licensure by endorsement, reregistration of one's license, licenses for postgraduate education, and special licenses.

The Federation of State Medical Boards of the U.S., Inc. *Exchange—Section 3: Licensing Boards, Structure and Disciplinary Functions.* Euless, TX: FSMB. (published biannually) Describes the basic structure and operation of each state medical board, their review and disciplinary functions, and contacts for both of these functions.

National Board of Medical Examiners and The Federation of State Medical Boards of the U.S., Inc. *USMLE Step 1 (or 2, or 3) General Instructions, Content Outline, and Sample Items.* Philadelphia, PA: USMLE Secretariat. (published annually) These valuable booklets list the current examination dates and eligibility requirements for all three Steps, as well as certification and registration procedures. Most important, there are subject/content outlines for all three Steps of the exam. The Step 3 booklet can be obtained from the state licensing board through which you will take the examination.

Schwenker JA. *Pass USMLE Step 1: Practice by Assessing Study Skills.* Boston: Little Brown, 1995, 140 pp. Sharpen your test-taking and study skills for the USMLE Step 1 examination with this unique review book. The author draws on her abundant experience working with medical students to teach you how to learn rather than simply telling you what to learn. Following a detailed explanation of what to expect on the Step 1 exam, she helps you: assess your skills through a special 150-question practice exam, review some of the testing traps you may have fallen into and learn how to avoid them in the future. She also helps you to design a personalized review plan and study schedule, and improve your reasoning skills on multiple-choice tests using a 350-question post-test with Step 1-type questions. (+)

Internship and Residency

Marion R. *Learning to Play God.* New York: Fawcett Crest, 1991, 272 pp. We enter medical school filled with idealism and compassion, wanting to do something with our lives to help our fellow man. And what happens? Dr. Marion draws on his own experiences to recreate the dehumanizing, slightly insane, and often brutal process of medical training. He leads readers on a tour of a modern teaching hospital, encountering sleep deprivation while on call as an intern, the hysteria of the ER, and patients such as the "Turtle Man." More importantly, he offers suggestions on how to assure that humanity and idealism survive the grueling path to technical competency. (+)

Marion R. *The Intern Blues: The Private Ordeals of Three Young Doctors.* New York: Fawcett Crest, 1989, 362 pp. The story, taken from their diaries, of three pediatric interns as they wend their ways through a tumultuous year of discovery, sleepiness, and heartbreak. This book has become a classic—the real stories of internship. In addition to being a great read, you can use this book to learn medical terminology—an editor has explained all the medical terms right in the text. (+)

Other Health-Related Careers

American Chiropractic Association. *The Chiropractic College Directory* (annual). 220 pp. This book contains information about chiropractic and about the individual schools. KM enterprises, P.O. Box 25978, Los Angeles, CA 90025.

American Association of Colleges of Pharmacy. *Pharmacy School Admission Requirements* (annual). Similar to the book on medical school requirements. AACP, 1426 Prince Street, Alexandria, VA 22314-2841; (703) 739-2330.

American Association of Dental Schools. *Admission Requirements of U.S. and Canadian Dental Schools.* Similar to the book on medical school requirements. AADS, 1625 Massachusetts Avenue, N.W., Washington, DC 20036-2212; (202) 667-9433.

American Medical Association. *Allied Health Education Directory,* (annual). A listing of non-physician opportunities in medicine. AMA, P.O. Box 109050, Chicago, IL 60610-9050.

American Physician Therapy Association. *Directory of Physical Therapy Education Programs* (annual). A listing and description of all approved physical therapy programs. APTA, 111 North Fairfax Street, Alexandria, VA 22314-1488.

Corder BW, ed. *Medical Professions Admission Guide: Strategy for Success, 3rd ed.* Champaign, IL: *National Association of Advisors for the Health Professions.* 1994, 142 pp. A thorough overview of the path to various careers in the health professions. It includes dentistry, medicine, nursing, nurse practitioners, occupational therapy, optometry, pharmacy, physical therapy, physician assistants, podiatry, and veterinary medicine. Written by undergraduate advisers to these health professionals. NAAHP, P.O. Box 1518, Champaign, IL 61824-1518.

National Health Council. *200 Ways to Put Your Talent to Work in the Health Field.* Washington, DC: NHC, 1993, 35 pp. (free) An excellent overview of the many careers within medicine and the related biomedical fields. You will not be familiar with some of the listed careers, although they do exist. The booklet, divided by job category, also contains sources for additional information. NHC, 1730 M Street, N.W., Suite 500, Washington, DC 20036.

Survival: Thinking, Eating, Doing

Archer J, Jr. *Managing Anxiety & Stress, 2nd ed.* Muncie, IN: Accelerated Development, 1991, 214 pp. Premeds and medical students are under a lot of stress. Adjust your habits and your thinking to cope with stress before it is too late. This self-help book provides information about stress (positive and negative types) and stress management. Each chapter includes written activities to determine your own stress level, and appropriate stress reduction methods to lower it. The book presents different theories, all within the framework of a simple stress interaction model, including the effects of stress and anxiety on relationships, values, transitions, time use, and spirituality. (+)

Cohen GD, Gladstone W. *How to Test & Improve Your Own Mental Health.* Rocklin, CA: Prima, 1995, 231 pp. In most cases you know whether you are getting sick (a cold, the flu, etc.), but what if you doubt your sanity? Are you just stressed, or are you beginning to wonder if it might be something more serious? This book allows you to test your personal mental health and discover your ability to adapt to and cope with life stresses. It includes over 120 questions covering every area of your life, with a complete analysis of what your answers mean. The text also explains the characteristics of normal mental health, causes of instability, and concepts of mental healing. (+)

Edwards P. *Cheap Eating: How to Feed Your Family Well and Spend Less.* Hinesburg, VT: Upper Access, 1993, 201 pp. The author understands the pressures of a small budget. This book not only provides many cheap-but-tasty meals, but also tells you how to shop and even how to grow your own vegetables. The author discusses nutrition, buying in bulk, using leftovers, and other money-saving strategies. Learn to feed a family of four for $30 a week, control your weight without counting calories, and improve your nutrition while cutting costs. (+)

Fitzgerald M. *On Campus Cookbook: For the Non-Kitchen Cook!* New York: Workman, 1984, 128 pp. This book is the no-hassle answer to having no kitchen—food for any occasion, from all-nighters to a picnic date. It contains more than 70 easy recipes to make in your dorm room, using only hot-pots, blenders, and toaster ovens. The recipes take advantage of what is readily available, some even including food items from the cafeteria line. (+)

Fobes R. *The Creative Problem Solver's Toolbox.* Corvalis, OR: Solutions Through Innovation, 1993, 345 pp. Too often we tell ourselves (or are told by others) that our ideas won't work before we even try them. This book provides the inspiration to listen to yourself more often and teaches you how to maximize your problem-solving potential. Fun to browse through, it has icons highlighting interesting anecdotes of real-life problem solvers, such as the story of two Kodak researchers, working before the days of luminescent clocks and red safety lights, who would sing certain songs to time their darkroom developing chemicals. This book shows you how to recognize useful new applications for ideas that were discarded as useless, think in creative ways that schools commonly neglect to teach, how to identify easily overlooked alternatives, and handle criticisms of your creative ideas. (+)

Frandsen BR., Franndsen KJ, Fransden KP. *Where's Dad Now That I Need Him?* Sandy, UT: Aspen West, 1995, 322 pp. What type of oil do you need for your car? Do you know the best way to start charcoal? This book provides the information that Dads often know best. Chapter topics include: using good consumer sense, managing your money and credit cards, succeeding on the job, travel and vacation tips, dad's recipes (sandwiches, eggs, barbecue, chili, popcorn, etc.), maintaining your care and home, buying and selling a car, crime prevention, and holiday safety. It even tells you how to hold a yard sale. (+)

Frandsen BR, Franndsen KJ, Fransden KP. *Where's Mom Now That I Need Her?* Sandy, UT: Aspen West, 1983, 298 pp. Quick! How long does it take to hard boil an egg? Does the red stripe on your sweatsock mean you should sort it with the whites or the colored laundry? If you're not sure about the answers to these questions, this book is for you. It contains all the essential household trivia that only Moms seem to know. Learn how to make household cleaners, buy a cantaloupe, and cook "comfort" foods, such as pancakes, meatloaf, and cheesy potatoes. (+)

Messner E. *Resilience Enhancement for the Resident Physician.* Durant, OK: EMIS, 1993, 158 pp. The ravages of internship and residency have concerned the medical profession for decades, including the deterioration in patient care that may result from sleep deprivation, physical exhaustion, clinical depression and substance abuse. This book describes the common warning signals of stress and burn-out, and offers methods for self-treatment. Prepare yourself by reading this book. (+)

Michalko M. *Thinkpak: A Brainstorming Card Deck.* Berkeley, CA: Ten Speed Press, 1994. Stumped? These idea-stimulating cards help you generate new ideas, turn negatives into positives, and find solutions for "impossible" problems. Drawing on his own premise that "everything new is really an addition to or a modification of something that already existed," the author combines a deck of cards with a creative-thinking book to produce a method for jump-starting ideas. When you have a problem to be solved, you draw a card from the deck and try to apply the principle on the card to the situation. Excellent for brainstorming. (+)

Minninger J. *Total Recall: How to Boost Your Memory Power.* New York: Pocket Books, 1984, 307 pp. This book teaches you how to remember 20 things in less than two minutes using simple memory improvement techniques. Besides providing you with invaluable memory aids, it asks you to re-think your "inability" to learn certain subjects by explaining why emotions can block recall. You might find that you really can memorize mundane material, such as organic chemistry (if you want to). (+)

Ruchlis H. *Clear Thinking: A Practical Introduction.* Buffalo, NY: Prometheus, 1990, 271 pp. Do you ignore the facts if they get in the way of your "truths"? You aren't the only one. However, the ability to think critically is imperative in the Information Age, with its networked computers, global communications, and cleverly packaged ideas. This introduction to basic critical analysis shows how to evaluate evidence, isolate facts, and use sound reasoning skills in everyday situations. Chapters focus on: The Nature of Facts; The Reasoning Process; Common Errors in Reasoning; Conflicting Opinions; Stereotypes, Prejudice, and Discrimination; and How Opinions Are Influenced. (+)

Schelske R, Funk G. *Laundry 101.* Sandy, UT: Aspen West, 1987, 24 pp. Is laundry as big a mystery as quantum physics to you? This booklet describes step-by-step, in plain English, how to sort your clothes into correct piles (the key to success!), what type of detergent and fabric softener to use, and what dryer settings to use. Read this book so you don't turn your whites into pinks again. (+)

Tannen D. *Talking From 9 to 5—Women and Men in the Workplace: Language, Sex and Power.* New York: Avon, 1994, 368 pp. Workplace conversations are not idle chatter—they are the social cement that determines success and failure. How do women's and men's conversational styles affect who gets heard, who gets credit, and what gets done? This book answers those questions about miscommunication between the sexes. This world-famous linguist puts it all into practical terms with practical advice—and warnings. (+)

Ulene A. *The Nutribase Complete Fast Food Restaurant Nutrition Counter.* Garden City Park, NY: Avery Pub., 1996, 245 pp. It is no longer necessary to give up good nutrition for the sake of convenience. This guide allows you to quickly compare restaurant foods and eat smart. Nutritional information, including the carbohydrate, fat, protein, and sodium content, and much more, is listed for more than 3,000 menu items from over 65 restaurant chains. (+)

INDEX

—D—

—I—

—J—

—P—

ABOUT THE AUTHOR

Kenneth V. Iserson, M.D., M.B.A., FACEP, is a noted medical teacher, clinician, and researcher. A past-president of the Society of Teachers of Emergency Medicine and a Professor of Surgery, he directed the Residency Program in Emergency Medicine at the University of Arizona College of Medicine in Tucson for a decade. He frequently speaks to premedical student, and adviser groups throughout the country on the complex process of selecting a medical school, applying to, interviewing for, and obtaining a desired medical school slot. He also speaks to medical students, advisers, and residency director groups about selecting a medical specialty and the residency selection process.

Dr. Iserson is also the author of *Getting Into A Residency: A Guide for Medical Students* (Galen Press 1996), *Death to Dust: What Happens to Dead Bodies?* (Galen Press, 1994), and *Ethics in Emergency Medicine* (Galen Press, 1995).

GALEN

Galen of Pergamum (A.D. 130-201), the Greek physician whose writings guided medicine for more than a millennium after his death, inspired the name, Galen Press. As the father of modern anatomy and physiology, Galen wrote more than one hundred treatises while attempting to change medicine from an art form into a science. As a practicing physician, Galen first ministered to gladiators and then to Roman Emperor Marcus Aurelius. Far more than Hippocrates, Galen's work influenced Western physicians, and was the "truth" until the late Middle Ages when physicians and scientists challenged his teachings. Galen Press, publishing non-clinical health-related books, will follow Galen's advice that "the chief merit of language is clearness...nothing detracts so much from this as unfamiliar terms."

Books You Want to Own !!

Résumés and Personal Statements for Health Professionals
by James W. Tysinger, Ph.D.

House Calls, Rounds, and Healings: A Poetry Casebook
by David Schiedermayer

Getting Into A Residency: A Guide for Medical Students,
Fourth Edition
by Kenneth V. Iserson, M.D.

Companion Disk for Getting Into A Residency
DOS & Windows™ versions

The International Medical Graduates' Guide to U.S. Medicine
Negotiating the Maze
by Louise B. Ball

Death to Dust: What Happens to Dead Bodies?
by Kenneth V. Iserson, M.D.

Ethics in Emergency Medicine, Second Edition
Edited by Kenneth V. Iserson, M.D., Arthur B. Sanders, M.D., Deborah Mathieu, Ph.D.
with a legal introduction by Alexander M. Capron

After-Death Planner

Yes! . . . Please send me:

____ copies of **Get Into Medical School! A Guide for the Perplexed**
      @ *$31.95 each* $ _____

____ copies of **Death to Dust:What Happen to Dead Bodies?**
      @ $ 41.95 *each* $ _____

____ copies of **After-Death Planning Guide** @ $ 3.00 *each* $ _____

____ copies of **Résumés and Personal Statements for**
      Health Professionals   @ *$15.95 each* $ _____

____ copies of **Getting Into A Residency: A Guide For**
      Medical Students @ $ 31.95 *each* $ _____

____ copies of **The International Medical Graduates'**
      Guide to U.S. Medicine @ $ 28.95 *each* $ _____

____ copies of **Ethics In Emergency Medicine, 2nd ed.** @ *$39.95 each* $ _____

____ copies of **House Calls, Rounds, and Healings: A**
      Poetry Casebook @ *$12.95 each* $ _____

____ copies of _____ $ _____

____ copies of _____ $ _____

____ copies of _____ $ _____

____ copies of _____ $ _____

AZ RESIDENTS — ADD 7% Sales Tax $ _____

Shipping: $3.00 for 1st Book, $1.00 / each additional $ _____

Priority Mail: **ADD** $2.95 / book $ _____

TOTAL ENCLOSED   **$** _____

[ ] Check   [ ] Credit Card   [ ] Institutional Purchase Order   Payment is enclosed (U.S. Funds Only)

SHIP TO: Name: _____

        Address: _____

                 _____

        City/State/Zip: _____

        Phone: **(required)** (_____)_____

CREDIT CARD: ❑ **Visa**   ❑ **Mastercard**

Number:_____   Expiration date: _____

   Signature:_____   Phone: (_____)_____

Send completed form and payment to:

Galen Press, Ltd.   Tel (520) 577-8363
PO Box 64400-MS   Fax (520) 529-6459
Tucson, AZ 85728-4400 USA   Orders: 1-800-442-5369 (US/Canada)

Visit our Home Page at http:/www.galenpress.com

Also available through your local bookstore.

Yes! . . . Please send me:

____ copies of ***Get Into Medical School! A Guide for the Perplexed***
        @ $31.95 each $ _____

____ copies of ***Death to Dust:What Happen to Dead Bodies?***
        @ $ 41.95 each $ _____

____ copies of ***After-Death Planning Guide*** *@ $ 3.00 each* $ _____

____ copies of ***Résumés and Personal Statements for Health***
        Professionals   *@ $15.95 each* $ _____

____ copies of ***Getting Into A Residency: A Guide For Medical***
        Students *@ $ 31.95 each* $ _____

____ copies of ***The International Medical Graduates' Guide***
        to U.S. Medicine *@ $ 28.95 each* $ _____

____ copies of ***Ethics In Emergency Medicine, 2nd ed.*** *@ $39.95 each* $ _____

____ copies of ***House Calls, Rounds, and Healings: A Poetry***
        Casebook *@ $12.95 each* $ _____

____ copies of _____ $ _____

____ copies of _____ $ _____

____ copies of _____ $ _____

____ copies of _____ $ _____

AZ Residents — Add 7% Sales Tax $ _____

Shipping: $3.00 for 1st Book, $1.00 / each additional $ _____

Priority Mail: **ADD** $2.95 / book $ _____

TOTAL ENCLOSED   **$** _____

[ ] **Check**   [ ] **Credit Card**   [ ] **Institutional Purchase Order** Payment is enclosed (U.S. Funds Only)

SHIP TO: Name: _____

          Address: _____

                     _____

          City/State/Zip: _____

          Phone: **(required)** (_____)_____

CREDIT CARD: ❑ **Visa**   ❑ **Mastercard**

Number:_____   Expiration date: _____

  Signature:_____   Phone: (_____)_____

Send completed form and payment to:
Galen Press, Ltd.   Tel (520) 577-8363
PO Box 64400-MS   Fax (520) 529-6459
Tucson, AZ 85728-4400 USA   Orders: 1-800-442-5369 (US/Canada)

Visit our Home Page at http:/www.galenpress.com

Also available through your local bookstore.

Yes! . . . Please send me:

_____ copies of **Get Into Medical School! A Guide for the Perplexed**
     @ *$31.95 each* $ _____

_____ copies of **Death to Dust:What Happen to Dead Bodies?**
     @ $ 41.95 each $ _____

_____ copies of **After-Death Planning Guide** @ $ 3.00 each $ _____

_____ copies of **Résumés and Personal Statements for Health
     Professionals** @ $15.95 each $ _____

_____ copies of **Getting Into A Residency: A Guide For Medical
     Students** @ $ 31.95 each $ _____

_____ copies of **The International Medical Graduates' Guide
     to U.S. Medicine** @ $ 28.95 each $ _____

_____ copies of **Ethics In Emergency Medicine, 2nd ed.** @ *$39.95 each* $ _____

_____ copies of **House Calls, Rounds, and Healings: A Poetry
     Casebook** @ *$12.95 each* $ _____

_____ copies of _____ $ _____

_____ copies of _____ $ _____

_____ copies of _____ $ _____

_____ copies of _____ $ _____

AZ RESIDENTS — ADD 7% Sales Tax $ _____

Shipping: $3.00 for 1st Book, $1.00 / each additional $ _____

Priority Mail: **ADD** $2.95 / book $ _____

TOTAL ENCLOSED $ _____

[ ] **Check**   [ ] **Credit Card**   [ ] **Institutional Purchase Order**   Payment is enclosed (U.S. Funds Only)

SHIP TO: Name: _____

     Address: _____

     _____

     City/State/Zip: _____

     Phone: **(required)** (_____)_____

CREDIT CARD: ❏ **Visa**   ❏ **Mastercard**

Number:_____   Expiration date: _____

 Signature:_____   Phone: (_____)_____

Send completed form and payment to:

Galen Press, Ltd.   Tel (520) 577-8363
PO Box 64400-MS   Fax (520) 529-6459
Tucson, AZ 85728-4400 USA   Orders: 1-800-442-5369 (US/Canada)

Visit our Home Page at   http:/www.galenpress.com

Also available through your local bookstore.